P9-DTW-547

The Active Reader

Fourth Edition

The Active Reader

Strategies for Academic Reading and Writing

Eric Henderson

OXFORD

UNIVERSITY PRESS

OXFORD
UNIVERSITY PRESS

Oxford University Press is a department of the University of Oxford.
It furthers the University's objective of excellence in research, scholarship,
and education by publishing worldwide. Oxford is a registered trade mark of
Oxford University Press in the UK and in certain other countries.

Published in Canada by
Oxford University Press
8 Sampson Mews, Suite 204,
Don Mills, Ontario M3C 0H5 Canada

www.oupcanada.com

First Edition published in 2008
Second Edition published in 2012
Third Edition published in 2015

Library and Archives Canada Cataloguing in Publication
Henderson, Eric, author
The active reader : strategies for academic reading and writing / Eric
Henderson. — Fourth edition.

Includes index.
Issued in print and electronic formats.
ISBN 978-0-19-902592-3 (softcover). —ISBN 978-0-19-903066-8 (PDF)

1. English language—Rhetoric—Textbooks. 2. Academic writing—
Textbooks. 3. Report writing—Textbooks. 4. Reading comprehension—
Textbooks. 5. College readers. 6. Textbooks. I. Title.

PE1408.H385 2018   808'.042   C2017-905534-8
                                             C2017-905535-6

Cover image: Rubberball/Mike Kemp/Brand X Pictures/Getty Images
Cover design: Sherill Chapman
Interior design: Laurie McGregor

Oxford University Press is committed to our environment.
Wherever possible, our books are printed on paper which comes from
responsible sources.

Printed and bound in the United States of America
1 2 3 4 — 21 20 19 18

Contents

4   Critical Thinking

5   Reading Strategies

PART II | ACADEMIC WRITING

10   Writing Research Papers 123

PART III | THE READER   157

Section One | University Issues   158

Section Two | Canada in the World   191

Section Three | Voices within Canada   216

Sample Student Essays
and The Active Voice Essays

Sample Student Essays

The Active Voice Essays

From the Publisher

Oxford University Press is pleased to bring you *The Active Reader*, a practical and integrated approach to reading and writing effectively. **Now in full colour**, this text is a guide to rhetoric and research and is also a reader, providing students with everything they need to succeed in their post-secondary classrooms and beyond.

Exceptional Features of *The Active Reader*

Intersections with Science

The Social Dilemma of Autonomous Vehicles

Jean-François Bonnefon, Azim Shariff, and Iyad Rahwan
(2,767 words)

Pre-reading

1. What is a "social dilemma"? Using reliable sources, explain this term, giving examples situations in which a "social dilemma" is involved.
2. *Collaborative or individual activity:* What is your opinion of autonomous cars? Do y believe that their use will be commonplace in the near future? What are some pro lems to be overcome before self-driving cars become feasible on our roads? In grou discuss issues related to autonomous cars, or explore this topic in writing, answeri the above and other related questions.

Abstract

Autonomous vehicles (AVs) should reduce traffic accidents, but they will sometimes have to choose between two evils, such as running over pedestrians or sacrificing themselves and their passenger to save the pedestrians. Defining the algorithms that will help AVs make these moral decisions is a formidable challenge. We found that participants in six Amazon Mechanical Turk studies approved of utilitarian AVs (that is, AVs that sacrifice their passengers for the greater good) and would like others to buy them, but they would themselves prefer to ride in AVs that protect their passengers at all costs. The study participants disapprove of enforcing utilitarian regulations for AVs and would be less willing to buy such an AV. Accordingly, regulating for utilitarian algorithms may paradoxically increase casualties by postponing the adoption of a safer technology.

1 The year 2007 saw the completion of the first benchmark test for autonomous driving in realistic urban environments (1, 2). Since then, autonomous vehicles (AVs) such as Google's self-driving car covered thousands of miles of real-road driving (3). AVs have the potential to benefit the world by increasing traffic efficiency (4), reducing pollution (5), and eliminating up to 90% of traffic accidents (6). Not all crashes will be avoided, though, and some crashes will require AVs to make difficult ethical decisions in cases that

involve unavoidable harm (7). For example, harming several pedestrians by swerving, passerby, or the AV may be faced with the ch its own passenger to save one or more ped

2 Although these scenarios appear u probability events are bound to occur wit on the road. Moreover, even if these situati arise, AV programming must still include an what to do in such hypothetical situations. of decisions need be made well before AV commodity. Distributing harm is a decision considered to fall within the moral domain the algorithms that control AVs will need principles guiding their decisions in situati harm (10). Manufacturers and regulators w plish three potentially incompatible objecti ent, not causing public outrage, and not dis

3 However, pursuing these objectives inconsistencies. Consider, for example, t in Fig. 1A, and assume that the most con tude is that the AV should swerve. This w ian moral doctrine (11), according to whic of action is to minimize casualties. But case displayed in Fig. 1C. The utilitarian c that situation, would be for the AV to swer senger, but AVs programmed to follow thi might discourage buyers who believe their trump other considerations. Even thoug

---

9. Harris J, Pomeranz J, Lobstein T, Brownell KD. A crisis in the marketplace: How food marketing contributes to childhood obesity and what can be done. *Annu Rev Public Health* 2009;30:211–25.

10. Hastings G, McDermott L, Angus K, Stead M, Thomson S. The Extent, Nature and Effects of Food Promotion to Children: A Review of the Evidence. World Health Organization, 2007. Available at: www.who.int/dietphysical activity/publications/Hastings_paper_marketing.pdf (Accessed February 8, 2012).

11. Cecchini M, Sassi F, Lauer JA, Lee YY, Guajardo-Barron V, Chisholm D. Tackling of unhealthy diets, physical inactivity, and obesity: Health effects and cost-effectiveness. *Lancet* 2010;376(9754):1775–84.

12. Siegel M, Doner Lotenberg L. *Marketing Public Health: Strategies to Promote Social Change*, 2nd ed. Sudbury, MA: Jones and Bartlett Publishers, 2007.

13. McLaren L, McIntyre L, Kirkpatrick S. Rose's population strategy of prevention need not increase social inequalities in health. *Int J Epidemiol* 2010;39:372–77.

14. Eikimo TA, Bambra C. The welfare state: A glossary for public health. *J Epidemiol Community Health* 2008; 62:3–6.

15. Elliott C. Marketing fun foods: A profile and analysis of supermarket food messages targeted at children. *Can Public Policy* 2008;34(2):259–73.

16. Editeur officiel du Québec. *Consumer Protection Act.* 1978;248–49.

17. Jeffery B. The Supreme Court of Canada's appraisal of the 1980 ban on advertising to children in Québec: Implications for "misleading" advertising elsewhere. *Loyola of Los Angeles Law Review* 2006;39:237–76.

18. Wilson K. The complexities of multi-level governance in public health. *Can J Public Health* 2004;95(6):409–12.

Key and challenging words

unpalatable, cognizant, coercive, onus, differential, jurisdictional

Questions

1. Briefly discuss the importance of the studies mentioned in paragraph 2 to the authors' purpose.

2. Explain why the authors state that "even a robust evidence base often is not sufficient to ensure the adoption and implementation of specific policies" (paragraph 3).

3. Identify the authors' thesis, and comment on its rhetorical effectiveness; for example, you could consider language, tone, or appeals designed for the essay's audience.

4. Define *upstream* (paragraph 3) and *downstream* (paragraph 4) approaches and explain the difference between them. Try to use context to answer the question before referring to a business dictionary.

5. (a) Discuss the strategies the authors use to aid comprehension in the section "The why: 'Health' may not be the most effective rationale." You could consider organization, rhetorical patterns, transitions, and the like; (b) If you were to divide this long paragraph into three shorter paragraphs, where would you make the separations? Justify your choices and provide headings for each subsection.

6. Analyze the authors' use of precedent and one other argumentative strategy in their essay (see Kinds of Evidence in Argumentative Essays in Chapter 9, p. 105).

7. Analyze the authors' conclusion, keeping in mind the audience they are addressing.

Post-reading

1. As a group lobbying for health interventions for children, use the information and approaches discussed in this essay (along with other sources if appropriate) to create a brief report/presentation. Your audience will

not be health professionals but government representatives in a position to recommend or implement the kinds of interventions discussed in the essay.

High-interest readings offering a diversity of subjects and approaches.

Half of the essays in Part III: The Reader are new to this edition, reflecting the need for topical content in a fast-changing world. The readings continue to be accompanied by pre- and post-reading questions and vocabulary lists. More essays now feature a qualitative method, actively engaging today's students in interpreting the ideas, values, and theories being presented.

Thematic connections among the readings.

Thematic connections among the readings encourage comparative analyses. The many themes include racism, gender, disability, food and nutrition, and technology. Specific topics include political satire, autonomous vehicles, mental wellness in Aboriginal communities, and identity and belonging among Canadian-born children of immigrants.

Annotated sample essays.

Written by students and professional writers, annotated sample essays in the chapters help students to improve their analytical and writing skills.

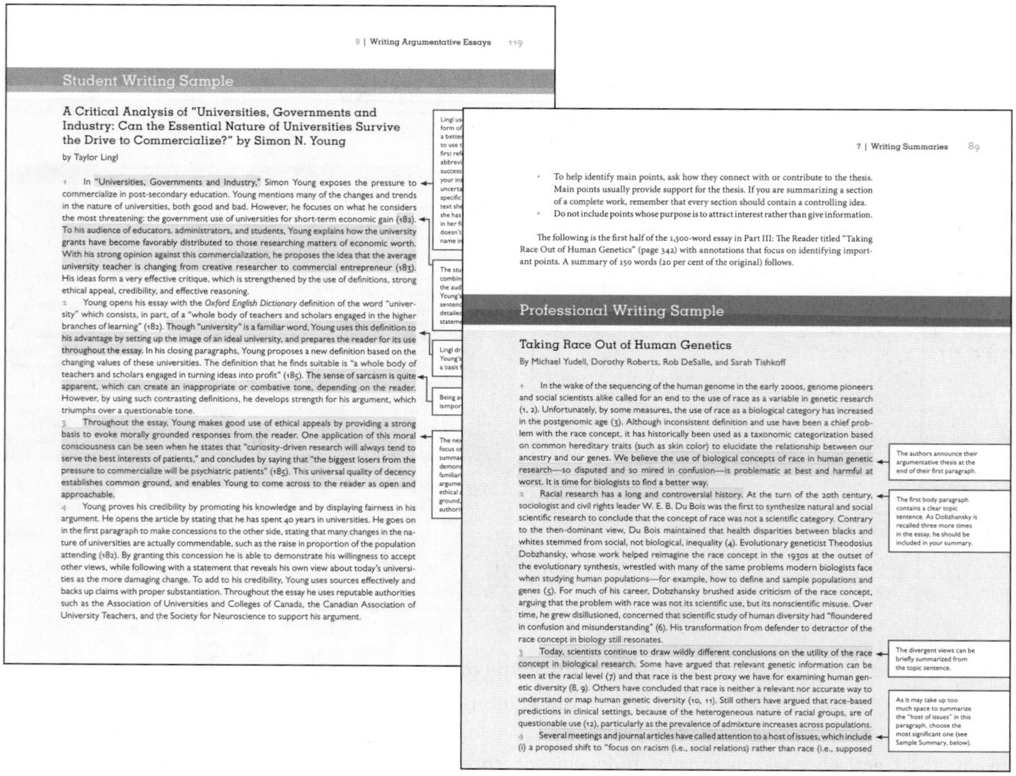

Voices within Canada

Mental Wellness in Canada's Aboriginal Communities: Striving toward Reconciliation

Patricia Boksa, Ridha Joober, and Laurence J. Kirmayer
(2,136 words)

Pre-reading

1. Access the website mentioned in note 1 (see References) in order to obtain an overview of the aims of the Truth and Reconciliation Commission of Canada, along with their reports. (You may have to use links at this site to get this information.)

With the presentation in Ottawa this spring of the report from the Truth and Reconciliation Commission (TRC) of Canada on Indian residential schools, the well-being of Canada's Aboriginal peoples took centre stage for a few days in the media and minds of the Canadian public. The TRC documented key historical issues that have contributed to major mental health disparities in Canada's indigenous population and pointed the way toward a larger process of national reconciliation.¹ Because *JPN* is the official journal of the Canadian College of Neuropsychopharmacology, a Canadian society devoted to understanding mental health and disease, we are taking the opportunity with this editorial to keep the discussion going forward by highlighting the mental wellness of Aboriginal peoples in Canada. We present a brief historical background of some of the factors recognized as contributing to current mental health challenges faced by the Aboriginal population and end with some suggestions on how mental health professionals might contribute to the reconciliation process. Although much of what we discuss in this editorial has been written before, it bears repeating to engage our readers. In addition to their importance in the Canadian context, many of the issues we discuss are relevant to indigenous peoples in other countries.

Historical Overview

Aboriginal people make up about 4% of the current population of Canada and comprise First Nations (60%), Métis (33%) and Inuit peoples (4%). More than half of Aboriginal people live in Canadian cities, with the remainder living largely in rural or remote small communities.

There is substantial cultural diversity among Aboriginal peoples in Canada; for example, First Nations comprise more than 600 major bands speaking 55 different languages from 11 major language groups. Historically, First Nations are derived from peoples with ancient roots in Canada. Ancestors of all First Nations indigenous peoples date back to 13 500 years ago, while archeological records clearly date numerous First Nations settlements in Canada originating as far back as 9000 to 10 000 years. By 500–1000 CE, First Nations peoples had established trade routes across what is now Canada, while the Inuit, descendants of the Thule in Alaska, migrated across the Arctic starting from around 1000 CE.

Starting in the sixteenth century, European colonization had catastrophic effects on the indigenous peoples of North America (for a review, see Kirmayer and colleagues⁴). About 90% of the population died by the mid-1850s due largely to the introduction of infectious diseases, but also due to warfare and forced displacement. Aboriginal persons remaining in Canada were subjected to "civilize," assimilate and eliminate their cultures. The creation of Indian reserves was to confine Aboriginal people to small settlements while appropriating their lands. The locations of these communities were decided by government and commercial interests with the main purpose of freeing more desirable land for the use of European settlers. The *Indian Act* of 1876 formalized the reserve system and made "status" Indians wards of the state, with the federal government financing and imposing structures for band administration, education and health care. The explicit purpose of this legislation was to eliminate indigenous cultures by

---

...l Justice and Social Determinants of Health: Lesbian, Gay, Bisexual, ...sgendered, Intersexed, and Queer Youth in Canada

...rah Dysart-Gale
...words)

Pre-reading

1. Access a support or informational website for LGBTIQ youth, such as the Lesbian Gay Bi Trans Youth Line (http://www.youthline.ca), mentioned in paragraph 18 of this essay, using the "About Us" or similar link. Write a summary of the site's aims and objectives.
2. After scanning the essay, including its headings, and reading the first section, "Nursing, Social Justice, and LGBTIQ," (a) identify the essay's purpose and intended audience; (b) construct a reading hypothesis of three or four sentences in which you include purpose, audience, and other factors relevant to your approach to the essay (see the Reading Hypothesis box in Chapter 5, p. 49).

While nurses address lesbian, gay, bisexual, transsexual, intersexed, and queer (henceforth LGBTIQ) ...' health needs, the professional nursing practice ... social justice provides a larger role for ...ing and minimizing social barriers faced by LGBTIQ ...

...e: This paper examines the social and health-related ...ences of LGBTIQ youth in Canada, a country which ...moved many of the social and legal barriers faced by ... in countries such as the United States. An aware...the Canadian LGBTIQ experience is instructive for ...in different countries, as it reveals both the possibil...d limitations of social legislation that is more inclu-...LGBTIQ youth.

...: Review of literature in PubMed, Academic Search ..., government documents.

...sion: The literature reveals that exclusion, isolation, ...r remain realities for Canadian LGBTIQ adolescents. ...nadian experience suggests that negative social atti-...ward LGBTIQ persist despite progressive legislation. ...The value of social justice positions nurses to constructively intervene in promoting the health and well-being of LGBTIQ youth in the face of social homophobia.

Nursing, Social Justice, and LGBTIQ Youth

Epidemiological evidence has established that lesbian, gay, bisexual, transsexual, intersexed, and questioning queer (henceforth LGBTIQ) youth face greater risks to their health and well-being than do their heterosexual age-mates. Although nurses therefore interact with LGBTIQ youth as patients, the values of professional nursing practice warrant a larger role for nurses beyond the treatment of these patients' medical issues. As articulated by the World Health Organization (WHO) and the American Association of Colleges of Nursing (AACN), the value of social justice obligates nurses to identify and minimize social barriers to health, faced by all vulnerable groups, including young people, especially vulnerable groups such as LGBTIQ youth. Canada, having eliminated many legal barriers faced by the LGBTIQ community in the United States, may serve as a model for a more just society concerning LGBTIQ youth (Elliott & Bonauto, 2005). However, feelings of exclusion, isolation, and fear persist for Canadian LGBTIQ youth despite such legal progress (Commission des Droits de la Personne et des Droits de la Jeunesse du Québec [Commission of the Rights of the Person and Rights of Youth of Quebec], 2007), as legislative acceptance of the civil and human rights of

---

Student Writing Sample

A Critical Analysis of "Universities, Governments and Industry: Can the Essential Nature of Universities Survive the Drive to Commercialize?" by Simon N. Young

by Taylor Lingl

1   In "Universities, Governments and Industry," Simon Young exposes the pressure to commercialize in post-secondary education. Young mentions many of the changes and trends in the nature of universities, both good and bad. However, he focuses on what he considers the most threatening: the government use of universities for short-term economic gain (182). To his audience of educators, administrators, and students, Young explains how the university is changing. With his strong opinion about this commercialization, he proposes the idea that the average university teacher is changing from creative researcher to commercial entrepreneur (183). His ideas form a very effective critique, which is strengthened by the use of definitions, strong ethical appeal, credibility, and effective reasoning.

2   Young opens his essay with the *Oxford English Dictionary* definition of the word "university" which consists, in part, of a "whole body of teachers and scholars engaged in the higher branches of learning" (182). Though "university" is a familiar word, Young uses this definition to his advantage by setting up the image of an ideal university, and prepares the reader for its use throughout the essay. In his closing paragraphs, Young proposes a new definition based on the changing values of these universities. The definition that he finds suitable is "a whole body of teachers and scholars engaged in turning ideas into profit" (185). The sense of sarcasm is quite apparent, which can create an inappropriate or combative tone, depending on the reader. However, by using such contrasting definitions, he develops strength for his argument, which triumphs over a questionable tone.

3   Throughout the essay, Young makes good use of ethical appeals by providing a strong basis to evoke morally grounded responses from the reader. One application of this moral consciousness can be seen when he states that "curiosity-driven research will always tend to serve the best interests of patients," and concludes by saying that "the biggest losers from the pressure to commercialize will be psychiatric patients" (185). This universal quality of decency establishes common ground, and enables Young to come across to the reader as open and approachable.

4   Young proves his credibility by promoting his knowledge and by displaying fairness in his argument. He opens the article by stating that he has spent 40 years in universities. He goes on in the first paragraph to make concessions to the other side, stating that many changes in the nature of universities are actually commendable, such as the raise in proportion of the population attending (182). By granting this concession he is able to demonstrate his willingness to accept other views, while following this with a statement that reveals his own view about today's universities as the more damaging change. To add to his credibility, Young uses sources effectively and backs up claims with proper substantiation. Throughout the essay he uses reputable authorities such as the Association of Universities and Colleges of Canada, the Canadian Association of University Teachers, and the Society for Neuroscience to support his argument.

- To help identify main points, ask how they connect with or contribute to the thesis. Main points usually provide support for the thesis. If you are summarizing a section of a complete work, remember that every section should contain a controlling idea.
- Do not include points whose purpose is to attract interest rather than give information.

The following is the first half of the 1,500-word essay in Part III: The Reader titled "Taking Race Out of Human Genetics" (page 342) with annotations that focus on identifying important points. A summary of 150 words (20 per cent of the original) follows.

Professional Writing Sample

Taking Race Out of Human Genetics

By Michael Yudell, Dorothy Roberts, Rob DeSalle, and Sarah Tishkoff

1   In the wake of the sequencing of the human genome in the early 2000s, genome pioneers and social scientists alike called for an end to the use of race as a variable in genetic research (1, 2). Unfortunately, by some measures, the use of race as a biological category has increased in the postgenomic age (3). Although inconsistent definition and use have been a chief problem with the race concept, it has historically been used as a taxonomic categorization based on common hereditary traits (such as skin color) to elucidate the relationship between our ancestry and our genes. We believe the use of biological concepts of race in human genetic research—so disputed and so mired in confusion—is problematic at best and harmful at worst. It is time for biologists to find a better way.

2   Racial research has a long and controversial history. At the turn of the 20th century, sociologist and civil rights leader W. E. B. Du Bois was the first to synthesize natural and social scientific research to conclude that the concept of race was not a scientific category. Contrary to the then-dominant view, Du Bois maintained that health disparities between blacks and whites stemmed from social, not biological, inequality (4). Evolutionary geneticist Theodosius Dobzhansky, whose work helped reimagine the race concept in the 1930s at the outset of the evolutionary synthesis, wrestled with many of the same problems modern biologists face when studying human populations—for example, how to define and sample populations and genes (5). For much of his career, Dobzhansky brushed aside criticism of the race concept, arguing that the problem with race was not its scientific use, but its nonscientific misuse. Over time, he grew disillusioned, concerned that scientific study of human diversity had "floundered in confusion and misunderstanding" (6). His transformation from defender to detractor of the race concept in biology still resonates.

3   Today, scientists continue to draw wildly different conclusions on the utility of the race concept in biological research. Some have argued that relevant genetic information can be seen at the racial level (7) and that race is the best proxy for examining human genetic diversity (8, 9). Others have concluded that race is neither a relevant nor accurate way to understand or map human genetic diversity (10, 11). Still others have argued that race-based predictions in clinical settings, because of the heterogeneous nature of racial groups, are of questionable use (12), particularly as the prevalence of admixture increases across populations.

4   Several meetings and journal articles have called attention to a host of issues, which include (i) a proposed shift to "focus on racism (i.e., social relations) rather than race (i.e., supposed

The authors announce their argumentative thesis at the end of their first paragraph.

The first body paragraph contains a clear topic sentence. As Dobzhansky is recalled three more times in the essay, he should be included in your summary.

The divergent views can be briefly summarized from the topic sentence.

As it may take up too much space to summarize the "host of issues" in this paragraph, choose the most significant one (see Sample Summary, below).

Updated coverage of documentation styles, now with colour coding.

The coverage of MLA, APA, and CMS documentation styles has been updated to include the most recent guidelines and more commentary (Chapter 10). The documentation section now also features colour coding of in-text and reference citations to help students recognize their common elements, assisting with their documentation process.

Active Voice essays.

Active Voice boxes contain mini-essays written by professors and students to explore practical topics, such as the aims and goals of report writing, how to develop research skills, and how to quote from the works of others.

Sample page 144

144   PART II | Academic Writing

Many of the distinguishing features of the styles are given below. Exam... common bibliographic formats are then provided.

signal phrase
Introduces a reference by naming the author(s) and usually includes a "signal verb" (e.g., states, argues, explains).

Note: A *signal phrase* names the author before the reference is given; APA styles, the parenthetical citation will not include the author's name if a ... cedes it.

Electronic formats in all styles should be cited using what information ... author's name is not given, use the name of the organization or sponsoring ... If there is no sponsor, use the work's title alphabetized by the first major ... number or section heading can sometimes be used to identify location, if ... page numbers are absent.

MLA (Modern Language Association) Style

- MLA uses an "author/number" referencing format. The basic par... includes author's last name and page number with no punctuation ...

  (Slotkin 75)
  (Rusel and Wilson 122)

- If a signal phrase is used, only the page number will be in parenthe...

  Slotkin states, ". . ." (75)

- For sources with two authors, give last names of both authors with "... three or more, give last name of first author followed by "et al."
- Block quotations should be used for important passages at least four ... They are indented 10 spaces from the left margin, double-spaced, a... quotation marks. The end period precedes the parenthetical citatio...
- The final page, titled "Works Cited," alphabetically lists by auth... works used in the essay. Entries are double-spaced with the first l... flush left and successive lines indented one-half inch (1.25 cm). A... titles begin with a capital letter. Titles of books and journals are ... titles of shorter works (such as articles or chapters) contained in l... in quotation marks.

MLA Sample Formats

Book (one author)

Begin with the author's last name and given name(s) followed by the title i... with publisher and publication year; you do not need to include publicatio... publisher (which is Transaction in the following example).

Berger, Arthur Asa. *Video Games: A Popular Culture P...*
Transaction, 2002.

Author   *Title*   Publication information   Electronic sou...

Sample page 146

146   PART II | Academic Writing

Website

The non-academic article was found online and includes the online publication date. The date when you accessed the site is optional, but can be included if no publication date is given or if required by your instructor.

Zhou, Steven. "Canada at 150: Is Common Decency the New Bar for National Pride?" cbc News, 6 May 2017, www.cbc.ca/news/canada/manitoba/canada-immigration-refugees-common-decency-1.4101913.

Video Post

In the following example, the first date in the entry refers to the year this play was published, while the second date is that of the upload. The first date is optional unless it will be helpful for a reader.

Synge, J. M. *Playboy of the Western World*. 1907. YouTube, uploaded by Brattleboro Community TV, 22 Nov. 2014, www.youtube.com/watch?v=tV_kYBeTatM.

Motion Picture (Film)/TV Episode

Begin with the film's title unless specific performers, director, etc. are stressed in your essay, in which case, you would begin with the relevant person's last name.

Alien: Covenant. Directed by Ridley Scott, Twentieth Century Fox, 2017.

For a TV episode, begin with the episode's name (in quotation marks), followed by the series name (italicized), and season and episode number. If the movie/episode were viewed on a network, this name is italicized and is followed by a comma and the location.

"The Mother Line." *The Honourable Woman*, season 1, episode 6, Sundance TV, 4 Sept. 2014. *Netflix*, www.netflix.com/ca/title/80018058.

APA (American Psychological Association) Style

- APA uses an author–year referencing format. One basic format includes author's last name and year of publication (general references and broad summaries); the other basic format also includes page number (direct quotations, paraphrases, and summaries of specific passages).
- Commas separate author's name from year, and year from page number (if required); "p." or "pp." (for more than one page) precedes page number(s):

  (Hassan et al., 2012, p. 224)
  (Bryson & de Castell, 1998, pp. 542–544)

- If a signal phrase is used, the year will follow the author's name in parentheses:

  Hassan et al. (2012) explore the longer-term effects of video games.

Author   *Title*   Publication information   Electronic source

---

Sample page 128

128   PART II | Academic Writing

The Active Voice

A Beginner's Guide to Research in the Academic Library

1   The twenty-first-century academic library can seem overwhelming to the undergraduate researcher. In addition to the traditional materials found in the library's online catalogue, there are numerous other electronic resources available, including databases, journals, and e-books, as well as other digital formats and media. The sheer volume of information resources in today's academic library need not be intimidating. On the contrary, an effective research strategy will enable you to take full advantage of all the wealth of print and electronic information resources available to you.

2   An effective strategy should include three important considerations:

1. Your *research topic*
2. The *information resources* most relevant to your topic
3. The *search strategy* you will use to obtain and retain information from those resources

3   When you understand how to choose a well-defined research topic, where to look for information on that topic, and how to construct an effective search in an academic library catalogue or database, you will have the basic tools required for most research projects at the first-year level. As you become a more confident researcher, you can expand on these basic skills and strategies by exploring more specialized resources and experimenting with advanced search methods.

The Research Topic

4   The starting point for your research will be your topic. When choosing your own topic, make sure to select one that is neither too broad nor too narrow. If your topic is too broad, you will have difficulty focusing your research and writing. Conversely, if your topic is too narrow or obscure, you may not be able to find

enough relevant information to support your re... question.

5   For instance, you may want to write about ... lessness or the homeless. It would be difficult to ... focused paper on such a broad topic. To narro... focus, you might want to research homelessness i... ticular age group, such as teenagers. However, thi... further by looking at particular health problems of ... less teens or risk factors associated with homeless... teens, such as poverty, addiction, or abuse.

Selecting Resources for Your Research Topic

6   Subject or Research Guides: Once you ha... cided on a research topic, you must choose your r... ces. The academic library is your ultimate destina... a diversity of scholarly and non-scholarly sources... academic libraries provide subject or research gu... their website. These guides are prepared by sub... brarians with specialized knowledge in the infor... resources of their particular subject areas. Most ... guides provide direct links to relevant online dat... scholarly websites, and primary source materials ... subject, as well as valuable information on referen... sources such as dictionaries, encyclopedias, biogr... and bibliographies, including subject headings a... number ranges.

7   Primary and Secondary Sources: Your re... may require that you investigate both primary a... ondary source information. The meaning of prim... secondary sources can vary across the disciplin... in the humanities and social sciences, primary s... generally provide *first-hand* information or dat... may include primary works such as autobiogr... interviews, speeches, letters, diaries, unpublish... scripts, data sources, government records, newsp...

Sample page 137

10 | Writing Research Papers   137

Summary: Because of the greater demands of university, compared to earlier schooling, students with add may not have to confront their disorder until university.

mixed format
A method of source integration in which you combine significant words of the source, placed in quotation marks, with your own words.

In a **mixed format**, you combine summary or paraphrase with direct quotation. Effective use of mixed format demonstrates both your understanding and your polished writing skills since it requires you to seamlessly integrate the language of the source with your own language. You can use this format when you want to cite part of an important passage in which key words or phrases occur, carefully choosing the significant words and excluding the less important parts.

Integrating Quotations

When you incorporate direct quotations into your essay, you must do so grammatically and smoothly; you must also provide adequate context for your reader. The following shows a poorly integrated quotation and its well-integrated alternative:

An unloving parent–child relationship can be characterized as "unaccepted, unacknowledged, or unloved" (Haworth-Hoeppner 216).

Well-integrated: An unloving parent–child relationship exists when the child feels "unaccepted, unacknowledged, or unloved" (Haworth-Hoeppner 216).

The Active Voice

To Quote or Not to Quote?: Strategies for Effectively Using the Words of Other Writers in Your Writing

1   Students are often given warnings about using quotations in academic essays. You may have received feedback such as "you are relying too much on quotations" or "quote only when necessary" and, as a result, be tempted not to quote at all.

2   However, the quickest glance at published essays will demonstrate that including direct quotations from other sources is standard academic practice. Writing handbooks and websites often provide practical advice about how to integrate quotations into your writing. But as a writer new to the conventions of academic discourse, you may be more concerned about choosing when to

quote, or not to quote, than with the practical details of how to do so.

3   As a starting point, it is worth considering why academic writers include the ideas and words of other writers in their writing. Remember that you are not writing in a vacuum: you are placing your ideas in the context of experts in the field and engaging in a form of indirect conversation with them. By including quotations or paraphrasing—hence, summarizing the ideas of others—you demonstrate that you have carried out relevant research and that you understand important issues or theories relevant to your points. Used judiciously,

Continued

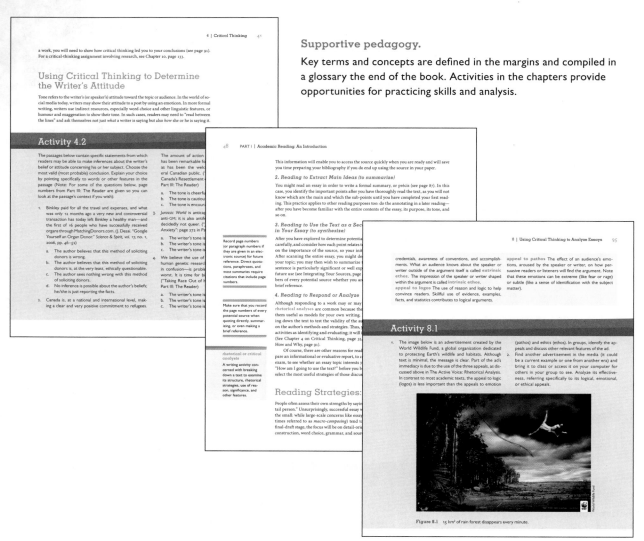

Supportive pedagogy.

Key terms and concepts are defined in the margins and compiled in a glossary the end of the book. Activities in the chapters provide opportunities for practicing skills and analysis.

Online Resources

For Instructors

- An instructor's manual provides answer keys to activities in Parts I and II of the book, and to the post-reading questions of selected readings in Part III: The Reader.

- PowerPoint slides are available for each chapter.

For Students

A student study guide includes chapter summaries, key terms, interactive chapter quizzes, and a list of suggested resources to support the readings in Part III: The Reader.

COMPANION WEBSITE

Eric Henderson

The Active Reader: Strategies for Academic Reading and Writing, Fourth Edition

ISBN 13: 9780199025923

Inspection copy request

Ordering information

Contact & Comments

About the Book

The Active Reader: Strategies for Academic Reading and Writing is a writing guide and reader designed to give students a practical, integrated approach to reading and writing at the university level. Part I explores academic reading, introducing students to the conventions of academic discourse, critical thinking, and reading strategies. Part II focuses on academic writing, beginning with the fundamentals of academic essay writing, followed by discussion of how to write reports, critical analyses, summaries, argumentative essays, and research papers. Part III is a reader comprised of 32 readings from various disciplines, organized into six thematic sections.

Instructor Resources

You need a password to access these resources. Please contact your local Sales and Editorial Representative for more information.

Student Resources

 www.oupcanada.com/Active4e

Preface

When preparing the Preface of the first edition of *The Active Reader*, I applied the term "new realist" to the student of that day. Some ten years later, I think the term is equally applicable to most of the students in my academic reading and writing courses. To this, I can add the quality of "earnestness," a determined commitment to confront underlying causes of our problems today and, in many cases, acknowledge human responsibility. Certainly, most students today are well aware of the challenges that their generation and future ones face. They also understand the role that communication, especially written communication, will play in meeting these challenges. This book was designed in response to the need both for problem-solvers and for good communicators, the two faces of today's (and tomorrow's) realists.

One of the reasons for studying the conventions of academic reading and writing is to direct the human need to explore and learn, to express and create, to discuss and debate, in writing, into useful and fulfilling channels. Although the immediate result might be a level of competence that will help students in their other courses and lead to improved grades, the acquisition of writing and reading skills serves many long-term goals. Language is one of the most powerful resources for ensuring our survival as individuals, as a society, and as a species. Through the medium of language, we can read about contemporary problems, ask a range of pertinent questions, and propose practical solutions to these problems. *The Active Reader: Strategies for Academic Reading and Writing* seeks to provide student readers, writers, and researchers with the tools to question, investigate, analyze, and communicate.

For the Fourth Edition

This edition includes several necessary adaptations of the previous ones, although selection criteria have remained the same: essays of high interest, relevance, and accessibility to today's student have been chosen.

The number of academic essays has been increased from the third edition, although non-academic essays continue to fulfill an important function by engaging students while illustrating the contrastive conventions of non-academic prose. This edition gives equal weight to four different kinds of academic essays, reflecting different purposes, formats, and styles: humanities essays that analyze texts; empirical studies that involve an experiment or survey; critical review essays; and editorial/argumentative essays. The humanities essay encourages the close reading (or viewing) of texts and stimulates critical thinking. The empirical study provides an apt model for science, business, and other students, who will be writing up reports, lab experiments and the like, while the critical review essay bears many similarities to the student research paper, in which students locate sources on a topic, organize them logically, and evaluate their contribution, forming conclusions or answering questions posed in their introductions.

In a world that seems, to some, increasingly beset by shrill rhetoric and biased opinion, studying reason-based arguments can greatly enhance critical thinking and thoughtful debate. Like student writers, academic writers often have opinions on the topics they investigate, and may stress their study's importance while making recommendations based on their findings. By studying the essays in Part III, students should find assurance that scholarly writing is a place for informed discussion and even enlivened debate, thus providing an efficacious model for argumentation.

The 32 readings, all published in journals or books, are divided into six categories of interest to today's students: "University Issues," "Canada in the World," "Voices within Canada," "Media and Image," "Society of Excess?", and "Intersections with Science." They embrace diverse disciplines, from economics to environmental studies, history to health sciences. The essays are integrated with a well-developed rhetoric—10 chapters covering the conventions of academic writing and reading, critical thinking, summarizing, argumentation, and writing rhetorical analyses and research papers. Plentiful examples from student writing, many of which include explanatory comments, illustrate the material covered.

Thematic links among several essays encourage comparative analyses. For example, the four essays between pages 207 and 303, along with an annotated essay on page 120 in Chapter 9, comprise a complete thematic unit on food production, consumption, and waste, showing diverse purposes and formats within a common topic.

Using many resources to assist in comprehension, *The Active Reader* actively challenges the stereotype that academic writing is dry and inaccessible to students today. The pages that follow will fully equip students to successfully read and write about challenging texts, the kinds of texts they will often be called on to read, understand, and model in many of their assignments.

As in previous editions, "The Active Voice" boxes provide informative essays by instructors, writing professionals, and students (see below) that alert readers to issues of practical concern today—from developing research skills to the challenges of report and online writing. Some of these essays flow seamlessly from the text, while others elaborate on or demonstrate the application of a point mentioned in the text. Many can be treated as mini-essays that can be discussed and analyzed.

The Active Voice

Homelessness 101

1   In a busy city, many people become so immersed in their daily routines and problems that they are unaware of their own surroundings. Most do not notice the many homeless people living on the streets and simply carry on with their day as if they didn't exist. In my final year of high school, I was able to participate in a unique and truly meaningful experience that allowed me to spend a day with the homeless people of Vancouver. My classmates

and I set up a "free-market" at Oppenheimer Park, an area inhabited by many of the homeless. We handed out donated clothing, toiletries, and household items, as well as holding a free barbeque where we served hot dogs. The most memorable experience, however, was playing soccer against a team of homeless people. Through the experience I learned that not all the homeless are "druggies" and that they are not scary or intimidating. Mostly, I learned the importance of acceptance and of giving back.

2   The term "homeless" instantly evokes many stereotypes, the most common of which is that homeless people all suffer from addictions or drug-related problems. Through my experience at the free-market, I learned that this is not true. Although many of them, unfortunately, have serious addictions, I met others who were homeless for different reasons. For instance, Devon is a woman in her twenties who ran away from an abusive family. She didn't have a job and was temporarily forced to live on her own on the streets. Luis came from Mexico with very little money and no place to live. Not everyone understands that drugs do not play a role in all their lives—many have never even done drugs before.

3   Second, I learned that the homeless are not scary or hard to approach. When playing soccer with the homeless team, we all had a great time. Not only were they much better than we were at the game, but they were also extremely friendly and fun to compete against. After the game, I struck up a conversation with a member of the victorious team. He told me he was an ex-Hell's Angel, which initially made me somewhat timid; however, during our conversation, I became aware how intelligent he was and how easy he was to talk to. I learned that it really is worth striking up a conversation with people living on the streets and hearing their stories.

4   Last, I learned the importance of giving back. It was an amazing feeling to see somebody pick up one of the shirts I donated and the smile on her face as she tried it on. Seeing the homeless competing as a team and showing off their considerable skills also showed me that we all have hidden talents that can be put to good use, that we are really all one community. Many people pass homeless people downtown on their way to work, trying to avoid eye contact or acknowledging them in any way. It is important to remember how lucky we are to live in a warm house with food and to remember to give back to the less fortunate—even if it means just giving them a smile to show you know they are there.

5   That day gave me an entirely new perspective on homeless people. By talking and engaging in a game with them, it became evident that there is nothing wrong with them; they just need our support. I found them approachable and their stories interesting. Mostly, I learned how important it is to help those in need. It was a unique and rewarding experience that opened me to a new world.

—**Ilona Mihalik**, first-year student

Acknowledgements

I wish to gratefully acknowledge the editorial staff at Oxford University Press Canada for their enthusiasm and expertise. I would particularly like to thank Leah-Ann Lymer, my helpful and patient developmental editor, for charting the course of the new edition; Heather Macdougall for her precise and expert copyediting; Steven Hall for making the proofing and production stages virtually frustration free; and Jodi Lewchuk for her ongoing support.

I much appreciate the help of my colleagues at the University of Victoria. I am especially indebted to Monika Rydygier Smith, who has contributed to all editions in numberless ways. I am grateful to suggestions and other input from Heidi Darroch, Brian Day, Rebecca Gagan, Sean Henry, Kylee-Ann Hingston, Brock MacLeod, Kim McLean-Fiander, Andrew Murray, and Harb Sanghara.

I am indebted to the generosity of those individuals who took the time to write new essays or update their original contributions for the fourth edition: Suzanne James, Erin Kelly, David Leach, Justin Harrison, and Dennis R. Nighswonger. All "Active Voice" contributors have enlarged the scope of this book significantly, imbuing it with their knowledge of and passion for their subject.

I would like to thank the named and anonymous reviewers who offered valuable feedback that helped to shape this and previous editions:

- Wisdom Agorde, MacEwan University
- Karin Collins, University of Winnipeg
- Frances Condon, University of Waterloo
- Rhiannon Don, Nipissing University
- Theresa Hyland, Huron University College
- Suzanne James, University of British Columbia
- Betsy Keating, University of Windsor
- Nicole Klan, Vancouver Island University
- Dennis R. Nighswonger, Lakehead University
- Cindy Soldan, Lakehead University
- Abdollah Zahiri, Seneca College

From its inception to the completion of the fourth edition, *The Active Reader: Strategies for Academic Reading and Writing* has been rooted in my teaching life at UVic, particularly the teaching of academic reading and writing to first-year students. I am indebted to the many students who allowed their writing to be represented in this book.

Above all, Madeline Sonik has been a constant and sustaining presence in my life, in which the aspirations for and planning of this book occupy a small—but vital—part.

Eric Henderson
November 2017

PART I

Academic Reading: An Introduction

As students, you will be introduced to many different kinds of writing during your post-secondary education. Your goal usually is to interact with these texts in various ways, such as the following:

- discuss the issues they raise with your classmates
- respond to them in writing, agreeing or disagreeing with the argument
- learn the ways they are put together and/or the rhetorical strategies used
- acquire the specialized knowledge they contain or become familiar with the procedures through which this knowledge can be acquired
- refer to their findings as part of a research project
- use them as models for your own writing, perhaps in preparation for other undergraduate courses

As you proceed in your program of study, the nature of this interaction will likely increase in complexity. New skill acquisition invites new challenges. By rising to these challenges early in your university career, you will be better prepared for the discipline-specific reading and writing challenges that lie ahead. Inevitably, some of these challenges will present themselves as academic readings, researched and documented essays by experts who seek to advance knowledge in their discipline. Part I is designed to help you interact with these essays.

Chapters 1 and 2 introduce the kinds of reading tasks you perform at the post-secondary level. They attempt to answer the questions, What can you expect when you read academic essays? Who are they written for and how are they written? In what ways is academic writing a distinct genre with its own rules and procedures? What do academic readings across the disciplines have in common?

In Chapter 3 we consider three distinct formats of academic essays. What can you look for when you read a humanities essay? How does a typical essay in the humanities differ from one in the social sciences or the sciences?

Of course, reading academic prose involves much more than identifying its main features and where to find them. Chapters 4 and 5 highlight the unique engagement between writers and readers of academic texts and the strategies that can enhance this engagement. Chapter 4 focuses on applying critical-thinking skills to academic reading. Although we exercise critical thinking in many everyday activities, the complex and diverse nature of academic writing requires us to be conscious of critical thinking before, during, and after reading academic texts. Chapter 5 is designed to help you understand challenging essays: to become familiar with their rules and procedures and to use them in practical ways throughout your university career. Questions addressed include, What kinds of thinking does academic reading require of you? What kinds of reading skills are required? What specific strategies can you use to make the reading process easier, increase comprehension, and develop the skills to analyze the text?

1 An Introduction to Academic Prose

What Is Academic Writing?

What is meant by *academic writing*? The answer depends on who is doing the writing (and the reading).

1. Academic writing can refer to the practices of scholars and researchers, the nature of the texts that you will be asked to read in many of your classes.
2. For students, academic writing could be considered writing at a level that demonstrates your literacy through clear, precise, and grammatical prose and that successfully conveys your ideas through appropriate structures and the use of critical thinking—in short, writing at the university level.

In Part I, we will be addressing the first meaning, while in Part II, we will be addressing the second one.

Collaborative Exercise 1.1

Defining Academic Writing

In groups of three, expand on the first definition of academic writing, incorporating any other features you believe are important. Your completed definition should be two sentences. Compare your group's definition with that of other groups.

Like most other writing, academic writing has a distinct purpose, in this case, to advance knowledge in a discipline. It is also intended for a specific audience: knowledgeable and interested readers. In most kinds of writing, including the kinds you will do in many of your courses, **purpose** and **audience** are two key variables that you must consider before you begin.

In order to be prepared for the kinds of sophisticated reading tasks that lie ahead, you need to become acquainted with academic discourse: its conventions and vocabulary, as well as the critical-thinking skills that enable you to respond fully to its challenges.

What Are Conventions?

You can think of conventions (the word means "come together") as a set of instructions. **Conventions** are recurrent patterns that direct and organize the behaviour of specific groups of people. One reason we follow conventions is to help us communicate with one another. For example, it is a convention in some cultures to bow when being introduced to a stranger or simple acquaintance, or to shake hands.

Academic writing also has its conventions, which help direct the reader and organize the essay, opening up a channel of communication between writer and reader. The next section focuses on general information applicable to most academic writing. We will discuss the conventions of academic writing closely in Chapter 2.

General Features of Academic Writing

Knowledge across the Disciplines

Although academic writing is generally written for knowledgeable readers, knowledge itself differs somewhat across the disciplines, as the following definitions suggest. (See Chapter 9 for more information on which research methods and procedures are best suited to the various disciplines.)

- *Humanities:* The branch of knowledge concerned with examining the ways that humans express and represent themselves. Humanities writing focuses on how ideas and values are used to interpret human experience, analyzing primary sources to draw conclusions about their literary themes, language, art and culture, historical significance, theoretical basis, or universality. Typical humanities disciplines are classical studies, history, linguistics, literature, modern languages, Native studies, philosophy, and religious studies, among others.
- *Social sciences:* The branch of knowledge concerned with the study of human behaviour within a well-defined order or system (e.g., society, human mind, economics, political system). Social science disciplines include anthropology, economics, geography, political science, psychology, and sociology, among others.
- *Sciences:* The branch of knowledge concerned with the study of natural phenomena using empirical methods to determine or validate their laws. The natural and applied sciences include biology, chemistry, engineering, environmental sciences, health sciences, mathematics, and many more.

purpose

Why you are writing; variables affecting purpose include your topic and your audience.

audience

Whom you are writing to: includes one or more readers with common interests, knowledge level, and/or expectations.

conventions

Recurrent patterns that direct and organize the behaviour of specific groups of people and that, applied appropriately, help us communicate with our audience.

The Active Voice

Why Study the Humanities?

1 Today's students are under a lot of pressure from many sources to attain a "useful" post-secondary degree. According to many media commentators, and some governments, the so-called useful areas of study could include science, technology, engineering, and mathematics (the STEM fields). Government funding often goes to enhance these programs so that more students can study them. But it is a mistake to ignore the value of the humanities—which traditionally includes languages (modern, classical, and linguistics), literature, philosophy, and history. There are two arguments I want to present.

2 The first is that studying in the humanities results in a knowledge and skill set that is valuable in many ways. Students will acquire the so-called soft skills of analytical reading, writing, and thinking which, as it turns out, are valued by many employers. John Manley (former deputy prime minister of Canada, and now leader of the Business Council of Canada) reports on the results of a survey of 100 leading companies which indicate the skills employers are looking for in new hires: (1) people skills, (2) communication, (3) problem-solving, (4) analytic abilities, (5) leadership, and, clocking in at (6), industry-specific skills. And these are the skills which will get you promoted in a job as well. These humanities skills, then, are good both for your job and for broader life satisfaction. We need to remember that so much of our life is outside of our jobs. In order to be an engaged citizen in today's complex world, we need to know the historical, cultural, and social contexts of current events. It is a reality that students today are much more likely to have multiple careers than youth in past generations. The key to success in such a world is flexibility. And that is where the notion of utility which I referred to earlier comes in. There is a temptation to assume that specific skills are useful: computer-assisted drafting, arc welding. But some skills run the risk of becoming obsolete: 35-mm film projection, carburetor repair. In the humanities, you learn how to learn, how to solve problems, how to analyze data, and how to work in teams. These are skills which are useful in many contexts. Utility is a slippery notion, indeed.

3 It's true that our graduates probably will not get jobs with titles like historian or philosopher, but if that was the logic behind our actions, why would we go to the gym or take a yoga class? We are unlikely to become professional lifters or stretchers. Nonetheless, the activity will enhance the quality of our lives. Similarly, humanities students will get jobs that draw on their knowledge and skills and allow them to acquire new knowledge and new skills which will, in turn, advance them up the job ladder while enriching them materially, cognitively, and spiritually.

4 My second argument is that the students themselves actually speak to the value of humanities: they vote with their feet and with their words. Over the past 50 years, the proportion of people studying the humanities as a percentage of population has remained quite constant (about 4 per cent of the population). Demand is not falling. At time of writing, the humanities students at my university have the highest high-school admission average of any faculty (that is to say, they have lots of choices but choose us), our first-year course enrolments are up, and our student body is the size of a small city—about the size of many small universities or colleges in North America. These are not members of some lost generation who slip thought the cracks and end up in the safety net of humanities. About 90 per cent of our fourth-year students say that if they had it all to do over again, they would choose the same program. So, students are coming, they like what they get, and they would do it all again. Who are we not to listen to the voices of our students?

5 By studying the humanities, you will discover the person you can become. The person you become will determine the world you live in.

References

Manley, John. "Jobs, Skills and Opportunities: Strengthening Canada's Human Capital Advantage." Notes for remarks by the Honourable John Manley, President and CEO Canadian Council of Chief Executives (now called the Business Council of Canada). Presented at the Canadian Club of Toronto. 28 November 2013.

—**Dr. John Archibald**, Professor of Philosophy, University of Victoria

Audience: Who Reads Academic Writing?

It will come as no surprise that the largest audience for academic writing is scholars, people with knowledge about and interest in a particular topic. However, not all writing in academic books and journals is intended for the same audience. The expert in cell biology will not necessarily be familiar with the same terms as the expert in theoretical physics. The biologist may read the academic journal *Cell* while the physicist may read every issue of *Communications in Mathematical Physics*. Yet both may read scientific journals like *Nature* or *Science* that publish articles of interest in the broad field of science and the social sciences, as well as the results of research. Academic journals and many academic presses vary in their readership, from highly knowledgeable readers to those with a general knowledge.

One way of gauging the intended audience is to note what criteria are used to determine the suitability of an article for publication. The most reliable academic journals are **peer-reviewed** (refereed). (See below, Where Academic Writing Is Found, for different categories of journals and magazines.) The aims of academic publications are summarized by John Fraser, a well-known journalist and educator:

peer-reviewed journal

A type of journal in which submissions are reviewed by experts before publication, an authoritative source for scholarly research.

> [T]he best academic publications extend our understanding of who we are in ways that trade publications and magazines and newspapers have largely abandoned. Canada's collective memory, our understanding of our social and economic conditions, aboriginal challenges to national complacency, the actual consequences of de-linking ourselves from the realities of our past . . . all find provocative and highly useful resonances from our academic publishers.
>
> —J. Fraser, "Academic Publishers Teach Mainstream Ones a Lesson,"
> *The Globe and Mail* 4 June 2005: F9.

In non–peer-reviewed journals, authors may summarize and rewrite technical prose for interested but not highly knowledgeable readers. Such journals are not usually considered academic: their stress is less on original research and more on making this research accessible to the non-specialist. However, they are different from consumer-type magazines in which writers must often adopt strategies to attract and maintain the interest of a general reader.

The Purposes of Academic Writing

The most obvious function of academic journals, particularly those in the social sciences and sciences, is to publish the results of experiments. However, many articles in humanities journals refer to previous studies and interpret them in light of a specific theory or framework. Still others review what is currently known about a particular topic, summarizing what has been written to date and its significance.

These distinctions suggest three basic kinds of academic texts:

1. those that present the results of original research
2. those that build on existing research, offering new interpretations
3. those that review and analyze the current state of knowledge about a topic (see Chapter 3)

An Exchange of Ideas

Academic writing operates as a shared or "open" system, *a medium for the exchange of ideas among experts*, in order to explore an idea, concept, or text; to answer an important question; to test a hypothesis; or to solve a problem. In spite of the occasional inconsistencies in results and disagreements among experts, it is this common objective—to help us better understand ourselves and our world—that unites those working in specialized fields. This objective undermines the stereotype of the "isolated scholar." Scholars, especially those involved in experimentation, seldom work alone. More often, they work in collaborative teams in which a breakdown in communication or a lack of co-operation could endanger the experiment's validity and damage their own credibility.

Analysis, Synthesis, and Academic Writing

Analysis

Another basic feature of academic writing is the emphasis on **analysis**. When you analyze, you "loosen [something] up." Analysis can be applied to all the disciplines: an earth scientist may literally "loosen up," or break down, the constituents of a soil sample to determine the concentration of its elements, while a nuclear physicist may study the behaviour of sub-atomic particles in a particle accelerator as they reach very high speeds and begin to break down into smaller units. A literary analysis could involve breaking down a poem's stanzas or a novel's narrative to study smaller units, such as metre (in a poem) or point of view (in fiction).

Analysis can serve several functions. Thus, there are various ways that an analysis can proceed:

- by attention to detail (description)
- by applying a timeline to events (chronology)
- by comparing and contrasting
- by dividing and subdividing a whole (division and classification)
- by looking at the pros and cons of something

There are many other methods as well (see Rhetorical Patterns and Paragraph Development, page 77).

Synthesis

Academic writers do not just break down; they also synthesize. **Synthesis** is the act of "putting together." The writer(s) of a scientific experiment presents the raw data that emerged in the study of a particular phenomenon. However, the data alone lack relevance until placed within a larger context—the hypothesis that the experiment was intended to test, for example, or results from similar experiments. In the final section of the write-up, the writer synthesizes his or her findings by connecting them with the hypothesis and/or the results of related studies.

In your research, you, too, will synthesize, combining the results of your research to reflect your purpose and approach to your topic. Synthesis can involve both the ideas you use and the language by which you express them. When you synthesize, then, you will make choices not just about which sources to use but also about whether to quote your sources directly, summarize the findings, or paraphrase important passages.

analysis
In analysis, you break up a whole in order to (1) closely examine each part individually and/or (2) investigate the relationships among the parts.

synthesis
Writing in which elements of a work or other studies about a work are brought together, usually in order to draw a conclusion or interpret a claim you wish to assert about the work.

Where Academic Writing Is Found

Academic writing is published in academic journals and in books published by academic (university) presses. When searching for research sources, you should pay particular attention to *who* publishes the work.

University presses disseminate the research of scholars. The decision to publish a work is based on the comments of "readers," or peer-reviewers, experts in the same subject as the work's author, who evaluate the manuscript. Although the work may be controversial—for example, if it challenges previous findings or interpretations—you can rely on it as a credible source. University presses also produce **monographs**, the term for highly specialized scholarly works or treatises in book form.

Trade books, published for profit and usually to appeal to a wider audience than books published by academic presses, may also be reliable sources, particularly if they have been received favourably by authorities. The best way to assess their reliability is by looking for reviews from independent sources. Many journals regularly include book reviews relevant to their subject area.

Academic (scholarly) journals are often more current sources than book-length studies because most journals publish several times a year, and the pre-publication process is quicker than with longer works; thus, journals can provide "leading-edge" research in rapidly developing fields. They can be accessed as hard copies or through your library's electronic databases and indexes. (Do not assume, however, that every article you locate in your library's database is an academic source. Databases often include both scholarly and non-scholarly material.)

Some academic journals publish only in online formats. **Open-access journals** permit free access by users. The publishers of such journals may wish to promote the use of their studies' findings in the interests of a more informed and knowledgeable public.

Figure 1.1 summarizes some of the different classifications of academic and non-academic writing. However, the categories are not always clear-cut; for example, some academic journals include material intended for a more general audience. (Note that **periodical** is a general term for the kind of publication that is issued periodically, at regular or semi-regular intervals.)

In this text, essays written for a prospective audience comprising scholars, researchers, and professors are referred to as academic or scholarly essays, whether they are in book or journal format, while essays written for an audience comprising non-specialists who share certain interests, beliefs, or ideologies are referred to as journalistic essays. Articles in mass-circulation magazines or newspapers are usually written for an audience with varied knowledge and interest levels.

Although the essays in this text are primarily scholarly, a few are written for a literate audience of non-specialists and do not conform in all respects to the conventions of scholarly writing. Furthermore, not all your assignments may be modelled on scholarly conventions or require you to use scholarly discourse. For example, you may be asked to respond online with other class members to an essay and be permitted to write more informally. In some of your assignments, your instructor may ask you to begin with a *hook*, a deliberate strategy to engage a reader, such as a catchy phrase, question, or brief narrative, a technique less frequently used in scholarly writing. Understanding the strategies professional writers use to "spice up" their prose or make it more concise will give you more options when scholarly conventions are less crucial.

---

university press

A university-affiliated publisher, usually of books or journals; they are authoritative sources for scholarly research.

monograph

A highly specialized scholarly work or treatise in book form.

trade books

Books published by non-academic presses for general readers about topics of interest to them.

academic (scholarly) journal

A type of periodical containing scholarly content (articles, reviews, and commentaries) by experts for a knowledgeable audience in related fields of study.

open-access journal

A kind of journal (usually scholarly) that is available online without a fee.

periodical

A kind of publication that is issued periodically, at regular or semi-regular intervals; academic journals and magazines are examples of periodicals.

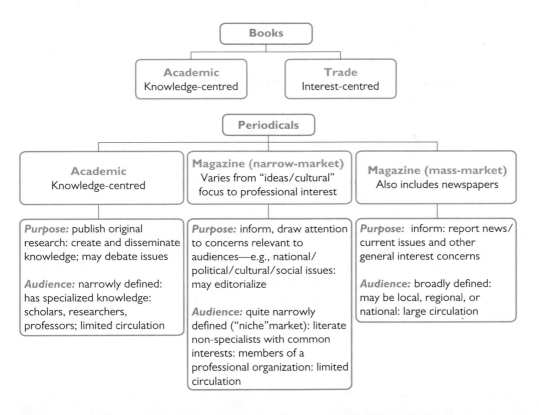

Books

Academic
Knowledge-centred

Trade
Interest-centred

Periodicals

Academic
Knowledge-centred

Magazine (narrow-market)
Varies from "ideas/cultural" focus to professional interest

Magazine (mass-market)
Also includes newspapers

Purpose: publish original research: create and disseminate knowledge; may debate issues

Audience: narrowly defined: has specialized knowledge: scholars, researchers, professors; limited circulation

Purpose: inform, draw attention to concerns relevant to audiences—e.g., national/political/cultural/social issues: may editorialize

Audience: quite narrowly defined ("niche"market): literate non-specialists with common interests: members of a professional organization: limited circulation

Purpose: inform: report news/current issues and other general interest concerns

Audience: broadly defined: may be local, regional, or national: large circulation

Figure 1.1 Published texts can be divided into categories depending on their purpose and audience.

Peer-reviewed journals have the most authority, but non–peer-reviewed journals could still be good scholarly sources. Most databases let you search for peer-reviewed articles only, excluding magazines, newspapers, and non–peer-reviewed scholarly sources.

The Influence of the Academic Community

Why study academic writing? What have the interests of the scholarly community to do with those outside this community? The academy and the world "outside" benefit from one another in unmistakable ways. The rigour of academia provides training for those who take the skills they acquired in university out into the world. They are better equipped to confront the large concerns of our society and world because of their exposure to the specialized skills, along with the general reading, writing, and critical-thinking skills that the academy seeks to instill.

In less obvious ways, the influence of academic research is far-reaching: the results of major academic studies often help shape our future by influencing government policies. Government agencies and independent think tanks may consult scholars or commission scholarly research before recommending a particular action. They may even provide the funds for research in areas of interest or concern.

Since 1990, governments and scientists, including many with connections to universities, have joined forces to produce four assessment reports and many special reports on climate change through the agency of the Intergovernmental Panel on Climate Change (IPCC). The creation of these non-binding but highly influential reports on "the current state of knowledge on climate change" suggests that, notwithstanding the tensions that can exist between governments and researchers, the relationship between them is symbiotic. Furthermore, the role of the media in publicizing the content of these reports underscores its vital relationship with the academic community.

A Self-Regulating Community

There is another important fact about the academic community that helps to make it a true community: academic writing, by its very nature, is self-regulating. Researchers question, test, and, in some cases, criticize one another's work. In 2010, a major British medical journal, *The Lancet*, fully retracted a study published a dozen years before that linked a common vaccine with an increased incidence of autism, finding flaws in the study's methodology as follow-up studies found no such link. Three of the study's thirteen authors continued to endorse the study and, consequently, found their careers as physicians in jeopardy.

Academic writers often anticipate criticism or, at least, challenges to their methods or findings. To assure readers that they are aware of a study's possible weaknesses, authors often include a section at the end of the article that addresses limitations. For example, they could note that the study used a small sample, which might mean that the findings cannot be generalized. Doing so extends an invitation to future researchers to conduct similar studies using a larger sample size in order to make the results more reliable, more applicable to larger or more diverse groups.

academic writer
A specialist in his or her subject area who is familiar with what has been written and is able to assess the strengths as well as the limitations of others' work. He or she can discriminate between a study that satisfies its objectives and one that does not, and between one whose methods are consistent with its aims and one whose methods are not. In other words, self-criticism is built into the model of research-oriented scholarship.

The Active Voice

Although self-criticism is fundamental to the scientific model, ensuring that only well-tested and reliable results are presented to the public and governments, the scientific community has sometimes reacted to criticism from those outside that community. In 2010, 255 scientists, including at least 11 Nobel laureates, wrote an open letter that was published in a prominent academic journal. In it, they explained how scientific theories become facts, how the attacks of "climate deniers" on scientists distort these facts, and why it is vital to act now against the consequences of global warming.

Climate Change and the Integrity of Science

Gleick, P.H. et al.

1 We are deeply disturbed by the recent escalation of political assaults on scientists in general and on climate scientists in particular. All citizens should understand some basic scientific facts. There is always some uncertainty associated with scientific conclusions; science never absolutely proves anything. When someone says that society should wait until scientists are absolutely certain before taking any action, it is the same as saying society should never take action. For a problem as potentially catastrophic as climate change, taking no action poses a dangerous risk for our planet.

2 Scientific conclusions derive from an understanding of basic laws supported by laboratory experiments, observations of nature, and mathematical and computer modeling. Like all human beings, scientists make mistakes, but the scientific process is designed to find and correct them. This process is inherently adversarial—scientists build reputations and gain recognition not only for supporting conventional wisdom, but even more so for demonstrating that the scientific consensus is wrong and that there is a better explanation. That's what Galileo, Pasteur,

Darwin, and Einstein did. But when some conclusions have been thoroughly and deeply tested, questioned, and examined, they gain the status of "well-established theories" and are often spoken of as "facts."

3   For instance, there is compelling scientific evidence that our planet is about 4.5 billion years old (the theory of the origin of Earth), that our universe was born from a single event about 14 billion years ago (the Big Bang theory), and that today's organisms evolved from ones living in the past (the theory of evolution). Even as these are overwhelmingly accepted by the scientific community, fame still awaits anyone who could show these theories to be wrong. Climate change now falls into this category: There is compelling, comprehensive, and consistent objective evidence that humans are changing the climate in ways that threaten our societies and the ecosystems on which we depend.

4   Many recent assaults on climate science and, more disturbingly, on climate scientists by climate change deniers are typically driven by special interests or dogma, not by an honest effort to provide an alternative theory that credibly satisfies the evidence. The Intergovernmental Panel on Climate Change (IPCC) and other scientific assessments of climate change, which involve thousands of scientists producing massive and comprehensive reports, have, quite expectedly and normally, made some mistakes. When errors are pointed out, they are corrected. But there is nothing remotely identified in the recent events that changes the fundamental conclusions about climate change:

i.   The planet is warming due to increased concentrations of heat-trapping gases in our atmosphere. A snowy winter in Washington does not alter this fact.

ii.   Most of the increase in the concentration of these gases over the last century is due to human activities, especially the burning of fossil fuels and deforestation.

iii. Natural causes always play a role in changing Earth's climate, but are now being overwhelmed by human-induced changes.

iv.   Warming the planet will cause many other climatic patterns to change at speeds unprecedented in modern times, including increasing rates of sea-level rise and alterations in the hydrologic cycle. Rising concentrations of carbon dioxide are making the oceans more acidic.

v.   The combination of these complex climate changes threatens coastal communities and cities, our food and water supplies, marine and freshwater ecosystems, forests, high mountain environments, and far more.

5   Much more can be, and has been, said by the world's scientific societies, national academies, and individuals, but these conclusions should be enough to indicate why scientists are concerned about what future generations will face from business-as-usual practices. We urge our policy-makers and the public to move forward immediately to address the causes of climate change, including the unrestrained burning of fossil fuels.

6   We also call for an end to McCarthy-like threats of criminal prosecution against our colleagues based on innuendo and guilt by association, the harassment of scientists by politicians seeking distractions to avoid taking action, and the outright lies being spread about them. Society has two choices: We can ignore the science and hide our heads in the sand and hope we are lucky, or we can act in the public interest to reduce the threat of global climate change quickly and substantively. The good news is that smart and effective actions are possible. But delay must not be an option.

—From *Science*, vol. 328, no. 5979, 7 May 2010, pp. 689–90. Reprinted with permission from AAAS.

Questions to Consider

1.   In your own words, explain what is meant by the statement, "When someone says that society should wait until scientists are absolutely certain before taking any action, it is the same as saying society should never take action" (paragraph 1).

2.   What is the difference between a theory and a fact? (paragraph 2)

3.   According to the authors, what is the fundamental difference between those who "gain recognition . . . for demonstrating that the scientific consensus is wrong" (paragraph 2) and those who believe that the theory of climate change is wrong?

4.   Among the opponents of the climate change theory, to whom do you believe the authors are referring in paragraph 6? What shows you this?

5.   Do you think the authors produced a strong argument in the letter? Why or why not? (For more information about argumentative strategies, see Chapter 9, pp. 100–122.)

2. Conventions of Academic Writing

The kind of writing you find in academic journals and books might present challenges to novice readers in both reading and understanding. Knowing what to expect and, especially, where to locate important information will ease the reading process for you.

Some of the conventions of academic writing described below apply more to scholarly journals than to books. However, academic essays on a related topic are often collected in edited volumes and follow formats similar to those described. Although essays in edited books are not preceded by abstracts (see Abstracts, page 17), an editor may summarize the purpose and content of each essay in a book's introduction and indicate how it contributes to the field of study.

Authors

empirically based study
Data or information based on an experiment or on observation; it can be verified.

Collaborative research is common in the sciences and social sciences. This is due to the nature of empirically based study, such as experimentation, which relies on direct observation under controlled conditions. Many people may be needed to observe the data or perform statistical operations on it; members of the research team contribute their expertise, as well as having input in the final version. For example, on the first page of "Tracking Affect and Academic Success across University," the responsibilities of each author are noted (see page 164 in Part III, The Reader).

In some studies, it is necessary to sample varied populations, so the authors may work in different provinces or countries. For example, a study on national stereotypes published in the journal *Science* lists 65 authors from 43 different countries; interestingly, the complete article is only five pages long! Most academic writing could be considered collaborative, in a sense, because the authors draw heavily on the work of their predecessors in the field.

Length

Academic essays vary in length. It is a truism, however, that good science writing is straightforward and concise. Scientific studies, in particular, may be as short as two or three pages; others are longer (see "Academic Language and the Challenge of Reading for Learning about Science" on page 158 in Part III: The Reader). Writing in some humanities disciplines, such as philosophy, history, and English, is more discursive (i.e., covers a wide area), partly because of the way that knowledge is defined in these disciplines: many fundamental ideas and concepts have been debated for generations, and writers continue to explore new subtleties in and variations on them.

Length is often a function of the depth and detail expected in academic writing. While you may be asked to include three main points in your essay and provide two examples each for support, academic writers gain credibility by being thorough and detailed. For example, writers in the humanities often make extensive use of primary sources, quoting from these texts to support their points. Many science and social science essays use tables, graphs, charts, and other illustrations as aids to understanding, and in most academic essays, authors summarize the work of other researchers and integrate it with their own analysis.

Research

Research Sources

The most authoritative research sources for an academic writer are previously published studies on the topic. Academic writers depend on the writing of scholars in their fields, which they summarize, partly in order to give background to their own topic; however academic writing consists of much more than just summaries of other scholars' work. Thus, when you are asked to write a research paper, you too must do more than summarize.

Most research, whether conducted by scholars or by scholars-in-training—students—involves analysis, which is often centred on first-hand or **primary sources**, *original material in a field of study.* Much research begins with primary source material; for example, it would be logical to study a literary work (primary source) before you looked at what other people had to say about it (secondary source). *Primary*, then, means "first in order," not necessarily first in importance. **Secondary sources**, by contrast, *comprise commentary on or interpretation of primary material.*

Kinds of primary sources vary from discipline to discipline. Here are a few examples from various disciplines:

- *Anthropology and archaeology:* artifacts, fossils, original field notes, reports resulting from direct observations
- *Literature:* poems, plays, fiction, diaries/letters of writers
- *Fine arts:* sheet music, recordings, photographs, sketches, paintings, sculpture, films
- *History:* contemporary documents from the period being studied—e.g., newspaper accounts, letters, speeches, photographs, treaties, diaries, autobiographies
- *Natural sciences:* data from experimentation, field/laboratory notes, original research reports
- *Sociology:* interviews, questionnaires, surveys, the raw data from these sources

discursive
Expansive, or covering a wide area.

Academic writers seek to add to the store of knowledge in their discipline; to do so, they analyze the findings of previous studies. In turn, future researchers will attempt to use the findings of these current studies to help answer a question, test a hypothesis, or solve a problem of their own. It would be very difficult to locate important studies if the writer failed to say where they appeared. Thus, the writer provides a bibliographic "trail" that future researchers can follow to the source.

primary sources
Original material in a field of study; examples include literary texts, historical documents, and interviews.

secondary sources
Commentary on or interpretation of primary material; examples include academic studies, reports, and presentations.

Of course, it is not just *writers of scholarly articles* who use research. Non-academic writers may also use research. But a journalist, unlike a scholarly writer, does not cite sources. *Using citations is a feature of academic writing.*

Documenting Sources

Scholarly writers use a set of established standards (conventions) for citing sources. Although these standards vary, there are four basic formats preferred by most book and journal publishers, which are described in detail in the major manuals published by university presses and research organizations:

- *MLA Handbook*, 8th ed. Published by the Modern Language Association of America (MLA).
- *Publication Manual of the American Psychological Association*, 6th ed.
- *The Chicago Manual of Style*, 16th ed. Published by the University of Chicago Press.
- *Scientific Style and Format: The CSE Manual for Authors, Editors, and Publishers*, 8th ed. Published by the Council of Science Editors.

See Chapter 10 for a summary of major documentation methods and formats.

Voice and Style

The voice in academic essays is generally objective and analytical, avoiding the expression of personal views. In this sense, most academic writing can be considered expository rather than argumentative, since academic writers do not usually try to persuade their audience of the rightness of a system of values or of a course of action. Still, academic studies often set out to investigate a real-life problem, and their authors may propose solutions to the problem at the end of the study. This may take the form of recommendations or areas that future research should focus on.

Furthermore, academic writing can be considered persuasive as it seeks to convince its reader of the validity and importance of the findings. Of course, academic writers also have opinions about and a stake in what they are investigating. Objectivity, then, is not synonymous with a lack of involvement but refers to the degree of detachment that ensures the writer will not be swayed by contrary or faulty evidence or by imprecise reasoning. Such a guarantee is necessary if the author is to be seen as reliable and the findings as credible.

Objectivity and Style

As observers and recorders of natural phenomena, scientists must assume a distance from the object of study to avoid influencing the results or raising the perception of bias. Thus, they may use voice in specific ways to convey distance. For example, writers may use **passive constructions**, in which the subject of the sentence is acted upon, rather than acting itself.

Abstracts, which precede many journal articles in the natural and social sciences (see page 17), typically use passive constructions to convey detachment and objectivity. In the following abstract from the journal *Child Development*, the writer uses the passive voice and

---

Most academic essays can be considered expository, or fact based. However, in their conclusions, writers may make recommendations or argue for the importance of their topic or the results.

---

passive construction (passive voice)

A way of constructing a sentence to show that the subject is being acted upon.

---

abstract

A condensed summary of the essay that follows; it is placed before the essay begins and includes at a minimum purpose, methods, and results. The function of the abstract is not to introduce the essay but to provide a concise overview so that readers can determine whether they should read the entire article.

displaces the authors of the study. The passive voice is italicized and the substituted subject is bolded:

> Using a genetic design of 234 six-year-old twins, **this study examined** (a) the contribution of genes and environment to social versus physical aggression, and (b) whether *the correlation between social and physical aggression can be explained by* similar genetic or environmental factors or by a directional link between the phenotypes. For social aggression, *substantial (shared and unique) environmental effects but only weak genetic effects were found.* For physical aggression, *significant effects of genes and unique environment were found.* . . .
>
> —M. Brendgen, G. Dionne, A. Girard, M. Boivin, F. Vitaro, and D. Pérusse. "Examining Genetic and Environmental Effects on Social Aggression: A Study of 6-year-old Twins." *Child Development, vol. 76, 2005, pp. 930–46.*

The Passive Voice and Other Common Constructions in Academic Writing

Student writers may be told to avoid the passive voice in their writing—for good reason, because it often results in a weaker sentence. However, if the purpose is to de-emphasize the subject, such as the researcher, or to stress the object (receiver of the action), such as that which is being studied, then a passive construction may be preferred to an active one. Note the difference between passive and active in the following examples:

Active voice: Researchers have carried out several studies to assess psychiatric risk factors in motor vehicle accidents.

Researchers is the active subject, but in this case, the *studies* (object of the verb) that assess risk factors are more important than the generic subject, *researchers*. By changing the construction of this sentence to the passive, the writer can replace an active but unimportant subject with a passive but important subject. Note that in passive constructions, the active subject may not appear in the sentence. Below, the original, unimportant subject is indicated by the use of brackets.

Passive voice: Several studies have been carried out [by researchers] to assess psychiatric risk factors in motor vehicle accidents.

If an active construction is used, writers may either use the first person, *I, we, our*, etc., or substitute *this study shows* or *the research confirmed.*

active construction (active voice)

A way of constructing a sentence to show that the subject performs the action of the verb.

Language and Academic Writing

Compared to literary writing, academic writing is characterized by a lack of ornamentation. Writing in the sciences, in particular, is marked by direct, straightforward prose with few modifiers (adjectives and adverbs). Academic writers are also much less likely to use figurative language, such as metaphors, similes, personification, and the like, than literary writers. They may, however, use analogies to help explain a point. An **analogy** is a systematic comparison between the topic item and another one that is like it in the relevant point but is otherwise unlike the first one. The analogy can be used to make the first item more easily understood. The authors of "The More You Play, the More Aggressive You Become" (see page 329 in Part III: The Reader) compare the effects of smoking to those of video game playing.

In spite of a lack of ornamentation, academic writing may strike beginning readers as hard to follow. This may be due to specialized vocabulary, or jargon, or elements of style, such as complex sentence and paragraph structure; the frequent use of citations can also hinder comprehension. Many of these obstacles can be overcome, though, by frequent exposure to this kind of writing and by learning the conventions of the various disciplines.

Inexperienced readers should read more closely, more slowly, and more consciously than when presented with simpler material. New reading habits can be developed by adopting specific strategies, such as learning to differentiate more important ideas from less important ones and using context to identify crucial words and concepts. Fortunately, clarity is a major aim of all successful academic writers, as it should be for writers in general, and academic writers employ deliberate techniques to achieve this goal. Inexperienced readers, with practice, can overcome most difficulties.

The three-pronged approach to reading challenging essays is summarized below:

- learn the conventions of academic writing and of your discipline (Chapters 2 and 3)
- develop an effective large-scale reading strategy based on the conventions and reading purpose (Chapter 5, pp. 47–48)
- learn to recognize words by their context; look up jargon and other words essential to meaning (Chapter 5, pp. 56–59)

See also "Academic Language and the Challenge of Reading for Learning about Science" on page 158 in Part III: The Reader.

Strategies for Approaching Academic Essays

Using pre-reading strategies, as discussed below, will help you determine an article's content. In the pages that follow, we consider information gained from looking at titles, abstracts, and markers, such as headings. We then look closely at common features of academic introductions and conclusions.

Previewing Content: Titles

Academic titles are often

- lengthy and informative
- divided into two parts with a colon in between
- composed mostly of nouns, many of them specific to the discipline

---

analogy
A systematic comparison between the topic item and another one that is like it in the relevant point but is otherwise unlike the first one; it can be used to make the first item more easily understood.

Academic studies, particularly in the sciences, may use various strategies to convey objectivity, such as passive constructions and displaced subjects. They may also include direct references to the authors. Such strategies are usually not appropriate in student essays.

The title of a scholarly article is designed to give the reader information about content at a glance. This is helpful not only for experts but also for student researchers because it enables them to gauge an article's potential usefulness simply by scanning a journal issue's contents. Typically, key terms in the article appear in the title; thus, searching by keyword in an electronic database often produces helpful results.

Many scholarly titles include two parts separated by a colon. In this example from the *Journal of Clinical Child and Adolescent Psychology*, the first part summarizes the study's finding while the second part reveals the method:

School Connectedness is an Underemphasized Parameter in Adolescent Mental Health: Results of a Community Prediction Study

If you turn to this book's table of contents and look at the titles in Part III: The Reader, you will often be able to predict an essay's topic and perhaps its findings or conclusion by looking at the detail in the title.

Previewing Content: Abstracts

An abstract is a kind of summary. Abstracts precede most journal articles, giving a preview of content by focusing on the study's purpose, method, results, and conclusion. They may also briefly explain background (for example, the need for the study) or consider the findings' significance. They often include keywords, which enable a researcher to find the article electronically when searching for words and phrases related to the topic. Abstracts are usually written by the study's author(s) and may range in length from 100 to 250 words.

Previewing Content: Section Markers

Section markers can be used to *re*view or to *pre*view content rather than provide new content. For example, in the introductory section, they can preview the essay's organization (see Thesis Statements below for information on the essay plan). They may also review what the writer has already covered. Section markers, in effect, indicate specific places in an essay where readers can get their bearings.

Used after complex material, they summarize content before the writer moves on to a new area. The following is a brief summary late in "Social Norms of Alcohol, Smoking, and Marijuana Use within a Canadian University Setting" that acts as a reminder about the purpose of the study (see page 175 in Part III: The Reader):

The primary objective of this study was to determine the relationship between perceived and actual substance use in a sample of Canadian university students.

The following is the first sentence of a paragraph that follows a detailed discussion on a government paper on the digital economy: it summarizes the main content before the author proceeds to her next point (see "Missing in Action" on page 235 in Part III: The Reader):

As is clear from the submissions and government paper on the digital economy, digital policy frames skill as the ability to participate in the labor force and to purchase and consume products and services. . . .

Writers often announce upcoming content by using headings. In empirical studies, these markers serve a *formal function* by dividing the essay into conventional categories, each having a

Empirical studies use formal headings: "Introduction," "Methods," "Results," and "Discussion." Authors of other kinds of studies may use descriptive or content headings, which make it easy for readers to determine the essay's main points or areas of discussion.

particular purpose, for example, "Introduction," "Methods," "Results," and "Discussion" (or "Conclusion"). Writers may include subsection markers as well.

In other kinds of academic writing, markers serve a *descriptive function*, enabling readers to preview content. **Descriptive headings** are one way that writers can make essay structure clearer to their readers. They orient the readers of long academic essays or those that deal with complex material. Because the essays students write for class are usually much shorter, headings are seldom necessary. However, if you are writing a scientific, engineering, or business report, you may be required to use formal headings to designate the sections of your report (see The Active Voice: Report Writing—Aims and Goals, Chapter 6: page 82).

descriptive headings

Headings usually consist of a phrase summarizing the content of the section that follows.

Activity 2.1

A good way to prepare for reading academic essays is to look at specific articles and see how they make use of the academic conventions discussed so far. Access a periodical index or electronic database and evaluate a sample issue of three different journals—one each from the humanities, social sciences, and natural sciences—noting some of the differences among them. You can answer the following questions by scanning the table of contents and a representative number of essays—say, three or four.

1. What kinds of articles does the journal contain? How long are they? What are some typical titles?
2. Were most articles written by a single author or by multiple authors?

3. Do the articles include abstracts?
4. What is the number of articles per issue?
5. Are book reviews included? Editorials?
6. How are the essays laid out (for example, note the use of formal/standardized or content/descriptive headings or other markers)?
7. Typically, how many sources are used per article (you can determine this by looking at the last pages of the article where references are listed alphabetically)?
8. Is specialized language used? Is the level of language difficult?

Features of Introductions in Academic Writing

This section discusses some common characteristics of introductions of academic essays, usually the first part of the essay you read after you preview or "pre-read" the whole essay for content. In the order you are likely to encounter them in academic writing, they include the literature review, the justification, and the thesis.

Like virtually all essays, academic essays begin with an introductory section. It may be titled "Introduction" or "Background" or have no heading, but its purpose is to prepare the reader for the body of the essay by introducing important concepts and summarizing previous studies on the topic.

Literature Review

literature review

A condensed survey of articles on the topic arranged in a logical order, usually ending with the article most relevant to the author's study. *Literature* here carries the broad meaning of something written; it does not refer only to literary works.

In the **literature review**, the author prepares the way for the unique contribution of his or her own study by summarizing related studies, which may be ordered chronologically and end with the most recent study or with that most closely related to the author's approach. Having a clear structure is vital because, typically, the literature review summarizes many studies concisely in a comparatively short space.

The authors of "Being CBC" (see page 203 in Part III: The Reader) begin their review by citing statistics on the numbers of Hong Kong immigrants arriving in Canada. In the second paragraph of their review, they narrow their focus to studies on immigrants who plan to return to Hong Kong. Their third paragraph introduces the less-studied generation of children born in Canada of immigrant parents. The literature review, then, moves from the general to the specific, the last paragraph providing the strongest link to the authors' own topic.

Justification

While students generally write essays to become stronger researchers and writers, academic authors need to convince their peers that their essay is worth consideration through a **justification**. Thus, they usually need to go one step further than student writers and announce *how*, specifically, their work will contribute to the field of study. The justification answers questions like

- Why is the study important?
- How will it advance knowledge about the topic?
- What gap will it fill?

Like many justifications, the following clearly states the gap that the study will attempt to fill:

[S]tudies examining the link between sleep and media use have largely been based on children and adolescents . . . , while little attention has been paid to emerging adults . . .

> —"Sleep Problems: Predictor or Outcome of Media Use among Emerging Adults at University?": page 257 in Part III: The Reader.

The literature review and the justification together demonstrate the writer's credibility, showing what others have written and where the author's own study fits in.

Thesis Statements

After the literature review and the justification, typically, comes the thesis. Student writers are familiar with the common practice of including a thesis statement in their introductions. Academic theses may take one of several forms, such as

- a hypothesis
- an essay plan
- a question

In experiments, the thesis may consist of a **hypothesis** or prediction. The experiment is designed to test the hypothesis, and the conclusion will announce whether it was proven or disproven. Another common form is an **essay plan**, a statement of intent. An essay plan outlines the areas to be explored in the order they will appear. Authors may refer to the plan throughout the essay to orient the reader as he or she is conducted through the different stages of the essay's development. Theses as questions are sometimes used when the author proposes to analyze an area in which there is debate or controversy.

Literature reviews with parenthetical names and years or a succession of numbers can be hard to read. A good strategy is to ignore the parentheses and pay attention to studies mentioned near the end of the introduction: they will likely be directly relevant to the review.

justification

Announces reason for undertaking the study; it may focus on what it will add to previous research or what gap in the research it will fill.

For more on thesis statements in student essays, see page 63.

hypothesis

A prediction about an outcome; it is used in essays in which an experiment is set up to prove/disprove the prediction.

essay plan

A form of a thesis in which main points are outlined in the order they will occur in the essay.

The following three-part hypothesis predicts the experiment's outcomes (see "Social Norms of Alcohol, Smoking, and Marijuana Use within a Canadian University Setting," page 175 in Part III: The Reader):

It was hypothesized that (1) the Canadian students surveyed would perceive more frequent alcohol, cigarette, and marijuana use among their peers than actually reported; (2) perceived use would predict actual use for all 3 substances assessed; and (3) actual use and perceived norms would be lower for Canadian post-secondary students than their US peers.

The following essay plan clearly sets out the essay's two main points in the order of their occurrence:

We present a brief historical background of some of the factors recognized as contributing to current mental health challenges faced by the Aboriginal population and end with some suggestions on how mental health professionals might contribute to the reconciliation process.

—"Mental Wellness in Canada's Aboriginal Communities":
page 216 in Part III: The Reader.

Longer essays often include more detailed essay plans.

In the following question thesis, the author makes it clear that he will challenge the findings of another study:

Clearly, some new drugs are valuable, but can [the authors'] conclusions be generalized in the way that Schnittker and Karandinos have done?

— "Pharmaceutical Innovation": page 310 in Part III: The Reader.

Other theses take the form of simple statements. Regardless of form, an important stage of pre-reading is identifying the thesis, while a focused reading of an essay's introduction will yield crucial information relevant to the essay as a whole.

Features of Conclusions in Academic Essays

Conclusions of academic essays seldom take the form of simple summaries. In their concluding paragraphs, academic writers

* explain the significance of their topic and their findings
* analyze their results in the context of those of other studies
* make recommendations for future research, emphasize the challenges ahead, or advocate actions

Conclusions may include all these purposes or stress one over another. Along with introductions, they should be part of your reading process before turning your attention to the essay's body paragraphs where the author develops his or her main points, providing support for the thesis.

The following passage from the last paragraph of "When Canada Goes Viral" (see page 194 in Part III: The Reader) stresses the topic's significance:

> Though the campaign lacks overtly activist aims, the Canada Party video and its reception open up important questions about the state of political satire in Canada and its relation to concurrent work in the U.S.

Although the authors of "Tracking Affect and Academic Success across University" (see page 163 in Part III: The Reader) stress the significance of their results and make recommendations for future research, in this passage, they situate their findings within the current research:

> The results contribute to the literature on self-regulation across the life course, specifically to the growing literature on psychological experiences that propel average gains in well-being across the transition to adulthood, a literature that until recently has been mainly descriptive in nature (Shulman & Nurmi, 2010).

Finally, this passage from "The Social Dilemma of Autonomous Vehicles" (see page 336 in Part III: The Reader) stresses future challenges and ends with a plea for the reader's attention to the issue:

> Figuring out how to build ethical autonomous machines is one of the thorniest challenges in artificial intelligence today (22). As we are about to endow millions of vehicles with autonomy, a serious consideration of algorithmic morality has never been more urgent.

The Active Voice

Issues in Education: Challenge to Conflict

Issue #1: Challenges

1   Student challenges are often discussed in faculty meetings and conferences. On such occasions, we often hear about those challenges from administrative and instructional perspectives. We do not, however, hear about those challenges as often from a student's perspective.

2   So, on a recent assignment I asked my students, "What, in your view, is the greatest problem, issue, or challenge for students pursuing post-secondary education in Canada?"

3   The challenges identified by these students fit into five categories: money, preparation, transition, self and personal issues, and other factors. It is interesting, although not surprising, that both Aboriginal and non-Aboriginal students identified the same kinds of challenges.

4   The *overwhelming* top challenge identified was money. If one has sufficient financial resources, all of the other challenges of being a student can be dealt with. If not, the rest is essentially irrelevant.

5   Previous experience with education came next. The emphasis here was on pressures to get a degree, including choosing a major and/or a career. Many students recognized a lack of sufficient experience or information in either life or education to make such choices. Add the perception of lifelong impact and large financial burdens: more pressure. Some students noted a lack of previous educational

Continued

preparation. It is difficult to meet the expectations of post-secondary performance if one has little knowledge or experience about what those expectations might be.

6   The emphasis for "transition" was on the experiential gap. The main challenge noted here was culture shock from changes in lifestyle caused by moving from the high school to university setting or moving from a reserve to the city: more pressure.

7   Challenges related to personal issues and concerns included goals, motivation, time management, balance, and commitment.

8   The final, miscellaneous category of "other factors" was directed toward other agents, inside and outside the system, that affected the experience of being a student: more pressure.

Issue #2: Audience and Purpose

9   Many writing texts tell us that the first thing we should do in the composition process is define our audience and purpose. Identifying the audience that makes up our courses is also important.

10   The typical first-year student in my class is, in logical sequence: 1) living away from home independently for the first time; 2) anxious about the new experience; 3) concerned about daily priorities and other social interests; 4) overwhelmed with expense requirements; 5) working one or more jobs; 6) expected to take a minimum of five courses, with six becoming more frequent; 7) pressured to attend university from a variety of sources; and, finally, 8) forced to take a writing course.

11   Besides their lack of motivation and commitment, students in my classes can at times constitute a hostile audience. So, I try to make the subject matter and purposes relevant to the students' interests, which tend to be much wider than many people might expect. I suggest that many texts do not do this very well.

Issue #3: Conflicting Purposes

12   The goal of writing for academic purposes is to inform the audience or explain something for the audience. This is the intellectual aspect of such work. There are, however, other aspects of the broader academic context that may embody other purposes.

13   This idea is fairly simple in outline. Each student has a purpose for taking a course. Each instructor has a purpose in presenting a course. Each department has a purpose in what may be offered. Each discipline embodies a purpose in the way subject matter is studied. This continues on through the academic hierarchy and may provide a potential source of confusion and conflict. For example, some students in first-year courses want to engage in primary research but are disappointed when they find that this is usually not allowed until they have become familiar with the language and theories of their discipline and have taken research methods courses at the upper level.

14   We all have purposes. For a professional academic, these purposes can be described as professional objectives. My own objectives include advocating and developing thinking skills and abilities to formulate coherent expressions of thought that contribute to the pursuit of autonomy through development of critical competence. Unfortunately, as worthwhile as this objective might seem to be, it does not always correspond to that of other agents in the academic context.

Final Thoughts

15   1) It seems clear that providing and maintaining transition support focused on the nature of post-secondary academics as well as the requirements, expectations, and skill performances could benefit many students.

16   2) When engaged by topics of interest, and with coaching, students can gain a better understanding of intellectual processes involved in academic purposes.

17   3) We need to be clearer about purposes for education. There are financial realities in education, as in many other aspects of life. But, let's face it, learning is messy and expensive. It is not efficient and cannot be done fast and cheap. However, simply providing more money will not necessarily solve the range of problems related to student needs.

18   In any case, interpreting education solely through a perspective of economic determinism provides a narrow focus that can diminish the value of the enterprise as a whole.

19   Moving forward, we need to explore alternative approaches to addressing the needs of students, all of which should be based on an informed foundation of purposes and perspectives.

—**Dennis R. Nighswonger**, Lecturer, Department of English, Lakehead University

3 Three Common Kinds of Academic Essays

Although academic writing shares many characteristics, most academic essays can be divided into one of three categories. You can think of them as Type A (for "*arts*," often referred to as the humanities), Type B (for "*biology*," an example of a discipline within the natural sciences), and Type C (for "*critical* review"). Since formats and other conventions vary among these different kinds of essays, being able to identify their type will enable you to access information more efficiently.

Type A: Humanities (Qualitative) Essays

Type A is common in the arts/humanities disciplines and in other disciplines in which the methodology is *qualitative*, concerned with ideas, values, or theories, rather than with data that can be measured and quantified. Typically, a Type A essay includes a thesis, an essay plan, or questions that the writer will attempt to answer; in longer essays, descriptive headings may be used to summarize section content. Primary sources are used extensively. See Characteristics of Type A, Type B, and Type C Essays in Appendix B, and the excerpt from a Type A essay, page 26, for more details.

> Authors of Type A essays use a qualitative methodology, concerned with the interpretation of ideas, values, or theories, which they may apply to specific primary sources.

Type B: Empirical (Experimental) Essays

In Type B essays, the writer's research design involves an experiment or some other empirical process through which primary sources, such as raw data, are generated. Research of this kind is sometimes called **original research** to distinguish it from the kind of research that depends heavily on underlying theories and perspectives.

> **original research**
> Research in which the author(s) conducts an experiment to generate raw data or uses available data to prove/disprove a hypothesis or answer a research question.

In addition to using quantitative methods, these essays use standardized divisions that replicate the chronological stages of the experiment, beginning with "Introduction," followed by "Methods," "Results," and "Discussion" and/or "Conclusion." The divisions may then be sub-divided. For example, "Methods" may be divided into "Subjects," "Participants," "Measures," "Procedures," "Statistical Analyses Used," and so on. See Characteristics of Type A, Type B, and Type C Essays in Appendix B, and the sample Type B essay, page 27, for more details.

Type B Sub-genre: Qualitative Methodologies

> Authors of Type B essays use quantitative data, often generated through an experiment, or qualitative data to test a hypothesis or answer a question.

Some essays use conventional Type B formats while employing qualitative methods to analyze evidence gathered from unstructured interviews, focus groups, forums, or written texts like print media. As contrasted with the sometimes artificial setting of the psychology lab, qualitative methods enable the researcher to examine human motivations and interactions within naturally occurring contexts. For example, Healey et al. analyze the results of collaborative research on climate change in northern Inuit communities by recording community perspectives and capturing everyday life experiences through photography (page 362 in Part III: The Reader). The essay by Kobayashi and Preston on page 203 of The Reader, as well as the essay by Elliott and Brierly on page 288, use focus groups and thus include primary sources (i.e., individual comments from focus group members).

In spite of the advantages of qualitative studies, data generated through these methods may be harder to generalize to larger populations than data generated through quantitative methods. In addition, data analysis requires careful and skilled interpretation to avoid researcher bias.

Type C: Synthesis/Critical Review Essays

> Authors of Type C essays synthesize and critically review published studies to reveal the progress toward solving a problem.

Common in the social sciences—especially psychology—and in the sciences, Type C essays synthesize and critically review (evaluate) relevant texts, such as scholarly articles. Type C essays reveal the progress toward solving a problem; they may also draw attention to inconsistencies or gaps in the research. In this sense, they look back to see how far research has come and look ahead to future directions for research; their authors may conclude by making recommendations. Review essays may be occasioned by a specific phenomenon, such as the prevalence of online gaming among adolescents (see "The More You Play, the More Aggressive You Become," page 329 in Part III: The Reader), or a significant social concern, such as "Addressing Driver Aggression," page 304 in The Reader. In format, Type C essays may resemble Type A essays with a thesis/essay plan and content divisions. See Characteristics of Type A, Type B, and Type C Essays in Appendix B, and the sample Type C essay, page 31, for more details.

Although not all academic essays conform precisely to the characteristics outlined here and in Appendix B, the majority closely resemble Type A, Type B, or Type C. Works published in books generally follow the formats of Type A or Type C, whereas experimental results (Type B) typically appear in journals. As well as much scientific writing, several kinds of public writing, such as case studies, proposals, and business and other kinds of formal reports, commonly use the methodology and structure of Type B essays.

Argumentative essays, such as editorials and commentaries, are discussed in Chapter 9.

Tables, Graphs, and Other Visuals

A **table** presents detailed information in matrix format, in columns and rows that are easily scanned. **Graphs** represent relationships between two variables. *Line graphs* show a relationship over time while *bar graphs* show values or trends within the data.

Writers may use tables, graphs, and charts (the last two are often represented by the abbreviation "Fig.," for "Figure") to present their raw data. They are especially common in the "Results" section of Type B essays where their primary function is to concisely summarize the quantitative results of the experiment. Writers may explain the most significant results in the text of the essay, reserving detail for the table to which the reader will be directed in the explanatory text.

Reading Tables and Graphs

- Read the text material first to understand specific terms and/or abbreviations used in the table/figure.
- If there is a heading, read it carefully; headings are sometimes given above the figure and explanatory material below it. At other times, the information is all in one place, and the first sentence summarizes the table's/figure's purpose, the following sentence(s) giving further explanation.
- If the table/figure is particularly detailed or complex, reread the relevant section(s) in the text. Text material will often direct you to specific parts of the table/figure deemed significant by the author(s).
- Read labels carefully, but do not be distracted by superscript numbers, letters, or symbols, which often refer to statistical significance of specific items.

table

Presents detailed information in matrix format, in columns and rows that are easily scanned.

graph

Represents relationships between two variables.

Activity 3.1

It can be helpful to be able to identify types of academic essays in order to determine your approach and the reading strategies most applicable to your assigned reading. Choose two essays of different types identified on pages 23–24 as A, B, or C. (Do not choose other types—for example, argumentative—though they may be similar in some ways to the kinds of essays discussed in this chapter.) Identify three features of each essay type as discussed in this chapter; if they apply to individual paragraphs, identify them by paragraph number. Note: For more detailed information about Type A, B, and C essays, see Appendix B.

Academic Essay Formats

In your career as a student, you will be asked to write essays and reports that conform to one or another of the essay types discussed. For example, you may be asked to write a lab report as a result of a specific experiment you performed. Such empirically based reports resemble the Type B academic essay. For information on how to write reports, see The Active Voice: Report Writing—Aims and Goals, Chapter 6: page 82.

Inevitably, you will write essays in several of your classes in which you generate a position about a literary text, historical event, or philosophical system and defend that position, citing from primary sources, as authors of Type A essays also do.

The use of research, synthesis, summarizing, and critical evaluation makes the student research essay much like the Type C essay. The following samples demonstrate features of the types of essays discussed in this chapter.

Type A

The first few paragraphs of the essay titled "Speed That Kills" (on page 346 in Part III: The Reader) is excerpted here to illustrate some of the conventions of Type A essays.

Professional Writing Sample

Excerpt from "Speed That Kills: The Role of Technology in Kate Chopin's 'The Story of an Hour'"

by Jeremy Foote. From *The Explicator* 71. 2 (2013), pp. 85–9.

> Foote begins directly by summarizing previous approaches to this classic short story, preparing the way for his own approach (thesis) later in the introduction.

> Foote uses two literary critics as secondary sources, choosing to quote the first one directly probably because it specifically supports the claim in his first sentence.

> An example of jargon, the word "protomodernist" means "original" modernist text. (Modernism was an artistic movement beginning in the late nineteenth and early twentieth centuries.)

> The simple thesis is appropriate for such a short essay, but might be insufficient for a longer one.

> Although Foote analyzes a story written about 125 years ago, here he addresses today's reader, making the text relevant to this reader, who may be unaware of the role of technology in Chopin's age.

1   Kate Chopin's "The Story of an Hour" has been taught and analyzed almost exclusively from a feminist perspective. As Lawrence Berkove writes, "There has been . . . virtual critical agreement on what the story says: its heroine dies, ironically and tragically, just as she has been freed from a constricting marriage and has realized self-assertion as the deepest element of her being" (152). Louise Mallard's sense of joy at her husband's apparent death, and her own death at his return, have become an archetype of feminine self-realization and the patriarchy that is always there to extinguish it (e.g., Harlow 501). Indeed, the feminist images of the story are so powerful that I believe critics have overlooked another theme. "The Story of an Hour" can be read as a protomodernist text. As also seen with later modernist writers, technology and the societal changes caused by technology play important roles in Chopin's story.

2   "The Story of an Hour" was first published in *Vogue* in 1894. More than a century later, now in the midst of our own technological revolution, it is difficult to grasp how fundamentally nineteenth-century technologies were altering the world in Chopin's time. Before the railroad, traveling was extremely difficult and dangerous. In the 1850s, it took an average of 128 days to traverse the Oregon Trail (Unruh 403), with a mortality rate of 4 per cent to 6 per cent (408). The transcontinental railroad, completed in 1869, allowed the same journey to be made, safely and much more comfortably, in less than a week (Cooper). Perhaps more importantly, during the 1890s trains started to become part of daily life. In 1889 the first interurban electric rail lines were laid, and by 1894 hundreds of miles of track were being added every year (Hilton and Due 186–87).

3   Communications underwent an even more dramatic acceleration. The completion of the first successful transatlantic cable in 1866 meant news that had previously taken a week or more to travel between Europe and the Americas could now be sent nearly instantaneously.

> Examples from secondary sources are used throughout the paragraph for support. A primary source is used at the end of paragraph 3.

Like the railroad, while the initial invention had occurred years earlier, in the 1890s telegrams went from novel to quotidian. In 1870, Western Union relayed 9 million telegrams. By 1893, they were sending more than 66 million telegrams annually (United States Bureau of the Census 788).

4   Later writers would explore the effects of these and other technologies. In his 1909 "Futurist Manifesto," Filippo Marinetti gushes, "Time and Space died yesterday. We already live in the absolute, because we have created eternal, omnipresent speed." Not all writers would be as optimistic as Marinetti. A few decades after "Hour" was published, World War I would provide striking evidence of the destructive power of new technologies, and writers like Ezra Pound and T.S. Eliot would lament the new world that man had created. In "Hugh Selwyn Mauberly," for example, Pound claims that the world experienced "Fortitude as never before / Frankness as never before, / Disillusions as never told in the old days" (81–83). Pound felt that technology led to a world "as never before" but that these changes led to a "botched civilization" instead of a technological utopia (89).

5   "The Story of an Hour" can be read as a precursor to these more technophobic works. The story begins with news of Mr Mallard's death in a railroad disaster—received by telegram. This may be a commentary on the literal danger of riding trains in the 1890s, but we can also see the railroad's role in the story as a more subtle warning. While we do not know for certain why Mr Mallard would have been riding a train that day, Chopin describes him later as "a little travel-stained, composedly carrying his grip-sack and umbrella," bringing to mind the image of a commuter returning home from a day at the office (Chopin).

> This paragraph is clearly structured, beginning with a topic sentence. Although Foote quotes a positive source, most of the examples here refer to technology in more cautious, even negative, terms, which ties in with his thesis.

> Unsurprisingly, many of the primary sources used by humanities writers are drawn from other texts in the writer's discipline.

> The author's analysis now focuses on Chopin's story. Notice that Foote combines brief plot summary (the beginning of this sentence) with analysis, supporting the analysis with a direct quotation from the story.

Type B

The following is a short example of a Type B essay, illustrating some of the conventions of this kind of essay.

Professional Writing Sample

Adaptive Responses to Social Exclusion: Social Rejection Improves Detection of Real and Fake Smiles

by Michael J. Bernstein, Steven G. Young, Christina M. Brown, Donald F. Sacco, and Heather M. Claypool. From *Psychological Science* by Association for Psychological Science. Reproduced with permission of SAGE Publications Inc. via Copyright Clearance Center.

1   Being excluded from social relationships poses numerous immediate and long-term threats (e.g., Baumeister & Leary, 1995). Consequently, it is not surprising that people are sensitive to cues that indicate potential rejection (Pickett & Gardner, 2005). For example, individuals who are dispositionally high in need to belong are better than others at identifying facial expressions and vocal tones (Pickett, Gardner, & Knowles, 2004), and ostracized participants have better memory for socially relevant information than do nonostracized participants (Gardner, Pickett, & Brewer, 2000). In both cases, individuals either fearing rejection or suffering actual rejection show increased attention to social cues.

> As is often the case in Type B essays, the two-part title includes the result of the study (following the colon). The first part of the title identifies the area studied. Unlike most Type B essays, there is no abstract. The literature review is a major focus in the introductions of most Type B essays. Here it begins in the first sentence and continues for much of the introduction.

Typically, the last study mentioned by the authors in the literature review is the one most relevant to their own research. In this sentence, the dependent clause summarizes the results of an important study while the independent clause suggests a gap in the research. The complete sentence justifies the need for the current study.

The hypothesis (prediction) occurs at the end of the introduction in most Type B essays. It arises out of previous research and the attempt to extend or refine the results of earlier studies in order to explain a phenomenon or solve a problem.

The "Method" section is divided into three short subsections, "Participants" (who took part), "Materials," (what was used), and "Procedure," (how the experiment was done). The precise detail is needed so that future researchers can replicate the study or build on it by varying the research methods.

2   Facial expressions of emotion can act as such social cues. A Duchenne smile, for example, involves the automatic activation of two facial muscles in response to the experience of pleasure and is generally considered a "true" smile (Ekman, Davidson, & Friesen, 1990), indicative of cooperation and affiliation (Brown & Moore, 2002). In contrast, non-Duchenne, or "masking," smiles can conceal the experience of negative emotions (Ekman, Friesen, & O'Sullivan, 1988). Knowing whether a facial expression is conveying an honest affiliation signal should help rejected individuals identify targets who are likely to offer the greatest opportunity for reconnection.

3   Although research has shown that individuals with greater belongingness needs (Pickett et al., 2004) are more accurate at discriminating among true, diagnostic facial-expression signals (e.g., discriminating between expressions of anger and happiness), no research has examined the extent to which rejected individuals are able to determine whether the expression being identified is genuine in the first place. Although being able to identify the qualitative emotional category of a facial display is of value to socially excluded individuals, distinguishing real from fake emotions seems especially important to ensure that reaffiliation efforts are maximally distributed toward people displaying genuine affiliative cues. Indeed, directing resources toward an individual faking an affiliative display would likely be a costly error for socially rejected individuals, who already find themselves in a perilous situation. Accordingly, we hypothesized that rejected individuals would show an enhanced ability to discriminate between real and fake smiles, presumably because they are more attuned than others to subtle social cues, including those present in Duchenne smiles (involuntary signals of cooperation) as opposed to non-Duchenne smiles (controllable and unreliable indicators of cooperation).

Method

4   Participants were randomly assigned to social-inclusion, social-exclusion, or control conditions. They were then shown faces exhibiting Duchenne or non-Duchenne smiles and were asked to decide whether each was "real" or "fake."

Participants

5   Thirty-two undergraduates (17 females, 15 males) participated in the study for course credit.

Materials

6   The facial stimuli were located on the BBC Science & Nature Web site (BBC, n.d.).[1] Respondents were asked to watch 20 color videos (approximately 4 s each) one at a time. Each depicted an individual who had an initially neutral expression and then smiled before returning to a neutral expression. Which faces exhibited real/fake smiles remained constant for all participants. Thus, there were 20 faces, 10 of which were always exhibiting real smiles and 10 of which were always exhibiting fake smiles. Thirteen men and seven women were depicted in the videos.[2]

Procedure

7   Participants were informed that they were to perform two ostensibly unrelated tasks concerning memory and face perception. The first was an essay task that constituted the

---

[1] The faces were pretested for equivalency of attractiveness and positivity. Ratings of neutral expressions of targets showing Duchenne smiles versus neutral expressions of targets showing non-Duchenne smiles revealed no differences (p > .2).

[2] The stimuli included three minority-group individuals. Removing data for these targets from analyses did not change any findings.

manipulation of social status. Participants, having been randomly assigned, wrote about a time they felt "rejected or excluded," a time they felt "accepted or included," or their morning the day before the study (control condition). This manipulation has been used previously with success (e.g., Gardner et al., 2000). As a manipulation check, participants responded to a scale assessing the degree to which they felt a threat to their sense of belonging, a common measure used to confirm the effectiveness of rejection manipulations (Williams, Cheung, & Choi, 2000).

8   Finally, participants watched each video and indicated, on a response sheet next to the computer, whether the smile was "genuine" or "fake." Upon completion of this task, participants responded to demographic questions before being probed for suspicion, thanked, and debriefed.

Results

Manipulation Check

9   To examine whether the manipulation of social rejection was successful, we conducted a one-way between-subjects analysis of variance (ANOVA) on the belongingness measure.

10   Results indicated that the manipulation had the intended effect (prep > .99); rejected participants experienced a greater threat to their sense of belonging.

Discrimination Scores

11   We calculated d', a signal detection measure examining the ability to discriminate stimuli—in this case, the ability to discriminate Duchenne smiles from non-Duchenne smiles. This measure simultaneously considers hits (correctly identifying a Duchenne smile as genuine) and false alarms (incorrectly identifying a non-Duchenne smile as genuine) in the calculation. The one-way ANOVA on these scores was significant, $F(2, 29) = 5.63$, $p_{rep} = .97$; compared with control participants ($M = 1.05$, $SD = 0.56$) and included participants ($M = 1.34$, $SD = 0.56$), rejected participants ($M = 1.88$, $SD = 0.62$) exhibited greater discriminability, $t(29) = 3.33$, $p_{rep} = .98$, $d = 1.35$, and $t(29) = 2.12$, $p_{rep} = .92$, $d = 0.87$, respectively. Discrimination ability did not differ between included and control participants ($p > .25$; see Fig. 1).

12   There was no effect of target or participant sex. Thus, these variables are not discussed further.

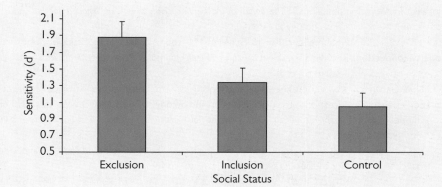

Figure 1   Mean ability to discriminate (sensitivity, d') Duchenne and non-Duchenne smiles as a function of social-status condition. Error bars indicate standard errors.

The citation underscores the reliance of researchers on prior studies. By using an established procedure, the authors add to their credibility.

The result of the manipulation check confirms that the manipulation worked as it was designed to do. If it had failed to confirm the validity of the social status manipulation, the researchers would probably have had to redesign their experiment. The check, then, acted as a backup, confirming the validity of the methodology.

Researchers often present their data by referring to complex statistical methods, and the "Results" section may be written by a specialist in statistics. Non-specialists, including students, can learn to read such sections carefully to extract the most important information while ignoring unneeded detail. The key finding, which is discussed more fully in the next section, is highlighted here. For more information about statistics, see Appendix A, A Note on Statistics p. 403.

Most Type B essays are accompanied by tables, graphs, or charts that summarize the study's results. In this case, a bar graph shows the relationship between social status and the ability to tell fake from genuine smiles. Note the clear labelling of both axes and the brief explanation below the graphic.

Discussion

13   We found that socially rejected individuals have enhanced ability to determine whether the "happy" facial expression of a target individual is genuine (a true indication of an affiliative opportunity) or deceptive (feigning the appearance of positive affect). This suggests that motivation to reaffiliate increases rejected individuals' sensitivity to other social cues indicating belongingness opportunities—specifically, facial displays that are honest signals of cooperation and affiliation.

14   Although the results of the current study are congruent with some of the rejection literature showing reaffiliative responses to social exclusion (Lakin & Chartrand, 2005; Maner, DeWall, Baumeister, & Schaller, 2007), these results are among the first to show that rejection can lead to increases in performance at a perceptual level, provided that the performance supports opportunities for affiliation. Once rejected, people are left with a strong desire to be accepted, which leads them toward interaction partners with whom they might affiliate. Therefore, it seems essential to detect legitimate signs of positivity that indicate possible reaffiliation with other people. Otherwise, rejected individuals could miss out on new chances for acceptance or "waste" affiliation efforts on people who are not receptive. Future research should examine whether other faked emotions can be differentiated from true emotions, as well as how these perceptual skills may guide subsequent behavioral choices.

References

Baumeister, R.F., & Leary, M.R. (1995). The need to belong: Desire for interpersonal attachments as a fundamental human motivation. *Psychological Bulletin*, 117, 497–529.

BBC. (n.d.). Spot the fake smile. Retrieved October 1, 2007, from http://www.bbc.co.uk/science/humanbody/mind/surveys/smiles

Brown, W.M., & Moore, C. (2002). Smile asymmetries and reputation as reliable indicators of likelihood to cooperate: An evolutionary analysis. In S.P. Shohov (Ed.), *Advances in psychology research* (Vol. 11, pp. 59–78). Huntington, NY: Nova Science Publishers.

Ekman, P., Davidson, R.J., & Friesen, W.V. (1990). The Duchenne smile: Emotional expression and brain physiology II. *Journal of Personality and Social Psychology*, 58, 342–353.

Ekman, P., Friesen, W.V., & O'Sullivan, M. (1988). Smiles when lying. *Journal of Personality and Social Psychology*, 54, 414–420.

Gardner, W.L., Pickett, C.L., & Brewer, M.B. (2000). Social exclusion and selective memory: How the need to belong influences memory for social events. *Personality and Social Psychology Bulletin*, 26, 486–496.

Lakin, J.L., & Chartrand, T.L. (2005). Exclusion and nonconscious behavioral mimicry. In K.D. Williams, J.P. Forgas, & W. von Hippel (Eds.), *The social outcast: Ostracism, social exclusion, rejection, and bullying* (pp. 279–296). New York: Psychology Press.

Maner, J.K., DeWall, C.N., Baumeister, R.F., & Schaller, M. (2007). Does social exclusion motivate interpersonal reconnection? Resolving the "porcupine problem." *Journal of Personality and Social Psychology*, 92, 42–55.

Pickett, C.L., & Gardner, W.L. (2005). The social monitoring system: Enhanced sensitivity to social cues and information as an adaptive response to social exclusion and belonging need. In K.D. Williams, J.P. Forgas, & W. von Hippel (Eds.), *The social outcast: Ostracism, social exclusion, rejection, and bullying* (pp. 213–226). New York: Psychology Press.

Pickett, C.L., Gardner, W.L., & Knowles, M. (2004). Getting a cue: The need to belong and enhanced sensitivity to social cues. *Personality and Social Psychology Bulletin*, 30, 1095–1107.

Williams, K.D., Cheung, C.K.T., & Choi, W. (2000). Cyberostracism: Effects of being ignored over the Internet. *Journal of Personality and Social Psychology*, 79, 748–762.

Type C

The following is a short example of a Type C essay.

Professional Writing Sample

Why Ordinary People Torture Enemy Prisoners

by Susan T. Fiske, Lasana T. Harris, and Amy J.C. Cuddy. From *Science*, vol. 306, no. 5701, 26 November 2004, pp. 1482–3.

1   As official investigations and courts-martial continue, we are all taking stock of the events at Abu Ghraib last year. Initial reactions were shock and disgust. How could Americans be doing this to anyone, even Iraqi prisoners of war? Some observers immediately blamed "the few bad apples" presumably responsible for the abuse. However, many social psychologists knew that it was not that simple. Society holds individuals responsible for their actions, as the military court-martial recognizes, but social psychology suggests we should also hold responsible peers and superiors who control the social context.

2   Social psychological evidence emphasizes the power of social context; in other words, the power of the interpersonal situation. Social psychology has accumulated a century of knowledge about how people influence each other for good or ill [1]. Meta-analysis, the quantitative summary of findings across a variety of studies, reveals the size and consistency of such empirical results. Recent meta-analyses document reliable experimental evidence of social context effects across 25,000 studies of 8 million participants [2]. Abu Ghraib resulted in part from ordinary social processes, not just extraordinary individual evil. This Policy Forum cites meta-analyses to describe how the right (or wrong) social context can make almost anyone aggress, oppress, conform, and obey.

3   Virtually anyone can be aggressive if sufficiently provoked, stressed, disgruntled, or hot [3–6]. The situation of the 800th Military Police Brigade guarding Abu Ghraib prisoners fit all the social conditions known to cause aggression. The soldiers were certainly provoked and stressed: at war, in constant danger, taunted and harassed by some of the very citizens they were sent to save, and their comrades were dying daily and unpredictably. Their morale suffered, they were untrained for the job, their command climate was lax, their return home was a year overdue, their identity as disciplined soldiers was gone, and their own amenities were scant [7]. Heat and discomfort also doubtless contributed.

4   The fact that the prisoners were part of a group encountered as enemies would only exaggerate the tendency to feel spontaneous prejudice against outgroups. In this context, oppression and discrimination are synonymous. One of the most basic principles of social psychology is that people prefer their own group [8] and attribute bad behavior to outgroups [9]. Prejudice especially festers if people see the outgroup as threatening cherished values [10–12]. This would have certainly applied to the guards viewing their prisoners at Abu Ghraib, but it also applies in more "normal" situations. A recent sample of U.S. citizens on average viewed Muslims and Arabs as not sharing their interests and stereotyped them as not especially sincere, honest, friendly, or warm [13–15].

Titles of Type C essays are often shorter than those of other types, containing a statement of the problem under investigation.

The authors of this study introduce the problem in the first paragraph, understanding the behaviour of American troops at an Iraqi prison. In the next paragraph, they explain how social psychology can help us understand the complexities of the factors involved.

The paragraph begins by briefly outlining the study's methodology and concludes with the simple thesis.

The review is divided into four categories or sub-topics. Typically, categories in Type C essays include content headings; however, because three of the categories are only one paragraph long, the authors probably thought headings were unnecessary.

The Council of Science Editors (CSE) documentation method, used here, consists of numbers in the text, which correspond to a list of sources at the end of the essay arranged by their order in the text.

Review essays contain a large number of concise summaries.

The category or sub-topic of outgroups is analyzed in paragraphs 4–6.

5   Even more potent predictors of discrimination are the emotional prejudices ("hot" affective feelings such as disgust or contempt) that operate in parallel with cognitive processes [16–18]. Such emotional reactions appear rapidly, even in neuroimaging of brain activations to outgroups [19,20]. But even they can be affected by social context. Categorization of people as interchangeable members of an outgroup promotes an amygdala response characteristic of vigilance and alarm and an insula response characteristic of disgust or arousal, depending on social context; these effects dissipate when the same people are encountered as unique individuals [21,22].

6   According to our survey data [13,14], the contemptible, disgusting kind of outgroup—low-status opponents—elicits a mix of active and passive harm: attacking and fighting, as well as excluding and demeaning. This certainly describes the Abu Ghraib abuse of captured enemies. It also fits our national sample of Americans [14] who reported that allegedly contemptible outgroups such as homeless people, welfare recipients, Turks, and Arabs often are attacked or excluded [14].

In this paragraph, the authors introduce two important research areas to help explain the prevalence of prisoner mistreatment. The first, "conformity to peers," is analyzed in this paragraph; the second, "obedience to authority," is discussed in the following one. Clear organization is vital in Type C essays.

7   Given an environment conducive to aggression and prisoners deemed disgusting and subhuman [23], well-established principles of conformity to peers [24,25] and obedience to authority [26] may account for the widespread nature of the abuse. In combat, conformity to one's unit means survival, and ostracism is death. The social context apparently reflected the phenomenon of people trying to make sense of a complex, confusing, ambiguous situ-ation by relying on their immediate social group [27]. People rioted at St. Paul's Church, Bristol UK, in 1980, for example, in conformity to events they saw occurring in their immediate proximity [28]. Guards abuse prisoners in conformity with what other guards do, in order to fulfill a potent role; this is illustrated by the Stanford Prison Study, in which ordinary college students, randomly assigned to be full-time guards and prisoners in a temporary prison, nevertheless behaved respectively as abusers and victims [29]. Social psychology shows that, whatever their own good or bad choices, most people believe that others would do whatever they personally chose to do, a phenomenon termed false consensus [30,31]. Conformity to the perceived reactions of one's peers can be defined as good or bad, depending on how well the local norms fit those of larger society.

8   As every graduate of introductory psychology should know from the Milgram studies [32], ordinary people can engage in incredibly destructive behavior if so ordered by legitimate authority. In those studies, participants acting as teachers frequently followed an experimenter's orders to punish a supposed learner (actually a confederate) with electric shock, all the way to administering lethal levels. Obedience to authority sustains every culture [33]. Firefighters heroically rushing into the flaming World Trade Center were partly obeying their superiors, partly conforming to extraordinary group loyalty, and partly showing incredibly brave self-sacrifice. But obedience and conformity also motivated the terrorist hijackers and the Abu Ghraib guards, however much one might abhor their (vastly different) actions. Social conformity and obedience themselves are neutral, but their consequences can be heroic or evil. Torture is partly a crime of socialized obedience [34]. Subordinates not only do what they are ordered to do, but what they think their superiors would order them to do, given their understanding of the authority's overall goals. For example, lynching represented ordinary people going beyond the law to enact their view of the community's will.

Compare and contrast, a common pattern of development in Type C essays, is used in this paragraph.

9   Social influence starts with small, apparently trivial actions (in this case, insulting epithets), followed by more serious actions (humiliation and abuse) [35–37], as novices overcome their hesitancy and learn by doing [38]. The actions are always intentional, although the perpetrator may not be aware that those actions constitute evil. In fact, perpetrators may see themselves

as doing a great service by punishing and or eliminating a group that they perceive as deserving ill treatment [39].

10   In short, ordinary individuals under the influence of complex social forces may commit evil acts [40]. Such actions are human behaviors that can and should be studied scientifically [41,42]. We need to understand more about the contexts that will promote aggression. We also need to understand the basis for exceptions—why, in the face of these social contexts, not all individuals succumb [43]. Thus, although lay-observers may believe that explaining evil amounts to excusing it and absolving people of responsibility for their actions [44], in fact, explaining evils such as Abu Ghraib demonstrates scientific principles that could help to avert them.

> The focus of this paragraph is on research needed in specific areas. Identifying gaps in the literature is a common feature of Type C essay conclusions.

11   Even one dissenting peer can undermine conformity [24]. For example, whistle-blowers not only alert the authorities but also prevent their peers from continuing in unethical behavior. Authorities can restructure situations to allow communication. For example, CEOs can either welcome or discourage a diversity of opinions. Contexts can undermine prejudice [1]. Individual, extended, equal-status, constructive, cooperative contact between mutual outgroups (whether American blacks and whites in the military or American soldiers and Iraqi civilians) can improve mutual respect and even liking. It would be harder to dehumanize and abuse imprisoned Iraqis if one had friends among ordinary Iraqis. A difficult objective in wartime, but as some Iraqis work alongside their American counterparts, future abuse is less likely. The slippery slope to abuse can be avoided. The same social contexts that provoke and permit abuse can be harnessed to prevent it. To quote another report [(45), p. 94]: "All personnel who may be engaged in detention operations, from point of capture to final disposition, should participate in a professional ethics program that would equip them with a sharp moral compass for guidance in situations often riven with conflicting moral obligations."

> Type C essays usually have a clear practical focus on the progress of research in clarifying and solving a problem. Authors may address possible research applications at the end of specific sections or at the end of the essay, as Fiske et al. do here.

References and Notes

> Typically, Type C essays include more sources than other types, as the purpose is to critically analyze all studies in the field in order to fully show how researchers have investigated a problem.

1.   S.T. Fiske, Social Beings (Wiley, New York, 2004).
2.   F.D. Richard, C.F. Bond, J.J. Stokes-Zoota, Rev. Gen. Psychol. 7, 331 (2003).
3.   B.A. Bettencourt, N. Miller, Psychol. Bull. 119, 422 (1996).
4.   M. Carlson, N. Miller, Sociol. Soc. Res. 72, 155 (1988).
5.   M. Carlson, A. Marcus-Newhall, N. Miller, Pers. Soc. Psychol. Bull. 15, 377 (1989).
6.   C.A. Anderson, B.J. Bushman, Rev. Gen. Psychol. 1, 19 (1997).
7.   A. Taguba, "Article 15–6. Investigation of the 800th Military Police Brigade," accessed 30 June 2004 from www.npr.org/iraq/2004/prison%5fabuse%5freport.pdf
8.   B. Mullen, R. Brown, C. Smith, fur. J. Soc. Psychol. 22, 103 (1992).
9.   B. Mullen, C. Johnson, Br. J. Soc. Psychol. 29, 11 (1990).
10. J. Duckitt, in Advances in Experimental Social Psychology, M.P. Zanna, Ed. (Academic Press, New York, 2001).
11. When their own mortality is salient, as in wartime, people particularly punish those from outgroups seen to threaten basic values (12).
12. S. Solomon, J. Creenberg, T. Pyszczynski, Curr. Dir. Psychol. Sci. 9. 200 (2000).
13. S.T. Fiske, A.J. Cuddy, P. Click, J. Xu, J. Person. Soc. Psychol. 82. 878 (2002).
14. A.J. Cuddy, S.T. Fiske, P. Click, "The BIAS map: Behaviors from intergroup affect and stereotypes," unpublished manuscript (Princeton University, Princeton, NJ, 2004).
15. L.J. Heller, thesis. Princeton University, 2002.
16. H. Schütz, B. Six, Int. J. Intercult. Relat. 20, 441 (1996).

17. J.F. Dovidio et al., in Stereotypes and Stereotyping, C.N. Macrae, C. Stangor, M. Hewstone, Ed. (Guilford, New York, 1996).

18. C.A. Talaska, S.T. Fiske, S. Chaiken, "Predicting discrimination: A meta-analysis of the racial attitudes—behavior literature," unpublished manuscript (Princeton University, Princeton, NJ, 2004).

19. A.J. Hart et al., Neuroreport 11, 2351 (2000).

20. E.A. Phelps et al., J. Cogn. Neurosci. 12, 729 (2000).

21. Neuroimaging data represent college student reactions to photographs of outgroup members. These data should not be interpreted to mean that such reactions are innate or "wired in"; they result from long-term social context [9] and vary depending on short-term social context [46].

22. M.E. Wheeler. S.T. Fiske, Psychol. Sci., in press.

23. J.P. Leyens et at., Eur. J, Soc. Psychol. 33, 703 (2003).

24. R. Bond, P.B. Smith, Psychol. Bull. 119, 111 (1996).

25. S. Tanford, S. Penrod, Psychol. Bull. 95, 189 (1984).

26. J. Tata et al., J. Soc. Behav. Pers. 11, 739 (1996).

27. J.C. Turner, Social Influence (Brooks/Cole, Pacific Grove, CA, 1991).

28. S.D. Reicher, Eur. J. Soc. Psychol. 14, 1 (1984).

29. C. Haney, C. Banks, P. Zimbardo, Int. J. Criminol. Penol. 1, 69 (1973).

30. B. Mullen et at., J. Exp. Soc. Psychol. 21, 262 (1985).

31. B. Mullen, L. Hu, Br. J. Soc. Psychol. 27, 333 (1988).

32. S. Milgram, Obedience to Authority (Harper & Row, New York, 1974).

33. T. Blass, J. Appl. Soc. Psychol. 29, 955 (1999).

34. H.C. Kelman, in The Politics of Pain: Torturers and Their Masters, R.D. Crelinsten, A.P. Schmidt, Eds. (Univ. of Leiden, Leiden, NL, 1991).

35. A.L. Beaman et al., Pers. Soc. Psychol. Bull. 9, 181 (1983).

36. A.L. Dillard, J.E. Hunter, M. Burgoon, Hum. Commun. Res. 10, 461 (1984).

37. E.F. Fern, K.B. Monroe, R.A. Avila, J. Mark. Res. 23, 144 (1986).

38. E. Staub, Pers. Soc. Psychol. Rev. 3, 179 (1999).

39. A. Bandura, Pers. Soc. Psychol. Rev. 3, 193 (1999).

40. L. Berkowitz, Pers. Soc. Psychol. Rev. 3, 246 (1999).

41. J.M. Darley. Pers. Soc. Psychol. Rev. 3, 269 (1999).

42. A.G. Miller, Ed., The Social Psychology of Good and Evil (Guilford, New York, 2004).

43. Although social context matters more than most people think, individual personality also matters, in accord with most people's intuitions: Social Dominance Orientation (SDO) describes a tough-minded view that it is a zero-sum, dog-eat-dog world, where some groups justifiably dominate other groups. People who score low on SDO tend to join helping professions, be more tolerant, and endorse less aggression: they might be less inclined to abuse. People choosing to join hierarchical institutions such as the military tend to score high on SDO, in contrast [47]. Right-Wing Authoritarianism (RWA) entails conforming to conventional values, submitting to authority, and aggressing as sanctioned by authority. People who score low on RWA would be less prone to abuse. [48] High SDO and RWA both predict intolerance of outgroups social groups outside one's own.

44. A.G. Miller, A.K. Gordon, A.M. Buddie, Pers. Soc. Psychol. Rev. 3. 254 (1999).

45. J.R. Schlesinger, H. Brown, T.K. Fowler, C.A. Homer, J.A. Blackwell Jr., Final Report of the Independent Panel to Review DoD Detention Operations, accessed 8 November 2004, from www.informationclearinghouse.info/article6785.htm

46. L.T. Harris, S.T. Fiske, unpublished data.

47. J. Sidanius. F. Pratto, Social Dominance: An Intergroup Theory of Social Hierarchy and Oppression (Cambridge Univ. Press, New York, 1999).

48. B. Altemeyer, Enemies of Freedom: Understanding Right-Wing Authoritarianism (Jossey-Bass, San Francisco, 1988).

4 Critical Thinking

If you look up the words *critical*, *critic*, and *criticism* in a dictionary, you will see that each word has several meanings, including making a negative judgment, or criticizing. However, the root of *critical* comes from a Greek word that means "to judge or discern," to weigh and evaluate evidence. It is this meaning that is implied in the term *critical thinking*.

Much of what we do today is done quickly. This is true not only of video games, text messages, Twitter, and email but also of leadership roles where "instant" decisions are valued (especially if they turn out to be good decisions!). However, because critical thinking involves many related activities, speed is not usually an asset. Leaders may sometimes need to make quick decisions, but more often, their decisions arise after carefully weighing an issue and receiving input from diverse sources. Since critical thinking is a process, the best way to succeed is to slow down, to be more deliberate in your thinking so you can complete each stage of the process.

Academic essays call on the reader's careful use of critical thinking. Other kinds of writing, such as literary works, do this as well, but exercising the range of critical-thinking skills is crucial when you read academic prose because academic arguments are frequently based on tight logic or a series of claims that increase in complexity. Questioning and testing these claims is at the heart of critical thinking.

> Critical thinking is a process of engagement. It consists of a series of logical mental processes that lead to a conclusion.

Writing at the post-secondary level also requires readers to make inferences, to draw valid conclusions based on evidence. What is common to all forms of interactive reading is a reliance on critical thinking, which can involve any of the following:

* analyzing
* questioning
* hypothesizing
* evaluating
* comparing
* judging

- reconsidering
- synthesizing
- weighing the evidence
- drawing a conclusion

When Do You Use Critical Thinking?

Critical analyses, research, and many everyday activities involve critical thinking.

In many of your assignments, you will have to form conclusions about what you have read. You might employ critical thinking to decide whether to use a secondary source in your research essay. Then, you will need to judge the reliability of the sources and the validity of the findings—critical thinking, again.

Critical-thinking skills are also triggered whenever you read a work in order to comment on it in a classroom discussion or for a written assignment. When you use research, you will have to assess the reliability and usefulness of your sources, compare their claims, and organize them logically in your essay.

Critical skills are also used in many everyday situations, like those described below (Inferences and Critical Thinking), and in fieldwork projects, like those discussed in The Active Voice: Silent Witnesses to the Past (see page 42) in which the fieldworker observes phenomena in his or her surroundings and draws conclusions from these observations.

For a writer, critical thinking is stimulated whenever analysis is involved, as it is in most kinds of problem-solving. A writer asks a question about a relevant topic in his or her discipline and uses the methods and processes of the discipline to answer it. For example, P. Whitney Lackenbauer uses critical thinking, a historical perspective, and relevant sources to explain the "dual messaging" he sees in Canada's attitude to its northern regions ("Sovereignty and Security in the Canadian North": page 199 in Part III: The Reader). Using critical thinking can involve questioning the findings of peers. For example, Joel Lexchin in "Pharmaceutical Innovation: Can We Live Forever? A Commentary on Schnittker and Karandinos" (page 310 in Part III: The Reader) challenges the conclusions of a scholarly study; he uses questioning, evaluating, comparing, and weighing the evidence to help him reach his conclusion.

Although critical thinking involves typical activities, they vary somewhat from discipline to discipline:

- Empirical studies in the natural and social sciences often identify problems, generate hypotheses, predict occurrences, create raw data, analyze using cause and effect, and attempt to generalize from their findings.
- Studies in the arts and humanities often identify problems, ask questions, propose a thesis, interpret primary and secondary sources, and analyze using definitions, examples, comparison and contrast, and other patterns.

Inferences and Critical Thinking

inference
A conclusion based on what the evidence shows or points to. More than one inference might be possible in a given situation, but the most probable one is said to be the best inference.

Context clues can be used to infer the meaning of an unfamiliar word (see Word Meanings, page 56). More broadly, inferences apply to ideas and the way we use them to form conclusions. Writers do not always explicitly state their points but may leave it to the reader to infer meaning.

Many research methods rely on inferences: astronomers, for example, study the phenomenon of black holes by observing the behaviour of the matter that surrounds them. They know that before gas is swallowed up by a black hole, it is heated to extreme temperatures and accelerates. In the process, X-rays are created, which escape the black hole and reveal its presence. Scientists cannot actually *see* black holes, but they can *infer* their existence through the emission of X-rays.

We practise critical thinking every day, inferring causes or consequences from what we observe—the evidence. If you are impatiently waiting for a bus and someone at the bus stop tells you that the buses are running 15 minutes late, you might be more interested in inferring the consequence than the cause: you will be late for class. However, if the bus immediately arrives, you might revise your original conclusion, which was based on the testimony of the person at the bus stop. You might also infer that this person is not a reliable source.

You use critical thinking as you read whenever you evaluate evidence and draw conclusions about claims (assertions) or the writer. Although critical thinking can involve all the activities mentioned above, there are three general activities that will promote critical-thinking skills as you read a text:

- reading closely and objectively,
- asking questions,
- and drawing logical conclusions.

It is important to remember that critical thinking is a *process of rigorous but flexible engagement* with a text (or a non-textual situation) that may change as you read (or learn more about the non-textual situation).

More than one inference might be possible in a given situation—that is, an inference could be a *possible* conclusion, but not the *most probable* one. A more probable inference is said to be a better one. However, an incorrect inference could occur if you drew a hasty conclusion without thinking something through or if you had a bias (for example, if you prejudged someone based on appearance). In reading, you might make an incorrect inference if you failed to read the instructions for an assignment or read them too quickly. Making correct inferences is essential in responding to everyday situations and to the reading challenges and writing of your university career.

Activity 4.1

When students move away from home to go to a college or university, the new environment promotes critical thinking, and making correct inferences can be a key to survival. In groups, evaluate the evidence and discuss the best of the possible conclusions (inferences); try to make specific inferences based on the evidence rather than general ones. Share your group's conclusions with those of other groups. (The scenarios below were based on first-year students' experiences.)

1. Evidence:

   a. I noticed bottles of iron and Vitamin C pills beside my roommate's bed.
   b. She had complained of being tired and had talked about visiting the campus medical centre.

   Conclusion: _____

Continued

2. Evidence:
   a. When I came home from classes, I noticed that the fridge was nearly empty.
   b. The reusable grocery bags were gone.
   c. The grocery list was still on the fridge door.

   Conclusion: _____

3. Evidence:
   a. My roommate and I were planning to see a movie if he finished his essay by 3:00 p.m.
   b. At 1:30 p.m., he texted me to say that he was working on his last paragraph.
   c. At 3:00 p.m., I still had not received another text from him.

   Conclusion: _____

4. Evidence:
   a. My roommate is hard-working and often complains about the noise on our floor of the rez.
   b. She told me as I left for classes that she had an important exam coming up.
   c. When I returned home after class, she was not there, and her laptop was gone.

   Conclusion: _____

5. Evidence:
   a. My roommate works long hours at a restaurant after his last class and on weekends, so I do not see him until late at night.
   b. He has always taken a bus to work, and if it is behind schedule, he occasionally arrives late for work, which causes him much anxiety.
   c. Last night he came back, smiling, earlier than usual and told me to look in the driveway.

   Conclusion: _____

In the following scenarios, based on student experiences, you are given a short description and need to pick the best inference (conclusion) among the choices. Remember that there may be more than one possible inference; choose the most probable one.

1. My roommate is a bit of an "exercise freak." I have noticed that when she returns from a workout class at a nearby gym, she is always more sweaty and tired than when she works out on her own.
   a. She is having trouble with the routines during the workout classes.
   b. The workout classes push her harder than she pushes herself on her own.
   c. She is probably low in energy when she attends the workout classes.

2. When I went for lunch yesterday at our Commons cafeteria, in addition to the usual two options of a meat entree and a chicken and pasta one, there was a third entree on the menu: vegetarian stir fry.
   a. It was probably decided that the students should be offered more options for their lunch.
   b. It was probably decided that an option for vegetarians should be offered.
   c. Someone had probably forgotten to take down one of the options from a previous serving.

3. Last night at about 9:00 p.m., I heard the muffled sound of orchestral music coming from the room next door.
   a. My neighbour probably likes going to sleep to the sound of orchestral music.
   b. My neighbour probably likes studying to the sound of orchestral music.
   c. My neighbour was probably watching a movie.

4. Every Friday, my roommate, who is one of the most motivated and hard-working people I know, meets with a group of students to review math concepts. This Friday, she said she was going to study by herself instead.
   a. Her best friend decided she wasn't going to go, so my roommate decided she wouldn't go either.
   b. She didn't find that studying as part of a group really helped her understand the concepts.
   c. Her class had already been tested on the concept that was going to be reviewed.

5. I was waiting in line at the bus terminal to use the ticket machine. There were six machines, but people were lined up at only four of them, and the lineups were very long.
   a. People knew that these four machines were faster than the other two.
   b. People lined up were probably members of the same family or on a tour.
   c. Two machines were broken.

Critical Thinking and Skepticism

Focused reading is a systematic method that can be used in reading for content (see Focused Reading, page 50). By reading a text very closely, by attending objectively to its claims, to the details that support these claims, and to the writer's language and tone, you will be in a position to go beyond simple comprehension and apply critical-thinking skills.

Reading closely, then, means becoming conscious not only of content but also of how you interact with a text—for example, being open to challenges to your own ways of thinking but not being swayed by other views unless they stand up to the tests of logic and consistency. One attitude often used to describe this state of readiness is *skepticism*. Adopting an attitude of healthy skepticism does not mean you should mistrust everything you read or are told. It is different from being a cynic, as explained in the philosophical statement of the Skeptics Society, a group of scholars who publish the quarterly magazine *Skeptic*:

> Some people believe that skepticism is the rejection of new ideas, or worse, they confuse "skeptic" with "cynic" and think that skeptics are a bunch of grumpy curmudgeons unwilling to accept any claim that challenges the status quo. This is wrong. *Skepticism is a provisional approach to claims.* It is the application of reason to any and all ideas—no sacred cows allowed. In other words, skepticism is a method, not a position. Ideally, skeptics do not go into an investigation closed to the possibility that a phenomenon might be real or that a claim might be true. When we say we are "skeptical," we mean that we must see compelling evidence before we believe.

> —www.skeptic.com/about_us

In critical thinking, you constantly test and assess the evidence presented, considering how it is being used and where the writer is going with it. Key activities in a close reading of a text are questioning, evaluating, and reconsidering.

The Spirit of Inquiry

The popular tabloid *National Enquirer* promotes itself as a magazine "for enquiring minds." In fact, a typical tabloid reader believes anything he or she is told or, at least, finds humour in improbable claims.

A truly inquiring mind analyzes what it reads and does not take everything at face value. The critical thinker questions assumptions, tests the evidence, and accepts (or rejects) conclusions after careful analysis. When questions arise, the critical thinker first seeks for answers within the text itself but may also consider relevant knowledge from outside sources or from personal experience.

In analyzing arguments, the critical thinker should ask, Does the writer reason consistently? Does he or she do justice to the argument's complexity? Are there inconsistencies or oversimplifications? (See Failures in Reasoning, Chapter 9, page 108). The critical thinker should also be aware of the counter-arguments, especially those unacknowledged by the writer. Is the writer avoiding certain issues by not mentioning them? By considering all sides and angles and by questioning all easy answers, the critical thinker sets logical boundaries within which the text can be understood.

Critical Factors in Critical Thinking

A writer might make a claim that directly contradicts what our knowledge or common sense tells us—for example, that cats are more intelligent than humans. More commonly, a writer might make a claim about an often debated topic—for example, that cats are smarter than dogs. Such a claim would probably cause you to use critical thinking to evaluate the following:

Logical fallacies are failures or distortions in reason or logic. See Chapter 9.

- *The writer's credibility:* Is the writer an expert? A researcher into animal behaviour? A veterinarian? An animal trainer? Someone who has owned dogs and cats? Someone who has owned cats only? Could the writer have a bias? Are there any logical fallacies in the argument? Has fact been carefully distinguished from opinion?
- *The writer's audience:* In other words, who is his or her audience? How might the audience affect the claim? Is he or she addressing pet owners? Just dog owners? Animal behaviour experts?
- *Nature of the claim (assertion):* Specific claims are stronger than general ones and often easier to prove. Since there are many varieties of dog breeds, it would be difficult to generalize about the intelligence of *all* dogs.
- *Basis of the claim:* A claim may depend on an underlying assumption, such as a definition. Intelligence can be defined or measured in different ways: physiologically (e.g., the weight of the brain in proportion to the weight of the body) and behaviourally (e.g., trainability, adaptability, independence). Advocates of a dog's superior intelligence may point to trainability as the intelligence factor, while advocates of cat intelligence may point to adaptability or independence.
- *Method:* How does the writer attempt to prove the claim? A method that sought to measure intelligence scientifically would be more credible than one that relied only on personal observation. However, not all valid arguments make use of scientific evidence. Deductive methods are based on general statements, such as beliefs or values, which are then applied to specific cases. Does the statement seem reasonable/logical? (See Chapter 9, page 108, for more about deductive reasoning.)
- *Support:* In critical thinking, you must evaluate the nature of the evidence and the way the writer uses it. Typical questions might include the following: What kind of evidence did the writer use? Has the writer relied too much on one kind of evidence? How many sources were used? Were they current ones? Did the writer ignore or minimize some sources (e.g., those that found dogs more intelligent than cats)?

Drawing Conclusions

Drawing a conclusion about a work you have read usually involves more than making one inference; it results from the *incremental process of reading critically*. In arriving at a conclusion, you weigh the factors involved in your analysis of the text. As you complete your reading, you will synthesize the evidence you analyzed in order to say something definitive about it, about its presentation, and/or about the writer.

In the end, *your goal is to determine whether the accumulated weight of evidence supports the writer's claim*, or, as members of the Skeptics Society would ask, Is the weight of evidence "compelling"? If you have been using your critical-thinking skills to write a critical analysis of a work, you will need to show how critical thinking led you to your conclusions (see page 91). For a critical-thinking assignment involving research, see Chapter 10, page 133.

Using Critical Thinking to Determine the Writer's Attitude

Tone refers to the writer's (or speaker's) attitude toward the topic or audience. In the world of social media today, writers may show their attitude to a post by using an emoticon. In more formal writing, writers use indirect resources, especially word choice and other linguistic features, or humour and exaggeration to show their tone. In such cases, readers may need to "read between the lines" and ask themselves not just *what* a writer is saying but also *how* she or he is saying it.

Activity 4.2

The passages below contain specific statements from which readers may be able to make inferences about the writer's belief or attitude concerning his or her subject. Choose the most valid (most probable) conclusion. Explain your choice by pointing specifically to words or other features in the passage (Note: For some of the questions below, page numbers from Part III: The Reader are given so you can look at the passage's context if you wish):

1. Binkley paid for all the travel and expenses, and what was only 12 months ago a very new and controversial transaction has today left Binkley a healthy man—and the first of 16 people who have successfully received organs through MatchingDonors.com. (J. Desai. "Google Yourself an Organ Donor." *Science & Spirit, vol. 17, no. 1,* 2006, pp. 46–52)

    a. The author believes that this method of soliciting donors is wrong.
    b. The author believes that this method of soliciting donors is, at the very least, ethically questionable.
    c. The author sees nothing wrong with this method of soliciting donors.
    d. No inference is possible about the author's beliefs; he/she is just reporting the facts.

2. Canada is, at a national and international level, making a clear and very positive commitment to refugees.

The amount of action taken in the last few months has been remarkable for a national government body, as has been the welcoming response by the general Canadian public. ("Causes and Consequences of Canada's Resettlement of Syrian Refugees": page 213 in Part III: The Reader)

    a. The tone is cheerful.
    b. The tone is cautious.
    c. The tone is encouraging.

3. *Jurassic World* is anticapitalist, antimanagerialism, and anti-GM; it is also antifeminist, racist, species-ist, and decidedly not queer. ("*Jurassic World* and Procreation Anxiety": page 272 in Part III: The Reader)

    a. The writer's tone is comic.
    b. The writer's tone is serious.
    c. The writer's tone is self-assured.

4. We believe the use of biological concepts of race in human genetic research—so disputed and so mired in confusion—is problematic at best and harmful at worst. It is time for biologists to find a better way. ("Taking Race Out of Human Genetics": page 342 in Part III: The Reader)

    a. The writer's tone is indignant.
    b. The writer's tone is objective.
    c. The writer's tone is sarcastic.

Continued

5. They're the impulse buys piled up next to the cash register. They're the books stocked by Urban Outfitters and hipster gift stores. They're the books you pick up, laugh at, and figure would be just about right for that co-worker who's into sci-fi (*The Space Tourist's Handbook*) [or] the friend who watches too much TV (*Hey! It's That Guy!: The Fametracker.com Guide to Character Actors*). . . . Pop-culture-inspired handbooks for situations you're never going to face featuring information you're never going to need, these gimmicky, kooky, sometimes just plain stupid books have at least one thing in common: There are more and more of them out there, because they sell. (Hal Niedzviecki. "Publishers Feel Smart about Selling People Stupid Books." *The Globe and Mail*, 17 Dec. 2005, R1.)

    a.   The writer's tone is respectful.
    b.   The writer's tone is amused.
    c.   The writer's tone is contemptuous.

The essay in the Active Voice feature below demonstrates how critical thinking can be used to "reconstruct" the past. The questions that follow it stress the application of critical thinking to the essay itself.

The Active Voice

Silent Witnesses to the Past

1   No academic subject can claim a greater longevity in the Western educational system than the study of Greek and Latin. From the Renaissance on, it was thought that the mastery of these two difficult languages would provide a mental training without equal. The consequences of this belief were still apparent until quite recently. During the Second World War, for instance, classicists came second only to mathematicians in the recruitment of code-breakers, having intellectual capabilities, it was believed, perfectly honed to tackle complex problems. That said, despite their formidable reputation, classical languages have of late suffered an astonishingly rapid decline. Dominant for some 500 years, the study of Latin all but disappeared from schools in a single generation, while Greek is in an even more perilous state.

2   University departments of classics (now usually called something along the lines of "Greek and Roman Studies") have generally shown themselves to be highly adept at adjusting to the changing circumstances. Their new mission is to introduce students to classical civilization through non-linguistic media. None has proved more successful than archaeology.

3   Classical archaeology is, of course, much more than an inferior substitute for the ancient languages. It is a highly effective way for students to gain a direct and tangible connection with antiquity, in many ways far more direct than they ever could from the written text. I might illustrate this from my own experience with a training excavation conducted on behalf of the University of British Columbia. The practicum, conducted for academic credit at the Lunt Roman Fort, near Coventry, England, from 1985 to 2002, was in each of those years attended by 35 or so students from UBC and elsewhere in North America.

4   The Lunt Fort was first built in the early sixties AD (during the reign of Nero) and remained under occupation for about 30 years. Our work concentrated on its defensive system, in the form of a turf rampart fronted by a series of ditches. In the course of excavation, the students brought to light objects that had remained untouched since they were discarded nearly 2,000 years ago by the fort's original occupants. The term *discarded* is deliberate, since most of the material was there because its owners had thrown it away: pieces of pot, old nails, a

belt buckle, a broken brooch, and the like. For students sensitive to the spirit of history, the thrill of gaining this direct physical contact with the ancient Romans proved to be a life-transforming experience.

5   Archaeology is not, of course, a mere treasure hunt. The students, usually from faculties of arts, were obliged to acquire a whole new set of skills. They were given thorough training in the techniques required of the modern archaeologist. They learned to plan, to survey, to enter items into a systematic database. They were taught to date fragments of pottery, to identify different types of corroded metal, to distinguish between natural strata in sandy soil and deposited material compacted over hundreds of years. This last is not an easy task but a crucial one on a site like ours, where no stone construction was used and the residual material is often detectable only through variations in the colour of the soil.

6   More importantly, however, beyond these essentially technical skills, the students developed crucial expertise in applying logical thought processes to the investigation of complex evidence. Archaeological remains are silent witnesses to the past. Like other witnesses, they surrender their testimony only under skilful cross-examination. Let me illustrate this with a concrete example. The most useful features on any Roman fort are the "V"-shaped defensive ditches. When forts were demolished to give way to civilian settlements, the ditches were filled, and the material deposited in them came primarily from the fort's upper structures. In the ensuing centuries, the surface area would almost invariably be subject to human activity, usually plowing. The evidence at ground level would thus often be destroyed or damaged. But the fill of the ditches would survive intact, and much of the history of the site can be recovered from it. Students noticed when they drew a plan of a section of a ditch that there was, at the bottom, at the point of the "V," a roughly square-shaped slot. What had caused this? They soon learned to dismiss such fanciful ideas such as "ankle-breakers" by observing what happened in the newly excavated ditches when it rained: they filled with silt.

7   The slots were clearly made by Roman soldiers dragging buckets along the ditch-bottom to remove the silt.

Students were then told to observe whether the excavated slot was silt-free or full of silt. What could that observation tell us? We made the students try to think in Roman terms. In the case of a silted-up ditch, why would the Romans have stopped removing silt from the bottom of the ditch? Almost certainly, it means that the occupants anticipated that they would be abandoning the fort at some point in the near future and saw no need to keep the ditch clean. In other words, it suggests an orderly redeployment. Conversely, a meticulously cleaned ditch suggests that the fort was abandoned and the ditches filled in as the immediate result of an order to move, perhaps because of some military crisis.

8   Archaeology thus involves not only the collection of material from which evidence is derived but, most importantly, the interpretation of that evidence by a series of logical mental sequences. It is a never-ending process. Examination of surviving material will reveal the size and nature of wall foundations. Foundations of a certain size token walls of a certain size. Why do walls have to be so high, so thick? Would that size have been needed for storage? If not, it presumably means that the walls were needed for defence. But, let us suppose, the period was peaceful and the region settled, at least according to Tacitus and the like. Does the evidence on the ground suggest that we have to question the literary evidence (written, after all, in Rome, usually by historians who never set foot in a military camp and almost certainly had never been to Britain)? There are numerous permutations of this kind of questioning.

9   Interestingly, the very mental discipline that the detailed knowledge of the ancient languages reputedly bestowed on previous generations is now well matched by what archaeology offers the students of today. The vast majority will not become professional archaeologists. But after their training, they see their world differently and will have developed considerable proficiency as problems-solvers, acquiring broad skills that stand them in excellent stead in their chosen future careers.

—**Anthony Barrett**, Professor, Department of Classical, Near Eastern and Religious Studies, University of British Columbia

Continued

Questions to Consider

1. Why do you think that the study of classical languages was considered "a mental training without equal"? Can you infer reasons for its decline after the Second World War?

2. Explain how the specialized skills mentioned in paragraph 5 equip students to draw more accurate conclusions about the objects they will be studying. How do the skills described in paragraph 6 differ from those in paragraph 5?

3. What are "ankle-breakers," and why does the writer dismiss them as "fanciful"?

4. What is the function of the questions in paragraph 8? Does the writer answer the last question in this paragraph? Why or why not?

5. Paraphrase (put in your own words) the last sentence, in which the writer summarizes the value of the skills students gain through the experience at the excavation of the Lunt Fort.

5 Reading Strategies

Interacting with Texts

Reading is not just a passive process. It is an active or, more accurately, an *interactive* one involving a relationship *between* you and the text you are reading (*inter-* is a prefix meaning "between"), which can change as you read and apply critical-thinking skills. That is why when you read a text for the second and a third time, you uncover new meanings and make new inferences.

Each reader approaches a text in a different way: your ideas, beliefs, and specific knowledge about the topic reflect who you are and your unique experiences. You will therefore interact with the text in a unique way.

In addition, the nature of the text itself, the purpose of the author in writing, the audience it was intended to reach, and the reason for reading it all play a role in the way you interact with it, as do the author's own ideas, beliefs, background, and the specific choices—in diction, style, and tone—that he or she makes.

Consider, for example, what you might find yourself thinking about as you began reading an essay by David Suzuki on wind farms as an alternative energy source:

> Off the coast of British Columbia in Canada is an island called Quadra, where I have a cabin that is as close to my heart as you can imagine. From my porch on a good day you can see clear across the waters of Georgia Strait to the snowy peaks of the rugged Coast Mountains. It is one of the most beautiful views I have seen. And I would gladly share it with a wind farm.
>
> But sometimes it seems like I'm in the minority. All across Europe and North America, environmentalists are locking horns with the wind industry over the location of wind farms.
>
> —D. Suzuki. "The Beauty of Wind Farms." *New Scientist, vol. 186* no. 2495, 2005, pp. 20–1.

Questions about the subject itself: What do I know about wind farms? Where did my knowledge come from (the media, teachers or textbooks, conversations with friends, my own observation)? Have I any personal experience that might affect my reading? Do I have opinions about the topic? What might change them?

Questions about the writer: Is the author's name familiar? What do I associate with him and his writing? Where did these associations come from (previous work by the author or by another author, something mentioned in class or in general conversation)? Is he an authority? How would the average Canadian respond to an essay written by this writer?

While readers have different knowledge and opinions about wind farms, many know something about the author, a noted Canadian scientist and environmentalist. The following comments on his essay illustrate the different ways that reader and writer can interact with a text: each reader's point of view is shaped, at least somewhat, by his or her experience with the subject of wind farms and, in one case, with the author. Each reader, therefore, has likely approached the essay in a different way. Reflecting on your knowledge of the subject and author(s) is a practical pre-reading activity that will make you more conscious of the background, opinions, and possible biases that could come into play as you read. Many of the pre-reading questions in Part III: The Reader ask you to do exactly that.

Student Comments

Katherine W.: I was not very knowledgeable about the "windmill issue" before I read this article, but by the end, I was pretty much convinced that it is an important issue. Of course, my viewpoint might have been a little biased because I have always been a fan of windmills (no practical reason) and have a lot of respect for David Suzuki. I guess that is the main reason I was convinced.

Tristan H.: Since I grew up in southern Alberta, I am no stranger to windmills, but I never imagined they were an issue with certain groups. Whenever we talked about windmills, it was not to say how ugly or unpleasant they were. They were more of an accent to the background. Without reading this essay, I would never have thought they were an environmental issue at all.

Andrew M.: In the first paragraph, David Suzuki speaks of his cabin on Quadra Island and the fact he would "gladly share it with a wind farm." I have flown over and around Quadra Island numerous times as well as across the Georgia Strait to the Coastal Mountains referred to in his article. The island is covered by forest, as are the mountains across the strait. I have seen wind farms in various parts of Alberta, all of them in non-forested areas. I don't see his point as credible, as it is impractical to set up wind farms in forested areas.

Annotating Texts

One way to explore a topic in a text, then, is to write about it from your own point of view, to reflect on it and respond in writing. While this can be a valuable experience, university-level assignments often require a more formal approach to a text. However, whether writing a response or a more formal analysis, you will need to jot your ideas down, to **annotate** the essay (*ad* = to + *nota* = note).

Making annotations about the text you are reading is an important (perhaps the *most* important) reading strategy, not just because it enables you to return to the essay later and have your questions and other responses fresh in your mind but also because when you annotate an essay, you are *beginning your actual work on the assignment*: you are translating abstract ideas and impressions into concrete language, solidifying those ideas. Annotating a text could involve any of the following, among many others:

- underlining main ideas and/or ones most relevant to your reading purpose (see Reading Purpose, below)
- determining meanings of unfamiliar words by context or by looking them up in a dictionary
- asking questions about the text
- reflecting on your own experiences and observations
- identifying points you agree or disagree with and asking yourself why you agree/disagree; how can you support your view?
- noting connections between one passage and other ones or one section and another one
- identifying rhetorical strategies and commenting on their use

Pre-reading Strategies: Reading Purpose

It is important to know why you are reading a text; the reason affects the way you respond to it. Are you reading it to determine whether the essay is related to your topic? To extract the main ideas? To use the text as a secondary source in your essay? To write a rhetorical or critical analysis? Each of these questions affects the way you respond to the essay and the reading strategies you adopt. Becoming familiar with some general reading strategies, then, can make the reading process more manageable, ensuring that you remain in control of the reading situation, rather than the other way around.

1. Reading to Determine Whether the Essay Is Related to Your Topic (to explore)

When you search for potential sources for a research essay, you look for essays that seem promising, perhaps from their titles or the fact that they are listed in bibliographies of general works such as textbooks or in encyclopedias, indexes, or subject directories. If you are using an online resource, you might search for articles or books by keywords related to your topic. Since you are exploring, you do not want to waste time by closely reading each text, so a specific strategy is essential.

Once you find a potentially useful essay title, you can read the abstract, if available, the introduction, and headings. If it still looks promising, turn your attention to the main parts of the essay, scanning for topic sentences and other content clues (see Reading Paragraphs: Locating Main Ideas, page 52). Finally, read the conclusion. Scanning prevents wasting time on what might not be useful, giving you more time to scan other potential sources.

It is vital, however, that you record all relevant bibliographic information for every potential source—title, author, journal or book title (and include names of editors if the source is an edited book), journal volume and issue numbers, and page range, or website details.

annotation (verb annotate)

A note that explains, expands on, or comments on a written text.

See the annotated writing samples on pages 26–34 in Chapter 3 for examples of annotations.

This information will enable you to access the source quickly when you are ready and will save you time preparing your bibliography if you do end up using the source in your paper.

2. Reading to Extract Main Ideas (to summarize)

You might read an essay in order to write a formal summary, or précis (see page 87). In this case, you identify the important points after you have thoroughly read the text, as you will not know which are the main and which the sub-points until you have completed your first reading. This practice applies to other reading purposes too: do the annotating in a later reading—after you have become familiar with the entire contents of the essay, its purpose, its tone, and so on.

3. Reading to Use the Text as a Secondary Source in Your Essay (to synthesize)

> Record page numbers (or paragraph numbers if they are given in an electronic source) for future reference. Direct quotations, paraphrases, and most summaries require citations that include page numbers.

After you have explored to determine potential sources, you must now read closely, annotate carefully, and consider how each point relates to your thesis. How much you annotate depends on the importance of the source, so your initial task is to attempt to answer this question. After scanning the entire essay, you might decide that only one section directly pertains to your topic; you may then wish to summarize this section to use in your essay. If a phrase or sentence is particularly significant or well expressed, you can record its wording exactly for future use (see Integrating Your Sources, page 136). Make sure that you record the page numbers of every potential source whether you are quoting directly, summarizing, or making a brief reference.

> Make sure that you record the page numbers of every potential source when quoting directly, summarizing, or even making a brief reference.

4. Reading to Respond or Analyze

Although responding to a work may or may not be an assignment at the university level, rhetorical analyses are common because they reveal how an essay is put together, making them useful as models for your own writing. In an analysis, you are concerned with breaking down the text to test the validity of the author's claims and inferences, and to comment on the author's methods and strategies. Thus, your interaction with the text will involve such activities as identifying and evaluating; it will involve critical thinking and objective analysis. (See Chapter 4 on Critical Thinking, page 35, and The Rhetorical Analysis: Explaining the How and Why, page 91).

> **rhetorical or critical analysis**
>
> A writing activity concerned with breaking down a text to examine its structure, rhetorical strategies, use of reason, significance, and other features.

Of course, there are other reasons for reading: to write a review of a book or film, to prepare an informational or evaluative report, to compare and contrast two essays, to study for an exam, to see whether an essay topic interests you, for pure pleasure, and many more. Asking "How am I going to use the text?" before you begin can orient you appropriately and help you select the most useful strategies of those discussed below.

Reading Strategies: The Big Picture

People often assess their own strengths by saying, "I like to look at the big picture" or "I'm a detail person." Unsurprisingly, successful essay writing requires attention to both the large and the small: while large-scale concerns like essay organization and paragraph structure (sometimes referred to as *macro-composing*) tend to occur in the early and middle stages, by the final-draft stage, the focus will be on detail-oriented tasks (*micro-composing*), such as sentence construction, word choice, grammar, and source integration.

Selective Reading: Scanning and Focused Reading

In **selective reading**, your reading strategy is determined by your pre-reading choices, which can depend on what you are reading (for example, an introduction, a book chapter, an academic essay, or a book review) and your purpose for reading, as discussed above. It is therefore very different from simply sitting down with a book or essay and closely reading every word from beginning to end. Unlike reading for pleasure, then, selective reading is planned, conscious reading.

Scanning

Scanning is a form of selective reading. In a *general scan*, you read to get the gist of a text, looking for content markers, such as headings and places in which the author summarizes material (this summary could include tables, graphs, and other visual representations used to condense textual explanation). You try to identify main ideas in the essay by locating topic sentences, often, but not always, the first sentence of the paragraph. Thesis statements, plans, or hypotheses are found in academic essays at the end of the introduction. For now, you can skip details such as examples. General scanning is a good way to start reading a text since it gives you an overview of content. From a general scan, you might then move on to another selective reading method.

In a specific scan, or *target scan*, you look for *specific* content, for words and phrases related to your topic. If you are looking for information in a book, you can consult the **subject index** (or author index) at the back of the book. These indexes may give you many page references, requiring you to scan several pages to access the information you seek. If you are accessing a text online, you can use your browser's Find function to locate significant words or phrases. (For more about searching by keywords, see "Search Strategies," which is in the Active Voice essay titled "A Beginner's Guide to Research in the Academic Library," Chapter 10: page 128).

A *general scan* is helpful if you know you will be using the whole text—for example, if you are going to summarize a work or refer to it often in your essay—since it can give you an overview of content. A *target scan* is helpful if you want to assess the usefulness of a text; if you decide that it does contain relevant content, you can then apply another method of selective reading, such as focused reading.

Reading Hypothesis

After scanning an essay's title, abstract, headings, list of sources, and introduction, you might construct a reading hypothesis that can guide you throughout a first reading of an essay. In essence, a reading hypothesis is a prediction about the essay's content or other elements, such as the writer's style or tone. Its main purpose is to solidify your expectations about the essay and shape the way you approach your reading of it.

You can make the hypothesis concrete by writing it up as a short paragraph. Essentially, the reading hypothesis answers questions like, What is the essay about? What is the author trying to prove and how does he or she accomplish this? How might the essay be similar to or different from others on the same topic? Of course, your hypothesis is a starting point and may well change as you read more closely.

A reading hypothesis could also list the specific strategies you will use to read the text, such as those discussed in the next few pages.

selective reading
A reading strategy designed to meet a specific objective, such as scanning for main points or reading for detail.

scanning
A form of selective reading in which you skim sections or an entire text. In a general scan, you try to determine the gist of a text—for example, by locating main ideas; in a target scan, you look for specific concepts or topics by key words or phrases. In research, a target scan typically occurs after you have narrowed your general topic.

subject index
A list of important words in a printed text, ordered alphabetically and usually placed at the end of the text.

In order to successfully scan academic essays, you should be familiar with their conventions—in particular, where to find important information (see Chapter 2).

Focused Reading

Because focused reading is close reading, it is best to scan a text beforehand to find the most relevant portions, which you then read in detail. University-level reading across the disciplines often involves both scanning and focused reading.

Activity 5.1

Below are several reading situations with two variables for each—reading purpose and kind of text. Consider how the variables would help you decide on the most appropriate reading strategy (or strategies) to use in each situation.

Reading Purpose	Kind of Text	Reading Strategy(ies)?
to provide an overview or a general summary	journalistic essay	
to see whether the topic interests you sufficiently to write an essay on it	informative essay	
to summarize results	journal study that describes original research (an experiment)	
to write a character or thematic analysis	novel	
to prepare for an exam question with a topic assigned in advance	essay you have never read	
to study for a final exam	your class notes	
to write a critical response to an essay about a recent controversial topic (e.g., face transplants)	journalistic essay accessed online	
to compare/contrast two essays (e.g., two tax systems)	edited collection of essays with differing points of view published by an academic press	
to write a critical analysis	argumentative essay	
to pass the time before your dentist appointment	popular magazine	
to check the accuracy of a direct quotation you used in your essay	academic essay	

focused reading

A reading strategy in which close attention is paid to sentences and words in order to extract detail, tone, style, relevance, etc.

As the term **focused reading** implies, you read the text closely line by line and word by word not just to understand content—for example, main ideas—but also to identify the text's rhetorical strategies, tone, or stylistic elements. You apply critical thinking skills by questioning the writer's claims or inferences (conclusions drawn from the evidence). Many of the strategies for focused reading are discussed below under Dividing the Whole and Reading Strategies: The Detail Work.

In a focused reading, you often concentrate on one or more short or medium-length passages and relate them to a main idea or to other sections of the text. For example, if you are writing an essay for a history class, you might concentrate on specific passages from a primary text, such as a historical document, in order to connect key ideas in the passage to a historical event or other historical element. The purpose of analyzing the specific passage(s) is to support your thesis about the significance or interpretation of the event.

Reading Strategies in Action

Adopting reading strategies means adopting a plan for reading, a logical sequence of steps once you know your reading purpose. Of the four main reading purposes discussed above, let's assume that you are looking for sources for an essay on street youth and schizophrenia (reading purpose 1). It is a good, specific topic, but not all potentially useful articles will include your keywords in their title. You could follow a sequence to evaluate the usefulness of the source:

Step 1 What is the title of the article? "Incidence of mental illness among the unemployed"

Action: Potentially useful; proceed to step 2 (general scan).

Step 2 General scan: What further information is contained in the abstract and headings? One of the headings is titled "Youth Unemployment and Mental Illness."

Action: As it is a lengthy section, repeat step 2 (general scan), identifying paragraph content by topic sentences.

Action: No relevant information obtained; proceed to step 3 (target scan).

Step 3 Target scan: Do any of the following keywords result in hits? "homeless," "street youth," "schizophrenia"

Action: In a section titled "Dire Consequences," several results are found for "homeless"; proceed to step 4 (focused reading).

Step 4 Focused reading: What is this section about? Are any points relevant to your topic?

Action: Reading closely, you identify one substantial passage that discusses mental illness among unemployed youth in homeless shelters. Although the article does not address your specific topic (schizophrenia), you summarize the passage and record two direct quotations for potential use in your essay.

Dividing the Whole

Information is more easily grasped if it is separated into logical divisions. Experiments may be divided into formal sections, each labelled according to convention; formal reports also use standardized headings. Such categories tell you where specific information can be found; for example, in the "Methods" section, the writer describes how the study was set up, the number of participants, how they were chosen, what measurements were applied, and similar details. If you are interested in whether the author proved a hypothesis, you would read the abstract or the introduction and then read the "Discussion" section.

Fortunately, most academic writers are aware of the importance of structure and organize content in the body of their essays logically. In the absence of an essay plan, formal or content headings, additional spacing, or similar aids, your job is to determine that logic and use it to create manageable subdivisions. As well as making the essay easier to read, when you do this you are also familiarizing yourself with the parts of the essay that are going to be useful to you.

Rhetorical Patterns and Transitions

Information can often be organized by **rhetorical patterns**. Identifying these patterns makes the text easier to follow. For example, in the chronological pattern, the writer traces a development over time, usually from old to new. In the problem–solution pattern, problems or solutions, or both, are proposed, as in the example below (also see Rhetorical Patterns and Paragraph Development, page 77).

In addition, the relationship between ideas is often shown through **transitional words and phrases**. These transitions can indicate whether an idea is going to be expanded, qualified, or emphasized, or whether a new idea will be introduced. Transitions can occur between one paragraph and the next or between parts of a paragraph (e.g., between sentences), linking smaller parts of the text. Paying attention to organizational patterns and transitions can help you break down an essay into smaller, more manageable units.

Reading Paragraphs: Locating Main Ideas

A **topic sentence** states the main idea of the paragraph and is often the first sentence; it can be developed by examples or analysis throughout the rest of the paragraph. Occasionally, a writer may build *toward* the central idea, in which case the topic sentence may be a middle or even the last sentence in the paragraph. Wherever it occurs in the paragraph, the function of the topic sentence is partly structural—providing a foundation for the paragraph.

In the passage below, the author addresses Canadian governmental bodies, proposing solutions to ease the challenges of learning disabilities for Canadians. The author announces the rhetorical pattern in the topic sentence and uses transitions to help guide the reader from one idea (solution) to the next. (Ellipses show that some words have been omitted):

The LDAC recommends a number of actions to be taken by federal and provincial governments to address the problems noted above. . . . First, awareness and education are fundamental for medical, mental health, and educational professionals. . . . Second, early universal screening and intervention for preschool and primary school children could increase literacy rates, reduce healthcare costs, improve family life, and enhance employment outlook. Further, the LDAC recommends that universal health insurance plans cover screening, assessment, and intervention costs. Ultimately, all of these initiatives would serve to "reduce the short- and long-term economic costs of failure (special education, unemployment, health, welfare, and corrections)" (Learning Disabilities Association of Canada, 2007, p. 8).

The following paragraphs illustrate different methods of paragraph construction. In the first, the opening sentence announces the paragraph's main idea, that Canadians have much to be proud of but are often unaware of their heroes; it is the topic sentence, which is developed through examples. This paragraph can be said to have been developed *deductively*: the topic sentence makes a general statement after which more specific statements are used for support:

Canadians have lots to celebrate, aside from hockey and Medicare, though we tend not to celebrate very loudly. How many Canadians even know that Nancy Huston, a Calgarian by origin but writing in French, won France's prestigious Prix Fémina, or that Canadian composer Howard Shore has won three Oscars, three Golden Globes and four Grammies for his film scores? . . .

—Toope, "Of Hockey, Medicare and Canadian Dreams": page 191 in Part III: The Reader.

In contrast to the first example, the paragraph below begins with a quotation from a Canadian senator on the Chinese Head Tax proposal. After a second quotation by another senator, there is a general statement, then finally the topic sentence, which reflects the main idea in the paragraph as a whole. The paragraph can be said to have been developed *inductively*: the topic sentence (in italics below for emphasis) is a general statement arrived at after specific "evidence" has been considered:

> Even George W. Allan, who introduced the amendments in the Senate for the government, said that he had "no special leaning towards this Chinese legislation." Given the level of agreement against the proposals, it would be, Richard W. Scott averred, "a service to the empire if we allow this question to stand over another year." By that time, he hoped, passions in British Columbia might have calmed somewhat and a more reasonable examination of the question might be assayed. *Thus, the same Senate that had seemed to sanction the 1885 Chinese Immigration Act now let the debate on its amendment stand for six months, thereby signaling an unwillingness to allow the law to be changed in a more restrictive manner.*
>
> —Anderson, "The Senate and the Fight against the 1885 Chinese Immigration Act": page 228 in Part III: The Reader.

If you are having difficulty locating the topic sentence, ask yourself which sentence best describes what the paragraph is about. Not all paragraphs contain topic sentences: a paragraph, especially a short one, may expand on the main idea in the previous paragraph, rather than introduce a new idea.

> When you scan an essay, a section, or a paragraph, try to identify the topic sentence(s)—often, but not always, the first sentence of paragraphs.

Activity 5.2

Identify the topic sentence in the following paragraph. If you wish to get a sense of paragraph context, page numbers where the full essay is found have been given.

1. "The Story of an Hour" was first published in Vogue in 1894. More than a century later, now in the midst of our own technological revolution, it is difficult to grasp how fundamentally nineteenth-century technologies were altering the world in Chopin's time. Before the railroad, traveling was extremely difficult and dangerous. In the 1850s, it took an average of 128 days to traverse the Oregon Trail (Unruh 403), with a mortality rate of 4% to 6% (408). . . .

    —Foote, "Speed That Kills": page 346 in Part III: The Reader.

Using Strategic Repetition and Prompts in Reading

Important words and phrases tend to recur throughout related paragraphs, and writers may use such keywords to stress important content. Although needless repetition should be avoided, strategic repetition places the stress where the writer wants it to be, helping the reader grasp essential concepts. However, strategic repetition does not just apply to words: a **paragraph wrap**, usually the last sentence of a paragraph, sums up the main idea in the paragraph, recalling the topic sentence.

> **paragraph wrap**
> Sums up the main idea in the paragraph, recalling the topic sentence. It usually appears in the last sentence of a paragraph.

prompt

A word, phrase, or clause that directs readers to important content rather than containing important content itself.

Thinking of transitions, strategic repetition, prompts, and other strategies for reading reinforces the importance of using them to create coherence in your own writing. Although they are usually discussed as *writing* rather than as *reading* strategies, thinking of them as *reading* strategies highlights the essential relationship between writing and reading. Writing consciously by using strategies for coherence helps conscious readers to decode a difficult text. See Writing Middle Paragraphs (Chapter 6, page 73), which discusses strategies for coherent writing.

In the following introductory paragraph, the authors repeat the key word in the paragraph (and the essay), using it as a noun and a verb. Strategic repetition, keywords, and a paragraph wrap referring back to the first sentence are highlighted below:

Ensuring a sufficient supply of quality food for a growing human population is a major challenge, aggravated by climate change and already-strained natural resources. Food security requires production of some food surpluses to safeguard against unpredictable fluctuations *(1)*. However, when food is wasted, not only has carbon been emitted to no avail, but disposal and decomposition in landfills create additional environmental impacts. Decreasing the current high scale of food waste is thus crucial for achieving resource-efficient, sustainable food systems *(2)*. But, although avoiding food waste seems an obvious step toward sustainability, especially given that most people perceive wasting food as grossly unethical *(3)*, food waste is a challenge that is not easily solved.

— Aschemann-Witzel, "Waste Not, Want Not, Emit Less": page 301 in Part III: The Reader.

Rhetorical patterns, transitions, topic sentences, and strategic repetition, then, give structural and content cues about where important information can be found. **Prompts** are another kind of cue that direct readers to important content in the next sentence or paragraph. Thus, brief summaries and questions can act as prompts to what lies ahead.

In the following paragraph excerpt, the first sentence refers to a "myth" about cyberbullying: it acts as a prompt for the main idea, the "reality," discussed in the second sentence, the topic sentence (in italics):

Many individuals may believe that they already fully understand and can recognize what cyberbullying is. *The reality, however, is that there exists much variability in the way cyberbullying is defined and considered—even among cyberbullying researchers.*

—Sabella, Patchin, and Hinduja, "Cyberbullying Myths and Realities": page 314 in Part III: The Reader.

Activity 5.3

Analyze the following paragraphs, identifying strategies such as rhetorical patterns, topic sentences, transitions, strategic repetition, and prompts.

1. Given all of this research, one might ask: Why is it a myth that "cyberbullying causes suicide?" The answer to this question lies in the important difference between the nature of correlation and causation. While it is true that there exists a relationship between bullying and suicide (a connection or correlation), no conclusive statistical evidence has shown that a cyberbullying experience directly "leads to" or causes suicide. As previously stated, most youth who are cyberbullied do not take their own lives. So, the best that we can confidently say is that, among some young people, cyberbullying and suicide may be co-occurring (or are "co-related") with at least one of many other factors such as depression, social withdrawal, disability, social hopelessness,

or other psychiatric morbidity (Skapinakis et al., 2011). That is, cyberbullying may aggravate the victim's already existing vulnerabilities.

—Sabella, Patchin, and Hinduja, "Cyberbullying Myths and Realities": page 314 in Part III: The Reader.

2. Many people do resist the temptation to engage in self-serving behaviours that contribute to climate change. Yet, admittedly, many do yield to the temptation. What will it take to change these people's behaviour? As a start—but only a start—understanding environment-related motivations, attitudes, social and organizational perceptions, rationales, biases, habits, barriers to change, life-context, and trust in government will help. Certainly, psychologists are already engaged in the effort on their own. For example, some have investigated the psychological dimensions of global warming (e.g., Dresner, 1989–90; Heath & Gifford, 2006; Nilsson, von Borgstede, & Biel, 2004). However, the major thesis of the present article is that we psychologists must do more.

—Gifford, "Psychology's Essential Role in Alleviating the Impacts of Climate Change": page 350 in Part III: The Reader.

3. The United States and Canada are 2 countries that have many shared values. However, there are important differences between these 2 countries that may be reflected in different normative beliefs about health behaviors. For example, the legal drinking age in Canada is much younger (18–19 years) than in the United States (21 years). In terms of drug control policies, the United States has a greater conservatism towards legalizing drugs such as marijuana than Canada. Under current Canadian legislation, possession of small amounts of marijuana for personal use (i.e., ≤ 15 g) will not typically result in a criminal record. In terms of smoking, such differences may inevitably be reflected in cross-cultural differences in post-secondary students' use of alcohol and drugs and normative beliefs regarding such health behaviors. . . .

—Arbour-Nicitopoulos et al., "Social Norms of Alcohol, Smoking, and Marijuana Use within a Canadian University Setting": page 175 in Part III: The Reader.

Reading Strategies: The Detail Work

Sooner or later readers find themselves grappling with the elements of the sentence—words, phrases, and clauses. In their focused reading, students may encounter challenges with word meanings (vocabulary) or with the author's style or tone.

Connotations and Denotations

Readers need to know *how* a writer is using words before making inferences about meaning. Individual words carry connotations, or implications, beyond those of their dictionary meanings, or denotations. Paying careful attention to context—the surrounding words—can help you determine a word's connotation and help you figure out its meaning. Sometimes dictionaries suggest a word's connotations, although often, when you look up a word in a dictionary, you find one or more of its common definitions and have to look at the passage itself to know exactly how it is being used (its connotation).

A word can acquire different connotations through its use over time or by a specific group. In some cases, positive or negative values have become associated with the word. Many common words have several connotations. Consider, for example, the implications of the words *slender, slim, lean, thin, skinny, underweight, scrawny,* and *emaciated,* which suggest a progression from positive (graceful, athletic . . .) to negative (. . . weak, sickly). Sometimes only context will make a word's connotation clear.

connotation (verb connote)

The implications or additional meanings of a word; a word's context may suggest its connotations.

denotation (verb denote)

The meaning of a word, for example, as defined in a dictionary.

Activity 5.4

In groups or individually, make a list of 10 common adjectives. Then, for each word, come up with five words similar but not identical in meaning to the original word and use them in sentences. The sentences should reveal the word's connotation, so ensure that you provide adequate context for each word's exact meaning in the sentence. This exercise could also be done after reading Word Meanings, below.

Linguistic Resources

Writers may indirectly signal their intended meaning to their readers, and if readers fail to pick up the signals, they will fail to "read" the work correctly. Thus, reading an essay might involve more than figuring out contextual clues: it might involve asking questions like, What response is the author looking for from me? Does the author want me to read literally, or does the surface level of the words hide another meaning? Although these kinds of questions relate to the author's purpose, the author's use of language is the place to find answers.

Such questions are especially relevant to essays written to persuade. For example, a writer might adopt an ironic tone to make the reader question a commonly accepted or simplistic perspective. In **irony**, you look beyond the literal meaning of words to their deeper or "true" meaning. The object might be to make you aware of another perspective, to poke fun at a perspective, or to advocate change.

irony

The existence in a text of two levels of meaning, one surface and literal, the other deeper and non-literal.

Word Meanings

Dictionaries are an indispensable part of the writing life whether you are a professional writer or a student writer. They are also an essential part of the reading life. But while a good dictionary is part of the key to understanding challenging texts, it is not the only one—sometimes it is not even the best one.

This is because the texts you read at the post-secondary level may be more challenging than what you are used to. To look up every unclear word would require too much time and interrupt the reading process, reducing your understanding. Thankfully, you do not need to know the precise meaning of every word you read; you need to know the exact meanings of the most important words but only approximate meanings for many of the others.

Our largest vocabulary is our reading vocabulary, consisting of words we would not use in our writing but that we would recognize, though not necessarily be able to define, when reading. We recognize these words, then, only within the contexts of our reading. Still other words may be unfamiliar, but their basic meaning can be grasped by utilizing context clues, as discussed below.

Context Clues

Important nouns, verbs, adjectives, and adverbs are often revealed through context—the words around them. Writers may define difficult words or may use synonyms or rephrasing to make their meanings clear; such strategies are used if the author thinks the typical reader may not know them. On the other hand, authors may use an unfamiliar word in such a way that the meanings of the surrounding words clarify the meaning and connotation of the unfamiliar word. There are various ways of using these context clues, as we see in the examples below.

Specialized words, such as words borrowed from another language or culture, are defined for general audiences:

Shikata ga nai, as the saying goes—what's done is done.

> —Miyagawa, "A Sorry State": page 221 in Part III: The Reader.

Even in highly specialized writing, the writer may define terms the reader might not know:

Young female larvae of bees, wasps, and ants are usually *totipotent*, that is, they have the potential to develop into either a queen or a worker.

> —F.L.W. Ratnieks and T. Wenseleers. "Policing Insect Societies."
> *Science, vol. 307*, no. 5706, 2005, p. 54.

Rather than being stated directly in a clause or phrase that follows, a word's meaning may be inferred from a word or phrase elsewhere in the sentence:

Minoxidil has some benefit in male pattern *alopecia*, but baldness is not a fatal disease.

> —Lexchin, "Pharmaceutical Innovation: Can We Live Forever? A Commentary on
> Schnittker and Karandinos": page 310 in Part III: The Reader.

When a writer does not define a word, you may be able to infer its meaning by determining the idea the writer is trying to express. In the following example, consider the word *contiguous*: the preceding word, *parts*, and the following word, *whole*, help reveal the word's meaning as "touching" or "adjoining." The previous part of the sentence also suggests that *contiguous* means something stronger than *linked*:

Since at least the end of the 19th century, cartoonists in Canada . . . have depicted North America as a collection of territories whose identities are linked, and sometimes even as parts of a *contiguous* whole.

> —A.J. Green. "Mapping North America: Visual Representation of Canada and the United
> States in Recent Academic Work and Editorial Cartoons." *The American Review of Canadian
> Studies, vol.* 37 no. 2, 2007, p. 134.

In addition to looking at nearby words to guide you to meaning, you can often look at relationships expressed in the sentence or a previous one, like those showing contrasts. In the sentence below, a contrastive relationship can help you infer the meaning of the italicized word:

The availability of pornographic material at the library . . . represents the *defilement* of something regarded by Mali'hah as "pure."

> —T.F. Ruby. "Listening to the Voices of *Hijab.*" *Women's Studies
> International Forum, vol.* 29, 2006, pp. 54–66.

Similarly, if a writer uses examples, they can sometimes be used to infer the meaning of a previous word. In this sentence, the author gives the example of *dressmaker* used as a substitute for *prostitute*; a *euphemism* is a kind of substitution:

> When prostitutes were recorded on nominal census schedules, the space beside their names for "occupation, trade or calling" was left blank, or some innocuous term or *euphemism*—such as dressmaker—was entered in the space.
>
> —P.A. Dunae. "Sex, Charades and Census Records: Locating Female Sex Trade Workers in a Victorian City." *Histoire sociale/Social History*, vol. 42, 2009, pp. 267–97.

What follows *innocuous* could also help define that word, especially if it occurs to you that *innocuous* has the same first five letters as the word *innocent* (see Family Resemblances, below).

In the passage below, examples of *changes across* the spectrum of light are given (it also helps to look at the etymology of the word; *trans* = across + *mutare* = change):

> [N]atural philosophers assumed that coloured rays of light were *transmutable*. To change blue into red, white into yellow, or orange into violet, they reckoned that one simply had to find a way to quicken or retard the speed at which the pulses moved through the aether.
>
> —J. Waller. *Leaps in the Dark: The Forging of Scientific Reputations*. Oxford University Press, 2004.

Family Resemblances

If context does not help with a word's meaning, you can look for resemblances, recalling words that look similar and whose meanings you know. A "family" of words may arise from the same Latin or Greek root. (Most English words of more than one syllable are derived from Latin; others come from Greek.) Thus, you may be able to infer the meaning of a new word by recalling a known word with the same word element. For example, you can easily see a family resemblance between the word *meritocracy* and the familiar word *merit*. You can take this a step further by looking at the second element and recalling that *meritocracy* and *democracy* contain a common element. In a *democracy*, the *people* determine who will govern them. In a *meritocracy*, then, *merit* determines who governs.

Specialized Language

The strategies discussed above for understanding unfamiliar words apply to all kinds of writing. However, the academic disciplines have their own specialized vocabularies that scholars use to communicate with each other. This language is known as **jargon**, and even the jargon of two subdisciplines, such as plant sciences and zoology, can vary. When you take courses in a discipline, you begin to acquire this specialized vocabulary. To acquire knowledge about a subject is to simultaneously acquire its language, in addition to the other conventions of the discipline.

Although some highly technical articles may use jargon that baffles the undergraduate, both novice and more experienced readers can make use of the variety of discipline-specific dictionaries, encyclopedias, and research guides that can be accessed through many libraries. For example, Oxford University Press publishes a series of subject dictionaries in art and architecture, the biological sciences, classical studies, computing, earth and environmental sciences, and many other disciplines.

jargon
Discipline-specific language used to communicate among members of the discipline.

Activity 5.5

Using contextual or word resemblance strategies whenever necessary, determine the meanings of the italicized words in the following passages, all of which are taken from readings in Part III of this book:

1. Frequencies were calculated in the demographic characteristics, which were subsequently *dichotomized* into the following categories. (From Arbour-Nicitopoulos et al., "Social Norms of Alcohol, Smoking, and Marijuana Use within a Canadian University Setting" (paragraph 10): page 175 in Part III: The Reader)

2. These influences [on a person's decisions] are presumed to determine the different strategies or *heuristics* that individuals as decision-makers actually employ. (From Gifford, "Psychology's Essential Role in Alleviating the Impacts of Climate Change" (paragraph 23): page 350 in Part III: The Reader)

3. In the *Jurassic Park* films there was a sense of capitalism enabling the pursuit—albeit foolhardy and *hubristic*—of science and wonder. (From Dyer, "*Jurassic World* and Procreation Anxiety" (paragraph 4): page 272 in Part III: The Reader)

4. [I]n North America there has been an upsurge of political satire since the early 2000s—a trend that can be traced to a number of factors, including America's increasingly *polarized* culture and the *proliferation* of accessible and affordable digital tools. (From McLeod, "When Canada Goes Viral" (paragraph 4): page 194 in Part III: The Reader)

5. The BBC, for example, helped pioneer the *hybridization* of documentary and entertainment. (From Ouellete, "Reality TV Gives Back" (paragraph 2): page 266 in Part III: The Reader)

6. Homophobia represents a major cause of social injustice, and nurses are therefore professionally mandated to be *vigilant* in *eradicating* it from all phases of the healthcare encounter. (From Dysart-Gale, "Social Justice and Social Determinants of Health" (paragraph 11): page 241 in Part III: The Reader)

7. At first, the reception of the Chinese was relatively *cordial*: "Colonial British Columbians were initially remarkably tolerant of the thousands of Chinese who came." (From Anderson, "The Senate and the Fight against the 1885 Chinese Immigration Act" (paragraph 3): page 228 in Part III: The Reader)

8. Responsive action to these effects must *transpire* at multiple socio-ecological levels. (From Healey et al., "Community Perspectives on the Impact of Climate Change on Health in Nunavut, Canada" (paragraph 23): page 362 in Part III: The Reader)

9. Our findings indicate that it may be worthwhile to promote more effective sleep habits to assist university students in getting good quality sleep given the *pivotal* role that sleep plays across the lifespan. (From Tavernier and Willoughby, "Sleep Problems" (paragraph 21): page 257 in Part III: The Reader)

10. Conventional wisdom would have us believe that since technology has *proliferated* over the last decade and stories of cyberbullying are frequently mentioned in the news, it is likely more *prevalent* than traditional, schoolyard bullying. (From Sabella et al., "Cyberbullying Myths and Realities" (paragraph 16): page 314 in Part III: The Reader)

PART II
Academic Writing

Academic discourse can be thought of as *a set of oral and written procedures used to gener-ate and disseminate ideas within the academic community.* Most of the classes you take in university focus on written discourse: by writing down your thoughts, you are recording them to be analyzed by others (and, yes, usually graded). Familiarity with the conventions of written discourse will be valuable to you throughout your academic career and beyond because, in spite of the uses of modern technology, it is primarily through writing that knowledge is trans-mitted. (See The Active Voice: Brave New Words, page 75.)

You will probably be writing essays and reports in your courses, which, while they share similarities, may be markedly different. To write a lab report for a chemistry class, for ex-ample, you use different procedures, or conventions, from those you use in a literary analysis for an English class, which, in turn, are different from those you use to write a marketing plan for a business class or a feasibility study for an engineering class.

Despite these differences, there are two relatively distinct forms that academic writing can take: the essay and the report. You will be required to write essays in many of your under-graduate courses. Writing reports may be limited to your science courses, some of your social sciences courses, along with business, engineering, or health sciences courses. Chapter 6 re-views the fundamentals of writing academic essays, followed by an overview of report writing (The Active Voice: Report Writing—Aims and Goals, page 82).

Chapters 7–9 discuss specific kinds of writing assignments. Learning summarization skills (Chapter 7) enables you to represent in your essays the ideas and words of other writers. When you summarize, then, you focus more on *re-presenting* than on analyzing. When you write a rhetorical analysis—discussed in Chapter 8—you use your critical-thinking skills to "break down" one or more specific texts.

In Chapter 9, you will learn about applying general academic writing skills to the mode of argument: in argumentative essays, you assert and defend a claim. When you try to convince someone that something is good or bad or persuade them to adopt a particular action, you consider the use of specific strategies in order to support your claim; outside sources may also strengthen your claim.

Research papers, discussed in Chapter 10, display the fullest range of skills for student readers and writers because they combine various skills, including summarizing, analysis, synthesis, and critical thinking. They call on your skills of locating, evaluating, and integrating outside sources.

6 An Overview of the Essay

The Stages in Writing

Essays, like most projects, are written in chronological stages. Although academic writing may emphasize revising and editing the rough draft more than you are used to, students approach academic writing knowing that it is a chronological process that usually begins with a broad topic.

The stages in writing an essay are

- coming up with a thesis
- finding support for the thesis
- relating parts and discovering structure (outlining)
- composing the essay
- revising

Coming Up with a Thesis

Using pre-writing techniques, you explore the topic, asking what you know and what you want to find out about it. The objective is to narrow the topic to express your specific focus or approach in a **thesis statement**. (See page 70.)

Many different methods can be used to narrow a topic. These include association techniques, such as freewriting, brainstorming, and clustering, or mapping. A good beginning point is to use the "subject test" and consider how the topic would apply to various disciplines: for example, dance is considered a subject or subdiscipline within the fine or performing arts, yet this subject could be explored from a number of different angles within other disciplines:

- dance as self-expression (humanities—fine arts)
- dance as entertainment (humanities—fine arts)

thesis statement
A statement that includes the main point of your essay or what you will attempt to prove; it is placed at the end of your introduction.

- the history of dance (humanities—history)
- the function of dance in other cultures (humanities—cultural studies; social sciences—anthropology)
- dance as the expression of a collective identity (social sciences—sociology)
- dance as therapy (social sciences—psychology)
- dance as physical movement (science—kinesiology)
- dance as an area of skill acquisition and study (education)

Each of these approaches suggests a way of narrowing the broad subject of dance in order to write on it for different classes or as an assignment for your English class. In fact, the approaches could already be considered topics, but they are, as yet, undeveloped. *What would you like to know about it?* Let us say that you are planning to major in psychology. Therefore, the topic of dance as therapy is something you would like to know more about. One option is to begin your research now by finding out what has been written about this topic. Accordingly, you could check out your library's databases, such as *Humanities Index* or *Periodical Contents Index*, which cover journals focusing on the performing arts. However, this might be the time to try one of the pre-writing strategies, such as brainstorming, to narrow the topic further. The goal is to sum up your specific approach in a thesis statement.

Pre-writing Techniques

freewriting
A pre-writing technique in which you write on a subject without stopping to edit

Freewriting utilizes your associations with something. To freewrite, begin with a blank piece of paper or a blank screen and start recording your associations with a subject. Do not stop to reflect on your next thought or polish your writing: simply write continuously for a predetermined time—such as five or ten minutes. A good starting point is a sentence that includes the subject you want to find out more about, such as a tentative definition: "Dance as therapy is. . . ."

In the **questioning** technique, you ask questions pertinent to the topic. Initially, these questions could be the basic *What?*, *Who?*, *Where?*, *When?*, *Why?*, and *How?*

questioning
A pre-writing technique in which you ask relevant questions about the topic.

- What is dance therapy? What are its basic elements/divisions/stages? What are its goals?
- Who would use dance as therapy? Who would benefit from it?
- Where can you go to study dance therapy? Where is it practised?
- When did dance therapy begin? Why?
- How does it work? How is it similar to/different from other kinds of creative healing techniques?

Each question suggests a different approach to the topic and a different rhetorical pattern. For example, the first question might lead you to the definition pattern; the second question might lead you to divide dance therapy into different types or other subcategories (division/classification). The last question could lead you to focus on comparison and contrast (e.g., dance therapy versus music therapy) or to analyze the costs and benefits of different creative healing techniques (see Rhetorical Patterns and Paragraph Development, page 77).

brainstorming
A pre-writing technique in which you list your associations with a subject in the order they occur to you.

In **brainstorming**, you list your associations with a topic, writing down words and phrases until you feel you have covered the topic thoroughly. Although you do not intentionally look for connections when you generate your list, you can later look back to explore possible connections between the items.

Clustering is a spatial technique that generates associations and seeks connections among them. You begin by writing a word or phrase in the middle of a blank page and circling it. As associations occur to you, you write them down and circle them, connecting them by a line to the word or phrase that gave rise to the association. As you continue this process, you will develop larger clusters in some places than in others. The well-developed clusters may suggest the most promising ways to develop your topic.

Whatever method you use, the thesis statement you come up with should reflect your purpose in writing. For example, if you were writing a personal essay on dance as part of your application to a performing arts program, it would be very different from what you would write for a research essay.

> **clustering**
>
> A pre-writing technique that works spatially to generate associations with a subject and connections among them

Activity 6.1

Three sample thesis statements on dance follow. Determine which one would be applicable to

a. a personal essay
b. an argumentative essay that attempts to persuade the reader to take a particular course of action
c. a research essay concerned with the historical development of dance therapy

1. With its roots in modern dance and its stress on self-expression over performance, dance therapy has evolved into a vibrant profession that today serves such diverse groups as disabled people and employees of large corporations.

2. One of my earliest memories is of pulling myself up close to the TV so I could follow the intricate moving shapes before my eyes, trying to make sense of the patterns they formed. Now, at 18, I want to personally explore what it is like to be a part of the visual pattern called dance.

3. Cuts to the operating budgets of performing arts programs at this university must be curtailed so these students can feel the security they need to succeed in their studies and the university community can experience the benefits of the performing arts on campus.

Finding Support

In the next stage, you attempt to back up your thesis. Thesis statements are claims of some kind. A claim must have **support**. For example, although you could claim that the dog ate your homework, your instructor is not likely to take such a claim seriously. But if you produced your vet bill, the claim would at least have some support and may merit your instructor's consideration. If you were writing a critical analysis of a poem, the support would need to come from the poem itself (a primary source). If you were writing a research paper, you would need to find out what other people have discovered about your topic (secondary sources).

See Kinds of Evidence, page 80, and also Kinds of Evidence in Argumentative Essays, page 105.

> **support**
>
> Evidence to help prove a claim.

Relating Parts and Discovering Structure

When you have found enough support, it is time to begin thinking about how you will use it in your essay. Thus, you begin organizing claims and support in a logical and consistent way, one that clearly expresses the relationship between each claim and its support. One way to clarify

outline

A linear or graphic representation of main and sub-points, showing an essay's structure

these relationships is to construct an **outline**, a diagrammatic representation of the essay and a plan you can use in the composing stage so you stay on track.

An outline can be a brief listing of your main points, a *scratch* or *sketch outline*, often used for in-class or exam essays when you do not have time for detailed planning. With longer essays, an outline can be developed to include levels of sub-points (developments of main points) along with details and examples. The *formal outline* uses a number/letter scheme to represent the essay's complete structure. The conventional scheme goes like this:

I.   First main point (topic sentence of paragraph)
   A. First sub-point (development of main point)
      1. first sub-sub-point (development of sub-point: detail or example)
      2. second sub-sub-point
   B. Second sub-point
      1. first sub-sub-point
      2. second sub-sub-point

This example represents a paragraph with a three-level outline—the main point is the top level, followed by the sub-points, with the sub-sub-points on the lowest level; each level supports the one above it. Some paragraphs may be less developed, while overly long paragraphs can be subdivided in the most logical place.

When you are considering your outline, especially if it is a formal outline, remember that it serves as the blueprint for the essay itself. Therefore, to construct a useful outline, you should ask questions like the following:

The topic sentence states the topic or the main point of the paragraph. It is often the paragraph's first sentence.

- How do the main points in my outline relate to my thesis statement?
- How do the sub-points relate to my main points?
- Do I have enough main points to support my thesis and enough sub-points to support each topic sentence?
- Do any points seem irrelevant or out of place? (If the latter, where do they belong?)
- What is the most effective order for my points?
- Are my points logically related to each other (i.e., each one should naturally follow from the previous point)?
- Can points be expanded? Have I covered everything my reader would expect me to cover?

Composing

Making the commitment to the first draft is difficult for many people—students and non-students alike. It is important to realize that a first draft is inevitably "drafty"—in need of revising. But this should not hold you back from fully recording your thoughts—imperfectly expressed as they may be. When you compose an essay, you draft the introduction, middle paragraphs, and conclusion. Techniques and strategies for these tasks are described in detail in The Structure of the Essay (page 69).

Revising

Although in composing the first "rough" drafts your focus is on getting ideas down, during the revision stage you should not expect to be simply dotting i's and crossing t's. The word *revise* means to "see again." First, look at your essay's purpose and audience, its structure, support, and clarity. Review these areas as if you are seeing them for the first time. Waiting at least several hours after you have completed a rough draft before revising is sensible. Ask the kinds of questions you originally asked when you were creating an outline (see above, page 66), and see if you are satisfied with the results.

Next, check for grammatical correctness and concision. *Then*, it will be time to dot the i's and cross the t's—checking for spelling errors and typos and ensuring that the essay conforms to the required format.

The importance of these end-stage activities cannot be underestimated, though they sometimes are. After all, when you have finished the rough draft, the paper looks physically complete. But try to see your essay through the eyes of your instructor. What often strikes a reader first are the very things you may have glossed over as your deadline approached: grammatical errors, lack of coherence, faulty word choice, wordiness, typos, and mechanical errors that are simple to fix.

Though nothing will replace careful attention to every detail, here is a checklist that will help you "re-see" your essay.

Content and Structure

- Is the essay's purpose clear from the introduction? Is it consistent throughout the essay?
- Is it written for a specific audience? What would show a reader this (for example, level of language, voice or tone, kinds of evidence, citations)?
- Is the thesis statement consistent with the focus of the essay and its main points? If not, consider adjusting the thesis so that it is.
- Are all paragraphs adequately developed and focused on one main idea?
- Are any paragraphs noticeably shorter or longer than others? If so, can you effectively combine short paragraphs or break up longer ones?
- Have different kinds of evidence been used for support? Does any part of the essay seem less well supported than other parts?
- Would an example or illustration make an abstract point more concrete or a general point more specific?
- Could a reader misunderstand any point? If so, would this be due to the way it is expressed? If your draft has been commented on or edited by a peer, pay particular attention to passages noted as unclear. If one reader has difficulties in comprehension, others will too.

Grammar and Style

- Are there sentence fragments (i.e., "sentences" missing a subject or predicate), run-on sentences (two "sentences," or independent clauses, with no punctuation between them), or comma splices (two "sentences" separated only by a comma)?
- Is punctuation used correctly? For example, are commas used (1) to separate independent clauses with a coordinating conjunction (*and, or, but, for, nor, yet, so*) and to separate an introductory word, phrase, or clause from a following independent clause; (2) to separate items in a list or series; (3) to separate non-essential information from essential information? Are semicolons and colons used correctly? Are dashes and parentheses used correctly and sparingly (dashes for emphasis, parentheses for asides)?
- Are apostrophes used correctly to indicate possession and similar relationships in nouns and indefinite pronouns (e.g., *the book's author*—one book; *the books' authors*—more than one book; *anyone's opinion*—indefinite pronoun)?

- Do verbs agree in number with their subjects and pronouns with their antecedents (the noun they replace)?
- Is the relationship between a noun and its antecedent clear (i.e., every pronoun should refer back to a specific noun)?
- Has the principle of pronoun consistency been maintained (i.e., pronouns should not arbitrarily change from third person [*he/she, they/them*] to first or second person [*I/me, we/us, you*])?
- Is parallelism present in sentences with elements that must be parallel (lists, compounds, correlative conjunctions, and comparisons)?
- Are there any misplaced or dangling modifiers, confusing sentence meaning?
- Are you satisfied that every word you have used is the best word and expresses precisely what you want to say? Is the level of language appropriate and have you avoided contractions and slang?
- Have you avoided repetition? Have you managed to eliminate unnecessary words and phrases?

Mechanics

- Have all outside references been cited correctly? Have you used the documentation style favoured by your instructor or by your discipline?
- Have you met word count, essay/page format, and other specific requirements?
- Have you proofread the essay at least twice (once for content and flow, once for minor errors such as typos—breaking each word into syllables and reading syllabically throughout is the best way to catch minor errors)?

The Process-Reflective Method

Although most essays are written in stages, most writers do not engage with their topic mechanically but by moving back and forth—from composing to outline, for example, if they need to rethink their structure, or from composing back to the research stage to check on a source or find more support for a point. Some writers, in fact, do not follow a linear process but begin composing without any firm plan in place, trusting their instincts and realizing that it is sometimes only by writing something down and taking the risk of going off-topic occasionally that they can discover what they really want to say. In the exploratory model, your intentions and goals are revealed through the act of writing itself, and an outline is less important than in the linear approach. Below, Frans de Waal, primatologist and author of *Our Inner Ape*, describes his personal process. It illustrates the importance of revising and the necessity of finding the approach that works best for you:

> I write my books without much of an outline except for the chapter titles. My main strategy is to just start writing and see what happens. From one topic follows another, and before you know it I have a dozen pages filled with stories and thoughts. . . . I have a very visual memory, and remember events in great detail. When I write, my desk fills up with ever higher piles of papers and books used for reference, until it is a big mess, which is something I cannot stand. I am very neat. So, at some point I put all that stuff away, print out the text I've

written, and sit down comfortably with a red pen. By that time I have already gone over the text multiple times. With pen in hand, I do a very rigorous rereading and again change things around.

—http://www.emory.edu/LIVING_LINKS/OurInnerApe/book.html

When de Waal reveals, above, that he has "gone over the text multiple times" before he considers large-scale changes, he is revealing his preference for a writing process in which he pauses to reflect, re-examine, and change, if necessary, before continuing—a kind of revision on the fly, or paragraph-by-paragraph approach. As with the traditional-linear approach, however, you should not be concerned with mechanical correctness as you write.

Typical activities in **process-reflective drafts** are rephrasing, clarifying, expanding, and connecting: you concern yourself with making logical transitions from one thought to the next and checking to see that your developing points are consistent with your general plan. You should begin with a few rough points and "reminders," such as important authors or quotations you want to use, but you do not need to have a detailed plan. Rather, the plan evolves as you write. Process-reflective writing can also be used for in-class and exam essays in which there is seldom time to outline your points in detail.

> **process-reflective draft**
> A draft that emerges from a flexible engagement with what you are writing, one that reflects the connections between thinking and writing.

The Structure of the Essay

Most essays are divided into an introduction, middle or body paragraphs, and a conclusion. Each part contributes in a different way to the essay. In this section you will learn techniques and strategies for drafting each part.

Writing Introductions

The introduction is more than just a starting place. Its primary function is to inform the reader about the essay's purpose, topic, and approach to the topic (usually through the thesis statement); it may include the essay's main points. As well, the introduction may indicate the primary organizational scheme (rhetorical pattern) for the essay. In all these ways, the introduction previews what is forthcoming.

A good introduction is persuasive: it must sufficiently interest the reader, encouraging him or her to read on, perhaps by conveying the importance of the topic. The introduction not only introduces the essay but also introduces its writer; therefore, you must come across as credible and reliable. (See Issues of Credibility, page 81.)

Student writers are often advised to write the introduction last because they will not know precisely how the topic will develop until the body of the essay is written. On the other hand, many writers like to have a concrete starting point. If the latter describes you best, you should return to the introduction after you have written your middle paragraphs to ensure that it fits well with them.

[handwritten margin notes:]
intro:
-purpose
-main points
-your position

come across as credible & reliable

Writing Thesis Statements – *a promise to your reader*

The Greek word *thesis* refers to the act of placing or setting down. *A thesis statement, then, is a formal assertion, a generalization that is applicable to the entire essay.* However, this generalization can take different forms depending on purpose and audience. Student and academic writers usually place the thesis statement in the introduction; journalistic writers often do not. For kinds of theses in academic essays, see Chapter 2 (page 19).

Thesis statements vary in what they include:

no surprises

- A *simple thesis statement* announces the topic and includes a comment about it.
- An *expanded thesis statement*, or essay plan, includes the main points in the order they will appear in the essay. *3-4 main points*

Simple thesis: Xenotransplantation, the transplantation of organs across a species barrier, is emerging as a possible alternative to transplants from human donors.

Expanded thesis: In order to understand the extent of bullying today, we must consider who is affected by bullying, what are its impacts, and how we can prevent it.

explain   argue
fact-based, or action-driven

claim

An assertion about the topic appearing in the thesis statement and topic sentences.

The thesis statement usually embodies a **claim**, the nature of which depends on the essay's purpose:

- Claims of *fact* are common in expository essays in the sciences and social sciences in which reliable studies and factual information are used for support.
- Claims of *value* or *policy* are common in argumentative essays. Such claims argue that something, such as a law, is good or bad or that it needs to change.
- *Interpretive* claims are common in humanities essays in which the writer sets out to analyze one or more primary sources by using a specific frame of reference, such as a critical theory. For example, a poem could be analyzed through its literary motifs or through the lens of feminist theory. When you write a rhetorical or critical analysis, you will also use an interpretive claim (the essay you analyze is your primary source).

Fact-based claims are common in exposition. Claims of value or policy are common in argument. Interpretive claims are common in the humanities, in which primary sources are analyzed.

The following statements demonstrate different kinds of claims:

expository

Thesis with factual claim: **Cultural, psychological, and economic factors are contributing to an increasingly prevalent phenomenon, hikikomori, or the withdrawal from society by extreme isolation.**

Thesis with policy claim: **More sustainable, shade-grown coffee plantations need to be established in order to counter the effects of habitat destruction and help maintain the planet's diversity.**

Thesis from a rhetorical analysis with interpretive claim: **In his essay, Robidoux presents a strong argument through the use of historical documentation, examples, and appeals to ethos.**

The thesis you write must not just state your topic but also show the reader how the essay will be developed. Once you have narrowed your topic, you should work on your thesis to ensure it is

logical opening / dramatic opening
→ tell a story
→ must relate to argument

- informative
- well-focused
- clearly expressed

Creating Reader Interest

Readers need to be convinced at the outset that your essay is worth reading. The most traditional way to generate interest and persuade your reader of the topic's importance is to use a **logical opening**: to begin with a universal statement that becomes more specific and ends with the most specific claim, the thesis itself; this method is called the inverted triangle method.

One risk in this approach is that in making the first sentence too broad or familiar, it fails to interest the reader. Therefore, student writers are sometimes encouraged to use a **dramatic opening**. Examples of dramatic openings include the use of personal experience, description, narration, or a pertinent question that intrigues the reader. An opening could also make an emotional appeal; however, use these appeals cautiously because you cannot always assume that a typical reader will respond in the way you wish. The following examples illustrate two different ways of attracting reader interest. Note that, in both cases, the last sentence is the thesis statement.

Logical opening: The writer begins with a statement about her subject area, health and nutrition. In sentence 3, she mentions the importance of reliable research. Her specific topic is addressed in sentence 4, and her thesis is her final sentence (italicized):

The field of health and nutrition is evolving fast, which can make it confusing as experts often disagree on what is healthy and what is not. The average citizen is easily influenced by media claims, which may be part truth and part "hype." A good way to ensure that what is being consumed is beneficial to health is to research exactly what it is and how its constituents affect the human body; this research enables educated health decisions and personalized diets. Coffee is an example of a controversial health topic today. Millions of people drink coffee every day, yet few know its true effect on health. In Canada alone, 14 billion cups of coffee are consumed each year (Hales & Lauzon, 2008). Despite old studies which show coffee as detrimental to health, new research on the health benefits of coffee have begun to emerge. *While certain health concerns still exist based primarily on quantity of consumption and any pre-existing health conditions, new evidence suggests that caffeine as well as other compounds present in coffee offer surprising health benefits.*

—student writer Clara Buttemer

Dramatic opening (questions): The writer begins with two questions, referring to the popular connotation of perfectionism. Using the reversal strategy, she then cites the definition of

logical opening

A technique for creating reader interest by beginning with a generalization and narrowing to the thesis.

dramatic opening

A technique for creating reader interest by beginning with a question, illustration, anecdote, quotation, description, or other attention-grabbing technique.

experts. Her final sentence (italicized) makes it clear that her essay will focus on the problems of the "maladaptive perfectionist":

> What does it mean to say that one is a perfectionist? Does it mean that one does everything perfectly? In common language, the term "perfectionist" carries the connotation that the perfectionistic individual does everything perfectly, but according to perfectionism experts in social psychology, perfectionism is a term referring to a mentality, or set of cognitions, that are characteristic of certain people. According to Hollender (as cited in Slade & Owens, 1998), perfectionism refers to "the practice of demanding of oneself or *others* a higher quality of performance than is required by the situation" (p. 384). Although the name suggests to the layperson that perfectionism would be a desirable trait, this quality is in fact often unrecognized for its detrimental effects on the lives of people who are maladaptively perfectionistic. *Perfectionism is associated with mental illness and can contribute to problems in areas of life such as academic success and intimate relationships.*
>
> —student writer Erin Walker

Activity 6.2

In the following paragraphs

a. identify the method for creating interest
b. discuss how the writer establishes his or her credibility
c. identify the thesis statement and whether it is a simple thesis or an expanded one

You can also pre-read Rhetorical Patterns and Paragraph Development, page 77, to determine the essay's main organizational method.

1. Women in society have come a long way, from earning the right to vote to becoming political leaders, and from riding horses side saddle to riding motorcycles. Today, with more dual-income families and an increasing number of wives whose salaries are higher than their husbands', the gender wage gap has improved significantly. However, women are still not treated equally in the workplace, and women's salaries remain a very relevant issue as, on average, women make only seventy-two cents for every dollar that men make (Drolet, "Why has the gender wage gap narrowed?"). In a society that has promoted gender pay equality since 1956 by implementing the *Female Employees Equal Pay Act* (Canadian Human Rights Commission "Federal Government adopts the *Female Employees Equal Pay Act*"), how can such a large disparity still exist? By examining the gender wage gap and its causes, the problem is clear, but what are the solutions? Action must be taken to overcome this disparity by an extensive education program that informs society about the gender wage gap and its contributing factors.

   —student writer Jacqueline Greenard

2. As of September 2016, Facebook had 1.18 billion daily users (Facebook, "Company Info: Facebook Newsroom"). American adults visit Facebook for 21 minutes a day on average (Price, par. 1). A survey conducted by the Pew Research Center found that 62 percent of Americans consume their news through social media, and 44 percent get their news through Facebook (Gottfried and Shearer, pars. 1–5). These statistics paint a picture of a website with a significant hold over the population's attention. Facebook uses the algorithm EdgeRank to manage the complex array of multimedia content that gets uploaded to their website, and some experts believe that this helps create a cycle of misinformation for unknowing Facebook users. How does Facebook deliver its news via this algorithm? What are its potential problems, and how can users bypass this algorithm?

   —student writer Jordan Manning

topic sentence (thesis for a paragraph)
— normally first sentence
— unified one main topic
— coherent   — support!

6 | An Overview of the Essay   73

Writing Middle Paragraphs

The structure of middle paragraphs is often said to mirror that of the essay itself: the paragraph begins with a generalization that is supported by the sentences that follow. In its structure and function, the essay's thesis statement is equivalent to the **topic sentence** of a paragraph, which announces the main idea (topic) of that paragraph. This analogy is useful because it stresses the importance of a predictable order for both essays and paragraphs.

When a writer uses a topic sentence to announce the central idea, the rest of the paragraph provides support, such as examples, reasons, statistical data, or other kinds of evidence. It illustrates, expands on, or reinforces the topic sentence. In the following paragraph, student writer Leslie Nelson expands on the main idea, first by explaining the function of talking therapies and then by dividing them into three different subcategories and explaining the function of each (the topic sentence is italicized):

> *Talking therapies—especially when combined with medication—are common treatments of adolescent depression.* There are several kinds of talking therapies, including cognitive and humanistic approaches, and family and group sessions. Each of these therapy types confronts depression in a different way, and each is useful for adolescent treatment. Cognitive therapies confront illogical thought patterns that accompany depression; humanistic therapies provide support to the patient, stressing unconditional acceptance. Group therapies, on the other hand, encourage depressed patients to talk about their feelings in a setting with other people who are undergoing treatment for similar problems. This therapy can inspire different coping strategies, and it allows people to realize that they are not alone in their problems.

The common placement as the first sentence tends to make for a coherent paragraph, while similarly structured paragraphs contribute to a readable, coherent essay. (For more about the placement of topic sentences within paragraphs of academic essays, see Chapter 4, page 52).

Writing Strong Paragraphs

Effective paragraphs are unified, coherent, and well-developed. A **unified** paragraph focuses on only one main idea; when you move to another main idea, you begin a new paragraph. If, however, a paragraph is long, you should consider dividing it into two paragraphs even if each contains the same idea. Look for the most logical place to make the division. For example, you could divide the paragraph where you begin an important sub-point.

A **coherent** paragraph is easy to follow. Coherent paragraphs are both clear and carefully arranged to place the emphasis where you want it to be. Compositional theorists use the term **reader-based prose** to suggest a focus on the concerns of the reader. In reader-based prose, the writer carefully designs the paragraph for a specific audience by using understandable and well-organized prose, stressing what is most important and clarifying the relationships among the points and sub-points. Coherence can be achieved by considering the following points.

Strategies for Coherent Writing

1. *Logical sentence order:* In logical sentence order, one sentence follows naturally from the preceding one, and there are no sentences out of order or off-topic. There are no gaps in thought that the reader has to fill.

topic sentence
A sentence that states the main idea in the paragraph; it is usually the first sentence.

unity
A principle of paragraph construction in which only one idea is developed throughout the paragraph.

coherence
A principle of paragraph construction in which ideas are logically laid out with clear connections between them.

reader-based prose
Clear, accessible writing designed for an intended reader.

2. *Organizational patterns:* You can order the paragraph according to specific patterns (see Rhetorical Patterns and Paragraph Development, page 77).

3. *Precise language:* When you consider what words to use, remember that it is not always a case of the right word versus the wrong word. Always choose the *best word for the given context.* Whenever you use a word that is not part of your everyday vocabulary, you should confirm its meaning by looking it up in a dictionary.

4. *Appropriate adverbial transitions:* Transitional words and phrases enable you to convey precise relationships between one idea and the next.

5. *Selective rephrasing and reiteration:* Knowing the knowledge level of your audience will determine whether and when you should rephrase in order to clarify difficult concepts.

6. *Repetition of key words/phrases or the use of synonyms:* Repetition can be used to emphasize important ideas. Of course, *needless* repetition should always be avoided.

7. *Parallel/balanced structures:* Employing parallel/balanced structures creates coherence, in part, through the use of familiar syntactic patterns. Writers and politicians alike know the virtue of balanced structures: they are pleasing to the audience and often easy to recall.

Being aware of these strategies will make you a more conscious writer, focused on the needs of your readers. In the excerpt below, after defining the term *nanotechnology*, student writer Jeff Proctor makes effective use of transitions (noted by italics) to help explain a difficult concept to general readers. He uses a balanced structure in sentence 4 to make a comparison understandable and repeats the key word *precision* at strategic points in the paragraph (the beginning, middle, and end). Other words, too, can be considered near-synonyms for *precision* (synonyms and repetition are underlined):

> Consciously rephrasing ideas and specific passages as you write can help you to clarify your thoughts. Try following important points with transitions like *in other words, in summary,* or *to reiterate* and a paraphrase or expansion of the original. If your second attempt is clearer—and it often is—you can then consider crossing out the original to avoid needless repetition.

Nanotechnology will allow the construction of compounds at nanometre <u>precision</u>. *Essentially*, this capability would allow scientists to form a substance one atom at a time and to put each atom <u>exactly</u> where it needs to be. *Consequently*, any chemical structure that is stable under normal conditions could theoretically be produced.[4] In comparison to semiconductor lithography, which <u>could be imagined as</u> the formation of electrical circuits by joining large heaps of molecules, the techniques of nanotechnology <u>could be imagined as</u> the <u>careful</u> arrangement of molecules with a pair of tweezers. With this incredible degree of <u>precision</u>, electrical circuits could be designed to be smaller than ever before. *Currently*, each component in a computer is the size of thousands of atoms; *however*, if nanotechnological processes were used to produce it, one component could be on the scale of several atoms. This fact alone emphasizes the potential efficiency of next-generation computer circuits, for smaller components are closer together and, *thus*, able to communicate with each other in less time. *Furthermore*, it could be guaranteed that products are reproducible and reliable as a result of the absolute <u>precision</u> of these formation processes.

Transitions in the paragraph above convey various relationships:

- summary: *essentially*
- cause–effect: *consequently, thus*
- time: *currently*
- contrast: *however*
- addition: *furthermore*

Other relationships include

- concession or limit (e.g., *admittedly, although, though, it is true that, of course*)
- illustration (e.g., *for example, for instance, such as*)
- sequence (e.g., *first, second . . . ; then, next*)
- emphasis (e.g., *certainly, especially, in fact, indeed, undoubtedly*)

For more information on paragraphs, see Dividing the Whole, page 51, and Reading Paragraphs: Locating Main Ideas, page 52.

The Active Voice

Brave New Words: Technology and the Future of Writing

1 Google is making us stupid! Text messages ruin our spelling! Facebook and Twitter turn students into illiterate zombies!

2 Every month, a new report sounds the alarm that digital tools are reducing, not improving, our ability to communicate. Should we believe the gloomy headlines? Is the Internet *really* the enemy of good writing?

3 The truth is, teachers have always fretted that technology will corrupt our minds—ever since the dawn of writing itself. We don't usually think of the alphabet as a "technology," but when humans first devised systems to transcribe oral language onto physical media (from stone tablets to papyrus, paperbacks to e-readers), it had a profound effect on our civilization. And not everyone welcomed it.

4 The Greek philosopher Socrates preferred oral questioning to teach critical thinking. (It's what we now call the "Socratic Method".) Writing down facts and ideas, he argued, would turn the keen memories of his fellow citizens into mush. (Of course, we know Socrates' opinion only because Plato, his famous pupil, recorded his words for posterity.) Still, Socrates was probably right. Most people can't recite a 1,000-line epic poem by heart. Some of us need a list to remember which five ingredients to buy at the corner store.

5 Still, the benefits of writing outweighed the unintended consequences. Storing information in written records, rather than human memory, allowed us to transfer greater knowledge between generations. Manuscripts were the original form of ROM or "Read-Only Memory"—data preserved via a special code only a special few people could interpret.

6 Around 1493, when Johannes Gutenberg unveiled his movable-type printing press, his device—a combination of several pre-existing technologies—reduced the time and cost of duplicating manuscripts by hand and extended the power of the written word. Kings, popes, and other authority figures quickly regulated what got published. They were right to worry. The rise of literacy spread political revolution, democratic reform, and a scientific world view throughout Europe and beyond.

7 Not everyone benefitted equally from the right to write and the power to publish. In the mid-twentieth century, American journalist A. J. Liebling quipped: "Freedom of the press is limited to those who own one." The printing press may have ushered in modern democracy, but it was never a truly "democratic" technology. In the 1970s and 1980s, copy machines and desktop publishing lowered duplication costs and opened the potential of self-publishing to everyone from dissidents in Soviet-era Russia (who secretly distributed *samizdat* literature) to punk-rock fans (who produced music "zines").

8 Then along came the Internet—and everything changed.

9 The original ARPANET was designed by the US military to withstand a nuclear attack. Who could have predicted

Continued

the explosion of creativity unleashed when this global computer network was opened to public access? Since the 1990s, the Internet has evolved into a wide-reaching platform to share writing (and other media) via websites, blogs, and social media by removing middle managers from the publication process. "That's not a *job* anymore," observed New York University professor Clay Shirky of the skills needed to publish in the twenty-first century. "That's a *button*."

10   Thanks to the Internet, students today write *more* than ever. But do they write *better*?

11   Teachers have always complained that their current crop of pupils can't compose as well as previous generations. (We also think the music was better back in our day.) Before, comic books or TV rotted their grammar. Now, the taint of "text-lish"—digital slang and hashtagged acronyms, like *IMHO* or *#yolo*—creeps into their prose from Facebook messages, texting apps or Instagram tags.

12   In fact, so-called "digital natives" of the "millennial generation" can write as well as their great-grandparents, who composed in longhand or on touch typewriters. Andrea Lunsford, a scholar of writing at Stanford University, compared first-year composition papers from 2006, 1986, 1930, and 1917. She found no meaningful change in the error rate over the past 90 years.

13   Sali Tagliamonte and Derek Denis, linguists at the University of Toronto, analyzed a million words of instant messages written by 72 teenagers. They concluded the students' online writing reflects the "same dynamic, ongoing processes of linguistic change that are currently under way on contemporary varieties of English." Our language is constantly evolving, and new additions to our vocabulary, taken from digital culture, are a natural part of that evolution.

14   Computers might have an impact, though, on how we read. Studies suggest that students comprehend longer texts better when read on paper versus an LCD screen. Journalist Nicholas Carr has argued the Internet has created a cultural "shallows" in which we're constantly surfing from fact to fact, across a surface of hypertext, without the deep understanding of immersing ourselves in a book.

15   We certainly aren't helped by the temptations to multi-task while writing on a Net-connected device. Rather than focus on the assignment at hand, we often scroll through news feeds, glance at Facebook updates, and click tempting links that catch our eye. Inevitably, our writing gets caught in this crossfire of shifting contexts. Some people hopefully claim the Internet is "rewiring" our brains for the digital age, but psychological research suggests we remain clumsy at such cognitive juggling acts.

16   Finally, the power of instantaneous publication also comes with great responsibility. All writers on the Internet must think carefully before they press "Send" or "Post." (Unfortunately, most don't.) Our online "global village" is built on a paradox: What might feel like a casual exchange (or argument) between friends (or strangers) is often broadcast around the world to a potential audience far wider than a typical newspaper. Your words are preserved as a digital breadcrumb trail that can be traced back to your name long after you close your laptop.

17   Students have lost scholarships or faced discipline for posting inappropriate or offensive content online. Professors have had tweets or blog posts come back to damage their careers. Even if you delete a poorly considered thought, an anonymous troll might screen-cap your digital musing for later abuse. Authors have always needed to master spelling and grammar, style and content, research and rhetoric. Now we must mind our "digital footprint," too. Writing, Socrates worried, would ruin our memories. But the Internet, it seems, never forgets. It's hard to know what's worse.

18   It would be foolish to speculate on what technological change might come next. Will Google still dominate our quest for information? Will we continue to compress thoughts into 140-character "micro-blogs"? Or will the very act of writing be transformed as we compose on holographic keyboards or even blink messages (or whole novels!) using virtual-reality headsets?

19   In the end, it won't make a big difference. The skills of effective written communication will remain universal, whatever the medium: The right words, in the right order, for the right reasons, to the right reader. We must still learn to focus on the vision—and revision—necessary to make our sentences as meaningful as possible, even as we accelerate into the future.

—**David Leach**, Chair of the Department of Writing, University of Victoria

Rhetorical Patterns and Paragraph Development

Rhetorical patterns are systematic ways to organize and present information. They apply both to the essay itself and to individual paragraphs. That is, while a writer may focus on the benefits of coffee throughout the essay, he or she might begin by defining caffeine and develop another paragraph by contrasting the new research stressing benefits with older research stressing costs.

Thus writers also use rhetorical patterns to help organize and develop individual paragraphs, supporting the specific claims in the topic sentences. Part of an essay's success lies in choosing the most appropriate rhetorical pattern(s) to develop a claim. One way to help narrow down a general topic is to think of different ways it can be developed by using rhetorical patterns.

Most topics can be developed by using one or more of the methods listed in Table 6.1 or the two methods discussed below. For example, if you were looking for ways to develop the topic "fighting in hockey," you could use description or narration to convey the excitement of a hockey brawl. Conversely, you could use either method to convey it as an unseemly spectacle. You could use the process analysis pattern to depict the step-by-step procedures officials use to break up a fight, the chronological pattern to trace the history of rules governing fighting, or the pattern by example to call attention to notorious fighting incidents in recent years.

> **rhetorical pattern**
> A method of organizing and presenting information in essays and paragraphs; examples include cause–effect, classification, comparison and contrast, cost–benefit, and definition.

> One way to help narrow down a general topic is to think of different ways it can be developed by using rhetorical patterns.

Table 6.1 Rhetorical Patterns

Purpose	Rhetorical Pattern	Description/Explanation
	definition	• see page 78 for a detailed explanation of definition
	comparison and contrast	• see page 79 for a detailed explanation of comparison and contrast
to create an image or picture of something	description	• uses images related to sight or the other senses to create immediacy and involve the reader • uses modifiers (adjectives and adverbs) to add detail • may systematically focus on a scene, using a logical method such as from left to right, top to bottom, etc.
to tell a story	narration	• relates an occurrence, usually in chronological order • stresses action through the use of strong verbs • provides anecdotes—brief narratives that introduce or illustrate a point
to show how something works or is done	process analysis	• breaks down a (usually) complex process into a sequence of successive steps, making it more understandable • provides instructions or directions
to show the way something changed/ developed	chronology	• uses time order to trace something, often from its beginning to the present day • can be applied to people, objects (like inventions), or situations
to particularize the general or concretize the abstract	example	• gives particular instances of a larger category, enabling readers to better understand the larger category • gives immediacy and concreteness to what can seem otherwise broad or abstract

Continued

Table 6.1   (continued)

to analyze why something happened or a result/outcome	cause–effect	• uses inductive methods to draw conclusions • works from causes to effects or from effects to causes, for example, to determine whether smoking leads to (causes) heart disease or to determine whether heart disease results from (is an effect of) smoking
to account for or justify something	reasons	• uses deductive methods that draw on one's knowledge or experience (which may ultimately be derived from inductive findings), for example, you should not smoke because it often leads to heart disease (reason derived via empirical evidence)
to analyze by dividing into subcategories	classification/division	• Classification: groups items according to shared characteristics (e.g., types of bottled water: purified, mineral, sparkling) • Division: separates large category into constituent parts (e.g., the essay into introduction, middle paragraphs, conclusion)
to look at two sides/views of something	cost–benefit analysis	• weighs the pros and cons of an issue, question, or action, usually to decide which is stronger • in argument, is used to support a value or policy claim and/or refute an opposing claim
to identify a problem or solve/resolve it	problem–solution	• analyzes or explains a problem or proposes a solution • may incorporate other methods, such as reasons, cause–effect, or cost–benefit analysis.
to better understand something	analogy	• shows how one subject is similar to another to clarify the nature or a feature of the first subject

Definition

Using definition as a rhetorical pattern is common in expository essays written for a general audience unfamiliar with specialized terms. Thus, definitions often precede large sections that focus on explaining or analyzing, as in this introduction to an essay on the effects of trans fat on human health:

> In the early 1900s, William Normann invented the hydrogenation process in which trans fat, short for trans-fatty acid, is the by-product. A tiny amount of trans fat is found naturally, usually in animal fat; however, the majority of trans fats are made when hydrogen is added to vegetable oil in a process called hydrogenation. Hydrogenation is the modification of vegetable oil to allow it to be a solid at room temperature. The way the atoms of the fatty acids are bonded shows whether the fat is saturated or unsaturated: saturated fats have only single bonds while unsaturated fats have double bonds. A trans fat is a fat that was once an unsaturated fat but has had its double bonds weakened through the process of hydrogenation.
>
> —student writer Kim Snyder

Using definition can also be an effective strategy in argument. Value claims, in particular, often rely on definition: after explaining what you mean by something, you can link the definition to your evidence. For example, if you were arguing that gymnastics should or should not be considered a sport, you would need to state what you meant by a *sport*. Ensuring that this was a definition with which most readers would agree, you could then use the definition as a springboard into your claim and main points by showing how gymnastics does or does not fit this definition.

Comparison and Contrast

When you compare, you look at how two items are similar; when you contrast, you consider their differences. However, the term *compare* is generally used to refer to both similarities and differences. You can compare ideas, issues, people, places, objects, or events—as long as bases of comparison exist to make such comparisons valid. For example, you can compare two jobs by looking at their salaries, workweeks, levels of responsibility, and so on. However, if you were comparing two things in order to evaluate them, you would have to ensure that the same evaluation standards could be fairly applied to each. For example, you could not evaluate two universities that were vastly different in size. That is why the compilers of *Maclean's Guide to Canadian Universities* categorize universities by their size before applying their performance measures, such as student body, classroom size, and calibre of faculty, which serve as the bases of comparison.

Organizing a comparison and contrast essay can be more complicated than organizing essays that use another primary rhetorical pattern. Consider using the three-step organizational approach:

1. Determine whether the two items you want to compare *can* logically be compared. The health-care system in the United States cannot be compared to the education system in Canada. Although the health-care systems in the two countries are comparable, such a large undertaking might prove unmanageable. More reasonable would be a comparison between two provincial health-care or education systems.

2. Carefully select the bases of comparison, or criteria for comparing (choosing at least three should help make the comparison valid). Each basis can serve as a main point in your essay.

3. Choose one of two possible methods for organizing your main points: the *subject-by-subject (block)* method or the *point-by-point (topics)* method. In the first, you begin with the first subject of comparison and apply your bases of comparison to it; you then do the same for the second subject, keeping your points (criteria) in the identical order. In the more commonly used point-by-point method, you begin with a basis of comparison and apply it to the first, then the second subject. You continue to do this until you have represented all your bases of comparison.

The following paragraphs use one basis of comparison, human health benefits, as part of an essay that compares organic and locally grown foods to determine which is better for human and ecosystem health. The paragraph that discusses the benefits of organic food is longer because more studies have been done on this. Nevertheless, the second paragraph on locally grown foods is well-developed through logical reasoning. Notice that both paragraphs present different contrasts: the first between organic and non-organic food and the second between locally grown and imported foods. Thus, the essay's main organizational method is comparison and contrast, while individual paragraphs are also developed through this pattern:

The demand for organically produced food in supermarkets across North America has steadily increased over the past decade (USDA, 2008). A big reason for this is the widely held belief that organic food is better for our health than "conventional" food, largely based on differences in how the food is grown. Organic food is produced naturally and has no contact with synthetic inputs, such as pesticides, chemical food additives, or chemical fertilizers. "Conventional" food, by contrast, is grown in conditions where synthetic chemicals are used. Naturally, this has led many people to believe that there is more nutritional value in organic than in non-organic food (Williams, 2002). However, a critical review of past research shows an inconsistency in data regarding the relationship between organic food and increased nutrients (Magkos, Arvaniti, Zampelas, 2006). Short-term studies have shown mixed results regarding the health benefits of conventional and organic food; long-term studies, due to time and money constraints, have been too difficult to undertake. It remains unclear if organic is indeed more nutritious than conventionally grown food.

There have been substantially fewer scientific studies on the health effects of eating local food, but it has garnered no shortage of public awareness. In a wave of new food initiatives, regimens that stress eating locally, like the 100-mile diet, have become extremely popular. Although people tend to buy local food for political reasons, it can be argued that it is actually better for your health than exotic food. Fruits and vegetables that travel a great distance before being consumed are harvested early to allow time to ripen during transportation. Local food travels a very short distance before being consumed, which allows for it to ripen in its natural environment. With shortened food chains (Feagen, 2007), produce that is ripened by the sun and consumed soon after harvest will not only taste better but also retain more nutrients than produce grown at a distance.

—student writer Stephen Littleford

For examples of essays in *The Active Reader* that employ different rhetorical patterns, including definition and comparison and contrast, see Classification of Readings by Rhetorical Mode/Pattern (inside back cover).

Kinds of Evidence

Although it is good to use various kinds of evidence in your essay, some are likely going to be more important than others. The choices you make depend on the type of essay you are writing and on your purpose, audience, topic, and claim. For example, if you are writing a rhetorical or critical analysis, you will focus on the essay you are analyzing as a primary source; if you are writing a research essay, your focus will likely be on secondary sources. For kinds of evidence typically used in argumentative essays, see page 105.

Some kinds of evidence can be more authoritative than others. In fact-based writing, "hard" evidence—facts, statistics, and the findings of empirical research—provides the strongest grounds for support. "Soft" evidence, such as expert opinion, examples, illustrations, and analogies, may also be important to help explain a concept but will likely be less important than "hard" evidence. Argumentative essays may use analogies, precedents, expert opinion, and even, perhaps, personal experience.

One kind of example that is often pertinent to fact-based social sciences writing, as well as writing in business and education, is the **case study**, a detailed exploration of one particular case, such as a real-life situation, in order to gain a depth of understanding of the issue being investigated. Case studies use empirical methods of observing and recording, although

---

Common kinds of evidence may vary from discipline to discipline. Humanities writing often uses extensive direct quotation from primary sources. Social sciences writing tends to focus on statistics, interviews, questionnaires, case studies, and interpersonal observation. The sciences rely on direct methods that involve experimentation.

case study

A carefully selected example that is analyzed in detail in order to support a writer's claim.

typically the data produced and then analyzed is qualitative rather than quantitative, based, for example, on interviews, questionnaires, and personal observation. Because of their systematic methodology and the wealth of detail that is analyzed, the findings from case studies can often be generalized, while ordinary examples cannot.

Issues of Credibility

Credibility factors include *knowledge*, *reliability*, and *fairness*. You exhibit your knowledge by appearing well informed about your topic and supporting each claim with solid and substantial evidence. You convey reliability in several ways:

- by using the accepted conventions of the discipline in which you are writing; this includes using the appropriate citation style, being aware of the specialized language of the discipline, and following format requirements, such as the use of an abstract and formal sections (report writing)
- by writing effectively and following the rules of grammar, punctuation, syntax, sentence structure, and spelling
- by writing efficiently, using precise words
- by using credible and authoritative sources (research essays)
- by reasoning logically and avoiding logical fallacies (argumentative essays)

Although fairness applies particularly to argumentative essays, it can also be important in research essays, since synthesis could involve acknowledging sources whose findings contradict your claim or hypothesis; this means explaining contrary evidence. The following criteria, however, apply mostly to argument. You convey fairness in several ways:

- by using an objective voice and not showing bias
- by acknowledging and accurately representing the opposing view
- by looking for common ground
- by avoiding slanted language and emotional fallacies

Writing Conclusions

Like introductions, **conclusions** can vary depending on the kind of essay and other factors. While conclusions are always a vital part of essays, their functions differ. They may refer back to the thesis statement, reasserting its importance and usually rephrasing it. They may also look ahead by considering a way that the thesis can be applied or the ways that it could be further explored.

Although the essay conclusion may both look back to the thesis statement and look ahead to the thesis's implications, the stress often falls on one or the other. A **circular conclusion** is primarily concerned with reminding the reader of your thesis and with reinforcing it. Even so, if you want to emphasize these functions, you should not repeat the thesis word for word, nor should you simply summarize what you have already said in your introduction. You should draw attention to the significance of the paragraphs that follow your introduction and precede your conclusion—after all, they are probably the most substantial part of the essay. One way you can do this is to summarize the most important point, connecting it to your thesis.

credibility
Credibility can be demonstrated by an author's knowledge, reliability, and fairness.

[handwritten marginal notes:]
circular
— restates, but doesn't repeat
— reinforce the thesis
— paraphrase yourself

spiral
— offer applications, suggestions for further study, potential next step

conclusion
The last paragraph or section of an essay whose function is to summarize the thesis and/or main points in the body of the essay.

circular conclusion
Reinforces the thesis.

spiral conclusion
Suggests applications or
further research.

A **spiral conclusion** is more concerned with the significance of the thesis. In argumentative essays, you may want to make an emotional or ethical appeal or, especially if your purpose is to reach a compromise, to suggest common ground between your view and the opposing one. Other strategies in spiral conclusions include ending with a relevant anecdote or personal experience (informal essays) or a question or hypothesis that extends from your research (formal essays or reports). If your focus has been on a problem, you could suggest solutions by making recommendations. If your topic was applicable to a small number of people, you can suggest how it could be generalized to a larger group, one that would include the reader.

The paragraph below uses the circular pattern. Although it repeats some information from the introduction, it uses different words and introduces a new term, *adaptive perfectionism*, from the middle paragraphs of the essay. In the final sentence, the writer advocates further research in the field to benefit people who are maladaptive perfectionists. You can compare the conclusion to the introduction, above on page 72:

As an infiltrating personality characteristic, perfectionism is often deleterious and psychologically harmful. Although adaptive perfectionism has been associated with positive elements such as a proclivity for excellence, it has also been associated with increased levels of depression as compared to non-perfectionists. Maladaptive perfectionism is that much more detrimental to an individual's life in that it is associated with more elements of mental illness and with difficulty in academics and intimate relationships. Since, as Costa and McCrae (1986) point out, personality is relatively stable, research on perfectionism is a warranted endeavour to better understand, and to better help people suffering from, this quality.

—Student writer Erin Walker

The Active Voice

The following essay gives guidelines relevant to students writing reports in the sciences, social sciences, engineering, and other disciplines in which an adaptation of the Type B essay is required. Note the emphasis on clear, direct, and active writing.

Report Writing—Aims and Goals

1   Of all types of writing, report writing is the most categorically active. It is built on *doing something*, then writing about what was discovered as a result of doing it—a lab experiment, for instance, or a survey, or a site visit. *Planned, designed, measured, saw, researched, interviewed, calculated, analyzed, evaluated, solved*: verbs—dynamic action or "doing" words—lie at the heart of all report writing. That is because reports record the results of a study undertaken to *find out something specific*: answer a question, clarify an issue, solve a problem, analyze a policy, establish a cause or consequence, decide on a course of action, evaluate possible outcomes, make a recommendation, or give an update on a project. In all these cases, reports "write up" the results of a study conducted to yield specific, concrete information that is otherwise missing, unknown, or incomplete.

2   Original findings based on original research—that is what reports typically deal with. In fact, "report of original research" is a common name for this type of writing in the science and social science disciplines, where the principal goal is to expand the field of knowledge—to fill gaps in the current state of research. The audience for such reports is typically other scientists or scholars. The report writer's job is to convince experts in the field that the findings are valid, making an original contribution to knowledge.

3   In other situations, however, report writing may answer more practical goals. Engineers, for example, may write investigative reports, recommendation reports, feasibility reports, or progress reports. The information compiled in these types of reports is usually intended to promote a specific course of action—for example, to implement (or scrap) a policy, develop a community program, approve an expansion of medical facilities, upgrade a highway, purchase new educational software, build a new gas line, or restore polluted waterways. As a result, they tend to be written for a mixed audience—other engineers as well as managers, policy-makers, public administrators, budgeting personnel, or company clients. Consequently, while they are generally technical in scope, they are often written so as to make sense to non-experts as well, with the goal of persuading them to act on the findings.

Organizing Reports

4   We have said that the goal of report writing is to provide specialized, concrete information, based on empirical research, in response to a question, problem, or project. At the same time, to ensure the report is sufficiently persuasive—allowing important decisions to be made on the information presented—reports also record *how* the information was compiled. They provide a methodology. This is a key way in which science and much social science writing differs from humanities writing. It explains not only the facts but how the facts were derived. This is important because knowing *how* the data was compiled means readers can gauge its trustworthiness for themselves.

5   Report writers therefore organize reports with an eye to showing *how* the information was found so they can demonstrate its reliability. Luckily, organizational *templates* make this a relatively easy task. Formal reports have a rigidly defined structure that report writers are expected to follow to meet disciplinary demands for clarity and accountability. The American Psychological Association (APA), the disciplinary body that regulates report writing in the social sciences and some of the sciences, requires an IMRAD style of organization: introduction, methods, results, and discussion, with each section clearly signalled by headings.

Introduction

6   Introductions provide context and needed background, explaining topic and purpose, and describing what the study was intended to find out and why. In the academic disciplines, this usually involves giving an opening literature review, an overview of current research in the field. A research question that the study is designed to answer may also be stipulated.

7   The introduction often ends with a hypothesis, a "prediction" about expected results that the study is designed to test.

Methodology

8   This section explains *how* the study was conducted. It outlines steps taken to compile the data, giving details about *where*, *when*, and *how*. In many cases, this section may also explain *why* the study was designed the way it was. The methodology section, in short, stipulates the techniques used to gather information:

- lab experiment
- fieldwork
- "on-site" observations
- tests, surveys, or questionnaires
- primary and secondary sources (print and electronic)
- interviews
- technical descriptions or specifications
- mathematical formulas or calculations
- computer modeling

Continued

Results

9   This section objectively describes the findings yielded by the study. The focus is on presenting the "raw data": no discussion of its significance takes place yet. What the data *means* (interpretation and evaluation) is reserved for the next section.

Discussion

10   The *APA Publication Manual* is very specific about key functions of a conclusion (usually called "Discussion") of an APA report. Primarily, this is where the study's findings are evaluated or interpreted. Their significance is explained. This section answers the questions, What do the results mean? What conclusions can we derive from them? If a hypothesis has been presented, the discussion should likewise state whether it is been confirmed or not, always bearing in mind that a negative result can be as valuable as a positive one. In either case, something new has been discovered.

11   Finally, a discussion usually ends with a closing peroration, a final "heightened appeal" for the significance or worth of the study. The goal here is to avoid a "so what?" response. The *APA Manual* suggests that report writers should aim to answer the following questions:

- What have I contributed here?
- What has my study helped resolve?
- What broader theoretical implications can I draw from my study?
- Can meaningful generalizations be drawn?
- Does further research need to be done to clarify any remaining uncertainties?

—**Monika Smith**, Assistant Teaching Professor, Academic and Technical Writing, University of Victoria

7 Writing Summaries

Student researchers are often told that when they use secondary sources in their research essays, they must do more than simply summarize them. Similarly, when students analyze literature, they may be advised to "avoid plot summary." From these examples, it might seem that summarization should play a minor role in academic discourse. Nothing could be further from the truth: although there are specific times and places for summaries, they are a major part of research-related writing.

Times and Places for Summaries

When you **summarize**, you represent another writer's ideas in a condensed form in your own words. The key words in this definition are *representing*—"*re*-presenting"—and *condensed*—"concentrated." A summary does not interpret or analyze but presents the essence of the original. The summary is more concentrated than the work being summarized because it contains only the main ideas, and sometimes only *the* main idea, of the original.

If you are reviewing a novel, you will typically summarize its plot or characters before you begin your analysis. If you are critiquing a text in order to argue against the author's position, you might begin by summarizing the author's arguments before replying with your own points. Similarly, in a critical analysis, you may briefly summarize a point before applying your critical-thinking skills to it. (There is an example of a student critical analysis in Chapter 9, page 119; a student rhetorical analysis can be found in Chapter 8, page 98.) The following are specialized summaries; their functions are discussed below:

- abstract
- literature review
- annotated bibliography

summary (*verb* summarize)

A broadly inclusive term for representing the ideas of a writer in a condensed form, using your own words.

abstract

A condensed summary used in an empirical study; it is placed before the essay begins and includes at a minimum purpose, methods, and results.

literature review

A condensed survey of articles on the topic arranged in a logical order, usually ending with the article most relevant to the author's study.

annotated bibliography

An expanded bibliography that includes not only the information of standard bibliographies but also highly condensed summaries of related works.

In many academic essays, a concentrated summary called an **abstract** precedes the essay, giving an overview of what follows (see page 17). Another form of summary is the **literature review**, in which the author concisely summarizes relevant studies before stating his or her own thesis or hypothesis (see page 18).

Another kind of summary, an **annotated bibliography** is an expanded bibliography that includes the information of both standard bibliographies and condensed summaries of works. These include studies referred to in the text, but may also include significant studies not cited there. Typically, each entry in the bibliography includes the thesis, main points, and a brief analysis, such as a comment on what it contributes to the field as a whole—where it fits in. Annotated bibliographies may form appendices to book-length studies.

Some authorities in a subject compile such bibliographies as independent projects. For example, *The World Shakespeare Bibliography Online* is a massive compilation of annotated entries for "all important books, articles, book reviews, dissertations, theatrical productions, reviews of productions, audiovisual materials, electronic media, and other scholarly and popular materials related to Shakespeare" created in the last 65 years. It includes more than 146,000 annotated entries in many languages.

Students may be assigned a more modest annotated bibliography as part of a research project or as an independent project. In either case, the purpose will be to demonstrate your ability to research, summarize, and evaluate relevant works on a topic.

In the annotated bibliography entry below, Lorinda Fraser summarizes one of the studies she used in her research essay and provides a brief assessment of its significance:

Sublette and Mullan analyzed 471 studies on Massively Multiplayer Online Games (MMOGS) addiction or "problematic game play," narrowing themselves down to only 16 studies that they felt met their criteria for unbiased data to evaluate the reliability of the evidence. These studies were then combined, compared, and discussed; recommendations for future research directions were proposed. In their review, Sublette and Mullan satisfy an important need by providing an extensive, objective review of current evidence-based research removed from the fear-based hype and sensationalism frequently offered in this field today.

Summarizing and Research

Summary is an important feature of scholarly discourse, whether practised by students or academics, because it enables writers to situate their own points relative to those of others. By presenting the main idea(s) of your sources and synthesizing them with your own ideas, you are developing and supporting your thesis. Writers of academic essays rely on this form of development. Academic writers summarize the ideas of other writers

- to support their own point
- to disagree with a relevant study
- to explain a concept or theory relevant to their topic
- to compare/contrast a study's findings with those of other studies

The amount of space you devote to a summary depends on how you want to use it and on its importance to your thesis. If you are summarizing an author's position with which you disagree, you probably will do no more than briefly mention the main arguments on the other side. If one source is particularly important to your research essay, your summary should be longer than those of less important sources. Summaries, then, can range greatly in length, as well as in purpose.

The Stand-Alone Summary: The Précis

Summaries can also serve as ends in themselves. A stand-alone summary, sometimes called a précis (meaning something precise), represents all the main points in a complete work or section(s) of a work. It is a miniature version of the original, following the same order of points as the original but omitting detail and less important sub-points; it is usually about 15 to 25 per cent the length of the original.

The specific guidelines that apply to stand-alone summaries do not apply to all types of summaries, but learning these guidelines and practising them is the best way to master summary writing. The important skills required in précis writing include the following:

Comprehension skills: Because summaries require you to change the wording of the original, you focus more closely on comprehension than if you quoted the words of the source directly: you must be clear on content in order to write a successful summary.

Prioritizing skills (establishing a hierarchy): Distinguishing the main ideas from the less important ideas is a fundamental part of the reading process. In précis writing, you need to think about the importance of a point relative to other points, the importance of a sub-point relative to other sub-points, and so on.

Concision skills: Wherever possible, too, you should try to tighten up the writing of the original without sacrificing clarity. Focusing on conciseness will serve you well in any writing you do, making you a more disciplined writer.

> Stand-alone summaries help develop three main skills basic to reading and writing at the university level: comprehension, prioritizing, and concision skills.

Ten Pointers for Précis Writing

When writing précis-style summaries, you should keep the following guidelines in mind:

1. Be accurate. Use focused reading strategies to ensure you do not misrepresent a fact, idea, or opinion.
2. Follow the order of the original. Begin the summary with the thesis or first main point.
3. Include only the most important points. You may include the most important sub-point(s) as well, depending on space. Most sub-points develop a main point.
4. Avoid detail. If a reader wants detail, he or she can read the original. Do not include examples unless they are very important.
5. Avoid repetition. However, writers may emphasize a point by repeating it. Ideas stressed in the original should be stressed in your summary, but without creating redundancy.
6. Do not repeat the author's name or the work's title any more than necessary.
7. Do not add your own opinions. Do not analyze or interpret. Summaries require you to objectively represent, not to respond to the writer or his/her views.
8. Use your own words, minimizing direct quotations. If a brief passage cannot be easily paraphrased, you may quote it directly, but *ensure that you use quotation marks to show the reader that those exact words occurred in the source.* You can also use direct quotation if a word or phrase is significant or well expressed. Common everyday words from the original do not have to be placed in quotation marks unless they occur in longer phrases (for the number of consecutive words that can be used without quotation marks, check with your instructor).

9. Write economically. Use no more words than you must, stressing basic words—nouns and verbs, adjectives and adverbs if they are important and can be expressed concisely, and transitions (sparingly) to create a logical flow between one idea and the next.

10. Ensure that the verbs you use reflect the author's rhetorical purpose. For example, if the writer is arguing rather than explaining a point, use a verb that reflects this: The author *argues* . . . *claims* . . . *criticizes* . . . (argument); the author *states* . . . *explains* . . . *discusses* . . . (exposition).

When summarizing, remember to be SPACE conscious. Be

- **S**pecific
- **P**recise
- **A**ccurate
- **C**lear
- **E**fficient

A How-To of Précis Writing

Reading strategies: Reading to summarize means you should use the appropriate forms of selective reading (see Chapter 5, p. 49). Begin by scanning the text to get its gist—its thesis—and to determine its structure—that is, how the author has divided the text. Then it is time for focused reading. When you summarize, you are uncovering the work's structure, so the logical method to use when summarizing is the *outline method:*

Identify main ideas by double underlining them. In *paragraphs*, for important ideas, look for topic sentences (often, but not always, the first sentence of the paragraph). In *sentences*, look for independent clauses, which contain the main idea. Identify the most important sub-points (developments) by single underlining. For information about using contextual cues, such as transitions and prompts, to lead you to main ideas, see Reading Paragraphs: Locating Main Ideas, page 52.

1. Next, prepare an outline with all main points and important sub-points. You can indent sub-points as in a formal outline.
2. Change the wording as much as possible and estimate word count. If above the desired length, omit the least important main point; if below, add the least important main point or the most important sub-point.
3. Write your summary from the outline, changing more wording so that it is mostly or entirely in your own words; add transitions for coherence. If the summary is above the desired length, omit the least important main point.

Some Summary Writing Strategies

In addition to the guidelines discussed above, consider the following strategies:

- Read through the essay at least twice before beginning to identify main points and important sub-points.
- Look for main points in topic sentences, often the first sentence in the paragraph; some paragraphs may not contain topic sentences. Use prompts and other context cues to direct you to main points and important sub-points.
- Place parentheses around non-essential details and examples that will not be included in your summary.

- To help identify main points, ask how they connect with or contribute to the thesis. Main points usually provide support for the thesis. If you are summarizing a section of a complete work, remember that every section should contain a controlling idea.
- Do not include points whose purpose is to attract interest rather than give information.

The following is the first half of the 1,500-word essay in Part III: The Reader titled "Taking Race Out of Human Genetics" (page 342) with annotations that focus on identifying important points. A summary of 150 words (20 per cent of the original) follows.

Professional Writing Sample

Taking Race Out of Human Genetics

By Michael Yudell, Dorothy Roberts, Rob DeSalle, and Sarah Tishkoff

1   In the wake of the sequencing of the human genome in the early 2000s, genome pioneers and social scientists alike called for an end to the use of race as a variable in genetic research (1, 2). Unfortunately, by some measures, the use of race as a biological category has increased in the postgenomic age (3). Although inconsistent definition and use have been a chief problem with the race concept, it has historically been used as a taxonomic categorization based on common hereditary traits (such as skin color) to elucidate the relationship between our ancestry and our genes. We believe the use of biological concepts of race in human genetic research—so disputed and so mired in confusion—is problematic at best and harmful at worst. It is time for biologists to find a better way.

The authors announce their argumentative thesis at the end of their first paragraph.

2   Racial research has a long and controversial history. At the turn of the 20th century, sociologist and civil rights leader W. E. B. Du Bois was the first to synthesize natural and social scientific research to conclude that the concept of race was not a scientific category. Contrary to the then-dominant view, Du Bois maintained that health disparities between blacks and whites stemmed from social, not biological, inequality (4). Evolutionary geneticist Theodosius Dobzhansky, whose work helped reimagine the race concept in the 1930s at the outset of the evolutionary synthesis, wrestled with many of the same problems modern biologists face when studying human populations—for example, how to define and sample populations and genes (5). For much of his career, Dobzhansky brushed aside criticism of the race concept, arguing that the problem with race was not its scientific use, but its nonscientific misuse. Over time, he grew disillusioned, concerned that scientific study of human diversity had "floundered in confusion and misunderstanding" (6). His transformation from defender to detractor of the race concept in biology still resonates.

The first body paragraph contains a clear topic sentence. As Dobzhansky is recalled three more times in the essay, he should be included in your summary.

3   Today, scientists continue to draw wildly different conclusions on the utility of the race concept in biological research. Some have argued that relevant genetic information can be seen at the racial level (7) and that race is the best proxy we have for examining human genetic diversity (8, 9). Others have concluded that race is neither a relevant nor accurate way to understand or map human genetic diversity (10, 11). Still others have argued that race-based predictions in clinical settings, because of the heterogeneous nature of racial groups, are of questionable use (12), particularly as the prevalence of admixture increases across populations.

The divergent views can be briefly summarized from the topic sentence.

4   Several meetings and journal articles have called attention to a host of issues, which include (i) a proposed shift to "focus on racism (i.e., social relations) rather than race (i.e., supposed

As it may take up too much space to summarize the "host of issues" in this paragraph, choose the most significant one (see Sample Summary, below).

innate biologic predisposition) in the interpretation of racial/ ethnic 'effects'" (13); (ii) a failure of scientists to distinguish between self-identified racial categories and assigned or assumed racial categories (14); and (iii) concern over "the haphazard use and reporting of racial/ethnic variables in genetic research" (15) and a need to justify use of racial categories relative to the research questions asked and methods used (6). Several academic journals have taken up this last concern and, with mixed success, have issued guidelines for use of race in research they publish (16). Despite these concerns, there have been no systematic attempts to address these issues and the situation has worsened with the rise of large-scale genetic surveys that use race as a tool to stratify these data (17).

5   It is important to distinguish ancestry from a taxonomic notion such as race. Ancestry is a process-based concept, a statement about an individual's relationship to other individuals in their genealogical history; thus, it is a very personal understanding of one's genomic heritage. Race, on the other hand, is a pattern-based concept that has led scientists and laypersons alike to draw conclusions about hierarchical organization of humans, which connect an individual to a larger preconceived geographically circumscribed or socially constructed group.

6   Unlike earlier disagreements concerning race and biology, today's discussions generally lack clear ideological and political antipodes of "racist" and "nonracist." Most contemporary discussions about race among scientists concern examination of population-level differences between groups, with the goal of understanding human evolutionary history, characterizing the frequency of traits within and between populations, and using an individual's self-identified ancestry to identify genetic risk factors of disease and to help determine the best course of medical treatments (6).

> The first sentence in this paragraph compares early and later arguments about race, acting as a prompt. The relevant point (topic sentence) concerns today's discussions.

Sample Student Essay

Sample Summary of "Taking Race Out of Human Genetics"

1   Since the human genome was sequenced, experts have agreed that race should no longer be a genetic research variable, yet it continues to be used in genetic research. The authors argue that its use is potentially harmful and that race should be discarded as a biological concept. The history of racial research is controversial: an influential geneticist, Theodosius Dobzhansky, defended race as a scientific category, but later changed his opinion. Today's scientists are divided. They have debated related issues, including the need to link racial categories to research methodologies; proposing appropriate guidelines, however, has not solved the problem. The authors stress the difference between "ancestry" and "race," which, unlike ancestry, is a "pattern-based concept" used to link individuals to larger hierarchical structures. Race is often used today to help explain human evolution by examining population-level divergences between groups, whereas ancestry is used to identify individual genetic risks and diagnostic options.

Activity 7.1

Summarize in 150 words the second half of the essay "Taking Race Out of Human Genetics," page 342 in Part III: The Reader.

8 Using Critical Thinking to Analyze Essays

The Rhetorical Analysis: Explaining the How and Why

A rhetorical analysis is usually focused on one text. When you analyze a work, you break it down in order to examine its parts and the author's rhetorical strategies, using your critical-thinking skills and your knowledge of texts. The rhetorical analysis assumes you are familiar with how such texts are written and capable of evaluating the author's success in achieving his or her objectives. The main purposes of rhetorical analyses are (1) to explain how a text is put together and (2) to evaluate/critique the use of rhetorical strategies. A rhetorical analysis should be objective in both content and voice.

Writing a rhetorical analysis makes you more conscious of the way that texts written by academics and other professionals are put together, as well as the kinds of strategies you can use to make content clear and accessible. In this sense, you critically analyze a text to see what works—and why—in order to use some of its features as models for your own writing. Of course, the text under consideration could serve as a negative model too.

In a *rhetorical analysis*, you use critical thinking and your knowledge of texts to break down a work in order to examine its parts and the author's rhetorical strategies.

In a *critical analysis*, you analyze the writer's *argument* for its effectiveness. For more on critical analyses and the language of argument, see Chapter 9, pages 117–118. For an example of a critical analysis, see Chapter 9, page 123.

The Active Voice

Rhetorical Analysis: What, Why, and How

What Is Rhetoric?

1   Many people now use the term **rhetoric** to mean empty language or even as a synonym for lying. The long history of rhetorical studies, however, suggests that we should give this word more respect. In ancient Greece, formal education started with training in rhetoric, defined as persuasive speech. All participation in that society's civic institutions—such as defense of oneself in a court of law or engagement in a public debate about whether to go to war—required public speaking, so the ability to deliver stirring arguments was highly valued. By the fifth century BCE schools of rhetoric existed, and their instructors wrote manuals on the art of rhetoric. Rhetoric remained central to the training of educated people across Europe from the medieval period until well into the eighteenth century. Twentieth- and twenty-first-century scholars of rhetoric debate how arguments work in a variety of contexts ranging from political speeches to scientific studies to pop songs.

2   Perhaps the most influential of the ancient rhetorical theorists was Aristotle (born 384 BCE, died 322 BCE), a student at Plato's Academy who served as tutor to Alexander the Great. He wrote on a wide range of subjects, including imaginative literature (*Poetics*), logic (*Organon*), and philosophy (*Nicomachean Ethics, Metaphysics*). Still foundational to the work of contemporary rhetoric studies is his treatise *On Rhetoric*. Responding to already existing rhetorical handbooks, Aristotle defined the goal of rhetoric not merely as persuasion itself but as the discovery and consideration of all available means of persuasion. Rhetoric thus included not just style, the arrangement of points, and emotional impacts—the topics stressed by other writers on the subject. It also involved consideration of audiences, speakers, subject matter, occasions for speaking, logic, and the character of the speaker. With his discussion of rhetoric, Aristotle did not invent a new field or discover new concepts. Rather, he described in a systematic way what effective speakers already did and, in the process, created a set of specialized terminology on which rhetorical theorists still rely.

Rhetorical Appeals

3   If we agree with Aristotle that rhetoric involves all available means of persuasion, then a rhetorical analysis could take into account everything and anything that impacts persuasiveness. Argumentative patterns used to shape each paragraph, types of introductions, structures of sentences, and qualities of word choices—all of these are rhetorical elements that could be described and analyzed. But a discussion of every persuasive aspect of even a very short argument would be too long and wide-ranging to be easily understood. By focusing on the key means of persuasion identified by Aristotle, we can develop more focused, coherent evaluations of arguments.

4   According to Aristotle, an individual making an argument has three basic means of persuasion at his or her disposal. We usually refer to these means of persuasion as the three rhetorical appeals since they comprise different ways of appealing to and perhaps winning over an audience of listeners or readers. A particular argument might stress one more than the others, but all three are usually present. We use Greek terms for these appeals not in order to complicate matters unnecessarily; relying on Aristotle's specialized terminology allows an analysis to convey complex ideas concisely to any reader familiar with basic rhetorical theory.

5   Most readily understood is the appeal to **logos**, the persuasive impact of **logical** argumentation. Logos includes claims that an audience will perceive as probable as well as the reasons, examples, and evidence that support these claims. In the field of rhetoric, logical argumentation differs from that found in formal logic—as far as rhetoricians are concerned, it is sufficient for an audience to perceive a point as logical, not necessary for that point to be perfectly valid or true in all cases. As such, logos includes most of what we think of as the content of an argument such as the points it presents and the supporting statistics, cases, or testimonies it offers.

6   Aristotle recognized, however, that there were other factors than content that could lead an audience to find an argument persuasive. The emotional state of those

listening to or reading a set of points could influence the likelihood of their agreeing with the claims being presented. Speakers or writers who could invoke powerful feelings in their audiences had a useful tool at their disposal. Vivid description or even emotionally charged language might lead an audience to feel anger, grief, or pity and thus be moved to act in a particular way. More subtle emotions like friendliness or a general sense of belonging to a group could be created through the way a speaker addressed an assembled crowd. Influencing emotions as a means of persuasion is called the appeal to **pathos**, and emotionally charged arguments are said to be **pathetic**.

7   Finally, the extent to which an argument might persuade an audience depends upon who delivers that argument. Aristotle recognized that listeners were much more likely to believe a wise, virtuous, and well-meaning speaker than one who seemed ignorant or ruthless. He called the appeal based on the character of a speaker or writer **ethos**, the elements of a speech that established character **ethical** appeals.

8   The treatise *On Rhetoric* is particularly concerned with how a speaker can make effective ethical appeals within the argument itself. One can create the impression of being an expert by talking about personal experience of a field or simply by showing mastery of complex ideas; one can seem a moral person by speaking about having done good deeds; and one can appear open-minded and rational by being respectful towards opposing arguments. The character of the speaker or writer created within the argument is known as **intrinsic ethos**.

9   Aristotle recognized, though, that the impression an audience had of the speaker before the speech began could have an impact on its persuasiveness. A very old man might have difficulty convincing an audience that he would fight in the war for which he was advocating, but he could convince the same group of listeners that he had extensive experience of previous wars and thus authority to speak to this issue that no young soldier could possess. A jury might not accept an argument about having mistakenly taken a bracelet from a shop without paying for it from someone they knew as a thrice-convicted thief, but they could find the same argument very persuasive from a pious priestess. **Extrinsic ethos**, what is known about the speaker outside the argument itself, can powerfully alter the effectiveness of that argument.

Rhetorical Analysis

10   Aristotle was most concerned with public speeches, but many of the examples of arguments we encounter today, and most of the ones we analyze, come in other forms, either as broadcasts by radio, television, or online of speeches or, more commonly, in writing. Even so, the three appeals can be identified in arguments we might wish to analyze.

11   Advertising regularly uses all available means of persuasion to convince an audience that a product is worth buying. A television advertisement introducing a new hybrid car might appeal to logos by arguing the car is good because of its gas mileage. Simultaneously, the same ad could appeal to pathos by using bright colors and bouncy music, thus encouraging the audience to associate the car with happiness. It could also make an extrinsic ethical appeal by mentioning the name of the well-regarded company that makes this new car and an intrinsic ethical appeal by presenting the new car's name in an attractive script and having it read by a smooth-voiced announcer.

12   Academic arguments employ appeals for more limited audiences. Indeed, it might seem at first glance that a document like an article in a peer-reviewed sociology journal relies on only one appeal, offering logical arguments in the form of data and statistics generated by a study to persuade readers that its results are accurate and that its conclusions are true. Certainly logos is the primary appeal of most academic writing, but other appeals are present. The prestige of the journal in which the article appears can help establish strong extrinsic ethos. The quality of the writing in the article itself and the extent to which the authors have mastered the conventions of scientific discourse affect intrinsic ethos. Pathos is likely subtle in such an argument, but the extent to which an article's choice to define certain terms or explain particular points makes an audience feel either confidently well-informed or anxiously confused will determine the extent to which that group of readers is persuaded.

Why Study Rhetoric?

13   In addition to using the three appeals to analyze advertisements, speeches, blog posts, newspaper editorials, or academic articles, one can use these concepts to generate arguments that will effectively persuade those listening to or reading them. To create a new argument, it is important

Continued

that we start not with a choice of which appeal to emphasize but rather with consideration of whom we are trying to persuade. Rhetoric emphasizes practical considerations of what will be effective in the real world, not abstract thought about what would be best in an ideal situation. Begin by thinking about how each appeal might work on your actual audience in relation to a particular case, being sure to take into account what values, attitudes, and knowledge members of that group share. Then decide which appeals would be most appropriate to utilize.

14   Does this emphasis on effectiveness mean that a rhetorician is licensed to lie, or at least to bend the truth to say what an audience wants to hear? When you make an argument, how much should you consider whether your argument is valid and true, one you think is fundamentally right? These questions have long concerned philosophers and ethicists. Plato and Socrates saw rhetoric as dangerously immoral because of its tendency to stress persuasiveness in specific situations over the ideals of everlasting truth and virtue. Aristotle was more positive towards rhetoric in part because he was more cynical about the ability of audiences made up of uneducated people to be persuaded by philosophical argumentation. He specifically worried that if good people did not study and employ rhetoric then their true arguments could be defeated by untrue or immoral arguments carefully crafted by those who had studied rhetorical manuals. Nevertheless, Aristotle was still cautious about rhetoric, seeing it as a tool that could be turned towards either moral or immoral purposes.

15   It is because rhetoric is a tool that can be applied in a variety of situations to almost any subject matter that it remains helpful to those of us living in a complex, media-saturated culture. Understanding the rhetorical appeals enables one to analyze existing arguments and to consider why they are or are not effective for a particular audience—and to think critically about whether one should be persuaded by the writer's or speaker's ideas. These same concepts can serve as prompts for generating effective arguments. One can also consider the appeals when attempting what is perhaps the most ancient rhetorical exercise of all, writing a highly persuasive argument with which you disagree, a practice Aristotle recommends not just to hone skills but also to put strain on and thus test the limits of one's convictions. Learning about rhetoric places you into an ancient and enduring Western educational tradition while simultaneously preparing you to succeed in crafting effective personal, popular, and academic arguments.

—**Erin E. Kelly**, Associate Professor, Department of English, University of Victoria

Resources for Further Study

Aristotle. *On Rhetoric: A Theory of Civic Discourse.* Translated by George A. Kennedy, Oxford University Press, 1991.

- This English translation of Aristotle's treatise offers a lengthy introduction and extensive notes that make clear the originality and implications of key sections.

Plato. *Gorgias.* Translated by Walter Hamilton, Penguin Classics, 2004; and *Phaedrus.* Translated by Christopher Rowe, Penguin Classics, 2005.

- These dialogues present Socrates debating the morality and utility of rhetoric with two interlocutors and coming to slightly different conclusions.

Chaim Perelman and Lucie Olbrechts-Tyteca. *The New Rhetoric.* University of Notre Dame Press, 1991.

- For a sense of how contemporary rhetoric theorists reinterpret and apply Aristotle's ideas, see Perelman and Olbrechts-Tyteca's discussions of modern starting points and frameworks for argumentation.

The Forest of Rhetoric: *Silva Rhetoricae,* Brigham Young University, rhetoric.byu.edu.

- This excellent website created by Professor Gideon O. Burton offers overviews of basic and advanced rhetorical terms and concepts.

Key Terms

rhetoric The art of using language to persuade or influence an audience; the study of persuasive speech and writing.

appeal to ethos The impact, either positive or negative, of the audience's sense of the speaker or writer's character on the persuasiveness of his or her argument. While the speaker or writer's ethics come into play, so do expertise, credentials, awareness of conventions, and accomplishments. What an audience knows about the speaker or writer outside of the argument itself is called **extrinsic ethos**. The impression of the speaker or writer shaped within the argument is called **intrinsic ethos**.

appeal to logos The use of reason and logic to help convince readers. Skillful use of evidence, examples, facts, and statistics contributes to logical arguments.

appeal to pathos The effect of an audience's emotions, aroused by the speaker or writer, on how persuasive readers or listeners will find the argument. Note that these emotions can be extreme (like fear or rage) or subtle (like a sense of identification with the subject matter).

Activity 8.1

1. The image below is an advertisement created by the World Wildlife Fund, a global organization dedicated to protecting Earth's wildlife and habitats. Although text is minimal, the message is clear. Part of the ad's immediacy is due to the use of the three appeals, as discussed above in The Active Voice: Rhetorical Analysis. In contrast to most academic texts, the appeal to logic (logos) is less important than the appeals to emotion (pathos) and ethics (ethos). In groups, identify the appeals and discuss other relevant features of the ad.

2. Find another advertisement in the media (it could be a current example or one from another era) and bring it to class or access it on your computer for others in your group to see. Analyze its effectiveness, referring specifically to its logical, emotional, or ethical appeals.

Figure 8.1 15 km² of rain forest disappears every minute.

For more on logical, emotional, and ethical appeals as they can be used in argument, see Chapter 9.

Rhetorical analyses can be approached in different ways, depending on the nature of the source text. One kind of analysis applies to literary works. The literary analysis breaks down the elements of the text—in the case of fiction, these might include plot, character, setting, point of view, or language—showing how they relate to one another. Literary works contain no thesis but rather themes, which can be inferred from the interconnections among these elements. Like other kinds of texts, literary texts can be analyzed according to their conventions, which vary by genre (poetry, drama, fiction, creative non-fiction) and by subgenre (lyric, dramatic, and narrative poetry, for example).

Organizing a Rhetorical Analysis

A typical rhetorical analysis begins with an introduction that includes a generalization about the essay and/or the topic, such as its importance or relevance in today's world. It must also include a summary of the author's thesis and/or main points. You should also address the essay's purpose and its audience in your introduction.

Your introduction should end with your thesis statement, in which you address whether the text successfully fulfills its purpose and supports its claims. An effective thesis statement goes further than just stating whether the text is successful but also explains why and how; thus, your expanded thesis should include the rhetorical features of the text that you will develop in your body paragraphs.

An *expanded thesis statement*, or essay plan, includes the main points in the order they will appear in the essay.

In the body paragraphs, then, you provide support for your thesis by analyzing the specific features mentioned in your introduction, referring to specific passages from the essay you are analyzing. Consider how these features, such as the author's organization or rhetorical strategies, reflect his or her purpose, objectives, and audience.

In any analysis, being specific is vital. Support all claims you make about a text by referring specifically to examples that illustrate your point. As in literary analyses, use direct quotations for important examples, remembering to provide citations. The best rhetorical analyses proceed from a close and detailed reading of the source text (see Focused Reading, Chapter 5, page 50).

For citation formats, see Chapter 10, page 143–152.

The questions below, organized according to purpose, can be used to help generate points for a rhetorical analysis. The author's thesis, type of essay, purpose, and intended audience, along with other factors, will help determine which questions are the most relevant to your analysis.

For information on critical analyses, which analyze a writer's argument, see Chapter 9, page 117.

Explaining/Summarizing

- When was the essay written? Is it current?
- Why was it written? Is it intended to inform, explain, persuade?
- Who is the intended audience? How do you know this?
- What do you know about the author(s)? Does he or she appear to be an expert in his or her field or otherwise qualified to write on the topic? How is this apparent (if it is)? What makes the author credible (or not)?
- What is the writer's thesis or central question? What is the justification for the study? In what way(s) does the author propose to add to his or her field of knowledge? Is a literature review included?
- How does the author convey essay structure? Essay plan? Questions?
- What are the essay's main points?

- What format does the essay follow? How does the text reflect the conventions of the discipline for which it was written?
- What kinds of evidence does the author use? Are primary and secondary sources included?
- Is there a stress on either analysis or synthesis in the essay? On both equally?
- How is the essay organized? Is there a primary rhetorical pattern? What other kinds of patterns are used? (See Table 6.1, page 77.)
- What level of language is used? Does the author include any particular stylistic features (e.g., analogies, metaphors, imagery, unusual/unconventional sentence structure)?
- Is there a conclusion? What is its primary purpose?

Analyzing

- Does the author create interest in the topic? How is this done?
- Main points: Are they identifiable (in topic sentences, for example)? Are they well supported? Is supporting detail specific and relevant?
- If secondary sources are used, are there an adequate number? Are most of them current references?
- What kinds of sources were used? Books? Journal articles? Websites? Which are the most important? Have the author(s) published related works in the field of study?
- Are the kinds of evidence used relevant to the topic, audience, and discipline? Are examples and illustrations used to make points more concrete?
- What kinds of strategies and techniques does the author use to facilitate understanding? Are they effective? Are there other ways that organization or content could have been made clearer?
- What kinds of rhetorical features are used: logos? pathos? ethos? How are they used?
- Is the voice or tone appropriate, given the kind of essay and the audience?
- Does the conclusion answer the question that the author sets out to explore? Does it explain the relevance of the study, what it contributes to the field?
- Does the author appear reasonable? Has he or she used reason effectively, establishing a chain of logic throughout?
- Does the author succeed in making the issue relevant to the reader? Does he or she appeal to the reader's concerns and values?
- Is the order of points appropriate? Do points progress from weakest to strongest (climax order) or strongest to weakest (reverse climax)?

Activity 8.2

1. After reading one of the Type A or Type C essays in Part III (see Index of Essay Types on page 383 for essay types), choose at least five questions under Explaining/ Summarizing and five questions under Analyzing that would be relevant to a rhetorical analysis of the chosen essay.

2. Use these 10 questions to outline an analysis, identifying and answering other relevant questions to fill out your outline.

3. Determine the best order of points for your outline (see Relating Parts and Discovering Structure, Chapter 6, page 65).

Sample Student Rhetorical Analysis

A rhetorical analysis, like the one below on "Reality TV Gives Back," by Laurie Ouellette (page 266 in Part III: The Reader), highlights some of the main features of the source text, using some summary, but mostly analysis. The annotations refer to some of the points discussed above.

Student Writing Sample

Rhetorical Analysis of "Reality TV Gives Back: On the Civic Functions of Reality Entertainment"
by Sean MacLean

> MacLean introduces his topic and mentions the key critic that Ouellette responds to in her essay. He then addresses the essay's purpose and audience.

1   Media is a lens through which we see the world. Therefore, it is crucial to use critical thinking to evaluate the directions taken by both public and private broadcasting systems. Critics, such as John Corner, have shown concern about the decline of educational documentaries that serve to train citizens to be active participants in the democratic process. In Laurie Ouellette's article, "Reality TV Gives Back: On the Civic Functions of Reality Entertainment," she addresses such concerns for her audience of cultural studies experts and attempts to shed light on the civic functions of reality entertainment in its "reinterpreted and integrated" (285) form. She argues that, although the standards and purposes of reality TV have changed, it has adapted

> After briefly summarizing Ouellette's thesis, MacLean identifies the features he sees as crucial to the essay's success: credibility, use of rhetorical patterns, and emotional appeal.

to provide civic purpose. Ouellette effectively conveys her argument by demonstrating her credibility, while organizing her material by rhetorical patterns, notably compare and contrast, cause–effect, and examples, including a detailed analysis of Secret Millionaire, a Fox Network program. In addition, a subtle emotional appeal caps her effective conclusion.

> Much of this paragraph analyzes Ouellette's response to an influential (but, she suggests, an outdated) essay by John Corner. However, MacLean also refers to her use of other scholars' work, including Ouellette's own book, to increase her credibility.

2   Although reality TV is still a comparatively recent topic for scholarly discussion and debate, Ouellette is clearly an authority. She is familiar with relevant sources and cites major studies, in particular John Corner's "Performing the Real: Documentary Diversions." However, her intent is not necessarily to contradict the work of Corner but to fill in a gap of knowledge in this early (2002) study. According to Corner, documentary TV has become sidetracked, having abandoned its earlier goal of educating its citizens, which leads to the large question, "[will] democracy itself . . . survive?" (284). Ouellette replies to Corner's claim by showing how a new political landscape and sense of citizenry self-responsibility enable civic function (and, by extension, Western capitalist democracy) to "operate *within* market imperatives and entertainment formats" (285). In explaining how "good citizenship" relates to political change during the Clinton and Bush eras, Ouellette refers to a book she coauthored, *Better Living through Reality TV: Television and Post-Welfare Citizenship*. In addition, she cites a variety of other authorities, including Toby Miller, a cultural studies scholar (285), and David Vogel, a business historian (286). When accompanied by an objective voice and appropriate scholarly jargon, her credibility is firmly established.

> A simple topic sentence sets up MacLean's focus on rhetorical patterns. Note that he does much more than identify these patterns, but shows *how* they are used, supporting his points by cited textual references.

3   Ouellette's use of rhetorical patterns helps her organize her material. In particular, she uses compare and contrast and cause–effect in the first half of her essay to help explain the new roles taken on by reality TV and its viewers. She begins by contrasting the pre-1990s public broadcasting commitment to civic education with what Corner sees as reality TV's defining format, "documentary as diversion": "Envisioning the medium as an instrument of education, not a mover of merchandise, public broadcasters embraced democracy and other nonfiction

formats as a dimension of their broader mission to serve and reform citizens. . ." (284). Using cause–effect in paragraph 2, Ouellette explains how reforms and downsizing forced public broadcasters to retreat from their original mission to instill citizenship values. She links the call for volunteerism as part of the agendas of two US presidents to an influx of "do good" programs that retain an entertainment value while "[intervening] directly in social life, enacting 'can do' solutions" (286) for those in need.

4   Examples can provide concrete support for general claims, and Ouellette uses many examples of reality TV shows to support her claim about "do good" TV in paragraphs 6 to 12. Her strategy of mentioning some shows in passing (e.g., *American Idol Gives Back* and *Oprah's Big Give*) enables her to demonstrate the popularity of this new sub-genre (as many readers will have heard of and perhaps watched at least some of the shows mentioned); focusing on two shows for extensive commentary enables her to demonstrate precisely how these shows exemplify reality TV "giv[ing] back." She claims that *Extreme Makeover Home Edition* is the "template" (286) for "do good" programming. After briefly summarizing the show's premise, she gives examples of the ways viewers are encouraged "to practice compassionate citizenship" (286) through volunteering or other ways of becoming involved. Towards the end of her analysis, she transitions from the specific to the general by applying her comments on *Home Edition* to the sub-genre at large, thus demonstrating logical paragraph development: "More explicitly than other reality sub-genres, the helping trend acknowledges the limitations of self-maximization and pure market logic—and capitalizes on the result" (286).

> MacLean uses direct quotations effectively for support in this and other paragraphs. Here he quotes a word, a phrase, and a complete sentence from Ouellette's essay, integrating Ouellette's words with his own. (Note the use of the colon before the last quotation. A colon can be used before a direct quotation if preceded by a grammatically complete sentence.) "Do good" is not cited, as it occurs throughout the essay.

5   Ouellette proceeds similarly with her most developed example, *Secret Millionaire*, in which the debut episode is analyzed in detail and even includes brief narratives about the impoverished individuals the "secret millionaire" and his son listen to as they work in disguise as labourers. As Ouellette implies, *Secret Millionaire* takes "do good" programming to its limits by acknowledging that the plights of the characters encountered are not easily solved by glamorous gifts from corporate sponsors and by reversing the trend of more traditional "do good" shows of rewarding the poor; instead, *Secret Millionaire* proposes "to evaluate, educate, guide, enlighten, and transform the richest people in North America" (298). It is these aims that make *Secret Millionaire* a key example for Ouellette. Moreover, she ends her essay by making a subtle emotional appeal by predicting that this show will probably not survive because there are no big corporate giveaways, thus instilling a sense of regret and disappointment in the reader: "Alas, this lack of marketability will undoubtedly keep the civic possibilities opened up by programs such as *Secret Millionaire* in check" (288).

> Although the topic is the same as the previous paragraph (Ouellette's use of examples), MacLean likely felt that including it with the examples previously discussed would produce an overly long paragraph.

6   Ouellette has fashioned a successful essay that goes well beyond a critical evaluation of John Corner to "unravel the complexities of reality entertainment in its current forms" (287). She establishes her credibility to write on the topic through analysis of diverse sources, including her own studies. Although readers who are not well versed in cultural studies may find the lengthy sentences and paragraphs, along with the jargon of the discipline, somewhat challenging, Ouellette uses rhetorical patterns to organize and develop her points, especially compare and contrast, and examples, thus helping to make the essay comprehensible to the non-specialist reader.

9 Writing Argumentative Essays

Argumentative Purpose

Although argument today reflects its origins in classical thought and the theories of Aristotle, its contemporary uses are diverse. For example, today argument can serve several purposes:

- to defend a point of view
- to propose an action or better way to do something
- to interpret or critique a text
- to expose or raise awareness of a problem
- to strengthen/direct group opinion
- to reach a compromise

The most straightforward kind of argument is one in which you take a position on an arguable topic and defend it. However, argumentative purpose can extend beyond this. For example, you can analyze both sides to reach a compromise, finding common ground. Thus, in her essay on a section of the Criminal Code that permits corporal punishment under specific circumstances, student writer Danielle Gudgeon steers a middle ground between those who want the law upheld and those who want it abolished. Her middle position makes it likely that an audience on both sides will consider her points, making her argumentative goal more attainable:

Section 43 of the Criminal Code has a social utility for both teachers and parents, but it is an old law that must be amended to reflect society's progression. The addition of clear guidelines to the law regarding the severity of discipline and the use of objects as weapons will create a distinction between abuse and discipline. This will prevent subjectivity within the courts and discourage future abuse, while affording parents the option of disciplining their children.

Academic Arguments

Many academic arguments are written to a specific audience, usually a typical reader of the journal in which the essay appears. Although purposes vary here, too, two common purposes are to raise awareness and to strengthen/direct group opinion. For example, the authors of "Mental Wellness in Canada's Aboriginal Communities" (page 216 of Part III: The Reader) and "Social Justice and Social Determinants of Health" (page 241 of Part III: The Reader) argue to raise awareness and include recommendations for acting on this awareness. Similarly, the authors of "A Ban on Marketing to Children" (page 297 of Part III: The Reader) and "Taking Race Out of Human Genetics" (page 342 of Part III: The Reader) speak directly to their readers to encourage group action. Authors of essays in the humanities (Type A essays) usually interpret a text with the implicit argument that the author's interpretation is better than or takes more into account than other interpretations of the same text. (See Three Common Kinds of Academic Essays, Chapter 3.)

Authors of Type B essays may also use argument selectively, especially in their Introductions, where they justify their study's importance, and in their Discussion sections. For example, the authors of "Self-Reported Food Skills of University Students" (page 277 of Part III: The Reader) often link their results to specific "nutrition education interventions" that could fix or alleviate a problem. Clearly, authors of essays that include experimentation want to ensure that their study is taken seriously and that its results will be seen as significant. This is often where argumentation comes in, though such authors will typically not use the kinds of argumentative strategies discussed later in this chapter (see, in particular, Giving Life to Logic, page 110).

The kinds of evidence and the argumentative strategies you use depend on your purpose in arguing, your audience, and the topic itself. It is useful to look at three diverse forms that written argument can take in the media in order to see how these elements interact: the letter to the editor/blog, the review, and the editorial (see Table 9.1). Each has a different purpose, which is reflected in its structure, voice, language, kinds of evidence, and typical reader/viewer. The letter to the editor is the most subjective, in which writers can "have their say," whereas the voice of the editorial writer is usually objective and formal. Within these categories, there can be much variation; for example, although many reviewers are experts in their field, many forums exist online today for non-experts who may be less objective in their critiques.

Like the old letter-to-the-editor writer, "bloggers" range from opinionated novices to informed experts. Unlike letters to the editor, blogs often take the form of entries and are not restricted by length requirements. Another obvious difference is that bloggers can incorporate interactive elements in the design of their site, including direct feedback. Blogs have become a major part of many online publications, as well as print publications that want to reach a larger audience through their online presence.

Everyday Arguments

Consider the following scenario: you have moved into a residence at your university only to find the rules and regulations there particularly unfair (a 10:00 p.m. curfew for weekday social functions, for example). You might well discuss your disagreement with other residents and write a petition that argues for more reasonable rules—you are arguing your case, rather than engaging in conflict. The impulse to argue can easily arise if we perceive our values or beliefs

Table 9.1   Argument in Different Kinds of Writing

	Letter to the Editor/Blog	Book/Film Review	Editorial
Purpose	to sound off, state your viewpoint; other purposes are possible as well	to critique a text, film, or some other type of material	to critique a position, expose a problem, reach a compromise, or promote affiliation
Writer	any interested reader	is knowledgeable in the field; professional reviewers are named in bylines	member of an editorial board; writer's name is not given; represents the views of the publication
Audience	those with similar values and views	book readers, film-goers, readers with an interest in the subject matter, etc.	educated readers, often the politically informed
Structure	usually short; might be edited for length and for style	usually follows conventional structure of argument: generalization with value claim followed by supporting evidence from the film/book	usually short; tight structure: focused on one issue
Claim	value or policy; argument may present only one side	value; will consider the pros and cons but will come down on one side or the other—"thumbs up" or down	policy; will carefully weigh both sides; may argue for one side, but argument characterized by careful reasoning
Voice	subjective—*I*	sometimes uses first person—*I*	objective—the "editorial *we*"
Language/tone	may be colourful, emotional, or volatile: "I'm appalled by our political leaders"; conversational, informal	may use some specialized words and terms; may be ironic or sarcastic, direct or evocative	elevated, sophisticated; formal, detached
Evidence	personal opinion may predominate	mostly expert opinion on primary source (text); may use comparison; evaluates according to established standards	facts and figures; precedents; reason-based evidence

challenged; similarly, we may argue to defend our self-interest or that of a group with which we identify, such as our family, school, or community.

Whenever you send a résumé to a prospective employer, you are implicitly arguing that you are the best person for the job and supporting your claim by facts about your knowledge and experience. If you are asked during the interview why you believe you should be hired, you will have to marshal your strongest persuasive skills in response. Argument in its myriad forms is ingrained not only in our society—in our legal and legislative systems, for example— but also in our daily lives.

Facts versus Opinions

An *opinion* is not the same as a *fact*, which can be verified by observation or research; opinions are challengeable. Of course, facts can be interpreted differently and used for different purposes. Facts, therefore, can be used to support the thesis of an argumentative essay.

However, effective arguers are always clear about when they are using facts and when they are using opinion. In reading, use your critical-thinking skills to ask if the writer always clearly separates facts from opinion. If not, he or she might be guilty of faulty reasoning (see page 108).

> **Fact:** The moon averages 384,400 kilometres from earth's equator.

Now consider the following two pairs of statements, each consisting of a fact and a related opinion:

> **Fact:** According to moon-landing conspiracy theories, the 1969 *Apollo* moon landing was faked.
>
> **Opinion:** The *Apollo* moon landing didn't actually take place; it was all a hoax.
>
> **Fact:** On 13 November 2009, NASA announced that water had been found on the moon.
>
> **Opinion:** Now that water has been found on the moon, humans should set up colonies at the moon's poles by 2050.

See The Active Voice: Climate Change and the Integrity of Science, page 10 in Chapter 1, for more on the distinction between scientific fact and opinion.

Collaborative Exercise 9.1

Consider the two pairs of statements above on the topic of humans on the moon. Discuss the ways that fact differs from opinion in each case. Come up with two other topics and write two statements for each, one of which represents a fact and the other of which represents an opinion.

Claims in Argument

The term **claim** is particularly appropriate to argument: when you set up your position in the introduction of your argumentative essay, you are doing more than *stating* a thesis: you are *actively asserting* one. When you claim something, you assert your right to it. The claim is the assertion that you will support through valid evidence and logical reasoning in the body of your essay.

An argumentative claim is usually one of value or policy. In a **value claim**, you would argue that something is good or bad, right or wrong, fair or unfair, and so on. A **policy claim** proposes an action. In this sense, a policy claim goes further than a value claim. However, value claims may be appropriate if you wish to make your audience consider something in a more positive light. For example, if you argue in favour of euthanasia to a general or unreceptive audience, you might not want to use a policy claim, one that proposes a change in the law. A value claim instead would focus on changing attitudes, getting the reader to see, as a first step, perhaps, that euthanasia relieves the suffering of a terminally ill patient.

claim

An assertion that you will support through evidence and reason. Claims occur in thesis statements; many topic sentences also assert a claim about the topic of the paragraph.

value claim

An assertion about a topic that appeals to its ethical nature (e.g., good/bad or fair/unfair).

policy claim

An assertion about a topic that advocates an action (e.g., to fix a problem or improve a situation).

For the purposes of an academic essay—outside of formal arguments, of course, people can and will debate anything—successful argumentative claims must be *arguable*, *specific*, and *realistic*.

Arguable Claims

Most factual claims are not arguable because, as mentioned, a fact is different from an opinion. Facts can be questioned, and their interpretation is sometimes open to debate, but it is difficult for facts themselves to serve as the basis of an argumentative claim, though they may help support it. For example, you could not easily argue against the fact that the closest star to earth is 4.2 light years away. However, you could use this fact as evidence to support a policy claim, say, for allocating more (or fewer) financial resources to the space program.

In addition, a belief—for example, that God exists—is not arguable in a formal way, although you could argue for the interpretation of a passage from the Quran or other religious text. Similarly, you could not logically argue that one religion is better than another since there are no clear and objective standards that reasonable members of your audience could agree on (and on which to base your claim). *Arguable claims must be supported through objective evidence, not just opinion.*

Cost–Benefit Essays

You can argue that one method or system is better than another—for example, that the flat tax system is better than the progressive tax system. You could also write a comparison and contrast *expository* essay on this topic, but in that case, you would set the essay up as a question to be considered (e.g., which system most benefits taxpayers in the middle-income bracket?) and use facts and studies to evaluate the question. There can be a fine line between an argumentative and an expository cost–benefit essay; therefore, it is necessary to clearly announce your purpose—argumentative/persuasive or investigating/explaining—in your thesis.

Specific Claims

An overly broad or vague claim can be hard to support: "We need to change our attitude toward the environment"; "We need to do something about bullying." One way to make a broad claim more specific is to think about how it might apply to a subject you are knowledgeable about. For example, if you wanted to argue that the media promotes unhealthy weight loss in teenagers, a very big topic, and you were an athlete, you could consider what rules or procedures can lead to unhealthy weight loss in your sport. Many sports, such as rowing, have weight categories. In some provinces, the junior female lightweight category is 135 pounds and under. As a rower, you may be aware of unhealthy eating habits that can develop in rowers seeking to remain in a lower weight category in order to be competitive. Your thesis statement might take this specific form: *To help prevent unhealthy and dangerous eating habits in young rowers, junior lightweight categories should be eliminated from provincial regattas.*

A broad claim can also be made more specific (and manageable) if you can apply it to a particular group. It might be unwieldy to apply an anti-smoking claim to Canada or even to an entire province, since municipalities may have their own smoking bylaws; you might therefore restrict the focus to your city or even your campus.

Realistic Claims

Unrealistic claims are usually policy claims that have little chance of being implemented. One could argue for almost anything that would make life easier or that would fulfill a need, but if it is not realistic, the argument becomes moot. You may be able to muster some points in favour of a return to Prohibition or the legalization of all currently illegal drugs, but since such arguments would not take account of social conditions today, the claim would not be realistic. Unenforceable policy claims are also unrealistic.

Activity 9.1

In discussion groups, evaluate the 10 claims below, determining whether they would make good thesis statements for an argumentative essay. Are the claims arguable, specific, and realistic? If not, consider what changes would make them arguable. Revise them accordingly.

1. Cloning should be prohibited because it is wrong for humans to "play God."
2. In order to represent the interests of voters more accurately, give voters a wider selection of candidates, and provide a stronger voice for minority issues, the government should adopt the single transferable vote (STV) electoral model.
3. *The Simpsons* is a much funnier sitcom than *Family Guy*.
4. Having a Twitter account today is essential if you want to be successful in business.
5. The Wii is a more popular gaming system than the Xbox 360 or PlayStation 4.
6. Fighting should be banned from all levels of hockey.
7. Internet dating services are an innovative, convenient, and affordable alternative to the singles scene.
8. The culture of consumerism is responsible for many of the problems that our world faces today.
9. There need to be legal guidelines for genetic testing because it may threaten our privacy, lead to harmful gene therapy, and have dangerous social costs.
10. Because of the dangerousness of the sport utility vehicle, people should have to prove that they really need an SUV before being permitted to purchase one.

Kinds of Evidence in Argumentative Essays

Facts, Statistics, and Scientific Studies

Although an effective argument can be built around reasonable points with logical connections between them, specific kinds of evidence can bolster a claim. Some are more common to argument than to exposition, but most can be used in both. For example, most arguments will be more convincing if their points are supported by scholarly studies, facts, and statistics (see Chapter 10). In particular, policy claims can often benefit from factual support. Use the most current statistics available from the most reliable sources. These sources need to be acknowledged in your essay; your citations will reveal both the currency and the reliability of the source. Referring to a fact, statistic, or study that is outdated or otherwise lacking authority can damage your credibility (see Issues of Credibility in Chapter 6, page 81).

Some of the kinds of evidence discussed in Chapter 6 can also be used in argument; see Kinds of Evidence, page 80.

Experts and Authorities

Experts are directly involved in the issue you are arguing. You will usually use expert testimony to support your claim; however, the occasional use of experts with whom you disagree can make your argument more balanced. One way to stress experts who agree with you is to cite them directly (direct quotation), while putting the ideas of opposing experts in your own words (summarization or paraphrase), ensuring that you do so accurately and fairly. Because academic writers are often experts in their chosen field, they may refer to their own studies throughout their papers. Doing so gives them credibility.

Authorities can also lend credibility by virtue of who they are and what they say: even if they do not have direct experience in the issue you are arguing, they may make the reader pay more attention to it. Citing Robert Louis Stevenson's comment that "politics is the only occupation for which no preparation is thought to be necessary" could be used in an argument on what makes a good politician, though Stevenson was not a politician.

Examples and Illustrations

Using examples can make a general claim more concrete and understandable, enabling the reader to relate to it. An illustration could take the form of an *anecdote* (a brief informal story) or other expanded example. In the essay "Social Justice and Social Determinants of Health," the authors give two anecdotes of the mistreatments of LGBTIQ adolescents (see page 241 in Part III: The Reader). Such examples used alongside statistics help the authors give a human face to objective facts. In his essay, "Of Hockey, Medicare and Canadian Dreams," Stephen J. Toope gives examples of less-known Canadians and their accomplishments to help make the point that Canadians have much to celebrate other than hockey and Medicare (see page 191 in Part III: The Reader).

Precedents

precedent
A kind of example that refers to the way a situation was dealt with in the past in order to argue for its similar use in the present.

In law, a **precedent** is an important kind of example: to *set a precedent* means to establish a procedure for dealing with future cases. In argument, appealing to precedents—the way something was done in the past—can be particularly effective in policy claims. To use a precedent, you must show (1) that the current situation (what you are arguing) is similar to that of the precedent, and (2) that following the precedent will be beneficial. (Of course, you can use a precedent as a negative example as well, showing that it was not beneficial.)

Precedents can be used to argue controversial issues, such as decriminalizing marijuana or prostitution or providing universal access to post-secondary education. The authors of "A Ban on Marketing of Foods/Beverages to Children" (see page 297 in Part III: The Reader) argue that their goal of banning marketing to children could be better achieved by using a precedent based on ethics rather than health.

Personal Experience introduction

The selective use of personal experience in argumentative essays can involve your reader and increase your credibility; for example, if you have worked with street people, you may be seen as better qualified to argue a claim about homelessness. Personal experience could take the form of direct experience, of observing something first-hand, or of reporting on something that happened to a friend. For example, Kimberley McLeod in "When Canada Goes Viral" explains that her ability to detect irony in a Canadian satiric video was likely due to the fact she is a Canadian, whereas non-Canadians often misunderstood the video's ironic tone (see page 194 in Part III: The Reader). She uses her direct experience to support her point about the role of context (i.e., in this case, being a Canadian) in interpreting satire.

However, simply announcing that you experienced something and benefited by it does not necessarily make your argument stronger; for example, saying that you enjoyed physical education classes in high school is not going to convince many people that it should be a required subject in schools.

Two Kinds of Reasoning

Two methods of reasoning are **inductive** and **deductive reasoning**. In inductive reasoning, you arrive at a probable conclusion by observing and recording specific occurrences. Flaws in inductive reasoning can occur if not enough observations have been made—that is, the evidence is insufficient to make a generalization—or if the method for gathering the evidence is faulty. Thus, researchers try to include as large a sample as possible within their target population; this makes their findings more reliable (see Appendix A, A Note on Statistics, page 375). Similarly, researchers reveal the details of their experiment's methodology. They need to show that their evidence-gathering methods are logical and unbiased.

While inductive reasoning works from detail to generalization, deductive reasoning begins with a general claim assumed to be true. The way deductive reasoning works can be shown by the **syllogism**, a three-part structure in which a conclusion is valid because both the general claim (major premise) and specific instance or case (minor premise) are true and are logically related:

> ***Major premise (generalization):*** **All students who wish to apply for admission to the university must submit their grade transcripts.**
>
> ***Minor premise (specific case):*** **Deanna wishes to apply for admission to the university.**
>
> ***Conclusion:*** **Deanna must submit her grade transcripts.**

Using Reason in Arguments

Most arguments will require you to reason both inductively and deductively. Inductive reasoning could involve the following:

- using factual and statistical evidence
- ensuring that your sources are credible, such as peer-reviewed articles
- providing lots of support for your points

inductive reasoning
Reasoning that relies on facts, details, and observations to draw a conclusion.

deductive reasoning
Reasoning based on a generalization, which is applied to a specific instance to draw a conclusion.

syllogism
A logical three-part structure that can be used to illustrate how deductive conclusions are made.

Deductive reasoning could involve the following:

- making appropriate and valid generalizations
- ensuring that your audience would agree with them
- ensuring that your specific points are logically connected to your general claims

Whatever the purpose in arguing—whether to settle an issue, expose a problem, or reach a compromise—it is vital that the reader believes you have presented enough evidence and that your claims are valid. Although using specific argumentative strategies is important (see page 110), *most successful arguments begin and end with your effective use of reason* or what Aristotle called appeals to logic, logos (see Chapter 8, The Active Voice: Rhetorical Analysis: What, Why, and How, page 92).

However, reason can also be misused in arguments. Consider the following statements. The first illustrates the misuse of inductive reasoning because there is inadequate evidence to justify the conclusion; the second illustrates the misuse of deductive reasoning because a false generalization has resulted in a faulty conclusion. Avoiding logical fallacies (failures in reasoning) in your own essays and pointing them out in the arguments of others will make your arguments stronger and more credible.

> **The premier broke a promise he made during his election campaign. He is a liar, and his word can no longer be trusted.**

It is not reasonable to distrust a politician because he broke one promise. If the premier broke several promises, there would be much stronger grounds for the conclusion. Thus, in most people's minds, there is not enough inductive evidence to support the claim. Furthermore, politicians do not always deliver on their pre-election promises (this could almost be considered a generalization peculiar to campaigning politicians!); thus, the statement also shows faulty deductive reasoning.

> **Eduardo is the only one in our family who has a PhD. He is obviously the one who inherited all the brains.**
>
> *Major premise:* **Possessing a PhD means you are very intelligent.**
>
> *Minor premise:* **Eduardo possesses a PhD.**
>
> *Conclusion:* **Eduardo is very intelligent.**

Possessing an advanced degree could be partly a measure of intelligence; it could also indicate persistence, a fascination with a particular subject, a love of learning, inspiring teachers, an ambitious nature, strong financial and/or familial support, and so on.

Failures in Reasoning

logical fallacies
Categories of faulty reasoning.

Errors in reasoning fall into several categories, termed logical fallacies. To argue effectively and to recognize weak arguments when you read them, it is not necessary to be able to categorize every failure in logic. Most errors are the result of sloppy or simplistic thinking—the failure to do justice to an issue's complexity (sometimes deliberate in the case of conscious distortions, but often unconscious). Developing your critical-thinking skills will make you alert to errors of logic. A few examples of fallacious reasoning follow:

- *Oversimplification:* An arguer may consider only two possibilities, one of which may be clearly unacceptable (*either/or fallacy*):

  If you do not get a university degree, you might as well resign yourself to low-paying jobs.

- *Cause–effect fallacy:* Among the many cause–effect fallacies is the one that argues a claim on the basis of a coincidental (non-causal) relationship between two occurrences:

  Re-elect your prime minister; the economy grew by 4 per cent while she was in office.

- *Slippery slope fallacy:* The arguer claims that a challenge to the status quo will lead to a breakdown of social order or of human values; it has been used as an argument against such practices as euthanasia, legalizing marijuana, and the screening of embryos. Of course, arguments can be made against these issues, but using "slippery slope" logic does not make for a sound argument:

  If gay marriage is legalized, the next thing people will want to do is marry their pets!

- *Circular reasoning:* An arguer may assume something is true simply by citing the premise as if it validated the claim, for example by appealing to a premise that has yet to be proven (i.e., "I'm an 'A' student"):

  I'm an "A" student. How can the teacher give me a B– on the assignment?

- *Irrelevance:* One type of fallacy of irrelevance is a non sequitur—literally, "it does not follow"—as in this example where the "evidence" (supposed questionable personal conduct) has no logical connection with the claim (trustworthiness as a public official); it does not *follow from* the claim:

  He can't be trusted for public office. After all, he admitted to an extramarital affair.

- Another fallacy of irrelevance is *name-dropping*, citing a famous person as if his or her personal opinion provides objective evidence; in the *guilt by association fallacy*, the arguer uses the fact that some allegedly disreputable person or group supports a view as an argument against it (or opposes it as an argument in its favour). For example, several celebrities and sports figures have become the focus of advertising campaigns (a form of name-dropping) only to be embroiled in a controversy and discarded. In these cases, the sponsor's decision was likely guided by a legitimate concern about the negative influence of the association.

- *False analogy:* In this fallacy, you make a comparison between two things that are not comparable because they are, in fact, not alike or they differ greatly in one respect. In the heat of the moment (see emotional fallacies below), people sometimes compare a perpetrator of a minor crime to Adolf Hitler or another bona fide tyrant. In the example below, the writer compares animals in zoos to those in people's homes. Calling pet owners "hypocrites" is also an example of slanted language (see below):

  People who complain about zoo animals but who also own pets are nothing but hypocrites.

- *Slanted language:* An arguer may use highly charged language to dismiss an opponent's claims. Simply characterizing an opponent as "ignorant" or "greedy" serves no constructive purpose. Of course, you may be able to show through unbiased evidence that the opponent has demonstrated these characteristics.
- *Emotional fallacies:* These statements appeal to the emotions of a reader in a manipulative or unfair way, such as a partisan appeal, guilt by association, name-calling (*ad hominem*), or dogmatism (simply asserting something without offering proof—often, over and over). They are very different from legitimate appeals to emotion:

  Don't believe the claims of those neo-liberals. They just want to take your hard-earned money away from you. (partisan appeal)

- A common emotional fallacy is the *bandwagon*, which asserts that because something is popular, it has value:

  All my friends' parents give them unrestricted curfews on Friday nights.

Giving Life to Logic: Strategies for Argument

Although effective arguments depend heavily on the use of reasonable claims supported by convincing evidence, logic alone will not necessarily convince readers to change their minds or adopt the writer's point of view. Student writers should consider using the following strategies, depending on topic, purpose, and audience, to shape a logical and appealing argument, one that will make readers more responsive to the claim.

Rhetorical Patterns

Definition and Comparison: Writers may define important terms early in their arguments, and connect these definitions to points later on in the essay. For example, in "Universities, Governments and Industry," Simon N. Young defines "university," then explains why the modern university fails to satisfy this definition, supporting his argument that researchers have become entrepreneurs rather than true teachers (page 182 in Part III: The Reader). In "Speed That Kills" (page 346 in Part III: The Reader), Jeremy Foote draws similarities between the influence of technology in the late Victorian era and its influence today.

Dramatic introductions: Dramatic introductions are used more often in argument than in exposition, because they may enable the reader to relate to a human situation or to set a scene. For example, the first-person introductory paragraph by Mitch Miyagawa in "A Sorry State" (page 221 in Part III, The Reader) introduces the author's family conflicts, appropriate in an essay that shows how racist decisions can disrupt families' lives. In "*Jurassic World* and Procreation Anxiety," Richard Dyer's first sentence attracts attention by being both direct and controversial: "*Jurassic World* is anticapitalist, antimanagerialism, and anti-GM; it is also antifeminist, racist, species-ist, and decidedly not queer" (page 272 in Part III: The Reader).

Establishing common ground: Getting your readers to see that you share many of their values can make them more receptive to you as an arguer. Although this strategy is dependent on knowing your audience, clearly most readers will respond favourably to universal qualities like generosity, decency, security, and a healthy and peaceful environment. The common ground strategy can be considered a form of ethical appeal. The authors of "Taking Race Out of Human Genetics" urge their readers to unite "for a simple goal: to improve the scientific study of human difference and commonality" (page 344 in Part III: The Reader), believing that most of their readers, scientists, would agree with this goal.

Making concessions: In granting concessions, you acknowledge the validity of an opposing point, demonstrating your fairness and willingness to accept other views, at least in part. After conceding a point, you should follow with a strong point of your own. In effect, you are giving some ground in an effort to get the reader to do the same. The concession can be made in a dependent clause and your own point in the independent clause that follows: "Although it is valid to say. . . [concession is made], the fact is. . . [your point]."

Concessions can be vital in cases in which there is a strong opposition or in which you wish to reach a compromise. Simon N. Young makes a concession in the first paragraph of his essay "Universities, Governments and Industry: Can the Essential Nature of Universities Survive the Drive to Commercialize?" (page 182 in Part III: The Reader), acknowledging a positive change in the direction that universities are taking before mentioning what he sees as a recent, more damaging change.

Appeal to reader interests: When you appeal to the interests of your readers, you show how they might be affected by your claim. For example, in a policy claim, you might show how they could benefit by the implementation of a particular policy—how it will be good for them—or what costs might result if it is not implemented—how it will be bad for them. Arguing in favour of a costly social program may be a hard sell to those whose approval and support are vital, such as business leaders. Therefore, you could explain how the program could benefit these leaders—for example, by helping to prevent a bigger problem, such as increased health-care costs or taxes. If you know the values and motivations of your readers, you may be able to use this knowledge to make your points directly relevant to them.

Offering solutions: Making recommendations, like appeals to reader interests (discussed above), focus on practical issues. Readers may see this as more beneficial and constructive than simply arguing that a problem exists. Jessica Aschemann-Witzel ends her essay, "Waste Not, Want Not, Emit Less" (page 301 in Part III: The Reader), by proposing solutions to food waste. Authors of argumentative and expository essays alike often conclude this way, leaving readers with a positive impression.

Emotional and ethical appeals: While dramatic openings can be successful in many argumentative essays, the success of an opening that includes an appeal to emotion depends greatly on your audience. Beginning an essay on animal testing by describing a scene of caged

common ground
An argumentative strategy in which you show readers that you share many of their values, making you appear open and approachable.

concession
An argumentative strategy in which you concede or qualify a point, acknowledging its validity, in order to come across as fair and reasonable.

Appeals are designed to evoke emotional or ethical (morally grounded) responses from your reader. For more about Aristotle's three appeals, see Chapter 8, pages 92–95.

animals at a slaughterhouse may alienate neutral readers. If you do use such an opening, you need to ensure that a typical reader will respond in the way you wish. Emotional and ethical appeals, however, are commonly used in conclusions. They provide an effective coda, a final way that the audience can reflect on the topic. In the following conclusion, student writer Mary McQueen appeals to landlords in order to subtly reinforce her claim advocating a more open policy toward pets in apartments:

> The human/animal bond is special and worth preserving and promoting. Landlords who allow pets make an important, generous contribution towards the solution of the pet-friendly housing problem and have the opportunity to make the partnerships of landlords, tenants, and companion animals so successful that they become role models to inspire others around the community, the province, and the country.

In the cases of neutral or opposing viewpoints, emotional and ethical appeals work best when they are subtle, not overstated. In the example above, the writer indirectly evokes the emotional bond that many owners have with their pets, showing how landlords can contribute to this bond. Ethical appeals focus on issues like fairness, equality, responsibility, and the like. Thus, the example also demonstrates a subtle ethical appeal since it evokes a hierarchical relationship (landlord and tenant) based on the demonstration of ethical qualities like respect.

Refutation Strategies

refutation
An argumentative strategy of raising opposing points in order to counter them with your own points.

In a **refutation**, or *rebuttal*, you show the weaknesses or limitations of opposing claims. Here are three general strategies to consider. Which one you use depends on the three factors that you need to take into account when planning your argumentative essay: your topic, purpose, and audience.

Refutations usually form a crucial part of your argument if your purpose is to defend your point of view. However, if your argumentative purpose is to raise awareness of an important issue, as Robert Gifford does in "Psychology's Essential Role in Alleviating the Impacts of Climate Change" (page 350 in Part III: The Reader), there may be no clear opposing view to refute. In his introduction, Gifford clearly states his thesis that psychology "has an important role to play in easing the pain caused by climate change" and that his essay is necessary because "the thesis is not broadly acknowledged." In many arguments, however, one of the three strategies below can be used.

Refutations can range from simply acknowledging the opposing viewpoint to focusing on one or two main opposing points to a systematic point-by-point critique. The refutation strategy you choose depends on your topic, your purpose in arguing, and your audience.

Acknowledgement: You may need to do no more than simply acknowledge the opposing view, for example if the argument on the other side is straightforward or obvious. In the case of arguing for more open policies toward pets (above), the position of landlords is simple: allowing pets increases the potential for property damage. After acknowledging the competing claim, the writer would go on to raise strong points that counter this claim without necessarily referring to it again.

Limited rebuttal: In a limited rebuttal, you raise and respond to the major point(s) on the other side, then follow with your own points without mentioning minor competing claims. One obvious reason for using a limited rebuttal is that in a short essay, you will not have space to respond to all the competing claims. This strategy may also be appropriate if the strength of the opposing view is anchored by one or perhaps two very significant claims. You would not want to give strength to the other side by raising and refuting less important issues unless you are trying to reach a compromise when both strengths and weaknesses might be considered. When you are analyzing the main argument on the other side, however, it is important to represent that position fairly, for example, by using concessions.

Full rebuttal: Point-by-point rebuttals can be very effective if the competing claims of an argument are well known, if there is strong opposition to your claim, or if you are critiquing a text, as is Joel Lexchin in "Pharmaceutical Innovation: Can We Live Forever? A Commentary on Schnittker and Karandinos" (page 310 in Part III: The Reader). If your argumentative purpose is to reach a compromise, you might also choose to use the point-by-point strategy. Here, however, you would try to reach out to the other side (or both sides), showing that you understand the points that define their position. This strategy would demonstrate your knowledge and fairness.

The paragraph below illustrates the effective use of the point-by-point strategy in an essay on mandatory physical education classes in high school. Notice how student writer Meghan Cannon skilfully uses a concession (second sentence, italicized) to help turn a competing claim into a point in her favour:

Some individuals argue against mandatory physical education because they believe that many teenagers feel self-conscious about their bodies and, therefore, self-conscious about physical activity. *While the initiation of physical activity may be difficult for one suffering from body image issues, the long-term effect is invariably one of satisfaction.* Students learn to appreciate what they can do with their bodies instead of being completely concerned with how they look. Physical activity promotes self-awareness and acceptance. Self-confidence soars from participation in sport and the social interaction induced by sport.

Organizing Your Argument

For most argumentative essays, deciding on your **order of points** will mean choosing between two options: the *climax order* or a *mixed order*. In the first, you begin with the weakest point and build toward the strongest; in the second, you could begin with a strong point—but not the strongest—follow with weaker points, and conclude with the strongest. It may not be advisable to begin with the weakest point if your audience opposes your claim, since an initial weak point may make your readers believe your entire argument is weak. Other orders are also possible. For example, if you are arguing to reach a compromise, you might need to focus the first part of your essay on one side of the debate, the second part on the opposite side, and the third on your compromise solution.

Whichever rebuttal strategy you use, you should consider outlining the points on the other side before writing the essay. Consider how someone who disagreed with your claim might respond to your main points. This could reveal the strengths on the other side and any weaknesses in your own argument. More important, perhaps, it should serve to keep the opposing view in focus as you write, causing you to reflect carefully on what you are saying and how you say it.

order of points
The way in which points are presented in an essay. Climax order is the order of points that proceeds from the weakest to the strongest; other orders include inverted climax order and mixed order.

Readers could agree with your argumentative claim, disagree with it, be neutral, or be composed of some who agree and some who disagree. The makeup of your audience will help determine which argumentative strategies are the most effective ones for your essay.

Collaborative Exercise 9.2

The Audience Plan

Taking the audience factor into account is very important as you prepare to write an argumentative essay. Constructing an audience plan will enable you to consider your approach to the essay, including the kinds of strategies to use. Team up with two other students and interview the other members of your group to determine their knowledge level, their interest level, and their orientation toward your position (agree, disagree, neutral, or mixed); they will serve as your "audience," the basis for an audience profile. Then, use this information to construct an audience plan based on your audience profile, your topic, and argumentative purpose. Discuss strategies you would use to persuade this audience. Include your topic and your writing purpose in the plan.

Sample Student Argumentative Essay (MLA Citation Style)

In the following student essay, the writer uses some of the argumentative strategies mentioned in this chapter, along with other strategies, in the interests of clarity and readability. Many of these strategies are mentioned in the marginal notes.

Student Writing Sample

Agroecology Essentials: Ecological Farming Alternatives for a Modern World

by Megan Wilson

1   Farming is an ancient process in human history whereby we have collectively cultivated an ability to grow our own food and gather the nutrients that we need in order to live healthily. This ability was first exercised around 10,000 BCE in the beginning of what is now known as the agricultural revolution, or neolithic revolution (Weisdorf 1). Quite simply, the ability to farm changed everything. This is the time when humans shifted from being nomadic to sedentary, established tiers of social class, and eventually formed civilizations (1). Perhaps the greatest turning point in human history began with the ability to cultivate the land in which we live. In the last 200 years, farming has been strongly influenced by the growing population (Hole 113). The widely practiced method of industrial, monoculture farming threatens the biodiversity of the area, reduces soil fertility, causes unnecessary use of chemicals, and inevitably will create social and economic problems for the next generations (Altieri 143). Therefore, more sustainable methods are becoming essential, such as agroecology, the concept of linking ecological

processes with modern agriculture (Gliessman 1). With a focus on diversification, design, and integration in global agriculture, we can create a more sustainable and wholesome practice of food cultivation with no compromise to yields.

2   The key ingredient to a successful agroecology is surprisingly simple on the surface: plot diversification (Wojtkowski 15). A good way of thinking about this concept is realizing that plants, like humans, thrive best when they are with their friends. In nature, the underlying biodiversity of the area is extremely important to the ecosystem's health (15). It is only natural that plants grown together will be happier, more reliable, and more productive. For example, the systematic and deliberate pairing of plant species in an agroecosystem is defined as complementarity. To be able to compare and contrast sustainability, yield and growth, scientists in the field use the Land Equivalent Ratio (LER). The formula for LER is the following:

$$LER = (Y_{AB}/Y_A) + (Y_{BA}/Y_B); \text{ where Y is yield}$$

3   Using the LER compares the yields of a polyculture (with both plant A and B) to identical monocultures of only A and only B (Wojtkowski 17). By pairing species that have a high LER, yields of both will increase as a result. This pairing, or complementarity, is essential to agroecology and could be considered the heart of the practice. However, just pairing two species together that do well is not sufficient. Indeed, crop patterns are intricately designed for specific climates, topographical situations, and plot sizes (25). Cover crops are an example of this level of complementarity. They range in types from grasses to alfalfa, and clovers to legumes. Introducing a cover crop protects the surrounding crops in harsh climates or in the winter (Gliessman 108). Cover crops are a good example of agroecological implementation because they have *several* benefits to the system, including managing weeds and regulating the soil temperature for other plants (108). Another example is introducing insect repellent marigolds as a substitute to using pesticides (Wojtkowski 33). The philosophy of agroecology is that to any agricultural problem, nature already has a solution, although implementing these sustainable solutions that exist in nature can be a serious challenge.

4   One attractive quality of agroecology is there are no rules with the design when it comes to location or size. In fact, agroecosystems usually have undefined beginnings and ends (Altieri 90). This translates into the ability to adapt to a variety of circumstances and conditions. Whereas most people think of rural environments when the subject of agriculture is mentioned, in fact urban agriculture is another example of a sustainable food system under the general umbrella of agroecology: we can practice agroecological principles in our own backyards. Buying local foods is growing in popularity whether it be to support local business or to obtain healthier produce. The ecological advantages to buying locally grown food are often overlooked. A study was conducted in Finland investigating the carbon footprint of their national food chain (Virtanen et al. 1849). Their research was gathered by monitoring the economy using the national economic input–output model (EIO-LCA). Regarding impacts to the climate, the share of agriculture comprises approximately 70% including CO_2 and other toxic emissions from transportation and practice. Virtanen concludes, "it is clear that when effective climate policies are sought, the focus should be on agriculture" (1853). One way to limit these emissions is to literally move the agriculture. With farms closer to cities, the carbon footprint of buying produce decreases dramatically as opposed to buying broccoli from California and oranges from South Africa. Eliminating foods as world travellers is a very real benefit of successfully integrating agroecology. Another positive aspect of introducing green space into cities is that locals have more

In her introduction, Wilson makes it clear she will be proposing an action and attempting to raise awareness. (See Argumentative Purpose, p. 100.)

Aware of her audience, Wilson uses an analogy here, one of several strategies in this paragraph to ensure understanding. She also uses many examples to render abstract or technical information concrete.

Wilson increases coherence by definition (complementarity, polyculture, and monoculture) and selective repetition ("This pairing, or complementarity. . . .")

Wilson uses mostly summary when referencing statistics, but follows with a direct quotation, perhaps because it is a clear statement that connects climate change and agriculture, stressing the need for healthy agricultural practices.

opportunity to buy local foods to support their families. Food insecurity is a major concern in the United States; it is defined as the inability to obtain food due to financial or accessibility problems (Goode 190). In 2013, 17.5 million households reported a period of food insecurity during that year (190). Introducing agroecology into our lives at the urban level will create ready access to local foods, and the benefits to buying locally grown food are two-fold: it will create more sustainable food systems while simultaneously improving the quality of life for city dwellers.

5   There are several challenging prerequisites to successfully integrating the practice of agroecology in modern society, but the following limitations are, in fact, the stepping stones in the path to sustainability. From an economic perspective, the inherent complexity of integrating agroecology can act as an impediment to the business community. Economic analysis is generally based on profitability and risk; however, the analysis should also encompass non-monetary yet invaluable benefits that sustainable agriculture provides (Wojtkowski, "Agroecological Economics" 8). These include the environmental impact, quality of surrounding life, and elimination of the use of harmful substances. In other words, the analysis requires an objective view with a magnifying glass, as opposed to a generalized overview. The second limitation is the social aspect. Agriculture is most widely practiced in small, rural communities in the tropics (Altieri 145), so converting from conventional agriculture in these small communities would be a major challenge if agroecology practices are to become widespread. Lastly, it is the government that regulates agricultural practices, which means that there are political implications involved in addition to economic and social ones. It is no secret that the government and farmers often have vastly different agendas (Wojtkowski, "Agroecological Economics" 251). Government policies on conventional agriculture such as crop-loss insurance, tax regulation, and price supports create a false sense of security (251) for farmers and consumers alike; a system that has been in place for a long time is not necessarily the best system for the needs of the present. In contrast, as an example of positive intervention, the government in the UK offers financial breaks that promote the organic sector of agriculture by providing organic farmers with monetary compensation (Hole 114). This could provide an example for other countries of how government policies can enhance the quality of agriculture. The path to complete agricultural sustainability is admittedly beset with challenges, but despite these drawbacks, the future of our communities and health of its citizens could depend on changing our way of thinking about past practices. At its core, agroecology is the sustainable pathway towards global food security and sustainability.

6   When you cross a curious farmer with a forward-thinking environmentalist, you get the principles of both agriculture and ecology in action, in other words, agroecology. The union of these two key players and their philosophies should be applied to modern agriculture to forever change our relationship with our food. The key features of agroecology involve plant diversity, variable plot design, and implementing *natural* solutions. However, as basic and practical as these practices might seem, the cotton fields continue to grow. The forest continues to be emptied by clear-cutting. Government policies continue to promote what is "tried and true" with the biodiversity of the planet slowly diminishing (Altieri 369). Agroecology incorporates a wide range of the environmental spectrum, from biodiversity preservation to limiting the use of toxic chemicals to grow our food. By definition conventional agriculture nourishes us today, while slowly malnourishing the environment in turn. By focusing on finding the ecological solution to our agricultural endeavours and integrating agroecology, we will be able to start giving back nourishment in return for our own.

When two works by the same author are used, the title of the relevant work (or an abbreviated form) is included in the citation, along with the author and page number.

Wilson uses the argumentative strategy of a precedent here to show how a positive outcome in the past could be applied beneficially in the present. (See Precedents, p. 106).

Repetition of the verb *continue* helps convey the urgency of the situation, according to the writer.

Wilson uses an ethical appeal in her final sentence, and also makes it memorable through word choice and rhythm.

Works Cited

Altieri, Miguel A. "Part Two: The Design of Alternative Agricultural Systems and Technologies." *Agroecology: the Science of Sustainable Agriculture.* 2nd ed., Westview Press, 1995, pp. 71–204.

Gliessman, Stephen R. "Chapter 15: Species Interactions in Crop Communities." *Agroecology: the Ecology of Sustainable Food Systems.* 2nd ed., CRC Press, 2007, pp. 205–217.

Goode, Lauren. "Society of the Quarter." *Journal of Agriculture and Food Information,* vol. 16, no. 3, 17 July 2015, pp. 189–195. doi:10.1080/10496505.2015.1048644.

Hole, D. G., and A. J. Perkins. "Does Organic Farming Benefit Biodiversity?" *Biological Conservation.* vol. 122, no. 1, Mar. 2015, pp. 113–130. doi: 10.1016/j.biocon.2004.07.018.

Schumacher, E. F. "Epilogue." *Small Is Beautiful: A Study of Economics As If People Mattered.* Blonde & Briggs, 1973.

Virtanen, Yrjö, et al. "Carbon Footprint of Food: Approaches From National Input–Output Statistics and a LCA of a Food Portion." *Journal of Cleaner Production,* vol. 19, no. 16, 2011, pp. 1849–1856. doi:10.1016/j.jclepro.2011.07.001.

Weisdorf, Jacob L. "From Foraging to Farming: Explaining the Neolithic Revolution." *Journal of Economic Surveys,* vol. 19, no. 4, Sept. 2005, pp. 561–586. 10.1111/j.0950-0804.2005.00259.x

Wojtkowski, Paul A. *Agroecological Economics: Sustainability and Biodiversity.* 1st ed., Elsevier/Academic Press, 2008.

———. *Introduction to Agroecology Principles and Practices.* Haworth Press, 2006.

For examples of essays in *The Active Reader* that use argument, see Classification of Readings by Rhetorical Mode/Pattern (inside back cover).

Using Critical Thinking to Analyze Arguments

Analyzing an argument involves a similar approach to that of analyzing an essay, as discussed in Chapter 8. However, while a rhetorical analysis breaks down an essay to look at its rhetorical features, which *may* include Aristotle's three appeals—logos, pathos, and ethos—a critical analysis breaks down the argument. A critical analysis, then, could be considered a specialized form of a rhetorical analysis, using concepts and terms applicable to argument, as described below.

In writing a critical analysis, you determine whether the argument is successful (or not) and why. A critical analysis of an argumentative essay, then, should focus on the hows and whys of the author's argument. It should not be used as a forum for expressing your personal agreement or disagreement with the author's opinions, as a critical *response* would do.

Literary writers do not necessarily stop to think about specific techniques, such as imagery or metaphors, as they write. Similarly, the techniques of argument are ingrained in experienced writers, and they are not always conscious of their persuasive strategies. However, student writers, like student arguers, benefit the most if they are consciously aware of the techniques used by successful writers (arguers). To produce a thorough and effective argument, then, it is necessary to be familiar with the *language* of argument. This also applies when you analyze someone's argument.

The Language of Argument

The following terms relevant to argument have been discussed in this or previous chapters. Using them, where appropriate, in analyzing an argument will not only enable you to explain your points clearly but also add to your credibility as an analyzer:

General Terms

claim (value, policy, and interpretation), page 70
credibility, page 81
deductive reasoning, page 107
inductive reasoning, page 107
purpose (argumentative), page 100

Kinds of Evidence

analogy, page 16
anecdotal evidence, page 106
authorities/expert opinion, page 106
examples/illustrations, page 106
precedent, page 106

Strategies

appeal to reader interests, page 111
common ground, page 111
comparison, page 79
concession, page 111
definition, page 78
emotional appeal, page 111
ethical appeal, page 111
rebuttal (acknowledgement, limited, full), page 112
recommendations, page 111

Fallacies

logical and emotional fallacies, page 110
slanted language, page 110

The kind of critical analysis that breaks down an argument is structured like the rhetorical analysis, discussed in Chapter 8 (see Organizing a Rhetorical Analysis, Chapter 8, page 96).

The following is a student critical analysis of "Universities, Governments and Industry: Can the Essential Nature of Universities Survive the Drive to Commercialize?" by Simon Young (page 182 in Part III: The Reader).

Student Writing Sample

A Critical Analysis of "Universities, Governments and Industry: Can the Essential Nature of Universities Survive the Drive to Commercialize?" by Simon N. Young

by Taylor Lingl

1   In "Universities, Governments and Industry," Simon Young exposes the pressure to commercialize in post-secondary education. Young mentions many of the changes and trends in the nature of universities, both good and bad. However, he focuses on what he considers the most threatening: the government use of universities for short-term economic gain (182). To his audience of educators, administrators, and students, Young explains how the university grants have become favorably distributed to those researching matters of economic worth. With his strong opinion against this commercialization, he proposes the idea that the average university teacher is changing from creative researcher to commercial entrepreneur (183). His ideas form a very effective critique, which is strengthened by the use of definitions, strong ethical appeal, credibility, and effective reasoning.

2   Young opens his essay with the *Oxford English Dictionary* definition of the word "university" which consists, in part, of a "whole body of teachers and scholars engaged in the higher branches of learning" (182). Though "university" is a familiar word, Young uses this definition to his advantage by setting up the image of an ideal university, and prepares the reader for its use throughout the essay. In his closing paragraphs, Young proposes a new definition based on the changing values of these universities. The definition that he finds suitable is "a whole body of teachers and scholars engaged in turning ideas into profit" (185). The sense of sarcasm is quite apparent, which can create an inappropriate or combative tone, depending on the reader. However, by using such contrasting definitions, he develops strength for his argument, which triumphs over a questionable tone.

3   Throughout the essay, Young makes good use of ethical appeals by providing a strong basis to evoke morally grounded responses from the reader. One application of this moral consciousness can be seen when he states that "curiosity-driven research will always tend to serve the best interests of patients," and concludes by saying that "the biggest losers from the pressure to commercialize will be psychiatric patients" (185). This universal quality of decency establishes common ground, and enables Young to come across to the reader as open and approachable.

4   Young proves his credibility by promoting his knowledge and by displaying fairness in his argument. He opens the article by stating that he has spent 40 years in universities. He goes on in the first paragraph to make concessions to the other side, stating that many changes in the nature of universities are actually commendable, such as the raise in proportion of the population attending (182). By granting this concession he is able to demonstrate his willingness to accept other views, while following with a statement that reveals his own view about today's universities as the more damaging change. To add to his credibility, Young uses sources effectively and backs up claims with proper substantiation. Throughout the essay he uses reputable authorities such as the Association of Universities and Colleges of Canada, the Canadian Association of University Teachers, and the Society for Neuroscience to support his argument.

Lingl uses an abbreviated form of the title. However, a better practice is to use the full title on first reference and an abbreviated title on successive ones; ask your instructor if you're uncertain. She uses many specific references to the text she is analyzing. As she has named the author in her first sentence, she doesn't need to repeat the name in her citation.

The student efficiently combines concerns with the audience, topic, and Young's stance in one sentence before her detailed yet concise thesis statement (last sentence).

Lingl draws attention to Young's use of definition as a basis for his argument.

Being aware of audience isimportant in analyses.

The next two paragraphs focus on analysis, not summary. They also demonstrate the writer's familiarity with various argumentative strategies: ethical appeals, common ground, concessions, and authorities.

Rather than touch briefly on several features, the writer selects only a few representative ones and uses critical thinking to analyze them. Here she explains the use of deductive reasoning in a specific paragraph. She makes it clear that her example is representative of Young's argument throughout.

5   Young's method of development and use of effective reasoning are strongly demonstrated in paragraph 9. In this paragraph, he uses deductive reasoning by beginning with a generalization and applying a concrete example. He opens with a quote from the Canadian Association of University Teachers stating, "the future of academic medicine is in danger" (184). From here, he incorporates a specific example of the treatment and prevention of depression, and proves that the unprofitable natural products and strategies receive little attention (184). He succeeds in producing a reasonable and valid generalization.

6   In the final paragraph, Young strongly reiterates his concern for the problem but expresses little hope for a positive ending. He makes reference to charitable organizations, one of the only sources of funding that maintain the sole purpose of providing benefits to society. However, he goes on to admit that though they are able to avoid the move to commercialization, they will have little effect on combatting it (185). By finishing up without a concrete solution, Young succeeds at making the problem even more paramount.

Young's inconclusive ending could just as easily be seen as a weaknesses. However, the writer explains why she sees it as a strength.

7   In conclusion, Young's essay presents an interesting view into the changing nature of universities. He succeeds in exposing the problems that have developed due to commercialization. Young combines strongly supported evidence and credibility with definitions and moral reasoning to construct a very convincing essay.

Sample Professional Argumentative Essay with Annotations

The following argument appeared in a journal for medical professionals. Specific strategies strengthen the argument, increasing the likelihood that readers will respond in the way the authors want them to. Bolded words in the notes refer to specific kinds of evidence and strategies mentioned in this chapter. They could be used as a basis for a critical analysis of "Added Sugar on Nutrition Labels."

Professional Writing Sample

Added Sugars on Nutrition Labels: A Way to Support Population Health in Canada

By Jodi T. Bernstein and Mary R. L'Abbé. From *CMAJ*, vol. 188, no.15, 2016, pp. 373–4. © Joule Inc. or its licensors. Copied under license from Access Copyright.

Unsurprisingly, the authors don't begin their academic argument with a catchy "hook," but with a straightforward fact that introduces their topic. They are clearly writing to an **audience** of medical/nutrition specialists as their essay appeared in the *Canadian Medical Association Journal*.

1   In June 2015, Health Canada published a proposal to redesign the nutrition label, mandatory on nearly all prepackaged foods.[1] Nutrition labelling is a tool intended to help Canadians make informed food choices to improve their health. Several of the proposed changes are focused on improving information about sugar content for consumers, because the current labels "do not currently provide sufficient information on sugars, to help assess whether there is a little or a lot of sugar in prepackaged food."[1] Currently, only total sugars, which refers to all

mono- and disaccharides, are declared on the nutrition label. Following a lengthy consultation process, in which Canadians voiced their concern and desire for the label to include information on added sugars, a proposal for the label to include a declaration of added sugars was made in 2014; however, it was not included in the final regulatory proposal.[1]

2   Excess intake of added sugars (the sugars and syrups added to foods and beverages[2])—not total sugars—is associated with an increased risk of diabetes, obesity, dental caries and cardiovascular disease.[3-5] Although total sugars include added sugars, they also refer to the sugar found naturally in whole fruits, vegetables and dairy products that are part of a healthy, balanced diet recommended in Canada's Food Guide.

3   In contrast to Canada, the US Food and Drug Administration proposed a declaration of added sugars on nutrition labels in March 2014.[6] In July 2015, the US proposal was amended to include a benchmark (% daily value) of a maximum of 10% of calories coming from added sugars, to help consumers interpret whether there is a little or a lot of sugar in a product.[6] Limiting intake of added sugars to less than 5% or 10% of calories is consistent with international guidelines from the World Health Organization (WHO), Public Health England and the US 2015 Dietary Guidelines, although the WHO and Public Health England use the more inclusive "free sugars" definition, which encompasses all sugars not found in their naturally occurring state, including juice, honey and syrup.[3,4,6] These guidelines were based on reviews of the latest scientific evidence from clinical trials, cohort studies and observational studies[3,6] and from modelling of dietary patterns.[6]

4   Health Canada's proposal includes the addition of a benchmark for total sugars of 100g or 20% of calories per day.[1] This value is based not on dietary recommendations but rather on Canadian intake patterns from 2004,[1] which may only encourage the status quo. However, the proposal also includes grouping all sugar-based ingredients in brackets after the general name "sugars." This will provide consumers with a clearer indication of all the sugars added to the product, but not the amount.

5   Added sugars are chemically indistinguishable from total sugars.[2] Several algorithms can be used to estimate the added-sugar content of foods.[7] However, they are time-consuming, require a thorough knowledge of the food supply, are limited by the use of assumptions in their development, and require corroboration with manufacturers' proprietary data to evaluate their validity.[7] Instead, food manufacturers can use their proprietary product formulations to provide levels of added sugar that are accurate and up to date.

6   With added sugars on the nutrition label, the onus would be on the manufacturers to keep sufficient records to substantiate the amount of added sugars claimed. Requiring disclosure of added sugars, with a benchmark that reflects current dietary guidelines, would be the most accessible and reliable way for consumers to obtain this important information. It would help them select foods and beverages to lower their intake of added sugars and lower their risk of many adverse health effects.[3,6] Without this declaration, consumers and patients would be unable to determine the amounts of added sugars in a product.[6]

7   There are also substantial population-level benefits. Reformulation of products to be lower in added sugars is a likely outcome of having to declare added sugar content on nutrition labels, as manufacturers strive for an advantage over their competition. According to the United Nations, reformulation is considered a "best buy" approach to reducing intakes of nutrients that increase risk of chronic disease, and it is an equitable approach because it benefits the whole population.[8] Such benefits have clearly been shown with labelling of trans fatty acids and efforts to reduce their intakes.[9] By not including added sugars on nutrition labels, it will be difficult to compare intakes in Canada and other countries, to monitor national intake trends over time and to assess industry's reformulation efforts.

In their **thesis**, the authors do not directly state that a declaration of added sugars *should* be included in the final proposal, but this can be inferred from the first part of the sentence in which the authors mention that Canadians were consulted and desired that the amount of added sugars should appear on food labels.

This brief paragraph uses **definition**, so readers understand the differences between added sugars, total sugars, and natural sugars.

The authors **compare** Health Canada's proposal with that of an equivalent branch of the US government, concluding the paragraph by citing three reputable organizations.

The authors go further than just mentioning **experts**: in this sentence, they identify how the guidelines were established, referring to two sources included in the list of References. Someone wishing for more specific information could consult these sources.

In this paragraph, the authors use logical reasoning to show why food manufacturers should provide the amount of added sugar on labels. Note the use of **transitions** to show relationships between ideas ("however" and "instead").

The authors **appeal to reader interests**, showing how they benefit by the disclosure of added sugars.

The authors use the introduction of labelling on trans fats as a **precedent**, showing how this successfully reduced its consumption.

In this concluding **ethical appeal**, Bernstein and L'Abbé encourage an action that will be good for Canadians.

8   Since the regulatory changes were proposed by Health Canada, a new federal government has been elected. This may present an ideal opportunity to alter the final regulations. In fact, the mandate letter from the prime minister to the new minister of health lists improving food labels to give more information on added sugars as a priority.[10] If included in the first overhaul of the nutrition label in nearly 15 years, the declaration of added sugars would be an important opportunity for improving the health of Canadians and should not be lost.

References

Articles in this journal use the Council of Science Editors documentation style in which in-text superscript numbers correspond to numbered sources in the References section.

1.   Regulations amending the food and drug regulations-nutrition labelling, other labelling provisions and food colours. Canada Gazette 2015 June 13;149(24).

2.   Hess J, Latulippe ME, Ayoob K, et al. The confusing world of dietary sugars: definitions, intakes, food sources and international dietary recommendations. Food Funct 2012;3:477–86.

3.   Guideline: sugars intake for adults and children. Geneva: World Health Organization; 2015.

4.   Sugar reduction: the evidence for action. London (UK): Public Health England; 2015.

5.   Scientific report of the 2015 Dietary Guidelines Advisory Committee. Washington (DC): US Department of Agriculture and Department of Health and Human Services; 2015.

6.   Food labeling: proposed rule for revision of the nutrition and supplement facts labels. Washington (DC): US Food and Drug Administration; 2014/15.

7.   Louie JCY, Moshtaghian H, Boylan S, et al. A systematic methodology to estimate added sugar content of foods. Eur J Clin Nutr 2015;69:154–61.

8.   Prevention and control of non-communicable diseases: report of the Secretary-General [no. A/66/83]. New York: United Nations General Assembly; 2011 May 19. Available: www.un.org/ga/search/view_doc.asp?symbol=A/66/83&Lang=E (accessed 2016 Feb. 25).

9.   Arcand J, Scourboutakos MJ, Au JTC, et al. trans Fatty acids in the Canadian food supply: an updated analysis. Am J Clin Nutr 2014;100:1116–23.

10. Minister of health mandate letter. Ottawa: Office of the Prime Minister of Canada; 2015. Available: http://pm.gc.ca/eng/minister -health-mandate-letter (accessed 2016 Jan. 6).

10 Writing Research Papers

Research essays call on various kinds of reading and writing skills, including developing effective introductions, middle paragraphs, and conclusions, as discussed in Chapter 6. Since research requires you to read your sources closely, it is wise to adopt specific strategies to make the most of your reading, as discussed in Chapter 5. Further, comprehension of the material depends on your use of critical thinking, as discussed in Chapter 4. Responding to texts in writing involves such processes as evaluating and comparing sources. In addition, identifying which ideas from a source are the most relevant to your topic and integrating them into your own essay are key research skills essential in summarization. These kinds of activities were discussed in Chapters 7 and 8.

However, the fundamentals of research extend beyond these skills. In this chapter, we focus on

- locating sources in the modern library
- assessing the reliability of sources, particularly electronic ones
- integrating ideas and giving credit to your sources

We begin with some brief comments on the nature of the research process.

Coming Up with a Topic

For many students, finding a topic to write on is the first challenge to overcome. Here are some questions to consider when you need to come up with a topic from scratch:

- Where do your interests lie (hobbies, leisure pursuits, reading interests, extracurricular activities)?
- What would you like to learn more about? Curiosity is a good motivator. A topic you are familiar with does not always make a good one for a research essay.

- What topic do you think readers might like to learn about? Thinking of *other* people's interests can guide you to a worthwhile topic. What topic could benefit society or a specific group (for example, students at your university)?
- Can you think of a new angle on an old topic? Neglected areas of older topics can be new opportunities for exploration.

Preparing for Research

Research often begins after you have come up with a research question or a statement of the problem to be investigated.

You could begin your research by consulting general reference works, such as textbooks, encyclopedias, or dictionaries, along with specialized indexes and guides in the fields related to your topic.

However, your research question or thesis will likely not be clear until you have conducted preliminary research. Typically, this begins with narrowing a general topic. If you began with a topic like "energy sources in today's world," you would soon find that the topic was much too large; the information available would be overwhelming. However, you can use any of the pre-writing strategies mentioned in Chapter 6 to make the topic more manageable (see Pre-writing Techniques, pages 64–65).

One way to narrow the topic of energy sources is to focus on alternatives to fossil fuels, for example nuclear power, with its safety and environmental concerns, or thermo-mechanical energy, which is often considered a less viable long-term energy source. This research can be done either in the library or online using your library's electronic resources.

Your reading will narrow the topic further. It could lead you to three specific energy sources: bio-diesel, solar energy, and hydrogen. However, writing on all three sources in one essay would probably prevent you from going into detail about any of them. Although you could randomly select one of the three alternative sources, a better option would be to ask what you or your audience might want to know about these energy sources: *Why are these sources important? Who would be interested in knowing about them, and what more do you need to find out about them in order to inform others? Whom could they benefit? What are the potential benefits? What are the potential costs?* Posing these kinds of questions may lead you to a research question or thesis statement.

All these energy sources offer a potential global solution to the energy crisis, but *Which of the three offers the best potential?* With this question in mind, you can recall what you have read about each or continue to browse general works for more background information—in particular, information concerning the costs and benefits of these three energy sources. In the end, you might decide that the most promising is hydrogen. Your thesis might take this form:

> **Current research into the development of alternative fuels provides hope for an oil- and nuclear-free future, but of the different types of alternative fuels, hydrogen is the most promising because it satisfies the requirements for a long-term energy plan.**

It could also be phrased as a research question:

> **Among the various alternative fuels being promoted today, does hydrogen live up to the claims of its proponents by being able to satisfy the requirements for a long-term energy plan?**

Now, with a tentative thesis and organizational pattern (cost/benefit analysis), you can conduct further research by turning to specific journals, especially peer-reviewed journals in which academics, scientists, and researchers publish their findings. This is where library search skills enter the picture. Knowing how the modern library works will save you a lot of time and help you find high-quality sources. By following the guidelines in The Active Voice: A Beginner's Guide to Research in the Academic Library (page 128), you will be able to locate specific sources directly relevant to a topic like energy sources.

As with most projects involving a combination of skills that develop through *doing them*, doubts and occasional frustrations are inevitable. The information that follows on research methods and sources is designed to make this process a more comprehensible and satisfying experience.

> **peer-reviewed journal**
> A type of journal in which submissions are reviewed by experts before publication; it is an authoritative source for scholarly research.

Research Proposals

Research proposals are a part of the professional world. For the student researcher, a proposal is usually written before your major research, but it can also be written after it and may include an essay outline. The main purpose of a proposal, whether for your instructor or for a potential employer, is to convince a reader that the project you propose is worth doing and that you are the right person to do it. For you, a successful proposal will persuade your instructor that you have done adequate preparation and are on the right track to a successful research paper.

Many research proposals require two parts: (1) a description of what you are undertaking and (2) your methodology. In the first part, you include your thesis and main points. In some proposals, you include your reason for wanting to research the topic; thus, you could mention your interest in the area or summarize the importance of research in this field to others. You will not be held to the specific terms of your proposal if you discover on further research that you need to amend your thesis or your main points. The proposal represents a *probable* plan: your thesis and main points can be revised if necessary.

In the second part of the proposal, you should include the sources you have found useful so far and the kinds of sources that you will look at as your research continues. Be as specific as possible, naming books, journals, websites, and so on, along with article titles. If you are planning other kinds of research, such as interviews or questionnaires, mention them too. The more detail you provide, the more your reader will be convinced. Being specific makes your proposal credible.

A final function of the research proposal is that it gives you a preliminary plan to follow; it solidifies your topic and your approach to the topic in your own mind.

A proposal may even include projected dates, such as the date you plan to begin your major research and the date you plan to complete it.

> The main purpose of a research proposal is to convince a reader that the project you propose is worth doing and that you are the right person to do it. Many research proposals require two parts: (1) a description of what you are undertaking, including your thesis and main points and (2) your methodology, including the kinds of sources you will be using.

Sample Proposal

The sample student proposal below uses main points in the form of questions, which can be used to generate possible research directions.

Student Writing Sample

Proposal for Research Essay on the Effects of Implementing Prison-Based Needle Exchange Programs in Canadian Federal Prisons

by Kate Newcombe

Topic: The benefits that introducing needle exchange programs into the Canadian federal prison system will have on inmates and employees.

Purpose: To investigate prison-based needle exchange programs and argue the benefits of implementing such a system in Canadian federal prisons.

Description: With the recent introduction of the safe injection site in downtown Vancouver, a growing interest in these sites has developed throughout the community, health services programs, and governments. Although it is a controversial topic, evidence from the Vancouver needle exchange site demonstrates the benefits of these programs. This issue is worth exploring because drug use continues to be widespread in Canadian prisons, and the increased health risks to intravenous drug users due to lack of proper injecting equipment are growing rapidly. Currently, no such programs exist in Canadian prisons. I am interested in discovering more about prison-based needle exchange programs and arguing for the benefits they provide to inmates as well as prison workers. The main organizational methods will be problem–solution and cause–effect.

Tentative Thesis Statement and Central Questions: Prison-based needle exchange programs are an effective, cost-efficient, and beneficial safety tool for public health officials to implement in Canadian prisons in efforts to control drug-related problems and the spread of HIV/AIDS.

- What are the health benefits to intravenous drug users by introducing a system such as this into Canadian prisons?
- Will the introduction of needle exchange systems increase drug use by inmates?
- How will its introduction affect prison employees? (i.e., will there be a physical threat to the health and safety of workers?)
- Have other countries implemented this system into their prisons? If so, what are the results?
- How, if at all, will the introduction of this system help control the spread of HIV/AIDS in the prison population?
- How has the Canadian government dealt with groups and individuals who argue for implementation?
- Is this truly a cost-effective system?

Methodology: In my preliminary research through my university database, I have found several reliable scholarly articles and reviews of prison-based needle exchange programs. They are peer-reviewed and diverse, from such journals as *Dalhousie Journal of Legal Studies, Substance Use & Misuse, The Lancet,* and *The New England Journal of Medicine.* Tentative articles include Iafrate (2015), "Canadian Prison Needle-Exchange Programs: Can the Health Benefits Overcome The Current Legal Barriers?," Van der Meulen (2017), "'It Goes on Everywhere': Injection Drug Use in Canadian Federal Prisons," and Bayoumi and Zaric (2008), "The Cost-Effectiveness of

Vancouver's Supervised Injection Facility"; other studies available also evaluate the success of the Vancouver program. The researchers' findings support the argument that the introduction of prison-based needle exchange programs is beneficial to inmates and employees, while it does not appear that the health benefits of clean syringes and needles increase intravenous drug use within prisons. Davies' "Prison's Second Death Row" (2004) also looks promising as the author accounts for the reluctance of some governments to institute harm reduction programs.

Recording Important Information

Keeping methodical and accurate records during the research phase of the essay-writing process allows you to read material efficiently as well as save time (and your sanity) when you write your paper. You should record *notes* as you research, ensuring that they include the following information:

- a direct quotation, a summary, or a paraphrase of the writer's idea (if it is a direct quotation, make sure you put quotation marks around it)
- the complete name(s) of the author(s), ensuring correct spelling
- the complete name(s) of any editors or translators
- the complete name of the book, journal, magazine, newspaper, or website
- the title of the specific article, chapter, section, or webpage
- full publication details, including date, edition, and translation (if applicable)
- the name of the publisher and the company's location (including province or state) for books
- in the case of an article accessed electronically, the day you viewed the page and either the URL or the **digital object identifier** (DOI); the date of the site or its most recent update should also be recorded
- the call number of a library book or bound journal (to help you find it again if necessary)
- the page numbers you consulted, both those from which specific ideas came and the full page range of the work (or some other marker, such as section headings and paragraph numbers, for unnumbered Internet documents)

Organizing Research Notes

There are many ways to organize information from your research in order to use it later, including the manual method—for example, notecards, which are portable and practical. Many software programs are designed to help with planning and organization. For example, *RefWorks* (www.refworks.com) is an Internet-based "citation manager" that allows you to import references from popular databases like *Academic Search Complete*, *MLA Bibliography*, and *EconLit*. Other useful software includes databases such as *EndNote* (www.endnote.com), *Bibliographix* (www.bibliographix.com), and *Nota Bene* (www.notabene.com). Students can usually take a tutorial for these programs on the websites or even through their own institution if it has purchased licences allowing students to use them. These programs offer many benefits, such as automatic formatting for a great variety of citation and bibliographic systems.

Ensure that you keep your research notes, such as summaries and direct quotations, separate from your personal annotations. Use a method that clearly distinguishes between the two; otherwise, you could end up plagiarizing by failing to attribute the idea or words of a source, thinking they were your own.

digital object identifier (DOI)
A number-letter sequence that begins with the number 10 often found on journal articles; it serves as a persistent link for digital material and should be cited rather than a URL when available.

The Active Voice

A Beginner's Guide to Research in the Academic Library

1   The twenty-first-century academic library can seem overwhelming to the undergraduate researcher. In addition to the traditional materials found in the library's online catalogue, there are numerous other electronic resources available, including databases, journals, and e-books, as well as other digital formats and media. The sheer volume of information resources in today's academic library need not be intimidating. On the contrary, an effective research strategy will enable you to take full advantage of all the wealth of print and electronic information resources available to you.

2   An effective strategy should include three important considerations:

1. Your *research topic*
2. The *information resources* most relevant to your topic
3. The *search strategy* you will use to obtain and retain information from those resources

3   When you understand how to choose a well-defined research topic, where to look for information on that topic, and how to construct an effective search in an academic library catalogue or database, you will have the basic tools required for most research projects at the first-year level. As you become a more confident researcher, you can expand on these basic skills and strategies by exploring more specialized resources and experimenting with advanced search methods.

The Research Topic

4   The starting point for your research will be your topic. When choosing your own topic, make sure to select one that is neither too broad nor too narrow. If your topic is too broad, you will have difficulty focusing your research and writing. Conversely, if your topic is too narrow or obscure, you may not be able to find enough relevant information to support your research question.

5   For instance, you may want to write about *homelessness* or *the homeless*. It would be difficult to write a focused paper on such a broad topic. To narrow your focus, you might want to research homelessness in a particular age group, such as teenagers. However, this would probably still be too broad. You could narrow your focus further by looking at particular health problems of homeless teens or risk factors associated with homelessness in teens, such as poverty, addiction, or abuse.

Selecting Resources for Your Research Topic

6   **Subject or Research Guides:** Once you have decided on a research topic, you must choose your resources. The academic library is your ultimate destination for a diversity of scholarly and non-scholarly sources. Most academic libraries provide subject or research guides on their website. These guides are prepared by subject librarians with specialized knowledge in the information resources of their particular subject areas. Most subject guides provide direct links to relevant online databases, scholarly websites, and primary source materials for the subject, as well as valuable information on reference resources such as dictionaries, encyclopedias, biographies, and bibliographies, including subject headings and call number ranges.

7   **Primary and Secondary Sources:** Your research may require that you investigate both primary and secondary source information. The meaning of primary and secondary sources can vary across the disciplines, but in the humanities and social sciences, primary sources generally provide *first-hand* information or data. This may include original works such as autobiographies, interviews, speeches, letters, diaries, unpublished manuscripts, data sources, government records, newspapers,

and government policy papers, among others. Secondary sources are works that analyze or provide criticism or interpretation of a primary work, source, or experience from a *second-hand* perspective. These can include scholarly journal articles, textbooks, collections of critical essays, biographies, historical articles, and films, to name a few examples.

8   **The Library Catalogue:** The library catalogue is the most important tool for finding secondary print sources like books, encyclopedias, dictionaries, and journals in your library, as well as any electronic versions of these materials that are available. Unlike an Internet search engine such as Google, the library's catalogue is a bibliographic index and provides a comprehensive list of the most relevant scholarly and non-scholarly sources related to your research topic through its combined use of subject headings and descriptors. For concise, general information on your topic, the academic library can also provide you with encyclopedias and

dictionaries, which are more scholarly sources of information than Wikipedia, and can help you to narrow your focus by highlighting key academic issues and concepts, as well as providing suggestions for further research. Scholarly books relevant to your topic are also important sources for you to explore. In addition to covering a subject in more depth than a journal article, they often provide important historical, biographical, literary, or cultural context that may not be available elsewhere. Books also feature images or tables of contents that can help you to identify important aspects of the subject that you may want to explore further and bibliographies to help you locate other resources. E-books are especially useful for browsing tables of contents and bibliographies and for keyword searching within the full text of a book.

9   **Online Databases:** Scholarly journal articles are a key secondary source for your research. Journal articles review what other scholars have said about your topic

Continued

and often provide important supportive or alternative perspectives relevant to your thesis. Online databases and indexes are your main tools for finding journal articles in both print and online formats. Your library's home page may provide a discovery search tool, such as *Summon*, for searching for information sources. In a single unified search box, the system retrieves a number of relevant articles from your library's catalogue and journal subscriptions, and allows you to limit your search, save or export your results, or link to the full text. This method is useful for quickly finding information on your topic, and can be further refined by using the additional filters and limiters available.

10   A good multidisciplinary online database like *Academic Search Complete* provides relevant information on most topics at the undergraduate level. However, you may also want to take advantage of the many subject and specialized databases available. Most subject areas feature a core database that indexes the key journals for that discipline, such as ERIC for Education, *Sociological Abstracts* for sociology, or the *MLA International Bibliography* for language and literature. It is important to get to know the core databases in your subject area. If your library has subject guides, these will list the core databases or "best bets" for each subject.

Most libraries will also allow you to select databases by subject in addition to providing an A–Z list. This can be helpful, particularly if the database indicates it includes full text, coverage dates available, authenticated links for mobile access, and anything else that may be pertinent.

11   You should also consider the type of information you require. For example, it is unlikely that you will find complex data or statistical information unless you search a statistical database. Historical government information, too, will require different search strategies, and may include specialized use of websites such as the Internet Archive. Again, the specialized subject guides, as well as consultation with your subject librarian, will help you in determining the right information resources you need for your research topic.

Search Strategies

12   **Determining Keywords:** Once you have chosen some relevant resources, the next step will be to identify the key concepts from your topic to use as keywords or search terms. For instance, if you want to search for information on risk factors associated with homelessness in youth, you will want to identify keywords that embody

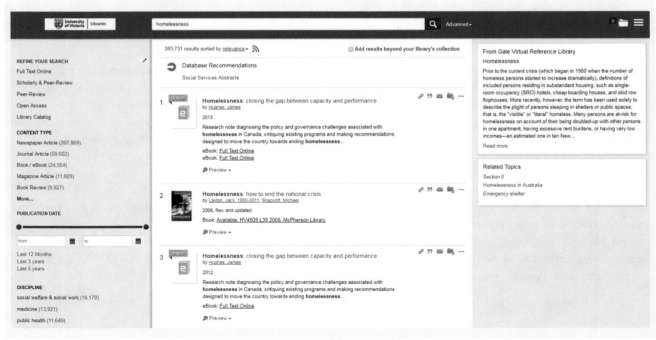

the concepts *risk factors*, *homelessness*, *youth*. Some risk factors might be *poverty*, *addiction*, or *abuse*. Using *risk* or *factors* as search terms would be too broad and would not provide good search results. Similarly, using *"risk factors"* as a single term would not find results unless the books or articles used this exact term.

13 Boolean Operators: To be effective, the actual search process should employ some form of Boolean strategy. The most common Boolean operators, AND, OR, and NOT, are used to combine, expand, or eliminate keywords in your search. For instance, AND combines the two different terms *homelessness* AND *youth*. A search conducted using AND will also narrow your results. This is more effective than searching for each of the keywords separately, since any sources retrieved must include both terms. The OR operator is used to expand your search results by including other concepts. These may be the same concepts or different aspects of a broader concept. In this example, you might want to search for results that include the keywords *youth* OR *teens* OR *adolescents*, which are synonymous concepts. Or you may want to search for *poverty* OR *abuse* OR *addiction* as different aspects of the risk factors. The NOT operator is used to eliminate results with that given keyword, such as *children* if you do not want results that discuss young children. The NOT operator should be used judiciously, however, because you may eliminate an article that discusses both children and teens, which may be relevant to your topic.

14 The Boolean terms are capitalized here for readability but this is not necessary in most databases. Also, many databases will now allow you to combine your keywords without using the Boolean operators at all. You simply enter your terms and choose the correct search mode. Using Basic Search in *Academic Search Complete* as an example, the search mode *Find all of my search terms* is equivalent to AND, and the search mode *Find any of my search terms* is equivalent to OR. Many other databases and catalogues now work similarly, including *Google Scholar*, which can be an important resource to consult either when you are in the beginning stages of your research or when you are looking for a specific article you are unable to locate elsewhere. When using *Google Scholar*, however, remember to access it through your academic library website, so that you can directly link to online resources in your library's catalogue, including open-access journals. Keep in mind

Continued

that *Google Scholar* is a search engine, and although it may be extensive, it is certainly not exhaustive. Your library's catalogue or discovery tool is still the best choice for scholarly academic sources related to your research topic.

15 Truncation and Wildcards: Boolean search strategy is often used with truncation and/or wildcard symbols. Truncation symbols enable you to include all variants of a search term. Using the asterisk as the truncation symbol in *teen** will ensure that your search results include all the terms *teen*, *teens*, and *teenager*. Wildcards are used within a word, for instance in *colo#r* to search for an alternative spelling (*colour* and *color*) or *wom?n* to search for any unknown characters (*woman* and *women*). Most databases and catalogues use the asterisk (*) or a question mark (?) for the truncation or wildcard symbol. Some databases may also use the pound sign (#) or another symbol.

16 Basic or Advanced Search: Online catalogues and databases usually feature simple or basic search and advanced search options. The basic search field can be used to enter single terms, as described above, or more complex search statements using Boolean operators. However, to construct a search statement using Boolean strategy in a basic search field, you must use parentheses to separate the OR terms from the AND terms as indicated below. The database will search for the terms in parentheses first, then from left to right.

(*Homeless** **OR** *runaway**) **AND** (*teen** **OR** *adolescen** **OR** *youth*) **AND** (*poverty* **OR** *abuse* **OR** *addict**)

17 Also, if you want to use a combined term such as "*risk factors,*" you must use quotation marks unless the field provides the option to search two or more words as a phrase.

18 The Advanced Search option allows you to insert your terms and then select AND, OR, or NOT to combine the fields and to add additional fields, if necessary. Advanced search also allows you to search for terms in various fields, such as *All Text*, *Abstract*, *Author*, *Title*, or *Subject Terms*. By selecting a specific field, you limit the search to that field alone. It is often best to try a search in the default field initially and then try other advanced strategies to refine your results, if necessary.

19 Subject Headings or Descriptors: Subject headings or descriptors are very useful for refining your search strategy. In an academic library, under the Library of Congress classification system, subject headings have been applied to each bibliographic entry to describe what it is about. A subject heading is not merely a keyword found in the article or abstract, and some online databases enable you to search the subject directly to show related subject headings. Sometimes, subject headings within the results list are linked, so you can either expand or narrow the results of your current search to all of the related records in the database with that subject term.

20 Another strategy is to take note of the subject headings in your initial keyword searches. Combining these terms again in the *Subject Terms* field will often yield more relevant results. Most online library catalogues will also provide related subject headings to other resources with the same heading. Additionally, there may also be a link to other items in the same immediate call number range. This will enable you to easily browse the collection for other relevant materials.

21 Limiters: Another search strategy is using the limiters available to you in a particular database. This strategy is generally used to limit your results if there are too many, or to limit to a particular date range, article type, format, or publication. One very useful limiter found in many databases is the scholarly or peer-reviewed limiter. Peer-reviewed articles are scholarly articles that have been reviewed by a board or panel of scholars from the same discipline for publication in academic journals. They are a more reliable source of information for your research than popular sources that are intended for a general audience. Some databases will limit to scholarly sources automatically and return the results under a *peer-reviewed* link or tab. *Academic Search Complete* provides a *Scholarly (Peer Reviewed) Journals* check box to the right of your search results list, or you can check the *Scholarly (Peer Reviewed) Journals* box in the *Limit your results* field before you execute your search, and the database will only retrieve scholarly articles.

22 Marking and Saving: Most online databases and library catalogues provide a marking and saving feature. You can select your most relevant results, mark them by checking a box or adding them to a folder, and then choose from several options—usually print, email, save, or export. Export often includes an option to download or export to the bibliographic management software of your choice, such as *RefWorks* or *EndNote*. These citation management tools allow you to create a customized personal account so that you can store and organize your citations, as well as create a bibliography conforming to a particular citation style, such as APA, MLA, or Chicago. Citation management tools can help you keep track of your search history, as well as store links to previously searched databases and full-text articles, and often include areas where you can write your own comments. As you scan abstracts and articles, and later during your readings, be sure to note the points and ideas you wish to quote and paraphrase. Remember, crediting sources is an essential part of academic writing.

23 **Refining Your Strategy:** One final consideration for effective academic library research is refining your strategy throughout the process. It may be necessary to re-evaluate your topic, choice of resources, or search strategy if your initial search efforts are unsuccessful. Do not feel frustrated: this is not an indication that your strategy is not a good one or that you have failed. On the contrary, conducting academic research is a naturally evolving process, and knowing how to access the resources at your academic library is a part of the learning experience. In the end, your goal is a strong research topic with thoughtful, meaningful research accompanied by accurate citations to scholarly resources. Therefore, it is important to start your library research early. This will allow you enough time to determine a manageable topic, consult your subject librarian, explore as many resources as possible, refine your search strategy as necessary, and obtain any materials that are not readily available online or in your academic library.

—Based on original text by **Danielle Forster** and updated by Justin Harrison, Caron Rollins, and Christine Walde, University of Victoria Libraries

Activity 10.1

Using one of your library's search engines or a general/science database, such as *Academic Search Complete* or *Medline*, answer the questions below. To make your search more efficient, you can use the search limiters *journal article only* and *peer-reviewed journals only*; you can also set the publication date to 2004 and/or enter the main author's name "Tatem" in the Search window.

Access the academic journal *Nature,* volume 432, issue 7014. Referring to the letter "Biology Students Find Holes in Gap Study" on page 147, answer the questions below, all of which stress the critical-thinking skills discussed in Chapter 4:

1. How do these students establish their credibility to critique a study in an academic journal?

2. How do the students use the study by Whipp and Ward?

3. What year did Tatem et al. begin studying women's times? How can you infer this?

4. How many points do the students use to support their claim? Which do you consider the strongest? Why?

5. Following the letters, the authors of the study responded to the criticisms (see "Mind the Gap: Women Racers Are Falling Behind," page 147). After reading all the letters on the page, along with the authors' response, consider whether the authors effectively answered the charges. What tone did they use in their response? Note: It is not necessary to be familiar with the models mentioned by the authors.

Using Credible Sources

In determining whether to use a source in your research essay, bear in mind the four "Re's" of research sources: reputable, reliable, recent, and relevant.

- *Re*putable: Reputable sources are usually associated with well-known organizations or acknowledged experts in their field.
- *Re*liable: Information from reliable sources can be trusted as accurate and free of bias.
- *Re*cent: Although currency is more important to some topics than others, recent information is generally superior to older information.
- *Re*levant: The information in relevant sources is directly related to your thesis and/or main points.

Credibility Issues in Online Sources

Of the four qualities mentioned above, the first two—reputable and reliable—are especially relevant to online searches. The explosion of information via the Internet has made it more difficult to assess the authority of written information today. Because the boundaries are sometimes blurred between knowledge and speculation and between fact and opinion, those who surf the net, reading indiscriminately, may sometimes find it hard to tell reliable from unreliable information. Today's student researcher must read carefully and ask questions about the source's sponsor(s) and/or author(s), along with the accuracy, currency, objectivity, and scope of the information.

The criteria below apply particularly to open-access resources, from Google Scholar to the array of commercial, governmental, and personal websites that anyone sitting in front of a computer screen can view. In contrast to these are the more authoritative resources accessed through your institution's library home page. The way you use open-access resources, or *if* you use them in your research, depends on what kind of information you are looking for.

You should first consider your purpose for seeking out a source. Is it for reliable information from an objective source with sound evidence-gathering methods (Statistics Canada, for example), or is it to learn about a particular viewpoint? If the latter, it might be acceptable to use a website that advocates a position or supports a cause. If you were writing an essay on animal rights, you might want to access People for the Ethical Treatment of Animals (PETA) or Animal Rights Canada, since their advocacy of animal rights is clear and above board—which is not to say that their information is always factual or accurate.

Not all websites, however, acknowledge their true stake in an issue, nor do all websites use quality control to ensure accurate content. Even seemingly reliable and objective websites, such as government-affiliated ones, may contain misleading or outdated information. The questions below are therefore relevant to most sources you access via the Internet.

Sponsors and Authors

- What group or individual has created the site or is responsible for its content? If the organization/individual is unfamiliar, try to find its parent organization, affiliated organizations, or a mission statement concerning the organization's and/or website's purpose. You should be suspicious of websites lacking self-identification.

- Who are the authors of the material on the site? Are names and affiliations given? Biographies? Is contact information provided? Mailing address, telephone number, email address?

Accuracy and Currency

- What is the source of the content? Are informational sources identified—by author, title, date? How has statistical information been calculated (e.g., through censuses, surveys, questionnaires by reliable organizations)? How are statistical information and other factual data being used?
- Are all claims and other statements reasonable and well supported?
- What is the original date of the site? Has it been updated recently? Does factual information appear verifiable? Can it be verified by checking a reliable and unaffiliated website?

Objectivity

- Does the content seem presented without bias? Is it politicized? Does it seem to address a specific reader (e.g., is the voice familiar and informal?) or directed toward a general reader? Is the tone neutral? Can you identify any slanted language or bias?
- If opinion exists, is it clearly differentiated from fact? Are other points of view besides those of the author/organization represented? How are they treated?
- Is there advertising?

Scope and Comprehensiveness

- Does the site include different views of and approaches to issues?
- Is there a menu or site map that provides an overview of content? (You could get an indication of scope from that.)
- Are there links to other sites? Do these sites appear reliable?
- Does content primarily consist of text? What is the approximate proportion of text to graphics (for research purposes, text should outweigh graphics)? Are there accompanying charts, graphs, or other illustrative material? If so, do they seem designed to explain and summarize (as opposed to being merely decorative)?

Other Issues

- Is the information on the website easy to access? Does it appear well organized? What specific resources are designed to enhance accessibility or navigation?
- Is the site appealing and attractive rather than just glitzy?

Integrating and Documenting Sources

When you integrate or synthesize your research into your essay, you can use one or more of several methods. When you document these sources, you use a standardized format to show your readers where you obtained this material. Typically, you integrate or synthesize your sources as part of the composing process, while documenting these sources is often the final stage in the composing process. The value in documenting as early as possible in the process, however, is that it will give you time to check and double-check the accuracy of your information.

Integrating Your Sources: Summary versus Paraphrase

summary

A method of integrating the main idea (or ideas) of an original source into your own words.

paraphrase

A method of source integration in which you put someone else's ideas in your own words, keeping the length of the original.

When you **summarize** a source, you use an idea (or multiple ideas) from the source that is directly relevant to your essay, putting it in your own words. If you wanted to summarize a large portion of the original, you would follow the guidelines for précis summaries (see page 87). What distinguishes a summary from a **paraphrase** is that summaries are selective: they focus on main ideas. When you paraphrase, you include *all of the original, putting it in your own words*. You could paraphrase anything from a part of a sentence to one or two paragraphs. Paraphrasing is reserved for important information.

Whereas a summary condenses and is thus an efficient method for synthesizing material, a paraphrased passage is about the same length as the original. Because you include so much in a paraphrase, you must be careful to use different wording or you may unknowingly be plagiarizing. Changing the order of the original will also help you avoid plagiarism (see Plagiarism, page 141).

Direct Quotation and Mixed Format

When you represent a source by direct quotation, you use exactly the same words as the original, enclosing them within quotation marks. Authors of empirical studies may use few direct quotations, but they are often used by authors of humanities essays, which analyze primary sources, such as literary or historical texts, and may depend on direct quotations for support. Researchers in the social sciences who use a qualitative methodology, such as interviews or focus groups, may also rely on direct quotations.

Direct quotations, used selectively, can enhance your credibility, as discussed below (The Active Voice: To Quote or Not to Quote). However, when you summarize or paraphrase, you show your comprehension of a source by "translating" it into your own words.

> *Direct quotation unnecessary:* "Pilot error accounted for 34 per cent of major airline crashes between 1990 and 1996, compared with 43 per cent from 1983 to 1989." [Statistical detail does not need be quoted directly.]

> *Paraphrase:* In the six-year period between 1990 and 1996, 34 per cent of major airline crashes were due to pilot error, a decrease of 9 per cent over the previous six-year period.

If factual material can be easily put in your own words, prefer summary or paraphrase to direct quotation.

> *Direct quotation unnecessary:* "Students often find ways to compensate for their symptoms of add in their earlier years so that the disorder reveals itself only with the increased intellectual and organizational demands of university."

Summary: Because of the greater demands of university, compared to earlier schooling, students with add may not have to confront their disorder until university.

In a mixed format, you combine summary or paraphrase with direct quotation. Effective use of mixed format demonstrates both your understanding and your polished writing skills since it requires you to seamlessly integrate the language of the source with your own language. You can use this format when you want to cite part of an important passage in which key words or phrases occur, carefully choosing the significant words and excluding the less important parts.

> **mixed format**
> A method of source integration in which you combine significant words of the source, placed in quotation marks, with your own words.

Integrating Quotations

When you incorporate direct quotations into your essay, you must do so grammatically and smoothly; you must also provide adequate context for your reader. The following shows a poorly integrated quotation and its well-integrated alternative:

An unloving parent–child relationship can be characterized as "unaccepted, unacknowledged, or unloved" (Haworth-Hoeppner 216).

Well-integrated: An unloving parent–child relationship exists when the child feels "unaccepted, unacknowledged, or unloved" (Haworth-Hoeppner 216).

The Active Voice

To Quote or Not to Quote?: Strategies for Effectively Using the Words of *Other* Writers in *Your* Writing

1   Students are often given warnings about using quotations in academic essays. You may have received feedback such as "you are relying too much on quotations" or "quote only when necessary" and, as a result, be tempted not to quote at all.

2   However, the quickest glance at published essays will demonstrate that including direct quotations from other sources is standard academic practice. Writing handbooks and websites often provide practical advice about how to integrate quotations into your writing. But as a writer new to the conventions of academic discourse, you may be more concerned about choosing when to quote, or not to quote, than with the practical details of how to do so.

3   As a starting point, it is worth considering why academic writers include the ideas and words of other writers in their writing. Remember that you are not writing in a vacuum: you are placing your ideas in the context of experts in the field and engaging in a form of indirect conversation with them. By including quotations or paraphrasing—hence, summarizing the ideas of others—you demonstrate that you have carried out relevant research and that you understand important issues or theories relevant to your points. Used judiciously,

Continued

quotations demonstrate to your reader that you are aware of the conventions of academic writing and that your ideas are worth paying attention to.

4   But now let's focus on how experienced writers decide when to quote, what to quote, and how much to quote. Clearly, there is no simple formula, but here are some guidelines for when you should consider quoting:

- Quote when you find that you cannot paraphrase the original words without a significant loss of meaning.
- Quote when the original phrase is especially powerful or significant.
- Quote to increase your credibility by situating your ideas within the context of claims made by an expert in the field.
- Quote for emphasis: a direct quotation suggests that a source is very significant to the development of your ideas or position, giving it more weight than ideas which are simply paraphrased.

5   Here is a quotation from the essay "Addressing Driver Aggression: Contributions from Psychological Science" effectively integrated into a sentence:

> Wickens, Mann, and Wisenthal argue that acts of driver aggression and violence are "not errors or lapses in judgment; they are aberrant driving behaviours." (see page 305 of Part III: The Reader)

Notice that this quotation includes powerful and distinctive phrases—"not errors or lapses in judgment" and a powerful clause, "they are aberrant driving behaviours"—which are central to the argument presented in the original essay. Paraphrasing this quotation would not be impossible, but the initial wording is effective and words such as "lapses" and "aberrant" are particularly striking. By using a quotation such as this, a writer gains credibility and is able to take advantage of the powerful language of published writers.

6   Quotations are most common (and appropriate) in sections of an essay which summarize the research of others, provide a literature review, and/or explain the theoretical background central to an issue being discussed or an argument presented. These will be commonly found at the beginning of an essay, but quotations can also be used effectively in the middle or concluding sections.

7   However, the most important advice about what to quote may well be what not to quote. Never quote just for the sake of quoting. Imagine encountering a statement like the following in an essay:

> In reference to mortality problems, Joel Lexchin indicates that those "are not addressed in this present paper."

Readers are likely to wonder why the writer has chosen to quote such an insignificant phrase, and may even question his or her competence. To avoid this perception, choose a phrase to quote which is striking, clear and significant, and which will improve—rather than detract from—the effectiveness of your own writing.

8   Finally, how much should you quote? As a general rule, quote only as much of the original as you need to clearly convey an author's idea(s). If at all possible, quote a phrase, rather than a sentence. For example, here is a sentence which includes a quotation from the essay "Psychology's Essential Role in Alleviating the Impacts of Climate Change":

> Robert Gifford presents a powerful argument that if psychology fails to promote an awareness of climate change and its devastating effects, in the future it may be perceived as "the science that fiddled whilst the planet burned." (see page 358 of Part III: The Reader)

9   Now compare that sentence with the following:

> Robert Gifford indicates that "If psychological science is to become recognized as an essential part of sustainability science and as an important player in the struggle to ameliorate the impacts of climate change, it must move towards a more serious engagement the problem. If we do not, we run the danger of being viewed by future citizens as the science that fiddled whilst the planet burned." (see page 358 of Part III: The Reader)

Admittedly, the longer quotation in the second example includes more detail; however, the shorter quotation is more focused, fits more smoothly within the sentence, and demonstrates that the writer has integrated ideas from Robert Gifford's essay, not merely copied words from the source.

10 If you need to quote an entire sentence or more, make sure that it is clearly introduced and followed by a comment indicating its significance, its relevance, and/or links to the ideas which follow. Only quote an entire paragraph when the content as originally stated is key to your discussion. (For a good example of the latter, see the final section of paragraph 33 of "Cyberbullying: Myths and Realities" in Part III: The Reader. The authors quote here from a first-hand account written from the perspective of a teacher involved in implementing an anti-bullying program. This lengthy quotation supports the previous argument with a pertinent and practical example.)

11 Finally, follow the golden rule of quoting: always include more of your own words in a piece of writing than words quoted from others.

12 So, should you include direct quotations in your essays? The simple answer is "yes," but do so judiciously.

—**Suzanne James**, Lecturer, Department of English, University of British Columbia

Omitting, Adding, or Changing Material

You may omit, add, or change quoted material, but must indicate such changes to the reader.

Omitting: You may omit part of a sentence if it is irrelevant or unimportant for your purposes. To indicate an omission of one or more words in the middle of a sentence, use an **ellipsis**, which consists of three spaced dots. If you leave out all the words to the end of the sentence—and if you leave out the following sentence(s) as well—add a fourth dot, which represents the period at the end of the sentence:

> **Original:** The present thesis is that psychology, in concert with other disciplines, has an important role to play in easing the pain caused by climate change. Were this thesis widely recognised, the present article would be unnecessary. Unfortunately, the thesis is not broadly acknowledged. (Gifford, "Psychology's Essential Role in Alleviating the Impacts of Climate Change," page 351).

> **Words omitted in the middle of the first sentence:** The present thesis is that psychology . . . has an important role to play in easing the pain caused by climate change.

> **The second sentence omitted:** The present thesis is that psychology, in concert with other disciplines, has an important role to play in easing the pain caused by climate change. . . . Unfortunately, the thesis is not broadly acknowledged.

Adding and changing: If you add or change material, you need to indicate this by using *brackets* (brackets are square; parentheses are rounded). Changes can be made for grammatical, stylistic, or clarification/explanation purposes. The following examples illustrate some of the different reasons for using brackets to add or change words:

> **Grammatical (provide a needed verb):** Researchers categorically state that we cannot "[become] tolerant to steroids" (student writer Pritpal Mann).

> **Clarification (to indicate words added to original):** The Federal Plan for Gender Equality stated that "the absence of equity and access-related research [regarding the information infrastructure] is of growing concern" (Status of Women Canada 1995, par. 270) (Shade, "Missing in Action," page 235 in Part III: The Reader).

ellipsis
Three or four spaced dots in a direct quotation, indicating that one or more words have been omitted.

Table 10.1   Integration Methods

Method	What It Includes	When and How to Use It
summary	only main ideas or most important points; is in your words	when you want to refer to main idea in a paragraph, findings of a study, and similar uses; you can summarize as little as a sentence, as much as an entire article
paraphrase	all of the original in your own words, often with the structure changed	when you want to refer to important material directly relevant to your point; paraphrases are used for small but significant passages
direct quotation	words and punctuation taken directly from the source; put in quotation marks	when material is both important to your point and/or well phrased, or is difficult to paraphrase; must be integrated grammatically and clearly
mixed format	significant words from source with your own words (i.e., summary or paraphrase)	when you want to include only the most significant words, omitting the inessential; integrate words from the source grammatically and clearly with your own prose, using brackets and ellipses as required

In addition to the uses of brackets within quotations, they can also be used to indicate parentheses within parentheses, similar to the use of single quotation marks to show quotations within quotations:

> "[T]he need for population-level intervention (i.e., intervention [policy or program] operating within or outside the health sector . . .) is increasingly recognized." (Dutton et al., "A Ban on Marketing of Foods/Beverages to Children," page 297 in Part III: The Reader).

To understand the reason for the changes to the sentence above, see page 297 (the direct quotation is taken from the first sentence of "A Ban on Marketing of Foods/Beverages to Children").

Table 10.1 summarizes some of the main features of the four integration methods discussed above. Note that whatever method you use, a citation is usually required. See below for the box Seven Common Questions about Source Citation.

Documenting Your Sources

documentation style

Guidelines for documenting sources put forth in style manuals and handbooks for researchers and other academic writers.

Documenting sources serves several practical purposes: it enables a reader to distinguish between your ideas and someone else's, and it makes it possible for any reader to access the source itself to ensure its accuracy or focus on its content. Documentation formats (called **documentation styles**) provide a coherent and consistent way for scholars to communicate with other scholars (and also with student researchers, who must learn the fundamentals of documentation formats in order to use them in their essays).

Plagiarism

Plagiarism is an extremely serious academic offence. Many students approaching post-secondary study believe that plagiarism is limited to cases in which they use direct quotations and fail to cite their sources. In fact, plagiarism encompasses much more than this: you *plagiarize* if you use any material that is not your own—whether you quote directly, summarize, paraphrase, or refer to it in passing in your essay—without acknowledging it.

But it is not only lack of acknowledgement that constitutes plagiarism: you plagiarize if you use the exact words of the source and do not put them in quotation marks. Finally, you plagiarize if you follow the structure of the original too closely.

Specifically, what kind of information must be acknowledged and what does not need to be? Two principles can guide you as you consider the question. You do not need to cite anything that falls under the category of *general knowledge*. If a typical reader is likely to know something, a citation may be unnecessary. Further, if a fact or idea is *easily obtainable*, a citation may also be unnecessary. (You may be told a specific number of sources that satisfies the "easily obtainable" criterion—often three.)

Both these categories depend on your audience; for example, if you were writing for an audience that is knowledgeable about the topic, your essay would probably contain fewer citations than if you were writing for a general audience that is less knowledgeable and would probably find it difficult to trace the information. If in doubt, err on the side of caution and make the citation.

The questions in the box below about citation are often asked by students beginning research projects at university.

> Common forms of plagiarism, beyond failing to properly acknowledge a source, include using the exact words of a source without putting them in quotation marks and following the structure of the original too closely.

Seven Common Questions about Source Citation and Plagiarism

Q: Do you need to cite information that you do not quote directly in your essay?

A: Yes. Specific content requires a citation, whether you use direct quotation, paraphrase, or summary to integrate it into your essay. Even general information may necessitate a citation.

Q: If you already knew a fact and you encounter it in a secondary source, does it need to be cited?

A: Probably. The issue is not whether you know something but whether your reader would know it. If you are writing for an audience familiar with your topic, you may not need to cite "common knowledge," that is, knowledge that all or almost all readers would be expected to know. If you are uncertain about the common knowledge factor, make the citation.

Q: What about specific information, such as a date, that is easy to look up, though it may not be common knowledge?

A: A fact that is easily obtained from a number of different sources (even if a typical reader would not know it) may not need to be cited. Other factors could be involved (for example, would a typical reader know where to look?). Your instructor may be able to tell you how many sources constitute "easily obtainable" information; a minimum number often given is three (i.e., at least three common, easily accessible sources).

Q: If you use a source that you have already used earlier in the same paragraph, do you need to cite it a second time?

A: Yes, you do if another source, or your own point, has intervened. If all the content of the paragraph is from one source, you may not have to cite it until the end of the paragraph. However, always make it clear to the reader what is taken from a source.

Q: Is it necessary to cite "popular" quotations, for example, the kind that appear in dictionaries of quotations? What about dictionary definitions?

A: Yes, these kinds of quotations should be cited unless the quotation has entered everyday use. For example, consider the following two quotations: "When the going gets tough, the tough get going"; "Making your mark on the world is hard. If it were easy, everybody would do it." The first quotation would not need a citation, though the second would— even though it is unlikely a reader would know either source. (Joan W. Donaldson is the author of the first quotation; Barack Obama is the author of the second). Dictionary definitions should always be cited.

Q: Does a list of your sources on the final page of your essay mean that you do not have to cite the sources within the essay itself?

A: No. All major documentation methods require both in-text and final-page citations. (In some formats, the in-text citations consist only of numbers.)

Q: What can you do to guarantee that the question of plagiarism never arises in your essay?

A: Honesty alone may not be enough, but it is a good start. Knowledge about what needs to be and what may not need to be cited is also essential and can be learned. Finally, being conscious of "grey areas" and checking with your instructor or another expert, such as a librarian, should almost guarantee that this serious issue doesn't arise.

Note: A good strategy for avoiding plagiarism (and consciously integrating the information) is to carefully study the passage you want to use; then, close the text and write the passage from memory completely in your own words. Finally, look at the passage again, ensuring that it is different in its structure as well as in its language— and that you have accurately restated the thought behind it. Don't forget to include the citation.

Changing Words and Structure in a Paraphrase

As mentioned, when you paraphrase, try to change as much of the original wording as you can, along with the structure of the passage. The original passage below is followed by two paraphrases that are too close to the original in wording or structure. A successful paraphrase then follows.

Original passage: "The aim of the current study was to identify and link interacting patterns of positive and negative affect to academic success during the transition to adulthood." (Barker et al., "Tracking Affect and Academic Success across University," page 163 in Part III: The Reader); (26 words)

Words unchanged: This study attempted to determine and connect *interacting patterns of positive and negative affect* in those transitioning to adulthood.

Structure unchanged: This study attempted to determine the relationship between positive and negative emotions and academic achievement in those in their late adolescence.

Wording and structure changed: Defining patterns of positive and negative emotions in late adolescence and connecting them to academic achievement was the objective of this study. (22 words)

Major Documentation Styles

There are three major documentation (citation) styles but many variants on these styles. The Modern Language Association (MLA) style is used in many humanities disciplines, including English literature. The American Psychological Association (APA) style is more widely used and is the style of choice in many social science disciplines and some science disciplines, as well as in education and business. Both are parenthetical styles, meaning that a brief citation including the author's name and page number (MLA) or name and publication year (APA) follows the reference in the text of an essay. The Chicago Manual of Style (CMS) or a variant such as Turabian Style is used in history, as well as by some book publishers. Superscript (raised) numbers are placed after the in-text references; they correspond to the numbers at the bottom of the page or end of the document where full bibliographical information is given. MLA, APA, and CMS styles also require a final-page listing of sources alphabetically by last name.

Fortunately, there are an increasing number of online resources for the various documentation styles; university library sources are the most reliable. Each organization that produces the manuals also maintains websites with updates. Further, when you decide on an area of study, you will become familiar with the style used in your discipline.

Many of the distinguishing features of the styles are given below. Examples of the most common bibliographic formats are then provided.

Note: A **signal phrase** names the author before the reference is given; thus, in MLA and APA styles, the parenthetical citation will not include the author's name if a signal phrase precedes it.

Electronic formats in all styles should be cited using what information is available. If an author's name is not given, use the name of the organization or sponsoring group in its place. If there is no sponsor, use the work's title alphabetized by the first major word. Paragraph number or section heading can sometimes be used to identify location, if necessary, where page numbers are absent.

signal phrase

Introduces a reference by naming the author(s) and usually includes a "signal verb" (e.g., *states, argues, explains*).

MLA (Modern Language Association) Style

- MLA uses an "author/number" referencing format. The basic parenthetical format includes author's last name and page number with no punctuation in between:

  (Slotkin 75)
  (Rusel and Wilson 122)

- If a signal phrase is used, only the page number will be in parentheses:

  Slotkin states, ". . ." (75)

- For sources with two authors, give last names of both authors with "and" between; for three or more, give last name of first author followed by "et al."
- Block quotations should be used for important passages at least four typed lines long. They are indented 10 spaces from the left margin, double-spaced, and do not include quotation marks. The end period precedes the parenthetical citation.
- The final page, titled "Works Cited," alphabetically lists by author's last name all works used in the essay. Entries are double-spaced with the first line of each entry flush left and successive lines indented one-half inch (1.25 cm). All major words in titles begin with a capital letter. Titles of books and journals are italicized, but the titles of shorter works (such as articles or chapters) contained in larger ones are put in quotation marks.

MLA Sample Formats

Book (one author)

Begin with the author's last name and given name(s) followed by the title in italics. Conclude with publisher and publication year; you do not need to include publication place after the publisher (which is Transaction in the following example).

Berger, Arthur Asa. *Video Games: A Popular Culture Phenomenon.* Transaction, 2002.

Author   *Title*   Publication information   Electronic source

Book/Journal (multiple authors)

Only the first author's names are reversed. The edition (ed.) number is placed after the work's title as in the example below. If the source is a volume from a multi-volume work, the volume number (e.g., Vol. 2) replaces the edition number.

> Bolaria, B. Singh, and Peter S. Li. *Racial Oppression in Canada*. 2nd ed., Garamond Press, 1988.

More than three authors: Give the name of the first author, followed by a comma and "et al."

Selection in Edited Work

The page range of the selection is preceded by the abbreviation for "pages." UP is the abbreviation for University Press in the following example. Note that you must provide the page range of the entire article or chapter, even if you quote from only one or two pages.

> Wright, Austin M. "On Defining the Short Story: The Genre Question." *Short Story Theory at a Crossroads*, edited by Susan Lohafer and Jo Ellyn Clarey, Louisiana State UP, 1989, pp. 46–63.

Journal Article

Notice that commas separate publication details and that abbreviations for volume and issue numbers are used. If the season or month of publication is given (e.g., Spring, Jan.), include it before the year with no comma separating it from the year.

> Bakshy, Eytan, et al. "Exposure to Ideologically Diverse News and Opinion on Facebook." *Science*, vol. 348, no. 6239, 2015, pp. 1130–32.

Journal Article in a Database (with DOI or URL)

If a digital object identifier (DOI) is available, include it preceded by the database you used to access the article.

> Haitzinger, Nichole. "Afro-Futurism or Lament? Staging Africa(s) in Dance Today and in the 1920s." *Dance Research Journal*, vol. 49, no. 1, Apr. 2017, pp. 24–36. Project Muse, doi:10.1017/S014976771700002X.

When a digital object identifier is unavailable, use the complete URL, preceded by the database you used to access the article.

> Ishiguro, Laura. "Histories of Settler Colonialism: Considering New Currents." *BC Studies*, vol. 190, Summer 2016, pp. 5–13. ProQuest, http://search. proquest.com.ezproxy.library.uvic.ca/docview/1836867142.

Author   *Title*   Publication information   Electronic source

Website

The non-academic article was found online and includes the online publication date. The date when you accessed the site is optional, but can be included if no publication date is given or if required by your instructor.

> Zhou, Steven. "**Canada at 150: Is Common Decency the New Bar for National Pride?**" cbc News, 6 May 2017, www.cbc.ca/news/canada/manitoba/canada-immigration-refugees-common-decency-1.4101913.

Video Post

In the following example, the first date in the entry refers to the year this play was published, while the second date is that of the upload. The first date is optional unless it will be helpful for a reader.

> Synge, J. M. *Playboy of the Western World.* 1907. YouTube, uploaded by Brattleboro Community TV, 22 Nov. 2014, www.youtube.com/watch?v=tV_kYBeTatM.

Motion Picture (Film)/TV Episode

Begin with the film's title unless specific performers, director, etc. are stressed in your essay, in which case, you would begin with the relevant person's last name.

> *Alien: Covenant.* Directed by Ridley Scott, Twentieth Century Fox, 2017.

For a TV episode, begin with the episode's name (in quotation marks), followed by the series name (italicized), and season and episode number. If the movie/episode were viewed on a network, this name is italicized and is followed by a comma and the location.

> "**The Mother Line.**" *The Honourable Woman*, season 1, episode 6, Sundance TV, 4 Sept. 2014. *Netflix*, www.netflix.com/ca/title/80018058.

APA (American Psychological Association) Style

- APA uses an author–year referencing format. One basic format includes author's last name and year of publication (general references and broad summaries); the other basic format also includes page number (direct quotations, paraphrases, and summaries of specific passages).
- Commas separate author's name from year, and year from page number (if required); "p." or "pp." (for more than one page) precedes page number(s):

(Hasan et al., 2012, p. 224)
(Bryson & de Castell, 1998, pp. 542–544)

- If a signal phrase is used, the year will follow the author's name in parentheses:

Hasan et al. (2012) **explore the longer-term effects of video games.**

Author   *Title*   Publication information   Electronic source

- If a page number is required, it will be placed in parentheses after the reference:

  Hasan et al. (2012) **explain, "Contrary to what Calvin thinks, experimental studies do allow for causal inferences"** (p. 224).

  If page and paragraph numbers are absent (e.g., many websites), include in parentheses the relevant heading within quotation marks and count by paragraphs to the cited passage.

  (Cook, 2016, **"A Message to Our Customers," para. 13**)

  For two authors, give both last names with an ampersand (&) between; for three to five authors, give all last names on first mention and first author's last name followed by "et al." for subsequent references; for more than five authors, give first author's last name followed by "et al." for all references.
- Works by the same author(s) from the same year are assigned different letters (e.g., 2004a, 2004b). They are also listed this way in "References" and are ordered alphabetically by title.
- Block quotations should be used for important passages more than 40 words long. They are indented five spaces from the left margin, double-spaced, and do not include quotation marks. The end period precedes the parenthetical citation.
- The final page, titled "References," lists all works used in the essay alphabetically by author's last name; authors' initials are used instead of given names. Entries are double-spaced with the first line of each entry flush left and successive lines indented five spaces. In article and book titles, only the first letter of first words, first words following colons, and proper nouns, along with all letters in acronyms, are capitalized.

APA Sample Formats

Book (one author)

Begin with the author's last name and initial(s) followed by the publication years in parentheses. Conclude with the place of publication and publisher.

Heyd, D. (1992). *Genetics: Moral issues in the creation of people.* Berkeley, CA: University of California Press.

Book/Journal (multiple authors)

All authors' names are reversed, with an ampersand before the last author's name.

Sahalein, R., & Tuttle, D. (1997). Creatine: Nature's muscle builder. Garden City Park, NY: Avery Publishing Group.

Three to seven authors: List all names.
More than seven authors: List the first six names followed by three points of ellipsis and the last author's name.

Author   *Title*   Publication information   Electronic source

Selection in Edited Work

The article title is followed by "In" and the names of editor(s) with the abbreviation "Ed." or "Eds." preceding the work's title in italics. The page range of the article follows in parentheses preceded by "pp." Note also that article titles are not in quotation marks.

> Chesney-Lind, M. & Brown, M. (1999). **Girls and violence: An overview.** In D. Flannery & C. R. Huff (Eds.), *Youth violence: Prevention, intervention and social policy* (pp. 171–199). Washington, D.C.: American Psychiatric Press.

Journal Article

The article title is followed by the journal name (italicized). The volume number is also in italics and is followed by the issue number if each issue begins with a page 1 (rather than continuing the page numbering from the previous issue). Note that there is no space between the volume and issue numbers and that the issue number is placed in parenthesis and not italicized.

> Clegg, S., Mayfield, W., & Trayhurn, D. (1999). **Disciplinary discourses: A case study of gender in information technology and design courses.** *Gender and Education, 11*(1), 43–55.

Journal Article in a Database (with DOI or URL)

If it is available for print and electronic articles, include the DOI (digital object identifier) as the last item; it is not followed by a period. Use the prefix http://dx.doi.org/ before the DOI.

> Skegg, K., Nada-Raja, S., Dickson, N., Paul, C., & Williams, S. (2003). **Sexual orientation and self-harm in men and women.** *The American Journal of Psychiatry, 160*(3), 541–546. http://dx.doi.org/10.1176/appi.ajp.160.3.541

If no DOI is available, use the home page of the journal in its place preceded by "Retrieved from."

> Barlas, S. (2017). **New user fee agreements aim at ensuring relief from high drug prices.** *P&T, 42*(5), 312–315. Retrieved from https://www.ptcommunity.com/

Website

A general reference to a website requires only an in-text citation. If there is no author, provide the title (or abbreviated form) in its place. If your reference is specific, it requires a listing on the References page. Conclude with the URL preceded by "Retrieved from."

> Kessler, S. (2017, May 7). **Algorithms are failing Facebook. Can humanity save it?** *Quartz.* Retrieved from https://qz.com/977297/facebook-live-murders-algorithms-are-failing-facebook-can-humanity-save-it/

Online Post

Begin with the name of the creator of the post and their screen name (if different) in parentheses. In the following example, only the screen name of the poster is known (Martian Archaeology).

Author   *Title*   Publication information   Electronic source

Identify the format type in brackets (e.g., video post, weblog) and conclude with the URL preceded by "Retrieved from."

> Martian Archaeology. (2016, November 21). *This is Mars 2017* [Video file]. Retrieved from https://www.youtube.com/watch?v=sWuUSX86390

Government Report (Corporate Author) Accessed Online

Reports are treated like books. If the report has an individual author, begin with that name; sometimes, however, a government department or branch acts as a group author which should be listed in the place of the individual name(s). Give the report or series number in parentheses if available and conclude with the URL preceded by "Retrieved from." Print format would conclude with place of publication and publisher (use "Author" if same as group author).

> Public Health Agency of Canada. (2011). *Family violence in Canada: A statistical profile* (Catalogue number: 85–224-X). Retrieved from www.statcan.gc.ca/pub/85-224-x/85-224-x2010000-eng.pdf

Motion Picture (Film)

Begin with the names of the producer and the director with "Motion picture" following the work's title in brackets. Conclude with the country of origin and the studio/distributor.

> Mac, D. (Producer), & Mac, D. & MacDougall, I (Directors). (2017). *Heel Kick* [Motion picture]. Canada: Rebel Arcade.

TV Episode

Begin with the names of the writer and the director with "Television series" if referring to the entire series or "Television series episode" if a specific episode. Conclude by naming the executive producer of the series and name of series, along with the place and the studio/distributor.

> Benioff, D., & Weiss, D. B. (Writers), & Sapochnik, M. (Director). (2016). *The winds of winter* [Television series episode]. In D. Benioff [Executive producer], *Game of Thrones*. New York, NY: HBO.

If there are more than one executive producers, as is often the case with high-budget series, give the names of all up to six. For more than six, give the first name only plus "et al."

CMS (Chicago Manual of Style) Style

- CMS uses the "note" referencing format with numbered footnotes (at the bottom of the page) or endnotes (at the end of the text) corresponding to superscript numbers in the text of the essay. Each entry is single-spaced with the first line indented five spaces and successive lines flush left.
- Full bibliographic details are given for first references, beginning with author's first name(s), followed by surname, work's title, and (in parentheses) place of publication,

---

Author   *Title*   Publication information   Electronic source

publisher, and date, and ending with page number(s). For example, the text may look like this:

In *To the Ends of the Earth,* historian T. M. Devine explains that "the myth of the successful Scot was partly built up in opposition to the racial stereotype of the supposedly inadequate Irish."[15]

The corresponding note would look like this:

15. T.M. Devine, *To the Ends of the Earth: Scottish Global Diaspora 1750–2010* (Washington, D.C.: Smithsonian Books, 2011), 150.

Successive references to the same source are condensed forms of the first citation:

18. Devine, *To the Ends of the Earth,* 129.

Consecutive references to the same work and page look like this:

19. Ibid.

(the page number would follow if it differs from the preceding note)

- Block quotations should be used for important passages at least four typed lines long. They are indented five spaces from the left margin, single-spaced, and do not include quotation marks. The end period precedes the parenthetical citation.
- On the final page, titled "Bibliography," entries are listed alphabetically by author's last name. Entries are single-spaced with double-spacing between them; the first line is flush left, and successive lines are indented five spaces.

CMS Sample Formats

Book (one author)

Note: The note begins with the author's full name in non-reversed order with a comma separating it from the title (italicized). Publication information is in parentheses with page number outside the parentheses.

1. Alistair Horne, *Hubris: The Tragedy of War in the Twentieth Century* (New York: Harper, 2015), 64.

Bibliography: The bibliographic entry provides the same information as the note in a different format.

Horne, Alistair. *Hubris: The Tragedy of War in the Twentieth Century.* New York: Harper, 2015.

Author   *Title*   Publication information   Electronic source

Book/Journal (multiple authors)

Note: Include all authors up to three. For four or more authors, give the name of the first author plus "and others" or "et al."

> **2.** Bob Beal and Rod Macleod, *Prairie Fire: The 1885 North-West Rebellion* (Edmonton: Hurtig Publishers, 1984), 104.

Bibliography: Only the name of the first author is reversed. For more than three authors, name all.

> Beal, Bob, and Rod Macleod. *Prairie Fire: The 1885 North-West Rebellion.* Edmonton: Hurtig Publishers, 1984.

Selection in Edited Work

Note: Begin with the relevant author and the selection, followed by a comma and "in" followed by the title of the volume in italics. The page(s) in the note refer only to what is being quoted or paraphrased in the text.

> **3.** Marcia K. Lieberman, "'Some Day My Prince Will Come': Female Acculturation through the Fairy Tale," in *Don't Bet on the Prince*, ed. Jack Zipes and Ingrid Svendsen (New York: Routledge, 1987), 189.

*Bibliography:*The bibliographic entry provides the same information in a different format. Always include the full page range for the selection.

> Lieberman, Marcia K. "'Some Day My Prince Will Come': Female Acculturation through the Fairy Tale." In *Don't Bet on the Prince*, edited by Jack Zipes and Ingrid Svendsen, 185–200. New York: Routledge, 1987.

Journal Article

Note: The issue number is only required if each issue begins with page number 1; otherwise, the volume number is sufficient:

> **4.** Robert Garner, "Political Ideologies and the Moral Status of Animals," *Journal of Political Ideologies* 8 (2003): 235.

Bibliography: The bibliographic form repeats most of the information of the note in a slightly different format, and includes the full page range of the article.

> Garner, Robert. "Political Ideologies and the Moral Status of Animals." *Journal of Political Ideologies* 8 (2003): 233–46.

Journal Article in a Database (with DOI or URL)

Note: If the DOI is available for an electronic article, include it as the last item, followed by a period for both the note and the bibliographic entry. If there is no DOI, include a URL.

Author   *Title*   Publication information   Electronic source

4. Robert Garner, "**Political Ideologies and the Moral Status of Animals,**" *Journal of Political Ideologies* 8 (2003): 235, doi:10.1080/13569310306087.

Bibliography: The bibliographic form repeats most of the information of the note in a slightly different format, and includes the page range. The date of access of an article in a database is not usually required. If included, the access date precedes the DOI.

Garner, Robert. "**Political Ideologies and the Moral Status of Animals.**" *Journal of Political Ideologies* 8 (2003): 233–46. Accessed March 7, 2017. doi:10.1080/13569310306087.

Website

If the website article lacks a date, you should include your access date. The bibliographic entry closely resembles the note, with author first and last names reversed and with periods rather than commas separating the items.

5. Jeffrey Gottfried and Elisa Shearer, "**News Use across Social Media Platforms 2016,**" Pew Research Center, last modified 26 May 2016, http://www.journalism.org/2016/05/26/news-use-across-social-media-platforms-2016/.

Author   *Title*   Publication information   Electronic source

Sample Student Expository Research Essay

The essay below uses APA documentation style.

Student Writing Sample

Curing the Incurable: Understanding Addiction beyond the Disease Factor

by Sam Perreault

Perreault's introduction develops logically. She begins dramatically by describing an all-too-common scenario. She provides background by summarizing the previous view on the cause of addiction, using the transition *however* to introduce the direction of current research. She then expands on this statement, cites a research study, and concludes with an expanded thesis that lays out the essay's structure.

1   Imagine living in a cycle of psychological and physical suffering where coping with emotions or others' needs is unbearable, physical pain and discomfort ail the body, and without the next "hit," functioning effectively for the day is impossible. This description might typically describe some individuals who abuse psychoactive substances to lessen their long-term psychological pain. For some time, addictions professionals have been trying to answer the question, "Why do people abuse drugs?" and the answer has led to the biological model as paramount. The view of the biological model explains addiction as caused by a specific gene or permanent brain damage due to drug exposure. However, current research has been moving toward an understanding of addiction as a bio-psycho-social triad; in addition to biological factors, psychological and social influences contribute to the likelihood of an individual becoming addicted. Barlow and Durand (2015) found examples of bio-psycho-social factors that increase the risk of addiction: an individual may inherit a fast metabolism, which could increase drug tolerance; substances may be used to cope with mood disorders or anxiety; and pressures that

increase stress put one at greater risk (pp. 424–425). For a better understanding of addiction, the bio-psycho-social perspective may prove to be more effective in assessing definitions of drug addiction, incorporating psychological and social influences as causes, and devising quality treatment plans for those factors.

2   Several definitions of addiction exist, but not without disagreement (Barlow & Durand, 2015, p. 399). The 5th edition of the *Diagnostic and Statistical Manual of Mental Disorders* considers addiction as a significant disruption in areas such as employment, education, relationships, or personal safety (p. 399). When drug use notably interferes with several of these, an individual is considered addicted. Other researchers have come up with three main classifications: disease, choice, and self-medication (Lewis, 2015, p. 1). Historically, the dominant biological model in medicine and government has viewed drug addiction as a disease (p. 11), which is caused by drug exposure and results in irreversible changes in the brain (p. 1). The disease model deems the addicted patient as incurably ill.

3   In contrast, addiction as a choice and self-medication views drug abuse as a decision that seems sensible to the addict to provide short-term satisfaction or relief and exceeds other choices: drugs can relieve anxiety or increase well-being, so addicts may use drugs to self-medicate (Lewis, 2015, pp. 2–3). Khantzian, an addictions researcher, stated that addiction follows self-regulation problems, and in order to manage those issues, one copes with drugs (Fletcher, Nutton, & Brend, 2015, p. 112). Self-regulation difficulties may manifest as depression, anxiety, post-traumatic stress, or personality disorders. Individuals who struggle with these psychological states might find it very burdensome so turn to substances as a coping mechanism. Considering these alternative definitions, treating addiction solely on the basis of biological causes may limit a full account of the influences that contribute to drug abuse. Incorporating the bio-psycho-social approach may result in a greater appreciation for the causes of addiction.

4   What explanations could account for addiction if it is not caused by a specific gene and not due to permanent brain damage from drug exposure? Some specialists have uncovered common experiences in the lives of many addicts: (1) poor infant and caregiver attachment bonding, (2) underdeveloped neurotransmitter systems, and (3) high scores on the Adverse Childhood Experiences Scale (ACEs). Some forms of ACEs include family alcoholism; sexual, emotional, and physical abuse; and severe parental depression (Lewis, 2015, p. 178). A failure to form healthy attachments and experiencing ACEs are hypothesized to be factors in the underdevelopment of the neurotransmitter system; all of these are connected and increase the likelihood of addiction.

5   Firstly, if infants learn that their caregiver's attention is unpredictable or harmful, they may form unstable attachments to him or her; as a result, normal coping mechanisms cannot develop for self-regulation and the infant may be insecure, dismissing, and fearful of others (Fletcher et al, 2015, p. 111). Human beings have a fundamental need to belong and connect with others, but when attachments are impaired and there is no comfort from social bonding, one might discover the psychological comfort of drugs (p. 114) as a replacement for damaged relationships. Additionally, through caregiver neglect in childhood, a child may develop a sense of helplessness because his or her basic needs had not been met, resulting in uncontrollable feelings of powerlessness and the decision later in life to use drugs to reclaim personal control (Dodes, 2009, p. 382). Thus, "a cycle of addiction is set in motion" (Fletcher et al., p. 114).

6   Secondly, current research has shown that early childhood deprivation affects the brain by preventing certain structures and systems from fully developing. A disruption in attachment bonding in infancy may affect the brain's biochemical structures, leading one to be less resilient to stressors and increase one's vulnerability to the positive outcomes of drugs (Maté, 2012, p. 58).

The topic of the first body paragraph corresponds to the first topic in Perreault's expanded thesis.

Perreault uses a question prompt to direct the reader to more important information in this paragraph. In the successive three paragraphs, she numbers her points to create coherence before using a question again in paragraph 8 as her first sentence.

Although some of her paragraphs are short, they are nonetheless sufficiently developed.

In the first reference to this source, all authors were named. In subsequent references, the first author's name + "et al." is used. If the source is used again in the same paragraph, the year can be dropped (see the last sentence).

Perreault effectively summarizes Dodes's explanation, but uses a short direct quotation to stress the ongoing nature of addiction, making an effective paragraph conclusion.

Comparably, the development of a normal neurotransmitter system requires attachment that is of sufficient quality and quantity, whereas the lack of that contact heightens one's vulnerability to "needing drugs … to supplement what the brain is lacking" (p. 57).

Unneeded words have been left out of this sentence, as indicated by an ellipsis.

7   Thirdly, it makes sense that ACEs may increase the likelihood of drug abuse since social attachment and brain development seem to play a crucial role in addiction. Correlational studies found greater instances of drug abuse when one's ACE score was high, meaning that an individual had several significant childhood experiences that were traumatizing and also abused drugs. An individual's high ACE score can predict a 500% increase in likelihood of alcoholism and a 4600% higher occurrence of intravenous drug use compared to control groups with low or no ACE score (Lewis, 2015, p. 179). Correspondingly, Maté (2012) proposed that ACES might affect one's psychological capability for responding to stress throughout the rest of one's life: how one responds to stress increases one's vulnerability to abuse drugs (p. 60). The trauma of ACEs, and poor regulation of the emotions and stress resulting from ACES, may cause an individual to seek psychological relief through drugs.

8   If some addicts abuse drugs to cope with emotions, then how do professionals treat drug abuse as a symptom of psychological suffering? If drug abuse is perceived as a disease, then professionals treat an addict as incurable (Lewis, 2015, p. 110). The disease model allows no room for treatment development and leaves the sufferers hopeless, but when addiction is perceived as a choice, the individual has the capacity to change his or her outlook on drug abuse (pp. 3–4). Changing one's perspectives can be accomplished through Cognitive Behavioral Therapy (CBT) or Motivation Interviewing (MI). CBT helps to change the problematic thinking that contributes to drug use and the recovery outcomes have proved to be beneficial, whereas MI's goal is to alter one's indecisiveness about changing drug use (Fletcher et al., 2015, p. 110) because the willingness to change may be the first challenge toward overcoming addiction. However, although these treatments can be effective, they only help a small percentage of the population, leaving many addicts still suffering. The problem with CBT and MI is that treatment is short-term and the focus is on the symptoms and behaviours of drug abuse; this approach may prove insufficient since many addicts revert to drug abuse, especially in times of stress, and may continue the abuse for long periods of time (Fletcher et al., p. 110). Exclusively treating the symptoms and behaviours may not be enough to keep one away from drugs long-term to establish new behaviours. Perhaps addiction is deeper rooted in the psyche and involves emotional issues that require extensive and intense therapy.

The writer uses a question to introduce her third topic. Unlike most of the first sentences in her body paragraphs, here the topic sentence occurs later in the paragraph (highlighted).

Here the writer uses a prompt to direct the reader to the main idea in the next paragraph.

9   Attachment focused treatment may be effective as it targets the client's social development history that influenced drug abuse because addiction is a search for the connection that was disrupted by poor social bonding (Fletcher et al., 2015, p. 112). This treatment could bring professionals to a fuller understanding of addiction; it addresses interpersonal relationships relative to the addict's drug use by building safe and rewarding relationships to replace the comfort found in drugs (p. 112). Bruce K. Alexander's research supports the reasoning behind attachment focused treatment in the studies of "Rat Park": when rats were caged in isolation, with nothing but a choice between pure water or morphine water, the rats would always drink the morphine water; when the same addicted rats were placed in cages with other rats, they refrained from drinking the morphine water and only drank pure water; that is, social bonding provided enough fulfillment to keep an addicted rat away from taking the drug (Lewis, 2015, p. 21). This study showed that once rats were placed with others to socialize, drug use stopped. Perhaps the same result could occur in humans when one replaces drug abuse with rewarding relationships.

Perreault's phrasing suggests that the experiment described in this paragraph is promising, though speculative.

10   A worthwhile approach to advance could be one that includes social attachment disruptions and ACES as legitimate causes that lead to addiction. Calling it a disease may undermine one's recovery, resulting in more emotional damage and increasing the likelihood of relapse (Lewis, 2015, p. 9). Lewis reports that Miller was able to predict an addict's relapse by the degree in which he or she believed that addiction is a disease, but if the addict did not believe the condition was incurable, recovery rates increased (p. 10). There is hope, and with the courage to examine one's mind and work hard, one can build self-efficacy and recover indefinitely; self-empowerment is a useful tool for long-term recovery (p. 10). Addiction is not going away, and people will continue to use drugs, especially as a way to cope with life difficulties. Researchers ought to expand their treatment methods to the bio-psycho-social approach in an attempt to decrease the suffering addicted people face by considering the psychological and environmental influences more seriously.

> Although students may be told not to introduce a new point in their conclusion, here it contributes to the hopeful tone the writer wants to establish.

> Perreault ends her essay with a brief recommendation in light of conclusions based on her research.

References

Barlow, H. D., & Durand, V. M. (2015). *Abnormal psychology: An integrative approach*. Delhi, India: Cengage Learning.

Dodes, M. L. (2009). Addiction as a psychological symptom. *Psychodynamic Practice, 15*(4), 381–393. http://dx.doi.org/10.1080/14753630903230468

Fletcher, K., Nutton, J., & Brend, D. (2015). Attachment, a matter of substance: The potential of attachment theory in the treatment of addictions. *Clinical Social Work Journal, 43*(1), 109–117. http://dx.doi.org/10.1007/s10615-014-0502-5

Lewis, M. (2015). *The biology of desire: Why addiction is not a disease*. New York, N.Y.: PublicAffairs. Retrieved from http://www.eblib.com

Maté, G. (2012). Addiction: Childhood trauma, stress and the biology of addiction. *Journal of Restorative Medicine, 1*(1), 56–63. https://dx.doi.org/10.14200/jrm.2012.1.1005

> As Perreault discusses a new approach to addiction research, it is appropriate that she uses mostly current sources.

> Perreault uses the format for an online book that was also published in print format.

PART III

The Reader

University Issues

Academic Language and the Challenge of Reading for Learning about Science

Catherine E. Snow

(2,409 words)

Pre-reading

1. What are your perceptions of or associations with "academic language" or "academic reading"? Write down some of these perceptions in point or bulleted form. Where do your perceptions come from (e.g., high school classes, university instructors, textbooks, general knowledge)? As a pre-reading activity, you could exchange your list with another person's and discuss some of the similarities and differences.

1　A major challenge to students learning science is the academic language in which science is written. Academic language is designed to be concise, precise, and authoritative. To achieve these goals, it uses sophisticated words and complex grammatical constructions that can disrupt reading comprehension and block learning. Students need help in learning academic vocabulary and how to process academic language if they are to become independent learners of science.

2　Literacy scholars and secondary teachers alike are puzzled by the frequency with which students who read words accurately and fluently have trouble comprehending text (1, 2). Such students have mastered what was traditionally considered the major obstacle to reading success: the depth and complexity of the English spelling system. But many middle- and high-school students are less able to convert their word-reading skills into comprehension when confronted with texts in science (or math or social studies) than they are when confronted with texts of fiction or discursive essays. The greater difficulty of science, math, and social studies texts than of texts encountered in English language arts (mostly narratives) suggests that the comprehension of "academic language" may be one source of the challenge. So what is academic language?

3　Academic language is one of the terms [others include language of education (3), language of schooling (4), scientific language (5), and academic English (6, 7)] used to refer to the form of language expected in contexts such as the exposition of topics in the school curriculum, making

arguments, defending propositions, and synthesizing information. There is no exact boundary when defining academic language; it falls toward one end of a continuum (defined by formality of tone, complexity of content, and degree of impersonality of stance), with informal, casual, conversational language at the other extreme. There is also no single academic language, just as there is no single variety of educated American English. Academic language features vary as a function of discipline, topic, and mode (written versus oral, for example), but there are certain common characteristics that distinguish highly academic from less academic or more conversational language and that make academic language—even well-written, carefully constructed, and professionally edited academic language—difficult to comprehend and even harder to produce (8).

4　Among the most commonly noted features of academic language are conciseness, achieved by avoiding redundancy; using a high density of information-bearing words, ensuring precision of expression; and relying on grammatical processes to compress complex ideas into few words (8, 9). Less academic language, on the other hand, such as that used in emails, resembles oral language forms more closely: Most sentences begin with pronouns or animate subjects; verbs refer to actions rather than relations; and long sentences are characterized by sequencing of information rather than embeddings. The two excerpts in Fig. 1, both about torque (a topic included in many state standards for seventh grade science), display the difference between a nonacademic

---

Source: From *Science*, vol. 328, no. 5977, pp. 450–2. Reprinted with permission from AAAS.

text (from the website www.lowrider.com) and an academic text (from the website www.tutorvista.com).

5   A striking difference between more informal and more academic language exemplified in the Lowrider/TutorVista text comparison is the greater presence of expressive, involved, interpersonal stance markers in the first Lowrider posting (". . . guys get caught up . . . ," "I frequently get asked . . . ," "Most of us . . . ,") and in the response ("Jason you are right on bro"). Though both the Lowrider authors are writing to inform, they are not assuming the impersonal authoritative voice that is characteristic of academic language. They claim their authority to provide information about the advantage of torque over horsepower adjustments on the basis of personal experience. The scientist's authoritative stance, on the other hand, derives from membership in a community committed to a shared epistemology; this stance is expressed through a reduction in the use of personal pronouns, a preference for epistemically warranted evaluations (such as "rigorous study" and "questionable analysis") over personally expressive evaluations (such as "great study" and "funky analysis"), and a focus on general rather than specific claims. Maintaining the impersonal authoritative stance creates a distanced tone that is often puzzling to adolescent readers and is extremely difficult for adolescents to emulate in writing.

6   Perhaps the simplest basis for comparing the Lowrider and TutorVista texts is to consider how rare in other contexts are the words they use most frequently. The rarest words used in the Lowrider text are the special term "lolo" and its alternative form "lowrider," "upgrade," "carb," "HP," "exhaust," "spin," and "torque." Only two words from the Academic Word List (10), a list of words used frequently across academic texts of different disciplines, appear in this passage. The TutorVista text rare words include "magnitude," "perpendicular," "lever," "pivot," "hinge," "fulcrum," and "torque," and it uses the academic words "task," "maximum," "significance," and "illustration." The difference in word selection reflects the convention in the more academic text of presenting precise information in a dense, concise manner.

7   Nominalizations are a grammatical process of converting entire sentences (such as "Gutenberg invented the printing press") into phrases that can then be embedded in other sentences (such as "Gutenberg's invention of the printing press revolutionized the dissemination of information"). Nominalizations are crucial to the conciseness expected in academic language. In the TutorVista sentence "We may increase the turning effect of the force by changing the point of application of force and by changing the direction of force," "application" and "direction" are nominalizations representing entire propositions. "Application" is shorthand for "where we apply," and "direction" is shorthand for "how we direct." Thus, although this sentence has the same apparent structure as "We can get a smile from a baby by changing his diaper and by patting his back," the processing load is much higher. "Increase" in the original sentence is a verb referring to a relation between two quantities, whereas "get" in the baby-sentence adaptation refers to an action or effect in the real world. "Diaper" and "back" are physical entities subjected to actions, whereas "application" and "direction" are themselves actions that have been turned into nouns. Part of the complexity of academic language derives from the fact that we use the syntactic structures acquired for talking about agents and actions to talk about entities and relations, without recognizing the challenge that that transition poses to the reader. In particular, in science classes we may expect students to process these sentences without explicit instruction in their structure.

8   Science teachers are not generally well prepared to help their students penetrate the linguistic puzzles that science texts present. They of course recognize that teaching vocabulary is key, but typically focus on the science vocabulary (the bolded words in the text), often without recognizing that those bolded words are defined with general-purpose academic words that students also do not know. Consider the TutorVista definition of torque: "Torque is the product of the magnitude of the force and the lever arm of the force." Many seventh graders are unfamiliar with the terms "magnitude" and "lever"; and some proportion will think they understand "product," "force," and "arm" without realizing that those terms are being used in technical, academic ways here, with meanings quite different from those of daily life. Yet this definition, with its sophisticated and unfamiliar word meanings, is the basis for all the rest of the TutorVista exposition: the trade-off between magnitude and direction of force.

9   Efforts to help students understand science cannot ignore their need to understand the words used to write and talk about science: the all-purpose academic words as well as the discipline-specific ones. Of course some students acquire academic vocabulary on their own, if they read widely and if their comprehension skills are strong enough to support inferences about the meaning of unknown words (11). The fact that many adolescents prefer reading Web sites to books (12), however, somewhat decreases access to good models of academic language even

From www.lowrider.com/forums/10-Under-the-Hood/topics/183-HP-vs-torque/posts (spelling as in the original posting)

Often times guys get caught up in the hype of having a big HP motor in their lolo. I frequently get asked whats the best way to get big numbers out of their small block. The answer is not HP, but torque. "You sell HP, you feel torque" as the old saying goes. Most of us are running 155/80/13 tires on our lolo's. Even if you had big HP numbers, you will *never* get that power to the ground, at least off the line. I have a 64 Impala SS 409, that i built the motor in. While it is a completely restored original (I drive it rolling on 14" 72 spoke cross laced Zeniths), the motor internals are not. It now displaces 420 CI, with forged pistons and blalanced rotating assembly. The intake, carb and exhaust had to remain OEM for originality's sake, and that greatly reduces the motors potential. Anyway, even with the original 2 speed powerglide, it spins those tires with alarming ease, up to 50 miles per hour!

In my 62, I built a nice 383 out of an 86 Corvette. I built it for good bottom end pull, since it is a lowrider with 8 batteries. And since it rides on the obligitory 13's, torque is what that car needs. It pulls like an ox right from idle, all the way up to its modest 5500 redline. But I never take it that high, as all the best power is from 1100 to 2700 RPM.

So when considering an engine upgrade, look for modifications that improve torque. That is what your lolo needs!

Posted by Jason Dave, Sept 2009

Jason you are right on bro. I have always found an increase in torque placement has not only provided better top end performance but also improved gas mileage in this expensive gas times.

Posted by Gabriel Salazar, Nov 2009

Figure 1   Examples of nonacademic text (Lowrider, above) and academic text (TutorVista, right).

for those interested in technical topics. Thus, they have few opportunities to learn the academic vocabulary that is crucial across their content-area learning. It is also possible to explicitly teach academic vocabulary to middle-school students. Word Generation is a middle-school program developed by the Strategic Education Research Partnership that embeds all-purpose academic words in interesting topics and provides activities for use in math, science, and social studies as well as English language arts classes in which the target words are used (see the website for examples) (13). Among the academic words taught in Word Generation are those used to make, assess, and defend claims, such as "data," "hypothesis," "affirm,"

"convince," "disprove," and "interpret." We designed Word Generation to focus on dilemmas, because these promote discussion and debate and provide motivating contexts for students and teachers to use the target words. For example, one week is devoted to the topic of whether junk food should be banned from schools, and another to whether physician-assisted suicide should be legal. Discussion is in itself a key contributor to science learning (14) and to reading comprehension (15, 16). Words learned through explicit teaching are unlikely to be retained if they are taught in lists rather than embedded in meaningful texts and if opportunities to use them in discussion, debate, and writing are not provided.

From www.tutorvista.com/content/physics/physics-iii/rigid-body/torque.php

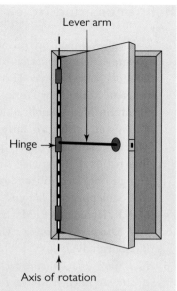

Torque is the product of the magnitude of the force and the lever arm of the force.

What is the significance of this concept in our everyday life?

Dependence of torque on lever arm

To increase the turning effect of force, it is not necessary to increase the magnitude of the force itself. We may increase the turning effect of the force by changing the point of application of force and by changing the direction of force.

Let us take the case of a heavy door. If a force is applied at a point, which is close to the hinges of the door, we may find it quite difficult to open or close the door. However, if the same force is applied at a point, which is at the maximum distance from hinges, we can easily close or open the door. The task is made easier if the force is applied at right angles to the plane of the door.

When we apply the force the door turns on its hinges. Thus a turning effect is produced when we try to open the door. Have you ever tried to do so by applying the force near the hinge? In the first case, we are able to open the door with ease. In the second case, we have to apply much more force to cause the same turning effect. What is the reason?

The turning effect produced by a force on a rigid body about a point, pivot or fulcrum is called the moment of a force or torque. It is measured by the product of the force and the perpendicular distance of the pivot from the line of action of the force.

Moment of a force = Force x Perpendicular distance of the pivot from the force.

The unit of moment of force is newton metre (N m). In the above example, in the first case the perpendicular distance of the line of action of the force from the hinge is much more than that in the second case. Hence, in the second case to open the door, we have to apply greater force.

10   It is unrealistic to expect all middle- or high-school students to become proficient producers of academic language. Many graduate students still struggle to manage the authoritative stance, and the self-presentation as an expert that justifies it, in their writing. And it is important to note that not all features associated with the academic writing style (such as the use of passive voice, impenetrability of prose constructions, and indifference to literary niceties) are desirable. But the central features of academic language—grammatical embeddings, sophisticated and abstract vocabulary, precision of word choice, and use of nominalizations to refer to complex processes—reflect the need to present complicated ideas in efficient ways. Students must be able to read texts that use these features if they are to become independent learners of science or social studies. They must have access to the all-purpose academic vocabulary that is used to talk about knowledge and that they will need to use in making their own arguments and evaluating others' arguments. Mechanisms for teaching those words and the ways that scientists use them should be a part of the science curriculum. Collaborations between designers of science curricula and literacy scholars are needed to develop and evaluate methods for helping students master the language of science at the undergraduate and high-school levels as well as at the middle-school level that Word Generation is currently serving.

References and Notes

1. Carnegie Council on Advancing Adolescent Literacy, *Time to Act: An Agenda for Advancing Adolescent Literacy for College and Career Success* (Carnegie Corporation of New York, New York, 2010); http://carnegie.org/fileadmin/Media/Publications/PDF/tta_Main.pdf.

2. J. Johnson, L. Martin-Hansen, Sci. Scope **28**, 12 (2005).

3. M.A.K. Halliday, paper presented at the Annual International Language in Education Conference, Hong Kong, December 1993.

4. M.J. Schleppegrell, *Linguist. Educ.* **12**, 431 (2001).

5. M.A.K. Halliday, J.R. Martin, *Writing Science: Literacy and Discursive Power* (Univ. of Pittsburgh Press, Pittsburgh, PA, 1993).

6. A. Bailey, *The Language Demands of School: Putting Academic English to the Test* (Yale Univ. Press, New Haven, CT, 2007).

7. R. Scarcella, *Academic English: A Conceptual Framework* (Technical Report 2003-1, Univ. of California Linguistic Minority Research Institute, Irvine, CA, 2003).

8. C. Snow, P. Uccelli, in *The Cambridge Handbook of Literacy*, D. Olson, N. Torrance, Eds. (Cambridge Univ. Press, New York, 2008), pp. 112–133.

9. Z. Fang, *Int. J. Sci. Educ.* **28**, 491 (2006).

10. A. Coxhead, *TESOL Q.* **34**, 213 (2000).

11. J. Lawrence, *Read. Psychol.* **30**, 445 (2009).

12. E.B. Moje, M. Overby, N. Tysvaer, K. Morris, *Harv. Educ. Rev.* **78**, 107 (2008).

13. C. Snow, J. Lawrence, C. White, J. *Res. Educ. Effectiveness* **2**, 325 (2009); www.wordgeneration.org.

14. J. Osborne, *Science* **328**, 463 (2010).

15. J. Lawrence, C. Snow, in *Handbook of Reading Research IV*, P.D. Pearson, M. Kamil., E. Moje, P. Afflerbach, Eds. (Routledge Education, London, 2010).

16. P.K. Murphy, I.A.G. Wilkinson, A.O. Soter, M.N. Hennessey, J.F. Alexander, J. *Educ. Psychol.* **62**, 387 (2009).

17. Preparation of this paper was made possible by collaborations supported by the Strategic Education Research Partnership and research funded by the Spencer Foundation, the William and Flora Hewlett Foundation, the Carnegie Corporation of New York, and the Institute for Education Sciences through the Council of Great City Schools. Thanks also to www.TutorVista.com for permission to reprint their lesson on torque.

Key and challenging words

discursive, proposition, redundancy, animate (adj), epistemology, emulate, syntactic, proficient, impenetrability

Questions

1. In your own words, explain the problem discussed in paragraph 1.

2. (a) Why do you think the author believes that narrative texts are less difficult for high school students to understand than those in the sciences or social studies? (b) Are narratives, such as novels, the only kinds of texts studied in English language arts?

3. How does academic language differ from non-academic (informal) language? Give two examples of everyday writing situations in which you would use non-academic language.

4. What is the function of the two excerpts in Figure 1? How would you describe a typical reader of each excerpt? How could audience and purpose affect the way both excerpts are written?

5. Several phrases in this article demonstrate "a high density of information-bearing words" (paragraph 4). Using a dictionary if necessary, explain in your own words the meaning of one of the following phrases from paragraph 5: "epistemically warranted evaluations"; "impersonal authoritative stance."

6. (a) In your own words, define *nominalization* (paragraph 7); (b) Change the following verbs into nouns that could be embedded in a sentence (e.g., *classify* [verb] → *classification* [noun: how we classify]): associate, combine, observe.

7. Explain why putting all your effort into learning the meanings of bolded terms in textbooks might be of limited usefulness. What else can be done to make comprehension of academic language easier?

8. Why might it be particularly important to address the issue of academic language at the middle-school level?

Post-reading

1. Find an encyclopedia entry of at least 200 words on one topic and a comparable entry from the Internet, ensuring that the Internet entry is not from an educational or similar authoritative source. Using the same criteria as discussed in "Academic Language and the Challenge of Reading for Learning about Science," compare the entries, noting the kinds of detail referred to in paragraphs 4–5.
2. Write a paragraph in informal (non-academic) prose that explains a topic you're knowledgeable about. Rewrite the paragraph in academic language. Use the guidelines given in paragraph 3. For example, you can use a "chatty" tone and first- and second-person pronouns in the non-academic example but an impersonal tone and nouns originating as verbs (nominalizations) in the academic example.

3. The following are verbs from the Academic Word List (see paragraph 6). Change five verbs below into corresponding nouns and use each in a sentence on a topic you're interested in (e.g., identify → *identification*. The use of DNA identification to establish guilt in a criminal case has been subjected to recent legal challenges.).

acquire	estimate
assume	interpret
compute	regulate
conclude	specify
define	vary

Tracking Affect and Academic Success across University: Happy Students Benefit from Bouts of Negative Mood

Erin T. Barker, Nancy L. Galambos, Andrea L. Howard, and Carsten Wrosch
(4,898 words)

Pre-reading

1. After reading the authors' brief abstract (see Chapter 2 for information about abstracts), match the sentences in the abstract with the corresponding division typically represented in articles in the sciences (i.e., Introduction, Method, Results, and Discussion).
2. Reflect on your expectations coming into college/university. What are/were your academic goals? What specific academic challenges do/did you believe you have/had to overcome in order to pursue a successful academic career?

Abstract

We examined how positive and negative affect covary within individuals over time and how patterns of association between affective traits and states relate to academic success across 4 years of university. Participants were 187 full-time first-year students at a large Canadian university who completed questionnaires about recent affective experiences in 6 waves across 4 years. Grade point average for each year of study was provided by the registrar's office. Our analysis identified an adaptive pattern characterized by the maintenance of high positive affect ("chronic happiness") and the co-occurrence of time-limited bouts of negative affect. Our results are consistent with findings

Source: From *Developmental Psychology*, vol. 52, no. 12, 2016, pp. 2022–30. Copyright © 2016, American Psychological Association.

showing productive consequences of experiencing positive and negative affect in tandem and the development of emotion regulation capacity across the transition to adulthood.

———

1   In their developmental account, Diamond and Aspinwall (2003) define emotion regulation capacity as the ability to flexibly coactivate, coordinate, and direct (i.e., manage) emotional states toward goals that arise within particular developmental contexts. In the current study we examine how positive and negative affective traits and states interact and predict academic success during the transition to adulthood. Patterns or combinations of positive and negative affect that are linked to academic success should reflect adaptive emotion regulation capacity.

2   In the developmental literature most research on emotion regulation capacity emphasizes either early or late periods of the life course (Diamond & Aspinwall, 2003). For example, across infancy and early childhood, research highlights the role of parents in supporting the development of adaptive emotion regulation skills that lead to later prosocial outcomes (e.g., Spinrad et al., 2006). At the other end of the life course, research has focused on the implications of age-related changes in emotional experience (e.g., emotional reactivity or functions) for social relationships in midlife and old age (e.g., Charles, Piazza, Luong, & Almeida, 2009; Kunzmann, Kappes, & Wrosch, 2014). Although there is a large literature on the regulation of negative emotions and particularly depressive symptoms during adolescence and the transition to adulthood (e.g., Burwell & Shirk, 2007; Silk, Steinberg, & Morris, 2003; Zimmermann, & Iwanski, 2014), fewer studies have examined emotion regulation capacity more generally across this period.

3   The transition to adulthood places high demands on individual emotion regulation capacity; adolescents are required to move from a position of dependence on one's family of origin to a position of self-reliance and adult forms of interdependence (Carstensen, Isaacowitz, & Charles, 1999; Tanner, 2006). Increased cognitive control and associated maturation of the prefrontal cortex between adolescence and the mid-20s support adaptive emotion regulation, and emotional well-being tends to improve (Riediger & Klipker, 2014). For example, on average, positive affect increases (Ross & Mirowsky, 2008) and negative affect decreases (Galambos, Barker, & Krahn, 2006) from the late teens into the 20s. Likewise, normative patterns of personality development reflect gains in emotion regulation capacity. These include increases in conscientiousness, agreeableness, and emotional intelligence and decreases in neuroticism (Parker, Saklofske, Wood, Eastabrook, & Taylor, 2005; Soto, John, Gosling, & Potter, 2011).

4   Many adolescents in Western countries initiate the transition to adulthood at college or university (Bureau of Labor Statistics, 2014; Galarneau, Marissette, & Usalcas, 2013), which usually involves goals for academic achievement. Academic success (Parker, Summerfeldt, Hogan, & Majeski, 2004) and student retention (Parker, Hogan, Eastabrook, Oke, & Wood, 2006) are predicted by improvements in university students' capacity to manage their emotional experiences. Furthermore, academic success is enhanced in students who are capable of experiencing positive emotional states related to academic achievement goals (positive academic emotions, Pekrun, Elliot, & Maier, 2009) and related to student engagement (e.g., vigor and dedication, Schaufeli, Martínez, Pinto, Salanova, & Bakker, 2002). Indeed, when positive affect is actively valenced and high in approach motivation (e.g., energetic), attentional resources narrow in on goal-relevant information, which can contribute more generally to success (Harmon-Jones, Gable, & Price, 2013).

5   Positive emotions also contribute to successful outcomes by broadening and building behavioral and psychological resources (e.g., coping resources; Fredrickson, 2001). In the university context, positive emotions contribute to gains in academic self-efficacy (Ouweneel, Le Blanc, & Schaufeli, 2011) and are associated with perceptions of high control (Goetz, Frenzel, Stoeger, & Hall, 2010), both of which have a strong relation to grade point average (GPA; see meta-analysis by Richardson, Abraham, & Bond, 2012). Thus, students who are able to manage their emotions to maintain high levels of positive affect during university may be building broad psychological resources such as agency and self-efficacy along the way while at the same time focusing those resources on specific tasks that will ultimately lead to academic success.

6   That said, positive emotions alone may not tell the whole story of academic success. Although the chronic experience of negative emotions (e.g., depressive symptoms), if paired with low levels of positive emotions, may contribute to low academic performance (Eisenberg, Gollust, Golberstein, & Hefner, 2007; Wintre & Yaffe, 2000), negative affect that is elicited in response to specific problems may also alter cognitive scope (Harmon-Jones et al., 2013) and build regulatory capacity (Wrosch & Miller, 2009).

For example, among adolescent girls, periods of negative affect preceded enhanced abilities to regulate goals (e.g., disengagement from unattainable goals), which in turn predicted improvements in affect (Wrosch & Miller, 2009). Alternatively, negative affect may likewise motivate psychological and behavioral change in service of academic success if the experience of negative emotions indicates insufficient progress with a particular goal and triggers a behavioral response aimed at overcoming goal-related problems (Carver & Scheier, 1990; Frijda, 1988; Nesse, 2000).

7   In support of these arguments, results from a daily diary study showed that university students who regularly experienced positive affect and occasionally experienced negative affect across one semester achieved the greatest academic success (Oishi, Diener, & Lucas, 2007). Likewise, university students with learner profiles that included high positive affect and moderate negative affect achieved the greatest academic success (Shell & Husman, 2008; for empirical evidence with regards to other life outcomes, see also Diener & Seligman, 2002). These results reflect short-term associations between affective experiences and academic success and suggest that students who are able to sustain elevated levels of positive affect and experience only occasional bouts or moderate levels of negative affect may be particularly able to achieve academic success.

The Current Study

8   The aim of the current study was to identify and link interacting patterns of positive and negative affect to academic success during the transition to adulthood. We considered this association between long-term patterns of self-reported affect and academic success as reflecting adaptive emotion management. This novel conceptualization provides an indirect or implicit examination of emotion regulation capacity and its consequences and a robust test of the hypothesis that students who are able to maintain positive affect and elicit negative affect in certain circumstances may be particularly able to achieve academic success across the university years.

9   We accomplished our aim statistically by examining how different combinations of within-person reports (time-limited bouts or states) and between-person reports (individual differences or traits) of affect were associated with academic success across 4 years of university. We expected that individuals who, on average, sustained high levels of positive affect across their university years (i.e., happy students;

trait-level) and who also experienced only average levels of negative affect (trait) or time-limited bouts of elevated negative affect (state) would have the highest GPAs over time. This pattern could reflect an academically successful student who managed his or her emotions over the long term to maintain high levels of positive affect in tandem with either average levels or time-limited increases in negative affect. This profile is consistent with findings showing productive consequences of experiencing elevated positive and negative affect in tandem.

10   Second, we expected that students who sustained high levels of negative affect across their university years and who also reported either low trait or state positive affect would have the lowest GPAs (i.e., unhappy students). This pattern may reflect an academically unsuccessful student who managed his or her emotions over the long term to maintain high levels of negative affect along with low levels of positive affect. This profile is consistent with the association between depressive experiences and low GPA (e.g., Eisenberg et al., 2007; Wintre & Yaffe, 2000).

Method

Participants

11   Participants were 187 full-time first-year students at a large Canadian university taking part in Making the Transition II, a web-based study of health-related behaviors and ongoing academic performance. Sixty percent of students were women ($n = 113$), and students' ages ranged from 17.5 to 19.8 years ($M = 18.4$, $SD = 0.44$). On the basis of self-reports, the ethnic distribution was 72% White, 16% Asian/South Asian, 5% mixed ethnicity, and 5% another visible minority (two students declined to report). Students lived at home with parents (53%), in campus residence (28%), in an apartment alone or with roommates (13%), or with nonparent relatives (5%). Most lived in two-parent households while growing up (86%), and most students' mothers (73%) and fathers (75%) had completed 2-year college or 4-year university degrees. Given these characteristics, this sample is representative of the university from which it was drawn and is not substantially different from other large Canadian universities. University enrolment in Canada is strongly associated with having lived in two-parent families in high school and with parents' postsecondary education. Furthermore, the percentage of students in the current sample enrolled in various university faculties (i.e., colleges, such as Arts or Science) closely matched the actual faculty distribution of first-year students at the university.

Procedures

12   The study was approved by the university research ethics review committee in accordance with the Government of Canada's Tri-Council Policy Statement: Ethical Conduct for Research Involving Humans. In Fall 2005, participants were recruited from compulsory first-year classes across campus. Research assistants described the study to students who were present on the day of their recruitment visit, and students interested in participating in the study provided contact information to the research team. Students were then contacted by email and invited to complete an initial paper-and-pencil questionnaire in groups at the beginning of the semester (baseline: September or October); 198 students attended, close to our goal of 200 participants. Participants were then invited to complete web-based questionnaires each month across their first year (through April 2006); they were invited to participate again near the end of their second (March 2007; paper-and-pencil questionnaire), third (February 2008; web-based questionnaire), and fourth (March 2009; web-based questionnaire) years of university. Data for the current study are taken from six waves: baseline, December 2005; April 2006; and the 2007, 2008, and 2009 surveys.

13   Although changes in survey mode can result in changes in response rates and data quality (e.g., via social desirability), these concerns are greater when survey delivery changes from an aural procedure (e.g., telephone or in-person interview) to a visual procedure (e.g., paper-and-pencil or web-based; Dillman et al., 2009). Results from two comparisons of data quality between web-based and paper-and-pencil survey modes found that personality inventories were equivalent in several respects across modes (e.g., measurement invariance, mean differences; Bjornsdottir et al., 2014; Chuah, Drasgow, & Roberts, 2006). Furthermore, a recent meta-analysis showed that the influence of social desirability was equivalent between paper-and-pencil and web-based survey administration (Gnambs & Kaspar, 2016). With regards to the measure of affect used in the current study, the Positive and Negative Affect Schedule (PANAS; Watson, Clark, & Tellegen, 1988), the subscales showed high and consistent internal reliability across waves (as reported in the measures sections). In addition, principal components analysis of the PANAS at each wave of measurement revealed the same two-factor structure corresponding to the positive affect and negative affect subscales. Correlations between the factors across waves were similar in direction and magnitude, ranging from −.17 to −.30. Thus, the changes in survey mode across waves in the current study likely had a minimal effect on the validity of our measures of positive and negative affect.

14   Eleven students had missing data on study predictor variables at every wave and were dropped from the analyses, reducing our final analytic sample to n = 187. In the final sample, study retention was good, with 60% ($n = 112$) of students participating at four, five, or all six waves of assessment. Twenty-seven percent participated at three waves ($n = 51$), and 13% participated once or twice ($n = 24$). We used full-information maximum likelihood estimation to perform our analyses. This procedure computes an individual likelihood function for each participant on the basis of his or her available data, provided that complete predictor data are present (positive and negative affect) for each wave of available outcome data (GPA). Importantly, cases contributing partial outcome data are retained and leveraged to improve the accuracy of the model estimates.

Measures

15   Positive and negative affect were measured with the PANAS in the December 2005; April 2006; and the 2007, 2008, and 2009 surveys (Watson et al., 1988). The response time frame was adapted to assess students' affect over a 2-week period. Participants were asked, "Over the last 14 days, on how many days did you feel . . .?" followed by 10 items assessing positive affect (e.g., interested, proud) and 10 items assessing negative affect (e.g., distressed, hostile). Two-week retrospective reports of emotional experience corresponded well with actual daily diary reports of emotional experience collected across the same 2-week period (Brown, Williams, Barker, & Galambos, 2007). Across waves of assessment, Cronbach's coefficient CY estimates ranged from .92 to .95 for positive affect and from .87 to .93 for negative affect. On average, students reported positive affect on 5.66 ($SD = 2.93$) to 6.31 ($SD = 3.06$) days out of 14 days across waves, with correlations ranging from .39 to .82. On average, students reported negative affect on 2.94 ($SD = 2.66$) to 3.71 ($SD = 2.41$) days out of 14 days across waves, with correlations ranging from .44 to .79. For positive and negative affect, correlations between repeated measures were generally strongest for adjacent assessments and weakest for assessments spaced further apart.

16   Academic performance was measured with students' official GPAs, which were supplied by the registrar's office. GPAs were on a four-point scale, ranging from 0 (*letter grade* *of F*) to 4 (*letter grade of A or A+*). Baseline GPA was based on students' admission averages ($M = 3.52$, $SD = 0.36$). GPAs for the fall and winter semesters of the first year and winter semesters of second through fourth years were calculated for each student as the average of grades in all classes taken each semester, weighted by course credit value. GPAs ranged from 2.84 ($SD = 0.76$) in the fall semester of first year to 3.29 ($SD = 0.55$) in the winter semester of fourth year.

Analysis Strategy

17   Analyses for the current study were performed using multilevel linear modeling in SAS PROC MIXED. We modeled change over time in students' GPAs as a cubic trend, following preliminary tests to establish the optimal function of change in the outcome variable. Positive and negative affect were included as person-mean–centered time-varying covariates (states), and the means of these variables across all waves of assessment were included as person-level covariates (traits). Time-varying effects of positive and negative affect represent students' affective states or "bouts" of affect. These effects indicate, for a given time of assessment, whether reporting higher or lower affect than one's own average is associated with GPA that semester. Person-level effects of positive and negative affect represent students' overall or average levels of positive affect and negative affect (i.e., traits). These effects indicate that students who feel more positive affect (happy students) or negative affect (unhappy students) compared with other students tend to achieve higher or lower GPAs across the study period. Thus, repeated measures of positive and negative affect are separated into distinct and uncorrelated within-person (bouts or affective states) and between-person (affective trait) components[1] (Curran & Bauer, 2011; Hoffman & Stawski, 2009).

18   We built our models in stages. First, we tested a model containing time trends and time-varying (state) and person-level (trait) measures of positive and negative affect. Second, we added interactions between positive and negative affect and linear time to assess whether associations between affect and GPA became stronger or weaker over time (interactions between affect and polynomials of time were considered, but none were significant). Third, we added interactions between positive and negative affect (e.g., time-varying negative affect × person-level positive affect) to assess whether specific combinations of jointly experienced levels of positive and negative affect predicted changes in GPA.

Results

19   Table 1 shows the results of our multilevel model predicting students' GPAs over time from time-varying positive and negative affect (states; *PA, NA*), average levels of positive and negative affect across all years (traits; *Mean PA, Mean NA*), and their interactions (e.g., *Mean PA × NA*). Results show that students' GPAs declined through the first year of university, rebounded by the end of second year, and stabilized in third and fourth years. This cubic trend is shown in Table 1 as effects for linear, quadratic, and cubic rates of change in GPA over time (*Time, Time²,* and *Time³*). Table 1 also shows a main effect of average negative affect. Students who reported higher levels of negative affect on average over all years generally achieved lower GPAs ($\gamma = -.043$, 95% confidence interval [CI] = $-.079$ to $-.006$). There were no effects of time-varying positive affect. Significant effects of time-varying negative affect and average positive affect manifested through interactions.

20   Table 1 and Figure 1 show a significant effect of average positive affect on changes in GPA over time (*Mean PA × Time*). Students who reported higher positive affect on average across all semesters began their studies with slightly lower GPAs, but increased their GPAs at a faster rate compared with students with lower average positive affect ($\gamma = .018$, 95% CI = .006 to .031). Significant differences favoring students with higher average positive affect ("happier" students) begin in third year, and by the end of fourth year, the difference between the GPAs of students reporting higher versus lower average positive affect is about equal to achieving a GPA of B + versus B (simple effect = .263, $SE = .098$, $p = .008$).

21   Table 1 and Figure 2 further show a significant interaction effect, indicating that the association between average positive affect and GPA also depends on the extent to which students experienced bouts of negative affect during a given semester (*Mean PA × NA*). For students reporting higher positive affect on average, GPAs were higher during times of heightened negative affect and lower during times of reduced negative affect.

22   Follow-up analyses of the simple slopes (see Preacher, Curran, & Bauer, 2006) showed that this effect only occurs for students whose average positive affect is at least two thirds of a standard deviation higher than the grand mean—specifically, only "happy" students' GPAs varied during times of heightened or reduced negative affect. At or above this threshold, happy students had better grades during semesters in which they experienced bouts of heightened negative affect. For students who report average positive affect below this threshold, bouts of heightened or reduced negative affect were unrelated to GPA in the same semester. In addition, happy students' GPAs were lower during semesters in which they experienced bouts of reduced negative affect.

23   Follow-up analyses indicated that happier students' GPAs were significantly higher than less happy students' GPAs (1 SD above and below the mean of average positive affect) at times when they experience bouts of negative affect at least half of a standard deviation above their own average (*simple effect* = .105, *SE* = .047, *p* = .026; at least 1.25 additional days of negative affect in a 2-week period). Furthermore, negative affect exceeding a person's own average by this amount or greater should have occurred 30.8% of the time—approximately 5 weeks per 16-week semester, or approximately 2.5 semesters over the course of a 4-year university career. By contrast, happier students' GPAs were significantly lower than less happy students' GPAs only when negative affect was at least 1.5 *SD* below their own average (simple effect = −.161, *SE* = .079, *p* = .042). Negative affect at these low levels should have occurred 6.7% of the time—approximately 1 week per 16-week semester, or approximately half a semester over the course of a 4-year university career.

24   We included several covariates in our model that are not shown in Table 1. Weighted effects codes for students' biological sex (women, men), parent education (whether or not students reported at least one university-educated parent), and ethnicity (White, Asian, another ethnicity) showed no associations with GPA. We also included measures of the numbers of courses taken each semester. There were no time-varying effects of number of courses (i.e., students' GPAs did not vary in semesters when they took more courses than usual), but students who took more courses on average reported slightly higher GPAs on average (γ = .132, 95% CI = .001 to .262)

Discussion

25   The aim of the current study was to identify patterns of emotional experience indicative of adaptive emotion regulation capacity with respect to achieving academic success during the transition to adulthood. We tested the hypothesis that students who are able to manage their emotions to experience general positive affect and occasional negative affect in tandem over the long term, across their university years, may be particularly able to achieve the greatest levels of academic success.

26   First, we found that students in the current sample whose pattern of emotional experience was characterized by high average positive affect across their university years earned the highest GPAs by the end of the 4-year period. That is, generally happy students showed the greatest improvements in academic success over time. This finding supports Lyubomirsky, King, and Diener's (2005) conclusion that "chronic happiness" can be cast as a psychological strength that supports goal-oriented success. That said, two other findings qualify our "happy student" finding. First, this effect was not evident in the first year; rather, it emerged later across the 4-year period. This finding corresponds with increases in emotion regulation capacity afforded by maturation of the prefrontal cortex and related to gains in cognitive control, emotional intelligence, and related personality development (Parker et al., 2005; Riediger & Klipker, 2014; Soto et al., 2011).

27   Second, the association of high average positive affect with high GPA was further qualified by the within-person effect of negative affect. Particularly happy students (those two thirds of a standard deviation or higher on average positive affect) experienced the greatest academic success (i.e., highest GPA) in semesters when within-person negative affect was elevated. In fact, happy students benefited only when within-person negative affect was high. In semesters when negative affect was much lower than average, happy students had lower GPAs than students with lower average levels of positive affect. For happy students, time-limited periods of elevated negative affect may reflect stressful but productive periods of investment in academic pursuits whereas time-limited periods of relative low negative affect may reflect coasting (Carver & Scheier, 1990).

28   These results more generally suggest that happy students' academic success could be derived from their ability to adaptively manage motivational benefits of time-limited periods—or bouts—of heightened negative affect. This finding supports the view that negative affect is a necessary component of effective self-regulation (Carver & Scheier, 1990; Diener & Seligman, 2002; Harmon-Jones et al., 2013; Heckhausen, Wrosch, & Schulz, 2010). We also found that "unhappy students"—those with high average negative affect across 4 years of university—earned the lowest GPAs across that period. These students did not appear to adaptively manage either negative or positive affect, a profile consistent with depressive disorders, symptoms of which are associated with lower GPA (Eisenberg et al., 2007; Wintre & Yaffe, 2000). In sum, our analysis of long-term temporal patterns of state and

Table 1   Multilevel Model Results Predicting GPA Over 4 Years of University from Time-Varying (State) and Person-Level (Trait) Positive and Negative Affect

Fixed effects	γ (SE)	95% CI LL, UL	p
Intercept (baseline GPA)	3.369 (0.048)	3.275, 3.464	
Rate of change in GPA over time:			
Linear (*Time*)	-1.387 (0.114)	$-1.611, -1.162$	<.001
Quadratic (*Time²*)	0.924 (0.082)	0.763, 1.086	<.001
Cubic (*Time³*)	-0.152 (0.015)	$-0.182, -0.122$	<.001
Positive affect			
Time-varying (*PA*)	0.008 (0.018)	$-0.028, 0.044$	.659
Average (*Mean PA*)	-0.011 (0.017)	$-0.044, 0.023$	.536
Negative affect			
Time-varying (*NA*)	0.040 (0.038)	$-0.034, 0.114$	.293
Average (*Mean NA*)	-0.042 (0.018)	$-0.078, -0.006$	.022
Affect × time interactions			
PA × Time	-0.000 (0.010)	$-0.019, 0.019$	.983
Mean PA × Time	0.020 (0.006)	0.007, 0.032	.002
NA × Time	-0.028 (0.026)	$-0.080, 0.023$	.276
Mean NA × Time	0.006 (0.007)	$-0.008, 0.019$	.412
Positive × negative affect interactions			
PA × NA	-0.006 (0.015)	$-0.035, 0.024$	.703
PA × Mean NA	-0.008 (0.005)	$-0.017, 0.001$	.099
Mean PA × NA	0.029 (0.011)	0.008, 0.050	.007
Mean PA × Mean NA	-0.004 (0.007)	$-0.019, 0.010$	.546
Random effects			
Between-person residual (τoo)	0.215 (0.029)	0.168, 0.285	<.001
Within-person residual ($<\sigma^2>$)	0.207 (0.012)	0.185, 0.233	<.001

Note. γ = Unstandardized multilevel regression coefficient. *SE* = standard error of estimate, LL = lower limit, UL = upper limit. Coefficients reported in this table adjust for demographic covariates (sex, ethnicity, parent education) and students' average and per-semester course loads.

trait positive and negative affect identifies a pattern indicative of adaptive emotion regulation capacity characterized by the long-term achievement of "chronic happiness" and time-limited bouts of negative affect.

29   The current study has several methodological strengths. The prospective longitudinal design adds a novel perspective on emotion regulation capacity by treating repeated measures of affective states as a reflection of long-term management of emotions and relating these patterns to a developmentally salient goal as the outcome. This approach provides an indirect or implicit evaluation of emotion regulation capacity. Furthermore, using repeated measurement of emotional states collected over long periods of time avoids pitfalls associated with common method variance and collecting general ratings of typical or usual ways of regulating emotions and subjective assessments of current or past success. Strategies for measuring the components of emotion regulation capacity often confound emotional experience and regulatory predictors with emotional competence outcomes (e.g., asking someone how they cope with negative emotions to relieve stress when they feel badly; John & Eng, 2014).

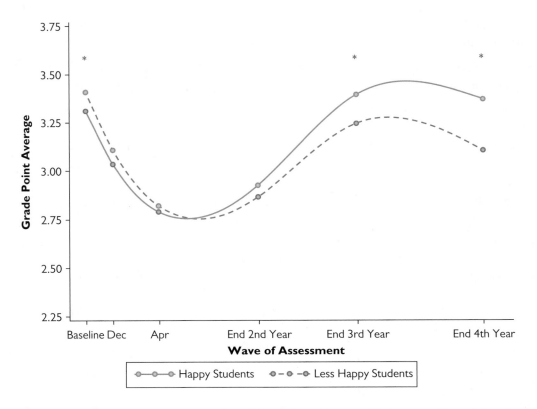

Figure 1   Interaction between average positive affect (*Mean PA*) and time predicting GPA. Dotted line shows trajectory for students who, on average, reported *Mean PA* at levels 1 *SD* below the mean of all students. Solid line shows trajectory for students who, on average, reported *Mean PA* at levels 1 *SD* above the mean of all students. Asterisk marks significant differences (*p* < .05) between students reporting high and low PA at baseline, end of third year, and end of fourth year.

30   A further strength of the current study is the fact that the measure of success, GPA, was obtained directly from the university registrar, providing an objective and official assessment of progress with a relevant developmental task. Thus, the current analysis tested an ecologically and developmentally valid model of emotional competence (Aldao, 2013; Diamond & Aspinwall, 2003). The results contribute to the literature on self-regulation across the life course, specifically to the growing literature on psychological experiences that propel average gains in well-being across the transition to adulthood, a literature that until recently has been mainly descriptive in nature (Shulman & Nurmi, 2010).

31   The main limitations of the current study were, first, that we did not measure the self-regulatory mechanisms, personality dimensions, or contextual factors that could underlie participants' emotional experiences and mediate or moderate the obtained associations between affective patterns and success (e.g., goal regulation processes, Heckhausen et al., 2010; reappraisal vs. suppression strategies, Gross & John, 2003; trait-consistent affect, Tamir, Robinson, & Clore, 2002). For example, circumstances unrelated to academic development may have elicited the affective states reported at each wave and could account for the associations between affect and GPA. Across the transition to adulthood, there are certainly many challenges to navigate that will elicit different emotional responses. Although our results suggest that the association between academic success and the adaptive pattern of emotional experience identified in the current study may reflect an ability to manage one's emotions such that individuals may be able to derive motivational benefits from the cooccurrence of positive and negative affect, we were not able to test these specific pathways.

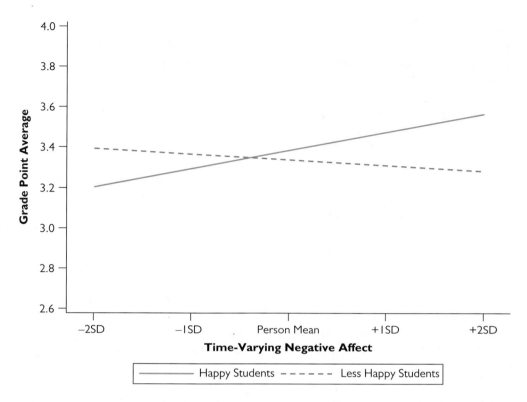

Figure 2   Interaction between average positive affect (*Mean PA*) and time-varying negative affect (*NA*) shows GPAs for happy and less happy students when they experience varying levels of negative affect. *x*-axis shows *NA* when students are at their own average (person mean) and when they are up to 2 *SD* above or below their own average. Solid line shows the relation between *NA* and GPA for students who report *Mean PA* at levels 1 SD above the mean of all students ("happy" students). Dotted line shows the relation between *NA* and GPA for students who reported *Mean PA* at levels 1 *SD* below the mean of all students ("less happy" students).

32   In sum, the results of the current study illustrate a promising approach for understanding the complex interplay between emotional experience and competence in the transition to adulthood. They further provide direction for future research on adaptive emotion regulation capacity in relation to other important life goals at other points in the life course. Thus, future research should (a) use this approach with respect to other life course goals and stages; (b) explore which specific affects in which particular combinations motivate one toward or away from particular life course goals; and (c) examine the specific self-regulatory mechanisms, personality correlates, and contextual demands (e.g., specific academic challenges, relationship challenges) that mediate or moderate associations between affective states and success at different points across the life course.

Notes

1. Person-mean centering is a valid strategy for separating within- and between-person components of a time-varying covariate (TVC), provided the TVC itself does not change over time (the within-person effect of a TVC is underestimated if it exhibits a time trend). Negative affect showed modest change over time; thus, we applied Curran and Bauer's (2011) detrending procedure to remove the influence of time.

References

Aldao, A. (2013). The future of emotion regulation research: Capturing context. *Perspectives on Psychological Science, 8,* 155–172. http://dx.doi.org/10.1177/1745691612459518

Bjornsdottir, G., Almarsdottir, A. B., Hansdottir, I., Thorsdottir, F., Heimisdottir, M., Stefansson, H., . . . Brennan, P. F. (2014). From paper to web: Mode equivalence of the ARHQ and NEO-FFI. *Computers in Human Behavior, 41,* 384 –392.

Brown, N. R., Williams, R. L., Barker, E. T., & Galambos, N. L. (2007). Estimating frequencies of emotions and actions: A web-based diary study. *Applied Cognitive Psychology, 21,* 259 –276. http://dx.doi.org/10.1002/acp.1303

Bureau of Labor Statistics U.S. Department of Labor. (2014, April 22). *College enrollment and work activity of 2013 high school graduates. Economic news release.* Retrieved from http://www.bls.gov/news.release/ hsgec.nr0.htm

Burwell, R. A., & Shirk, S. R. (2007). Subtypes of rumination in adolescence: Associations between brooding, reflection, depressive symptoms, and coping. *Journal of Clinical Child and Adolescent Psychology, 36,* 56–65. http://dx.doi.org/10.1080/15374410709336568

Carstensen, L. L., Isaacowitz, D. M., & Charles, S. T. (1999). Taking time seriously. A theory of socioemotional selectivity. *American Psychologist, 54,* 165–181. http://dx.doi.org/10.1037/0003-066X.54.3.165

Carver, C. S., & Scheier, M. F. (1990). Origins and functions of positive and negative affect: A control-process view. *Psychological Review, 97,* 19 –35. http://dx.doi.org/10.1037/0033-295X.97.1.19

Charles, S. T., Piazza, J. R., Luong, G., & Almeida, D. M. (2009). Now you see it, now you don't: Age differences in affective reactivity to social tensions. *Psychology and Aging, 24,* 645–653. http://dx.doi.org/10.1037/a0016673

Chuah, S. C., Drasgow, F., & Roberts, B. W. (2006). Personality assessment: Does the medium matter? No. *Journal of Research in Personality, 40,* 359 –376.

Curran, P. J., & Bauer, D. J. (2011). The disaggregation of within-person and between-person effects in longitudinal models of change. *Annual Review of Psychology, 62,* 583–619. http://dx.doi.org/10.1146/annurev.psych.093008.100356

Diamond, L. M., & Aspinwall, L. G. (2003). Emotion regulation across the life span: An integrative perspective emphasizing self-regulation, positive affect, and dyadic processes. *Motivation and Emotion, 27,* 125–156. http://dx.doi.org/10.1023/A:1024521920068

Diener, E., & Seligman, M. E. (2002). Very happy people. *Psychological Science, 13,* 81–84. http://dx.doi.org/10.1111/1467-9280.00415

Dillman, D. A., Phelps, G., Tortora, R., Swift, K., Kohrell, J., Berck, J., & Messer, B. L. (2009). Response rate and measurement differences in mixed-mode surveys using mail, telephone, interactive voice response (IVR) and the Internet. *Social Science Research, 38,* 1–18.

Eisenberg, D., Gollust, S. E., Golberstein, E., & Hefner, J. L. (2007). Prevalence and correlates of depression, anxiety, and suicidality among university students. *American Journal of Orthopsychiatry, 77,* 534–542. http://dx.doi.org/10.1037/0002-9432.77.4.534

Fredrickson, B. L. (2001). The role of positive emotions in positive psychology. The broaden-and-build theory of positive emotions. *American Psychologist, 56,* 218–226. http://dx.doi.org/10.1037/0003-066X.56.3.218

Frijda, N. H. (1988). The laws of emotion. *American Psychologist, 43,* 349–358. http://dx.doi.org/10.1037/0003-066X.43.5.349

Galambos, N. L., Barker, E. T., & Krahn, H. J. (2006). Depression, self-esteem, and anger in emerging adulthood: Seven-year trajectories. *Developmental Psychology, 42,* 350–365. http://dx.doi.org/10.1037/0012-1649.42.2.350

Galarneau, D., Marissette, R., & Usalcas, J. (2013). What has changed for young people in Canada? In *Statistics Canada.* Retrieved from http://www.statcan.gc.ca/pub/75-006-x/2013001/article/11847-eng.htm

Gnambs, T., & Kaspar, K. (2016). Socially desirable responding in web-based questionnaires a meta-analytic review of the candor hypothesis. *Assessment.* Advance online publication.

Goetz, T., Frenzel, A. C., Stoeger, H., & Hall, N. C. (2010). Antecedents of everyday positive emotions: An experience sampling analysis. *Motivation and Emotion, 34,* 49–62. http://dx.doi.org/10.1007/s11031-009-9152-2

Gross, J. J., & John, O. P. (2003). Individual differences in two emotion regulation processes: Implications for affect, relationships, and well-being. *Journal of Personality and Social Psychology, 85,* 348–362. http://dx.doi.org/10.1037/0022-3514.85.2.348

Harmon-Jones, E., Gable, P. A., & Price, T. F. (2013). Does negative affect always narrow and positive affect always broaden the mind? Considering the influence of motivational intensity on cognitive scope. *Current Directions in Psychological Science, 22,* 301–307. http://dx.doi.org/10.1177/0963721413481353

Heckhausen, J., Wrosch, C., & Schulz, R. (2010). A motivational theory of life-span development. *Psychological Review, 117,* 32– 60. http://dx.doi.org/10.1037/a0017668

Hoffman, L., & Stawski, R. S. (2009). Persons as contexts: Evaluating between-person and within-person effects in longitudinal analysis. *Research in Human Development, 6,* 97–120. http://dx.doi.org/10.1080/ 15427600902911189

John, O. P., & Eng, J. (2014). Three approaches to individual differences in affect regulation: Conceptualizations, measures, and findings. In J. J. Gross (Ed.), *Handbook of emotion regulation* (pp. 321–345). New York, NY: Guilford Press.

Kunzmann, U., Kappes, C., & Wrosch, C. (2014). Emotional aging: A discrete emotions perspective. *Frontiers in Psychology, 5,* 380. http://dx.doi.org/10.3389/fpsyg.2014.00380

Lyubomirsky, S., King, L., & Diener, E. (2005). The benefits of frequent positive affect: Does happiness lead to success? *Psychological Bulletin, 131,* 803–855.

Nesse, R. M. (2000). Is depression an adaptation? *Archives of General Psychiatry, 57,* 14–20. http://dx.doi.org/10.1001/archpsyc.57.1.14

Oishi, S., Diener, E., & Lucas, R. E. (2007). The optimum level of well-being: Can people be too happy? *Perspectives on Psychological Science, 2,* 346–360. http://dx.doi.org/10.1111/j.1745-6916.2007.00048.x

Ouweneel, E., Le Blanc, P. M., & Schaufeli, W. B. (2011). Flourishing students: A longitudinal study on positive emotions, personal resources, and study engagement. *The Journal of Positive Psychology, 6,* 142–153. http://dx.doi.org/10.1080/17439760.2011.558847

Parker, J. D., Hogan, M. J., Eastabrook, J. M., Oke, A., & Wood, L. M. (2006). Emotional intelligence and student retention: Predicting the successful transition from high school to university. *Personality and Individual Differences, 41,* 1329–1336. http://dx.doi.org/10.1016/j.paid.2006.04.022

Parker, J. D., Saklofske, D. H., Wood, L. M., Eastabrook, J. M., & Taylor, R. N. (2005). Stability and change in emotional intelligence: Exploring the transition to young adulthood. *Journal of Individual Differences, 26,* 100–106. http://dx.doi.org/10.1027/1614-0001.26.2.100

Parker, J. D., Summerfeldt, L. J., Hogan, M. J., & Majeski, S. A. (2004). Emotional intelligence and academic success: Examining the transition from high school to university. *Personality and Individual Differences, 36,* 163–172. http://dx.doi.org/10.1016/S0191-8869(03)00076-X

Pekrun, R., Elliot, A. J., & Maier, M. A. (2009). Achievement goals and achievement emotions: Testing a model of their joint relations with academic performance. *Journal of Educational Psychology, 101,* 115–135. http://dx.doi.org/10.1037/a0013383

Preacher, K. J., Curran, P. J., & Bauer, D. J. (2006). Computational tools for probing interactions in multiple linear regression, multilevel modeling, and latent curve analysis. *Journal of Educational and Behavioral Statistics,*

31, 437–448. http://dx.doi.org/10.3102/10769986031004437

Richardson, M., Abraham, C., & Bond, R. (2012). Psychological correlates of university students' academic performance: A systematic review and meta-analysis. *Psychological Bulletin, 138,* 353–387. http://dx.doi.org/10.1037/a0026838

Riediger, M., & Klipker, K. (2014). Emotion regulation in adolescence. In J. J. Gross (Ed.), *Handbook of emotion regulation* (pp. 187–202). New York, NY: Guilford Press.

Ross, C. E., & Mirowsky, J. (2008). Age and the balance of emotions. *Social Science & Medicine, 66,* 2391–2400. http://dx.doi.org/10.1016/j.socscimed.2008.01.048

Schaufeli, W. B., Martínez, I. M., Pinto, A. M., Salanova, M., & Bakker, A. B. (2002). Burnout and engagement in university students a cross-national study. *Journal of Cross-Cultural Psychology, 33,* 464–481. http://dx.doi.org/10.1177/0022022102033005003

Shell, D. F., & Husman, J. (2008). Control, motivation, affect, and strategic self-regulation in the college classroom: A multidimensional phenomenon. *Journal of Educational Psychology, 100,* 443–459. http://dx.doi.org/10.1037/0022-0663.100.2.443

Shulman, S., & Nurmi, J.-E. (2010). Understanding emerging adulthood from a goal-setting perspective. *New Directions for Child and Adolescent Development, 130,* 1–11. L10.1002/cd.277

Silk, J. S., Steinberg, L., & Morris, A. S. (2003). Adolescents' emotion regulation in daily life: Links to depressive symptoms and problem behavior. *Child development, 1869* –1880. Retrieved from http://www.jstor.org/stable/3696309

Soto, C. J., John, O. P., Gosling, S. D., & Potter, J. (2011). Age differences in personality traits from 10 to 65: Big Five domains and facets in a large cross-sectional sample. *Journal of Personality and Social Psychology, 100,* 330–348. http://dx.doi.org/10.1037/a0021717

Spinrad, T. L., Eisenberg, N., Cumberland, A., Fabes, R. A., Valiente, C., Shepard, S. A., . . . Guthrie, I. K. (2006). Relation of emotion-related regulation to children's social competence: A longitudinal study. *Emotion, 6,* 498–510. http://dx.doi.org/10.1037/1528-3542.6.3.498

Tamir, M., Robinson, M. D., & Clore, G. L. (2002). The epistemic benefits of trait-consistent mood states: An analysis of extraversion and mood. *Journal of Personality and Social Psychology, 83,* 663–677. http://dx.doi.org/10.1037/0022-3514.83.3.663

Tanner, J. L. (2006). Recentering during emerging adulthood: A critical turning point in life span human development. In J. J. Arnett & J. L. Tanner (Eds.), *Emerging adults in America: Coming of age in the 21st Century* (pp. 21–55). Washington, DC: American Psychological Association. http://dx.doi.org/10.1037/11381-002

Watson, D., Clark, L. A., & Tellegen, A. (1988). Development and validation of brief measures of positive and negative affect: The PANAS scales. *Journal of Personality and Social Psychology, 54,* 1063–1070. http://dx.doi.org/10.1037/0022-3514.54.6.1063

Wintre, M., & Yaffe, M. (2000). First-year students' adjustment to university life as a function of relationships with parents. *Journal of Adolescent Research, 15,* 9–37. http://dx.doi.org/10.1177/0743558400151002

Wrosch, C., & Miller, G. E. (2009). Depressive symptoms can be useful: Self-regulatory and emotional benefits of dysphoric mood in adolescence. *Journal of Personality and Social Psychology, 96,* 1181–1190. http://dx.doi.org/10.1037/a0015172

Zimmermann, P., & Iwanski, A. (2014). Emotion regulation from early adolescence to emerging adulthood and middle adulthood: Age differences, gender differences, and emotion-specific developmental variations. *International Journal of Behavioral Development, 38,* 182–194. http://dx.doi.org/10.1177/0165025413515405

Key and challenging words

self-efficacy, in tandem with, salient, confound, elicit

Questions

1. In your own words, explain the relationship between "emotional regulation capacity" and academic success.

2. In the Introduction (paragraphs 1–10), identify the following common features of academic introductions: (a) the justification for the study, (b) the paragraphs containing the literature review, (c) the hypothesis.

3. Focusing on two paragraphs from the essay's Introduction (see above), discuss their purpose within this section as a whole, showing how they contribute to its development. Refer specifically to the text.

4. Discuss the ways that the authors are able to increase coherence and reader understanding in two of the following: paragraph 3 (if not used in question 3); paragraph 26; and one other paragraph of your choice. (See Writing Strong Paragraphs on pp. 73–75 in Chapter 6, for strategies often used to help create coherent paragraphs.)

5. Why would the change in survey mode (see paragraph 13) not likely affect the validity of the study's findings, according to the authors?

6. (a) Identify by paragraph number the following common features of Discussion sections in the Discussion section of this essay: (i) restatement of the hypothesis, (ii) paragraphs in which the authors use synthesis to relate their findings to those of other researchers, (iii) limitations of the study; (b) Of the two specific strengths mentioned in paragraphs 29 and 30, which do you think is the more significant or contributes more to the field of study? Explain your answer.

7. For one of the suggestions for future research in paragraph 32, come up with a tentative hypothesis that would enable a researcher to expand on the findings of Barker et al.

Post-reading

1. *Collaborative activity*: As part of a new initiative on your campus called Planning for Academic Student Success (PASS), you are responsible for designing a poster and pamphlet to assist first- and second-year students by proposing practical strategies for successful learning. Drawing partly on the findings of Barker et al., as well as your own experiences, observations, and critical thinking, come up with specific tips and guidelines that will facilitate academic success. Among the strategies, you could include advice on how to "adaptively manage motivational benefits of time-limited periods—or bouts—of heightened negative effects" (see paragraph 28). Ensure your writing is geared to a student audience.

Social Norms of Alcohol, Smoking, and Marijuana Use within a Canadian University Setting

Kelly P. Arbour-Nicitopoulos, Matthew Y.W. Kwan, David Lowe, Sara Taman, and Guy E.J. Faulkner
(2,496 words)

Pre-reading

1. *Collaborative activity:* (a) Reflect on the problems of alcohol and drug consumption on your university campus. Do they affect you or people you know? (b) Does your university have a policy on drinking or drug use? Do you believe it is a good policy? How could it be improved in order to help reduce alcohol and drug consumption?

Abstract

Objective: To study actual and perceived substance use in Canadian university students and to compare these rates with US peers. **Participants**: Students (N= 1,203) from a large Canadian university. **Methods**: Participants were surveyed using items from the National College Health (NCHA) Assessment of the American College Health Association questionnaire. **Results**: Alcohol was the most common substance used (65.8%), followed by marijuana (13.5%) and cigarettes (13.5%). Substance use and norms were significantly less than the NCHA US data. Overall, respondents generally perceived the typical Canadian student to have used all 3 substances. Perceived norms significantly predicted use, with students more likely to use alcohol, cigarettes, or marijuana if they perceived the typical student to use these substances. **Conclusions**: Similar to their US peers, Canadian university students have inaccurate perceptions of peer substance use. These misperceptions may have potentially negative influences on actual substance use and could be a target for intervention. Further research examining the cross-cultural differences for substance abuse is warranted.

---

1   Excessive alcohol consumption, smoking, and drug use are all identified as modifiable risk factors associated with heart and liver diseases, and cancer.[1] However, young adults, specifically college students, do not attribute such health-risk behaviors to the development and progression of these diseases.[2] Transition from late adolescence to young adulthood is often associated with greater autonomy and independence. It is conceivable that previous inhibitions to some health-risk behaviors, such as smoking and alcohol consumption, may weaken due to reductions in parent–guardian influence, and the perception that these behaviors become socially "normal" and "acceptable" within the campus setting.[3]

2   Group norms are characterized as the attitudes, expectations, and behaviors within regular group members, and are seen as a powerful agent that can often account for, and even determine, an individual's behavior.[4] Peer norms may be particularly salient within a collegiate population, as students find themselves situated within a peer-dominated environment, with less frequent contact with parents, siblings, or other previous reference groups. Moreover, college students generally tend to overestimate the degree to which their peers are engaging in normative behaviors. For example, Perkins and colleagues[5] found nearly 75% of US college students overestimated the amount of alcohol being consumed by their peers at social events. These misperceptions are consistent with the findings from 2 review papers that examined student norms of alcohol consumption,[4,6] as well as findings from a nationwide survey, which found most students from each of the US colleges surveyed perceiving more frequent alcohol consumption among their peers than actually reported.[7]

3   The United States and Canada are 2 countries that have many shared values. However, there are important differences between these 2 countries that may be reflected in different normative beliefs about health behaviors.

Source: From *Journal of American College Health*, vol. 59, no. 3, 2010, pp. 191–6. Published by Taylor & Francis Ltd. www.informaworld.com

For example, the legal drinking age in Canada is much younger (18–19 years) than in the United States (21 years). In terms of drug control policies, the United States has a greater conservatism towards legalizing drugs such as marijuana than Canada. Under current Canadian legislation, possession of small amounts of marijuana for personal use (i.e., ≤ 15 g) will not typically result in a criminal record.[8] In terms of smoking, such differences may inevitably be reflected in cross-cultural differences in postsecondary students' use of alcohol and drugs and normative beliefs regarding such health behaviors. National data on the usage of alcohol and drugs among Canadian[9] and US[10] postsecondary students indicate substantially lower cigarette, marijuana, and alcohol use among Canadian students (12.7%, 16.7%, and 77.1%, respectively) than their US peers (39.8%, 38.2%, and 84.8%, respectively). However, no study has compared peer norms for substance use among Canadian and US postsecondary students. Understanding misperceptions of peer norms is particularly important because they may have strong implications towards students' engagement in health-risk behaviors.

4   Most of the research on health-risk behavior norms within the campus setting has been conducted in the United States,[5,7,11–14] with the primary focus on alcohol use.[6] The purpose of this study was to extend the findings on substance use norms to a Canadian sample of university students by (1) examining the relationship between Canadian postsecondary students' actual and perceived use of alcohol, cigarettes, and marijuana; and (2) comparing substance use and perceived norms between Canadian and US postsecondary students. It was hypothesized that (1) the Canadian students surveyed would perceive more frequent alcohol, cigarette, and marijuana use among their peers than actually reported[7]; (2) perceived use would predict actual use for all 3 substances assessed[7,12–14]; and (3) actual use and perceived norms would be lower for Canadian postsecondary students than their US peers.[9,10]

Methods

Design and Sample

5   Data were collected during the Spring of 2006 using the National College Health Assessment of the American College Health Association (NCHA-ACHA; for further information, see ACHA 2006[10]). The NCHA-ACHA consists of 58 questions and approximately 300 items primarily assessing student health status and health behaviors, access to health information, impediments to academic performance, and perceived norms across a variety of health risk behaviors such as alcohol, tobacco, and other drug use.[10] It has been evaluated extensively for reliability and validity in US college students.[15,16] To the best of our knowledge, this is the first study to use the NCHA-ACHA in a sample of Canadian university students.

6   Five thousand students (from a student body of approximately 50,000) at the largest campus of the University of Toronto, Ontario, Canada, were randomly chosen to receive an invitation by e-mail to participate in the survey. Over a period of 1 month, each potential participant received 3 such invitations t`o go to a secure Web site, maintained by the ACHA, to complete the NCHA-ACHA Web version of the survey. Participants were also entered into a draw to receive bookstore coupons as an incentive. Approval for the research protocol was granted by the university research ethics board.

Measures

Demographics

7   Participants provided demographic information, including age, sex, living situation, relationship status, ethnicity, body mass index (BMI; determined from self-reported weight [kg] and height [m]), and student status (i.e., undergraduate versus graduate/full-time versus part-time).

Self-reported Substance Use

8   Participants were asked to respond to the following question: "*Within the last 30 days, on how many days did you use the following. . .*" In line with our research objectives, data were extracted for cigarettes, alcohol, and marijuana use. Response options ranged from *never used* and *have used but not in the last 30 days* to *used all 30 days*.[10]

Perceived Substance Use Norm

9   Perceived substance use was assessed by the question, "*Within the last 30 days, how often do you think the typical student at your school used. . .*" Consistent with our research objectives, data were extracted for perceived cigarettes, alcohol, and marijuana use. Response categories were *never used, used one or more days, used daily.*[10]

Statistical Analyses

10   Frequencies were calculated in the demographic characteristics, which were subsequently dichotomized

into the following categories: *sex*—male versus female; *residence*—living at home (parental/guardian's home) versus away from home (college residence, fraternity or sorority, off campus housing); *relationship status*—single (not in a relationship) versus other (married, divorced, engaged or in a committed relationship); *student status*—undergraduate versus graduate student; *full-time status*—full-time versus part-time; and *ethnicity*—white versus other (aboriginal, Arab, black, Chinese, Filipino, Japanese, Korean, Latin American, South Asian, Southeast Asian, West Asian, multiracial, other).

11   Logistic regression was conducted to examine the relationship between perceived and self-reported substance use. Hence, responses to the 2 substance use variables were recoded into 2 categories: *not used in the past 30 days* versus *used in the past 30 days*. Demographic variables (age, BMI, sex, relationship status, student status, residence, full-time status, ethnicity) were entered first (Block 1) as covariates, whereas perceived substance use was entered second (Block 2). All models showed nonsignificant Hosmer-Lemeshow statistics, and significant omnibus chi-squares, indicating good model fit.[17]

Results

Demographics

12   A total of 1,203 students were surveyed, representing a 24% response rate. This response rate is slightly lower than the 31% to 35% response rate reported in other college studies that have used the NCHA.[10,15] Median age of the sample was 22 years (range 18–45). Participants were primarily white (60%), female (60%), single (51%), full-time (60%) undergraduate (65%) students, who were living away from home (68%). Mean BMI was 22.73 kg/m^2, which is indicative of a healthy body weight.

Actual and Perceived Substance Use in Past 30 Days

13   Data on self-reported and perceived substance use are shown in Figure 1. In the past 30 days, alcohol was the most commonly used substance (65.8%), followed by marijuana (13.5%) and cigarettes (13.5%; Figure 1a). National data on the usage of alcohol, cigarettes, and marijuana among 54,111 US college students drawn from 71 institutes (ACHA)[10] is also shown in Figure 1a. In comparison to the US data, cigarette, alcohol, and marijuana use in the current sample were lower.

14   Perceived substance norms are presented in Figure 1b. Despite the lower substance use, the majority of respondents in the present study had indicated that the typical student on their campus had used alcohol (95.6%), cigarettes (86.6%), or marijuana (76.7%) in the past 30 days (see Figure 1b). However, these perceptions were slightly lower than those reported previously for alcohol, cigarettes, and marijuana in the US data (i.e., 99%, 96%, and 94%, respectively).[10]

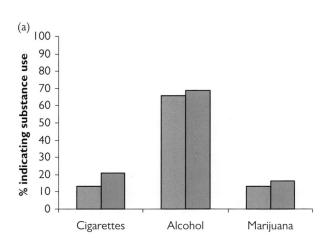
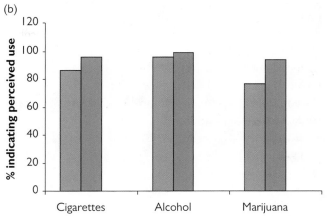

FIGURE 1   Reported (a) versus perceived (b) alcohol, cigarette, and marijuana use in the past 30 days. Actual substance use is based on respondents' self-reported use of cigarettes, alcohol, and marijuana within the past 30 days. Perceived substance use is based on respondents' perceptions of the *typical students'* use of the 3 substances within the past 30 days. *n* = 54,111 for the US[10] sample. ■ Current sample; ■ US data.

Do Substance Norms Predict Self-reported Substance Use?

15   Results from the logistic regression predicting self-reported cigarette, alcohol, and marijuana use are presented in Tables 1 to 3, respectively. For all 3 substances, ethnicity was a common predictor of actual 30-day use. Students of a white ethnicity were twice as likely to use cigarettes and alcohol, and were over 3 times as likely to use marijuana in the past 30 days, than students of a nonwhite ethnicity. For alcohol use, residence and relationship status were also found to be significant predictors, such that actual 30-day use was one-half times as likely for students currently in a relationship and almost twice as likely for students living away from their parents' or guardians' home. After controlling for demographic characteristics, perceived substance use remained a significant predictor of actual 30-day substance use. Students were twice as likely to use cigarettes, over 3 times as likely to use marijuana, and 7 times as likely to consume alcohol in the past 30 days if they perceived the typical student to have used these substances in the past 30 days (see Tables 1, 2, 3).

Table 1   Logistic Regression Predicting Self-reported Cigarette Use

Predictor	B	SE	Wald	Significance	OR	95.0% CI (OR)	
						Lower	Upper
Ethnicity	.89	.21	17.49	< .001			
White					2.44	1.61	3.72
Other					1.00		
Smoking norm	.66	.33	3.93	< .05			
Perceived use					1.93	1.01	3.69
Perceived nonuse					1.00		

Note. OR indicates the likelihood of using cigarettes in the past 30 days. Data only shown for significant predictors (*p* < .05).

Table 2   Logistic Regression Predicting Self-reported Alcohol Use

Predictor	B	SE	Wald	Significance	OR	95.0% CI (OR)	
						Lower	Upper
Relationship status	0.38	.14	7.02	< .01			
In a relationship					1.46	0.52	0.91
Single					1.00		
Residence	0.56	.15	14.48	< .001			
Away from home					1.75	0.43	0.76
Parents'/Guardian's home					1.00		
Ethnicity	0.64	.14	21.87	< .001			
White					1.90	1.45	2.49
Other					1.00		
Alcohol norm	1.96	.37	28.73	< .001			
Perceived use					7.12	3.47	14.60
Perceived nonuse					1.00		

Note. OR indicates the likelihood of using alcohol in the past 30 days. Data only shown for significant predictors (*p* < .05).

Table 3   Logistic Regression Predicting Self-reported Marijuana Use

Predictor	B	SE	Wald	Significance	OR	95.0% CI (OR) Lower	Upper
Ethnicity	1.36	.24	31.01	< .001			
White					3.89	2.41	6.27
Other					1.00		
Marijuana norm	1.30	.34	14.48	< .001			
Perceived use					3.68	1.88	7.21
Perceived nonuse					1.00		

Note. OR indicates the likelihood of using marijuana in the past 30 days. Data only shown for significant predictors ($p < .05$).

Comment

16   The primary objective of this study was to determine the relationship between perceived and actual substance use in a sample of Canadian university students. Similar to previous research,[4–7,10] students overestimated the use of substances on campus, specifically cigarettes, alcohol, and marijuana, relative to their own self-reported use. Perceived substance use was found to be a significant predictor of actual use for all 3 substances measured, with the strongest relationships shown for alcohol and marijuana. In addition to perceived substance use, ethnicity was a common predictor of actual use, with students of a white ethnicity at a greater risk of using cigarettes, alcohol, and marijuana than their nonwhite peers. For the alcohol model, being in a relationship and living away from home were also associated with greater alcohol use.

17   A secondary objective was to compare substance use and norms between Canadian and US postsecondary students. As hypothesized, substance use and norms were much higher in the US data[10] in comparison to data from the present study. Earlier research has shown greater cigarette use among US versus Canadian postsecondary students.[18] The current study findings suggest that, in addition to cigarette use, Canadian university students also use alcohol and marijuana less so than their US peers. Similar to the US data,[4–6,10] students in the current study had overestimated the use of all 3 measured substances, with the greatest discrepancies seen amongst cigarette and marijuana use. As shown in Figure 1, over 75% of students perceived the "typical" student to use cigarettes or marijuana, whereas only 13.5% actually reported using these substances. Although the discrepancy was smaller for alcohol

consumption (~30%), it still remains noteworthy. Together, these findings suggest that Canadian university students, similar to their US peers, have a bias towards overestimating the prevalence of cigarette, alcohol, and marijuana use on campus. Future research should examine the factors underlying students' misperceptions of peer substance use as well as the cross-cultural differences for substance use and normative beliefs between Canadian and US postsecondary students.

18   As hypothesized, perceived use was a common predictor of actual use for all 3 substances assessed. These results parallel what has been found in previous research on campus substance use norms in both the United States[7,12,13] and Canada.[14] However, our findings also suggest that perceived norms may have a stronger influence, and therefore act as a moderator, on students' use of some substances (e.g., alcohol, marijuana) over other substances (e.g., cigarettes). One implication of this moderating effect is that future substance use interventions should consider the relationship between social norms and the targeted substance. For substances where the social norm–substance use relationship is strong (e.g., alcohol), social norms campaigns may be an effective strategy for changing students' actual substance use. Meanwhile, social norm interventions may be less effective for preventing and/or treating postsecondary students' use of other substances (e.g., smoking) where this relationship is small.

Limitations

19   As with other studies, our study has some limitations that warrant mention. First, the use of survey invitations to a random group of students influences the generalizability of the results to the larger Canadian university population.

In particular, the current sample was predominately white so the findings regarding ethnicity must be interpreted with caution. Second, measures of actual and perceived use were self-report, and therefore may be influenced by response biases. Furthermore, these measures only focused on a 30-day period, which may not be representative of students' actual behavior. However, the substance use rates reported in the current sample are similar to those reported in a previous national data set,[9] which used data from over 6,000 Canadian university students. Lastly, the study design was cross-sectional, hence causation cannot be inferred.

Conclusions

20   These results contribute to the student norm research by examining the relationship between actual and perceived use across a variety of substances, within a Canadian sample of university students. The findings suggest that Canadian university students, similar to their US peers, have inaccurate perceptions of substance use by their campus peers. Moreover, these misperceptions may have potentially negative influences on students' actual substance use, although this needs confirmation through experimental research. These findings are particularly relevant to campus health services, as they suggest incorporating social norms in future interventions or campaigns that focus on altering students' engagement in health-risk behaviors. For example, campaigns that highlight the discrepancies between actual and perceived student health behaviors (e.g., cigarette use, incidences of binge drinking) may help to alter students' perceptions and possibly their own engagements in those behaviors. Future research should examine the feasibility of social norms campaigns for different health-risk behaviors, as well as the possibility of a "synergistic effect" of targeting one substance norm, specifically alcohol, on other related health-risk behaviors.

Acknowledgements

The research was supported by a Postdoctoral Fellowship (to K.A.-N.) and a Doctoral Scholarship (to M.K.) from the Social Sciences and Humanities Research Council of Canada.

References

1. World Health Organization. *The World Health Report: Reducing Risks, Promoting Healthy Life*. Geneva, Switzerland: World Health Organization; 2002.

2. Poortinga W. The prevalence and clustering of four major lifestyle risk factors in an English adult population. *Prev Med*. 2007;44:124–128.

3. Colder CR, Flay BR, Segawa E, Hedeker D, TERN members. Trajectories of smoking among freshmen college students with prior smoking history and risk for future smoking: data from the University Project Tobacco Etiology Research Network (UpTERN) study. *Addiction*. 2008;103:1534–1543.

4. Perkins HW. Social norms and the prevention of alcohol misuse in collegiate contexts. *J Stud Alcohol*. 2002; (suppl 14):164–172.

5. Perkins HW, Haines M, Rice R. Misperceiving the college drinking norm and related problems: a nationwide study of exposure to prevention information, perceived norms and student alcohol misuse. *J Stud Alcohol*. 2005;66:470–478.

6. Borsari B, Carey KB. Peer influences on college drinking: a review of the research. *J Subst Abuse*. 2001;13:391–424.

7. Perkins HW, Meilman P, Leichliter JS, Cashin JR, Presley C. Misperceptions of the norms for the frequency of alcohol and other drug use on college campuses. *J Am Coll Health*. 1999;47:253–258.

8. House of Commons of Canada. Bill C-38: An act to amend the Contraventions Act and the Controlled Drugs and Substances Act. Ottawa, Ontario, Canada: House of Commons; 2003.

9. Adlaf EM, Demers A, Gliksman L. *Canadian Campus Survey 2004*. Toronto, Ontario, Canada: Centre for Addiction and Mental Health; 2004.

10. American College Health Association. The American College Health Association National College Health Assessment (ACHA-NCHA), Spring 2003 Reference Group data report (Abridged). *J Am Coll Health*. 2005;53:199–210.

11. Martens MP, Page JC, Mowry ES, Damann KM, Taylor KK, Cimini MD. Differences between actual and perceived student norms: an examination of alcohol use, drug use, and sexual behavior. *J Am Coll Health*.2006;54:295–300.

12. Kilmer JR, Walker DD, Lee CM, et al. Misperceptions of college student marijuana use: implications for prevention. *J Stud Alcohol*. 2006;67:277–281.

13. Neighbors C, Geisner IM, Lee CM. Perceived marijuana norms and social expectancies among entering college student marijuana users. *Psychol Addict Behav*. 2008;22:433–438.

14. Perkins HW. Misperceptions of peer drinking norms in Canada: another look at the "reign of error" and its consequences among college students. *Addict Behav*. 2007;32:2645–2656.

15. American College Health Association. The American College Health Association National College Health Assessment (ACHA-NCHA), Spring 2005 Reference Group data report (Abridged). *J Am Coll Health.* 2006;55:5–16.

16. American College Health Association. The American College Health Association National College Health Assessment (ACHA-NCHA), Spring 2007 Reference Group data report(Abridged). *J Am Coll Health.* 2008;56:469–479.

17. Tabachnick BG, Fidell LS. *Using Multivariate Statistics.* 4th ed. Boston, MA: Allyn & Bacon; 2001.

18. Adlaf EM, Gliksman L, Demers A, Newton-Taylor B. Cigarette use among Canadian undergraduates. *Can J Public Health.* 2003;94:22–24.

Key and challenging words

normative, protocol, dichotomize, synergistic effect, discrepancy

Questions

1. Summarize the purpose and justification for the study.
2. Analyze the essay's Introduction, paying particular attention to organization and other strategies leading to comprehension (for example, topic sentences, transitions, and use of rhetorical patterns).
3. In your own words, explain the significance of Figure 1, using the information in the text section "Results" as well as the bolded text below the graphs.
4. What are the main findings in the section "Do Substance Norms Predict Self-reported Substance Use?" Paraphrase one of these findings.
5. In the "Comment" section, usually titled "Discussion" in Type B essays, identify by paragraph number and briefly summarize the following: (a) a main result; (b) the way it compares to a prior study; (c) a suggestion for further research. Note that there is more than one example of (a), (b), and (c) in the "Comment" section.
6. (a) Explain the importance of the "Limitations" section to the study as a whole; (b) briefly analyze the authors' effectiveness in addressing *one* of the study's limitations.

Post-reading

1. Referring to one of the study's findings, such as the bias of Canadian students to overestimate substance use by other students on campus (see paragraphs 16–18), come up with a hypothesis that could be the basis of an experiment to extend the findings of the current study. Then, give a two-sentence description of the design of such a study—i.e., give a brief description of its methodology. (See "Methods" in paragraphs 5–6, or Chapter 3, Type B essays.)
2. *Collaborative activity:* In the "Comment" and "Conclusions" sections, the authors suggest interventions to help reduce substance use on Canadian campuses. Design an intervention campaign for use by your institution's Health Services in which you consider the "relationship between social norms and the targeted substance" (paragraph 18). (Your campaign should take into account recent changes to marijuana's legalization in Canada.) The campaign could consider other strategies and interventions in addition to those mentioned by the authors, but you must refer to the key finding in the study (see "Comment" section, paragraph 16). Summarize the main features of your campaign.

Universities, Governments and Industry: Can the Essential Nature of Universities Survive the Drive to Commercialize?

Simon N. Young

(2,622 words)

> ### Pre-reading
>
> 1. Based on the essay's title, come up with a reading hypothesis of two sentences that includes (a) the kind of essay to follow (i.e., argumentative or expository) and (b) the author's thesis. Do not use any major words from the title.

1   Having spent 40 years in universities, I have had sufficient time to consider some of the idiosyncrasies, foibles, and problems of these academic institutions. The purpose of this editorial is to discuss the current state of university research and explain why I find some aspects of the current situation disturbing. Changes that started during the second half of the twentieth century and that have continued into the twenty-first threaten to bring about fundamental changes in the nature of universities. Some of the changes are commendable, for example, the large expansion in the proportion of the population attending universities, at least in the richer nations. Other trends are disturbing, especially the increasing tendency of governments and industry to view universities as engines for short-term economic gain. While universities certainly cannot ignore the context in which they function and the needs of society, responding purely to short-term economic considerations threatens to subvert the very nature of universities and some of the benefits they provide to society.

2   So what exactly is a university, and what is its purpose? I much prefer the *Oxford English Dictionary* definition of the word "university" to some of the more utilitarian definitions in other dictionaries. The Oxford definition reads, in part, "whole body of teachers and scholars engaged in the higher branches of learning." Thus, it is the community of faculty and students that is the essence of a university. The higher branches of learning in which teachers and scholars engage have two important products: the educated minds that are essential for the well-being of society and new knowledge and ideas. Some of that new knowledge will enrich society by producing economic growth, directly or indirectly, but the benefits of new knowledge go far beyond economic gain.

3   Universities have always been subjected to outside influences. The oldest European university, the University of Bologna, has existed at least since the 1080s. Some time before 1222, about 1,000 students left Bologna and founded a new university in Padua because of "the grievous offence that was brought to bear on their academic liberties and the failure to acknowledge the privileges solemnly granted to teachers and students."[1] The outside interference came from the Roman Catholic Church, and for several centuries, Padua was home to the only university in Europe where non-Catholics could get a university education. Both Bologna and Padua were student-controlled universities with students electing the professors and fixing their salaries. However, in spite of marked differences, there are similarities between what happened then and what is happening today, with important outside influences—then the dogma of religion, now the dogma of business—threatening to change the activities of the community of teachers and scholars.

4   The seeds of what is happening now were sown in the years following World War II. Before the war, the most important influence on a faculty member was probably the departmental chair, who in those days had power to influence in an important way what went on in the department. Nonetheless, a faculty member would have had access to departmental resources and would not necessarily have required outside research funding (although such funding was sometimes available from private foundations). The

mechanism of funding research, and the amount of money available for research, changed greatly in the postwar years. In 1945, Vannevar Bush's landmark report to President Harry Truman, *Science the endless frontier,*[2] had an important influence on university research. In this report, Bush stated, "The publicly and privately supported colleges, universities, and research institutes are the centres of basic research. They are the wellsprings of knowledge and understanding. As long as they are vigorous and healthy and their scientists are free to pursue the truth wherever it may lead, there will be a flow of new scientific knowledge to those who can apply it to practical problems in Government, in industry, or elsewhere." Bush supported the idea that the US government should provide strong financial support for university research but also supported the idea that the individual investigator should be the main determinant of the topics for investigation, with statements such as "Scientific progress on a broad front results from the free play of free intellects, working on subjects of their own choice, in the manner dictated by their curiosity for exploration of the unknown."[2]

5   In the latter half of the last century, many countries adopted the model of granting councils, which used a system based on peer review to distribute money for investigator-initiated research. This model has been a great success, but it has also contributed to important changes in universities. Much more money has been available to support medical research, basic science research, and engineering research than has been available for the social sciences or arts. Thus, decisions about support for different disciplines devolved from the universities to governments, who decided on the budgets of their various grant-giving bodies. Also, individual researchers who were successful in obtaining grants no longer depended as much on departmental facilities. In my opinion, this not only weakened the power of departmental chairs but also decreased collegiality within departments.

6   With increased enrolments, as a university education became accessible to a greater proportion of the population, and an increased need for infrastructure for the larger student population and for complex research equipment, administrators became more concerned about sources of funding and consequently more detached from the faculty. There is always a tendency for senior academic administrators to speak and behave as though they *were* the university (when of course they are there to serve the community of teachers and scholars). This is of course a normal human trait, no different from the tendency of politicians to forget that they are elected to serve the people. However, this increasing detachment of senior university administrators from the faculty has facilitated the erosion of collegiality within departments and universities. The individual personalities of university faculty probably also facilitated this change. I learned recently, when looking at the literature on personality, that an inverse correlation between intelligence and conscientiousness has been demonstrated in a number of studies (see, for example, Moutafi et al[3]). Thus, it might be more than just my paranoia leading me to believe that the small proportion of university faculty who lack conscientiousness and collegiality is larger than in some other walks of life. The erosion of collegiality is not a matter of great significance, except that it probably played a role in making researchers more open to the efforts of governments to transform them into entrepreneurs.

7   The most recent and possibly the most important change in university research resulted from the push by governments to commercialize the results of such research. In the United States, the Bayh-Dole Act of 1980 encouraged universities to license to private industry discoveries made with federal funds.[4] The push by governments for commercialization of new knowledge grew during the 1980s and 1990s and continues to have an important influence on universities. Recently, Lord Sainsbury, the science and innovation minister in the United Kingdom, boasted that there had been a cultural change in universities there, which has resulted in a substantial increase in university spin-offs.[5] In 2002 the Association of Universities and Colleges of Canada entered an agreement with the government to double the amount of research performed by these institutions and to triple their commercialization performance by 2010.[6] Although this agreement was reached in the absence of any broad consultation with the faculty who are supposed to commercialize their work, the universities seem to be well on track to achieve this objective, with a 126 per cent increase in revenues from licence royalties between 1999 and 2001.[7] Most major universities now have a technology transfer office, and at many universities success in commercialization is taken into account when faculty are considered for tenure. Will there come a time when success in commercialization carries the same weight as (or more weight than) teaching and research in the awarding of tenure?

8   The end result of all the changes discussed above is that individual faculty members have become much more like entrepreneurs whose main allegiance is to the

maintenance or growth of their own research programs and not infrequently to the commercialization of their research. The researcher exploring Vannevar Bush's "endless frontier" could be considered the modern equivalent of the homesteader taming the seemingly endless frontier of the nineteenth-century American West.[8] This is not necessarily detrimental if a new generation of university research entrepreneurs provides the new knowledge that will benefit patients and society. However, the change in culture that made university faculty more like entrepreneurs also made them more open to the desire of governments to make them entrepreneurs in the economic sense. Although the nature of universities has been changing, there was no threat to the fundamental nature of universities until the drive for commercialization began.

9   A recent report of the Canadian Association of University Teachers[9] states that university administrators have been "building increasingly hierarchical management structures" that "place the future of academic medicine in danger." The report's main concern is that "incentives to create commercializable products push economic concerns, rather than scientific and ethical considerations, to the forefront."[9] In the fields of biologic psychiatry and behavioural neuroscience, the emphasis on commercial applications has already, to some extent, moved research priorities away from an emphasis on mental well-being to an emphasis on commercial products. There are many examples of this shift. For example, more research is being carried out on antidepressant drugs than on psychotherapy, even though in mild to moderate depression (the majority of cases) drugs and psychotherapy are approximately equal in efficacy. There is increasing evidence for the efficacy of exercise[10,11] and fish oils[12,13] in the treatment and prevention of depression. However, these strategies receive much less attention than antidepressant drugs. Even an established antidepressant treatment such as S-adenosylmethionine (SAMe)[14] receives little attention. Searching the abstracts of the 2004 meeting of the Society for Neuroscience, I found 179 with the keyword "antidepressant" and only four with the keyword "S-adenosylmethionine," and none of those four was concerned with the antidepressant action of SAMe. SAMe is a major methyl donor and seems to work in a fundamentally different way from any product being investigated by drug companies. Surely we could expect that an antidepressant acting through a different mechanism would be a popular topic of investigation. However, SAMe is a natural product and not of commercial interest. Similarly, insights into what exercise or fish oils do to the brain may provide important insights into the pathophysiology of depression and its treatment, but these subjects receive little attention.

10   Many basic science researchers investigating the mechanisms of antidepressants produced by drug companies do not receive funding from those companies. However, enough are lured by drug company research funds into working on topics of interest to the companies to significantly influence what are fashionable topics of research. Laboratories with funding from industry can often afford more trainees, who may then adopt a more industry-centred approach in their own research. While the availability of funds from industry has certainly influenced research, the pressure on university faculty to commercialize the results of their research will undoubtedly cause even greater distortion in the areas of research that are most popular.

11   Granting agencies have increasingly tried to foster research in neglected areas by allocating funds to specific areas of research and requesting applications in those areas. Although this approach is certainly necessary, it has not done much to alter the effects of drug company money on research output. Also, in some ways it moves research even further away from the ideal in Vannevar Bush's report that "Scientific progress on a broad front results from the free play of free intellects, working on subjects of their own choice, in the manner dictated by their curiosity for exploration of the unknown."[2] This model was notably successful in the last half of the twentieth century, but it may not survive the pressure to commercialize. While there is still much scope for curiosity-driven research, the curiosity of researchers is likely to be aligned increasingly with the interests of drug companies. As mentioned above, a cultural change has accompanied the increasing commercialization of university research. The pressure to commercialize has been critiqued in some quarters, but many university faculty have nonetheless embraced commercialization or at least remained unconcerned about it. Are we far from a time when a researcher without a patent that is being commercialized will be regarded in the same way as those who do not publish regularly in the top journals? And how long will it be before governments make commercialization a mandate of granting councils and a requirement for the majority of grants?

12   A fascination with the workings of the brain and how it can malfunction in mental illness is the usual motivator for researchers in neuroscience and psychiatry research. As a result, curiosity-driven research will always tend to serve the

best interests of patients. Although research driven by commercial interests will certainly benefit psychiatric patients in some ways, it cannot serve their overall needs, as it is much too narrowly focused. The designation of funds by granting agencies for specific neglected topics will help but is unlikely to produce any large changes in the direction of research. Thus, the biggest losers from the pressure to commercialize will be psychiatric patients. In addition, I am concerned whether students who are trained to focus on the short-term commercial implications of their research will be able to maintain the breadth of vision that is a characteristic of the majority of creative researchers.

13   Changes due to pressure from governments to commercialize are not limited to researchers. The increased emphasis on commercialization in universities has in some ways distorted the perceptions of senior university administrators about the purpose of the institutions. For example, there seems to be a lack of concern about some of the sources of funds that universities receive. Universities now hold patents on many life-saving drugs. These patents sometimes limit access to the drugs, particularly in low-income countries.[15] In Canada, one-quarter of the faculties of medicine receive funding from the tobacco industry.[16] Perhaps a suitable future definition of a university will be a "whole body of teachers and scholars engaged in turning ideas into profit."

14   In thirteenth-century Italy, the response to interference by the Roman Catholic Church in the work of scholars was a move to another location to escape the interference. In the twenty-first century, that option is not available even to the minority who are concerned about the drive to commercialize. However, the picture is not entirely bleak. Charitable foundations will remain immune to commercial interests. In addition, even though charitable foundations will probably remain relatively small players in the funding of research, there are promising signs. For example, the Bill and Melinda Gates Foundation, created in 2000, has an endowment of about US$27 billion and is striving to use its money for the benefit of humankind in areas neglected by governments. This foundation is not involved in psychiatric research, but its focus on preventive approaches may help to direct interest to that important area. Research on prevention in psychiatry is still in its infancy and will certainly remain that way if short-term commercial considerations stay paramount. However, charitable foundations cannot be expected to have any large effect on the change in university culture brought about by the drive to commercialize. Although I would like to be able to end this editorial on a more hopeful note, I am concerned about these cultural changes, and I do not see any solution. Still, one lesson from history is that the communities of teachers and scholars making up universities have adapted to many changes over the centuries without changing the fundamental nature of universities, and they will surely continue to do so. I am just not sure how.

References

1. *History.* Padua (Italy): Università Degli Studi di Padova. Available: www.unipd.it/en/university/history.htm (accessed 2004 Dec 13).

2. Bush V. *Science the endless frontier. A report to the President by Vannevar Bush, Director of the Office of Scientific Research and Development, July 1945.* Washington: US Government Printing Office; 1945. Available: www.nsf.gov/od/lpa/nsf50/vbush1945.htm (accessed 2004 Dec 13).

3. Moutafi J, Furnham A, Paltiel L. Why is conscientiousness negatively correlated with intelligence? *Pers Individ Differ* 2004;37:1013–22.

4. Thursby JG, Thursby MC. Intellectual property. University licensing and the Bayh-Dole Act. Science 2003;301:1052.

5. Sainsbury L. A cultural change in UK universities [editorial]. *Science* 2002;296:1929.

6. Allan Rock welcomes framework on federally funded university research [press release]. Toronto: Industry Canada; 2002 Nov 19[modified 2003 Jun 16]. Available: www.ic.gc.ca/cmb/welcomeic.nsf/558d63659099294285 2564880052155b/85256a220056c2a485256c76004c7d44 (accessed 2004 Dec 13).

7. Berkowitz P. Spinning off research: AUCC sets new tool to measure universities' commercialization performance. *Univ Aff* [serial on-line] 2004; June/July. Available: www.universityaffairs.ca/issues/2004/june july/print/spinning-off.html (accessed 2004 Dec 13).

8. Kennedy D. Enclosing the research commons [editorial]. *Science* 2001;294:2249.

9. Welch P, Cass CE, Guyatt G, Jackson AC, Smith D. *Defending medicine: clinical faculty and academic freedom.* Report of the Canadian Association of University Teachers (CAUT) Task Force on Academic Freedom for Faculty at University-Affiliated Health Care Institutions. Ottawa: Canadian Association of University Teachers; 2004 Nov. Available: www.caut.ca/en/issues/academicfreedom/DefendingMedicine.pdf (accessed 2004 Dec 21).

10. Salmon P. Effects of physical exercise on anxiety, depression, and sensitivity to stress: a unifying theory. *Clin Psychol Rev* 2001; 21:33–61.

11. *Depression: management of depression in primary and secondary care.* Clinical guideline 23. London (UK): National Institute for Clinical Excellence; 2004 Dec. Available: www.nice.org.uk/pdf/CG023NICEguideline.pdf (accessed 2005 Mar 8).

12. Nemets B, Stahl Z, Belmaker RH. Addition of omega-3 fatty acid to maintenance medication treatment for recurrent unipolar depressive disorder. *Am J Psychiatry* 2002; 159:477–9.

13. Su KP, Huang SY, Chiu CC, Shen WW. Omega-3 fatty acids in major depressive disorder. A preliminary double-blind, placebo controlled trial. Eur *Neuropsychopharmacol* 2003;13:267–71.

14. Papakostas GI, Alpert JE, Fava M. S-Adenosyl-methionine in depression: a comprehensive review of the literature. *Curr Psychiatry Rep* 2003;5:460–6.

15. Kapczynski A, Crone ET, Merson M. Global health and university patents [editorial]. *Science* 2003;301:1629.

16. Kaufman PE, Cohen JE, Ashley MJ, Ferrence R, Halyak AI, Turcotte F, et al. Tobacco industry links to faculties of medicine in Canada. *Can J Public Health* 2004; 95:205–8.

Key and challenging words

dogma, collegiality, infrastructure

Questions

1. Explain why it is important for Young to define the common word "university" in paragraph 2.

2. Do you believe that the comparison in paragraph 3 between what happened at Italian universities before 1222 and what is occurring at today's universities is valid? Why or why not?

3. Name two negative consequences that resulted from adoption of the "model of granting councils" in the second half of the twentieth century.

4. Analyze paragraph 9. Among the factors you could consider are the method(s) of development (rhetorical patterns), the kinds of support, and the writer's credibility.

5. Who does Young believe will ultimately be most affected if research in neuroscience and psychiatry continues to be "driven by commercial interests?"

6. Comment on the author's use of *two* of the following argumentative strategies in the essay (see Chapter 9, pp. 110–113): (a) establishing common ground with the reader; (b) making concessions to the other side; (c) using an emotional appeal; or (d) appealing to reader interests.

7. Could Young have ended his editorial more positively or assertively than he did? Does the concluding paragraph add or detract from the strength of the essay?

8. Would you say that Young's main purpose is (a) to expose a problem, (b) to change a situation, (c) to critique a position, or (d) to reach a compromise? How might his audience affect his purpose?

Post-reading

1. *Collaborative activity:* As students who may be going on to intensive undergraduate work or perhaps graduate school, are you concerned about the increasing ties of university research to commercial interests? How do you think it could affect you or students like you in the next few years?

2. *Collaborative activity:* It is well known that substantially more money is given today to research in science, engineering, and medicine than to research in the arts. Do you think this allocation is inevitable? Do you think it is fair? Do you believe that students, administrators, or society should be concerned about the possible consequences to arts programs throughout the country?

3. Reflect on the idea of a "student-controlled university" (see paragraph 3). Write up a one- to two-page proposal in which you urge your government to finance such a university. In your proposal, you should outline the need for the project, along with goals and objectives, and provide a few specific features of such a university.

Intellectuals and Democracy

Mark Kingwell
(2,238 words)

1   You might think judges would make diverting dinner companions, but I can tell you that on the whole they don't. The judge sitting next to me, who shall go nameless, condemned all modern art as overpraised child's play. She railed against graduated income tax. She told me I would outgrow my socialist tendencies (I was 48 at the time). She left without contributing to the bill.

2   So I was not surprised when, after hearing what I did for a living, she said, "But what will your students *do* with that?"

3   There is a special intonation to this use of the verb 'do', familiar to anyone who has studied classics or considered a graduate degree in mathematics, with its long vowel of contempt honeyed over by apparent concern. When I was in my second postgraduate year, a woman in an Edinburgh bus queue delivered the best version I have so far encountered: "Philosophy! Really! Do you have any idea what you'll *do* with that?" (Poor sod: useless *and* out to lunch!)

4   I could have told the judge something she ought to have known already, which is that *philosophy students usually rock the* LSAT. They get into prestigious law schools, even sometimes make it onto the bench. Statistically speaking, there is no better preparation for success in law than an undergraduate degree spent thinking about the nature of knowledge, the meaning of being and, especially, what makes a valid argument.

5   But even though this is itself a valid argument, it is not a good one. I mean that the success of the argument actually conceded a greater failure; it gives away the game of justification to a base value. A degree in philosophy, or humane study more generally, does not require validation in the court of do-with usefulness. It is a convenient reality that such validation is sometimes gained, but the victory is really a surrender performed on the enemy's ground.

6   What's surprising is how many of today's university administrators are rushing to do just this, hyping the 'competitiveness' and 'pragmatism' of higher education. The annual higher education supplement published by *Maclean's*, the Canadian weekly magazine, is ground zero for the transactional reduction of learning. The latest version of the supplement included this representative claim from Robert Campbell, president of Mount Allison University in Sackville, New Brunswick. Parents of prospective students, he told a reporter, "are looking for a return on investment" in their child's tuition.

7   And so professors are told that they need to justify their activities according to a market model of 'research effectiveness', where quantifiable 'impact indicators' and 'external research use values' can be totted up and scanned. Students respond by assuming a consumer stance to their own education, swapping tuition dollars not for the chance to interact with other minds but to acquire a postgraduate market advantage. When a 2010 survey of 12,500 students asked, "What was the single most important reason in your decision to attend university," just 9% picked "a good general education" as their answer, while almost 70% had enrolled to "get a good job" or "train for a specific career."

8   Historically, median earning power for university graduates is indeed higher than that of college or high school grads, and over their lifetimes university graduates earn substantially more—75% by some estimates—than non-graduates. And yet, paradoxically, recent years have

Source: From *Unruly Voices: Essays on Democracy, Civility, and the Human Imagination*. Windsor, ON: Biblioasis, 2012. pp. 131–6. Published by Biblioasis and reprinted by permission of the publisher.

witnessed an avalanche of over-qualification. "[M]ore than a quarter of a million Canadian university students are about to graduate into the workforce this spring," *Maclean's* noted. "Yet studies show that fifty percent of Canadian arts and science grads are working in jobs that don't require a university credential two years after graduation."

9   All is not lost, however. "As the knowledge economy continues to grow—and manufacturing jobs disappear—there's more demand for university grads in the workforce than ever." Rest easy, parents. Pony up, students. There's still reason to get an education! It's just not anything to do with education.

10   Call this familiar mixture of doom and market optimism the *standard position*. It can be summarized this way: university education must be judged according to its ultimate usefulness. That usefulness will be understood as career success of one sort or another, especially as measured by wealth. The position then adds the *soft option*: get a degree because the "knowledge economy" will otherwise crush you.

11   The soft option is favoured by presidents as well as university presidents. Barack Obama, giving a speech at a college in 2011, noted that America's need to 'remain competitive' was an argument for higher education: "If we want more good news on the jobs front then we've got to make more investments in education." He offered no other arguments in its favour.

———

12   For all its currency, the standard position strikes me as wrong-headed, if not dangerous. It is a philistine position, obviously; it works to hollow out the critical possibilities of education. Holders of this position regard real humanistic educations as a dispensable luxury of idiosyncratic and purely personal value, and that makes them, in turn, dangerous.

13   They are correct, however, that the standard position is now so deeply presupposed that even calling attention to it can be enough to brand one an ivory-tower whackjob, tilting at windmills. The 2011 *Maclean's* authors noted with some satisfaction that nobody would nowadays express the indignation that greeted similar reductive accounts of education a decade ago, not apparently aware of the role *Maclean's* and its consumer-style surveys have played in that reduction.

14   As far as I'm concerned the judge and all those in the standard-position camp are the enemy. They are not enemies of philosophy, or me, or my students; they are enemies of democracy, and insofar as we refuse to admit that—insofar as we soft-pedal the value of the humanities when confronted by a scale of value keyed only to wealth—we are not being serious about what democracy means. As with the democratic narratives discussed in relation to Francis Fukuyama (see "The Tomist," in this collection) and the electoral system (see "Throwing Dice"), we are witnessing nothing less than the regulatory capture of universities under the general influence of a market model that can only be challenged by arguments rooted in another, human code of value.

15   Most defences of the humanities fall back on preaching to the choir: they assume the value of the very thing they need to defend, namely the cultivation of self and world that marks genuine study, what Aristotle called *skholé*, or leisure (hence the word 'school'). At that point, there is usually a predictable spinoff into denunciations of elitism and counter-denunciations of its reverse-snobbery evil twin, anti-intellectualism. The net result is either an impasse or a trail into absurdity: witness the 2006 *National Post* reader poll which concluded that bombastic hockey commentator Don Cherry was the nation's "most important public intellectual". . . .

16   But there's not need to go through any of that, because the standard position is actually self-defeating.

———

17   Let's do a little casual philosophical analysis. What are the unspoken premises of the standard position?

18   Most obviously, it assumes (1) that we know what *use* is. Something is useful when it has instrumental value. Things of instrumental value serve needs other than their own, either some higher instrumental value or an intrinsic value. And yet, in practice 'use' almost always comes down to money, which is itself a perfect example of a *lower* instrumental value. Money is just a tool, but we talk and act as if it were an end in itself.

19   So the position likewise assumes (2) that we know how to value things that contribute to use. We can convert any activity or human possibility into some quantified assessment, and thus dispose of the question of whether it is worth doing. Not only does this make a mockery of human action, quickly narrowing the scope of what is considered worth doing, but it simultaneously narrows the scope of argument about the nature of worth. This leads to a market monopoly on the notion of the 'real': anything that is not in play in a market is irrelevant or imaginary.

20   The position in turn presupposes (3) that education is in thrall to this 'real world' of market value—actually a massive collective delusion as abstract as anything in Hegel's

Phenomenology—because according to (2) all human activities are. The market's monopoly on reality reinforces the dominant value of competition and selfishness, incidentally converting education into a credential-race that can (and rationally should) be gamed rather than enjoyed itself.

21   Lurking nearby are two other implicit ideas about life after graduation: (4) education must be intimately linked to work; and (5) doing work while 'over-qualified' is a bad thing. This link between education and work is a nifty piece of legerdemain which preys on the uncertainties all humans have about the future, even as it leaves untouched the general presumption that one must have a job to be human. Parents and children alike fall for it.

22   Finally, at least in the soft option, there is (6): the assumption that education can find its match in white-collar work of the knowledge economy, and so justify doing a degree after all. This completes the regulatory capture of education. What was once considered a site of challenge to received ideas and bad argument, even to entrenched power and pooled wealth, is now a not particularly successful adjunct to the pursuit of that power and wealth.

23   Unfortunately the facts do not bear this out, and this is where the entire arrangement collapses.

24   While the number of jobs asking for a degree has increased over the past two decades, the fact is that, since 1990 or so, the North American job market has not been characterized by a smooth rise in demand for cognitive skills to match growth in technology. Instead, there has been a hollowing out of the market's middle, such that top-level jobs (creating technologies, playing markets, scoring touchdowns) have risen in overall wealth but not numbers, while low-end jobs (fixing pipes, driving semi-trailers, pouring lattes) have remained steady or grown slightly. In between, there is a significant depression of the very middle-class occupations that most university graduates imagine will be their return on investment.

25   The consequences of this economic reality are twofold. First, it explodes the assessment of education in terms of economic reality. There is no prospect of the competitive 'knowledge economy' future to underwrite a decision to go to university. The soft option is gone.

26   Second, and more profoundly, the standard position now exhibits its full contradictions. If you cannot value education in terms of money, then education has no value. That means that, if you decide to pursue such an education, it has to be for reasons other than value. But that would mean doing something that has no use, and surely that is silly.

27   There is an ironic benefit to this collapse. Sure, some people will conclude that university is not for them: it doesn't confer the market benefit it used to, so to hell with it. For others, though, the land beyond use might continue to beckon, a place where there is no easy decline into the disengagement of merely personal interests.

28   The standard position was founded on a paradox: university graduates are overqualified for the jobs they do; but you should still go because there is a statistical link between a degree and higher income. This is now replaced with a new paradox, the paradox of philosophy in the general sense: there is no use in pursuing a university education; but you should pursue it anyway because it's the only way to see any use beyond what is everywhere assumed.

———

29   What does any of this have to do with democracy? Again, a twofold conclusion. First, wider university admission isn't going to result in prosperity for everyone. If we want to have more equitable distributions of wealth and opportunity, we can't rely on markets to do it, even or especially markets flooded with dazed graduates looking for work in a depression created, in part, by high-flyers gaming the abstract markets. And no, more business schools are not the answer.

30   Second, though, we actually need graduates more than ever precisely because democracy depends on a population of engaged, critical thinkers who have general humane knowledge of history, politics, culture, economics, and science, citizens and not consumers who see that there exist shared interests beyond their own desires. Once the link between higher education and work has been broken, the value of the humanities and non-applied sciences becomes clear. Education is not there to be converted into market value; it is there to make us better and more engaged citizens, maybe even better and more virtuous people. There, I said it! The entailed benefit is that these citizens are ones who will challenge the reduction of all consideration to the price of everything and the value of nothing.

31   Aristotle again: usefulness is not virtue. He meant to ask us each to consider how and why we come to value things, to consider them relevant, to think them worth doing. "What are you going to do with that?" asks the concerned fellow diner or transit passenger.

32   But as Socrates said, philosophy concerns no small thing, just the tricky matter of *wondering how best to live*. So the answer is: I'm already doing it. And you should be too.

Key and challenging words

philistine, idiosyncratic, intrinsic, legerdemain, paradox, equitable

Questions

1. (a) Using your own words, explain what Kingwell means in paragraph 5; (b) explain what Kingwell means by the "regulatory capture of universities" (see paragraphs 14 and 22).
2. Identify, then paraphrase, Kingwell's thesis.
3. Analyze the essay's introduction (paragraphs 1–11) to determine the purpose of his essay and intended audience. Factors you could consider include language level, diction, tone, use of anecdotes and dialogue, and other rhetorical strategies.
4. Explain Kingwell's extensive use of *Maclean's* as a source in paragraphs 6–13. Do you think he believes its annual university rankings serve a useful purpose? Support your answer by specific references to Kingwell's essay.
5. Identify at least one example each of humour and irony in the essay. Discuss what either humour or irony contributes to the essay.
6. In the third section of the essay, identify a paragraph in which Kingwell uses deductive reasoning and one in which he uses inductive reasoning. (See Chapter 9, Writing Argumentative Essays, for the differences between deductive and inductive reasoning.)
7. Discuss the function and effectiveness of the concluding section. In your discussion, consider how it is connected to the introduction and to the essay as a whole.

Post-reading

1. Look back at how you answered pre-reading question 1. Has your response changed after studying the essay? Depending on your response to the essay, write one or two paragraphs that consider (a) how or why the essay made you question or change your original assumptions or (b) why the essay did not change your original assumptions. What would Kingwell need to do to make his argument more convincing to you?
2. Analyze Kingwell's use of ethical appeals in his essay. (See Chapter 8, The Active Voice: Rhetorical Analysis: What, Why, and How.)

Canada in the World

Of Hockey, Medicare, and Canadian Dreams

Stephen J. Toope
(1,968 words)

> ### Pre-reading
>
> 1. *Collaborative or individual activity:* In addition to hockey, what other accomplishments do Canadians deserve to be celebrated for or credited with? Individually or in groups, brainstorm a list. Choose one or two items from the list and write specifically on the unique nature of these accomplishments (or discuss one or two items if done in groups).
> 2. Who is Stephen J. Toope? Using at least two reliable sources, write one or two paragraphs that outline his biography and his qualifications for writing "Of Hockey, Medicare and Canadian Dreams."

Abstract

As Canada approaches its 150th anniversary, Canadians need to decide what we want to be when we grow up. Our national sport and Medicare alone will not define us. Understanding our strengths and facing our problems squarely, what visions could Canadians be dreaming of as we face a stormy future?

———

1 Hockey is a great, fast-paced sport, and it has served well as an emblem for Canadians' sense of self. Set in winter snows, demanding agility and fortitude in the face of harsh conditions, and requiring a robust competitive spirit, hockey speaks both to what Canadians have inherited from a frontier history and to what we hope to be.

2 It is too bad that the national game is dominated by an NHL that seems greedier, insensitive to the expectations of fans and dominated by the need to satisfy a US market. And the increasingly obvious risks associated with out-of-control violence may one day bring the current hockey regime to account.

3 Medicare is a great social policy achievement, and it has served well as an emblem for Canadians' sense of self. Emerging from the wide plains of Saskatchewan, and reflecting a desire to protect the vulnerable amongst us, Medicare speaks to an open spirit and an aspiration towards social equality.

4 Too bad the system underperforms less costly systems in Europe and fails to produce health outcomes that an advanced society should expect to see. The costs keep rising, crowding out other social expenditures of both federal and provincial governments. And access seems to depend too often on who you know.

5 Is this the best we can do as Canadians? Are hockey and Medicare our defining features? Do they best represent who we are and what we hope to become? As Canada approaches its 150th anniversary, we Canadians need to push ourselves a little to figure out what we want to be when we grow up.

6 It may seem strange to say that we aren't grown up yet, for we are among a handful of countries that has managed democratic rule for so long. Yet our democracy has, for much of its history, been a dependent one, first on the United Kingdom and then on the United States. It was only after the First World War that Canada began to develop an independent set of relationships with foreign states, and only in 1931, with the passing of the Statute of Westminster, that the Canadian Parliament was accorded status equal to the Parliament of the UK. Our economic policy was long constrained by our absolute dependence upon the United States in foreign trade. From the 1960s through to the early 2000s, the share of Canadian trade with the US rose from roughly 60 per cent of total trade to over 80. With more attention to Asia in the last few years, the concentration of trade with the US has fallen, but remains over 70 per cent. For much of our history in the twentieth century, Canada hid behind the US on major matters of foreign policy as well. Although we liked to think of ourselves as "honest brokers," much of the world saw us merely as somewhat gentler versions of Americans.

Source: From *Canadian Issues*, Summer 2013, pp. 58–61. Reprinted with permission.

7   These hard-sounding comments should not be mistaken for self-loathing. Canadians have much to be proud of, as our country has evolved through the last century. We have created a society marked by relative openness to immigration, especially in comparison with most of Europe. Our ability to attract large numbers of people from foreign shores, respecting and even borrowing from many of their traditions, while encouraging social integration, is enviable. It is practically unmatched in other liberal democracies. It is a truism, for example, that Vancouver is now the largest Asian city outside Asia, but what is truly remarkable is the ability of immigrants from China, Korea and elsewhere to build lives that are still connected to their histories and to have other Canadians acknowledge that history. UBC has the largest Mandarin language programme in North America, and many of its students are Anglo-Canadian, of Korean and Japanese origin, or foreign students from around the world.

8   Canadians should also be proud of our history of social mobility. Today, when many influential Americans, like Nobel Prize-winning economist Joseph Stiglitz, worry that the US is no longer a "land of opportunity," Canada is out-performing the US as a place where it is possible to rise from distinctly modest backgrounds to find economic security. A major reason for that continuing mobility is that education is publicly financed to a large extent, from day care right through to doctoral programmes. University and college education is still relatively affordable in Canada, opening up worlds of opportunity for new generations of students, from here and from around the globe.

9   On the cultural front, Canada has also seen an explosion of talent and global recognition over the last few years. Canadian authors like Atwood, Gallant, Hagi, Huston, Laferrière, Martel, Munro, and Ondaatje are international best-sellers and prize winners. Canadian actors star in major Hollywood films. Although English-Canadian cinema is not in its strongest period, Quebec cinema continues to produce inventive and influential films, including three nominated for best foreign-film Oscars in the last three years. In pop music, airwaves and iPods around the world are filled with the likes of Drake, Justin Bieber, Celine Dion, Carly Rae Jepsen, and Leonard Cohen. The Vancouver school of conceptual and post-conceptual photography is globally influential, with artists like Jeff Wall offered retrospectives at major galleries world-wide.

10   Canadians have lots to celebrate, aside from hockey and Medicare, though we tend not to celebrate very loudly. How many Canadians even know that Nancy Huston, a Calgarian by origin but writing in French, won France's prestigious Prix Fémina, or that Canadian composer Howard Shore has won three Oscars, three Golden Globes and four Grammies for his film scores? Just last year, Canadians could have celebrated the thirtieth anniversary of the *Canadian Charter of Rights and Freedoms*, a constitutional text that has influenced legal systems around the world, in part through direct borrowing and in part through the work of the Canadian Supreme Court which, since the advent of the *Charter*, has proven to be one of the most internationally cited courts in the world. Small-minded politics out of Ottawa precluded much attention to this anniversary.

11   But amidst the many reasons that we should celebrate, there are also reasons to worry. While we continue to target for roughly 250,000 new immigrants each year, their integration into our economy has faltered, even though they are better educated than ever before. Between 2000 and 2005, according to Statistics Canada, the income gap between Canadian-born workers and recent immigrants with university degrees widened significantly. Our productivity as a nation has also stagnated. Over the last thirty years, the productivity gap between Canadian and US workers has increased to almost $10,000 a person per year. This is not because Canadians don't work hard, but because our business performance in innovation is tepid at best. The Jenkins Panel on Canadian innovation reported to the federal government in 2010 that the expenditure of Canadian business on research and development had fallen since 2006, declining to the level of 2000, when Canada was already merely at the average of Organization for Economic Cooperation and Development (OECD) countries.

12   Consider also what has happened to real wages over the last thirty years. Statistics Canada reports that average real wage rates increased by only 14 per cent in Canada from 1981 to 2011, failing to match the rising cost of living. Even though social mobility is better than in the United States, it is less robust than in many European countries, which have traditionally been seen as bastions of privilege. The Conference Board of Canada laments that from 1990 to 2013, the wealthiest Canadians have significantly increased their proportion of total national income, while the poorest, and even middle-income groups, have lost ground.

13   Like the inhabitants of many other advanced economies, Canadians may live through a slow-moving demographic train wreck over the next few years. Not only are there likely to be too few working people to support the social safety net for the Boomer generation, but even now a growing gulf is opening between generations, with younger Canadians

worrying that they won't ever find meaningful jobs or be able to afford their own homes. UBC's Professor Paul Kershaw demonstrates that the average household income for young Canadian couples has stagnated since the mid-1970s, adjusting for inflation, while average housing prices in Canada have skyrocketed by 76%. Culturally, many of our once-treasured institutions and organizations are in perilous straits. In 2012 to 2013, funding cuts to arts organizations kicked in at the federal and provincial levels. The Playhouse Theatre in Vancouver closed, The Toronto Symphony operated in deficit, one of the last major Canadian independent publishers, Douglas & McIntyre, filed for bankruptcy protection, and the National Gallery of Canada cut staff to address a budget crunch.

14   Incanting the names of Sidney Crosby, Roberto Luongo and Carey Price just won't be good enough to protect Canadians from the storms to come, or to ground a rich sense of identity. Nor will Medicare alone be our sure port. Understanding our strengths and facing our problems squarely, Canadians need to figure out who we are, now that we really are quite close to grown up. What visions could Canadians be dreaming to as we face a stormy future? What might a robust sense of Canadianness, of pride in our society, look like 50 years or so from now, at the 200th anniversary of Confederation?

15   The social inclusion that we have offered to generations and generations of immigrants will continue, and be buttressed by better economic integration. That inclusive spirit will finally be matched by a respect for the traditions of the First Nations and other aboriginal Canadians, and society-wide efforts to help ensure their economic, social and cultural vitality. We will have recaptured our fundamental, if demanding, connections to the land and the landscape, defined so clearly in Margaret Atwood's *Survival* or Margaret Laurence's *The Stone Angel*. Those connections will imply a profound commitment to understanding and upholding the delicate balancing required in the exploitation of resources and treasuring the natural environment.

16   Canadians will have re-imagined our place in the world, recognizing that our social and economic links to Asia are an important trade strength, but that the greatest source of long-term opportunity might well be in Africa. We will admit that we cannot secure our future through military adventures because we will never have the staying power required to deal with internal conflicts and guerrilla-style war on foreign shores. Our focus, instead, will be on entrepreneurial social, cultural and economic engagement around the world, matched with military training missions and limited participation in collective security efforts designed to protect vulnerable populations. We will finally have cracked the code on Canadian-style social and economic innovation, innovation that draws on the diverse talents of an astonishingly intercultural and multilingual society with deep family, social, cultural and economic connections that span the globe. To spur that innovation in all fields of endeavour, Canadians will have found the will to risk for the great, rather than settling for the good.

17   And yes, hockey will still matter, but a hockey that has re-found its connection to people more than dollars, and a hockey that doesn't sacrifice the well-being of players in an attempt to mimic ultimate fighting. Canadians will have employed our 'new-found social innovation mojo to re-engineer Medicare to ensure its fiscal sustainability and improve health outcomes.

18   Canadians' dreams will be about hockey, healthy kids and pensioners, friends from all parts of the world, gorgeous natural vistas and culturally rich urban neighbourhoods, and work in far-away places where Canadians are welcomed as partners in creative social and economic initiatives. Adult dreams.

Note

1.   The views expressed are personal and should not be attributed to the University of British Columbia.

Key and challenging words

truism, preclude, retrospective (n), tepid, incant, buttress

Questions

1.   Identify, then paraphrase, Toope's thesis (recall that not all theses take the form of a statement).

2.   Analyze the author's brief introduction, commenting on any stylistic features, such as repetition, that

contribute to its effect or that suggest the essay's purpose.

3. Summarize paragraph 6, in which Toope explains why he believes Canada is not "grown up yet."

4. Discuss Toope's use of (a) examples and (b) statistics in developing his argument. Refer specifically to the text.

5. Discuss the strategies that Toope uses to avoid coming across as too negative in his essay. You could discuss his language, tone, rhetorical/argumentative strategies or any other relevant features.

6. Explain the purpose of the following paragraphs and their function in the essay: (a) 15–16; (b) 17–18.

Post-reading

1. Do you think that Toope is essentially an optimist or a pessimist in his vision of Canada—present and past? Provide textual evidence to support your claim.

When Canada Goes Viral: The Canada Party and the Circulation of Political Satire

Kimberley McLeod

(3,105 words)

> ### Pre-reading
>
> 1. Based on your observations and/or experiences (e.g., through reading works of satire in literature classes), come up with a one- to two-sentence definition of *satire*, which includes its purpose(s).

1   A man in a dress shirt and tie sits by a roaring fire reading a book. He is surrounded by a collection of stereotypical Canadian objects: flags, a picture of Queen Elizabeth II, red Olympic mittens, and National Hockey League merchandise. Yet the book he is reading—*Going Rogue* by Sarah Palin—is definitely not Canadian. He gives a perplexed look and puts the book down. Now he stares directly into the camera and introduces himself, stating, "Hello America, it's us, Canada" (Calvert and Cannon, "The Canada Party—'Meet'"). Canadian actor and comedian Brian Calvert then goes on to say that Canada is worried about the current state of American politics and declares that, because of this, Canada has decided to run as a candidate in the 2012 American presidential election.

2   Created by Calvert and writer Chris Cannon, the "The Canada Party—'Meet the Canada Party'" video was part of a prank performance project in which the two proposed that Canada would be a better presidential option than either Barack Obama or any of the Republican Party candidates. In the video, which uses the aesthetics of a campaign advertisement, Calvert lists the ways America would benefit from being run by Canada. Posted to *YouTube* in January 2012, the satirical performance went viral, receiving over a million views and considerable media attention in Canada and abroad. It was the most popular piece in the larger performance project, which included additional videos, a campaign website, and a published book.

3   After it was posted to *YouTube*, Calvert and Cannon's satirical performance drew the attention of traditional news media outside Canada, particularly in the UK and US. Responses to the prank reveal some of the challenges activist performers face when dealing with mass media, which can shift the message of tactical interventions and misread irony. Major international news outlets assumed the prank was primarily about nationalistic perceptions of differences between Canada and the US. Though tensions between the countries—and stereotypes of both nations—appear in the video, the artists also embed a scathing critique of Canada's then Conservative government and its leader, Stephen Harper, into their content. In addition, the international

Source: Reprinted with permission from University of Toronto Press (www.utpjournals.com) from *Canadian Theatre Review*, vol. 166, Spring 2016, pp. 28–33. https://doi.org/10.3138/ctr.166.005.

media's focus on national differences overlooked the most prominent influence on the video: satirical newscasters in the US. In contrast to the nationalistic bent of these news stories, the form and content of the Canada Party campaign highlight a fluid cross-border circulation of news media, political culture, and satire.

4   While satire has been popular for millennia, in North America there has been an upsurge of political satire since the early 2000s—a trend that can be traced to a number of factors, including America's increasingly polarized political culture and the proliferation of accessible and affordable digital tools (Boler 13–14; Day 4, 24). In particular, prank performance has gained traction as a way to critically engage with dominant political structures. Performers such as Stephen Colbert, Sacha Baron Cohen, and the Yes Men have popularized this form, which uses satire and irony to challenge mainstream practices and beliefs. Their pranks build on the work of a diverse range of earlier satirists. For example, their use of mimicry relates to the work of prank political candidates, such as the members of the Rhinoceros Party of Canada. This party was officially registered and ran candidates who made obviously undeliverable promises during federal elections from 1963 to 1993. Today's prank performers also extend forms developed on television during the 1960s. The BBC's *That Was the Week That Was* (1962–1963) generated many of the political satire forms we see in film and television today. The show also ran in the US from 1964 to 1965 and inspired the CBC's *This Hour Has Seven Days* (1964–1966). Contemporary prank artists also poach off mainstream capitalist culture in order to critique from within. This approach follows Gabriella Giannachi's argument that "radical artistic practices need to be utilising the very processes of empire, globalisation and capitalist production that they aim to critique" (11). In prank performances, this frequently involves the use of mimicry, as pranksters impersonate newscasters or agents of government organizations and large corporations.

5   The Canada Party campaign connects to a specific kind of prank performance that L.M. Bogad names "electoral guerrilla theatre" (2). This type of performance responds to the limitations of democratic electoral systems via the appropriation of signs and parodying of electoral norms. Bogad notes this is a fairly recent phenomenon that has become increasingly popular in liberal democracies since the sixties (2–8). In the past decade, one of the most prominent examples of this type of intervention has been election coverage by American comedian Stephen Colbert, who Calvert and Cannon acknowledge is one of their main influences (Ward).

6   Colbert twice used formal electoral processes as fodder for his comedy show, *The Colbert Report*. In 2007, Colbert tried to run in the South Carolina presidential primaries for both the Republicans and the Democrats but was unable to get on either ballot. In 2011, he continued to critically satirize American electoral norms through the legal formation of the Colbert Super Political Action Committee (PAC). Super PACs came into being after two controversial 2010 Supreme Court decisions, which opened the door for political organizations to raise unlimited amounts of money from both individuals and corporations. These funds can be used for political purposes as long as the Super PAC does not directly coordinate with a registered political campaign. Following this decision, there was fear that the new rules would allow corporations and the rich to further influence elections. Using funds donated by viewers, the Colbert Super PAC created and aired a number of satirical campaign videos. Eventually, Colbert announced his intention to run for office again. In order to continue to use his Super PAC funds, Colbert signed over control of the now-renamed The Definitely Not Coordinating with Stephen Colbert Super PAC to Jon Stewart, his longtime comedy collaborator and executive producer. Colbert's prank—which was awarded a Peabody—exemplifies the potential efficacy of prank campaigns as he drew attention to an important issue and had the more quantifiable effect of raising $773,704.83 from viewers. This money was eventually donated to charities, including organizations advocating for transparency in elections.

7   Like Colbert, Calvert and Cannon use electoral guerrilla tactics to satirize the American presidential race. While they do not go as far in their blurring of the fictional and the real—since Canada as a country is of course ineligible to run for President—the Canada Party uses a similar mode of mimicry to poke fun at the lack of enthusiasm many Americans had for their presidential choices. Both Calvert and Colbert mimic political candidates' look and manners, using a tactic that Bogad describes as "candidate drag." He notes that candidate dragging, like other forms of mimicry, leads to a "mimetic excess" (165) with political potential. In the video "The Canada Party—'Meet the Canada Party,'" Calvert drags as a proxy for the entire nation of Canada. This act is a form of performative excess that highlights the very improbability of the premise. At the same time, the video's visual aesthetics and use of campaign phrases expose the constructedness of actual political campaigns. For example, the video's setting mimics the advertisement

trope of candidates sitting at home, talking directly to the camera. Both Barack Obama and Mitt Romney released advertisements like this during the 2012 campaign (Romney; *Wall Street Journal* Digital Network).

8   The Canada Party's viral video intervenes in election discourse by playfully mimicking and mocking dominant political tropes. However, the ways the video content circulated expose some of the challenges satirical performers face when the mass media take up their work. I first heard about the Canada Party through a video and short article on the *BBC News* website, which gave me the impression that the prank campaign was uncritically pro-Canadian and anti-American. The BBC video—which was the site's most-watched on 13 September 2012—follows Calvert and Cannon as they ask New Yorkers whether they would vote for Canada for President and includes short clips from their viral video. The clips selected include Calvert's list of what Canada has accomplished ahead of the US, such as legalizing gay marriage and enacting strict gun laws. The interviews also focus on the failure of the American political system and even include Calvert stating that "most of our followers are actually based in the States. Some are just sick of the political situation and some of them just appreciate that there's a group there to laugh at the whole situation" (Bressanin). The American news network CNN also covered the Canada Party's campaign. In the segment, reporter Jeanne Moos—known for her reporting of offbeat stories—discusses the viral video and interviews Calvert and Cannon. Like the BBC article and video, her story focuses on Calvert and Cannon's critiques of American politics. However, she does acknowledge that Cannon is actually an American and a former US Marine—facts that challenge assumptions about the performance's uncomplicated nationalistic sentiments.

9   When watching the original *YouTube* video, I view Calvert and Cannon's work as equally critical of American and Canadian politics. While Calvert begins "The Canada Party—'Meet the Canada Party'" by laying out how progressive Canada is, he goes on to contradict these claims in an attempt to convince Americans of Canada's "redneck cred." In reference to then Prime Minister Stephen Harper, he argues, "Our Prime Minister is a Muppet version of George [W.] Bush." He also claims, "Our oil sands are so dirty it makes Texas look like a Greenpeace retreat," and "We have been known to club a baby seal now and then, but we could just as easily waterboard them." These statements show that while Canadians often situate themselves as separate from or superior to the US, many of our practices and beliefs are closely connected.

10   Calvert continues to critique Canada's political climate in the duo's second most popular video, "The Canada Party—'The Candidates.'" In this clip, he provides some biting descriptions of the Republican contenders—characterizing Rick Perry as "execute the gays" and Rick Santorum as "pretend not to be gay"—before going on to critique Obama for being too polite. Yet his judgment of Obama actually functions as a critique of Canada's environmental policies. He claims Obama can "take a lesson from the most passive aggressive country on Earth. Just agree to whatever they want and then when it's time to put up, drop the mike and Slim Shady right off the stage—or as we call it up here, pulling a Kyoto." These statements intentionally subvert the Canada Party's own tag line of "America, but Better" and undermine the nationalistic sentiment that Canada is superior to the US.

11   By setting up an opposition between the two countries and then highlighting conservatism in Canadian politics, the prank highlights the lack of distinction between Canadian and American values, citizenship, and media consumption. In interviews, Cannon confirms that this was a goal of the campaign. He states the video is not about "Canadians' smugness or on the other hand Canadians' sense of inferiority—standing next to the big guy on the block. It's much more of a coming together and helping our citizens and American citizens" (qtd. in Ward). In addition, the video's format exposes how Canadian comedy—while also influenced by homegrown shows like *This Hour Has 22 Minutes* and *The Mercer Report*—has been impacted by the widespread success of *The Daily Show* and *The Colbert Report*.

12   The use of *YouTube* to subvert assumptions about national superiority and difference invokes Alan Filewod's view that digital tools and aesthetics may enable Canadian performers to move away from dominant discourses on nationalism. He argues that "digitalization . . . disturbs the traditional narrative structures of national culture" (292). However, reading into this "disturbing" of "national culture" relies on context. My ability to discern the video's irony may partly relate to my own status as a Canadian, which follows Diana Taylor's argument that, even with globally circulated performances and images, reception still occurs in terms of local contexts (157). Yet, like their international counterparts, some Canadian media responses to the campaign played up a nationalistic Canada–America tension. A *Globe and Mail* article, entitled "Yes We Canada," cites only the duo's suggestions that are clearly critical of American policies (Chowdhry). However, the online version of the article embeds the original video, which encourages readers to

view the whole piece. Several other Canadian news articles follow this approach by either including the video or explicitly acknowledging Calvert and Cannon's critiques of the Canadian government (i.e., McQuigge; Ward).

13   Calvert and Cannon acknowledge the problematic assumptions many outlets made about their video's goals. They point out this kind of response was not limited to the mainstream press or international viewers as some Canadian YouTubers used the video to reinforce a sense of national pride. Calvert claims, "Even though [the video is] in a very Canadian, helpful tone, Canadians really rallied behind that to say, 'yeah, we really are better than America!' when that wasn't it at all. . . . We were really pointing out our own shortcomings, as much in our minds, as we were America's" (qtd. in McQuigge). Calvert's comment points to the danger of irony misfiring. Bogad notes, following Linda Hutcheon, that irony is subjective and transideological; thus, it can be interpreted in unexpected ways (11). Henry Jenkins explains how this is particularly true for *YouTube* videos since external sites can easily embed them. This removes videos from the larger context of their *YouTube* pages, including their uploaders' descriptions. Jenkins claims that "this uncontrolled flow of media content creates ambivalences and anxieties—not simply for commercial rights holders but also among amateur media makers" (116–117). This statement is true for Calvert and Cannon, whose critique of Canadian political culture got lost in its circulation beyond the space of the original prank on *YouTube*. While the video opens up the issue of Canadian–American political discourse and how it circulates, many readings of it subsume the Canadian part of the equation into the arguably already more dominant American political discourse.

14   That said, this misreading of Calvert and Cannon's irony also reflects artistic decisions the duo made and thus raises questions about how to make effective political art online. While Colbert and Stewart's Comedy Central shows were arguably limited by the corporate interests of their owner, Viacom, Calvert and Cannon are not beholden to a corporation. Michel de Certeau argues that this lack of proximity to major power structures can allow for what he defines as "tactics" (xix). Amber Day notes, following de Certeau, that tactics "do not have a base from which to operate," as opposed to strategies, which are "employed by power structures that have a place from which to generate relations with an external group" (183). In Day's opinion, this difference enables radical performance groups like the Yes Men to be "more unmistakably activist" (86) than satirical newscasters, who often have

to consider the corporate interests of the networks they are on. However, political agitators must take up this potential, and, in my view, Calvert and Cannon's split personal and political motivations hinder the Canada Party's activist potential.

15   While critical of contemporary political discourse, Calvert and Cannon also hoped the campaign would further their own careers as comedians. When asked about the future of the party, Calvert claims, "We just stay measured for the sake of our sanity about what may or may not happen. But to be on Stewart or Colbert would be great. Obviously, they are both inspirations" (qtd. in Ward). This desire to be noticed by the two comedians extends to poaching off their success. In several interviews and on the Canada Party's *Twitter* and *Facebook* pages, the two claim they are going to run again in 2016 and invite Colbert onto their ticket as Vice-President. The Canada Party campaign was a creative way to get noticed in a highly competitive field, and I do not intend to fault Calvert and Cannon for their savvy; however, it is possible the desire for mainstream recognition overshadowed their political aims.

16   In addition, the form of their election intervention limits its utopian possibilities. Several performance theorists, including Day, Boler, and Jill Dolan, note that activist performances can open up alternative modes of being and modify discourses, even if minutely. Boler and Day argue that irony and satire are valuable tools that can offer utopian possibilities in an increasingly spectacularized society. While Calvert and Cannon make fun of existing practices, they do not have a clear target, which makes it difficult to untangle what exactly they see as a viable alternative to the status quo. They take on several issues at once, including political campaigns, the hateful rhetoric of Republican candidates, and the hypocrisy underlying certain modes of Canadian patriotism. Calvert notes that this generalized critique has potential, as they do not attach themselves to any particular political party. He claims, "It's gotten kind of ridiculous which is why we attack the absurdity and the hypocrisy rather than siding with the political parties" (qtd. in "America"). However, the lack of a clear target makes their work a form of what Bogad calls "soft satire" (31)—satire that is not overly controversial and has broad appeal. Part of the "softness" of the intervention stems from its lack of impact on the real. When Calvert interviews Americans on the streets of New York City in the *BBC News* video, he simply repeats jokes from the viral clip. By keeping their campaign contained within pre-scripted bits and pre-recorded videos, Calvert and Cannon lower the intervention's stakes.

17   Though the campaign lacks overtly activist aims, the Canada Party video and its reception open up important questions about the state of political satire in Canada and its relation to concurrent work in the US. The fake campaign carved out a space for a Canadian voice in relation to the American presidential campaign—an event that Canadian citizens and news media follow closely. The Canada Party prank reflects a desire for a say within this event, which only American citizens can directly influence but which nevertheless has a global impact. It co-opts the attention given to the presidential race to critique not only American election culture but also the state of Canadian politics. By including a criticism of Canadian smugness, Calvert and Cannon situate Canada as an equal, but not culturally superior, player in hemispheric politics. In addition, the prank shows how difficult it is to produce satire for audiences in dispersed contexts, a situation that is increasingly the norm with the proliferation of distributed, online responses to political culture.

Works Cited

"America, but Better: Canadian Comedians Take On US Politics." *The World*. Public Radio International, 14 Aug. 2012. Web. 20 Apr. 2014.

Bogad, L. M. *Electoral Guerrilla Theatre: Radical Ridicule and Social Movements*. New York: Routledge, 2005. Print.

Boler, Megan. Introduction. *Digital Media and Democracy: Tactics in Hard Times*. Ed. Megan Boler. Cambridge, MA: MIT P, 2008. 1–50. Print.

Bressanin, Anna. "Canada for President: Can the US Learn from the North?" Online video clip and web page. *BBC News*. 19 Sept. 2012. Web. 21 Mar. 2013.

Calvert, Brian, and Chris Cannon. "The Canada Party—'The Candidates.'" Online video clip. *YouTube*. 17 Jan. 2012. Web. 24 Apr. 2014.

———. "The Canada Party—'Meet the Canada Party.'" Online video clip. *YouTube*. 3 Jan. 2012. Web. 21 Mar. 2013.

Chowdhry, Affan. "'Yes We Canada': Comedians Encourage Americans to Let Canada Run the U.S." *The Globe and Mail* 20 Sept. 2012. Web. 21 Mar. 2013.

CNN. "Canada for U.S. President?" Online video clip. *YouTube*. 23 Jan. 2012. Web. 24 Apr. 2014.

Colbert, Stephen. *Stephen Colbert's Super PAC*. Americans for a Better Tomorrow, Tomorrow, 2012. Web. 21 Mar. 2013.

Day, Amber. *Satire and Dissent: Interventions in Contemporary Political Debate*. Bloomington: Indiana UP, 2011. Print.

de Certeau, Michel. *The Practice of Everyday Life*. Berkeley: U of California P, 1984. Print.

Dolan, Jill. *Utopia in Performance: Finding Hope at the Theatre*. Ann Arbor: U of Michigan P, 2005. Print.

Filewod, Alan. *Committing Theatre: Theatre Radicalism and Political Intervention in Canada*. Toronto: Between the Lines, 2011. Print.

Giannachi, Gabriella. *The Politics of New Media Theatre*. London: Routledge, 2006. Print.

Jenkins, Henry. "What Happened before *YouTube*?" *YouTube: Online Video and Participatory Culture*. Ed. Jean Burgess and Joshua Green. Cambridge: Polity, 2009. 109–125. Print.

McQuigge, Michelle. "From Gay Marriage to Oil Spills, Canada Hopes to Solve America's Woes." *National Post* 30 Dec. 2012. Web. 24 Apr. 2014.

Romney, Mitt. "Too Many Americans." Online video clip. *YouTube*. 27 Sept. 2012. Web. 24 Apr. 2014.

Taylor, Diana. *The Archive and the Repertoire*. Durham: Duke UP, 2003. Print.

Wall Street Journal Digital Network. "Obama Campaign Ad: Read My Plan." Online video clip. *YouTube*. 27 Sept. 2012. Web. 24 Apr. 2014.

Ward, Doug. "The 'Canada Party' Invasion of America Begins Here." *The Tyee* 10 Sept. 2012. Web. 24 Apr. 2014.

Key and challenging words

tactical, scathing, polarize, proliferation, fodder, efficacy, performative, subsume, concurrent

Questions

1. Analyze the essay's first three paragraphs. Include in your analysis the answers to the following questions: (a) What is the function of the opening paragraph; is it effective?; (b) Where is the thesis and what kind of thesis is it (i.e., simple thesis, hypothesis, essay plan; see p. 19 in Chapter 2)?

2. (a) Using reliable sources, briefly identify and describe two of the following examples from paragraph 4: The Yes Men, the Rhinoceros Party of Canada, *This Hour Has Seven Days*; (b) Discuss the role of examples in paragraph 4, explaining their connection to the purpose of the paragraph as a whole.

3. Discuss the author's use of the first-person perspective in paragraphs 8, 9, and 12. Why might McLeod have chosen to use the first person here? Does it enhance her argument or detract from it? How, specifically?

4. Analyze paragraph construction in paragraph 10, along with another paragraph of similar length; you could consider the use of topic sentences and paragraph wraps, paragraph development and strategies for coherence, along with other features.

5. Drawing from information in paragraphs 4–6, which analyzes the influences on Calvert and Cannon's project, explain the importance of the work of Stephen Colbert. Do you consider Colbert the major influence on Calvert and Cannon? Why or why not?

6. (a) Analyze McLeod's use of L.M. Bogad as an important secondary source for the author (see paragraphs 5, 7, and 16); analyze the use of one other critic/theorist among the following: Alan Filewood (paragraph 12), Henry Jenkins (paragraph 13), or Amber Day (paragraphs 14 and 16).

7. Analyze the last four paragraphs of McLeod's essay. In your analysis, you could consider the specific functions of these paragraphs and their connection to the essay as a whole; McLeod's approach or tone and the way it differs from that of previous paragraphs; the use of synthesis to integrate McLeod's points; paragraph structure; and other rhetorical features to increase comprehension.

Post-reading

1. *Collaborative or individual activity*: Using your experiences and observations, along with critical thinking and specific examples, analyze or respond to one of the following: (a) Why is satire such a popular form today across various media?; (b) As Kimberley McLeod shows in her essay, one problem for the satirist is getting the audience to see the true target of the satire. Do you believe that this, in fact, is a problem, and, if so, how could it be resolved?

2. *Collaborative activity*: Design a satirical/spoof video on a subject of interest to students (ideally, it should feature Canadian content) and describe/explain its purpose, intended audience, and satirical target. Describe, narrate, or present the video's opening, as the writer of this essay does, and include some additional text from your video.

Sovereignty and Security in the Canadian North: (Re)learning the Lessons

P. Whitney Lackenbauer
(1,543 words)

Pre-reading

1. (a) Scan the essay to determine whether it is an academic or a non-academic essay and explain, in one paragraph, how you reached your conclusion; (b) Using reliable sources, write a two- or three-sentence biography of the author of this essay, determining his qualifications for writing on this topic.

2. Using a reliable source, such as a current government website, summarize the goals of Canada's *Northern Strategy* (see paragraph 3).

Abstract

Understanding the history of the Canadian North is key to comprehending our peculiar mindset about Arctic issues—particularly when it comes to sovereignty. History can give us confidence, allowing us to break away from a narrow fixation on sovereignty loss, as well as yielding valuable lessons about the unintended consequences of sovereignty and security practices conceived in southern political centres and deployed in the North without sufficient regard for local impacts.

———

1   "Canada's Arctic is central to our national identity as a northern nation. It is part of our history. And it represents the tremendous potential of our future." Prime Minister Stephen Harper's words, proclaimed in Inuvik, Northwest Territories, in 2007, connected the past, present, and future. Canada boasts the world's longest coastline, and most of it is in the Arctic. It has extensive jurisdiction and sovereign rights in the region, which it sees as a resource frontier, a homeland for its northern peoples, and a source of national identity.

2   Over the last decade, the changing Arctic has become front page news in Canada and around the world. Uncertainty over climate change, international interest in Arctic resources, undefined continental shelf boundaries, potentially viable maritime transportation routes (particularly the Northwest Passage which Canada considers its internal waters, not an international strait), and perceived sovereignty and security threats make Canadians keen observers of geopolitical dynamics related to the Arctic and what these mean for their foreign, defence, and domestic policies.

3   At the highest political levels, the Canadian government has intertwined sovereignty and security issues with strong rhetoric asserting Canada's status as an "Arctic superpower." On the other hand, a more optimistic message emerges in Canada's official *Northern Strategy* and its statement on Canadian Arctic foreign policy, which express clear confidence in Canada's sovereignty position and place a high priority on improving the social and economic well-being of northern residents, protecting the environment, and improving Arctic governance—regionally and internationally. This dual messaging emphasizing sovereignty, security, and national interests, as well as international cooperation and stewardship, reveals Canada's complex perspective and position on Arctic issues.

4   Understanding the history of the Canadian North is key to comprehending our peculiar mindset about Arctic issues—particularly when it comes to sovereignty.

5   Scholars have gone to great lengths to emphasize vulnerabilities in or uncertainties about our sovereignty claims in the Arctic over time—not Canada's remarkable achievement of consolidating its Arctic sovereignty position since 1880 through diplomacy and state action.

6   The Alaska Boundary dispute serves as a prime example of American bullying and expansionist tendencies, Britain's acquiescence, and our fledgling dominion's need to take control over its own destiny—because no one else would uphold our interests. Did Canada have the stronger case? Probably not, but such considerations do not matter much in nationalist myth-making.

7   Historians often cite the Second World War and early Cold War as examples of how American security imperatives forced Canada to take strategic notice of its Northwest and then the High Arctic, threatening Canadian sovereignty and control. But the Alaska Highway bolstered rather than eroded Canada's position in the end, and bilateral agreements to build and operate the Joint Arctic Weather Stations on remote Arctic islands in the late 1940s and the Distant Early Warning (DEW) Line from 1955–57 similarly confirmed Canadian sovereignty. Neither Canada nor the United States compromised core principles, but acted as respectful neighbours and allies with shared interests in continental defence.

8   Since the 1960s, when sovereignty and security discussions shifted to Arctic waters, differing Canadian and American positions on the legal status of the channels through Canada's Arctic Archipelago have proven more vexing. The transits of the oil tanker S.S. *Manhattan* in 1969 and the U.S. Coast Guard cutter *Polar Sea* in 1985 affirmed that the United States considers the Northwest Passage an international strait, open to navigation like other strategic straits around the world. Canada insists that these are internal waters, subject to full Canadian sovereignty and control. Bridging this legal chasm has proven impossible, but the two countries have managed it in constructive ways—such as the 1988 Arctic Cooperation Agreement, brokering a practical compromise on U.S. icebreaker transits while "agreeing to disagree" on the legal status.

9   How we understand history shapes how we perceive the Canada–U.S. relationship in the Arctic, and

Source: From *Canadian Issues*, Winter 2013, pp. 7–9.

expectations about Canada's place in the circumpolar world more generally. Political scientist Rob Huebert contends that we are entering a new era of the Arctic where climate change, newly accessible resources, and burgeoning global interest place Canada in a precarious sovereignty and security environment. At best, he asserts, history reveals Canada's limited capacity to protect its sovereignty and security in the region and explains why other nations have advanced Arctic claims at the expense of Canada's.

10   An emphasis on historical cooperation, however, suggests that Canada has benefited from a longstanding, responsible strategy that affords us as strong a sovereignty position as international law allows and also maintains constructive relations with our Arctic neighbours. Intermittent sovereignty and security "crises," however, have failed to provide the political and popular interest required to support a sustained, strategic investment in the region. History can give us confidence, allowing us to break away from a narrow fixation on sovereignty loss, as well as yielding valuable lessons about the unintended consequences of sovereignty and security practices conceived in southern political centres and deployed in the North without sufficient regard for local impacts.

11   While commentators such as Rob Huebert suggest that there is a "perfect storm" brewing today that will fundamentally destabilize Northern life, this is not a new scenario. Inuit and other Northern peoples felt the disruptive impacts of defence footprints on and in their homelands after the Second World War. The DEW Line stations were beachheads of modernism: sites of wage employment, new housing, access to social services, and Western technology and material culture. Although not primarily designed to bring Aboriginal peoples under state control, defence initiatives had far-reaching effects. Inuit political leader Mary Simon has summarized that "too often, military projects are centralized undertakings that are unilaterally imposed on indigenous peoples and their territories." Stated as such, the so-called "militarization" of the Arctic appears to fit within the framework of a coercive state interested in re-engineering Northern life to conform with modern (and military) priorities.

12   In other cases, however, the military learned how to engage in meaningful dialogue and value Northern perspectives to support sovereignty and security. The Canadian Rangers, a unique military organization established in 1947, are a case in point. Rather than committing full-time soldiers to defend remote northern and coastal regions against an unlikely invasion, the military recognized the value of having volunteers who already lived in isolated communities serve as its "eyes and ears." Over time, the military, the Rangers, and their host communities developed strong relationships rooted in respect and mutual learning. As a bridge between cultures and between the civilian and military realms, the Rangers grew to embody the successful integration of national security and sovereignty agendas with community-based activities and local stewardship. Today, this practical partnership, rooted in traditional knowledge and skills, serves as an important example of cooperation, communal and individual empowerment, and cross-cultural understanding.

13   Placing Northerners at the centre of the national conversation about sovereignty, security, and stewardship requires moving beyond political statements, media coverage, and "expert" academic opinion gleaned from archives and public documents. It means embracing various lenses to understand the historical and contemporary North, and requires commitment to an ongoing dialogue.

14   My travels throughout Canada's North over the last decade have taught me to ask new questions and to think in new ways. For example, in August 2010, when I was embedded with a Canadian military unit on Operation Nanook. On the first night, after we established camp on Bylot Island, Ranger Pauloosie Atagootak invited me for a walk. As we trudged over the tundra and down lush valleys, I asked him questions about the land, and he told me stories and shared his thoughts on living in the North.

15   After walking for about half an hour, Paul sat down on one of the downward slopes. After a couple of minutes of silence, he said the simple words: "I'm home." I felt it: the connection to the land, his homeland, his identity. He had spent much of his childhood in camps along this stretch of coastline. The land was as familiar to him as it was exotic and remote to me.

16   As we sat on the soft ground, we talked about community life. He worried about the younger generation who spent all their time plugged into iPods and playing video games. Paul pointed out that the clouds told of the weather coming in. How many children in Nunavut still looked to the skies each night, as his grandfather had taught him to do? Would climate change alter weather patterns so much that it would render such traditional knowledge moot? If resource development did spark a modern-day gold rush in Nunavut, how would the next generation of Nunavummiut fare? I dared not speculate. Nevertheless, Paul provided

a reassuring message. Inuit had faced challenges in the past, and they had proven resilient.

17   A "crisis" mentality conditions us to react hastily rather than to listen, discern, and act prudently. The idea of change at an "unprecedented pace" suggests that the past can no longer offer guidance. But it can, and it should. Canadian officials have had lots of experience managing sovereignty and security agendas in light of major geopolitical change since the Second World War. Balancing these considerations with domestic imperatives to improve the quality of life of Northerners, and translating our Northern strategy into deliverables that reinforce a constructive and secure circumpolar world, are real challenges facing Canada in the twenty-first century Arctic.

Key and challenging words

sovereign (adj.), jurisdiction, viable, acquiescence, fledgling, bolster, imperative, bilateral, burgeoning

Questions

1. In your own words, explain what the author calls "dual messaging" (i.e., demonstrating two contrary views on Canada's Arctic) (see paragraph 3).
2. Identify the justification of the essay and, in your own words, explain the approach to the topic that Lackenbauer proposes to take.
3. Using reliable sources, discuss the significance of one of the following historic events as it affected Canadian sovereignty and/or identity: (a) the "Alaska Boundary Dispute" (paragraph 6); (b) the building of the Alaska Highway (paragraph 7).
4. Analyze the author's argument, referring to three of the following strategies, plus at least one other strategy of your choice: common ground, comparison, concession, emotional appeal, fairness, or rebuttal (refutation). In addition to considering the use of argumentative strategies, consider the author's argumentative purpose and the effectiveness of the argument, along with, if appropriate, ways that the argument could have been improved.
5. Referring to two specific passages from the essay, show how Lackenbauer uses the transition "however" to qualify a previous point and introduce a point of his own.
6. Authors use direct quotations for different purposes (see The Active Voice: To Quote or Not to Quote, p. 137 in Chapter 10). Analyze the author's use of direct quotations in "Sovereignty and Security in the Canadian North," referring to three examples from the essay and at least two different purposes.
7. Analyze the use of personal experience in paragraphs 14–16. You could consider any of the following questions, among others, in your analysis: Is the use of personal experience appropriate in this essay or for this topic? Does it support the author's thesis? How? Is the placement of personal experience effective? Is the use of personal experience adequately prepared for by previous paragraphs?

Post-reading

1. *Collaborative or individual activity:* Using critical thinking, discuss or respond to the following quotation from "Sovereignty and Security in the Canadian North," considering its validity and coming up with other examples from your own experience or observations that support the claim: "A 'crisis' mentality conditions us to react hastily rather than to listen, discern, and act prudently" (paragraph 17).
2. Using reliable sources, create a timeline that shows the Canadian government's policy to Canada's North, beginning with the announcement mentioned in paragraph 1 up to the present.

Being CBC: The Ambivalent Identities and Belonging of Canadian-Born Children of Immigrants

Audrey Kobayashi and Valerie Preston
(5,048 words)

Pre-reading

1. Referring to the section called Type B Sub-genre: Qualitative Methodologies (Chapter 3, p. 24) and/or reliable online sources, consider the major features of essays that use elements of Type B essays but employ qualitative methodologies. Why might some authors choose to use this method rather than a quantitative one?

Abstract

Immigrants from Hong Kong are one of the largest recent cohorts of newcomers in Canada. We examine the processes through which the children of Hong Kong immigrants construct a sense of belonging in Canada, their only home. In focus group discussions, the participants express an unequivocal sense of Canadian citizenship and belonging. Yet their identities project an idealized Canadian body that wears "Canadian" clothing, plays "Canadian" sports, and, above all, speaks "Canadian" English. The projection is always relational and spatialized, variable according to place, and especially according to whether the other is viewed as family, as another "Canadian-born Chinese" (CBC), as a recent Chinese immigrant, or as a dominant Canadian. Often viewed as not Chinese enough by recent immigrants, in turn, they denigrate recent immigrants as not Canadian enough and resent them for reinforcing a concept of otherness held by dominant Canadians that often includes CBCs. Many participants feel more "Chinese" in family settings where parents uphold Chinese traditions. Their sense of belonging is a set of paradoxes, of between-ness, that they negotiate through a sense of place-ness: place as the homes in which they belong but also as a set of shifting public and private contexts in which they express their identities and relationships in variable ways.

---

1 Between 1987 and 1996, over 242,000 Hong Kongers, 14 percent of all immigrant arrivals, settled in Canada (Skeldon 1994; Mar 2005). With the 1997 handover of Hong Kong to China, the migration flow dropped abruptly, but not before these migrants transformed both Hong Kong and their Canadian destination cities of Vancouver and Toronto (Mitchell 2004; Preston, Siemiatycki, and Kobayashi 2006; Lo 2008; Ley 2010; Kobayashi, Preston, and Murnaghan 2011).

2 Hong Kong immigrants to Canada represent one of the most studied groups of transnationals, with strong ties to family, friends, and businesses in Hong Kong. Many established a trans-Pacific lifestyle, with some members of the family remaining in Hong Kong for work or business and others living in Canada, especially for the purpose of ensuring an international education for children, who later carry their cultural capital to Hong Kong (Waters 2003, 2006). International migration is a family strategy, with key decisions made along the life course according to demographic transitions from school to work to retirement (Kobayashi and Preston 2006). A return to Hong Kong was always planned, particularly for those who migrated as children. At the turn of the century, estimates of returnees living in Hong Kong ran over 100,000 (Ley and Kobayashi 2005). For these transnationals, migration involves constituting a sense of belonging in a new place while maintaining ties to the place of origin.[1] Research shows that this group has a strong attachment to Canada notwithstanding their high rate of return to Hong Kong (Skeldon 1994; Preston, Siemiatycki, and Kobayashi 2007; Kobayashi, Preston, and Murnaghan 2011).

3 Much less work has directly studied the Canadian-born children of Hong Kong emigrant parents. Here, we focus on the sense of belonging articulated by "Canadian-born Chinese" (CBCs), the children of Hong Kong emigrants who were born in Canada or who migrated to Canada before the age of sixteen.[2] As young adults who have grown up in

---

Source: From *Annals of the Association of American Geographers*, vol. 104, no. 2, 2014, pp. 234–42. © The Association of American Geographers, reprinted by permission of Taylor & Francis Ltd, www.tandfonline.com on behalf of The Association of American Geographers, www.aag.org.

Canada, we expect that their sense of belonging is different from that of their parents, shaped by different places and experiences (Aitken 2010; Aitken and Plow 2010). Research on second-generation Canadians from a variety of backgrounds has shown that they often have a sense of two cultures—one "Canadian," and the other that of their parents—but that they are "capable of interpreting and even re-framing the dominant narrative in a variety of ways to assert their own sense of identity and Canadianness" (Kobayashi 2008, 5). Racialized second-generation Canadians often feel the effects of everyday racism keenly, especially in educational and work contexts, and adjust their actions accordingly (Reitz and Somerville 2004; Reitz and Banerjee 2007; Brooks 2008). Our analysis explores these two processes: on the one hand, development of a sense of Canadian identity and reaction to acts of exclusion against themselves and, on the other, turning against recently arrived immigrant youth. We address the discursive production of belonging through focus groups designed to explore understandings of "Canadian" culture and identity and to find out how the CBCs experience and react to racism and discrimination.[3] Ours is not, therefore, a study of integration but of strategies of inclusion within the participants' own country.

Methodology

4   The eighty-six participants included in this study ranged in age from eighteen to twenty-six (Table 1), with a median age of twenty years. Approximately 45 percent were currently university students. Their parental homes were across Canada, but the largest number came from the suburbs of Toronto and Vancouver, especially the municipalities of Richmond Hill and Markham, Ontario, and Richmond, British Columbia. They were recruited with the assistance of Chinese-Canadian service groups and student clubs, and all conversations were in English. Discussions yielded more than 200 pages of rich conversation, which we recorded and transcribed before coding with N-Vivo software.[4]

5   We chose focus groups as the medium for collecting information because the interaction allows individuals to express, share, amplify, and sometimes even change their understanding. The focus group is not simply a group interview but a site of discursive production (Pratt 2000; Hopkins 2007). For this reason, we have selected a relatively small number of extended excerpts from focus group transcripts to illustrate in depth the interactions that occurred throughout these conversations.

6   We have adopted the term Canadian-born Chinese, or CBC, to refer to all our participants, because this terminology represents a socially constructed self-identity, not a literal statement of place of birth. The term is fraught, contested, variable, and in constant transformation, but early in the research we were told that many in the 1.5 generation also identify themselves as CBC, rather than as new immigrants from Hong Kong, for whom they have another acronym: FOB, or "fresh off the boat." Unlike FOB, which we discuss later, CBC does not have negative connotations either inside the community or outside. We stress, however, that all of the participants born in Canada and most of the 1.5 generation are Canadian citizens, although some of them hold dual citizenship (Table 1). Participants often emphasized that their Canadian identity derives from their status as citizens. Discussing their sense of belonging, however, they often expressed ambivalence, as a state of being in between their overseas-born parents and the dominant Canadian majority. Our analysis addresses that ambivalence.

Being CBC and Belonging Where?

7   As Yuval-Davis (2006, 2011) has emphasized, relationships to people and the material world, particularly family relationships, establish and reaffirm a sense of belonging. Indeed, the family, not the nation-state, might well be the primary unit for belonging (Waters 2006; Ho 2009; hooks 2009). For many contemporary migrants who actively maintain social connections and relationships across national borders, belonging is complicated, influenced by formal relations to multiple nation-states and economic, social, and political ties in several places (Preston, Siemiatycki, and Kobayashi 2007; Ho 2009).

8   Almost all of our CBC participants had thought about moving to Hong Kong for work after graduation, and a few who had parents in Hong Kong (known as "satellite kids"; see Waters 2003) were fairly certain that they would move there, but the majority believed that they would start their working lives in Canada. The focus group conversations nonetheless reveal a tension between feeling "Canadian," feeling "Chinese," and the places in which those feelings emerge. CBCs typically express belonging first to their Canadian childhood homes, the only homes they name when asked where they are "from." The from-ness of place has an inevitable and uncontested quality. As many of our participants were university students, from-ness is also an identity anchor to their families, a place of security against

Table 1   **Demographic characteristics of focus group participants**

	1.5 generation	Canadian-born
Year of birth		
1975–1979	14	3
1980–1984	43	26
Place of birth		
Hong Kong	52	0
Canada	0	29
Other (China)	5	0
Year of arrival		
Pre-1985	3	—
1985–1989	15	—
1990–1994	32	—
1995–1999	4	—
No response	3	—
Not applicable	0	29
Citizenship		
Canadian only	31	25
Canadian dual	14	1
Landed immigrant	6	0
No response	6	3
Education		
Less than high school	1	0
High school graduate	11	9
College/trades	0	1
Some university	31	17
Bachelor's degree	9	0
Postgraduate	1	0
Not stated	4	2
N	57	29

which the many social and cultural changes of university life were measured.

9   Despite their secure ties to Canadian citizenship, they also described their sense of belonging as contested and contradictory. Straddling what they often described as two cultures, they described never being fully accepted as Canadian or Chinese and therefore never fully at home. The following comment occurred during a focus group in Vancouver:

CBC1-2: I think it kind of goes back to the whole roots idea, like she said, y'know, you're born there

so that's where you belong in a way. You still feel like, oh my home's back there because I was born there and that's where—I was brought up there.

10   A discussion among Queen's University students from across Canada began with a round of stating fromness—Vancouver, Edmonton, Toronto, and so on—and then moved on to what it means to be tied to place:

KY2-5: ... The thing I noticed since I've come to Queen's, like back in Vancouver, most of my friends were Caucasian, but here it's more difficult to make friends because they didn't really know me, right? 'Cause they just saw an Asian face. It's kind of weird, like now, . . .

KY2-4: I think it depends on where you're from. I'm from Edmonton right? There's less Asians there. So people just see you as part of the regulars. I feel this way, I don't know if it's true or not. Like in Toronto or like Richmond, Vancouver, like you can be in somewhere and you won't see a white person for the whole day. And then Canada, like in Toronto or Vancouver, that's when people start labeling you.

KY2-11: I think white cultured people, they do label us. Yeah.

KY2-2: For sure. . . . It's just by how they live in, the style or culture that they live in. Say, they go to Richmond Hill, they're the only white guys. And like you go back to downtown and they're all like white guys. The Richmond Hill territory is kind of like Hong Kong.

11   A few minutes later, after more discussion of what it means to be from a place where identity is contested:

KY2-9: Well, we're not blend-in multicultural. . . . Blend-in. Like everyone seems like their own little. . . . Say in Toronto right? Woodbridge is all Italians. And Toronto, Richmond Hill and places like that, it's all Cantonese, Hong Kongnese. And Downtown I'd say is mostly Vietnamese. We just have our own areas, our own places. It's not really blended into one culture.

KY2-9: . . . Because it takes a lot of time for you to really be a part. Like to [KY2-4] how she said how it was different in Edmonton, right? Because there are so few immigrants there? So you don't see any sources of, you can't enter into your old lifestyle right? So I'm not saying you're forced to blend in, but then your core environment is different, so you have to adapt. So you slowly go into that, whereas in Toronto, the sources are there for you, so you don't see as much need to go into the mainstream.

KY2-7: . . . When you say mainstream, do you mean Canadian-Canadian? Like a piper person? [laughter and joking; the reference is to the "Scottish" heritage of Queen's University]. . . . I think everyone has the potential to get into this mainstream, but that would involve letting go of a lot of things which people, whether it's for themselves or for others, aren't willing to give up. When I say this, I mean like traditions, and maybe some benefits that being Chinese holds. That being Canadian might not hold. And that's the biggest barrier I see.

12   Sense of belonging is spatially differentiated just like the relationships from which it is constituted, not only by city and neighborhood but also by context, where participants act out place-based identities. Many feel more "Chinese" in family settings where parents uphold Chinese traditions. Going to Chinese restaurants and supermarkets on a Sunday, usually with one or both parents, was mentioned regularly. Participants emphasized that activities with their parents in the homes of family and friends and in Chinese commercial and residential enclaves reinforce and confirm their sense of belonging to a Chinese population, culture, and heritage, but even more so to a particular family.

13   Outside of what they view as Chinese cultural places, however, CBCs are very concerned about how they represent themselves in public places where many young adults are aware of the potential for discriminatory actions from other Canadians, including others from Hong Kong, who might label them as either CBC or recent immigrant. This topic came up in every focus group. Participants described manipulating their appearance by wearing different clothes in different places. One spoke of the clothes that her aunt in Hong Kong sent, which she refused to wear because she would be marked as foreign. Others described cars, even cell phones, as markers of difference. Language is a potent marker separating Canadians and non-Canadians, posing a challenge for CBCs who conduct different aspects of their lives in different languages. Their public identity is constructed in and through fluent English spoken with a Canadian accent, although many might speak Cantonese with their parents. Participants talked about speaking "Chinglish," a dialect that combines Chinese and English, with their friends to express connections with their Chinese and Canadian roots. Language as a place-marker is fraught,

however, for they are aware of the differences between themselves and recent immigrants:

CBC1-7: I don't know, there's one class where people think I don't know English well, or I won't understand it well. And there's another group who think that I won't know Cantonese well.

CBC1-3: I can remember back in high school I could like eavesdrop. Like I could hear Chinese people saying stuff about me, and I would just turn around and start yelling at them because I knew what they were saying. But they always saw me as someone who was only able to speak, understand English, so it just really surprised them of like how much we actually know.

14   Despite their claims of being at home in Canada, CBCs are very aware that parents and some older siblings feel differently:

CBC1-2: I feel the same way because the schools are better and the air is better and Hong Kong is now like my second home, but my parents aren't like that or even my brother because they came at an older age.

CBC1-4: . . . because they [older siblings born in Hong Kong] don't adjust as well as we do. I was here back in elementary so it's a lot easier. Especially now that there are so many Chinese people here it's harder to see it [is] an English-speaking place because everyone, like majority, is speaking Cantonese, right. It seems like Cantonese is more of a first language than English even though in school the teachers speak in English, they don't talk throughout the whole class. If they're in the classroom and you're working by yourself so you'll be talking in Cantonese with your own friends.

15   For our participants, however, the advantages of fluency in English, one of Canada's two official languages, are paramount, a shield against discrimination and exclusionary processes of othering:

KY2-5: But I grew up a Canadian so I think I would probably experience less racial prejudice than other people that immigrated here and stuff. But I still think to some degree that when I go to the work force one day, I will probably face it, too. But to a lesser extent because I could probably relate to them more, and I could probably try to slide into that role where they realize that in a lot of ways I am just like them, right? 'Cause they could probably relate to me, too, 'cause I play a lot of sports. I could socially hang out with them. And I think that's the way that I could break through that barrier. But I also see a lot of people not being able to do that too, right?

Facilitator: For what reasons?

KY2-5: I think that one of the keys is language. I think that's a big barrier. And maybe that's why some of our parents are finding it difficult here because of the language. And language, I think that's a big factor in trying to fit into the society, whatever society that you're living in.

Speaking of Being Racialized

16   Racialization is also a set of discursive relationships that often take distinctive linguistic forms (Essed and Trienekens 2008). The earlier comments show that CBCs often view racism as something that can be avoided by being the right kind of Canadian, speaking correctly, and thereby avoiding stereotypes. They also spoke of the hurtful experiences of everyday racism, which Essed (2002) described as the experiences that one recognizes on the basis of patterns of interactions with others. Conversations invariably turned to unpleasant public encounters, often involving classmates, store clerks, and strangers.

KY2-10: . . . Yeah, I remember once I was in grade eight or something, I was sitting in class, just sitting. And one guy came up to me and said, "Why don't you . . . go back where you came from?" Okay . . .

KY2-4: Yeah, . . . somebody told me that he was shopping at Cat Centre and some white guy just went up to him and goes, "Why don't you go back home?" Like out of the blue. He was just shopping. I think as a whole, we can't say all Canadians are racist, but it exists, but sometimes in a sense, I can say that my mom, she thinks everyone is racist. She always feels that she's discriminated, but I think it's because she lost her pride. . . . Some parents are just like that.

. . . Okay, just listen to this. This is so pathetic. There's this girl, like a nice, Canadian Caucasian girl. And I was hanging out with my Caucasian friends. And I would talk to her, and she would not talk to me. She would just talk to all my Caucasian friends. And there's like one or two Caucasian, and there's an Indian individual, and whatnot, and only talk to the Caucasian people. I ask them questions, they answer to them. And we're talking about discrimination. I've had enough discrimination. Since grade school,

. . . these kids would come up to me and teach me this song like, "Me Chinese, Me Know Dumb, Me Know .. ." I was like yo man, kid, I'm smacking your face. Sorry. Seriously, I had this kid in grade six, he used to pop the air out of my Nike Air's just because I was Chinese. He was like, "Go home you fool." And I'm like, "Where? Thornhill?" [laughter]

I don't know, I have to say that I've seen a lot of it and I felt a lot of discrimination, but I know for sure that not all Canadian people are like this. And just quite recently, on our school trip, we had a club trip to Montreal. And we're walking in Chinatown, there's this guy and he was like, "All you China men, you're all the same. You guys smell." And I'm like, "Yeah, Uncle Tom." I'm like, "Good luck with your pickup. That's a nice lumberjack jacket." [laughter]

KY2-5: Yeah, but there are like a lot of instances. I guess my mom had to deal with it too, 'cause like she'd come home and she'd be like, if this was Hong Kong you know, I would let somebody totally have it, right? But she just couldn't communicate to give them hell, you know what I mean? The guy, I don't know if it was a guy or a girl, but like if it was me, I would have totally just went nuts on them, just like verbally right? I would have told them off, like you know, I would have stood up for myself. But

I guess my mom just couldn't 'cause she didn't have the language. She couldn't defend herself verbally, you know what I mean? And I think a lot of people have to deal with that, that can't speak English that well.

Facilitator: How do they deal with it?

KY2-5: They don't. They take it and they go home most of the time.

KY2-1: I think name-calling and telling people to their face that, I don't know, to go back on the boat or something, these are very direct forms of racism or discrimination, and you can stand up for yourself if someone does call you to your face. But let's say, I would go shopping and then, you know how at the cashier they would say, "Oh hi, how are you?" And they would start having a conversation with the person in front of you who's Caucasian, and they're really, really friendly. And then you're next in line, all you do is pay and then go, right? I mean I would consider that discrimination, too, I mean, but how are you going to pinpoint it? Like yell at the person, like, why aren't you making a friendly conversation with me? I mean you can't do that. If someone does call you a name, then sure, you can stand up for yourself, but there are many subtle forms of discrimination, which I guess you just have to take it 'cause you can't yell at someone for no reason. Yeah, that's how I feel. Being called in the face, you can say something about that, but other forms, it's quite hard 'cause you know that you're being discriminated against and I guess you can see that with other people of color or other immigrants. . . . I think one of the best ways to combat it is to know Canadian culture so that when someone from the Canadian culture says something to you, you know you can just hit them back with it. And then they don't have anything else to say.

17   Agency and control are the main focus of these discussions. Participants spent very little time talking about the racists and their practices, although their descriptions highlight the painful nature of these experiences and their banality. Outright, overt racism is easier to address than

the everyday experience of being treated differently and unfairly. The patterns of disfluency, especially the frequent insertion of the filler term "like," occur most often when making direct reference to racism that cannot be easily controlled. The discussion focuses on how participants attempt to control situations, through dress, language, and knowing what they view as Canadian culture. Their cultural comfort and fluency with English are major advantages that CBCs feel equip them to deal with racism. For example, one participant argues that a quick response that emphasizes his residence in Canada, home is Thornhill, a Toronto suburb, deflects comments aiming to label him as a foreigner. The last participant also emphasizes that familiarity with Canadian culture allows him to respond effectively. CBCs consider themselves more equipped to deal with racism than their parents, who have less fluency in English and less knowledge of Canada. The discussions underscore the belief that having grown up in Canada, they have the power to effect change with their own actions and words and to dispel the words of others.

Being a CBC and Not Being a Recent Immigrant

18   The CBCs also deflect their experiences of racism by transferring their own prejudices to recently arrived immigrants, whom they label as FOBs. In nearly every group, the topic of relationships with recent immigrants came up, and it was always uncomfortable. The first time was at the end of a discussion about experiences of racism, when someone declared, "It's *their* fault that we experience racism." This comment invoked an immediate and vociferous response against "FOBs." Some people were visibly uncomfortable with this linguistic turn, literally squirming in their seats, avoiding eye contact with the speakers. But as the conversation shifted to follow up on why they did not want to be taken for recent immigrants, participation and consensus grew. The consensus was that they did not want to be taken for "Chinese" rather than "Canadian." What they viewed as the insistence of recent immigrants on creating a "Chinese" landscape consisting of certain kinds of cars, clothing, and, of course, language, made the CBCs vulnerable to racism and othering.

19   Some of the conversations were thoughtful, if fraught. The following conversation turns on calling recent immigrants "FOB," positioning the CBC self in relation to the foreign other:

KY5-10: . . . I did have a kind of reverse racism against more recent immigrants because I didn't understand when I was younger, why they couldn't assimilate into the Canadian culture. Like if you come to Canada, why aren't you learning to speak English properly, or make friends as opposed to being a little clique?

KY5-5: . . . I'm like, what's wrong with these people? Why can't they just assimilate into like everyone else? And stop being so segregated, 'cause that's what bothered me the most when it came down to it. Like do you guys always have to display that you guys are this group? And it really bothered me.

Facilitator: Why do you think it bothered you?

KY5-5: I guess partly because just the exposure to the Chinese culture. The only Chinese culture I've ever gotten was within my home, and I guess being bombarded with like so many different kinds of Chinese culture? Like you see the CBCs, you see the complete white-washed, you see the hard core Hong Kong people, and it's just like whoa, these people are all Chinese? . . . It's like, whoa, what's going on? . . .

KY5-1: I have to say, I never knew the term [FOB], like, like that's what people call [them]?

KY5-5: Yeah, I didn't know either until I came [here].

KY5-1: I didn't know until someone started, who didn't even know that it was bad, to tell me what it was. I didn't understand why people would like call people that, because originally all your parents are from the same place. And these students are coming here, and I find in a way, kind of racism. . . . So when I see people coming here, I kind of think, I understand why they're all together, and a lot of them are going to go back to Hong Kong, too? I kind of accept it.

Facilitator: Do you think that's a racist term?

KY5-1: I did initially, but it's kind of like now, it's used like more like . . .

KY5-5: Description.

KY5-1: Yeah, it's not like I see that people aren't trying to be racist when they say it. Not try, but they don't mean it to be like that? They say, uh . . .

Facilitator: It just becomes part of regular conversation?

KY5-1: Yeah, at first when I first heard it, I thought it was so weird. And I didn't understand how people could say it, because we're all like first-generation children of immigrants, and all our parents probably had the same . . .

KY5-4: Yeah, last year, . . . I made a bunch of Asian friends, and I was so shocked at how often they used that word to describe like people that just came from Hong Kong. They just like, I remember we were at bubble tea one time, and there was a group of like people just from Hong Kong, and I was sitting with my friends, and they were just saying that word out loud, and I was so embarrassed. And I was just like, I can't believe they were just saying that in front of them, . . .

KY5-5: Yeah, when I first moved to Toronto, my cousin had to explain all the different terminology, and I was like, why would they ever make up something like that? And it just kind of, made me think, like is that right or not right. . .

20   This four-way conversation contains many subtleties. It was one of the more sensitive and thoughtful interactions, revealing how CBCs learn and participate in racialization, how ubiquitous the denigration of recent immigrants is among their peers, the significance of coded language to differentiate the CBCs from the others, and the ambiguous guilt that accompanies language they know to be othering, the transition from shock to normal in a conversation about the other that is actually about the self.

Conclusions

21   CBCs are not immigrants. They are certainly not, as common parlance and even some scholarly literature (e.g., Portes and Rumbaut 2001) describes them,

"second-generation immigrants." They express an unequivocal sense of Canadian citizenship and belonging. They believe in a multicultural Canada in which they have a legitimate place. Yet their identities project an idealized Canadian body, one that wears "Canadian" clothing, plays "Canadian" sports, and, above all, speaks "Canadian" English. The projection is always relational and spatialized, variable according to place, and especially according to whether the other is viewed as family, as another CBC, as a recent Chinese immigrant, or as a dominant Canadian. Notwithstanding some recognition of the complexity of multiculturalism in Canada, their multiculturalism has only two dimensions: Chinese and Canadian. They are often viewed as not Chinese enough by recent immigrants. In turn, they denigrate recent immigrants as not Canadian enough, and they resent recent immigrants for reinforcing an otherness held by dominant Canadians that often includes them. They go to considerable lengths to differentiate themselves from recent immigrants. Yet they feel conflicted over what they see as a clash of cultures between the traditional expectations of their parents and their desire to be recognized within the Canadian mainstream. Their sense of identity and belonging is therefore a set of paradoxes of between-ness that they negotiate through a sense of place-ness: place as the homes in which they belong but also as a set of shifting public and private contexts in which they express their identities and relationships in variable ways.

22   Thomas (2005) described multiculturalism for American high school students as "banal," an uncontested, unexplained, and uncontextualized idealization that "racializes subjects within a narrow definition of cultural expression" (5). Our subjects echo this concept. CBCs are deeply racialized, in a relational, discursive project that involves not only the directly racist speech acts of the dominant group but also a range of conformist acts through which they position and create themselves. It is not only the attributes of speech, clothing, and the like but also the sense of agency, of controlling the situation through a secure sense of citizenship and knowledge of themselves as Canadian, that allows them to be confident of their identity and their place. Our findings are drawn from conversations with Canadian-born Chinese of Hong Kong ancestry, but additional research that investigates the strategies of inclusion deployed by children of immigrants from other origins, particularly those of Chinese background from Taiwan and the People's Republic of China, is warranted

to understand how these children place themselves in Canadian society.

Acknowledgments

This research was supported by a strategic grant from the Social Sciences and Humanities Research Council of Canada, No. 829-99-1012, to Drs. A. Kobayashi (Principal Investigator), D. Ley, G. Man, V. Preston, and M. Siemiatycki. We are grateful to Janine Rose, Susanne Cliff-Jungling, and Ann Marie Murnaghan for invaluable research assistance, The Rockefeller Foundation Bellagio Centre where Valerie Preston worked on this article, and two reviewers and the editor whose comments improved the article.

Notes

1. This research is part of a larger project investigating the transnational experiences of Hong Kong Canadians in Vancouver, Kingston, and Toronto, involving 257 participants in a total of thirty focus groups, conducted in Cantonese and English. Participants were recruited from a range of social and service organizations, most notably SUCCESS in Vancouver and CCIS in Toronto. All participants received reimbursement for travel costs to meetings that took place in various public places, including community centers and libraries. The social and economic characteristics of the Hong Kongers from Toronto and Vancouver were similar (Kobayashi, Preston, and Murnaghan 2011), and the same was true for the cbcs included in this analysis.

2. By combining these two groups, we follow Portes and Rumbaut (2001), who also group together the American-born children of immigrants and immigrants who arrive as children and receive some primary or secondary education in the United States; however, we disagree with labeling this group as second-generation immigrants. The second generation is by definition Canadian because they are born or naturalized in Canada.

3. Most focus groups included men and women; however, we conducted a few groups segregated by gender. Comparison of the transcripts revealed no consistent differences in the discussions.

4. Our codes are in two parts: The first is the number of the focus group; the second is the identifier given to each individual.

References

Aitken, S. C. 2010. Not bad for a little migrant working kid. *Children's Geographies* 8:363–71.

Aitken, S. C., and V. Plow. 2010. Overturning assumptions about young people, border spaces and revolutions. *Children's Geographies* 8:327–33.

Brooks, M. 2008. Imagining Canada, negotiating belonging: Understanding the experiences of racism of second generation Canadians of colour. *Canadian Diversity/diversité canadienne* 6:75–78.

Essed, P. 2002. Everyday racism: A new approach to the study of racism. In *Race critical theories: Text and context*, ed. P. Essed and D. T. Goldberg, 176–94. Malden, MA: Blackwell.

Essed, P., and S. Trienekens. 2008. "Who wants to feel white?" Race, Dutch culture and contested identities. *Ethnic and Racial Studies* 31:52–72.

Ho, E. L. E. 2009. Constituting citizenship through the emotions: Singaporean transmigrants in London. *Annals of the Association of American Geographers* 99:788–804.

hooks, b. 2009. *Belonging: A culture of place*. London and New York: Routledge.

Hopkins, P. 2007. Thinking critically and creatively about focus groups. *Area* 39:528–35.

Kobayashi, A. 2008. A research and policy agenda for second generation Canadians: An introduction. *Canadian Diversity/diversité canadienne* 6:3–6.

Kobayashi, A., and V. Preston. 2006. Transnationalism through the life course: Hong Kong immigrants in Canada. *Asia Pacific Viewpoints* 48:151–67.

Kobayashi, A., V. Preston, and A. M. Murnaghan. 2011. Affect and transnationalism through the voices of Hong Kong immigrants to Canada. *Social and Cultural Geography* 12:871–88.

Ley, D. 2010. Millionaire migrants: Trans-Pacific life lines. Malden, MA: Wiley-Blackwell.

Ley, D., and A. Kobayashi. 2005. "Back to Hong Kong": Return migration or transnational sojourn? *Global Networks* 5:111–28.

Lo, L. 2008. DiverCity Toronto: Canada's premier gateway city. In *Migrants to the metropolis: The rise of immigrant gateway cities*, ed. M. Price and L. Benton-Short, 97–127. Syracuse, NY: Syracuse University Press.

Mar, P. 2005. Unsettling potentialities: Topographies of hope in transnational migration. *Journal of Intercultural Studies* 26:361–78.

Mitchell, K. 2004. Crossing the neoliberal line: Pacific Rim migration and the metropolis. Philadelphia: Temple University Press.

Portes, A., and R. Rumbaut. 2001. *Legacies: The story of the immigrant second generation.* New York: Russell Sage Foundation.

Pratt, G. 2000. Research performances. *Environment and Planning D: Society and Space* 18:639–51.

———. 2010. Listening for spaces of ordinariness: Filipino-Canadian youths' transnational lives. *Children's Geographies* 8:343–52.

Preston, V., M. Siemiatycki, and A. Kobayashi. 2006. Transnational urbanism: Toronto at a crossroads. In *Negotiating borders and belonging: Identities and practices in Canada*, ed. L. Wong and V. Satzewich, 91–110. Vancouver, Canada: University of British Columbia Press.

———. 2007. The dual citizenship of Hong Kong Canadians: Convenience or commitment? In *Dual citizenship in global perspective: From unitary to multiple citizenship*, ed. T. Faist and P. Kivisto, 203–26. New York: Palgrave Macmillan.

Reitz, J. G., and R. Banerjee. 2007. Racial inequality, social cohesion, and policy issues in Canada. In *Belonging? Diversity, recognition and shared citizenship in Canada*, ed. K Banting, T. J. Courchene, and F. L. Seidle, 489–545. Montreal, Canada: Institute for Research on Public Policy.

Reitz, J. G., and K. Somerville. 2004. Institutional change and emerging cohorts of the "new" immigrant second generation. *Journal of International Migration and Integration* 5:385–415.

Skeldon, R. 1994. *Reluctant exiles?: Migration from Hong Kong and the new overseas Chinese.* Armonk, NY: M. E. Sharpe. Thomas, M. 2005. "I think it's just natural": The spatiality of racial segregation at a US high school. *Environment and Planning A* 37:1233–48.

Waters, J. L. 2003. "Satellite kids" in Vancouver: Transnational migration, education and the experiences of lone children. In *Asian migrants and education*, ed. M. W. Charney, B. S. A. Yeoh, and C. K. Tong, 165–84. Dordrecht, The Netherlands: Kluwer Academic.

———. 2006. Geographies of cultural capital: Education, international migration and family strategies between Hong Kong and Canada. *Transactions of the Institute of British Geographers* 31(2):179–92.

Yuval-Davis, N. 2006. Belonging and the politics of belonging. *Patterns of Prejudice* 40:197–214.

———. 2011. *The politics of belonging, intersectional contestations.* London: Sage.

Key and challenging words

enclave, paramount, disfluency, vociferous, ubiquitous, denigration, parlance, unequivocal, paradox

Questions

1. Explain in your own words the following statements: (a) "The focus group is not simply a group interview but a site of discursive production" (paragraph 5); (b) "We have adopted the term Canadian-born Chinese, or CBC, to refer to all our participants because this terminology represents a socially constructed self-identity, not a literal statement of place of birth" (paragraph 6).

2. In paragraphs 7–9, identify three near-synonyms the authors use to suggest the difficulty in defining Canadian-born Chinese sense of identity/belonging.

3. Analyze the use of secondary sources in paragraph 2, including in your analysis answers to the following questions: How does this paragraph function as part of the essay's introductory section? How do the sources help develop the paragraph's main idea? Does the use of sources in which Kobayashi and Preston are co-authors increase or decrease their credibility as writers?

4. Although the authors include a "Methodology" section, commonly found in Type B essays (see Chapter 3, pp. 23–24), their thesis does not take the form of a hypothesis as it usually does in a Type B essay: (a) Identify the thesis format and explain why the authors might have chosen to use this format; (b) Although the authors also do not include a "Results" section, identify the first paragraph in which the authors begin to discuss their results.

5. In paragraphs 9–10 or paragraph 13 ("Speaking of Being Racialized"), analyze the role the authors play

in synthesizing their primary sources (i.e., the words of the participants) in order to develop their points and achieve clarity. Refer to specific passages in your analysis.

6. It is common in qualitative studies involving unstructured interviews or focus groups to reproduce the exact words of the participants; (a) Why do you think it is important that the authors do this? (b) Briefly mention some of the pros and cons of this method of using direct quotations, referring specifically to at least two different participants to support your points. (Do not use the same passages that you used in Question 4.)

Post-reading

1. Referring to the pre-reading question after having read "Being CBC," explain some of the main features, benefits, and limitations of this method of research. Refer specifically to the essay to support your points.

2. *Collaborative activity*: Demonstrate the functioning of a "focus group" (see paragraph 5 of "Being CBC") by having one person act as a facilitator and the other members as participants. The topic(s) discussed should relate to the essay's content.

3. Identify one issue or problem that is discussed in the essay and propose concrete solutions/effective ways of resolving or reducing the problem.

Causes and Consequences of Canada's Resettlement of Syrian Refugees

Anne-Marie Bélanger McMurdo

(1,152 words)

> ### Pre-reading
>
> 1. Access the home page of the journal *Forced Migration Review* (http://www.fmreview.org) to determine the journal's aims and ambitions as well as its target audience.

1 Canada's pledge in late 2015 to accept 25,000 Syrian refugees for resettlement came at a time when certain other countries were considering measures such as confiscating assets of refugees, registering Muslim refugees entering their country or closing borders to refugees altogether. Why did Canada buck a growing trend and what have been the consequences?

2 A few factors can help explain Canada's action. First, Canadian public response to the Syrian refugee crisis had gathered a significant amount of momentum over time. This was further reinforced by the news of the death of three-year-old Alan Kurdi, a Syrian child who drowned while travelling by boat from Turkey to Greece with his family—a family who, it emerged, had previously been refused resettlement to Canada. This event marked a tipping point, strengthening the public outcry for the Canadian government to change its previously more restrictive policies towards refugees.

3 Secondly, national elections in Canada in October 2015 proved timely. During the pre-election phase, prime ministerial candidates responded to public opinion in favour of increased resettlement by each offering their own pledge to resettle Syrian refugees.

4 Thirdly, citizens wanted their government to match the rhetoric of Canadian identity as compassionate, actively engaged in the international community and open to newcomers. It was no surprise that citizens pushed the government to make an effort towards resettling Syrians, given the long-standing willingness of many citizens to be actively engaged in sponsoring refugees themselves. Civil society in Canada plays a significant role in resettlement as individuals can resettle refugees through what is known as the "Group of Five" scheme, whereby five or more Canadian citizens or permanent residents apply to sponsor refugees to come to Canada and take responsibility for supporting them after arrival.[1]

Source: From *Forced Migration Review*, no. 52, May 2016, pp. 82–4.

Resources for Resettlement

5   Resettlement is a form of responsibility sharing and a recognition of international cooperation between countries. However, there is no legal imperative to resettle refugees, and countries choose to accept refugees voluntarily and may set their own quotas and criteria. Canada's decision to accept 25,000 Syrian refugees[2] was, in this sense, its own choice.

6   The newly elected government's commitment to resettle Syrians was primarily driven by the momentum of the elections, and later by the need to demonstrate the new government's capacity to swiftly implement promises. In fact, once the government had been voted into power in October 2015, it was not clear how it would fulfil its promise to resettle 25,000 Syrian refugees to Canada. As a result, deadlines had to be pushed back from the end of 2015 to the end of February 2016. Since being elected, the federal government has made huge efforts to meet its target of resettling 25,000 Syrian refugees, but the focus on quantity to be resettled may have been at the expense of the quality of settlement services provided.

7   Disappointingly, settlement services in Canada have not yet received the same support from the government as was offered in physically resettling the refugees to Canada. In other words, with such a huge and rapid influx of refugees, settlement services have been stretched beyond capacity, without sufficient resources to adequately address the refugees' needs, or the time to invest in additional fundraising.

8   After repeated cuts in the settlement sector by the previous government, "newcomer" services—those engaged in welcoming and assisting resettled refugees and other immigrants—have been struggling to respond to the increase in arrivals. As a result of the scale of arrivals, enrolling the refugees in language classes and/or schools and allocating housing, to name but a few services, have proved challenging. For example, refugees have been staying in temporary accommodation for weeks longer than usual.[3] In response, the private sector and civil society have played an extremely active role in responding to the needs of the thousands of Syrian arrivals to fill this gap. Yet there is also a need for trained professionals to support this specific group of people and their varied and complicated needs, particularly for government-assisted refugees, who have greater needs and more vulnerabilities than other newcomer groups.

Fair Treatment?

9   In responding to popular opinion, the Canadian government has been offering special benefits to arriving Syrian refugees. For instance, Syrian refugees who arrived after the new government came to power do not—in contrast to refugees of other nationalities and previous Syrian refugees—have to repay the government's travel loan which enabled their journey to Canada. But what of Syrians who came while the previous government was in power? What about other refugees who are resettling at the same time as the Syrians? By trying to put forward a helpful and empathetic view towards the Syrian population, the government has effectively created two classes of refugees, disregarding fairness and equity. Others—including many in the private sector and social services—have followed suit in offering various benefits to newly arriving Syrians in Canada. Yet this welcome has the effect of making invisible any other refugees. Refugee experts, practitioners and advocates in Canada have been calling for fairness and equity in this response.

10   Canada is, at a national and international level, making a clear and very positive commitment to refugees. The amount of action taken in the last few months has been remarkable for a national government body, as has been the welcoming response by the general Canadian public. Furthermore, Canada has a high standard of settlement services given the country's priority to integrate newcomers and the existence of an already established settlement system. But what thought has been given to the long-term settlement implications of these refugees—and of others? Given that approximately 10,000 refugees resettle to Canada in any given year,[4] 25,000 Syrian refugees in the space of four months on top of the resettlement of 10,000 additional government-assisted Syrian refugees by the end of 2016[5] will surely put a substantial strain on the provisions of services to refugees for the next year and beyond.

11   With the recent attacks in Paris and Brussels, and subsequent waves of Islamophobia, the initiative to resettle Syrians to Canada has come in for increasing challenge by Canadians. Security in resettlement processing has become a point of public discussion and contention, with the new government undertaking regular information sharing about resettlement in order to ease the fears of Canadian citizens.

12   Only time will tell whether the new government will continue to bolster support to the settlement sector and demonstrate—after the deadlines have passed and targets

have been reached—that it values the successful integration of refugees. But if this much action can be successfully achieved, and ambitious quotas can be met given the right circumstances, many are hopeful that the momentum of this response can be maintained for future resettlement initiatives in Canada. The question now is whether this extraordinary support for refugees in Canada will translate into a full-scale, stronger post-arrival network of support and services for the refugee arrivals as well as into maintaining support for large-scale resettlement in the years to come.

References

1. www.cic.gc.ca/english/refugees/sponsor/groups.asp
2. A mix of government-assisted and privately sponsored refugees.
3. www.cbc.ca/news/canada/refugees-housing-moving-in-1.3476893
4. www.cic.gc.ca/english/refugees/canada.asp
5. www.cbc.ca/news/politics/liberals-immigration-levels-plan-2016-1.3479764

Key and challenging words

allocate, advocate (n), equity, bolster

Questions

1. (a) Why do you think the author chose to use a question as a thesis (see paragraph 1)? (b) Find another paragraph in which the author uses one or more questions and discuss their function within the paragraph and section in which they occur.
2. (a) What is the main rhetorical pattern in this essay? (b) Identify two other rhetorical patterns by paragraph number(s); (c) for one of these, explain its purpose within the essay.
3. (a) In paragraph 6, identify one verb that suggests the author's doubts about the resettlement of Syrian refugees in Canada; (b) How could you describe the author's tone in paragraph 7?
4. (a) Discuss the organization of the essay; (b) Select one section of the essay and comment on its organization, referring to paragraphs in which specific organizational strategies have been used.
5. Analyze the author's use of argument in the section "Fair Treatment?," referring to some of the argumentative strategies mentioned in Chapter 9. If appropriate, you could also consider ways that the argument could have been improved. Refer to specific passages in your analysis.
6. Who do you believe the author primarily credits with the successes of the Syrian resettlement in Canada? Who do you believe she primarily blames for the problems with the resettlement process? Support your points by referring to specific passages.

Post-reading

1. Using reliable sources, create a timeline that represents the Syrian "crisis," beginning with the antecedents to the crisis up to the present.

Voices within Canada

Mental Wellness in Canada's Aboriginal Communities: Striving toward Reconciliation

Patricia Boksa, Ridha Joober, and Laurence J. Kirmayer
(2,136 words)

> *Pre-reading*
>
> 1. Access the website mentioned in note 1 (see References) in order to obtain an overview of the aims of the Truth and Reconciliation Commission of Canada, along with their reports. (You may have to use links at this site to get this information.)

With the presentation in Ottawa this spring of the report from the Truth and Reconciliation Commission (TRC) of Canada on Indian residential schools, the well-being of Canada's Aboriginal peoples took centre stage for a few days in the media and minds of the Canadian public. The TRC documented key historical issues that have contributed to major mental health disparities in Canada's indigenous population and pointed the way toward a larger process of national reconciliation.[1] Because *JPN* is the official journal of the Canadian College of Neuropsychopharmacology, a Canadian society devoted to understanding mental health and disease, we are taking the opportunity with this editorial to keep the discussion going forward by highlighting the mental wellness of Aboriginal peoples in Canada. We present a brief historical background of some of the factors recognized as contributing to current mental health challenges faced by the Aboriginal population and end with some suggestions on how mental health professionals might contribute to the reconciliation process. Although much of what we discuss in this editorial has been written before, it bears repeating to engage our readers. In addition to their importance in the Canadian context, many of the issues we discuss are relevant to indigenous peoples in other countries.

Historical Overview

Aboriginal people make up about 4% of the current population of Canada and comprise First Nations (60%), Métis (33%) and Inuit peoples (4%). More than half of Aboriginal people live in Canadian cities, with the remainder living largely in rural or remote small communities. There is substantial cultural diversity among Aboriginal peoples in Canada; for example, First Nations comprise more than 600 major bands speaking 55 different languages from 11 major language groups. Historically, First Nations are derived from peoples with ancient roots in Canada. Ancestors of all North American indigenous peoples date back to 13 500 years ago, while archeological records clearly date numerous First Nations settlements in Canada originating as far back as 9000 to 10 000 years. By 500–1000 CE, First Nations peoples had established trade routes across what is now Canada, while the Inuit, descendants of the Thule in Alaska, migrated across the Arctic starting from around 1000 CE.

Starting in the sixteenth century, European colonization had catastrophic effects on the indigenous peoples of North America (for a review, see Kirmayer and colleagues[2]). About 90% of the population died by the mid-1850s due largely to the introduction of infectious diseases, but also due to warfare and forced displacement. Aboriginal persons remaining in Canada were subjected to systematic oppression by the Canadian government designed to "civilize," assimilate and eliminate their cultures. The creation of Indian reserves aimed to confine Aboriginal people to small settlements while appropriating their lands. The locations of these communities were decided by government and commercial interests with the main purpose of freeing more desirable land for the use of European settlers. The *Indian Act* of 1876 formalized the reserve system and made "status" Indians wards of the state, with the federal government financing and imposing structures for band administration, education and health care. The explicit purpose of this legislation was to eliminate indigenous cultures by

Source: From *Journal of Psychiatry and Neuroscience*, vol. 40, no. 6, 2015, pp. 363–5.

inculcating European values, as illustrated by the following quotation from an 1876 Department of Indian Affairs report:

> Our Indian legislation generally rests on the principle, that the aborigines are to be kept in a condition of tutelage and treated as wards or children of the State. ...the true interests of the aborigines and of the State alike require that every effort should be made to aid the Red man in lifting himself out of his condition of tutelage and dependence, and that is clearly our wisdom and our duty, through education and every other means, to prepare him for a higher civilization by encouraging him to assume the privileges and responsibilities of full citizenship.[3]

These views were in line with the colonial doctrines prevalent in other parts of the world during that historical epoch.

4   From 1883 until the mid-1980s, the Indian residential school system was another means used to inculcate Euro-Christian values, this time targeting Aboriginal children. The aim of this educational system was put bluntly by Duncan Campbell Scott, head of the Department of Indian Affairs from 1913–1932:

> I want to get rid of the Indian problem. I do not think as a matter of fact, that the country ought to continuously protect a class of people who are able to stand alone … Our objective is to continue until there is not a single Indian in Canada that has not been absorbed into the body politic and there is no Indian question, and no Indian Department, that is the whole object of this Bill.[4]

5   Under Scott, in 1920 it became mandatory for every Indian child between the ages of 7 and 15 years to attend school. Since many reserves in remote areas had no schools, this meant the residential schools, which approximately 150 000 Aboriginal youth attended over several generations. Children were often removed from their communities; isolated from their families, ways of living and language; and expected to take on a completely foreign demeanor in an atmosphere of strict regimentation. The schools were often sorely underfunded and plagued by overcrowding, poorly trained staff, poor sanitation and heating, and inadequate nutrition and health care. Lack of human warmth and physical abuse as enforcement were standard, while many children also experienced outright neglect and psychological and sexual abuse. This large-scale removal of children disrupted family and community structures, so that cultural tradition and values could not be passed on, often leading to intergenerational loss of parenting skills and fragility in forming attachments. The final report of the TRC concluded that Canada had committed cultural genocide in its dealings with Aboriginal peoples.[1]

Current Challenges and Strengths

6   The historical trauma of the Indian residential school system has had ongoing intergenerational effects on the psychological well-being of Aboriginal communities.[5] For example, higher rates of depressive symptoms, suicidal thoughts and attempts, and childhood abuse and neglect are reported among adults with a parent or grandparent who attended an Indian residential school in Canada (termed IRS offspring) than in those whose parents and grandparents did not.[6-8] The IRS offspring reported greater depressive symptoms associated with stressors, such as childhood adversity, adult trauma and perceived discrimination, suggesting an enhanced sensitivity to such stressors.[6] Additional challenges include higher rates of illicit and prescription drug use and abuse that have been observed among Aboriginal youth and adults compared with non-Aboriginal Canadian populations.[9-11] Social determinants of health, such as poverty, unemployment, housing and food security, social exclusion and discrimination, almost certainly play a role in the mental health challenges faced by Aboriginal peoples given that they remain, on the whole, among the poorest and most socially disadvantaged people in Canada. However, identifying these enduring social structural and historical causes of adversity in Aboriginal communities does not obviate the need to address current mental health. As noted in *Feathers of Hope, a First Nations Youth Action Plan*[12] from Ontario, labelling mental health issues as social issues is sometimes used as an unacceptable excuse for neglecting to provide adequate services.

7   While certain historical realities have affected and continue to affect virtually all Aboriginal peoples in Canada, as with any diverse population, there are variations in rates of psychiatric disorders and symptomatology among individual communities. Research points to factors such as cultural identity and overall community

self-determination and vitality as potentially important resiliency factors accounting for some of these variations. For example, while overall rates of suicide and suicidal ideation for Aboriginal youth are higher than in the general population of Canada,[13,14] Chandler and Lalonde[15] found wide variations in rates of completed suicide in a study of 80 First Nations bands in British Columbia (BC). Most notably, these rates of suicide among the various BC communities correlated strongly with an index of "cultural continuity" or local control based on the presence of several community factors, including self-government; involvement in land claims; and band control of education, health services, cultural facilities, and police and fire services.[15] In a recent study examining drug misuse among urban Aboriginal adults living in Edmonton, Canada, Currie and colleagues[11] found that enculturation, defined as "the degree to which Aboriginal peoples identify with, feel a sense of pride for, and integrate the values and norms of their Aboriginal heritage culture," was associated with reduced illicit and prescription drug problems. In agreement with these findings, the recently released First Nations Mental Wellness Continuum Framework—jointly developed by the First Nations and Inuit Health Branch of Health Canada, the Assembly of First Nations, and indigenous mental health leaders from various First Nations—highlights culture and the use of culturally specific holistic interventions incorporating indigenous knowledge as a cornerstone to achieving individual, family and community mental wellness.[16]

8   Across the country, some Aboriginal communities are devising innovative and effective mental wellness programs based on a strong sense of community and family, and often integrating elements of Western medicine with local cultural approaches to resilience, such as land-based and other traditional activities. Yet a major challenge to achieving mental wellness for many Aboriginal people is a general lack of appropriate and engaging mental health services. With the current jurisdictional division of Aboriginal health care between federal and provincial governments, there is a lack of dedicated long-term funding for mental health services. Funding is often project-based and time limited, and sustainability is a continual challenge. Many smaller, remote communities have limited or no access to mental health services. There is a dearth of trained mental health workers of Aboriginal origin and a high turnover of non-Aboriginal health workers leading to a lack of continuity of services and a lack of connection to specialized services for persons with severe mental illness or excessively long wait lists. Stigma and discrimination remain as major barriers to accessing mental health services. In mainly non-Aboriginal mental health settings, the values and traditions of Aboriginal persons may be poorly understood and their concepts of wellness and ways of knowing undervalued. Thus services may be inadequate or inappropriate owing to a lack of culturally competent and knowledgeable mental health care providers.

Mental Health and the Reconciliation Process

9   What can mental health professionals reading this editorial do to contribute to bridging the rift wrought by history and supporting mental wellness for Aboriginal communities? In fact, there are many opportunities for action by practitioners, whatever their interests, cultural backgrounds, resources and locations. The following are some suggestions.

- Take opportunities to talk with people of Aboriginal origin to learn about their diverse perspectives on these issues.
- Read and become informed on the history of Canada's Aboriginal peoples to better understand the current context. (Some readily available online resources are included in the reference list.[12,16–18])
- Bear witness to the facts of history and acknowledge that effects are still deeply felt today by all.
- Become culturally competent, with an understanding of historical legacy and current challenges that impact mental health in some Aboriginal communities. The Indigenous Physicians Association of Canada and the Royal College of Physicians and Surgeons of Canada have prepared basic training materials in cultural safety.
- Remember there is not a single pan-Aboriginal identity. Learn about the issues but be open to becoming acquainted with the large diversity of Aboriginal communities and with individuals with their own personal stories.
- Provide mental health services in culturally responsive ways and working respectfully within

Aboriginal frameworks of mental wellness. Given the history of trauma and high level of adversity experienced by some First Nations people, a "trauma-informed approach" to mental health care, "based on compassion, placing priority on a trauma survivor's safety, choice, and control" is recommended by the 2015 First Nations Mental Wellness Continuum Framework.[16] Yet caution must also be taken in perpetuating cultural stereotypes.

- Engage in respectful collaborations with traditional healers and knowledge holders.
- Acknowledge that local indigenous knowledge must guide the development of relevant mental health programs. There is much that Western mental health professionals can learn from some of the innovative, comprehensive and humanistic approaches to mental wellness and mental health care delivery that have been developed in some Aboriginal communities.
- As a practising psychiatrist, consider serving Aboriginal communities to address lack of services and long wait lists, preferably within the community itself. For early-career psychiatrists interested in social justice and cultural diversity, this may be a rewarding opportunity. (Note: DSM-5 contains a semi-structured interview, the Cultural Formulation Interview, which is a 16-item questionnaire designed to tap into cultural topics for clinicians to consider in patient assessment, diagnosis and treatment.[19])
- Support Aboriginal mental wellness workers in navigating and collaborating with mental health services.
- Encourage and actively support the training of young Aboriginal health professionals.
- Support and lobby for cooperation among federal, provincial and territorial governments to provide sustainable, dedicated funding for clinical mental health services in Aboriginal communities.

References

1. *Honouring the Truth, Reconciling for the Future: Summary of the Final Report of the Truth and Reconciliation Commission of Canada.* Truth and Reconciliation Commission of Canada; 2015. Available: www.trc.ca/websites/trcinstitution/index.php?p=890 (accessed 2015 Sept. 23).

2. Kirmayer LJ, Brass GM, Tait CL. The mental health of Aboriginal peoples: transformations of identity and community. *Can J Psychiatry* 2000;45:607–16.

3. Department of the Interior. Annual Report for the year ended 30th June, 1876 (Parliament. Sessional Papers, No. 1877;11:xiv.

4. National Archives of Canada, Record Group 10, vol 6810, file 470-2-3, vol 7, pp. 55 (L-3) and 63 (N-3).

5. Kirmayer LJ, Gone JP, Moses J. Rethinking historical trauma. *Transcult Psychiatry* 2014;51:299-319.

6. Bombay A, Matheson K, Anisman H. The impact of stressors on second generation Indian Residential School survivors. *Transcult Psychiatry* 2011;48:367-91.

7. Elias B, Mignone J, Hall M, et al. Trauma and suicide behaviour histories among a Canadian indigenous population: an empirical exploration of the potential role of Canada's residential school system. *Soc Sci Med* 2012;74:1560-9.

8. Bombay A, Matheson K, Anisman H. The intergenerational effects of Indian residential schools: implications for the concept of historical trauma. *Transcult Psychiatry* 2014;51:320-38.

9. Currie CL, Wild TC. Adolescent use of prescription drugs to get high in Canada. *Can J Psychiatry* 2012;57:745-51.

10. Fischer B, Argento E. Prescription opioid related misuse, harms, diversion and interventions in Canada: a review. *Pain Physician* 2012;15(Suppl):ES191-203.

11. Currie CL, Wild TC, Schopflocher DP, et al. Illicit and prescription drug problems among urban Aboriginal adults in Canada: the role of traditional culture in protection and resilience. *Soc Sci Med* 2013; 88:1-9.

12. *Feathers of Hope, a First Nations Youth Action Plan.* Provincial Advocate for Children & Youth. Toronto, ON; 2014. Available: http://digital.provincialadvocate.on.ca/i/259048-foh-report (accessed 2015 Sept. 24).

13. Lemstra M, Rogers M, Moraros J, et al. Risk indicators of suicide ideation among on-reserve First Nations youth. *Paediatr Child Health* 2013;18:15-20.

14. Kirmayer L, Brass G, Holton T, et al. Suicide among Aboriginal people in Canada Ottawa: Aboriginal

Healing Foundation 2007. Available: www.ahf.ca/publications/research-series (accessed 2015 Sept. 24).

15. Chandler MJ, Lalonde CE. Cultural continuity as a hedge against suicide in Canada's First Nations. *Transcult Psychiatry* 1998;35:191-219.

16. First Nations Mental Wellness Continuum Framework. Health Canada; 2015. Available: http://health.afn.ca/uploads/files/24-14-1273-fn-mental-wellness-framework-en05_low.pdf (accessed 2015 Sept. 24).

17. University of Manitoba National Centre for Truth and Reconciliation. Available: http://umanitoba.ca/centres/nctr/index.html (accessed 2015 Sept. 24).

18. University of British Columbia: Indigenous Foundations. Available: http://indigenousfoundations.arts.ubc.ca (accessed 2015 Sept. 24).

19. Lewis-Fernandez R, Aggarwal N, Hinton L, et al., eds. *DSM-5 Handbook on the Cultural Formulation Interview.* Washington, DC: American Psychiatric Press.

Key and challenging words

inculcate, illicit, obviate, resiliency, ideation, enculturation, dearth, stigma, humanistic

Questions

1. After reading paragraph 1, consider the essay's topic, purpose, and audience. In one sentence each, identify the topic, purpose, and audience.

2. Explain the importance of *The Indian Act* in the attempt to "'civilize', assimilate and eliminate [Aboriginal] cultures" (paragraph 3).

3. Analyze the role of primary sources in the section "Historical Overview," providing specific examples to support your points. (You could include the source indicated in note 1 at the end of the section, which is also a primary source.)

4. Discuss the role of two of the following rhetorical patterns in their respective sections as well as in the essay as a whole: (a) chronology in "Historical Overview," (b) cause–effect in "Current Challenges and Strengths," (c) problem–solution in "Mental Health and the Reconciliation Process."

5. Explain how "cultural community" and "enculturation" can alleviate some of the social problems associated with Aboriginal mental health (see paragraphs 9 and 10).

6. (a) Discuss the rhetorical purpose of the last section of the essay, "Mental Health and the Reconciliation Process"; (b) Explain why the use of bullets might be appropriate in this section; (c) What reader is addressed in this section, and why might the suggestions be relevant to this specific audience?

Post-reading

1. *Collaborative or individual activity:* Write or present to your class a report on the residential school system as described in paragraphs 4 and 5. Your report should include an overview of the purpose and history of residential schools in Canada, as well as their effects on Aboriginal peoples.

2. Using reliable academic sources, such as documents published by the Truth and Reconciliation Commission of Canada, or non-academic ones, such as newspaper/online articles related to the Commission's Final Report (see note 1), (a) develop a timeline of events that led up to the Final Report, and (b) include at least two related articles after the Report's publication in June 2015.

A Sorry State

Mitch Miyagawa
(5,043 words)

Pre-reading

1. Using reliable sources, such as media coverage, create a timeline of Canadian government apologies to minority groups in Canada, starting with the 1988 apology to Japanese Canadians for internment during World War II. Summarize in a couple of sentences each the nature of the apology and the response of the group to which the apology was directed.
2. How important do you think it is that governments issue apologies for past injustices? Have too many or too few apologies been made by Canadian governments? Reflect on this issue and its importance today in one or two paragraphs.

1   The government of Canada gave my family our first apology, for the internment of Japanese Canadians during World War II, in 1988. I was seventeen, and I don't remember any of it. I had other things to worry about. My mom had just left my dad, Bob Miyagawa. She'd cried and said sorry as my brother and I helped her load her furniture into the back of a borrowed pickup. Her departure had been coming for a while. At my dad's retirement dinner the year before, his boss at the Alberta Forest Service had handed him a silver-plated pulaski, a stuffed Bertie the Fire Beaver, and a rocking chair. My mom, Carol—barely forty years old and chafing for new adventures—took one look at the rocking chair and knew the end was near.

2   Three months after she left, on September 22, Brian Mulroney rose to his feet in the House of Commons. The gallery was packed with Japanese Canadian seniors and community leaders, who stood as the prime minister began to speak. "The Government of Canada wrongfully incarcerated, seized the property, and disenfranchised thousands of citizens of Japanese ancestry," he intoned. "Apologies are the only way we can cleanse the past." When he finished, the gallery cheered, in a most un-Japanese Canadian defiance of parliamentary rules.

3   The clouds may have suddenly parted in Ottawa; the cherry blossoms in Vancouver may have spontaneously bloomed. I missed it all. It was graduation year. Every day after school, I worked at West Edmonton Mall, diving elbow deep in Quarterback Crunch ice cream so I could save up for a pool table. Weekends, I visited my mom at her new place, a small apartment within walking distance of the tracks by Stony Plain Road.

4   Up until then, and perhaps to this day, being half Japanese had just been something I used to make myself unique. A conversation starter. A line for picking up girls. The internment my dad and 22,000 others like him suffered was something to add to the story. It increased the inherited martyr value.

5   I didn't get many dates.

6   Four years earlier, when Brian Mulroney was leader of the Opposition, he'd asked Pierre Trudeau to apologize to Japanese Canadians. Exasperated, Trudeau shot back, "How many other historical wrongs would have to be righted?" It was Trudeau's last day in Parliament as prime minister. He finished his retort with righteous indignation: "I do not think it is the purpose of a government to right the past. I cannot rewrite history."

7   Trudeau must have known that the apology door, once opened, would never be closed. Mulroney might have known, too. Redress for Japanese Canadians was the beginning of our national experiment with institutional remorse—an experiment that has grown greatly over the past twenty years, intertwining itself with my family's story.

8   I like to look at the glass as half full: my parents' divorce was not so much a split as an expansion. They both remarried, so my kids now have more grandparents than they can count. And I've gained the most apologized-to family in the country—maybe the world.

Source: © Mitch Miyagawa. First published in *The Walrus*, December 2009. Reprinted with permission of the author.

9   I watched Stephen Harper's apology for Indian residential schools with my dad's wife, Etheline, on a hot night in the summer of 2008. Etheline was the third generation of her Cree family to attend an Indian mission school. She went to Gordon Residential School in Punnichy, Saskatchewan, for four years. Gordon was the last federally run residential school to be closed, shutting down in 1996 after over a century in operation.

10   When I talked to my mom in Calgary afterward, she casually mentioned that her second husband Harvey's father had paid the Chinese head tax as a child. Harper apologized to head tax payers and their families in 2006.

11   I was aware that my family had become a multi-culti case study, but when I realized the government had apologized to us three times it went from being a strange coincidence to a kind of joke. (*Q: How does a Canadian say hello? A: "I'm sorry."*) Soon, though, I started wondering what these apologies really meant, and whether they actually did any good. In seeking answers, I've mostly found more questions. I've become both a cynic and a believer. In other words, I'm more confused than ever before. I'm no apology expert or prophet. I'm so sorry. All I can offer is this: my apology story.

12   In the fall of 2008, I travelled from my home in Whitehorse to Vancouver. The National Association of Japanese Canadians had organized a celebration and conference on the twentieth anniversary of Redress. It rained as I walked toward the Japanese Hall on Alexander Street in East Vancouver, in what was once the heart of the Japanese community. In the distance, giant red quay cranes poked above the buildings along Hastings, plucking containers from cargo ships anchored in Burrard Inlet. The downpour soaked the broken folks lined up outside the Union Gospel Mission at Princess and Cordova, a few blocks from the hall. Some huddled under the old cherry trees in Oppenheimer Park, beside the ball field where the Asahi baseball team, the darlings of "Japantown," played before the war.

13   Inside the hall, a few hundred people milled about, drinking green tea and coffee served from big silver urns by bluevested volunteers. The participants on the first panel of the day, titled Never Too Late, took seats on the wide stage at the front. They represented the hyphenated and dual named of our country: a Japanese-, Chinese-, Indo-, Black, Aboriginal, and Ukrainian-Canadian rainbow behind two long fold-out tables. Their communities had all been interned, or excluded, or systematically mistreated. Apology receivers and apology seekers. A kick line of indignation, a gallery of the once wronged. (*A Japanese-, Chinese-, Indo-, Black, Aboriginal, and Ukrainian- Canadian all go into a bar. The bartender looks at them and says, "Is this some kind of joke?"*)

14   In the fictional world of *Eating Crow*, a "novel of apology" by Jay Rayner, the hottest trend in international relations is something called "penitential engagement." To deal with the baggage from the wars, genocides, and persecutions of the past, the United Nations sets up an Office of Apology. The protagonist of the novel, Marc Basset, is hired as Chief Apologist, partly because of his tremendous ability to deliver heartfelt apologies, but also because of his "plausible apologibility." His ancestors captained slave ships, ran colonies, slaughtered natives, and waged dirty wars. Backed by a team of researchers and handlers, Basset circles the globe, delivering statements of remorse.

15   Penitential engagement is closer to reality than you'd think. The Japanese government has made at least forty "war apology statements" since 1950. All of Western Europe remembers German chancellor Willy Brandt's famous *Kniefall* in 1970, when he fell to his knees on the steps of the Warsaw Memorial, in silent anguish for the victims of the Warsaw Ghetto uprising. During the past twenty years, Italian prime minister Silvio Berlusconi has apologized for the colonial occupation of Libya, South African president Frederik W. de Klerk has apologized for apartheid, and the Queen has issued a Royal Proclamation of regret to the Acadians in the Maritimes and Louisiana. In 1998, the Australian government began its annual National Sorry Day for the "stolen generations" of aboriginal children. In 2005, the US Senate apologized for its failure to enact federal anti-lynching legislation. And both houses of Congress have now passed apologies for slavery.

16   At the 2001 UN World Conference against Racism, Racial Discrimination, Xenophobia and Related Intolerance, held in Durban, more than 100 countries called "on all those who have not yet contributed to restoring the dignity of the victims to find appropriate ways to do so and, to this end, appreciate those countries that have done so." Working toward this goal is the International Center for Transitional Justice in New York, which "assists countries pursuing accountability for past mass atrocity or human rights abuse." As if in response, jurisdictions across Australia, the United States, and Canada are passing apology acts designed to allow public officials to apologize without incurring legal liability.

17   Concerned about our precious self-image as a peace-making, multicultural country, Canada has been making every effort to lead the sorry parade. In addition to the residential school and Chinese head tax apologies, the federal government has also now said sorry for the *Komagata Maru* incident, when a ship full of immigrants from India was turned away from Vancouver Harbour, and established a historical recognition program "to recognize and commemorate the historical experiences and contributions of ethno-cultural communities affected by wartime measures and immigration restrictions applied in Canada." And we became the first Western democracy to follow South Africa in establishing a truth and reconciliation commission, for the residential schools.

18   Not surprisingly, other groups have come knocking on Ottawa's door. Among them are Ukrainian Canadians, on behalf of those interned during World War I, and the residents of the bulldozed Africville community in Halifax, now a dog park. Some who have already received an apology clamour for more, or better. Harper's *Komagata Maru* apology was issued to the Indo-Canadian community outside Parliament. Now they want the same as every other group: an official, on-the-record statement.

19   I sat down on a plastic-backed chair in the deserted second row. Seconds later, an old *Nisei*, a second-generation Japanese Canadian named Jack Nagai, plunked down beside me. He sighed and lifted the glasses hanging around his neck to his face. "Gotta sit close for my hearing aid," he said, then looked at me and grinned. I pulled out a notebook, and he watched me out of the corner of his eye, fingering the pen in his breast pocket.

20   *Black scuffs*, I wrote. The pearly walls and floor of the Japanese Hall auditorium were marked and streaked. A fluorescent light fifteen metres above my head flickered and buzzed. The hall had a school gym wear and tear to it. Jack noticed my scribbling and jotted down something on the back of his program.

21   The brown spots on his bald head reminded me of my Uncle Jiro, who passed away suddenly in 2005 at the age of seventy-seven. As it turned out, Jack was from Lethbridge as well, and had known my uncle from the city's Buddhist Church. My Uncle Jiro, "Jerry" to his non-Japanese friends, had helped the blind to read, bowled every Sunday, and kept a meticulous journal of the prices he'd paid for groceries and the sorry state of his golf game. He'd been a bachelor, mateless and childless, like several others on my dad's side.

22   Those few of us in my family who now have kids have Caucasian spouses, so our strain is becoming less and less Asian. The Miyagawa name may disappear here with my two sons, and with the name would go a story seeded a hundred years ago.

23   My grandmother and grandfather farmed berries on three hectares of rocky slope in Mission, BC, starting in the 1920s. They were their own slave-drivers, labouring non-stop to clear the land and get the farm going. Grandmother produced the workforce, delivering a baby a year for a decade. My dad was near the end, the ninth child of ten. By 1941, the Japanese controlled the berry industry in BC. My grandparents' farm expanded and flourished.

24   Then came Pearl Harbor, war with Japan, and the dislocation of more than 20,000 Japanese Canadians from the West Coast. On a spring day in 1942, my dad and his family carried two bags each to the station and boarded a train bound for the sugar beet fields of southern Alberta. They never made it back to Mission. The Japanese Canadians weren't allowed to return to BC until four years after the war was over, so the family instead settled in Lethbridge. Dad moved away soon after he came of age, and ended up in Edmonton, where I was born.

25   For my dad, the apology was pointless. Like many others in the Japanese Canadian community, he had already turned the other cheek. *Shikata ga nai*, the saying goes—what's done is done.

26   I admire and marvel at his ability to let go of the past. He even calls his family's forced move across the Rockies a "great adventure." For a ten-year-old, it was a thrill to see the black smoke pouring from the train engine's stack as it approached the Mission station.

27   Mist softens a train platform in the Fraser Valley. Last night's rain drips from the eaves of the station, clinging to the long tips of cedar needles. All over the platform, families are huddled together by ramshackle pyramids of suitcases. Children squat around a puddle on the tracks, poking at a struggling beetle with a stick. A distant whistle; their mother yells at them in Japanese; they run back to stand beside her. Their father stands apart, lost in thought. He's trying to commit to memory the place where he'd buried his family's dishes the night before, in one of his berry fields a few kilometres away.

28   Clickety-clack. Clickety-clack. A screech of brakes, a sizzle of steam. The train pulls in, the doors open, each one sentinelled by a Mountie with arms crossed.

29   The families become mist, along with their suitcases and the Mounties. Everything disappears except the train. It's quiet. An old conductor in a blue cap sticks his head out the window. No need for tickets on this train, he says. Step right up. Welcome aboard the Apology Express.

30   The conference began, and Jack and I leaned forward to hear. The panellists took their turns bending into low mikes, paying homage to the hallowed ground zero of apologies. Chief Robert Joseph, a great bear of a man in a red fleece vest, hugged the podium and said, "The Japanese Canadian apology was a beacon." Everyone at the tables looked tiny, posed between the high black skirting framing the stage and the minuscule disco ball that hung above them.

31   The people telling the stories of their communities were the same ones who had put on their best shoes to walk the marbled floors of Parliament, who had filed briefs for lawsuits. They spoke in the abstract—reconciliation, compensation, acknowledgement—and kept up official outrage as they demanded recognition for their causes. "We have to remember, so it will never happen again" was the panel's common refrain. After an hour, Jack's eyes were closed, and he'd started to lean my way. I could hear soft snoring from the other side of the room, where a group of seniors slumped and tilted in their chairs.

32   This wasn't what I'd come to hear either. After studying and listening to official expressions of remorse to my family and others, after reading the best books on the subject (*The Age of Apology*; *I Was Wrong*; *On Apology*; *Mea Culpa*), I'd come to believe that government apologies were more about forgetting than remembering.

33   I righted Jack as best I could, and snuck out the back of the hall for some fresh air.

34   I've always imagined that my mom met Harvey Kwan in a room full of light bulbs. They both worked for the Energy Efficiency Branch of the provincial government. She wrote copy for newsletters; he did tech support. In my mind, Mom would watch the way Harvey methodically screwed the bulbs into the bare testing socket. She appreciated his size. Not quite five feet tall, my mom likes her husbands compact (though she did dally for a time with a rather tall embezzler from Texas). She was further attracted to Harvey's quiet voice, his shy smile as he explained wattages and life cycles. Perhaps they reached for the same compact fluorescent and felt a jolt as their fingers touched.

35   Mom and "Uncle Harv" were both laid off soon after they started dating, so they moved from Edmonton to Calgary,

closer to their beloved Rockies, and became true weekend warriors, driving past the indifferent elk on Highway 1 to Canmore and Banff to hike and camp and ski. Mom was afraid of heights; Harv took her hand and led her to the mountaintops.

36   Harvey's father had sailed to Canada aboard the *Empress of Russia* in 1919, at the age of fourteen. He paid the $500 head tax, then rode the CPR with his father to the railroad town of Medicine Hat, on the hot, dry Alberta prairie. Around the time he became an adult, in 1923, the Canadian government passed a *Chinese Immigration Act*, which remained in force for twenty-five years. Under the act, no new Chinese immigrants could come to Canada, so a young bachelor like him could only have a long-distance family. He managed to sire three sons with his first wife in China during that time, but she never made it to Canada, dying overseas. He eventually took a second wife, Harvey's mom, who had to wait several years before she could enter the country. In the meantime, she lived unhappily with Harvey's father's mother, probably waiting on her like a servant.

37   And that's all Harvey knows. He doesn't know about his father's life, those twenty-five years away from his first wife and their children, then his second. He doesn't know his grandfather's name. He doesn't know what his grandfather did. He doesn't know where the man is buried. They never spoke of that time.

> Mr. Speaker, on behalf of all Canadians and the Government of Canada, we offer a full apology to Chinese Canadians for the head tax and express our deepest sorrow for the subsequent exclusion of Chinese immigrants . . . No country is perfect. Like all countries, Canada has made mistakes in its past, and we realize that. Canadians, however, are a good and just people, acting when we've committed wrong. And even though the head tax—a product of a profoundly different time—lies far in our past, we feel compelled to right this historic wrong for the simple reason that it is the decent thing to do, a characteristic to be found at the core of the Canadian soul.

> —Stephen Harper, June 22, 2006

38   Apology comes from the Greek *apo* and *logos* ("from speech"), and as every first-year philosophy student who reads Plato's *Apology* knows, it originally meant a defence of one's position. But somewhere along the line, it became a Janus word, adopting its opposite meaning as well. Rather than a justification of one's position or actions, it became an admission of harm done, an acceptance of responsibility. When Harper spoke on the head tax, you could see both faces of the word at work: *Those were different times. We're not like that now. We should, in fact, be proud of ourselves. Pat ourselves on the back. Reaffirm our goodness today by sacrificing the dead and gone.*

39   Rather than bringing the past to life, statements like these seem to break our link with history, separating us from who we were and promoting the notion of our moral advancement. They also whitewash the ways in which Canadians still benefit from that past, stripping the apologies of remorse. Rendering them meaningless. Forgettable.

40   I wasn't the only one taking a break from the conference. I followed a Japanese Canadian woman with short grey hair down the street to Oppenheimer Park, watching from a distance as she placed her hand, gently, on the trunk of one of the old cherry trees. I later learned that these were memorial trees, planted by Japanese Canadians thirty years ago. The City of Vancouver had been planning to chop them down as part of a recent redevelopment scheme, but the Japanese Canadian community rallied and saved them (though the old baseball diamond will still be plowed under).

41   I arrived back at the hall in time for lunch. Ahead of me in line was the author and scholar Roy Miki, one of the leading figures in the movement for Japanese Canadian redress and a member of the negotiating committee for the National Association of Japanese Canadians. Miki was an "internment baby," born in Manitoba in 1942, six months after his family was uprooted from their home in Haney, BC. He laughed when I told him about my family and, intrigued, pulled up a chair beside me for lunch. He had neat white hair, parted to one side, and wore blue-tinted glasses. We balanced bento boxes on our knees, and he told me something that astounded me: the negotiators hadn't wanted an apology very badly.

42   "We wanted to shine a light on the system—to show its inherent flaws," he said. "Our main concern wasn't the apology or the compensation. The real victim was democracy itself, not the people." What those pushing for redress wanted was an acknowledgement that democracy had broken down, and that people had benefited from the internment of Japanese Canadians. They wanted to change the system in order to protect people in the future.

43   Miki remained wary of government expressions of remorse, concerned that the emotional content of apologies—the focus on "healing"—distracted from the more important issue of justice. "Now the apology has become the central thing," he said. "It allows the government to be seen as the good guy. But there's a power relationship in apologies that has to be questioned; the apologizer has more power than the apologized-to."

44   Mulroney, in his apology to Japanese Canadians, said the aim was "to put things right with the surviving members—with their children and ours, so that they can walk together in this country, burdened neither by the wrongs nor the grievances of previous generations." Both the victimizer and the victim are freed from their bonds. Japanese Canadian internment "went against the very nature of our country." With the apology, so the redemption narrative went, Mulroney was returning Canada to its natural, perfect state. Cue music. Roll credits. The lights come up, and all is right with the world again. I find the storyline hard to resist, especially when the main characters are long gone. But of course not all of these dramas took place once upon a time.

45   My dad met his second wife, Etheline Victoria Blind, at a south Edmonton bingo. Yes, he found a native bride at a bingo, in front of a glass concession case where deep-fried pieces of bannock known as "kill-me-quicks" glistened under neon light.

46   I was working for an environmental organization at the time. Like most Alberta non-profits, we depended on bingos and casinos as fundraisers. Dad was one of our A-list volunteers. He was retired, reliable, and always cheerful, if a bit hard of hearing. Etheline, on the other hand, was on the long-shot volunteer list. She was the mother of the high school friend of a colleague. I didn't know her, but I called her one night in desperation.

47   I don't remember seeing any sparks fly between Dad and Etheline. He was sixty-five at the time, and not seeking to kick at the embers of his love life. But Etheline invited him to play Scrabble with her, and so it began.

48   Dad and Etheline had a cantankerous sort of affair, from my point of view. They lived separately for many years—Dad in a condo on Rainbow Valley Road, Etheline in an aging split-level five minutes away—but moved gradually toward each other, in location and spirit, finally marrying a few days after Valentine's Day, eight years after

they met. I flew down from Whitehorse with my son, just a year old then. He was the only person at the wedding wearing a suit, a one-piece suede tuxedo.

49   And so Etheline became my Indian stepmother.

50   Stephen Harper's apology to residential school survivors was a powerful political moment. You had to be moved by the sight of the oldest and youngest survivors, side by side on the floor of Parliament—one a 104-year-old woman, the other barely in her twenties. The speeches were superb, the optics perfect. Yet personally, I felt tricked. Tricked because the apology distilled the entire complicated history of assimilation into a single policy, collapsing it like a black hole into a two-word "problem": residential schools. Here was the forgetful apology at its best. By saying sorry for the schools, we could forget about all the other ways the system had deprived—and continued to deprive—aboriginal people of their lives and land. The government had created the problem, sure, but had owned up to it, too, and was on its way to getting it under control, starting with the survivors' prescription for recovery. If they were abused, they merely had to itemize their pain in a thirty-page document, tally their compensation points, stand before an adjudicator to speak of their rape and loneliness, and receive their official payment. All taken care of.

51   And yet. And yet.

52   Etheline, I apologize. I knew you for ten years and never really knew where you came from. I'm educated, postcolonial, postmodern, mixed race, well travelled, curious, vaguely liberal, politically correct. "You're the most Canadian person I know," I've been told. And yet I never once asked you about your time in residential school. I never really related until that night, after we'd watched Harper's shining moment, that powerful ceremony—and I'd watched how it moved you, felt the hair on my arms rise and a shiver in my back when we talked late and you told me how your grandfather was taken from his family when he was four, the same age my oldest son is now; told me how he'd never known his parents, but relearned Cree ways from his adopted family and became a strong Cree man even after his own children were taken away; how he'd raised you when your mother couldn't; how you were in the mission school, too, for four years, and your grandfather wouldn't let them cut your braids, and you'd feel the cold brick walls with your hands, and the laundry ladies would only call you by your number, and you would stare out the window toward the dirt road that led away from the

school and cry for your *Kokum* and *Meshom*. I never knew. Or if you told me, I only listened with half an ear. And I apologize again, for bringing it all up, for writing down your private pain. But I know we need to tell it again and again. It has to be there; it has to get into people's hearts.

53   And here I make an apology for the government apology. For whatever I feel about them, about how they can bury wrongs in the past instead of making sure the past is never forgotten, about how they can use emotion to evade responsibility, they have indeed changed my life. They've made me rethink what it means to be a citizen of this country. They've brought me closer to my family.

54   Near the end of the conference, the woman with short grey hair stood up and told a story. After World War II, when she was a schoolgirl, she'd one day refused to read out loud from a textbook with the word "Jap" in it. She was sent home, where she proudly told her father what she'd done. He slapped her across the face. The apology, she told everyone at the hall, had restored her dignity. The conference ended the next day, and I returned home with something to think about.

55   It's summer as I write, almost a year since the conference, and the apologies have kept coming. The state of California apologized for the persecution of Chinese immigrants last week. Thousands of former students of Indian day schools, feeling left out of the residential school apology, filed a statement of claim at the Manitoba legislature yesterday.

56   I'm sitting on the beach of Long Lake, just outside Whitehorse. Though it's hot outside, the water here always stays cold, because the summer's not long enough to heat it. Still, my two boys are hardy Yukoners, and they're running in and out of the water, up to their necks. I watch their little bodies twist and turn, then look at my own thirty-eight-year-old paunch and search the sky. What will we be apologizing for when my children are adults? Temporary foreign workers? The child welfare system?

57   Tomio bumps into Sam, knocking him to the ground. Sam cries. "Tomio," I tell my oldest, "say sorry to your brother." "Why?" he asks. "I didn't mean to do it."

58   "Say sorry anyway," I reply.

59   We say sorry when we are responsible and when we are not. We say sorry when we were present or when we were far away. We are ambiguous about what apologies mean in the smallest personal interactions. How can we expect our political apologies to be any less complicated?

60   A long time ago—or not so long ago, really, but within our nation's lifetime—another train hustled along these tracks: the Colonial Experiment. She was a beaut, shiny and tall. Ran all the way from Upper Canada; ended here in this lush Pacific rainforest. The Colonial Experiment was strictly one way, so it's up to the Apology Express to make the return trip.

61   Watch as we go by: a Doukhobor girl peeks out from under her house, her head scarf muddy. The police officers who took her sister and her friends away to the school in New Denver are gone and won't be back for another week. A Cree boy, hair freshly shorn into a brush cut, stares out the window of a residential school in the middle of the Saskatchewan grasslands, watching his parents' backs as they walk away. A Japanese fisherman hands over the keys to his new boat. A Ukrainian woman swats the mosquitoes away, bends to pick potatoes at Spirit Lake, and feels her baby dying inside her. A Chinese man living under a bridge thinks about his wife at home and wonders if he'll see her again.

62   But take heart: at every stop on the way back, someone important will say sorry for their lot. Just like the man in the top hat on my son's train engine TV show, he'll make it all better, no matter how much of a mess there's been.

63   All aboard. If you feel a little sick, it's just the motion of the cars. Close your eyes. Try not to forget.

Key and challenging words

redress, Janus word, grievance, cantankerous

Questions

1. How much of the essay would you consider the introduction? Explain.
2. Comment on Miyagawa's use of personal experience in his essay, referring specifically to at least one example from the introduction and at least one from another part of the essay.
3. Why does Miyagawa use an example from fiction (paragraph 14)? How does it help support his point?
4. Find one example each of a passage that uses narration, description, and analysis. Briefly explain how the use of each contributes to the essay as a whole.

5. Why does the author consider himself an authority on apologies? How does he show his expertise? Find an example of another authority and discuss how he or she is used to develop a point.
6. Identify two passages in which Miyagawa uses a specific or distinct tone (the tone should not be the same in both). How do the different tones affect the reader? How do they help develop the part of the essay in which they occur?
7. After reading the essay, analyze Miyagawa's attitude toward apologies. Use specific textual references in your analysis.

Post-reading

1. Find two individual reactions from members of the same racial/cultural group to whom Canadian governments have apologized. Using summary and analysis, compare and contrast their reactions.
2. The federal and provincial governments have made several apologies for racist behaviours in the past. Choose one example of a government apology other than that made by the government to Aboriginal peoples in 2008. In one paragraph, summarize the issue(s) that occasioned the apology; in another paragraph, summarize the responses of those to whom the apology was made.

The Senate and the Fight against the 1885 Chinese Immigration Act

Christopher G. Anderson

(4,254 words)

> ### Pre-reading
>
> 1. Anderson's essay is occasioned by the apology of Prime Minister Stephen Harper to Chinese Canadians for the Head Tax of 1885 and other discriminatory policies of the late nineteenth and early twentieth centuries in Canada. (a) Using a reliable source, such as an encyclopedia or recent government document, research the history of Chinese immigration to Canada from 1885 to 1923, including the laws enacted to limit or exclude Chinese immigration; (b) Using a reliable dictionary, find a definition for *racism* or *racial discrimination*.

1   *On June 22, 2006, the Prime Minister rose in the House of Commons to "offer a full apology to Chinese Canadians for the head tax and express our deepest sorrow for the subsequent exclusion of Chinese immigrants." After recalling the fundamental role that Chinese Canadians had played in the nation-building construction of the Canadian Pacific Railway (CPR), the Prime Minister observed how—once the line was completed—"Canada turned its back on these men" as it imposed a $50 Head Tax on Chinese migrants in 1885, increased this to $100 in 1900 and then to $500 in 1905, and finally expanded the scope of its exclusionary measures in 1923 to make it all but impossible for Chinese immigrants to resettle legally in Canada through into the post–Second World War period. Although the various race-based measures instituted to exclude Chinese migrants were deemed to be legal at the time, they were, according to the Prime Minister, "inconsistent with the values that Canadians hold today." This article argues that at the time of the 1885 legislation, and for some time after, there were voices that spoke out against these discriminatory policies. Most specifically, this sentiment dominated debates on the question in the Canadian Senate between 1885 and 1887, and it did so to such an extent that government supporters had to resort to some clever procedural maneuvers to see the law passed and amended against the will of the majority of Senators. In an important sense, then, these restrictive measures are not only "inconsistent with the values that Canadians hold today," but also conflict with values held by Canadians in the late*

nineteenth century, values that can be traced to a set of liberal beliefs on the rights of non-citizens inherited from Britain. The debates that took place in the Senate are, therefore, both interesting and important because they provide greater depth to our understanding of the historical record of race relations in Canada. They also speak to the more general issue of the role of the Senate in Canadian politics.

2   Although Chinese migrants had lived in Canada since as early as 1858, it was not really until the 1880s that their numbers began to rise appreciably. Thus, while 4,383 were identified in the 1881 Canadian census, the population is then thought to have grown to around 10,550 by September 1884 as the construction of the Canadian Pacific Railway picked up steam. More generally, some 16,000 to 17,000 Chinese migrants probably came to Canada during the early 1880s to work on the rail line.[1] For economic and geographic reasons, Chinese migrants generally arrived and lived in British Columbia, and it is from there that the most persistent and vocal cries were heard for greater control from the late nineteenth century onward.

3   At first, the reception of the Chinese was relatively cordial: "Colonial British Columbians were initially remarkably tolerant of the thousands of Chinese who came. British officials refused to countenance any discrimination, and whites, rather than pressing for hostile action, boasted of the British justice enjoyed by the Chinese."[2] Although there were certainly incidents of racism, including violence, against the Chinese, British liberalism formed the basis of

Source: From *Canadian Parliamentary Review, vol.* 30, Summer 2007, pp. 21–6. By permission of the author.

the government's response to their presence in the colony. While Britain itself had had very limited experience with receiving Chinese migrants, the country's official position on the presence of non-citizens was primarily defined at this time by a recognition of the right of foreigners to enter and remain, which precluded any wholesale restriction.[3] However, after British Columbia joined Confederation in 1871, local politicians (first at the provincial level and then at the federal level) began to pressure Ottawa to pass legislation to restrict the ability of the Chinese to immigrate to or—for those who had already arrived—find work in Canada.[4]

4   The first major effort in the House of Commons was undertaken by Arthur Bunster (Vancouver Island), who sought and failed to convince his fellow MPs in 1878 to make it illegal to hire people to work on the construction of the CPR if their hair was greater than 5.5 inches in length—an obvious attack on the Chinese, whose hair was generally worn in long queues.[5] In words that recalled those famously used by Lord Palmerston some 20 years earlier in the defence of the rights of foreigners in Britain,[6] Prime Minister Alexander Mackenzie stated that the motion "was one unprecedented in its character and altogether unprecedented in its spirit, and at variance with those tolerant laws which afforded employment and an asylum to all who came within our country, irrespective of colour, hair, or anything else."[7] Mackenzie did not "think it would become us, as a British community, to legislate against any class of people who might be imported into, or might emigrate to, this country."[8]

5   Although calls for "repressive measures" against the Chinese—including their forced removal from the country—were made time and again in Parliament through into the 1880s, Prime Minister John A. Macdonald, while he personally opposed such immigration, appointed two separate commissions of inquiry to investigate the situation in 1879 and 1884. Once the CPR was completed, however, the government introduced changes in May 1885 to the proposed *Electoral Franchise Act* before Parliament to deny any person of Chinese origin the right to vote in federal elections.

6   John A. Macdonald justified this action on the grounds that the Chinese migrant "is a stranger, a sojourner in a strange land . . . [H]e has no common interest with us . . . [H]e has no British instincts or British feelings or aspirations, and therefore ought not to have a vote."[9] Moreover, if given the vote, he warned, the Chinese would likely elect a sufficient number of Chinese-origin MPs in British Columbia to force the rest of the country to adhere to their

"eccentricities" and "immorality."[10] The Prime Minister's move received strong support from a number of MPs (especially those from British Columbia), but it also sparked some vocal opposition. For example, L.H. Davies (Queen's) argued that "If a Chinaman becomes a British subject it is not right that a brand should be placed on his forehead, so that other men may avoid him."[11] For his part, Arthur H. Gillmor (Charlotte), while he did "not think they are a desirable class of persons," argued all the same that "as British subjects, we ought to show them fair play."[12] Despite such protests, however, the motion was carried. For reasons that are not clear, such voices became mute when the House turned to consider the government's legislation to restrict Chinese immigration two months later.

7   It was left to Secretary of State Joseph A. Chapleau to explain Bill 125 (later renumbered Bill 156) "to restrict and regulate Chinese Immigration into the Dominion of Canada" to the House, and he did so with such an expression of regret as to lead one MP to comment that "one would almost imagine [that he] were in opposition to the Bill rather than in favour of it."[13] Chapleau began by declaring that he had been surprised when

> a demand was made for legislation to provide that one of the first principles which have always guided the English people in the enactment of their laws and regulations for the maintenance of the peace and prosperity of the country, should be violated in excluding from the shores of this great country, which is a part of the British Empire, members of the human family.[14]

8   Although he agreed that it was a good thing to ensure the continuance of a "white" British Columbia, he took issue with the way in which the Chinese had been demonized. As co-chair of the 1884 commission, he had found little evidence to support the uniformly negative image put forward by those who wanted to prevent their arrival; moreover, he had concluded that such migration had had a generally positive impact on the regional economy. Chapleau had come to see, however, that when it came to the Chinese people Canadians were "naturally disposed, through inconscient prejudices, to turn into defects even their virtues."[15]

9   The law would not only impose a $50 "Head Tax" (or "Capitation Tax") on Chinese migrants before they could

be landed, but would also put in place several other restrictions. For example, only one Chinese passenger was to be allowed per each 50 tons weight of the arriving vessel (s.5), and a system of certificates was to be put in place to control those who desired to leave and return without paying the Head Tax again (s.14). Those most in favour of restriction were not wholly satisfied by these proposals but saw in them "the thin end of the edge" in the creation of a more extensive system of control.[16] Indeed, amidst concerns over the administration of the legislation, the only opposition came from those who wanted to make it more restrictive, although these critics supported Bill 156 all the same as it passed easily through the House.

10   Subsequently, amendments were introduced to the *1885 Chinese Immigration Act* during the next two years. In 1886, the government sought to enforce compulsory registration of those already in Canada (with penalties for non-compliance), expand the scope of the law to cover trains as well as ships, and remove merchants from the list of those exempt from paying the Head Tax. Although the bill was passed in the Lower Chamber with little dissent, it was ultimately held up in the Senate by the opponents of restriction. In 1887, the government introduced new amendments that were notable for the absence of any further restrictions, save a change to allow the Chinese only three months leave from the country before having to repay the Head Tax.[17] Even these proposals, however, barely made it through the Upper Chamber, and that lone restrictive feature was ultimately removed.

11   There was an intimation of the level of support that the Chinese might receive in the Senate during its debate on the 1885 *Electoral Franchise Act*. "I cannot myself see the propriety," Alexander Vidal commented, "of excluding the Mongolians, who have shown themselves to be patient, industrious and law-abiding, from privileges which are given to every other member of the human family in this country."[18] For his part, Lawrence G. Power did not think "the Parliament of Canada should make any distinction of race at all; that the Chinese, Negroes, Indians and Whites should be on the same footing; that no exceptions should be made in favour of one or against another race."[19] Striking a position that would be repeated by a number of his colleagues when Bill 156 arrived not long thereafter, Richard W. Scott observed that having sought to open up China to the world, Canada should not "set up a Chinese wall on our side," for to do so would be "entirely contrary to the principles of the

Empire."[20] Despite such objections, however, the franchise legislation was passed. The protests that were made over denying the Chinese the right to vote paled, however, in comparison to the outrage expressed by the many Senators who spoke against the restriction of Chinese migration.

The Senate in Defence of the Chinese (1885–87)

12   Early on in the debate, Alexander Vidal set the tone for the majority in the Senate when he declared: "I think it is entirely inconsistent with the very fundamental principle of the British constitution that legislation of this kind should find a place on the statute book."[21] To pursue such a course as that proposed in Bill 156, observed James Dever, would tarnish the reputation of the country:

> We, who pride ourselves on the freedom of our institutions, and the abolition of slavery in the United States, and who fancy we are going over the world with our lamp in our hand shedding light and lustre wherever we go—that we should become slave-drivers, and prohibit strangers from coming to our hospitable shore because they are of a different colour and have a different language and habits from ourselves, in deference to the feelings of a few people from British Columbia, is a thing I cannot understand.[22]

13   To the extent to which the law would discriminate against a particular group, concluded William Almon, it remained "contrary to the genius of the nineteenth century."[23] Moreover, it was suggested that if the Chinese did not seem to adapt well to Canadian society, then this was in part the fault of Canadians themselves when they instituted such barriers as disenfranchisement and the prevention of family reunification. Indeed, it was observed that the Chinese became further excluded from European Canadian society by the stereotypes that the latter employed.

14   Although the opponents of restriction were unable to prevent the passage of the bill, the way in which it was returned to the House is worth noting, for it was only on account of some fancy procedural footwork on the part of the government side that it happened with so little disturbance. William Almon had "given notice that

[he] would oppose it at the third reading, and that [he] would move that it be read the third time three months hence"—thereby making it impossible for the legislation to pass that session.[24] The Senator, however, apparently committed a procedural error that allowed the legislation to emerge from the committee stage unscathed and pass through Third Reading without any discussion. Not only did Almon not give notice in writing, but he also wrongly assumed that debate could not pass through two stages on the same day. As a result, his efforts to scuttle the bill were sidestepped and it was returned to the House of Commons without a word altered, despite the considerable opposition to the very principles on which it was based that had been expressed. Almon's frustration comes through quite clearly, as does his firm conviction that it was a fundamentally illiberal piece of legislation:

> I think such legislation is a disgrace to humanity. I think it is rolling back civilization from the end to the beginning of the nineteenth century. The early part of this century did away with the Slave trade, with the *Test Act,* and gave Catholic emancipation and abolished slavery in the West Indies. We now enact a law which is as vile as any of those to the repeal of which I have just alluded, and I think it will impress an indelible disgrace on this House and on the Dominion.[25]

15   The chances that Almon's effort might otherwise have succeeded would seem to be slim—after all, it was fairly rare for a government bill to be turned back in the Senate, especially when the same party controlled both chambers—but the fate of the government's attempt to amend the 1885 *Chinese Immigration Act* by passing Bill 106 the following year makes it difficult to claim that there were none. As noted above, the proposed amendments in 1886 were mostly restrictionist in nature, but rather than simply debate these measures, opponents attacked the law itself. While much of the criticism trod upon familiar ground (e.g., "It is so repugnant to all that is English, and honourable or right that one can hardly discuss it in a proper frame of mind"),[26] there were important developments as well.

16   For example, Alexander Vidal raised the question of Canadian sovereignty and the country's right to restrict entry at its borders, and he suggested that this should not be held to be absolute but rather ought to conform to the principles on which the land had come to be settled. He began by inquiring as to the foundations of Britain's occupation of North America:

> By what royal right have we and our fathers crossed the ocean and taken possession of this western continent? What right had we to come here and dispossess the Indians, native proprietors of this country, and take possession of their lands? . . . [Do we] not only consider that we have a better right to it than they have, but to consider it so exclusively our own as to shut out from sharing in the advantages of this country others of God's people who have as much right to it as we have?[27]

17   The land was taken not by right, he claimed, but "because we believed that where our civilization and enlightenment have been introduced we have carried with us the blessings of Christianity to the people amongst whom we have settled."[28] To restrict other people now from coming to live in the country on the basis of race, he concluded, was so "utterly inconsistent with our professions as Christians and with the vaunted freedom we profess to cherish as a British people" that it undermined the basis on which the land had been occupied—the superiority of "the Anglo-Saxon race."[29] Thus, while Senators often still viewed the issue from a race-based and even missionary perspective, they also operated within a rights-based framework, with potentially quite important policy implications for Chinese Canadians.

18   Even George W. Allan, who introduced the amendments in the Senate for the government, said that he had "no special leaning towards this Chinese legislation."[30] Given the level of agreement against the proposals, it would be, Richard W. Scott averred, "a service to the empire if we allow this question to stand over another year."[31] By that time, he hoped, passions in British Columbia might have calmed somewhat and a more reasonable examination of the question might be assayed. Thus, the same Senate that had seemed to sanction the 1885 *Chinese Immigration Act* now let the debate on its amendment stand for six months, thereby signaling an unwillingness to allow the law to be changed in a more restrictive manner.

19   The government's second attempt to amend the law, Bill 54, responded to some of the criticisms that had been expressed in the Senate by removing the restrictive

elements included in the previous bill. Moreover, the one aspect of the new bill that would have made it more difficult for Chinese migrants—the three-month return clause—was first extended to six months and then dropped altogether. Nonetheless, the legislation received extended criticism ("a diabolical Bill . . . [that] has not a shadow of justice or right on its side"),[32] out of which emerged—amidst the old complaints—other lines of argumentation. For example, Almon asked: "How will it be now if we pass [this] Act to say that there is a dividing line between Canada and the United States? . . . Can we any longer point with pride to our flag and say that under that emblem all men, be they Mongolian, Circassian or Caucasian, are equally free?"[33]

20   The Senator who sponsored the bill on the government's behalf, future Prime Minister John J.C. Abbott, agreed that the principle that lay behind the 1885 *Chinese Immigration Act* was offensive to the chamber, but he argued all the same that the amendments on the floor might help to temper the harshness of the law. If too many alterations to the proposed bill were presented to the House, he cautioned, then it would reject them, with the result that the modest positive alterations that could be made would not come into effect, leaving the Chinese worse off than they might otherwise have been. This line of reasoning found some sympathy but little support, as "the sentiment of the Senate seemed to be that the Act should be wiped off the Statute Book."[34] Indeed, Vidal introduced Bill P to do just that, and he had such backing that Abbott himself admitted that it would likely pass on a vote. The justification for repeal was succinctly expressed by Robert Haythorne, who declared that "it is a difficult thing to amend a Bill based upon a wrong principle, and the principle upon which [the 1885 *Chinese Immigration Act* is] based is a bad and cruel one."[35] Even if the House would not accept it, Vidal argued, passage of Bill P would "show that we have proper views of British freedom and the responsibilities that are attached to our professions as Christians."[36]

21   The government side, however, was once again able—through procedural means—to steer its legislation through the chamber. It argued successfully before the Speaker that since the law involved the collection of revenue—the Head Tax—the Senate could not seek to repeal it. The Speaker based his ruling on s.53 of the 1867 *BNA Act* ("Bills for appropriating any Part of the Public Revenue, or for imposing any Tax or Impost, shall originate in the House of Commons") and on the 47th Rule of the Senate according to *Bourinot* ("The Senate will not proceed upon a Bill appropriating public money that shall not within the knowledge of the Senate have been recommended by the Queen's representative"). The question of the Senate's authority to amend money bills would long trouble Parliament and was eventually the subject of a Special Committee of the Senate in 1917. In response to this decision, Vidal argued: "I can easily understand that if we found the word 'Chinese' between cheese and cigars in the tariff bill that we could not touch it, but it is an extraordinary thing that we cannot amend a public Bill simply because there is a penalty attached for which the Government derives a revenue."[37] Although the purpose behind the Head Tax was clearly one of policy (that is, to restrict the entry of Chinese migrants) rather than one of generating revenue, the Speaker supported the government's line of reasoning. Thus, not only was Vidal's initiative ruled out of order but any chance of pursuing meaningful change to the bill seemed to have been thwarted. With the wind so completely and effectively taken out of the opposition's sails, Third Reading was speedily accomplished. It would be some years before the Senate would again exhibit such a rights-based outlook on the issue of migration control, even as the government expanded the scope of its restrictions towards Chinese migration as well as all other non-white, non-Christian, and non-British groups.

22   After coming into effect in January 1886, the 1885 *Chinese Immigration Act* doubtless contributed to the low levels of Chinese migration to Canada that occurred during the remainder of the 1880s. It is difficult, however, to assess the effect of the new law as there was an anticipated reduction in arrivals due to the completion of the CPR, which led many to leave the country, either to return to China or to try their fortunes in the United States. However, throughout the 1890s the number of entries recorded each year grew, if somewhat erratically, sparking a new wave of restrictive measures towards Chinese migration that culminated in the extremely effective 1923 *Chinese Immigration Act*. Indeed, according to official tallies, only eight Chinese immigrants were landed in Canada between 1924–25 and 1938–39—less than one every two years.

Conclusions

23   This examination of the response in the Senate to the government's first attempts to control Chinese immigration between 1885 and 1887 is instructive in at least two major respects. First, it uncovers an important feature of the

history of Canadian state relations with Chinese migrants that has too long been overlooked. While it is certainly true that the Chinese had few friends willing to support them in Canada, they could count a large number of Senators amongst them. Thus, Senator William J. Macdonald, himself a representative of British Columbia, took note of the role that many of his colleagues were playing:

> I wish to express my satisfaction at the fact that a people who have been treated so rigorously and ungenerously, who are unrepresented, and who have been hunted to the death, should have found representatives to stand up on the floor of this House and speak on their behalf.[38]

24 Of course, rights-based British liberalism was not the sole motivation for opposition to the 1885 *Chinese Immigration Act*. Indeed, there were traces of distrust of organized labour, alongside a desire that business should have access to such—as one Senator would put it a few years later—"good labour-saving machines."[39] Moreover, an opposition to discrimination did not necessitate admiration for the Chinese either as individuals or as a group (although it often was joined to such sentiments).[40] It also was at times connected to an opinion that "whites" were superior to the Chinese,[41] and for some Senators accepting such migrants in Canada was an important means by which the Chinese might be converted to Christianity.[42] Nonetheless, there is a clearly expressed respect for the individual rights of the Chinese that comes through in these debates, one that found widespread support amongst the opponents of restriction. Their racism, in short, did not fully displace their belief in equality, and they were able to support, as a result, radically different policy options from those that were being pursued by the government, and that would ultimately be transformed into a source of national shame.

25 As well as recalling an important piece of Canadian history, one that has been completely ignored or overlooked in the literature, the relevance of these Senate debates today can also be seen in the extent to which members of that institution sought to institute a policy position that is much more in keeping with what we understand to be modern values held by Canadians. This not only suggests that Canadians possess a much richer and more complex political history than is often recognized, but it also underlines the potential role for the Senate in broadening our political ideas and language, of providing the sort of sober second

thought that was supposed to be one of its central functions in the Canadian political system.

Notes

1. Patricia E. Roy, *A White Man's Province: British Columbia Politicians and Chinese and Japanese Immigrants, 1858–1914* (Vancouver: University of British Columbia Press, 1989), x–xi.
2. *Ibid.*, 4. See also W. Peter Ward, *White Canada Forever: Popular Attitudes and Public Policy Toward Orientals in British Columbia* [Second Edition] (Montreal and Kingston: McGill-Queen's University Press, 1990), 24–29.
3. See Colin Holmes, *John Bull's Island: Immigration and British Society, 1871–1971* (London: Macmillan Education Ltd., 1988).
4. See Bruce Ryder, "Racism and the Constitution: The Constitutional Fate of British Columbia Anti-Asian Immigration Legislation, 1884–1909," *Osgoode Hall Law Journal*, Volume 29, Number 3 (1991), 619–76.
5. 1207. See also James Morton, *In the Sea of Sterile Mountains: The Chinese in British Columbia* (Vancouver: J.J. Douglas Ltd., 1973), 43–44.
6. "Any foreigner, whatever his nation, whatever his political creed, whatever his political offences against his own Government may, under this Bill, as he does today, find in these realms a safe and secure asylum so long as he obeys the law of the land." Quoted in T.W.E. Roche, *The Key In The Lock: A History of Immigration Control in England from 1066 to the Present Day* (London: John Murray, 1969), 58.
7. Canada, House of Commons, *Debates*, March 18, 1878, p. 1209.
8. *Ibid.*
9. *Ibid.*, May 4, 1885, p. 1582.
10. *Ibid.*, p. 1588.
11. *Ibid.*, p. 1583.
12. *Ibid.*, p. 1585.
13. *Ibid.*, Edgar C. Baker (Victoria), July 2, 1885, p. 3013.
14. *Ibid.*, p. 3003.
15. *Ibid.*, p. 3006.
16. *Ibid.*, Noah Shakespeare (Victoria), July 2, 1885, p. 3011.
17. The new bill kept a provision to allow Chinese travelers in transit to pass through Canada without paying the Head Tax, while it added a clause to allow the

Chinese wife of a white man to enter without paying the Head Tax, and another that would ensure that a portion of the Head Tax was sent to provincial coffers in Victoria.

18. Canada, Senate *Debates,* July 13, 1885, p. 1276.
19. *Ibid.,* p. 1280.
20. *Ibid.*
21. *Ibid.,* p. 1297.
22. *Ibid.,* p. 1298.
23. *Ibid.,* p. 1295.
24. *Ibid.,* July 18, 1885, p. 1411.
25. *Ibid.*
26. *Ibid.,* Richard W. Scott, January 30,1886, p. 692.
27. *Ibid.,* May 21, 1886, p. 687.
28. *Ibid.*
29. *Ibid.*
30. *Ibid.*
31. *Ibid.,* May 26, 1886, p. 747.

32. *Ibid.,* William J. Macdonald, June 10, 1887, pp. 311–12.
33. *Ibid.,* p. 299.
34. *Ibid.,* Richard W. Scott, June 13, 1887, p. 349.
35. *Ibid.,* June 10, 1887, p. 313.
36. *Ibid.,* p. 307.
37. *Ibid.,* June 14, 1887, p. 396.
38. *Ibid.,* June 10, 1887, p. 311.
39. *Ibid.,* Henry A.N. Kaulbach, July 8, 1892, p. 497.
40. See W. Peter Ward, *White Canada Forever: Popular Attitudes and Public Policy Toward Orientals in British Columbia* [Second Edition] (Montreal and Kingston: McGill-Queen's University Press, 1990), Chapter 1.
41. According to Vidal, for example, the "superior civilization" of the "Anglo-Saxon race" meant that whites should have no fear of being overpowered by the Chinese; see Canada, Senate, *Debates,* July 13, 1885, p. 1297.
42. See *ibid.,* William Almon, p. 1296.

Key and challenging words

exclusionary, cordial, demonize, intimation, propriety, disenfranchisement, illiberal, indelible, restrictionist, aver, succinctly, appropriate, culminate

Questions

1. Identify in Anderson's introduction the justification for his essay and his thesis; paraphrase the thesis.
2. Construct a timeline for the most significant events referred to in the essay from 1878 to 1887.
3. (a) Identify a primary source used in the first three paragraphs of the essay; (b) Select a primary source that is set up in the block format and show its importance to the passage in which it occurs and the essay as a whole.
4. Briefly discuss the function of paragraph 11, which focuses on a time before Bill 125 (156) was introduced.
5. Explain in your own words the basis of the government manoeuvre that prevented Bill 54 from being repealed. How was faulty reasoning involved?
6. Explain how the views expressed by the senators who opposed the Head Tax exemplified a "rights-based" outlook (paragraphs 17 and 21) that characterized British thought in the nineteenth century.
7. According to the author in his conclusion, what can be learned from the debate in the Senate from 1885 to 1887?

Post-reading

1. *Collaborative or individual activity:* After coming up with a working definition of "racism" or "racial discrimination," consider whether the views expressed by the senators who opposed the Chinese Head Tax were, in fact, racist or discriminatory. Defend your point of view, making specific references to the senators' speeches.
2. Essays in the humanities often put forward a new interpretation of primary source material, arguing that the new interpretation is more valid than older interpretations or represents a significant perspective that is worthy of consideration. In 500 words, analyze the effectiveness of Anderson's argument; what made it convincing or not?

Missing in Action: Gender in Canada's Digital Economy Agenda

Leslie Regan Shade

(2,355 words)

Pre-reading

1. After reading the title and first paragraph and noting the name of the journal in which the essay appeared, (a) write a one-paragraph reading hypothesis that includes purpose, audience, and rhetorical mode; or (b) paraphrase paragraph 1.
2. *Collaborative or individual activity:* Were you aware that online gender equity was an issue for some Canadians? Reflect on/discuss the importance of this issue and possible ways to increase women's digital inclusion.

---

1   Global public interest advocates have hailed Canada, which has been developing federal policy and programs to increase citizens' Internet access since the 1990s, as an early promoter of online gender equity. But twenty years later, market fundamentalism and a retreat from the public interest by the Conservative-led federal government have diminished this progressive agenda, and concern with gender—especially the notion of gender equity—has palpably dissipated. Yet digital inclusion is still a persistent issue in Canada. As Internet governance becomes more globally implicated, feminist interventions in activism and scholarship are key to creating and sustaining innovative strategies of inclusion.

2   Perhaps the biggest policy sellout in the past decade in Canada has been the hollowing out of the principle of universality and a concomitant withering of public interest in social welfare. This includes digital policy, as evidenced by the gradual yet crucial disinvestment in funding for programs for Internet access. Consider how the rhetoric surrounding digital technologies has evolved: In the mid-1990s, hyperbole about information highways had politicians boasting that Canada would be the most wired nation in the world. The "roaring nineties" were characterized by the mantra of the marketplace (Stiglitz 2003) but also by the recognition that government funding for community Internet projects could ameliorate digital divides, notably through Industry Canada's Community Access Program (CAP). The dot-com euphoria of the late 1990s, critical policy research on the knowledge-based economy, and dreams of media convergence were quickly eclipsed by more sobering analyses of the tech crash amid the widely hyped new economy. Information highways transformed to broadband and fiber-to-the-home applications, while public concerns over privacy and security after September 11, 2001, created new policy and legislative regimes that often trumped human rights.

3   Modernizing the telecommunications landscape was the objective of the 2005 Telecommunications Policy Review Panel, which was tasked with formulating recommendations for a globally competitive regulatory environment; its final report called for market forces to prevail, bringing into question whether Canadians would be entitled to an affordable, universally accessible, and democratically accountable telecommunications system (Longford, Moll, and Shade 2012). In his 2010 Throne Speech before Parliament, the prime minister launched a strategy to "drive the adoption of new technology across the economy," to reintroduce copyright reform legislation, and to discuss increasing foreign ownership in the telecommunications sector, thus "giving Canadian firms access to the funds and expertise they need" (Government of Canada 2010).

4   Despite the documented boon it provided for community economic and cultural development, the CAP program was terminated in 2012 (*CBC News* 2012). Until recently, Canada could bask in its reputation as an international innovator in broadband access, but Canada now has the embarrassing distinction as a broadband laggard, sparking contentious debates between industry, government, the Canadian Radio-television and Telecommunications Commission, and public interest groups over whether regulatory intervention can increase competition in the broadband sector.

Source: From *Signs* 39.4 (Summer 2014), pp. 887–96. Published by: The University of Chicago Press, © University of Chicago Press 2014. Stable URL: www.jstor.org/stable/10.1086/67554

5   Concern with women's equality has also diminished in the past decade. Status of Women Canada became a federal departmental agency in 1976, with a mandate to coordinate policy and programs with respect to the status of women. Over the years the agency provided core funding for women's groups working in areas such as health care, education, antipoverty initiatives, and antiracism. In 2006, however, the Conservative federal government announced that Status of Women Canada would no longer fund groups engaged in advocacy, lobbying, or research. Following the government's directive, Status of Women closed regional offices; canceled the Policy Research Fund, which had supported independent policy research; changed funding eligibility criteria to allow for-profit organizations to apply alongside nonprofit groups; and, most notoriously, dropped the word "equality" from its mandate (Standing Committee on the Status of Women Canada 2007).

6   The rise and fall of CAP, the persistence of the market mantra, and a palpable contempt for equality issues are salient examples of discursive and material shifts in social and digital policy in the past decade, from promoting Internet access so as to foster and nurture participatory citizenship toward a discourse that merely advantages consumers' access to goods and services.

In the Good Old Days . . .

7   Early Internet policy recommendations regarded gender as an essential component for universal access, with Status of Women Canada funding research on Internet usage by women's groups and the potential of the Internet to foster women's citizenship (Shade 1996). Several declarations were issued in 1995 alone: the Federal Plan for Gender Equality stated that "the absence of equity and access-related research [regarding the information infrastructure] is of growing concern" (Status of Women Canada 1995, par. 270); the Coalition for Public Information (CPI), a nongovernmental organization aligned with the Ontario Library Association, integrated gender issues into its public policy framework (Skrzeszewski and Cubberley 1995); and the final report from the federally mandated Information Highway Advisory Council recognized that an attention to gender disparities was necessary to ensure equitable and universal Internet access (Industry Canada 1995).

8   In the 2000s, Canada played an international role in promoting gender equity in access to the Internet. The Canadian International Development Agency worked with the International Telecommunications Union's Task Force on Gender Issues to include gender mainstreaming in telecom programs and policies (ITU 2008). During the drafting of the World Summit on the Information Society (WSIS)'s "Declaration of Principles" (2012), the Canadian government collaborated with the summit's Gender Caucus to include a paragraph on gender equality (see also Gallagher 2011). And as part of Canada's participation in the second phase of WSIS, the Canadian Commission for UNESCO organized a conference that produced the "Canadian Civil Society Communiqué," affirming human rights, equality, cultural diversity, freedom of expression, privacy, and gender equality as Canadian values (CPSR 2005).

Digital Skills for Whom and for What?

9   The issue of social inclusion has been almost absent from recent digital policy, although the government's consultation paper on the digital economy did consider "digital skills": "the ability to locate, organize, understand, evaluate, create and share information using digital technology" (Industry Canada 2010a; see also Industry Canada 2010b). Emphasized was the need for a "sufficient quantity of qualified ICT [information and communication technology] workers" to form the "backbone" of a "strong, globally competitive information and communications technology sector," and one barrier to this goal was identified as the emergent "digital skills divide," which affected not just labor participation but "all . . . Canadians, be they homemakers, students or seniors" (Industry Canada 2010a).

10   In analyzing how digital skills are framed in the consultation paper, and in public submissions strategizing about best practices for addressing the digital divide, it becomes clear that digital skills were primarily couched in economic terms.[1] Infused with the technological imperative, submissions argue that digital skills are needed to function, participate, be productive, compete globally, spark innovation, prosper, prepare Canadians for the jobs of tomorrow, and meet the demands of market forces. Digital skills make for better workers. Better workers equate with better consumers, who create prosperity. More prosperity equates with global competitiveness—a veritable virtuous circle. Missing, however, is a more holistic vision that sees building digital skills as an element of citizenship and social justice. A blind spot in the submissions is a nuanced consideration of race, class, and gender inequalities.

11   More than two hundred organizations submitted briefs on digital skills, including an array of universities, colleges, and their associations; libraries and library associations; cultural groups; and a sprinkling of independent media companies, public interest groups, literacy organizations, and small Internet service providers. Themes that emerge from an analysis of submissions include identification of the educational sector as the conduit for training, strategies for increasing access to technology through libraries and community sites, increasing digital literacy, and ensuring broadband access for rural and remote communities, especially for First Nations communities.

12   Two organizations concerned with integrating women into the technological workforce submitted comments. Women in Film and Television—Toronto is a nonprofit professional organization that promotes, mentors, and trains women in the screen-based media industry and has a mandate to promote digital literacy skills. Its brief urges the government to conduct large-scale surveys on employment trends and skills gaps in the digital sector in order to ascertain gender disparities (WFTT 2010). The Canadian Advanced Technology Alliance (CATA; the largest high-tech professional association in Canada) and its Women in Technology Forum recommended redressing the gender imbalance in science and technology through education for young girls, promoting the participation and advancement of women in the tech sector, and improving work-life balance (CATA WIT Forum 2010). While these are laudable goals, the diverse echelons and practices within digital work—from paid higher-level programming, managerial skills, and lower-level data entry to the more contingent and affective labor practices of "prosumers" (online brand consumers and influencers) need to be differentiated, as many feminists argue (Scott-Dixon 2008; Gill 2010; Fortunati 2011).

13   Two other submissions also considered gender. OCAD University commented on gender representation in screen-based programming, including video games, and on the dearth of women serving as owners and workers in small technology companies, the mobile phone industry, and the social media industry (OCAD University 2010). A consensus document on the digital economy—the result of a roundtable organized at the University of Toronto and signed by over eighty academics, public interest stakeholders, and citizens—is notable because it highlights a citizen-based strategy emphasizing affordable, universal access, including a legal right to broadband Internet access, participatory citizenship and social inclusion, and promotion of privacy and other civil liberties ("Consensus Submission" 2010).

14   As is clear from the submissions and government paper on the digital economy, digital policy frames skill as the ability to participate in the labor force and to purchase and consume products and services. It emphasizes consumer rights rather than the rights of citizens to access ICTs in order to create content and participate meaningfully in democratic public life. Contemporary communications-policy discourse makes the terms "citizen" and "consumer" interchangeable, such that the "ubiquitous discourse of choice and empowerment" relegates the citizen solely to the market (Livingstone and Lunt 2007, 53). Indeed, Canadian digital policy has shifted from a semblance of citizen-based universality to a regime of market-generated rules for consumers. Programs and policies fixate on the technical, rather than social, infrastructure. Missing is a consideration of the nexus of technology, citizenship, and social justice. Despite the Canadian government's siren call for market forces to meet accessibility needs, numerous digital divides and differentials in digital skills persist, demarcated by socioeconomic status, demographics (including gender and generation), and geographic location (rural vs. urban). It is thus crucial to address these digital fissures and examine the relationships among four key variables in the adoption of digital skills: accessibility, affordability, usability, and value. Needed is a move from digital divides to digital capabilities, an approach that interrogates the texture of communication rights and entitlements. Digital skills can strengthen citizens' rights—the ability to create and participate meaningfully in democratic, social, and public life and thus contribute to social inclusion.

15   In her incisive feminist intersectional critique and analysis of the deployment of digital technologies in US society through federal programs, Virginia Eubanks (2011, xv) argues that optimistic "magical thinking" about technology disguises and heightens digital inequalities and that investments in technology, without simultaneous investment in social justice, merely increase inequalities at the structural, political, and sociocultural levels. As she argues, digital policy too often assumes middle-class values and experiences, neglecting or obscuring the

insights and struggles of poor and working-class people. The shuttering of the CAP program in Canada is also a gender equity issue. Community networks serve the economically disadvantaged, with women in the lower socioeconomic strata using the facilities to improve their situation and overcome technological disadvantages (Moll and Fritz 2012).

16   During the 2011 federal election, social media was widely deployed to raise awareness about the erosion of social welfare programs and policies. A popular website, ShitHarperDid.com, featured short informational videos delivered by low-key comedic hipsters. One video asked, "Do you know the pickup line that goes over the best for Canadian women?" The answer: "I am not Stephen Harper." Featuring a montage of young women addressing the camera, the script reads as follows:

> Harper has closed twelve out of sixteen Status of Women offices in Canada. He eliminated funding for Legal Voices for Women, including the National Association for Women in Law. He eliminated funding for Sisters in Spirit, an internationally praised organization, leading an investigation into six hundred murdered Aboriginal women and girls. Since 2006 Stephen Harper has cut funding for women's advocacy by 43 per cent. That's why, as a proud Canadian woman, I will be voting. And I will *not* be voting for Stephen Harper's Conservatives.[2]

17   The 2011 election did usher in an antiequality majority government, and as political scientist Sylvia Bashevkin ruefully comments, "Harper's track record of implementing regressive changes will probably continue now that his party controls both houses of parliament" (2012, 5). This does not bode well for digital inclusion. The ability to track key indicators of household and workplace Internet access that have been collected since the mid-1990s by Statistics Canada, the primary source of Canadian socioeconomic data, is imperiled now that the government has made cuts that affect thirty-four surveys (Bednar and Stabile 2012).

18   What is now needed more than ever is funding for collaborative research on digital inclusion that brings together academics and advocacy groups. Evidence-based policy making does not have to be merely quantitative, and qualitative work that engages community members

and intermediaries who serve as gateways to the Internet and broadband for many low-income Canadians can add much richness and depth to policy evidence. Aligning with Eubanks's research, a focus on social inclusion can enable us to learn from the media justice movement's awareness of wider social justice issues and attention to systemic issues of race, class, and gender. Feminist gender justice advocacy around policy issues within the media reform movement is crucial (Dougherty 2010; Shade 2011).

19   Ensuring a broadband-enabled digital society will take, as Catherine Middleton argues, "engaged, informed and digitally literate citizens" (2011, 11) and will involve the participatory development of applications and services that are valuable, affordable, and accessible. This, I argue, is a priority for feminist activism and scholarship, which can be at the vanguard of critiques and constructions of the digital economy.

Notes

1. For public submissions regarding the digital skills divide, see the "Building Digital Skills" page of Industry Canada's website for the Digital Economy in Canada at www.digitaleconomy.gc.ca/eic/site/028.nsf/eng/h_00492.html.
2. ShitHarperDid, "Canadian Women's Favourite Pick-Up Line," YouTube video. 1:09, posted by "ShitHarperDid," April 20, 2011, www.youtube.com/watch?v5KmthTKSWFWw&feature5bf_prev&list5UUz6NBjskefofNb8wXqLlD5A.

References

Bashevkin, Sylvia. 2012. "Regress Trumps Progress: Canadian Women, Feminism and the Harper Government." Perspective paper, Friedrich Ebert Stiftung, Washington, DC, July. http://library.fes.de/pdf-files/id/09205.pdf.

Bednar, Vass, and Mark Stabile. 2012. "Statistics Canada Cuts Compromise the Tools Used to Understand the State." *Toronto Star*, July 10. www.thestar.com/opinion/editorialopinion/article/1224561-statistics-canada-cuts-compromise-the-tools-used-to-understand-the-state.

CATA WIT Forum (Canadian Advanced Technology Alliance Women in Technology Forum). 2010. "Addressing the Shortage of Women in ICT." Report submitted to the Government of Canada, The Digital Economy in Canada,

Industry Canada, Ottawa, July 12. www.digitaleconomy.gc.ca/eic/site/028.nsf/eng/00362.html.

CBC News. 2012. "Ottawa Cuts CAP Public Web Access Funding." April 6. www.cbc.ca/news/canada/calgary/story/2012/04/06/ns-cap-funding-cut.html.

"Consensus Submission to the Federal Government Consultation on a Digital Economy Strategy for Canada." 2010. Report convened by Andrew Clement and Karen Louise Smith with support from the University of Toronto Faculty of Information, Identity, Privacy and Security Institute, and the Knowledge Media Design Institute, submitted to the Government of Canada, The Digital Economy in Canada, Industry Canada, Ottawa, July 13. www.ic.gc.ca/eic/site/028.nsf/eng/00284.html.

CPSR (Computer Professionals for Social Responsibility). 2005. "Canadian Civil Society Communiqué." Document WSIS-II/PC-3/CONTR/13-E, prepared on behalf of Canadian Civil Society, World Summit on the Information Society, Winnipeg. www.itu.int/wsis/docs2/pc3/contributions/Co13.pdf.

Dougherty, Ariel. 2010. "Snapshot of Foundation Support for Feminist Gender Justice Media." Media Equity Collaborative, Truth or Consequences, NM. http://old.gfem.org/sites/gfem.org/files/FNJn2010_SNAPSHOT_FdnFGJM_MEC.pdf.

Eubanks, Virginia. 2011. *Digital Dead End: Fighting for Social Justice in the Information Age.* Cambridge, MA: MIT Press.

Fortunati, Leopoldina. 2011. "ICTs and Immaterial Labor from a Feminist Perspective." *Journal of Communication Inquiry* 35(4):426–32.

Gallagher, Margaret. 2011. "Gender and Communication Policy: Struggling for Space." In *The Handbook of Global Media and Communication Policy*, ed. Robin Mansell and Marc Raboy, 451–66. Malden, MA: Wiley-Blackwell.

Gill, Rosalind. 2010. "'Life Is a Pitch': Managing the Self in New Media Work." *In Managing Media Work*, ed. Mark Deuze, 249–62. London: Sage.

Government of Canada. 2010. "Addressing the Shortage of Women in ICT." Speech from the Throne, March 3. www.ic.gc.ca/eic/site/028.nsf/eng/00362.html.

Industry Canada. 1995. "Connection, Community, Content: The Challenge of the Information Highway." Final report, Information Highway Advisory Council, Industry Canada, Ottawa.

———. 2010a. "Building Digital Skills for Tomorrow." Consultation paper, Industry Canada, Ottawa. www.ic.gc.ca/eic/site/028.nsf/eng/00041.html.

———. 2010b. "Shaping Canada's Strategy for the Digital Economy." Report, Industry Canada, Ottawa. www.ic.gc.ca/eic/site/ich-epi.nsf/eng/02090.html.

ITU (International Telecommunications Union). 2008. "Gender Mainstreaming Activities." Working document, International Telecommunications Union, Geneva. www.itu.int/ITU-D/gender/gender_mainstreaming_activities.html.

Livingstone, Sonia, and Peter Lunt. 2007. "Representing Citizens and Consumers in Media and Communications Regulation." *Annals of the American Academy of Political and Social Science*, no. 611, 51–65.

Longford, Graham, Marita Moll, and Leslie Regan Shade. 2012. "There and Back to the Future Again: Community Networks and Telecom Policy Reform in Canada, 1995–2010." In *Connecting Canadians: Investigations in Community Informatics*, ed. Andrew Clement, Michael Gurstein, Graham Longford, Marita Moll, and Leslie Regan Shade, 439–69. Edmonton: Athabasca University Press.

Middleton, Catherine. 2011. "From Canada 2.0 to a Digital Nation: The Challenges of Creating a Digital Society in Canada." In *The Internet Tree: The State of Telecom Policy in Canada 3.0*, ed. Marita Moll and Leslie Regan Shade, 3–13. Ottawa: Canadian Centre for Policy Alternatives.

Moll, Marita, and Melissa Fritz. 2012. "Keeping in Touch: A Snapshot of Canadian Community Networks and Their Users—Report on the CRACIN Survey of Community Network Users." In *Connecting Canadians: Investigations in Community Informatics*, ed. Andrew Clement, Michael Gurstein, Graham Longford, Marita Moll, and Leslie Regan Shade, 61–89. Edmonton: Athabasca University Press.

OCAD University. 2010. "Digital Economy/Digital Society." Report submitted to the Government of Canada, The Digital Economy in Canada, Industry Canada, Ottawa, July 13. http://digitaleconomy.gc.ca/eic/site/028.nsf/eng/00330.html.

Scott-Dixon, Krista. 2008. "Long (Standing) Digital Divisions: Women's IT Work in Canada." *Atlantis* 32(2):18–32.

Shade, Leslie Regan. 1996. "Report on the Use of the Internet in Canadian Women's Organizations." Report, Status of Women Canada, Ottawa.

———. 2011. "Wanted, Alive and Kicking: Curious Feminist Digital Policy Geeks." *Feminist Media Studies* 11(1):123–29.

Skrzeszewski, Stan, and Maureen Cubberly. 1995. "Future-Knowledge: A Public Policy Framework for the Information Highway." Report prepared for Canada's Coalition for Public Information, Coalition for Public Information/Ontario Library Association, Toronto.

Standing Committee on the Status of Women Canada. 2007. "The Impacts of Funding and Program Changes at Status of Women Canada." Report, House of Commons Canada, Ottawa, May. www.parl.gc.ca/HousePublications/Publication.aspx?Language5E&Mode51&Parl539&Ses51&DocId52876038&File55.

Status of Women Canada. 1995. "Setting the Stage for the Next Century: The Federal Plan for Gender Equality." Report, Status of Women Canada, Ottawa.

Stiglitz, Joseph E. 2003. *The Roaring Nineties: A New History of the World's Most Prosperous Decade*. New York: Norton.

WFTT (Women in Film and Television—Toronto). 2010. "Women in Digital Media." Report submitted to the Government of Canada, The Digital Economy in Canada, Industry Canada, Ottawa, July 6. www.digitaleconomy.gc.ca/eic/site/028.nsf/eng/00465.html.

WSIS (World Summit on the Information Society). 2012. "Declaration of Principles. Building the Information Society: A Global Challenge to the New Millennium." Report, December 12. www.itu.int/wsis/docs/geneva/official/dop.html.

Key and challenging words

concomitant, hyperbole, ameliorate, laggard, contentious, palpable, salient, veritable, echelon, contingent, dearth, relegate, nexus, demarcate, fissure, incisive, rueful

Questions

1. (a) Identify the main rhetorical patterns in (i) paragraphs 2–3 and (ii) in paragraphs 8–9; (b) For either (i) or (ii), discuss strategies that the author uses to increase comprehension, referring to the text.

2. Scan the essay for references to Industry Canada's Community Access program (CAP). Explain the importance of this organization to feminist goals of digital inclusion.

3. Analyze the rhetorical and stylistic effectiveness of paragraph 14. You could consider some of the features discussed in question 1 as well as those discussed in Chapter 6, p. 73, such as the use of repetition, parallel structures, and transitions.

4. Comment on the use of direct quotations in the essay. In your answer, refer to at least two direct quotations and analyze their function within the selected passages.

5. Using critical thinking and your knowledge concerning the differences between quantitative and qualitative sources (see Chapter 3), explain Shade's statement in paragraph 18 that more quantitative research is needed today.

6. Is Shade's essay about only gender inclusiveness? What groups lack an internet presence? Do you think her references to these other underrepresented groups help or hinder her credibility?

7. Analyze Shade's introduction (paragraph 1) and conclusion (paragraphs 18–19). In addition to analyzing the effectiveness of her argument there, explain whether you think they are too brief in an essay of this length, supporting your explanation by critical thinking and your knowledge of argument.

Post-reading

1. *Collaborative activity:* Design an information campaign that draws attention to the need and suggests practical means for increasing online gender equity in Canada or another specific place, such as your campus. Along with outlining the problem and proposing solutions, decide on a specific audience for the campaign (for example, a branch of government/administration, a citizens' action group, or other feasible target). Refer to Shade's essay at least twice in your presentation/report.

Social Justice and Social Determinants of Health: Lesbian, Gay, Bisexual, Transgendered, Intersexed, and Queer Youth in Canada

Deborah Dysart-Gale

(3,299 words)

Pre-reading

1. Access a support or informational website for LGBTIQ youth, such as the Lesbian Gay Bi Trans Youth Line (http://www.youthline.ca), mentioned in paragraph 18 of this essay, using the "About Us" or similar link. Write a summary of the site's aims and objectives.
2. After scanning the essay, including its headings, and reading the first section, "Nursing, Social Justice, and LGBTIQ," (a) identify the essay's purpose and intended audience; (b) construct a reading hypothesis of three or four sentences in which you include purpose, audience, and other factors relevant to your approach to the essay (see the Reading Hypothesis box in Chapter 5, p. 49).

Topic: While nurses address lesbian, gay, bisexual, transgendered, intersexed, and queer (henceforth LGBTIQ) patients' health needs, the professional nursing practice value of social justice provides a larger role for nurses in identifying and minimizing social barriers faced by LGBTIQ patients.

Purpose: This paper examines the social and health-related experiences of LGBTIQ youth in Canada, a country which has removed many of the social and legal barriers faced by LGBTIQ in countries such as the United States. An awareness of the Canadian LGBTIQ experience is instructive for nurses in different countries, as it reveals both the possibilities and limitations of social legislation that is more inclusive of LGBTIQ youth.

Sources: Review of literature in PubMed, Academic Search Premier, government documents.

Conclusion: The literature reveals that exclusion, isolation, and fear remain realities for Canadian LGBTIQ adolescents. The Canadian experience suggests that negative social attitudes toward LGBTIQ persist despite progressive legislation. The value of social justice positions nurses to constructively intervene in promoting the health and well-being of LGBTIQ youth in the face of social homophobia.

Nursing, Social Justice, and LGBTIQ Youth

1   Epidemiological evidence has established that lesbian, gay, bisexual, transsexual, intersexed, and questioning queer (henceforth LGBTIQ) youth face greater risks to their health and well-being than do their heterosexual age-mates. Although nurses therefore interact with LGBTIQ youth as patients, the values of professional nursing practice warrant a larger role for nurses beyond the treatment of these patients' medical issues. As articulated by the World Health Organization (WHO) and the American Association of Colleges of Nursing (AACN), the value of social justice obligates nurses to identify and minimize social barriers to health, faced by all vulnerable groups, including young people, especially vulnerable groups such as LGBTIQ youth. Canada, having eliminated many legal barriers faced by the LGBTIQ community in the United States, may serve as a model for a more just society concerning LGBTIQ youth (Elliott & Bonauto, 2005). However, feelings of exclusion, isolation, and fear persist for Canadian LGBTIQ youth despite such legal progress (Commission des Droits de la Personne et des Droits de la Jeunesse du Québec [Commission of the Rights of the Person and Rights of Youth of Quebec], 2007), as legislative acceptance of the civil and human rights of

Source: From *Journal of Child and Adolescent Psychiatric Nursing*, vol. 23, no. 1, Feb. 2010, pp. 23–8. © 2010 Wiley Periodicals, Inc.

sexual minorities has outpaced widespread social accept-ance of those rights. In the face of this situation, nurses must work to realize the value of social justice on a political, institutional, and personal level.

2   We will begin by discussing the social determinants of LGBTIQ adolescent health before discussing the social and political situation for LGBTIQ adolescents in Canada, and their ramifications for nursing practice. Throughout the discussion, these issues will be examined in the light of the nursing value of "social justice," understood as the pro-fessional obligation to fight disparities in health care that result from social bias or inequity.

Social Determinants of Health and LGBTIQ Youths

3   Biomedical models view disease as the result of factors such as infection, degeneration, or trauma. This perspective is complemented by another model, one that examines the social factors essential to the preservation and optimiza-tion of health, prevention of disease, and guarantee of max-imum quality of life. In the United States, such inequalities are typically regarded in terms of unequal access to medical prophylaxis and treatment. This tends to focus attention on the poor, ethnic and language minorities, native groups, and rural residents, leaving socially entrenched, "legitim-ated" inequities (such as those against sexual minorities) unchallenged (Muntaner, 1999). However, Lyman (2005) suggests that researchers in the UK and Canada approach the problem of unequal health status from a more product-ive perspective by looking at social rather than medical fac-tors in describing health disparities.

4   As defined by the WHO, the social factors that de-termine health are "peace, shelter, education, food, income, stable ecosystem, sustainable resources, social justice, and equity" (Raphael, 2006). While LBGTIQ youth are not the focus of the WHO's work, they nevertheless clearly confront serious challenges to these social determinants of health, with deleterious health consequences.

5   Peace and shelter needs of LGBTIQ children are frequently jeopardized, as they may be forced from their homes by verbal or physical abuse when their sexual-ity is acknowledged (Rew, Whittaker, Taylor-Seehafer, & Smith, 2005); studies suggest that over 60% of violence against LGBTIQ youth is inflicted by family members (Illingworth & Murphy, 2004). Even children who remain

at home are faced with bullying and marginalization in their schools and communities, risking the development of post-traumatic stress (DuRant, Krowchuk, & Sinal, 1998), disrupted access to education, and undermined social eco-systems. Economic security is jeopardized: LGBTIQ youth are overrepresented among homeless children (Whitbeck, Chen, Hoyt, Tyler, & Johnson, 2004) and frequently turn to prostitution for survival, putting themselves at risk for further violence and abuse, as well as sexually transmit-ted infections. Knowledge about prevention of infection is frequently inadequate. For example, Sullivan (1996) deter-mined that gay street youth aged 13–17 in his sample were poorly informed about human immunodeficiency virus (HIV), with 13% unable to provide any correct information at all about HIV and its transmission or prevention. Mental health care is also threatened: one result of this situation is that LGBTIQ youth are at a much higher risk for suicide and mental health disorders than their heterosexual age-mates (McAndrew & Warne, 2004; Garofalo, Wolf, Wissow, Woods, & Goodman, 1999).

6   Despite their increased healthcare needs, LGBTIQ adolescents are an underserved group. The extent to which misunderstanding, bias, and even homophobia among clin-icians contribute to a choice to avoid clinical treatment is unclear. There are instances of gross homophobia and neg-lect of professional duty to provide care, as in the case of the transgendered woman Tyra Hunter, whom a Washington DC court found had died of injuries after being abused by paramedics at the scene of a car crash and receiving ER care that did not "follow nationally accepted standards of care" (Fernandez, 1998). Similarly, attention to the issue of sex assignment was aroused by the case of David Reimer, whose questionable treatment by psychologists following a botched circumcision contributed to both his suicide death and that of his twin brother ("David Reimer," 2004).

7   Examples of less egregious but more endemic homo-phobia in health care were provided by several studies of nurses in the early 1990s that suggested homophobia was a factor in nurses' reluctance to care of HIV/acquired immune deficiency syndrome (AIDS) patients (Smirnoff, Erlen, & Lidz, 1991). In another older study, 33% of first-year medical students disagreed with the statement "that there is a broad range of normal sexual behavior and that homosexuality falls within this range" (McDaniel & Carlson, 1995, table 2). These studies contrast with a more recent one that suggests that the majority of nurses have positive or neutral attitudes

toward sexual minority patients (Roendahl, Innala, & Carlsson, 2004) and that student nurses expressing reluctance to work with AIDS patients showed no homophobic bias (Stewart, 1999).

8   Nurses' attitudes may be especially critical in determining LGBTIQ adolescents' satisfaction with their health care. Nurses are frequently gatekeepers of the clinical encounter, administering the typically heteronormative nursing assessment ("Are you married, widowed, single, or divorced?"). Such inappropriate assessment instruments set the tone for the clinical encounter, and errors can be compounded when nurses utilize a heterosexual definition of family in regulating hospital visits, planning discharge, etc. Incorrect assumptions and unwillingness to make necessary adjustments to institutional procedures impede communication and reinforce heteronormativity (Roendahl, Innala, & Carlsson, 2006).

9   Within the clinic, heterosexuality appears to be the expected "default" norm. Neville and Hendrickson (2006) found that over 75% of the lesbians and gays in their survey reported that heath practitioners usually or always assumed their heterosexuality; more positively, the same proportion of those surveyed also reported that their practitioners seem completely comfortable with their subsequent disclosure. Among young LGB informants, 33% found that their practitioners' attitudes toward their disclosure positively influenced their care; 62% discerned no influence on their care.

Social Justice: A Nursing Value

10   Healthcare institutions reflect the culture in which they are situated (Foucault, 1994), and it must be anticipated that LGBTIQ youth will experience some degree of socially endemic homophobia in their clinical encounters. Nevertheless, research firmly suggests that the basis for a trusting, cooperative clinical relationship between nurses and LGBTIQ youth exists: gay and lesbian youth have been shown to be trustworthy and accurate when providing accounts of their sexual activity in their medical histories (Schrimshaw, Rosario, Meyer-Bahlburg, & Scharf-Matlick, 2006). Lesbian, gay, and bisexual patients value such trust, identifying practitioners' attitude toward their sexuality as the most important factor in choosing a healthcare provider (Neville & Hendrickson, 2006).

11   As with all therapeutic relationships, healthcare practitioners develop trust by viewing LGBTIQ youth as individuals, not solely as patients with health or social deficits. Mature nursing practice demands that therapeutic interactions with any client be based on more than the mere treatment or prevention of disease. Nurses work toward individual and community health on all levels. This mandate, articulated as *social justice*, guides nurses in eliminating disparities in health and in assuring equitable access to healthcare services (WHO, 2007). Homophobia represents a major cause of social injustice, and nurses are therefore professionally mandated to be vigilant in eradicating it from all phases of the healthcare encounter.

12   One goal is to ensure that vulnerable clients such as LGBTIQ youth receive adequate, culturally competent care. Social justice requires nurses to move beyond the clinical context and look at society as a whole to offset the social factors undermining the health and well-being of all LGBTIQ youth. As expressed in a policy statement by the AACN, "the value of social justice is particularly significant because it directly addresses disparities in health and health care… and serves as a prelude to influencing policy formulation at the systems level" (AACN, 2007, p. 9). While cultural competency and awareness of the social causes of health disparities must be promoted within the nursing curriculum, the AACN calls for a more comprehensive understanding of social justice, mandating nurses to work for social justice beyond the clinical setting, advocating for just policies within institutions, systems, and ultimately the nation.

13   There is much homosexual bias to be found in local and federal policies that affects LGBTIQ youth in the United States. In an obvious example, sex education programs funded by the U.S. government are obliged to teach abstinence until marriage in lieu of comprehensive, evidence-based programs that mention safer and alternative sex practices (Hopkins Tanne, 2005). While the questionable effectiveness of abstinence-only curricula jeopardizes all young people, such curricula pose particular dangers for LGBTIQ students, who are implicitly taught that heterosexuality is the only sanctioned sexual behavior and that their attraction to same-sex peers is illegitimate. This is particularly ironic, given the fact that these programs were implemented as a means of reducing the transmission of HIV/AIDS, which despite shifting epidemiological patterns, remains associated with homosexual activity. Locally, even religious discourse that makes a careful distinction between "the sinner and the sin" in an attempt to curb homophobic violence serves inexorably to reinforce the status of LGBTIQ youths' lifestyles as sinful and unacceptable (Illingworth & Murphy, 2004).

LGBTIQ Youth in Canada

14   As U.S. nurses look for ways to correct social injustice for the LGBTIQ youth in their communities, their attention may well turn north to Canada, where many of the restrictive laws that marginalize sexual minorities and limit young peoples' options have been repealed (Elliott & Bonauto, 2005). The legalization of same-sex marriage in 2005 has brought with it equality in the workplace, parenting, and family life. The move to legalization can be characterized as the natural result of the evolution of beliefs in Canadian society. Already by the 1980s, over 60% of Canadians viewed gay and lesbian equality in the workforce and private life as consistent with Canadian values of human rights. In the mid-1990s, Canadian courts recognized same-sex partners' rights to spousal and bereavement benefits (Matthews, 2005). Following the legalization of same-sex marriage in 2005, the 2006 Canadian census enumerated 45,300 same-sex couples, 53.6% of which are men (Milan, Vézina, & Wells, 2007).

15   More specifically addressing the concerns of LGBTIQ youth, Canadian public policies seek to identify and minimize the potential danger gay children may face from psychological abuse in schools, society, and even in homes where their orientation is not accepted (Saewyc, 2007). In the 1990s, provincial and local Boards of Education began implementing anti-homophobia interventions in schools, such as the Toronto Board of Education's resource guide, "Sexual Orientation: Focus on Homosexuality, Lesbianism and Homophobia" ("New Lessons,", 1997). Since 1995, Toronto has operated the Triangle Program, a high school program for LGBTIQ students suffering from homophobia in traditional classrooms (Triangle Program, 2007). Other provincial and local school districts have followed suit with programs of their own (Émond & Bastien Charlebois, 2007).

16   However, social acceptance has not kept pace with the law. Everyday life for Canadian LGBTIQ youth is still marked by slights, insults, or even physical attacks (Lemoire & Chen, 2005). Although the changes in Canadian law measurably influenced Canadians' acceptance of homosexuality (Matthews, 2005), attitudes have been slow to change among conservative social groups ("New Lessons," 1997). Van de Ven (1994) suggests that while individuals within the dominant culture learn that outright hostility toward homosexuals is unacceptable, such tolerance is not necessarily accompanied by introspection or coming to terms with cognitively unacceptable hostile feelings. "The result may be outward tolerance but underlying hostility, perpetuated in part by anti-discrimination policies . . . that put a premium on acceptable behaviours toward minorities . . . while all but ignoring 'inner' feelings" (p. 118). Homophobia thus remains a form of xenophobia, on par with racism or sexism. A sad lesson learned by Americans from the Civil Rights Era of the 1960s is that although people of color and women may be equal to white men before the law, the irrefutable truth is that women still earn between 75% and 95% of their male counterparts' salary in similar professions (Dey & Hill, 2007). Likewise, Canadian law is an imperfect mirror of civil society.

Promoting Social Justice for LGBTIQ Youth

17   As the literature suggests, ties of blood, long-standing friendship, and civic tolerance cannot guarantee LGBTIQ youth the social acceptance that inclusive legislation was intended to produce. Thus, it appears that nurses must work to realize the value of social justice on political and personal levels.

18   The Canadian Public Health Agency asserts that healthcare practitioners and institutions can act to influence the social determinants of health as knowledge brokers, leaders, communicators, and influencers (Public Health Agency of Canada, 2004). The first step toward becoming a knowledge broker is to assess one's own attitudes, beliefs, and level of knowledge. Nurses can begin by informing themselves about the experiences of young LGBTIQ patients. For example, browsing sites such as Amazon.com provides an overview of literature addressed both to LGBTIQ youth and those who care for them. Schrader and Wells' (2005) excellent and comprehensive annotated bibliography of English-language resources has been prepared for Canadian educators and is available from various web links. Likewise, Web sites geared to LGBTIQ youth also provide nurses with information about their experiences and concerns (e.g., Lesbian Gay Bi Trans Youthline at http://www.youthline.ca, or Youth Resource at http://www.youthresource.com). A Google search of the key words "gay and lesbian films" identifies filmographies that portray various aspects of LGBTIQ experience (e.g., *Longtime Companion*, *My Beautiful Launderette*, *Sex: Unknown*). The resulting familiarity with LGBTIQ issues as portrayed in the media will enable nurses to better open dialog with LGBTIQ adolescents, as well as serve as resources and knowledge brokers within their clinics and communities.

19   As influencers, nurses can model clinically and culturally sensitive care within the healthcare setting. Besides influencing colleagues' behavior, nurses can also influence LGBTIQ youth directly by "assisting homosexual adolescents to affirm their identity in the face of social devaluation. . . [through] knowledge and resources to provide a corrective alternative view and the social experiences to sustain that view" (Sullivan 1994, para. 12). Illingworth and Murphy (2004) note that LGBTIQ youth frequently lack positive role models, which, combined with continual attacks on self-image and self-esteem, may lead to developmental and emotional problems. Instrumental in developing autonomy, they suggest, is the ability to form bonds of trust. While trust within the intimate family circle is essential, *thin trust*, or that formed within the general community, is no less vital. Thin trust is understood as the provisional trust that one accords to strangers, assuming that they will act in unthreatening, civil, and predictable fashion. Nurses can provide this much-needed thin trust in the clinical encounter by providing reassurance, positive regard, and knowledgeable information.

20   As communicators, nurses act directly with LGBTIQ youth in therapeutic interaction. Working with LGBTIQ youth in Toronto, Lemoire and Chen (2005) have used Carl Roger's person-centered therapy as a starting point in working with LGBT adolescents. The Rogerian tenets unconditional positive regard, congruence, and empathy are directly relevant to nursing communication. Through unconditional positive regard, nurses encourage clients to disclose information without fear that disclosures will alter their positive judgment of the client as an individual. The principle of congruence guides nurses to be consistent in their thoughts and actions, acting in a nonjudgmental, authentic manner. Through the principle of empathy, a nurse's interactions with the LGBTIQ adolescent client is motivated by honest interest in the individual and his or her experience, not by the desire to place the client within the neat parameters of a specific diagnosis. Lemoire and Chen build upon Roger's person-centered therapy, introducing specific therapeutic concerns for nurses working with LGBTIQ youth. These clients must be reassured that their sexual identity, although shared by a minority of the population, is nevertheless normal, natural, and healthy. Once the sexual identity of LGBTIQ youth has been normalized and validated, nurses must also use their position of trust to help them assess the risks of disclosing their sexual identity and explore communication strategies for such disclosure.

21   Finally, as leaders, nurses can advocate for the health and social needs of their LGBTIQ youth in clinical, institutional, and community settings. Within the clinical context, nurses can provide leadership in such projects as the development of inclusive, accurate nursing assessments; "Do you live with a partner?" elicits the same information about social support as "Are you married?" In contrast, the knowledge that families frequently are a source of intentional and unintentional psychological abuse for young LGBTIQ demands further assessment of the nature of family relationships for this population. Furthermore, within the healthcare institution as a whole, spousal benefits programs and inclusive community health outreach programs send strong messages to LGBTIQ that they are valued members of the community. Finally, on a community level, nurses can actively advocate for programs that develop LGBTIQ youths' self-esteem and autonomy. For example, McAndrew and Warne assert that while homosexual adults develop positive mechanisms for coping with homophobia, adolescent homosexuals may only have limited interaction with socially successful homosexual adults and thus not benefit from such positive role models (2004, p. 430). Illingworth and Murphy (2004) note that LGBTIQ youth find their strongest social network among their peers, an option mostly only for those living in large urban areas. Nurses can serve as bridges in initiating this generational and intergenerational dialog.

Conclusion

22   Homophobia and prejudice exert a negative impact upon the health and well-being of all LGBTIQ individuals; young people whose sense of personal and sexual identity is still in development are particularly vulnerable. The legal right to marry, and legally guaranteed access to education, career choice, and the achievement of other personal milestones are essential in developing LGBTIQ youths' sense of self-esteem and faith in their future. These are outcomes of particular interest to the discipline of psychiatric nursing. The nursing value of social justice mobilizes members of the profession to work for political changes that will remove existing barriers for LGBTIQ youth. Furthermore, social justice can inform the nursing research agenda, guiding qualitative and quantitative research to describe the subjective experience of LGBTIQ youth, develop, and assess the effectiveness of communication techniques, life-skills curricula, and other interventions to improve the lives of individuals in this vulnerable population.

23   However, as the experience of Canadian LGBTIQ youth reveals, legislation alone will not rid a society of homophobia. Nurses are socially and professionally positioned to work against homophobia in the clinic and the community. In the clinic, they combat homophobia by informing themselves about the psychosocial needs of LGBTIQ clients as part of their ongoing professional development. They maintain open and positive communication, and advocate for institutional policies that are fair and inclusive. Nurses further utilize their ethos to combat homophobia in the community. They can correct misinformation, prejudice, and homophobic speech by sharing research and evidence from their nursing practice. Perhaps most importantly, nurses can be nonjudgmental, tolerant, and supportive of LGBTIQ in both the clinic and the community. Thus, in working for social justice, nurses can build bridges of trust to patients and extend those bridges into the community at large.

References

American Association of Colleges of Nursing. (2007). White paper on the education and role of the clinical nurse leader. (July update). Retrieved December 2, 2009, from http://www.aacn.nche.edu/Publications/WhitePapers/ClinicalNurseLeader.htm

Commission des Droits de la Personne et des Droits de la Jeunesse du Québec [Commission of the Rights of the Person and Rights of Youth of Quebec]. (2007). De l'égalité juridique à l'égalité social: Vers une stratégie nationale de lutte contre l'homophobie [Judicial equality and social equality: Toward a national strategy for the fight against homophobia]. Quebec: The Government of Quebec.

David Reimer, 38, Subject of the John/Joan case. (2004, May 12). The New York Times. Retrieved December 2, 2009, from http://query.nytimes.com/gst/fullpage.html?res=9A07E4DA103CF931A25756C0A9629C8B63

Dey, J. D., & Hill, C. (2007). Behind the pay gap. American Association of College Women Educational Foundation. Retrieved December 2, 2009, from http://www.aauw.org/research/behindPayGap.cfm

DuRant, R., Krowchuk, D., & Sinal, S. (1998). Victimization, use of violence and drug use at school among male adolescents who engage in same-sex behaviour. Journal of Pediatrics, 133, 113–118.

Elliott, R. D., & Bonauto, M. (2005). Sexual orientation and gender identity in North America: Legal contrasts. Journal of Homosexuality, 48(3/4), 91–106.

Émond, G., & Bastien Charlebois, J. (2007). L'homophobie pas dans ma cour! Rapport de recherché non publié, Montréal: GRIS-Montréal.

Fernandez, M. (1998, Dec 12). Death suit costs city $2.9 million. The Washington Post. Retrieved December 2, 2009, from http://pqasb.pqarchiver.com/washingtonpost/search.html?nid=roll_archives

Foucault, M. (1994). The birth of the clinic: An archaeology of medical perception. New York: Vintage.

Garofalo, R., Wolf, C., Wissow, L., Woods, E., & Goodman, E. (1999). Sexual orientation and risk of suicide attempt among a representative sample of youth. Archive of Pediatric Adolescent Medicine, 153, 487–493.

Hopkins Tanne, J. (2005). US state rejects federal funding for abstinence only sex education. British Medical Journal, 331(7519), 715.

Illingworth, P., & Murphy, T. (2004). In our best interest: Meeting moral duties to lesbian, gay and bisexual adolescent students. Journal of Social Psychology, 35(2), 198–210.

Lemoire, S. J., & Chen, C. P. (2005). Applying person-centered counseling to sexual minority adolescents. Journal of Counseling & Development, 83, 146–154.

Lyman, M. J. (2005). Health as a socially mediated process: Theoretical and practical imperatives emerging from research on health inequalities. Advances in Nursing Science, 28(1), 25–37.

Matthews, J. S. (2005). The policial foundations of support for same-sex marriage in Canada. Canadian Journal of Political Science/Revue Canadienne de Science Politique, 38(4), 841–866.

McAndrew, S., & Warne, T. (2004). Ignoring the evidence dictating the practice: Sexual orientation, suicidality and the dichotomy of the mental health nurse. Journal of Psychiatric and Mental Health Nursing, 11, 428–434.

McDaniel, J. S., & Carlson, L. M. (1995). A survey of knowledge and attitudes about HIV and AIDS among medical students. Journal of American College Health, 44(1). Retrieved December 2, 2009, from http://0-web.ebscohost.com

Milan, A., Vézina, M., & Wells, C. (2007). 2006 Census: Family portrait: Continuity and change in Canadian families and house-holds in 2006: Findings. Statistics Canada 2006 Census: Analysis Series. Retrieved December 2, 2009, from http://www12.statcan.ca/english/census06/analysis/famhouse/index.cfm

Muntaner, C. (1999). Teaching social inequalities in health: Barriers and opportunities. Scandinavian Journal of Public Health, 27, 161–165.

Neville, S., & Hendrickson, M. (2006). Perceptions of lesbian, gay and bisexual people of primary healthcare services. *Journal of Advanced Nursing, 55*(4), 407–415.

New Lessons in Homophobia. (1997). *Maclean's, 118*(13). Retrieved December 2, 2009, from http://0-web.ebscohost.com

Public Health Agency of Canada. (2004). The social determinants of health: An overview of the implications for policy and the role of the health sector. Retrieved December 2, 2009, from http://www.phac-aspc.gc.ca/ph-sp/oi-ar/01_overview-eng.php

Raphael, D. (2006). The social determinants of health: What are the three key roles for health promotion? *Health Promotion Journal of Australia, 17*(3): 167–170.

Rew, L., Whittaker, T., Taylor-Seehafer, M., & Smith, L. (2005). Sexual health risks and protective resources in gay, lesbian, bisexual and heterosexual homeless youth. *Journal for Specialists in Pediatric Nursing, 10*(1), 31–39.

Roendahl, G., Innala, S., & Carlsson, M. (2004). Nurses' attitudes towards lesbians and gay men. *Journal of Advanced Nursing, 47*(4), 386–392.

Roendahl, G., Innala, S., & Carlsson, M. (2006). Heterosexual assumption in verbal and non-verbal communication in nursing. *Journal of Advanced Nursing, 56*(4), 373–381.

Saewyc, E. (2007). Substance use among non-mainstream youth. In *Substance abuse in Canada: Focus on youth* (pp. 14–21). Ottawa: Canadian Centre on Substance Abuse. Retrieved December 3, 2009, from http://www.ccsa.ca/Eng/KnowledgeCentre/OurPublications/Pages/SubstanceAbuseinCanada.aspx

Schrader, A., & Wells, K. (2005). Queer perspectives on social responsibility in Canadian schools and libraries: Analysis and resources. *School Libraries in Canada, 24*(4). Retrieved December 2, 2009, from http://www.teachers.ab.ca/SiteCollectionDocuments/ATA/Issues%20In%20Education/Diversity%20Equity%20and%20Human%20Rights/Sexual%20Orientation/Queer%20Perspectives%20on%20Social%20Responsibility.pdf

Schrimshaw, E., Rosario, M., Meyer-Bahlburg, H., & Scharf-Matlick, A. (2006). Test-retest reliability of self-reported sexual behavior, sexual orientation, and psychosexual milestones among gay, lesbian, and bisexual youths. *Archives of Sexual Behavior, 35*(2), 225–234.

Smirnoff, L., Erlen, J., & Lidz, C. (1991). Stigma, AIDS and quality of nursing care: State of the science. *Journal of Advanced Nursing, 16*(3), 262–269.

Stewart, D. (1999). The attitudes and attributions of student nurses: Do they alter according to a person's diagnosis or sexuality and what is the effect on nurse training? *Journal of Advanced Nursing, 30*(3), 740–748.

Sullivan, T. R. (1994). Obstacles to effective child welfare service with gay and lesbian youths. *Child Welfare, 73*(4). Retrieved December 2, 2009, from http://0-web.ebscohost.com

Sullivan, T. R. (1996). The challenge of HIV prevention among high-risk adolescents. *Health and Social Work, 21*(1). Retrieved December 2, 2009, from http://0-web.ebscohost.com

Triangle Program (2007). Website. Retrieved November 22, 2007, from http://schools.tdsb.on.ca/triangle/index.html

Van de Ven, P. (1994). Comparisons among homophobic reactions of undergraduates, high school students, and young offenders. *Journal of Sex Research, 31*(2), 117–124.

Whitbeck, L., Chen, X., Hoyt, D., Tyler, K., & Johnson, K. (2004). Mental disorder, subsistence strategies, and victimization among gay, lesbian, and bisexual homeless and runaway children. *Journal of Sex Research, 41*(4), 329–342.

World Health Organization. (2007). The Ottawa charter for health promotion. Retrieved December 2, 2009, from http://www.who.int/healthpromotion/conferences/previous/ottawa/en

Key and challenging words

prophylaxis, egregious, endemic, equitable, eradicate, inexorable, introspection, xenophobia, congruence, autonomy, mobilize

Questions

1. In paragraph 1, identify the justification for the study and the thesis statement; what kind of thesis statement do the authors use (e.g., hypothesis, simple thesis, essay plan), and why might it be suitable for this essay?

2. (a) Explain the differences between the two "models" mentioned in paragraph 2; (b) Which do the authors believe is the more useful one, and why?

3. Discuss the use of the following kinds of sources in the section of the essay in which they occur: (a) experts and authorities in paragraph 1, (b) facts and statistics in paragraph 5, (c) examples in paragraphs 6 and 7, (d) academic studies in paragraph 16.

4. Explain the use of the compare-contrast rhetorical pattern in paragraphs 7–9.

5. (a) What is the purpose of the section "Social Justice: A Nursing Value" within the essay as a whole? (b) How does the author use writing style in this section to stress nurses' obligations in promoting social justice towards LGBTIQ youth (e.g., you could consider diction, such as verb choice and other linguistic techniques, sentence/paragraph structure, repetition, and the like).

6. (a) What specific audience does Dysart-Gale address in the section "Promoting Social Justice for LGBTIQ Youth"? (b) What rhetorical strategies does she use to address the reader? (You could consider some of the same strategies mentioned in question 5, along with tone, emphasis, and other relevant features.)

7. Show how Dysart-Gale uses appeals to logic, emotion, and/or ethics in paragraph 23 and one other paragraph of your choice. (Note: refer to at least two of these appeals in each paragraph.)

Post-reading

1. *Collaborative or individual activity:* Explore the role that student peers (whether LGBTIQ or not) can play in ensuring a healthy and safe environment for LGBTIQ youth at post-secondary Canadian campuses. Come up with specific strategies that would help promote such an environment.

Learning Disabilities in Canada

Kim Calder Stegemann

(3,581 words)

Pre-reading

1. The article below was published in the journal *Learning Disabilities: A Contemporary Journal.* From the journal's home page (http://www.ldw-ldcj.org), access the page that describes the journal's "Aims and Scope": (a) In one or two sentences, summarize the type of article typically published in the journal; (b) Why are authors required to explain how the term *learning disability* (LD) is used in their essay? (c) After scanning "Learning Disabilities in Canada," identify the type of article of the four types mentioned under the online "Aims and Scope" that best describes this essay (see also Chapter 3, pages 23–24).

2. Using your own words, come up with a one- to two-sentence definition of "learning disability" that reflects your understanding of the term through your knowledge, observation, experiences, etc.

Abstract

The status of learning disabilities within Canadian public schools and the wider population is both optimistic and, at the same time, worthy of great concern. Each individual province and territory in Canada is responsible for its own public education systems, leading to inconsistencies in definition, identification practices, funding for support, and intervention/support services. The changes to the DSM-5 diagnostic criteria have led to even more confusion and concern, particularly among Canadian educational leaders in the field of learning disabilities. The consequences of not addressing learning disabilities can be devastating. Despite these challenges, some innovative practices are being launched in identification (neurobiological) and intervention (universal design for learning and response to intervention frameworks) that hold great promise for children and youth with learning disabilities in Canada.

Introduction

1   The term "learning disability" (LD) within the Canadian context is fraught with discrepancies. Canada is geographically varied, and so too are the provincial and territorial educational jurisdictions. With 10 different provincial and 3 territorial educational jurisdictions, it is difficult to achieve a consistent use of definition for learning disability. Further, variations in funding lead to different approaches to program and service delivery. Prevalence rates vary, typically less than 5%. The movement toward inclusive educational practices has resulted in more children with LD being educated in the general education classroom, with changes in funding schemes. The consequence of not addressing LD in children, youth, and adults are negative and profound. Therefore, there are multiple challenges for family, parents, and the children and youth themselves in Canada, who have learning disabilities.

History and Current Use of the Term "Learning Disabilities"

History of Learning Disabilities in Canada

2   The concept of learning disabilities formally came to the awareness of Canadians in the late 1950s when psychiatrist Edward Levinson was "puzzled by children who appear to have only mild behavioral difficulties, seem to have average intelligence, but had significant problems with school functioning" (Wiener & Siegel, 1992, 341). With Levinson's efforts, the Montréal Children's Hospital Learning Centre was created in 1960 to explore the concept of learning disabilities and to develop effective interventions. In 1962, the first association in support of children with learning disabilities was founded by a group of concerned parents (originally the Association for Children With Learning Disabilities, now called the Learning Disabilities Association of Canada – LDAC). This subsequently led to the creation of chapters in 10 Canadian provinces by 1977. The development of the national learning disabilities associations played a significant role in furthering awareness and services for individuals with learning disabilities (Wong & Hutchinson, 2001).

Provincial and Territorial Jurisdictions

3   Since the confederation of Canada in 1867, education has largely been the responsibility of each province or territory rather than the federal government (unlike the United States, which has federal legislation regarding the education of individuals with learning disabilities). While this allows each jurisdiction to create policies that reflect the unique multicultural, linguistic, and socioeconomic conditions of its area (Wiener & Siegel, 1992), it has led to a less consolidated vision of the meaning of learning disabilities (Klassen, 2002). The Learning Disabilities Association of Canada (LDAC), however, proposed a definition in 1981 (later revised in 2002 and re-endorsed in March, 2015) (Fiedorowica, Craig, Phillips, Price, & Bullivant, 2015) (see Figure 1) that mirrors that of the National Joint Committee on Learning Disabilities in the United States. Key features include an impact on verbal and nonverbal processes; average intellectual ability; impairment which effects language, phonological, visual spatial processes, processing speed, memory and attention, and executive functions; manifestations in oral and written language, reading, mathematics, and social skills; lifelong impact; genetic or neurobiological etiology; disorder not due primarily to hearing or vision problems, socio-economic factors, cultural linguistic differences, lack of motivation, or ineffective teaching.

4   Kozey and Siegel's 2008 review of definitions of learning disabilities across Canada found that none of the provincial or territorial Ministry of Education documents indicated complete adherence to the key features of the definition. The situation in 2015 is quite different, however.

Source: From *Learning Disabilities: A Contemporary Journal*, vol. 14, no. 1, 2016, pp. 53–62.

Figure 1   Official definition of learning disabilities. (Adopted by the Learning Disabilities Association of Canada January 30, 2002, and Re-Endorsed on March 2, 2015.)

Learning Disabilities refer to a number of disorders which may affect the acquisition, organization, retention, understanding or use of verbal or nonverbal information. These disorders affect learning in individuals who otherwise demonstrate at least average abilities essential for thinking and/or reasoning. As such, learning disabilities are distinct from global intellectual deficiency.

Learning disabilities result from impairments in one or more processes related to perceiving, thinking, remembering or learning. These include, but are not limited to: language processing; phonological processing; visual spatial processing; processing speed; memory and attention; and executive functions (e.g. planning and decision making).

Learning disabilities range in severity and may interfere with the acquisition and use of one or more of the following:

- oral language (e.g. listening, speaking, understanding);
- reading (e.g. decoding, phonetic knowledge, word recognition, comprehension);
- written language (e.g. spelling and written expression); and
- mathematics (e.g. computation, problem solving).

Learning disabilities may also involve difficulties with organizational skills, social perception, social interaction and perspective taking.

Learning disabilities are lifelong. The way in which they are expressed may vary over an individual's lifetime, depending on the interaction between the demands of the environment and the individual's strengths and needs. Learning disabilities are suggested by unexpected academic under-achievement or achievement which is maintained only by unusually high levels of effort and support.

Learning disabilities are due to genetic and/or neurobiological factors or injury that alters brain functioning in a manner which affects one or more processes related to learning. These disorders are not due primarily to hearing and/or vision problems, socio-economic factors, cultural or linguistic differences, lack of motivation or ineffective teaching, although these factors may further complicate the challenges faced by individuals with learning disabilities.

Learning disabilities may co-exist with various conditions including attentional, behavioural and emotional disorders, sensory impairments or other medical conditions.

For success, individuals with learning disabilities require early identification and timely specialized assessments and interventions involving home, school, community and workplace settings. **The interventions need to be appropriate for each individual's learning disability subtype and, at a minimum, include the provision of:**

- specific skill instruction;
- accommodations;
- compensatory strategies; and
- self-advocacy skills.

LDAC, 2015

As jurisdictions move away from categorical funding models in favour of a needs-based approach, some do not mention learning disabilities at all in their key ministerial documents, which is the case for the Yukon, Northwest Territories, Nunavut, Saskatchewan, Manitoba, and Québec (almost half of all jurisdictions in Canada). The movement away from "categories" and diagnosis may impact the types of programs and services that are provided for children with specific learning disabilities.

Diagnostic Criteria for LD

5   In the past, two criteria have been used to guide the diagnosis of a learning disability in the public school system in Canada. First, the child or youth must have average or above-average intelligence, as determined by an intelligence test. Second, a significant discrepancy must exist between intellectual ability and academic achievement. The use of standardized tests to measure the discrepancy between

intelligence and academic achievement has been criticized, in particular for identification of a reading disability (Siegel, 1988; Stanovich, 1991, 2005). Authors like Siegel and Stanovich contend that all students who show disabilities in learning (i.e., word recognition, reading comprehension, reading fluency, math, computation or problem solving, or written expression) should be identified as having a learning disability (Hutchinson, 2014).

6   However, a discrepancy between ability and achievement is only one of several factors used by many school districts across Canada to determine a diagnosis of LD (Greg Pearce, personal communication, June 14, 2015). School psychologists also consider a number of areas to reveal the nature of the cognitive processing deficit or weakness (memory, attention, executive function, processing speed) and to ensure that school attendance and other conditions are not the primary reason for a student's difficulties (British Columbia Association of School Psychologists, 2007). These school district practices may shift in the future, given the change in definition of learning disabilities in the *Diagnostic and Statistical Manual of Mental Disorders – 5th Edition* (DSM-5; American Psychiatric Association, 2013).

7   The DSM-5 stipulates normal intellectual functioning to be an IQ score of 70 (+/- 5) (American Psychiatric Association, 2013). The LDAC does not agree with the DSM-5 description of normal intellectual functioning, instead recommending that IQ scores be "interpreted cautiously in the context of all of the other information gathered about the individual" (Fiedorowicz et al., 2015). The DSM-5 suggests a discrepancy of at least 1.5 standard deviations below the population mean for age group (American Psychiatric Association, 2013) but notes that a more lenient threshold of 1.0 to 2.5 standard deviations may be appropriate, given supporting evidence. These guidelines are broader than many diagnostic criteria currently used by school psychologists in Canada (Greg Pearce, personal communication, June 14, 2015). Regardless, the school or educational psychologist must rely on his/her own critical and professional judgment to make appropriate diagnoses.

Epidemiology and Current Theories of Etiology

8   The LDAC definition of a learning disability indicates that the etiology is genetic or neurobiologically based. Given recent advancements in brain imaging, it is now possible to identify structural and functional differences in individuals

with learning disabilities. Both the Universities of British Columbia (Dr. Lara Boyd) and Calgary (Drs. Catherine Lebel and James Hale) are currently conducting research to track neurological changes in individuals with LD who receive intensive and specialized academic remediation. Dr. Hale's research team at the University of Calgary is also investigating the use of brain scans (neuropsychological assessment), combined with cognitive assessment, for identifying individuals with specific learning disabilities.

9   It is difficult to accurately report prevalence rates, with estimates ranging as high as 10%. The chief public health officer in Canada (Butler-Jones, 2009) noted that data on the prevalence of LD among children is "not readily available at the national level" (p. 24) for a number of reasons, including lack of diagnosis and parent reluctance to identify because of stigmatization. He suggested that 10% is a low estimate but can apply to the childhood and adult populations, since LD is a lifelong condition. Also complicating the estimates of occurrence is the method of data collection. In many cases, national surveys are used to estimate prevalence, with parents reporting or adults self-reporting, which may or may not be based on a diagnosis by a qualified psychologist. Further, for some of the national surveys, the Yukon, Nunavut, and Northwest Territories were not included, and the administration of surveys is not conducted consistently, on an annual or biannual basis. The results of three national surveys are included below: National Longitudinal Survey of Children and Youth (NLSCY), Participation and Activity Limitation Survey (PALS), and the Canadian Survey on Disability (CSD).

National Longitudinal Survey of Children and Youth (NLSCY)

10   According to the NLSCY, prevalence rates of school-age children (ages 6 to 15) are estimated at 4.9% (Learning Disabilities Association of Canada, 2007). The NLSCY is an ongoing longitudinal survey conducted in Canada every two years (last administered in 2009). Prevalence rates vary slightly across jurisdictions. There is also a significant fluctuation in prevalence rates, depending upon the age of the child. For example, parents reported rates of 1.6% for 6-year-olds and 7.2% for 10-year-olds. This difference makes sense given that most children are not diagnosed during their first year of school. Other related health issues were also reported. For example, among children aged 6 and 7 with learning disabilities, 45.0% had had at least one inner-ear

infection since birth, compared to the nondisabled population with an incidence rate of 24.1%. The incidence of allergies diagnosed by health professional was also higher in the population with learning disabilities (ages 6 to 15), at a rate of 28.1% compared to 17.2% in the nondisabled population. Further, social and emotional well-being was reported to be lower among children and youth with learning disabilities. Within the province of Alberta, 8.6% of children 6 to 15 years of age were reported by parents to have emotional, psychological, or nervous difficulties (as diagnosed by a health professional), vs. 1.0% in the nondisabled population (Learning Disabilities Association of Canada, 2007). It is not uncommon for more boys than girls to be labelled LD (Whitley, Lupart, & Beran, 2007).

Participation and Activity Limitation Survey (PALS)

11   The PALS is designed to collect information on adults and children who have a disability and whose everyday activities are limited because of the condition or health problem. It is no longer administered on a regular basis, with the last administration in 2006. The PALS definition of learning disability includes dyslexia, attention problems, and hyperactivity, which obscures the reliability of the data. National estimates are reported as 3.1% for the 5- to 14-year-old age range (Statistics Canada, 2006).

Canadian Survey on Disability (CSD)

12   The CSD also includes attention deficit-hyperactivity disorder in the category of LD, and surveys youth and adult populations. Prevalence rates of 2.3% are reported for those 15 years and older (Statistics Canada, 2012).

Common Practices in Diagnosis and Assessment

13   With the movement toward full inclusion of children with exceptional learning needs, many children and youth in Canada receive the majority, if not all, of their education in the general education classroom. Typically, general education teachers utilize differentiated instruction (Tomlinson, 1999) or employ principles of universal design for learning (UDL) (CAST, 2015; Rose & Meyer, 2002) in order to meet the diverse needs of all students within the classroom, including students with specific learning disabilities. Only when these approaches fail to produce adequate improvements is a child referred to the learning assistance teacher (also often called the resource teacher or special education teacher) within the school. These professionals are responsible for providing teacher support, suggestions, and intervention/remediation, and may also perform level B assessments to better determine the nature of the learning difficulties. Learning assistance teachers are also partners in developing individual education plans (IEPs).

14   School-based team meetings may be convened to discuss issues and create a working plan, which would include the parent and student (as appropriate). Additional school district specialists such as the school psychologist, occupational therapist, speech-language pathologist, or behaviour consultant may be involved in these meetings. If the school-based team believes that there is a significant learning problem, the school psychologist completes a psychoeducational assessment. In those provinces/territories that continue to use categorical funding systems, school psychologists may recommend a learning disability designation. Funding is often closely tied with the iep that is created for the designated child.

15   15A common model of providing support services is response to intervention (RTI) (Fuchs & Fuchs, 2006; Sugai, 2007, n.d.), sometimes referred to a multitiered system of supports (MTSS). RTI was designed as a general problem-solving framework to address the needs of students who continue to experience barriers to the curriculum despite UDL applications. RTI is also used for diagnostic purposes. McIntosh et al. (2011) reported that Canada has been slower to adopt the RTI framework, particularly for the purposes of identification of LD.

Common Practices of Professionally Attending to the Needs of Individuals with Learning Disabilities

16   As noted above, general education teachers are, first and foremost, responsible for the education of children and youth with LD. Many school jurisdictions use an RTI or MTSS framework to address specific student needs. That is, they begin by making UDL adjustments in the general education classroom. If these do not resolve the barriers to learning, they may engage more intensive and specialized approaches, potentially grouping students for short periods of time within the classroom. Only when these methods are unsuccessful are more intensive and specialized interventions employed. These may or may not be provided within the general education classroom and are often delivered by the school's learning assistance teacher.

Putting a Canadian Face on Learning Disabilities

17   Learning disabilities that are not identified, or are not addressed successfully, can lead to acute negative outcomes, whether for child, adolescent, or adult. For this reason, early diagnosis and intervention is highly recommended (British Columbia Association of School Psychologists, 2007). To that end, parents and educators must be informed of the concept of learning disabilities, characteristics, and the negative consequences of failing to address learning, social, and emotional needs. To assist with this lofty goal, the government of Canada sponsored a ground-breaking applied research study titled *Putting a Canadian Face on Learning Disabilities* (PACFOLD), which was released in 2007 by the LDAC (PACFOLD, 2007).

18   As part of the mandate from LDAC, four Canadian researchers collected data from 10 data surveys from Statistics Canada in order to "find out what it means to be a child, youth or adult with learning disabilities in Canada" (Learning Disability Association of Canada, 2007, p. 1). The findings were startling, highlighting the disadvantage and negative impact of living with learning disabilities, particularly when undiagnosed and untreated (Learning Disabilities Association of Canada, 2007; Wilson, Furrie, Walcot-Gayda, & Deri, 2009).

19   The negative impact of learning disabilities is seen in families, parents, and the children and youth themselves. For example, parents of children aged 6 to 15 with learning disabilities were more likely to report instances of depression than parents with children without disabilities (87.5% vs. 79.5%) (Learning Disability Association of Canada, 2007). When asked about self-esteem and self-efficacy, children and youth with learning disabilities reported feeling less positive about themselves as individuals and less able to do well (63.8% and 75.3%, respectively) (Learning Disabilities Association of Canada, 2007). Further, almost one third of families with children with a learning disability reported being unable to pay for the necessary supports for their children to succeed (Philpott & Cahill, 2008). Among young adult and adult populations, individuals with learning disabilities were more likely than nonlearning disabled to report suicidal thoughts, depression, and stress, and to be unemployed or earning less than their nondisabled peers (Wilson et al., 2009). These individuals were also less likely to have completed postsecondary education or training (Learning Disabilities Association of Canada, 2007). Finally, based on these findings, the PACFOLD study (Learning Disabilities Association of Canada,

2007) speculates that "[h]igher unemployment and lower incomes may be the root cause of the health problems Canadians with learning disabilities face" (p. 5).

20   The recent CSD (Statistics Canada, 2012) confirmed these trends with disturbing findings related to adults with learning disabilities. Of the 15- to 24-year- olds, 93.6% reported mental health problems. Many did not pursue further education (40.4%) because they felt avoided or excluded (58.3%) during their school years, and 41% did not receive the technological supports that they required. Employment was also severely hampered, with only 28.8% participating in the labour force (vs. 73.6% of the nondisabled group, 15 to 64 years of age). Of those employed, the median total personal income per year was $12,200, compared to $33,800 for the non-disabled counterparts.

Addressing the Problems

21   The LDAC recommends a number of actions to be taken by federal and provincial government to address the problems noted above in the PACFOLD study, which are also mirrored by the PALS and CSD. First, awareness and education are fundamental for medical, mental health, and educational professionals. Adequate training is required both during initial professional training and after employment, in the respective fields. Training and awareness should include information about comorbidity issues such as allergies and mental health problems. The LDAC recommends that such training and awareness be extended into the labour market for human resource personnel. Second, early universal screening and intervention for preschool and primary school children could increase literacy rates, reduce healthcare costs, improve family life, and enhance employment outlook. Further, the LDAC recommends that universal health insurance plans cover screening, assessment, and intervention costs. Ultimately, all of these initiatives would serve to "reduce the short- and long-term economic costs of failure (special education, unemployment, health, welfare, and corrections)" (Learning Disabilities Association of Canada, 2007, p. 8).

22   Prominent figures in the field of learning disabilities in Canada have advanced other recommendations to enhance the education and life of individuals with LD. The issue of inconsistent definition and operationalization of learning disabilities across Canada must be addressed, according to Dr. David Philpott, one of the authors of the *Pan-Canadian Perspective on Professional Knowledge of Learning Disabilities* (2008) (personal communication,

April 28, 2015). The executive director of the Learning Disabilities Association of Canada, Claudette Larocque, points to a drastic reduction in funding for nonprofit organizations such as the LDAC, which has adversely impacted the delivery of programs and services to individuals with LD and their families (personal communication, April 30, 2105). At the school level, Ms. Larocque also notes that the movement toward inclusive education has resulted in a lack of appropriate funding and services for some children and youth who are struggling with LD. As a result, these individuals are often faced with long wait times for psychological assessments. Postsecondary issues, she continues, relate to the need for new university or college applicants to have updated assessments (not older than three years), in order to qualify for classroom accommodations. As she points out, most postsecondary students do not know that they need to access psychoeducational assessment prior to their program entry, nor do they have the necessary funds to do so. Without appropriate documentation, many students are not successful in the first semester of their postsecondary education because they struggle without the appropriate accommodations.

23   Gordon Bullivant, executive director of Foothills Academy, a designated special education school in Alberta (for students with severe LD), reiterates the concern for reduced government funding for education and also the revised definition of learning disabilities (now termed learning disorders) in the DSM-5 (personal communication, June 11, 2015).

Conclusion

24   Canada is a huge country with various geographical and cultural regions. Because education is the responsibility of individual provinces and territories, there is no consistency in definition, diagnostic criteria, or service delivery. Nevertheless, exciting new research projects are exploring effective means of intervening for those individuals with reading, writing, or mathematical learning disabilities. Effective and efficient methods of identification and remediation are imperative in order to reduce the negative impact of learning disabilities on students and their families. Grappling with the DSM-5 definition and criteria will be a necessary step for all educational jurisdictions in Canada, and in particular for school psychologists who are responsible for diagnosis.

References

American Psychiatric Association. (2013). *Desk reference to the diagnostic criteria from DSM–5*. Arlington, VA: Author.

British Columbia Association of School Psychologists. (2007). Best practice guidelines for the assessment, diagnosis and identification of students with learning disabilities. Retrieved from http://bcasp.ca

Butler-Jones, D. (2009). Chief public health officer's report on the state of public health in Canada, 2009: Growing up well—Priorities for a healthy future. Retrieved from http://www.Phac-aspc.gc.ca/cphorsphc-respcacsp/2009/fr-rc/pdf/cphorsphc-respcacsp-eng.pdf

CAST. (2015). *About universal design for learning*. Retrieved from http://www.cast.org/our-work/about-udl.html#.VWcd_ayD5uA

Fiedorowicz, C., Craig, J., Phillips, M., Price, A., & Bullivant, G. (2015). *To revise or not to revise: The official LDAC definition of learning disabilities versus DSM–5 criteria* (Position paper of the Learning Disabilities Association of Canada). Retrieved from http://www.ldac-acta.ca/downloads/pdf/media_release/LDAC-DSM-5-Statement- March-2015-FINAL-CL.pdf

Fuchs, D., & Fuchs, L. S. (2006). Introduction to response to intervention: What, why, and how valid is it? *Reading Research Quarterly, 1,* 93–99.

Hutchinson, N. L. (2014). Inclusion of exceptional learners in Canadian schools: A practical handbook for teachers (4th ed.). Don Mills, ONT, Canada: Pearson Canada Inc.

Klassen, B. (2002). The changing landscape of learning disabilities in Canada: Definitions and practices from 1989–2000. *School Psychology International, 23,* 199–219.

Kozey, M., & Siegel, L. S. (2008). Definitions of learning disabilities and Canadian provinces and territories. *Canadian Psychology, 49,* 162–171.

Learning Disabilities Association of Canada (LDAC). (2007). *Executive summary of Putting a Canadian Face on Learning Disabilities Study* (PACFOLD). Retrieved from http://www.pacfold.ca/download/WhatIs/en/executive-Summary.pdf

Learning Disabilities Association of Canada (LDAC). (2015). *Official definition of learning disabilities*. Retrieved from http://www.ldac-acta.ca/learn-more/ld-defined/official-definition-of-learning-disabilities

McIntosh, K., MacKay, L., Andreou, T., Brown, J., Matthews, S., Gietz, C., & Bennett, J. (2011). Response to intervention in Canada: Definitions, the evidence base, and future directions. *Canadian Journal of School Psychology, 26,* 18–43.

PACFOLD. (2007). *What is PACFOLD?* Retrieved from http://www.pacfold.ca/what_ is/index.shtml

Philpott, D. F., & Cahill, M. (2008). A pan-Canadian perspective on the professional knowledge base of learning disabilities. *International Journal of Learning Disability, Community and Rehabilitation, 7.* Retrieved from http://www.ijdcr.ca/VOL07_02_CAN/articles/ philpott.shtml

Rose, D. H., & Meyer, A. (2002). Teaching every student in the digital age: Universal design for learning. Alexandria, VA: ASCD.

Siegel, L. S. (1989). IQ is irrelevant to the definition of learning disabilities. *Journal of Learning Disabilities, 22,* 469–478.

Stanovich, K. E. (1991). Discrepancy definitions for reading disability: Has intelligence led us astray? *Reading Research Quarterly, 26,* 7–29.

Stanovich, K. E. (2005). The future of a mistake: Will discrepancy measurement continue to make the learning disabilities field as pseudoscience? *Learning Disability Quarterly, 28,* 103–106.

Statistics Canada. (2006). Profile of disability for children. *Participation and Activity Limitation Survey (PALS).* Retrieved from http://www.statcan.gc.ca/pub/89-628-x/2007002/4125020-eng.htm#a4

Statistics Canada. (2012). *Canadian survey on disability (CSD).* Retrieved from hppt://www.statscan.gc.ca/pub/89-654-x/89-654-x2014003-eng.htm

Sugai, G. (n.d.). School-wide positive behavior support and response to intervention. Retrieved from http://www.rtinetwork.org/learn/behavior-supports/schoolwidebehavior

Tomlinson, C. A. (1999). The differentiated classroom: Responding to the needs of all learners. Alexandria, VA: ASCD.

Whitley, J., Lupart, J. L., & Beran, T. (2007). The characteristics and experiences of Canadian students receiving special education services for learning disability. *Exceptionality Education Canada, 17,* 85–109.

Wiener, J., & Siegel, L. (1992). A Canadian perspective on learning disabilities. *Journal of Learning Disabilities, 25,* 340–350.

Wilson, A. M., Furrie, A., Walcot-Gayda, E., & Deri, C. (2009). The mental health of Canadian with self-reported learning disabilities. *Journal of Learning Disabilities, 42,* 24–40.

Wong, B. E., & Hutchinson, N. (2001). Learning disabilities in Canada. In D. P. Hallahan & B. K. Keogh (Eds.), *Research and global perspectives in learning disabilities: Essays in honor of William M. Cruikshank* (pp. 197–215). Mahwah, NJ: Erlbaum.

Key and challenging words

jurisdiction, consolidate, discrepancy, etiology, stigmatization, comorbidity

Questions

1. (a) Why is it particularly challenging to define the term *learning disability* (LD) in Canada? (b) Briefly explain the difference between a definition of LD and diagnostic criteria for LD (see the section "Diagnostic Criteria for LD").

2. In two of the following paragraphs, identify the rhetorical pattern and explain its effectiveness as an organizational strategy both within the paragraph and in the section of the essay in which it occurs: (a) paragraph 2, (b) paragraph 3, (c) paragraph 19.

3. Analyze the structure and organization of the essay, showing how structural/organizational features contribute to the reader's comprehension and accessibility of information. (For example, you could consider order of points; placement and use of headings, thesis,

and topic sentences; paragraph organization; and other structural features. If you think that structure/ organization could be improved, you can include suggestions for improvement in your answer.

4. Analyze the author's use of experts (see, in particular, paragraphs 6–7 and 21–22) as sources, commenting on what they contribute to the sections in which they are used. (Note that in APA documentation style, these sources are not listed on the References page, though they require in-text citations.)

5. Like many Type C essays, the author of "Learning Disabilities in Canada" uses summary and synthesis throughout her essay. Analyze her use of summary and synthesis in two non-consecutive paragraphs, commenting on their purposes and effectiveness. Refer specifically to the text.

6. In your own words, describe the special challenge for students with learning disabilities as they begin their post-secondary education? (See the subsection in the essay titled "Addressing the Problems.")

Post-reading

1. How might the challenges for students with learning disabilities at university be addressed (see #5 under Questions, above)? In one or two paragraphs, propose concrete ways to address these problems.

2. Outline an informational report (concerned with informing/explaining), or an analytical report (concerned with recommendations) directed to a specific group or groups of people (for example, parents of children in a specific age group, a specific body of educators, such as a school board) in which you draw attention to central issues and problems related to learning disabilities in Canada. The purpose is to raise awareness. As stated in the essay, "Parents and educators must be informed of the concept of learning disabilities, characteristics, and the negative consequences of failing to address learning, social, and emotional needs" (paragraph 17). Your report can be in outline form (i.e., it does not need to be written in standard report form with paragraphs and headings).

Media and Image

Sleep Problems: Predictor or Outcome of Media Use among Emerging Adults at University?

Royette Tavernier and Teena Willoughby

(4,145 words)

Pre-reading

1. *Collaborative or individual activity:* Have you personally experienced or do you know of others who have experienced sleep problems that sometimes affect performance in class? What do you believe accounts for such problems? To what extent, if any, is media to blame, in your opinion? Discuss these questions in groups or write a response that includes answers to these questions.

Summary

The pervasiveness of media use in our society has raised concerns about its potential impact on important lifestyle behaviours, including sleep. Although a number of studies have modelled poor sleep as a negative outcome of media use, a critical assessment of the literature indicates two important gaps: (i) studies have almost exclusively relied on concurrent data, and thus have not been able to assess the direction of effects; and (ii) studies have largely been conducted with children and adolescents. The purpose of the present 3-year longitudinal study, therefore, was to examine whether both sleep duration and sleep problems would be predictors or outcomes of two forms of media use (i.e. television and online social networking) among a sample of emerging adults. Participants were 942 (71.5% female) university students (M = 19.01 years, SD = 0.90) at Time 1. Survey measures, which were assessed for three consecutive years starting in the first year of university, included demographics, sleep duration, sleep problems, television and online social networking use. Results of a cross-lagged model indicated that the association between sleep problems and media use was statistically significant: sleep problems predicted longer time spent watching television and on social networking websites, but not vice versa. Contrary to our hypotheses, sleep duration was not associated with media use. Our findings indicate no negative effects of media use on sleep among emerging adults, but instead suggest that emerging adults appear to seek out media as a means of coping with their sleep problems.

Introduction

1   In 2010, over 75% of Canadians and Americans (Statistics Canada, 2010a; U.S. Census Bureau, 2010) reported having internet access in their homes. Among adolescents, prevalence rates of daily television and computer use are as high as 85 and 95%, respectively (Milde-Busch et al., 2010). Moreover, 72% of all internet users report using online social networking (Brenner, 2013). These high prevalence rates have led to increased concern that media use may be displacing important lifestyle behaviours, such as sleep (Zimmerman, 2008). This is an important issue, given the pivotal role that sleep is thought to play in psychosocial functioning across the lifespan (Galambos et al., 2009). Higher media use has been consistently associated with more irregular sleep patterns, shorter sleep duration, as well as more sleep problems (Chahal et al., 2013; Choi et al., 2009; Oka et al., 2008; Punamäki et al., 2007). Researchers have proposed that increased media use may be linked to poor sleep because time spent engaged in media use may directly displace sleep (Li et al., 2007; Oka et al., 2008; Owens et al.,

Source: From *Journal of Sleep Research*, vol. 23, 2014, pp. 389–96. By permission of John Wiley & Sons.

1999; Van den Bulck, 2004; Zimmerman, 2008). Highly arousing media content (e.g. a violent movie) also may lead to nightmares and poor overall sleep quality (Li et al., 2007; Owens et al., 1999; Zimmerman, 2008), particularly among individuals whose emotion regulation strategies are not yet fully developed.

2   There are two important gaps, however, within the literature: (i) a lack of studies examining bidirectional associations between sleep and media use; and (ii) a lack of studies examining these associations among emerging adults. Researchers generally have inferred that longer media use precedes poor sleep, but have based this interpretation on concurrent findings (Chahal et al., 2013; Punamäki et al., 2007; Wang et al., 2012) and thus are not able to determine whether poor sleep, in fact, may precede media use or whether the nature of the association is bidirectional (but see Johnson et al., 2004; for an exception). Poor sleep may predict increased media use over time, for example, as individuals with sleep problems (who generally have been found to report more negative emotional adjustment) may seek out media as a way to cope. In fact, negative emotional adjustment has been linked to media use in both children and older adults (Chen and Kennedy, 2005; Van der Goot et al., 2012). Additionally, given that technological advances have led to increased ease of accessing media (e.g. through cell phones; Jacobsen and Forste, 2011), poor sleep quality also may lead to greater media use over time as individuals now can more easily engage in media use when they have difficulty initiating or maintaining sleep (Kubey, 1986).

3   Furthermore, studies examining the link between sleep and media use have largely been based on children and adolescents (Chahal et al., 2013; Choi et al., 2009; Li et al., 2007; Oka et al., 2008; Van den Bulck, 2004), while little attention has been paid to emerging adults. Importantly, university students have been found to report higher prevalence rates of media use relative to both junior and senior high school adolescents (Wang et al., 2012). Moreover, in both Canada (Statistics Canada, 2010b) and the USA (U.S. Census Bureau, 2010), use of online social networking has been found to be most prevalent among emerging adults, relative to any other age group. As an extension of the literature, therefore, the purpose of the present 3-year longitudinal study was to examine whether both sleep duration and sleep problems would be predictors or outcomes of two forms of media use (i.e. television and online social networking) among a sample of emerging adults.

Materials and Methods

Participants

4   Participants were 942 (71.5% female) first-year university students at Time 1 (17–25 years; M = 19.01 years, SD = 0.90), who remained enrolled at a mid-sized university in Southern Ontario, Canada across three consecutive academic years. Parental education was used as a proxy for socioeconomic status, and averaged between "some college, university or apprenticeship program" and "completed a college/apprenticeship and/or technical diploma." The majority of participants were domestic-Canadian (88%).

Procedure

5   We recruited first-year university students from various academic disciplines to participate in a longitudinal survey study on stress, coping and adjustment to university by way of posters, classroom announcements, website postings and visits to on-campus student residences. Participants were given either 1-h course credit or monetary compensation (CAD $10.00) at Time 1, and monetary compensation at Time 2 (CAD $20.00) and Time 3 (CAD $30.00). Three assessments were conducted, each one year apart. Each year, assessments took place between January and March. The study was approved by the University Ethics board prior to survey administration at all three assessments, and participants provided informed active consent prior to participation.

Missing Data Analysis

6   Missing data occurred within each assessment time point because some students did not finish the entire questionnaire (average missing data = 1.5%). In addition, not all participants completed each of the three survey waves— that is, some participants completed the survey in Years 1 and 3, and others completed the survey in Years 1 and 2. Specifically, out of the original sample that completed the survey in Year 1, 82% completed the survey in at least 2 of the 3 years (i.e. 63% completed it in all 3 years; 10% completed it only in years 1 and 2; and 9% completed it only in years 1 and 3). Missing data analyses revealed that the probability of missingness on a given variable was not related to scores on that particular variable (i.e. data were missing at random; Enders, 2010), and thus missing data for the main model were estimated using the full information maximum likelihood (FIML) estimation method. FIML retains cases that have missing data, thus avoiding the biased parameter

estimates that can occur with pair-wise or list-wise deletion (Schafer and Graham, 2002).

Measures
Demographics

7   Age, gender and parental education were assessed at Time 1, and were used as covariates in the model. For parental education, scores (1 = did not finish high school to 6 = professional degree, r = 0.40) were averaged for participants who reported on both parents.

Sleep problems

8   An adapted version of the Insomnia Severity Index (Morin, 1993) was used to assess the severity of sleep problems (e.g. difficulty falling asleep, staying asleep, waking up too early, and staying awake), with responses ranging from 1 = no problem to 5 = very severe problems. An assessment of participants' overall satisfaction with their subjective sleep quality, as well as perceived daytime functioning as a result of sleep patterns, was also included in the sleep problems index. Higher scores indicate more sleep problems.

Sleep duration

9   Sleep duration was calculated from participants' bed times ("What time do you normally fall asleep?") and wake times ("What time do you normally wake up?"), averaged across the week and weekend. Higher scores indicate longer sleep duration (in hours).

Media use

10   Two indices of media use were assessed. (i) Television: (a) "On an average WEEK day, how many hours do you spend watching TV shows/movies either on TV or computer?" (b) "On an average day on the WEEKEND, how many hours do you spend watching TV shows/movies either on TV or computer?" (ii) Online social networking: (a) "On an average WEEK day, how many hours do you spend going on Facebook/MySpace/Twitter/E-mail/Messenger?" (b) "On an average day on the WEEKEND, how many hours do you spend going on Facebook/MySpace/Twitter/E-mail/Messenger?" Responses to these four items ranged from 1 = not at all to 5 = 5 or more hours. Two separate composite scores were created (i.e. for television and for online social networking) based on scores averaged across the week and weekend. Higher scores indicate longer media use.

Plan of analyses

11   The primary statistical analyses were carried out using path analysis in AMOS 20.0. Model fit was evaluated using the comparative fit index (CFI) and the root mean squared error of approximation (RMSEA). CFI values greater than 0.95 and a RMSEA value of less than 0.06 (simultaneously) were used as the criteria for determining a well-specified or close-fitting model (Hu and Bentler, 1999). We note that both media use variables (i.e. time spent watching television and time spent engaged in online social networking) were modelled as continuous variables instead of categorical variables as this approach was in keeping with the research question at hand (i.e. an examination of the nature of the association between media use and sleep quality, and not on how the specific amount of time spent engaged in media use relates to sleep quality). Descriptive analyses (e.g. histograms; skewness and kurtosis values) indicated that scores on the two media use variables were normally distributed.

12   The cross-lagged model was comprised of four variables assessed at three time points: sleep problems, sleep duration, time spent watching television, and online social networking. Across the three time points we included lag-1 cross-lag paths, as well as lag-1 and lag-2 autoregressive/stability paths. We also accounted for concurrent associations among all the study variables within each wave. Age, gender and parental education were included as covariates, with correlations specified between these three covariates and each of the four variables assessed at Time 1. Finally, paths were estimated between each covariate and each of the four variables assessed at Time 2 and Time 3.

Results
Descriptive statistics

13   Descriptive statistics (i.e. means, standard deviations, ranges and Cronbach's alpha values) for all study variables are presented in Table 1. Average sleep problems for the sample ranged from 13.81 to 14.16, suggesting that participants reported few sleep problems across the three assessments. Average sleep duration ranged from 8 h, 18 min to 8 h, 36 min, across the three assessments. Overall, participants reported spending, on average, between "1 and 2 h" and "3–4 h" a day on both online social networking and watching television across all three assessments.

Primary analyses

14   In terms of the main cross-lagged model, results of a chi-square difference test of relative fit, χ^2_{diff} (12) = 11.75,

Table 1　Correlations, means, standard deviations, scale ranges and Cronbach's alpha values for all key study variables

	1	2	3	4	5	6	7	8	9	10	11	12	13	14	15
1. SPROB1	—														
2. SPROB2	0.57	—													
3. SPROB3	0.53	0.63	—												
4. SDUR1	−0.24	−0.16	−0.14	—											
5. SDUR2	−0.19	−0.25	−0.18	0.46	—										
6. SDUR3	−0.17	−0.22	−0.27	0.39	0.48	—									
7. OSN1	0.08	0.07	0.06	0.02	0.02	0.01	—								
8. OSN2	0.12	0.10	0.10	−0.01	0.02	0.00	0.54	—							
9. OSN3	0.12	0.13	0.14	−0.02	−0.01	−0.04	0.48	0.57	—						
10. TV1	0.03	0.06	0.05	0.05	0.03	0.02	0.26	0.18	0.16	—					
11. TV2	0.08	0.10	0.11	0.04	0.06	0.03	0.16	0.28	0.20	0.37	—				
12. TV3	0.08	0.12	0.14	0.02	0.04	0.07	0.15	0.21	0.24	0.35	0.46	—			
13. AGE	0.02	0.00	−0.01	−0.05	−0.07	−0.06	−0.08	−0.06	0.03	−0.02	−0.09	−0.05	—		
14. GEN	0.18	0.09	0.06	−0.05	0.00	−0.02	0.21	0.22	0.20	0.03	0.04	0.09	−0.07	—	
15. PEDU	−0.12	−0.07	−0.06	−0.01	0.01	0.06	−0.03	−0.09	−0.04	−0.06	−0.01	0.01	−0.11	−0.12	—
M	13.81	14.16	13.92	8.60	8.31	8.27	3.47	3.29	3.20	3.28	3.29	3.24	19.01	1.72	3.68
SD	4.26	4.20	4.42	1.22	1.19	1.17	0.97	0.98	0.93	0.98	1.00	1.05	0.90	0.45	1.29
Range	6–28	6–29	6–29	4–15	4–12	4–12	1–5	1–5	1–5	1–5	1–5	1–5	17–25	1–2	1–6
α	0.76	0.76	0.79	NA	NA	NA	0.85	0.85	0.82	0.74	0.79	0.80	NA	NA	NA

AGE, age at Time 1; GEN, gender; OSN, online social networking; PEDU, parental education at Time 1; SDUR, sleep duration; SPROB, sleep problems; TV, television. Numbers 1, 2 and 3 represent Time 1, Time 2 and Time 3, respectively.

$P > 0.05$, indicated that the patterns of associations among the variables were the same from Time 1 to Time 2 and from Time 2 to Time 3. Thus, subsequent analyses of our research questions were based on the model that was constrained over time, and we report below only the regression coefficients for Time 1–Time 2 (note that the pattern of results among the variables is the same from Time 2 to Time 3). Results of the path analysis indicated that the associations between sleep duration and television, as well as between sleep duration and online social networking, were not statistically significant (Table 2). The associations between sleep problems and television, as well as between sleep problems and online social networking, however, were both statistically significant, such that more sleep problems predicted both longer time spent watching television ($\beta = 0.070$, $P = 0.005$), as well as more time spent engaged in online social networking ($\beta = 0.054$, $P = 0.013$; Fig. 1), but not vice versa. Both time spent watching television and online social networking did not predict sleep duration and sleep problems.

Discussion

15   As an important extension of the literature, the present 3-year longitudinal study was the first to examine the direction of effects between two important sleep characteristics (i.e. sleep duration and sleep problems) and two indices of media use (i.e. television and online social networking) among a sample of emerging adults at university. In the present study, sleep problems predicted both time spent watching television, as well as time spent on social networking websites. On the other hand, neither time spent watching television nor time spent on social networking websites predicted sleep problems. Thus, sleep problems was a predictor and not an outcome of media use among our sample of emerging adults. Contrary to our hypothesis, sleep duration was not associated with time spent watching television or engaged in online social networking over time. These results provide an important insight into the nature of the associations between sleep and media use among emerging adults at university.

16   In contrast to findings in the present study, theoretical models of sleep and media use have traditionally modelled sleep problems as the outcome of media use (Cain and Gradisar, 2010). Moreover, few studies have specifically examined the direction of effects between sleep problems and media use (but see Johnson et al., 2004), particularly among emerging adults at university. The unidirectional finding from sleep to time spent watching television in the present study is in contrast to the Johnson et al. (2004) study, which found that time spent watching television predicted more sleep problems over time but sleep problems did not predict time spent watching television. One reason for this discrepant finding is that Johnson and colleagues assessed the association between watching television in adolescence and subsequent sleep problems in emerging adulthood, whereas the present study assessed the association between watching television and sleep problems "within" the emerging adulthood period. As has been proposed by Johnson et al. (2004) perhaps the nature of the association between television and sleep problems changes across the lifespan. Indeed, Johnson et al. (2004) found that a reduction in time spent watching television at 14 years was associated with a reduced risk for sleep problems at 16 years but, interestingly, a reduction in the amount of time spent watching television at 16 years was "not" associated with a reduced risk for sleep problems at 22 years. Also the data for the Johnson study were collected between 1983 and 1993—a period of time when the ease of accessing television other than from a television set was not as prevalent as it is today (Brown, 2006). The current ease of accessing television (e.g. through mobile devices such as iPads and tablets) may have facilitated the use of television as a sleep aid as it has become easier to watch television in the bedroom.

17   Higher media use (both watching television and online social networking) may be one way in which emerging adults cope with sleep problems. Indeed, Eggermont and Van den Bulck (2006) found that 36.7% of individuals surveyed reported that they watched television specifically as a way to help them fall asleep. Given that sleep problems have been associated with negative affect (Galambos et al., 2009) and poor overall emotional adjustment (Tavernier and Willoughby, 2013), emerging adults who report more sleep problems may seek out media as a coping mechanism to help regulate their emotions (Chen and Kennedy, 2005; Van der Goot et al., 2012). Additionally, as an activity that requires little physical and mental effort, both television viewing (Kubey, 1986) as well as passive browsing on online social networking websites (Tosun, 2012) are prime candidates for individuals with sleep problems (e.g. difficulty falling asleep) wishing to fill in their time spent trying to fall asleep. Importantly, in the present study, sleep problems at one point in time predicted longer time spent on media use 1 year later. This long-term association between sleep quality and media use lends itself to intriguing questions

Table 2   Beta weights and standard errors for all cross-lagged and stability paths

Path	B	β	SE	P
Sleep problems 1 → Sleep problems 2	0.561	0.565	0.031	0.000
Sleep problems 1 → Sleep duration 2	−0.024	−0.088	0.007	0.000
Sleep problems 1 → Online social networking 2	0.012	0.054	0.005	0.013
Sleep problems 1 → Television 2	0.017	0.070	0.006	0.005
Sleep duration 1 → Sleep duration 2	0.423	0.435	0.032	0.000
Sleep duration 1 → Sleep problems 2	−0.090	−0.026	0.077	0.240
Sleep duration 1 → Online social networking 2	−0.004	−0.006	0.017	0.799
Sleep duration 1 → Television 2	0.023	0.028	0.021	0.259
Online social networking 1 → Online social networking 2	0.508	0.505	0.031	0.000
Online social networking 1 → Sleep problems 2	0.101	0.023	0.097	0.298
Online social networking 1 → Sleep duration 2	0.003	0.003	0.029	0.909
Online social networking 1 → Television 2	0.058	0.057	0.026	0.025
Television 1 → Television 2	0.361	0.356	0.034	0.000
Television 1 → Sleep problems 2	0.153	0.036	0.094	0.104
Television 1 → Sleep duration 2	0.006	0.005	0.028	0.839
Television 1 → Online social networking 2	0.044	0.045	0.021	0.038

β, standardized beta; B, unstandardized beta; SE, standard error.

Numbers 1 and 2 after variable names indicate Time 1 and Time 2, respectively – only two time points are shown as cross-lagged paths were invariant across the three waves. Results for covariates (age, gender and parental education) are not shown, but can be obtained from first author.

regarding possible mechanisms (e.g. emotion regulation) that may explain this link. Furthermore, given that findings from the present study differ from other studies with regard to the direction of effects between sleep quality and media use (e.g. longer media use was associated with an increased risk of developing sleep problems 1 year later in Thomée et al., 2012), it is critical that future studies explore possible factors (e.g. personality traits such as neuroticism, conscientiousness, etc.) that might moderate the link between sleep characteristics and media use.

18   Moreover, in contrast to studies with children and adolescents that have reported a link between sleep duration and media use, we found that sleep duration was unrelated to television or online social networking among our sample of emerging adults. First, it is important to note the relatively adequate sleep duration reported among our sample (i.e. more than 8 h of sleep per night across all three assessments). As class start times have been shown to be predictive of sleep–wake timing among university students, increased flexibility in selecting class schedules may facilitate longer sleep duration among emerging adults at

university (Onyper et al., 2012). Although past studies have found that shorter sleep duration is associated with longer media use, some of these studies did not assess sleep problems (Chahal et al., 2013; Oka et al., 2008; Van den Bulck, 2004). Past studies based on emerging adults that have assessed both sleep duration and sleep problems often have found that sleep duration tends to be a weaker predictor of psychosocial outcomes relative to sleep problems (Galambos et al., 2009).

19   Although the present study makes a significant contribution to the literature by addressing two important gaps, findings must be interpreted against the study's limitations. First, our measure of online social networking was based on time spent across a number of different social networking websites, lumped together (e.g. Facebook/MySpace/ Twitter). As these websites have slightly different components (e.g. options for video chat), we were not able to distinguish "how" individuals spent their time. Additionally, our measure of television use did not assess the content of television programmes. Future research should examine, therefore, the direction of effects between sleep problems

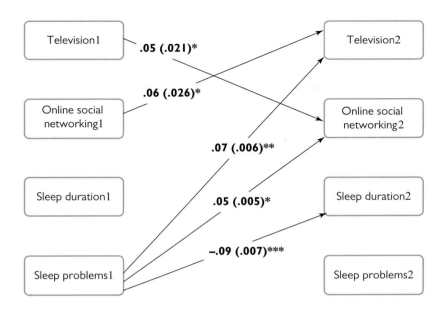

Figure 1 Significant cross-lagged paths. *Note.* *P < 0.05; **P < 0.01; ***P < 0.001. Values indicate standardized beta weights (standard errors are in parenthesis). For simplicity, only two time points are shown as cross-lagged paths were invariant across the three waves (i.e., pattern of significant cross-lagged paths for Time 1–Time 2 are the same for Time 2–Time 3). Numbers 1 and 2 after variable names indicate Time 1 and Time 2, respectively. Results for stability paths for each variable (all of which were significant) as well as covariates (age, gender, and parental education) are not shown but can be obtained from first author.

and time spent on particular activities on social networking websites, and should include an assessment of television content (e.g. degree of violence). Second, our assessments of television and online social networking were based on only two items per type of media activity. Future research should verify the associations found in the present study using multi-item, validated scales of media use in order to account for different aspects of media use (e.g. social context of media use—whether alone or with friends) and how they might relate to sleep characteristics.

20   Third, our assessment of sleep problems and sleep duration was based on participants' subjective self-reports. A worthwhile avenue for future research would be to assess the associations found in the present study using objective sleep measures (e.g. actigraph recordings). Fourth, it must be noted that although our sample was comprised of both domestic-Canadian and international students from a variety of different ethnic backgrounds, these students all came from the same university and thus results of our study may not be generalizable to other samples. Importantly, given the increased flexibility that university students have

in scheduling sleep–wake timing and daytime activities (Zimmermann, 2011), participants in this sample may not be representative of emerging adults in general, including those who are not enrolled at university and have full-time jobs with different scheduling constraints. Thus, it would be worthwhile for future studies to examine the nature of the association between sleep and media use among non-university emerging adult samples. Fifth, as the present study was based on a select sample of university students who generally reported few sleep problems and adequate sleep duration, it is crucial that future studies also examine the nature of the association between sleep and media use among clinical samples, including individuals diagnosed with insomnia. Sixth, although findings in the present study support a unidirectional association from sleep to media use, it remains to be determined whether the nature of the association between these two constructs may be reversed (i.e. from media use to sleep), or possibly bidirectional, given a different sample—such as clinically sleep-deprived individuals or individuals diagnosed with internet addiction.

21   A final noteworthy point concerns the fact that although the effect sizes (i.e. standardized beta weights) reported in the present study are deemed "small" by traditional standards (Cohen, 1992), it is important to highlight that a strength of the present study was the use of a conservative model, which controlled for autoregressive/stability paths, associations among all variables within a wave, as well as the effect of age, gender and parental education, while also simultaneously controlling for the effect of the other predictors in the model. Importantly, the present study has addressed two important gaps in the literature: (i) the need to assess bidirectional associations between sleep and media use; and the need to examine these associations among emerging adults. Our results provide evidence for a unidirectional association between sleep problems and media use, such that more sleep problems predicted both time spent watching television and engaged in online social networking. Sleep problems, therefore, was the predictor and not the outcome of media use among this sample. Establishing the direction of effects between sleep problems and media use holds important implications for the effective design and execution of intervention programmes aimed at targeting both sleep and waking behaviours among university students. Our findings indicate that it may be worthwhile to promote more effective sleep habits to assist university students in getting good quality sleep given the pivotal role that sleep plays across the lifespan. It will, therefore, be imperative for researchers to examine the effectiveness of media use as a sleep aid among university students.

References

Brenner, J. Who uses social networking sites. Pew Internet & American Life Project. Retrieved from http://pewinternet.org/ Commentary/2012/March/Pew-Internet-Social-Networking-full-detail.aspx#,2013.

Brown, J. D. Emerging adults in a media-saturated world. In: J. J. Arnett and J. L. Tanner (Eds) *Emerging Adults in America: Coming of Age in the 21st Century.* American Psychological Association, Washington, DC, 2006: 279–299.

Cain, N. and Gradisar, M. Electronic media use and sleep in school-aged children and adolescents: a review. *Sleep Med.*, 2010, 11: 735–742.

Chahal, H., Fung, C., Kuhle, S. and Veugelers, P. J. Availability and night-time use of electronic entertainment and communication devices are associated with short sleep duration and obesity among Canadian children. *Pediatr. Obes.*, 2013, 8: 42–51.

Chen, J. L. and Kennedy, C. Cultural variations in children's coping behaviour, TV viewing time, and family functioning. *Int. Nurs. Rev.*, 2005, 52: 186–195.

Choi, K., Son, H., Park, M. et al. Internet overuse and excessive daytime sleepiness in adolescents. *Psychiatry Clin. Neurosci.*, 2009, 63: 455–462.

Cohen, J. A power primer. *Psychol. Bull.*, 1992, 112: 155–159.

Eggermont, S. and Van den Bulck, J. Nodding off or switching off? The use of popular media as a sleep aid in secondary school children. *J. Paediatr. Child Health*, 2006, 42: 428–433.

Enders, C. K. *Applied Missing Data Analysis.* Guilford Press, New York, NY, 2010.

Galambos, N. L., Dalton, A. L. and Maggs, J. L. Losing sleep over it: daily variation in sleep quantity and quality in Canadian students' first semester of university. *J. Res. Adolesc.*, 2009, 19: 741–761.

Hu, L. and Bentler, P. M. Cutoff criteria for fit indexes in covariance structure analysis: conventional criteria versus new alternatives. *Struct. Equ. Modeling*, 1999, 6: 1–55.

Jacobsen, W. C. and Forste, R. The wired generation: academic and social outcomes of electronic media use among university students. *Cyberpsychol. Behav. Soc. Netw.*, 2011, 14: 275–280.

Johnson, J. G., Cohen, P., Kasen, S., First, M. B. and Brook, J. S. Association between television viewing and sleep problems during adolescence and early adulthood. *Arch. Pediatr. Adolesc. Med.*, 2004, 158: 562–567.

Kubey, R. W. Television use in everyday life: coping with unstructured time. *J. Commun.*, 1986, 36: 108–123.

Li, S., Jin, X., Wu, S., Jiang, F., Yan, C. and Shen, X. The impact of media use on sleep patterns and sleep disorders among school-aged children in China. *Sleep*, 2007, 30: 361–367.

Milde-Busch, A., von Kries, R., Thomas, S., Heinrich, S., Straube, A. and Radon, K. The association between use of electronic media and prevalence of headache in adolescents: results from a population-based cross-sectional study. *BMC Neurol.*, 2010, 10: 12.

Morin, C. M. Insomnia: Psychological Assessment and Management. Guilford Press, New York, NY, 1993.

Oka, Y., Suzuki, S. and Inoue, Y. Bedtime activities, sleep environment, and sleep/wake patterns of Japanese elementary school children. *Behav. Sleep Med.*, 2008, 6: 220–233.

Onyper, S. V., Thacher, P. V., Gilbert, J. W. and Gradess, S. G. Class start times, sleep, and academic performance in college: a path analysis. *Chronobiol. Int.*, 2012, 29: 318–335.

Owens, J., Maxim, R., McGuinn, M., Nobile, C., Msall, M. and Alario, A. Television-viewing habits and sleep disturbance in school children. *Pediatrics*, 1999, 104: 1–8.

Punamäki, R. L., Wallenius, M., NygOard, C. H., Saarni, L. and Rimpelä, A. Use of information and communication technology (ICT) and perceived health in adolescence: the role of sleeping habits and waking-time tiredness. *J. Adolesc.*, 2007, 30: 569–585.

Schafer, J. L. and Graham, J. W. Missing data: our view of the state of the art. *Psychol. Methods*, 2002, 7: 147–177.

Statistics Canada. Table 358-0171. Canadian internet use survey, households with access to the internet at home, Canada, provinces, and census metropolitan areas (CMA) CANDIM database. Government of Canada. Retrieved from http://www5.statcan.gc.ca/cansim/a26?lang=eng&retrLang=eng&id=3580171&pattern=internet+use&tabMode=dataTable&srchLan=-1&p1=1&p2=-1, 2010a.

Statistics Canada. Table 358-0155. Canadian internet use survey, internet use, by age group and frequency of use CANSIM database. Government of Canada. Retrieved from http://www5.statcan.gc.ca/cansim/a26?lang=eng&retrLang=eng&id=3580155& pattern=internet+use&tabMode=dataTable&srchLan=-1&p1=1&p2=-1, 2010b.

Tavernier, R. and Willoughby, T. Bidirectional associations between sleep (quality and duration) and psychosocial functioning across the university years. *Dev. Psychol.*, 2013.

Thomée, S., Härenstam, A. and Hagberg, M. Computer use and stress, sleep disturbances, and symptoms of depression among young adults – a prospective cohort study. *BMC Psychiatry*, 2012, 12: 176–189.

Tosun, L. P. Motives for facebook use and expressing "true self" on the Internet. *Comput. Hum. Behav.*, 2012, 28: 1510–1517.

U.S. Census Bureau. U.S. Department of Commerce. Computer and internet use in the United States. Retrieved from http://www.census.gov/hhes/computer/publications/2010.html, 2010.

Van den Bulck, J. Television viewing, computer game playing, and internet use and self-reported time to bed and time out of bed in secondary-school children. *Sleep*, 2004, 27: 101–104.

Van der Goot, M., Beentjes, J. W. J. and Van Selm, M. Meanings of television in older adults' lives: an analysis of change and continuity in television viewing. *Ageing Soc.*, 2012, 32: 147–168.

Wang, L., Luo, J., Gao, W. and Kong, J. The effect of Internet use on adolescents' lifestyles: a national survey. *Comput. Human Behav.*, 2012, 28: 2007–2013.

Zimmerman, F. J. Children's Media Use and Sleep Problems: Issues and Unanswered Questions. Research Brief. Henry J. Kaiser Family Foundation, Washington, DC, 2008.

Zimmermann, L. K. Chronotype and the transition to college life. *Chronobiol. Int.*, 2011, 28: 904–910.

Key and challenging words

prevalence, pivotal, concurrent, proxy, composite, constrain, discrepant

Questions

1. Explain how, in paragraph 1, the authors establish the significance of their topic.
2. Explain why the researchers' inference mentioned in paragraph 2 may be incorrect, according to Tavernier and Willoughby.
3. At the end of their Introduction, the authors describe the purpose of their study: (a) Paraphrase the last sentence in paragraph 3; (b) Why do you think the authors may have chosen not to phrase the last sentence of their introduction in the form of hypotheses? (For more about hypotheses, see p. 19 in Chapter 2).
4. In two or three sentences, explain the results of the study, referring both to the appropriate section of the essay and Table 2.
5. Taking one paragraph from the Introduction and one from the Discussion sections (such as paragraphs 2 and 17),

analyze the strategies used to create coherence and readability (see Strategies for Coherent Writing on pp. 73–75 in Chapter 6).

6. In the Discussion section, identify the following features by paragraph number(s) and briefly explain the importance of each: (a) the findings of the study, (b) synthesis of the authors' findings with those of other studies, (c) limitations of the current study, (d) "real-world" application of the findings.

7. How do the authors account for differences between their findings and those of Johnson et al. (see paragraphs 16 and 17)? Is their explanation successful in your view? Why or why not?

Post-reading

1. (a) Using reliable sources, define the term *longitudinal study*; (b) Briefly explain why college or university students might provide ideal subjects for these kinds of studies. (Note: In your answer, you could also refer to another longitudinal study; see "Tracking Affect and Academic Success across University" on p. 163 in Part III: The Reader.)

2. In their Discussion session, the authors explain several limitations of their study (see paragraphs 20 and 21). For two of the limitations, come up with one hypothesis for each that could be the basis of an experiment to remedy a limitation or extend the findings of the current study. Then, give a two-sentence description of the design of such a study—i.e., give a brief description of its methodology. (See the "Method" section of "The More You Play, the More Aggressive You Become" on p. 329 of Part III: The Reader. See also Type B essays in Chapter 3.)

3. *Collaborative or individual activity:* At the end of their study, Tavernier and Willoughby state, "Our findings indicate that it may be worthwhile to promote more effective sleep habits to assist university students in getting good quality sleep" (paragraph 21). Design an informational campaign to help bring awareness of the importance of sleep to students in post-secondary institutions, using appropriate strategies, such as mixed media, with this goal in mind.

Reality TV Gives Back: On The Civic Functions of Reality Entertainment

Laurie Ouellette
(3,029 words)

Pre-reading

1. Consider the documentaries you have watched. What were their names? What was their purpose? Their main features? Do they fit the description of the "documentary tradition" outlined in paragraph 1?

2. This essay has no descriptive (content) headings. Determine where the introduction ends and the body paragraphs begin. Read the first sentences of the first few paragraphs. Does it appear that they are topic sentences that can help you determine the essay's content?

Abstract

Reality TV is more than a trivial diversion. Civic aims historically associated with documentaries (particularly citizenship training) have been radically reinterpreted and integrated into current popular reality formats.

Keywords: citizenship, civic experiment, documentary, public service, reality TV.

————

1   In his influential 2002 essay "Performing the Real: Documentary Diversions," John Corner identified a *lack of civic purpose* as reality TV's defining attribute. His point of reference was the documentary tradition, from which the surge of "unscripted" entertainment since the late-1990s has selectively borrowed. Reflecting on the early stages of this development, Corner worried that if television programs like *Big Brother* drew from the look and style of serious documentary, they eclipsed its historical "civic functions," defined as official citizenship training, journalistic inquiry and exposition, and (from the margins) radical interrogation (48–50). Designed "entirely in relation to its capacity to deliver entertainment" and achieve "competitive strength" in a changing marketplace, reality TV repurposed "documentary as diversion," Corner argued (52). Serious techniques of observation, documentation, investigation, and analytic assessment were fused to the pleasure principles of soap opera and gaming—and focused inward. Cameras and microphones captured the performance of selfhood and everyday life within artificial settings and contrived formulas. For Corner, this interior play with the discourse of the real was symptomatic of a larger trend with troubling implications. Changing the whole point of documentary since the late-1800s, the new reality programming addressed TV viewers as consumers of entertainment instead of citizens. Would purposeful factual forms of television—and democracy itself—survive?

2   The broader institutional context for such concerns was—and is—the waning public service tradition. Public broadcasters such as the British Broadcasting Corporation (BBC) in the United Kingdom and to a lesser extent the Public Broadcasting Service (PBS) in the United States have played a major role in defining and developing television's civic potentialities (Scannell; Ouellette). Envisioning the medium as an instrument of education, not a mover of merchandise, public broadcasters embraced documentary and other nonfiction formats as a dimension of their broader mission to serve and reform citizens so they might better fulfill their national "duties and obligations" (Ang 29). Factual programming high in civic legitimacy but low in "exchange value" (Corner 52) was faithfully circulated as a "cultural resource for citizenship" as well as an instrument for enlightening and guiding national populations (Murdock 186). Since the 1990s, however, this commitment has been subject to reinterpretation and flux. As BBC scholar Georgina Born points out, the "concept and practice" of public broadcasting has been "radically transformed" across Western capitalist democracies by market liberalization, deregulation, digital technologies, and the post-welfare impetus to reform and downsize the public sector in general (Born, "Digitalising" 102; see also *Uncertain Vision*). Faced with budget cuts, entrepreneurial mandates, and heightened competition from commercial channels and new media platforms, many public broadcasters have backed away from traditional public service–inflected programming with limited audience appeal. At a juncture when citizens are increasingly hailed as enterprising subjects and consumers of do-it-yourself lifestyle resources, major European public broadcasters have embraced many of the popular reality conventions critiqued by Corner. The BBC, for example, helped pioneer the hybridization of documentary and entertainment, and is now a major player in the global circulation of unscripted formats. With fewer resources, PBS has also experimented with the popular reality show in an attempt to bolster ratings. With the market logic responsible for "documentary as diversion" operating across public and private channels, the conditions for fostering documentary as a civic project would appear to be closing down.

3   Although the further decline of journalistic and investigative documentary material on television is difficult to dispute, I want to suggest that the medium has not entirely withdrawn from civic engagement since Corner's essay was published—far from it. Many of the functions ascribed to the documentary and the public service tradition in general—particularly citizenship training—have been radically reinterpreted and integrated into popular reality formats. While the specific aims and techniques have changed, reality TV continues to be mobilized as a resource for educating and guiding individuals and populations. If the civic functions of reality entertainment are more difficult to recognize, it is partly because they now operate *within* market imperatives and entertainment formats, but also because prescriptions for what counts as "good citizenship" have changed. Unlike

Source: From *Journal of Popular Film & Television*, vol. 38, no. 2, 2010, pp. 67–71. DOI: 10.1080/01956051.2010.483347. Published by Taylor & Francis Ltd. www.informa world.com

the cultural resources for citizenship provided by the (partly) tax-funded public service tradition, reality TV's civic aims are also diffuse, dispersed, commercial (especially in the United States), and far removed from any direct association with official government policies or agendas.

4   In *Better Living through Reality TV: Television and Post-Welfare Citizenship,* James Hay and I argue that, particularly in the United States, reality TV does not "divert" passive audiences from the serious operations of democracy and public life, as much as it translates broader sociopolitical currents and circulates instructions, resources, and scripts for navigating the changing expectations and demands of citizenship. Many reality programs explicitly address TV viewers as subjects of capacity who exercise freedom and civic agency within (not against) entertainment and consumer culture. This is not particularly surprising, to the extent that reality TV took shape alongside the neoliberal policies and reforms of the 1990s, including the downsizing of the public sector, welfare reform, the outsourcing of state powers and services, the emphasis on consumer choice, and heightened expectations of personal responsibility. Within this context, we suggest, the application of documentary techniques to the demonstration, performance, and testing of self and everyday life makes reality entertainment potentially useful to new strategies of "governing at a distance" that deemphasize public oversight and require enterprising individuals to manage their own health, prosperity, and well being (Rose). From *The Apprentice* to *The Biggest Loser,* reality games command an indirect and unofficial role in constituting, normalizing, educating, and training the self-empowering the citizens beckoned by political authorities. However artificial and staged these programs appear on the surface, they help to constitute powerful truths concerning appropriate forms of civic conduct and problem-solving. To the extent that reality TV's civic functions are also marketable, affective, entertaining, and executed through dispersed partnerships among the television industry, sponsors, nonprofit agencies, celebrities, and TV viewers, they parallel with (and have helped to constitute) the "reinvention of government" in the United States (under Clinton and Bush) as a series of decentralized public-private partnerships on one hand, and self-enterprising citizens on the other (Ouellette and Hay 18–24).

5   Cultural studies scholar Toby Miller once theorized citizenship as an ongoing pull between the "selfish demands" of the consumer economy and the "selfless requirements" of the political order (136). This tension takes on an even greater degree of intensity as the line between consumerism and public politics further collapses, and the requirements of citizenship come to include the actualization of the self through consumer culture and the execution of compassion and ethical responsibility to others. We are expected to actualize and maximize ourselves in a world of goods and perform as virtuous subjects whose voluntary activities in the public world are, as George W. Bush explained during his inaugural address, "just as important as anything government does." In addition to calling on nonprofits, charities, and faith-based organizations to temper gaps left by the downsized welfare state, both the Bush and Clinton administrations promoted volunteerism as a preferred mode of privatized civic empowerment. Reality TV's contributions to what might be called post-welfare civic responsibility manifested within this milieu and are particularly evident in the "do-good" experiments that have flooded the airwaves since the millennium.

6   From *American Idol Gives Back* to *Oprah's Big Give,* a stream of high-profile helping ventures has appeared to redeem reality TV's scandalous associations with bug eating, navel gazing, and bed swapping. These programs (and the marketing discourses that surround them) make explicit claims about reality TV's civic importance. Do-good programs can take on a variety of formats—from the audience participation show to the competition to the makeover—but all reject the earlier notion of public service as education and preparation for participation in the official political processes. Reality entertainment instead intervenes directly in social life, enacting "can do" solutions to largely personalized problems within emotional and often suspenseful formats. The template was established by *Extreme Makeover Home Edition* (2002–present), a successful ABC program that mobilizes private resources (sponsors, experts, nonprofits, volunteers) in a "race against time" to revamp the run-down houses of needy families (see Ouellette and Hay 42–56). The participants are selected by casting agents who find the most "deserving" and marketable stories of hardship from tens of thousands of applications weekly. Products and brand names are woven into the melodramatic interventions, and as many critics have noted, complex issues and socioeconomic inequalities are simplified and downplayed. Still, to dismiss these ventures as trivial or somehow less than "real" would be to overlook their constitutive role as technologies of citizenship, private aid, and volunteerism.

7   On *Home Edition,* for example, TV viewers are "activated" to practice compassionate citizenship by volunteering for nonprofit partners such as Habitat for Humanity and

Home Aid. The ABC website provides direct links, publicity on sponsors and partners, advice on getting involved, and tips from volunteer agencies, thus further stitching the production and active consumption of reality TV into privatized networks of assistance and self-care. While often endorsed by public officials, do-good programs circulate as alternatives to the various ills (inefficiency bureaucracy, dependency, centralized control) ascribed to the welfare state. Needy subjects and their problems provide the raw material for the manufacture of entertainment commodities and circulation of advertising that cannot be zapped. The best and only solution to unmet needs and human hardships (private charity) is offloaded onto the private sector and TV viewers. More explicitly than other reality subgenres, the helping trend acknowledges the limitations of self-maximization and pure market logic—and capitalizes on the result.[1]

8   Do-good television is especially common on commercial channels in the United States. Although European public broadcasters offer reality-based lessons on living, most lack the resources to intervene directly in reality on a philanthropic scale. Why would the television industry take on such projects, given its historical avoidance of public service obligations? For one thing, do-good experiments are fully expected to be profitable. More importantly, they also allow media outlets to cash in on marketing trends such as "citizen branding" and corporate social responsibility (CSR). Because networks are offered as branded interfaces to suggested civic practices, good citizenship—and the ethical surplus it is assumed to generate—can be harnessed to build consumer loyalty. This makes it possible to differentiate brands of television in a cluttered environment and exploit what business historian David Vogel calls the burgeoning "market for virtue." For example, ABC (home to many do-good ventures) brands itself as a Better Community, while the reality-based cable channel Planet Green provides a branded interface to green citizenship and environmental problem-solving. Recently, MTV (owned by Viacom) announced its intention to replace trivial reality entertainment with issue-oriented and civic-minded material. Last year, the wealthy debutantes of *My Sweet Sixteen* were sent to impoverished global locations to improve their character and ethics in a program called *Exiled*. The contestants on the third season of sister channel VH1's *Charm School* are currently being instructed on the importance and procedures of volunteering and performing community service. The change is part of MTV and VH1's efforts to re-brand their programming—and their images—in the

wake of young people's overwhelming support of Barack Obama. Tellingly, *Charm School's* off-screen male narrator not only sounds a lot like Obama, he also punctuates the ongoing question of whether the show can transform party girls into "model citizens" with the slogan, "Yes, we can." As this example attests, the spirit of accountability public sector renewal ushered in by the election can easily be evoked as a new justification for the enactment of philanthropy and self-help—in part because of television's commercial investments in these solutions as branding devices and marketing strategies.

9   If CSR is becoming the new public service, we need critical frameworks for assessing its cultural output. My aim here is not to fault Corner's early evaluation of mainly British reality TV but to begin to unravel the complexities of reality entertainment in its current forms. I have been arguing that any attempt to theorize the civic functions and consequences of popular reality will need to also address its constitutive relationship to changing and colluding dynamics of commerce and governance. It also seems crucial to recognize the residual, emergent, and sometimes contradictory logics operating within the genre. For example, however market-driven and stitched into the circuitry of privatization, do-good reality programming does provide all-too-rare visibility on US television for the poor, the sick, the unemployed, the homeless, and the uninsured. As Anna McCarthy convincingly argues, it bears witness to the "trauma" of everyday life under neoliberal conditions, even as it deflects the causes and commodifies the consequences. Reality TV's helping interventions disrupt the calculated rationality of today's enterprise culture, encouraging visceral and affective reactions to poverty not unlike the industrial slum photographs of Jacob Riis or the gas company–funded social problem documentaries of John Grierson (see Winston). In the wake of the current financial crisis and recession, these dimensions of reality TV may be intensifying—as suggested by the recent Fox program *Secret Millionaire* (2008–09).

10   Developed by the UK company RDF Media, *Secret Millionaire* originated in 2006 on Channel 4, a publicly owned but commercially funded British channel. RDF developed the format for Fox Television last year, using US participants and locations but keeping the generic template and the series name intact. Conceived and marketed as reality entertainment, *Secret Millionaire* combines the techniques of the documentary, the social experiment, and the melodrama. Each week, a designated millionaire goes

"undercover" into impoverished communities to observe hardship firsthand and give away one hundred thousand dollars of his money (tellingly, the millionaire is almost always white and male) while the cameras roll. The benefactors are required to give up their mansions, fancy cars, expensive restaurants, electronic gadgets, and other taken-for-granted consumer privileges and subsist on "welfare wages" like the struggling individuals and families they encounter. They perform hard labour, eat cheap food, live in substandard housing, and interact socially with have-nots, often for the first time in their lives. Along the way, they scout around for people and projects to donate a chunk of their fortune to. Eventually, the expected "reveal" occurs: The millionaire unmasks his true identity and surprises the deserving recipients with a spectacular cash donation.

11   In the debut episode of the US version, a wealthy California lawyer who is also a successful business owner goes to live among the poor with his teenaged son. They perform temporary construction work, reside in a cheap motel, and quickly discover how much they have to learn about the "real world." What is innovative and potentially disruptive about the program is not its authenticity per se (the artificial conditions and staged aspects of other reality shows are readily apparent) but the alternative manner through which the intervention unfolds. In many respects, the formula draws from and exploits dominant representations of socioeconomic inequality: wealth is individualized, and only those "others" who are judged deserving on the basis of uncontrollable circumstances and/or exemplary character are candidates for assistance. Yet, unlike other do-good television programs, the *Secret Millionaire*'s purpose is ultimately *not* to evaluate or make over the poor. Nor is it to shower them with branded consumer goods (courtesy of sponsors) or to enact enterprising solutions to their complex social problems. Its point is to evaluate, educate, guide, enlighten, and transform the richest people in North America. Throughout the debut episode, father and son learn about routine dimensions of socioeconomic difficulties not from experts, but from the experiences and commiserations of people who mistakenly believe they share something in common with the main characters. A middle-aged, uninsured woman who became homeless for a time when she suffered a major back injury provides them breakfast and encouragement. She had subsequently found work at the same construction site and—unaware of their true identity (the cameras are ascribed to a documentary filming)—tries to help the best she can. Another family with a chronically ill child and no health coverage explains the everyday stresses and difficulties of making ends meet and their eventual slide into bankruptcy. While this constitution of the worthy poor is characteristic of other do-good reality experiments, *Secret Millionaire* also identifies the undernourished and collapsing public sector as a structural factor in their situations. TV viewers are allowed to identify with shared problems and difficulties that no television program can fix.

12   The millionaires perform extreme empathy and shock on hearing the hardship stories. As with all reality entertainment, their reactions are shaped and accentuated by casting, editing, camera work, and music. Yet, this artifice does not prevent the series from contributing in potentially useful ways to the "truth" about class and wealth in the current era. In the premiere, father and son undergo a process of self-recognition in which they become increasingly aware of their privilege. They come to see themselves as thoughtless and selfish and are unable to rationalize their "luxury spending" in the midst of unmet human needs and chronic suffering. While this recurring lesson can be easily dismissed as a cultural tempering of growing resentment against the business elites responsible for the current economic crisis, it also reworks the civic logic orienting of much of reality TV by reversing the process and subjects of transformation. Within this context, the millionaire's cash donation can be interpreted as a technology of private aid, but it can also be seen as enacting a reevaluation (if not quite a redistribution) of the allotment of resources and wealth in the United States. The lack of product placements in *Secret Millionaire* reinforces this possibility—not only because a consumer address is contained in the commercial breaks, but because the problem of uneven wealth cannot be resolved by a trip to Disney World or the installation of a free washing machine. Alas, this lack of marketability will undoubtedly keep the civic possibilities opened up by programs such as *Secret Millionaire* in check. Such are the limits of reality TV in its current form.

Note

1. For a more detailed analysis of the governmental dimensions of do-good TV (from which this article draws), see Ouellette and Hay ch. 1, "Charity TV: Privatizing Care, Mobilizing Compassion."

Works Cited

Ang, Ien. *Desperately Seeking the Audience*. London: Routledge, 2001. Print.

Born, Georgina. "Digitalising Democracy." *What Can Be Done? Making the Media and Politics Better*. Ed. J. Lloyd and J. Seaton. Oxford: Blackwell, 2006. 102–23. Print.

———. *Uncertain Vision: Birt, Dyke and the Reinvention of the BBC*. London: Secker and Warburg, 2004. Print.

Bush, George W. "Inaugural Address." *American Rhetoric Online Speech Bank* 20 Jan. 2001. Web. 11 May 2009. www.americanrhetoric.com/speeches/ gwbfirstinaugural.htm.

Corner, John. "Performing the Real: Documentary Diversions." *Television and New Media* 3 (2002): 255–69. Rpt. in *Reality TV: Remaking Television Culture*. Ed. Susan Murray and Laurie Ouellette. New York: NYU Press, 2009. 44–64. Print.

McCarthy, Anna. "Reality Television: A Neoliberal Theater of Suffering." *Social Text* 25.4 (2007): 17–41. Print.

Miller, Toby. *The Well-Tempered Self: Citizenship, Culture and the Postmodern Subject*. Baltimore: Johns Hopkins UP, 1993. Print.

Murdock, Graham. "Public Broadcasting and Democratic Culture: Consumers, Citizens and Communards." *A Companion to Television*. Ed. Janet Wasco. Malden: Blackwell, 2005. 174–98. Print.

Ouellette, Laurie. *Viewers Like You? How Public Television Failed the People*. New York: Columbia UP, 2002. Print.

Ouellette, Laurie, and James Hay. *Better Living through Reality TV: Television and Post-Welfare Citizenship*. Malden: Black-well, 2008. Print.

Rose, Nikolas. "Governing 'Advanced' Liberal Democracies." *Foucault and Political Reason: Liberalism, Neoliberalism and Rationalities of Government*. Ed. Andrew Barry, Thomas Osbourne, and Nikolas Rose. Chicago and London: University of Chicago Press, 1996. 37–64.

Scannell, Paddy. "Public Service Broadcasting and Modern Public Life." *Media Culture Society* 11 (1989): 135–66. Print.

Vogel, David. *The Market for Virtue: The Potential and Limits of Corporate Social Responsibility*. Washington, DC: Brookings Institute Press, 2005. Print.

Winston, Brian. *Claiming the Real: Documentary, Grierson and Beyond*. New York: Palgrave Macmillian, 2008. Print.

Key and challenging words

contrived, symptomatic, entrepreneurial, juncture, bolster, milieu, mobilize, constitutive, philanthropic, burgeoning, attest, collude, residual, visceral, benefactor, commiseration

Questions

1. (a) In two sentences, summarize the views of John Corner as expressed in paragraph 1; *or* (b) In two sentences, summarize the abstract of John Corner's article "Performing the Real: Documentary Diversions" (*Television and New Media* 3.3 [2002]: 255–69).

2. Explain the different uses for quotation marks around the following words in paragraph 1: "unscripted," "civic functions," and "entirely in relation to its capacity to deliver entertainment."

3. Explain how the view of public broadcasting today differs from the traditional view. What accounts for these differences?

4. Type A essays often make connections between forms of art or entertainment and the "real" world, claiming universal relevance for such art. Show how Ouellette connects reality TV in the 1990s to political, social, or economic forces at play during that time (see paragraph 4).

5. (a) Analyze Ouellette's use of synonyms, rephrasing, repetition, and sentence transitions to contribute to coherence in paragraph 5; (b) Analyze the effectiveness of paragraph transitions by looking at two of the following, considering how the last sentence of the earlier paragraph is connected to the first sentence of the following one: paragraphs 5–6, 6–7, 7–8, 8–9, or 9–10.

6. What is *branding* (paragraph 8)? Explain how branding can be applied to "do-good television" and why it is important, according to the author.

7. (a) In one paragraph, explain why *Secret Millionaire* (paragraphs 10–12) is a good illustration of what Ouellette discusses in the previous paragraphs; (b) Compare *Secret Millionaire* with other "do-good" reality shows discussed in the article, noting at least one similarity and difference.

8. Analyze the conclusion of the essay for its effectiveness.

Post-reading

1. *Collaborative activity:* (a) Discuss or debate the validity of Ouellette's main points about reality TV today. Refer to specific reality shows you have watched or are familiar with; *or* (b) Discuss or debate the concept of "reality" TV. How real is reality TV?

2. Access the home page of one of the TV shows mentioned in the article, such as *Secret Millionaire,* or another "do-good" reality TV show. Is there a summary of the show itself (rather than episode summaries)? Does the description of the show stress what Ouellette considers its citizenship function? Summarize the website's description of the show and its function or purpose.

3. Find an argumentative essay on some aspect of reality TV in a popular (non-academic) source, like a magazine or a blog. Analyze the argument, first summarizing its thesis and main points, and then evaluating the effectiveness of the argument.

Jurassic World *and Procreation Anxiety*

Richard Dyer

(3,201 words)

> ### Pre-reading
>
> 1. Read at least two reviews of *Jurassic World* in order to determine the film's connection to films in the *Jurassic Park* series as well as its reception by critics and viewers.
> 2. Who is Richard Dyer? Using reliable sources, write a one-paragraph summary of Dyer's career, including his areas of specialty and contributions to his fields of study, such as his major publications.

1   *Jurassic World* is anticapitalist, antimanagerialism, and anti-GM; it is also antifeminist, racist, species-ist, and decidedly not queer.[1] It is fun entertainment, with its thrills always accompanied by an immediate sense that all will be well. What underpins all this is the film's anxiety and ultimate reassurance about ideal reproduction, which has to be imagined as white, middle-class, heterosexual, male-led, and human.

2   It is not necessary to see the film to know that it is about a zoo-cum–theme park featuring prehistoric creatures, some of which get loose and create havoc until they are beaten back. Folded into this basic situation are two stories that offer a way into the wider spectacle: one tracks two brothers, Zach and Gray, who visit, and get lost in, the park; the other tracks two of the park's employees, Claire Dearing (Bryce Dallas Howard) and Owen Grady (Chris Pratt), who by the end the film become a couple; the two stories are connected because Claire is the brothers' aunt. All of these protagonists play a role in defeating the creatures run amok.

3   Procreation anxiety runs through both the story of the prehistoric creatures and that of the fraternal and heterosexual couples. The most dangerous creature is not just a pre-historic giant generated from dormant biological material, as are most of the other creatures and as was the case in the *Jurassic Park* films; rather, it is an "Indominus rex," a laboratory-produced combination of different genetic elements that have made it not only huge and powerful but also intelligent and predatory. This monstrous product of improper biological procreation is balanced by the two human dangers to the ideal vehicle of reproduction: the divorcing family (Zach tells Gray that most of the families he knows have separating parents) and the independent woman (Claire early on dismisses any idea that she wants children). The defeat of Indominus rex is swiftly followed by the arrival of Zach and Gray's mother and father, come to find them at the end of the mayhem, and by Claire and Owen's walking off together, "to survive" as he puts it, which surely implies their participation in the survival of the species.

4   This concern with reproduction makes *Jurassic World* progressive in some ways, but decidedly regressive in others. Its anticapitalism is based on a perception of the logic of capitalism being the pursuit of profit at whatever cost. In the *Jurassic Park* films there was a sense of capitalism enabling the pursuit—albeit foolhardy and hubristic—of science and wonder, a notion delivered to the audience through Richard Attenborough's warmly visionary performance as developer John Hammond (perhaps borrowing from his brother David's famed television promotion of the wonders of nature). This figure is reduced in *Jurassic World* to a maverick owner, Simon Masrani, for whom the park is a rich man's plaything, where he is not to be troubled with money matters. In the actual development and running of Jurassic World, however, money is the point, science and wonder merely the means to generate profit. This imperative is presented in the film itself by Claire, in practically Marxist terms: the necessity for profit to continue to expand by stimulating new demand based on ever more singular and spectacular product.

5   The director of *Jurassic World*, Colin Trevorrow, has couched the critique in more moralistic terms, identifying the Indominus rex as a consequence of "our greed and our desire for profit" which feeds off a constant desire for more "wonder . . . bigger, faster, louder, better," that is, the inherent greed of corporations is matched by the pathological needs of their consumers.[2] Monstrosities like Indominus rex, then, are a logical outcome of capitalism, both in their very existence and in the reluctance of capitalist organisations to curb their excesses. For example, Claire runs the park, yet takes quite some time to recognize the need to prioritize immediate human survival over the park's function as a business enterprise.

6   Of course, the film itself is founded on exactly that same promise of "bigger, faster, louder, better." Externally this promise is manifested in its relation not just to the *Jurassic* franchise but to the surrounding Hollywood narrative of ever-improving special effects. Internally, within the film, alongside Indominus rex, there's a swarm of pterosaurs breaking out of their aviary, picking off visitors and playing catch with them, as well as the behemoth/leviathan mosasaurus, a humungous sea creature out-mobying Moby Dick. The behemoth's size is made all the more breathtaking by being introduced in the context of a SeaWorld-style attraction, leaping out of the water to snaffle tidbits hung above it, but later grabbing a pterosaur with its human prey in its beak, and later still (spoiler alert) the Indominus itself.

7   Claire's reluctance to close down the park is the culmination of her parroting management-speak throughout the first part of the film. The creatures are "assets," security is about "asset containment," the park needs "the wow factor," Owen is employed to work with velociraptors to "evaluate patterns of vulnerability," the creatures' breakout is "a containment anomaly," and so on. I often wonder, when faced in life with the implacable mendacity and vacuousness of managerialism, whether I find it more appalling that managers actually believe what they say—or that they don't, and are just deeply cynical. Bryce Dallas Howard's performance suggests something even more disturbing: that questions of belief or cynicism don't even come into it, that the managers are on automatic pilot, perfectly turned-out Stepford people.

8   Indominus rex is referred to as a "genetically modified hybrid." Since the United States does not yet exhibit the anxiety about GM crops that is seen in Europe, where the sobriquet of "Frankenstein foods" has proved hard to dislodge from public consciousness, perhaps it is a stretch to suggest the film is altogether anti-GM. However, the notion of secretive meddling with nature, with no thought for the consequences, is deeply rooted in US science fiction. Although he is the sole character carried over from the *Jurassic Park* series, the chief geneticist, Dr. Henry Wu, is undeveloped in this film and shows no sign of conscience or remorse. When disaster strikes, he busies himself putting engineered embryos into safe containers, aided by Vic

Hoskins, nominally head of security but actually associated with the shadowy InGen organization, the very model of the military-industrial complex, which seeks to use the products of Wu's genetic engineering as weapons of war or other unimaginable forms of sinister social control.

9   Claire is made to bear the brunt of the film's progressive critiques, even though the actual, dangerously powerful figures are all male: the owner, the scientist, the military man. As the leading lady, she is central to the film and its vestigial romcom elements (she and Owen, ex-lovers, are at first antagonistic, then in each other's arms and finally walking off together to coupledom). She is also pivotal to the film's gender politics. Her immaculately groomed robotic presence furthers the goals of capitalism, managerialism, and genetic engineering and also underlines the distance of the independent, career woman from her proper role in reproduction. Not only does she explicitly reject the prospect of motherhood, she is even a lousy aunt, alternately forgetting how much time has passed since she saw her nephews and dispatching them straightaway to her assistant, Zara. The latter is no better: Zara is too busy with her cell phone to keep an eye on the boys, so they sneak off and into danger. It is Zara who becomes the human prey of the pterosaur, snatched by the mosasaurus; she's the genre's usual and useful snotty Brit, there to provide the spectacle of human sacrifice. And being a Brit, she allows the film to avoid the common (though increasingly politically incorrect) trope of offing the minor-character-of-color.

10   Claire in turn has to learn to be more like a man. The right kind of man. A joke is made of her becoming a macho action man like Owen, when, in response to his scorn of her not being much use to pursue the Indominus "in those ridiculous shoes," she adjusts her clothes to make them more practical. He's not convinced that such a cosmetic change will really hack it, but she proves able to handle herself almost as well as he can, even shooting dead a pterosaur pecking away at him. And in those shoes. The first shot of her starts from the shoes and cranes up, and the shoes are repeatedly shown in close-up before and after she becomes an action woman. When he holds his hand out to help her run away from one of the creatures, she bolts past him, high heels or not, and he does a double-take in surprise and admiration. But she has more to learn from him than traditional macho values. She has to learn ethics, to consider the wellbeing of people and animals above the profit motive.

11   Owen is the right kind of man par excellence. Partly by virtue of cinematography (elevator doors slide open to reveal him lolling center screen unfeasibly buff beneath the clothes), partly by virtue of the backstory of Chris Pratt's makeover from lovable chubby to stubbled hunk, he is the contemporary beau ideal of masculinity. Like any action hero, he can handle himself in a difficult situation, but he also has the ideal relationship to nature.

12   Owen lives on the island where the park is situated, but by himself, far from any other human habitation. When Claire goes to fetch him to take a look at the security of the Indominus rex enclosure, she finds him mending a motorcycle, that curious American emblem of the natural male's on-the-road freedom. He is at one with nature, rejecting Claire's view that the park's creatures are not real animals. He caresses raptors, gives comfort to dying dinosaurs.

13   However, he is also in charge of nature. His first scene has him training four velociraptors, later explaining that they have learned to treat him as their alpha male. Toward the end of the film, the raptors are called on to attack the rampaging Indominus. When it turns out that they share some DNA with the Indominus and begin to side with it against the humans, Owen reasserts his authority so that they turn on the Indominus. He may be with the animals, but he is in a commanding relationship to them (like Tarzan) and able to use them against each other in the interests of humanity.

14   Naturally, Owen and Claire are white, as are Zach and Gray and their parents. The proper whiteness affirmed at the end of the film is perhaps lightly reinforced by an almost daring moment earlier in the film, when adolescent Zach, always eyeing the girls, flirts with a young black woman, until interrupted by pre-adolescent Gray, who is worrying about the future of their parents' marriage. The black girl, however, disappears from the film after this moment in typical mainstream-movie fashion. The casting of the secondary parts in *Jurassic World* is nominally racially inclusive but the roles ensure that they remain subordinate. The only really dangerous man, Vic Hoskins, played by Vincent D'Onofrio, is white. The chief scientist is Chinese-American (B.D. Wong), the park owner Indian (Muslim actor Irrfan Khan). Barry, one of Owen's helpers with the raptors, is played by black French actor Omar Sy, but if not recognized he could be taken for a native of another island, with almost nothing to do except to be rescued at one point from the Indominus. If the casting was not explicitly intended as racist stereotyping, it certainly allows for it: the inscrutable Oriental, the playboy Indian, the good but incapable Black.

15   Khan and Sy are major stars in their countries of origin.[3] Casting them at once adds to the appeal of *Jurassic World* in the Indian and French (and perhaps, given Sy's parentage, African) markets, while also acknowledging a degree of global and specifically American recognition too. This inclusive but opportunistic casting goes hand in hand with their characters' extreme marginalization, as do the self-inflicted death of Khan's character (by recklessly taking the controls of a helicopter and crashing into the pterosaur aviary) and Sy/Barry's amiable helplessness. Their marginality affirms Hollywood's place at the top of the hierarchy of global cinema (somewhat misleadingly) while also suggesting that the fittest survivors to further the human race are not only white and gender- and sexuality-conformist but also American.

16   At the end of the film, all creatures quelled, Owen and Claire come together in silhouette against a shaft of light that is shining into a hangar where the survivors are all being attended to. There is a geometrically precise corridor separating the two crowds of wounded and worried victims and customers, as if it is the shaft of light itself that separates them. Then Owen and Claire walk up this corridor of light: they are the future, the white woman conscripted into the couple on the white man's terms.

17   Also present are Zach and Gray's parents, Karen and Scott, earlier revealed (in Gray's comment to Zach) to be on the verge of divorce. The strong bond finally forged between Owen and Claire stands in stark contrast to the weak one linking Karen and Scott, with him constantly in the background and her emoting in the foreground (and so overwrought when the boys are away that she keeps people waiting at a meeting at her workplace). They endanger proper reproduction, both by failing to provide the security necessary for the boys' growth and by threatening not to stick together. At the end, it's no longer clear that they will divorce: they are together and present for their sons at the end, with Owen and Claire on hand as the very model of what the ideal reproducing couple should be. This finale has already been anticipated in the archetypal grouping of Owen, Claire, and the boys: first, with Owen standing in front of them, stretching his arms out in symbolic protection, then standing behind them, the reassuring masculine ground for the display of woman and children.

18   Claire and Owen are pivotal to the film's entertainment value. All films are posited on reassurance: they are after all "only" films, and entertainment films must guarantee a happy ending. That is their presumed contract with the audience. However, some horror, action, and thrill films take the implicit promise of reassurance as an occasion to give their audience the possibility of safely experiencing and enjoying grimness, terror, pain, and an abandonment of secure coordinates, whereas others—James Bond, buddy franchises—maintain a jaunty, often humorous tone throughout. While *Jurassic World* may occasionally touch on terror for some audience members (one couple with a little girl hurried out before the end of a screening I attended), it mostly maintains a sense of fun, including a thread of verbal and visual jokes: Owen and Claire and the shoes; the boys' mother advising them merely to run from any marauding creatures and Claire similarly suggesting they hold hands for safety; self-reflexive in-jokes such as Gray looking at stills from the 1925 *The Lost World* on a ViewFinder, a guy wearing a *Jurassic Park* T-shirt bought on eBay and the boys escaping in an abandoned Jurassic Park jeep.[4]

19   The sense of fun is achieved partly through the very setting of the film, which combines two of the major forms of fun-for-a-day attractions, the zoo and the theme park. It is the former that is crucial here, for in many ways it embodies the human image of the animal world and humankind's relationship to it. While it may seem presumptuous, or just a sign of profit-driven escalation, to reclassify this Jurassic Park as a world, it is also consonant with the way that people have made of the actual world a zoo, complete with pens, fields, pastures, parks (local, national, safari), reserves, and designated wildernesses, a world that ensures human animals are separate from and in control of all other animals. True, as in *Jurassic World*, the animals may occasionally break out, but an escape only affirms how strong and reliable the system is most of the time. What the image of the world as zoo suppresses, of course, is the slaughter of so many other animals for food, adornment, aphrodisiacs, and sport, and the destruction of habitats that threatens the survival of most animals in the wild. Instead this is a world in which animals are petted, give rides, and above all provide literally spectacular entertainment.

20   As Owen embodies this ideal of the symbiotic relationship of human to all other animals, caring and at one with them and yet separate and in charge, Claire as his ideal mate learns to be the same. Their relationship, in its lovable romcom sparring, gags about Claire's clothes, and Owen's almost ridiculous hunkiness, is a major source of the film's sense of fun. Plus, they save the boys. And, looking to the future, they provide an impending model of ideal reproduction to ensure that, even if this particular unnatural,

genetically messed-up zoo world fails, Claire and Owen will continue to produce the world as a white, straight, American zoo for the future.

21   Perhaps there is just a hint of strain in this affirmation. The film's plotting is elliptical, vague about time and space and reliant on implausible coincidences and rushed explanations, no doubt assuming the thrill and threat of the stunningly realized creatures will carry it along. However, although less busy and physiologically impossible than much CGI cinema, *Jurassic World* is still careless about the coordinates of space and time, so that the happy ending is more a product of sleights of hand than resourcefulness or even luck. More to the point, the final shot of Claire and Owen has a quality of excessiveness to it: the forced abstraction of their coming together in silhouette, the unnaturalness of the shaft of light, the portentousness of Owen's manly words "To survive" and the silhouette-creating walk toward the light.

22   There is here a shard of uncertainty about whether the world as zoo really has a future, or the world with humans in it at all, and thus whether the underlying reassurance offered by the film really has much substance. The last shot of the film is not actually that of Owen and Claire walking to-ward the light, but one where the camera skims across the park. It has done so several spectacular times before, to lay out for the viewer the awesome scale of the place and the crowds visiting it. This time, however, the park is empty of humans, and the camera comes to rest on the Tyrannosaurus rex that earlier attacked the Indominus and thus saved Owen, Claire, and the boys and in effect most of the visitors to the park too. The Tyrannosaurus was engineered back to life but is not genetically modified, and unlike the Indominus, it's a male.

23   This, then, is a final shot that signifies an end to meddling and a start to leaving the creatures in peace on their island. It also reaffirms the rightful masculine possession of territory. But perhaps it also hints at the real future: not the bright light embracing Claire and Owen as they go forth to multiply, but one without humans at all, not just in a Jurassic World but in the darker, off-screen world itself.

Notes

1. GM is common shorthand for "genetically modified" foods or, in this case, animals.
2. Interview quotations are from: AFP, "How the Dinosaurs in *Jurassic World* Came to Life," *News Corp Australia*, June 10, 2015, at www.news.com. au/technology/innovation/how-the-dinosaurs-in-jurassic-world-came-to-life/story-fnjwucti-122739 1097262; and Kabita Maharana, "*Jurassic World*: Synthetic Indominus Rex Embodies the Worst Human Tendencies Teases Director Colin Trevorrow," *International Business Times*, "IBT Media," May 26, 2015, at www.ibtimes.co.uk/jurassic- world-synthetic-indominus-rex-embodies-worst-human-tendencies-teases-director-colin-1502955.
3. Hindi cinema is one of the largest in the world and Khan also had international success with the British-made, Hindi-language, Indian-set film *The Warrior* (Asif Kapadia, 2001) and in an impressive secondary role in *Slumdog Millionaire* (Danny Boyle, 2008). Sy is best known as a comedian in France but has also had a considerable international art house presence thanks to the success of a pair of films by Olivier Nakache and Eric Toledano: *The Intouchables* (2011), especially, and *Samba* (2014).
4. The second Jurassic film was of course called *The Lost World* in homage to this film, while the ViewMaster was an early stereoscopic device anticipating the immersive thrills of films like *Jurassic World*.

Key and challenging words

regressive, hubristic, maverick, behemoth, implacable, mendacity, vacuousness, sobriquet, vestigial, rampage, nominal, inscrutable, conscript, pivotal, jaunty, presumptuous, consonant, elliptical, portentousness

Questions

1. How would you describe the author's style in paragraph 1? (Style could be shown through word choice, sentence structure, tone, and other linguistic/rhetorical features.)

2. After reading the first three paragraphs, (a) identify the author's thesis; (b) explain the purpose of paragraph 2; (c) briefly analyze the author's support for the topic sentence in paragraph 3.

3. Analyze Dyer's use of the comparison–contrast rhetorical pattern in paragraph 4 for its effectiveness, explaining what it contributes to the essay as a whole.

4. In paragraph 6, identify the following: (a) one example of jargon, (b) two examples of informal diction, (c) one example of a neologism (made-up word), and (d) one example of an allusion. In paragraph 9, identify (a) one example of jargon, (b) two examples of informal diction.

5. Discuss the author's use of the first-person point of view (POV) in paragraphs 7 and 17. In your answer, address its purpose in each paragraph and what it contributes to the paragraph. Do you believe that this POV is justified? Why or why not?

6. Analyze Dyer's tone in paragraphs 13 and 14. Tone can be defined as the writer's attitude toward his/her subject and may be shown through language (e.g., playful, humorous, sarcastic, condemnatory, reflective, solemn tone). Point to specific words to support your claim.

7. Analyze the author's argument in the final three paragraphs of the essay. Show how the essay's conclusion is connected to the preceding paragraphs. Do you find it convincing and effective? Justify your answer by referring to Dyer's claims and their support in these paragraphs.

Post-reading

1. Discuss "*Jurassic World* and Procreation Anxiety" as a Type A essay, noting at least two ways in which it conforms to the conventions of this kind of essay and at least two ways in which it differs from it. (See p. 23 in Chapter 3, and Appendix B.)

2. Authors of Type A essays draw conclusions (i.e., make inferences) about the texts they study. Thus, these inferences often arise from the evidence they find in the texts, along with their knowledge of other texts. More broadly, they use critical thinking to make inferences (see Inferences and Critical Thinking in Chapter 4, p. 36). Find two inferences that Dyer makes and explore their validity using the text as well as your critical thinking skills. (One early example of an inference occurs in paragraph 3, where Dyer claims that Owen's invitation to Claire to go with him "to survive" implies the survival of the species [i.e., procreation]).

Self-reported Food Skills of University Students

Courtney K. Wilson, June I. Matthews, Jamie A. Seabrook, and Paula D.N. Dworatzek
(3,842)

Pre-reading

1. *Collaborative activity:* In groups of three or four, discuss the importance of a healthy diet while at university. Possible prompts could include these or other questions related to diet and acquiring food skills: How would you assess your eating habits in a typical week at university? Compared to other activities at university, such as academics, athletics and clubs, and social life, how important is a healthy diet? What are the main obstacles for you and/or your peers in achieving a healthy diet? How could these be overcome?

2. Using the self-evaluation scale referred to in the essay, evaluate your food skills and weekly meal preparation patterns. (See "Methods, Study Design" in the reading for the seven individual food skills and rating scale.) Calculate your Total Food Skills Score out of 700.

Abstract

University students experience a life transition that often results in poor dietary behaviors and weight gain. Adequate food skills may improve diet quality and prevent chronic disease. Research is limited, however, on students' food skills and food-related behaviors. The objective of this study was to assess whether self-perceived food skills and related behaviors of students at a large, Canadian university differed based on sex, having taken a Food and Nutrition (FN) course, and living conditions, using a cross-sectional online survey. The response rate was 21.9% (n = 6638). Students (age, M ± SD 19.9 ± 2.1 years) self-reported their abilities for seven distinct food skills. Students rated (out of 100) their ability for some skills significantly higher than others (79.7 ± 20.9 for peeling, chopping, and slicing vs. 56.1 ± 29.1 for weekly meal planning; p < 0.001). Females reported higher total food skill scores than males (487.0 ± 141.1 out of a possible 700 vs. 441.9 ± 151.8, respectively; p < 0.001). Respondents who had taken a FN course reported higher total food skill scores than those who had not (494.9 ± 137.0 vs. 461.9 ± 149.2; p < 0.001). Students who resided away from their parental home for longer than one year reported significantly higher total food skill scores than those living away for one year or less (488.9 ± 134.6 vs. 443.3 ± 153.0, respectively; p < 0.001). Results indicate that students' self-perceived food skills vary by sex, FN education, and living condition. Higher abilities were reported for mechanical food skills; conceptual skills were significantly lower. These results may assist in effectively targeting this population with nutrition education interventions.

---

1. Background

1 Many university students experience rapid weight gain, which is often related to poor dietary behaviors (Vella-Zarb & Elgar, 2009). Although students may intend to make healthy food choices, many lack the knowledge and self-efficacy to do so (Matthews, Doerr, & Dworatzek, 2016). Commonly-cited barriers to healthy eating in the student population include personal preferences (e.g., taste), self-discipline, finances, time, and convenience; however, academic demands and social and physical environments may create additional obstacles (Chenhall, 2010; Deliens, Clarys, De Bourdeaudhuij, & Deforche, 2014). Low self-efficacy and the perception of having

inadequate food skills also pose barriers to meal preparation (Health Canada, 2015; Larson, Perry, Story, & Neumark-Sztainer, 2006) and healthy food choices, resulting in an increased tendency to choose convenience foods (Chenhall, 2010). Regular consumption of ready-made convenience foods contributes to weight gain (Nelson, Story, Larson, Neumark-Sztainer, & Lytle, 2008; Vella-Zarb & Elgar, 2009), putting students at an increased risk of overweight and obesity in adulthood (Guo, Wu, Chumlea, & Roche, 2002). Since 1985, the prevalence of obesity in Canadian adults increased from 6.1% to 18.3% and is predicted to rise to 21% by 2019 (Twells, Gregory, Reddigan, & Midodzi, 2014). Food and nutrition (FN) education, ranging from practical cooking skills to critical assessment of nutrition information, could enable young adults to develop and sustain healthy eating behaviors, potentially addressing both the obesity epidemic and the "culinary deskilling" that is purported to have occurred over the same timeline (Chenhall, 2010; Nelson, Corbin, & Nickols-Richardson, 2013; Slater, 2013). Almost 2 million Canadians are enrolled in post-secondary education (Statistics Canada, 2013), representing a significant population for health promotion interventions, particularly since food preparation in this age group is associated with better diet quality (Larson et al., 2006).

2 There is a paucity of data on food skills among youth (Desjardins & Azevedo, 2013; Larson et al., 2006; Waterloo Region, 2010), in part due to a lack of standardized definitions and measurement tools (Chenhall, 2010; Desjardins & Azevedo, 2013; SafeFood, 2014). Food skills typically include planning, preparation, and storage, and each of these categories may include technical, mechanical, conceptual, and/or perceptual aspects (Chenhall, 2010; Waterloo Region, 2010). For example, doubling a recipe (preparation) would require technical skills to calculate ingredient amounts, mechanical skills to combine ingredients, conceptual skills to decide required yield, and perceptual skills to choose appropriately-sized mixing bowls. Self-assessment of personal food skills likely reflects a combination of a person's skills and self-efficacy towards meal planning, preparation, and storage (Waterloo Region, 2010). Understanding students' food skills abilities may help in developing effective nutrition education interventions.

3 The purpose of this study was to assess self-perceived food skills of undergraduate students at a large, urban, Canadian university. Differences in self-reported food skills were compared by sex, having taken a secondary or

postsecondary school FN course, living conditions, and years living away from their parental home.

2. Methods

2.1 Study Design

4   In 2012, using FluidSurveys Online Survey Software (Fluidware, Inc., Ottawa, ON, 2012), an original survey assessed the self-perceived food skills and weekly meal preparation patterns of students attending Western University in London, Ontario, Canada. Students reported their abilities for seven individual food skills (peeling, chopping, slicing; cooking dishes at same time; making meals with available ingredients; cooking in batches for future use; making a recipe healthier; choosing a spice/herb; and planning weekly meals) on an 11-point scale from 0 (no skill) to 100 (very good). Additionally, students' food skill scores were summed for a Total Food Skill Score (TFSS) out of 700. The survey contained 67 items, predominantly closed-ended, with categorical and scaled response categories. Questions related to students' knowledge of dietary recommendations, intentions, and coping self-efficacy have been reported elsewhere (Matthews et al., 2016). Survey questions were rooted in Social Cognitive Theory, as it aims to address the relationship between environmental, personal, and behavioral factors (including skills and self-efficacy) and how these may influence human behavior (Bandura, 2004). Survey items were informed by a review of the related literature, expert opinion, and evidence- and practice-based indicators. The survey was pilot tested with a group of undergraduate students who were not included in the final sample (Matthews et al., 2016). All 30,310 undergraduate students were invited to complete the survey. Recruitment involved an initial email invitation, followed by weekly reminder emails over the next two weeks (Dillman, 1978). The Non-Medical Research Ethics Board at Western University approved the study. Completion of the survey implied consent.

2.2 Statistical Analyses

5   Data were analyzed using SPSS Version 22.0 (IBM Corp., Armonk, NY). Means and standard deviations (M ± SD) were calculated for continuous variables; percentages for categorical outcomes. An independent samples t-test was used to compare mean differences between two groups, and a chi-square test assessed differences in proportions between categorical variables. Spearman's rank correlation coefficient assessed the strength of the relationship between students' current meal preparation and parental meal preparation habits. Correlation values were categorized as follows: 0.75 or greater was very good to excellent; 0.50–0.75 was moderate to good; 0.25–0.49 was fair; and 0.25 or less was indicative of little to no correlation (Colton, 1974). Students living in campus residences or with family were collapsed into one group because students in residence must purchase a meal plan and typically do not prepare their own meals and, similarly, students living with family may have most meals prepared for them. Repeated measures analysis of variance (RMANOVA) were conducted for food skills, as each subject reported seven food skills that would be related to each other. Additionally, RMANOVA with post-hoc analyses, were also computed for sex, FN course, living condition, and years away from parental home. Given the large sample size, $p \leq 0.01$ was considered statistically significant.

3. Results

6   The first email invitation garnered 4096 responses, with subsequent emails increasing responses to 7132. After removing respondents who followed the survey link but did not complete any questions, the final sample included 6638 respondents for a response rate of 21.9%. Final sample sizes vary by question as not all respondents answered all questions. Demographic characteristics of the sample are included in Table 1. The sample distribution by faculty/program of study/major (data not displayed) was representative of the Western University population; however, a higher percentage of female students completed the survey than was representative of the overall student population at the time of the survey (i.e., 56% female and 44% male students) (Western Office of Institutional Planning & Budgeting, 2014). The majority (65.2%) of respondents were 19–24 years of age, while 27.4% were 18 years of age or younger. The mean respondent age was 19.9 ± 2.1 years. This is representative of the typical Canadian postsecondary population (Statistics Canada, 2010).

3.1 Overall Cooking Ability

7   Given three categories of overall cooking ability, 62.5% of respondents reported they were comfortable preparing meals from basic ingredients, utilizing a recipe if required. Fewer (31.5%) reported only being able to put together ready-made ingredients to prepare a complete meal. Six percent reported having limited-to-no cooking ability. When analyzed by sex, 4.7% of female respondents

claimed to have limited-to-no cooking ability compared to 8.0% of males (Chi-square (2, 5794) = 30.35, p < 0.001). Females also rated themselves as being able to prepare meals from basic ingredients more often than males (64.8% and 58.9%; Chi-square (2, 5794) = 30.35, respectively; p < 0.001).

8   First-year students made up 53.5% of all students who indicated having limited-to-no cooking ability. Similarly, those living in residence/with family accounted for the majority (74.1%) with limited-to-no cooking abilities. Only 55.5% of students living in residence and 59.7% living with family reported being able to cook and prepare meals from basic ingredients, compared to 67.6% of those living independently (Chi-square (6, 5801) = 218.42, p < 0.001; Fig. 1).

3.2 Food Skills

9   Technical or mechanical skills that may be considered less complex, e.g., "peeling, chopping, or slicing", had the highest scores (79.7 ± 20.9), whereas those that may be considered more conceptual, e.g., "meal planning for the week's meals", were significantly lower (56.1 ± 29.1; F (5.3, 32,249) = 1119, p < 0.001; Fig. 2). For each food skill, females reported higher scores than males (F (5.3, 30,132) = 741, p < 0.001; Fig. 2). Only 38.8% of respondents reported having taken a FN course (42.0% females and 30.1% males; Table 1), and these respondents reported higher food skills than those who had not (F (5.3, 30,209) = 986, p = 0.002; Fig. 2).

10   First-year students reported significantly lower perceived food skill scores than all other students (p <0.001; Table 2), with the most notable differences for conceptual and perceptual skills (e.g., batch cooking for later use and healthy recipe adjustments). Furthermore, when taking into account living condition, students who lived in residence or with parents (dependent living) had lower self-reported food skills than those living independently (F (5.3, 30,091) = 1053, p < 0.001; Fig. 2). Students living away from home for one year or less reported lower food skill scores than students who had lived away from home for more than one year (F (5.3, 26,974) = 951, p < 0.001; Fig. 2). The majority (81.6%) of students reported access to kitchen facilities; however, when students in residence were eliminated from the analysis, 95.9% of students living off-campus reported having access. Students with access to kitchen facilities reported higher food skills compared to those without access (p < 0.001), with the greatest differences noted for batch cooking and making healthy recipe adjustments (data not displayed).

Table 1   Demographic data of Canadian university students (n = 6638) responding to an online survey regarding their self-perceived food skills and food-related behaviors.

Characteristics	% (n)
Age (n = 5838)	
< 18 years	27.4 (1598)
19–24 years	65.2 (3809)
> 24 years	7.4 (431)
Sex (n = 5809)	
Male	27.1 (1572)
Female[a]	72.9 (4237)
Years of Postsecondary Education (n = 5618)	
1	30.2 (1695)
2	23.5 (1321)
3	21.0 (1182)
4	15.9 (896)
5 or more	9.3 (524)
Years Away from Parental Home (n = 5194)	
≤ 1 year	49.1 (2552)
≥ 1 year	50.9 (2642)
Living Conditions (n = 5816)	
University residence	25.6 (1487)
With parents/family	17.1 (995)
Roommates/on own in a house or apartment	51.4 (2991)
With spouse in a house or apartment	5.9 (343)
Food or Nutrition Course Taken (n = 5829)	
Yes	38.8 (2259)
No	61.2 (3570)
International Student Status (n = 5814)	
Yes	7.6 (442)
No	92.4 (5372)
Access to Kitchen Facilities (n = 5815)	
Yes	81.6 (4747)[b]
No	18.4 (1068)

[a] Sample distribution includes a higher percentage of females than is representative of the overall student population at Western University (Western Office of Institutional Planning & Budgeting, 2014).

[b] 40% of students living in residence reported that they have access to kitchen facilities; however, it is atypical for them to use these facilities as the majority of student residents are required to purchase a campus meal plan.

3.3 Total Food Skill Score (TFSS)

11   The mean TFSS was 473 ± 146. Females had significantly higher TFSS than males (487 ± 141 vs. 442 ± 152, respectively; t (2556) = 10.11, p < 0.001). Students who took a FN course reported higher TFSS (495 ± 137) than those who had not (462 ± 149; t (4978) = −8.55, p < 0.001). Additionally, students living in residence/with family had TFSS (440 ± 155) that were significantly lower than students living independently off-campus (500 ± 133; t (4714) = −15.42, p < 0.001). Students who reported the highest level of cooking ability (i.e., "prepare meals from basic ingredients") had significantly higher TFSS (531 ± 114) than those who reported being able to use ready-made ingredients to prepare meals (401 ± 129) and those who reported limited-to-no cooking ability (233 ± 138; F (2, 6057) = 1481.97, p < 0.001). Students who had lived away from their parental home for one year or less had lower TFSS (443 ± 153) than students who had lived away from home for more than one year (489 ± 135; t (4928) = −11.24, p < 0.001). Lastly, students with access to kitchen facilities had higher TFSS (484 ± 141) than those without access (431 ± 157; t (1428) = −10.10, p < 0.001).

3.4 Weekly Meal Preparation

12   Meal preparation patterns differed significantly between students living in a university residence/with family compared to those living independently off-campus (Chi-square (4, 5809) = 1086.61, p < 0.001; Fig. 3). Fifty-one percent of students living independently reported preparing a meal 4–6 times/week or daily, compared to only 19.7% of students living in residence/with family. Of the latter group, 61.8% reported preparing a meal once per week or less. Infrequent meal preparation was also apparent in 24.2% of students living independently.

13   Of all female respondents, nearly 39% reported preparing a meal either 4–6 times/week or daily, compared to 35.5% of all male respondents (Chi-square (4, 5802) = 28.74, p < 0.001). Fewer females than males reported meal preparation less than once weekly (39.6% of females versus 41.9% of males; Chi-square (4, 5802) = 28.74, p < 0.001).

14   The majority (83.3%) of respondents indicated that their parents prepared meals either 4–6 times weekly or daily in their childhood home (Fig. 3). Half (50.8%) of respondents reported these same meal preparation frequencies, while the remainder prepared meals 2–3 times weekly

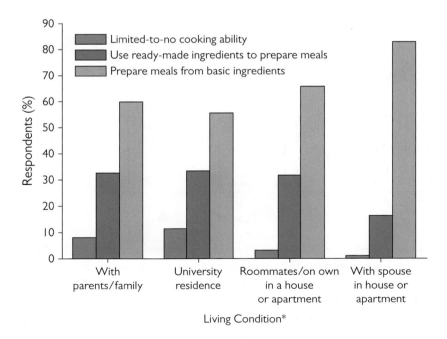

Figure 1   Students' Self-Reported Cooking Ability based on Living Condition, n = 5801. A chi-square test indicated that students' cooking ability differed significantly by living condition; p < 0.001. *Students were able to classify their living condition as "Other"; however, based on limited respondent selection (n = 20), this category was omitted.

or less. Students' current meal preparation habits showed little to no correlation with the patterns they reported for their parents (r_s (3327) = 0.22; p < 0.001).

4. Discussion

15   The current study identifies subpopulations of university students worthy of nutrition education interventions that focus on food skills. The skill-based deficit of university students is concerning, particularly in light of their susceptibility to weight gain and their tendency to develop poor dietary behaviors (Nelson et al., 2008; Vella-Zarb & Elgar, 2009).

16   First-year students made up more than half (53.5%) of respondents who reported limited-to-no cooking ability. This raises concerns about their readiness to independently make food choices and prepare meals. In addition, of those who reported having limited ability to cook and prepare meals, 50.3% were currently living in a university residence, suggesting this is an ideal environment for nutrition education interventions. This supports previous research indicating that living situations play an integral role in various lifestyle factors, including food choices (Brevard & Ricketts, 1996), and that colleges and universities should offer health promotion programs for students (Plotnikoff et al., 2015).

17   Distinct trends were observed in the food skills that students found to be easy or more challenging. For example, "peeling, chopping, or slicing vegetables or fruit" consistently received the highest scores, while "meal planning for the week's meals" received the lowest scores, suggesting that students are more confident in their mechanical abilities, but may need to develop their perceptual and conceptual food skills. These results are consistent with Canadian (Chenhall, 2010) and international reports (SafeFood, 2014). Students' self-reported food skill scores appear to decrease as the need for planning, conceptualization, and concept integration increases, suggesting specific knowledge gaps that can be targeted by experiential, skills-focused nutrition education interventions (Matthews, Zok, Quenneville, & Dworatzek, 2014).

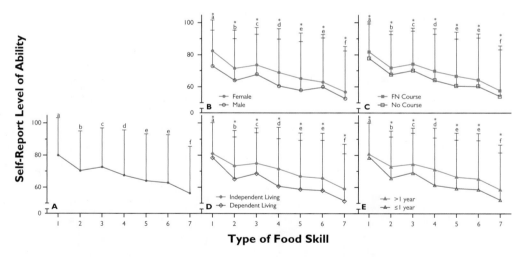

Figure 2   Students' Self-Reported Food Skills, where 1 = peeling, chopping, slicing; 2 = cooking dishes at the same time; 3 = making meals with available ingredients; 4 = cooking in batches for future use; 5 = making a recipe healthier; 6 = choosing a spice/herb; and 7 = planning weekly meals. (A) Overall Level of Ability, n = 6077 and by (B) Sex, n = 5668; (C) Having taken a Food and Nutrition (FN) course, n = 5687; (D) Living condition, n = 5674; and (E) Years away from their parental home, n = 5065. Students assessed their level of ability with respect to seven food skills on an 11-point scale ranging from 0 (no skill) to 100 (very good). Food skill scores were analyzed by RMANOVA with Tukey's post-hoc tests and are reported as M ± SD for each individual skill. Within each graph, food skills with different letters indicate significant differences among the food skills; p < 0.01. *Significant differences in food skills between categories i.e., sex, taking a FN course, living condition, and years away from parental home; p < 0.01.

Table 2   Food skills reported by first-year students vs. students of all other years of post-secondary education.

Food skill[a]	First-year students Mean ± SD (n)	All other years Mean ± SD (n)
Peeling, chopping, or slicing vegetables or fruit	77.9 ± 22.0[b] (1680)	81.1 ± 19.7 (3892)
Cooking of a few food dishes at the same time so that I can serve them together for a meal	65.5 ± 26.6[b] (1682)	72.9 ± 22.9 (3884)
Planning a quick, healthy meal using only foods already in my home	68.5 ± 25.8[b] (1679)	74.7 ± 22.5 (3882)
Cooking a large batch of a recipe so that it can be frozen in small portions for later use	60.7 ± 29.8[b] (1675)	70.8 ± 26.7 (3876)
Adjusting a recipe to make it healthier (e.g. decreasing the amount of fat, sugar, or salt)	58.3 ± 30.7[b] (1676)	67.0 ± 27.6 (3878)
Choosing a spice or herb that goes well with the food I am cooking/eating	57.8 ± 31.7[b] (1674)	65.5 ± 28.6 (3880)
Meal planning for the week's meals	52.1 ± 29.7[b] (1674)	58.7 ± 28.3 (3880)

SD, standard deviation.
[a] Students reported their food skill ability on an 11-point scale, ranging from 0 (no skill) to 100 (very good).
[b] Significantly different than all other years of postsecondary education, $p < 0.001$.

18   The tendency for females to report higher food skills than males is also consistent with other literature (Chenhall, 2010; Health Canada, 2015; Waterloo Region, 2010; SafeFood, 2014). This may be related to gender biases associated with traditional cooking roles (Daniels, Glorieux, Minnen, & van Tienoven, 2012), where females may spend more time developing food skills and, therefore, have higher self-efficacy in this area (Chenhall, 2010; Larson et al., 2006; SafeFood, 2014). If nutrition education interventions are to be successful in targeting skills, knowledge, and dietary behavior change, critical thought must be given to engaging male students in ways that resonate best with them. For example, improvements in dietary behavior and nutritional status have been achieved with male participants when interventions were not time-intensive (Plotnikoff et al., 2015).

19   Students who had taken a formal FN course had increased self-efficacy for food skills and, as previously reported, higher intentions and confidence toward healthy eating (Matthews et al., 2016). Other studies have found that a general nutrition course offered at the college level increased students' fruit and vegetable consumption (Ha

& Caine-Bish, 2009), and students themselves have indicated baseline nutrition knowledge is required for healthy food choices (Deliens et al., 2014). As FN courses are not mandatory in most Canadian jurisdictions, these findings support the call for the reinstitution of FN education at all school levels (Chenhall, 2010; Desjardins & Azevedo, 2013; Lichtenstein & Ludwig, 2010; Nelson et al., 2013; Slater, 2013).

20   The amount of time students had lived away from their parental home had an impact on their perceived food skills, with those who had lived away from home for more than one year reporting higher scores than those who had lived away for less time. This suggests the importance of targeting students during their first year living away from home and/or their first year of university (Colatruglio & Slater, 2016; Nelson et al., 2008; Vella-Zarb & Elgar, 2009). This transitional life stage is a vulnerable period during which students face significant challenges and form complex relationships with food (Colatruglio & Slater, 2016); therefore, this is a unique opportunity to improve students' food skills and related behaviors.

21   Students may gain self-efficacy and improved food skills as they move towards living independently,

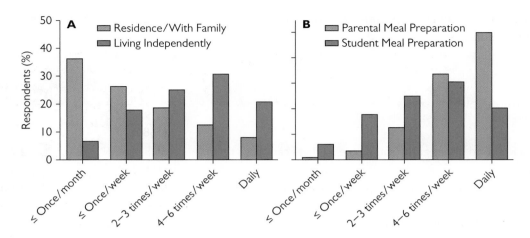

Figure 3   Students' Meal Preparation Patterns (A) By Living Condition, n = 5809. Students reported how often they prepared a main meal from basic ingredients. A chi-square test indicated that students' meal preparation habits varied by their living condition; p < 0.001. Students living in campus residences or with family were collapsed into one group because students in residence must purchase a meal plan and typically do not prepare their own meals and, similarly, students living with family may have most meals prepared for them. (B) Compared to Parents' Meal Preparation Patterns, n = 3334. Respondents who indicated living in a university residence/with family were excluded. A Spearman's rank correlation coefficient revealed a weak relationship (r = 0.22; p < 0.001).

particularly if they are engaged in meal preparation. Additionally, students may develop higher motivation towards cooking and higher self-efficacy for food skills as they become responsible for the nutritional wellbeing of others (e.g., spouses and/or children). Interventions must consider ways to evoke student interest and increase their motivation for these activities.

22   The majority of respondents indicated that they are comfortable preparing meals from basic ingredients; however, a quarter of those living independently are preparing meals less than once weekly. This trend is concerning because frequent meal preparation by young adults is correlated with better diet quality (Larson et al., 2006). Frequent meal preparation is also associated with less fast food consumption and a higher likelihood of meeting the dietary recommendations for fat, calcium, fruit and vegetables, and whole grains (Larson et al., 2006), as well as increased self-efficacy for cooking and food preparation techniques (Woodruff & Kirby, 2013). Despite witnessing parental meal preparation, many students are not adopting these behaviors, suggesting that parental influence may be insufficient for skill transference. Consideration must therefore be given to the barriers to students' meal preparation that are independent of parental influence (e.g., time,

cost, convenience, social and academic environments) (Deliens et al., 2014; Garcia, Sykes, Matthews, Martin, & Leipert, 2010). Nutrition education interventions must address these barriers to halt the "deskilling" phenomenon (Colatruglio & Slater, 2016; Slater, 2013) and increase the effort students put towards food planning, preparation, and storage.

23   For long-term improvements in students' food skills to occur, interventions must fill educational deficits encompassing the mechanical, conceptual, and perceptual skills required to plan and prepare healthy meals (Larson et al., 2006; SafeFood, 2014). "Hands-on" interventions targeting cooking skills may improve self-efficacy for meal preparation and improve dietary patterns (Garcia et al., 2014; SafeFood, 2014). Peer education has also been shown to enhance the effectiveness of health-related interventions targeted at students transitioning into university settings (Matthews et al., 2014; Nelson et al., 2013) and may be equally effective for nutrition and food skills education. Nutrition education curriculum could address misperceptions that food skills are not necessary and that food skills have to be performed to an expert standard to be useful. These and other potential avenues for intervention delivery should be considered collectively during program planning

and may offer the ability to target university students through multiple levels of influence.

24   The challenges that the university setting can present (e.g., food and social environments, academic demands, and the limited duration of the school year) must be anticipated when delivering nutrition interventions, as they may challenge students' abilities to make commitments to both the intervention and healthy food choices (Deliens et al., 2014; Nelson et al., 2008). Minimal surveillance, follow up, and evaluation have been documented, making it difficult to infer long-term behavior change (Nelson et al., 2008). A recent literature review identified that interventions of 12 weeks (one semester) or less have resulted in a greater number of significant health-related short-term outcomes than those spanning more than one semester (Plotnikoff et al., 2015), which is promising for future nutrition interventions targeting food skills in this population. Further research on food skills could also identify predictors of food skills (e.g., age, sex, BMI) as potential considerations for interventions.

4.1 Strengths and Limitations

25   The primary strength of this study is the large, diverse sample of university students. The response rate of 21.9% is similar to that of national college health surveys in this population (American College Health Association, 2014). Furthermore, 30.2% of respondents were first-year students, strengthening study findings regarding their identification as prime candidates for food skill intervention. The cross-sectional study design may be considered a limitation; however, to our knowledge this is the first study reporting on the food skills of a large sample of university students. While this study was conducted in a single university setting, it has a diverse student population. Although the sample consisted of a higher percentage of females than was representative of the student population, this could be due to self-selection, whereby female students are more likely to participate based on familiarity or interest in the topic. Nevertheless, the male subset still had a robust sample of 1572. The self-reported food skills data could be considered a limitation; however, self-assessment of personal food skills has been suggested to reflect an individual's perception of their own skills and self-efficacy, which could have a positive impact on behaviors (Waterloo Region, 2010). Lastly, the survey did not assess food safety knowledge, which is a critical aspect of food skills and should be considered in future work.

5. Conclusions

26   Emerging adulthood is a critical time during which youth become independent and adopt life-long health behaviors (Nelson et al., 2008). The current study adds to a growing body of research suggesting that young people have inadequate cooking skills and low involvement in food preparation (Chenhall, 2010; Desjardins & Azevedo, 2013; Larson et al., 2006). Results identified that students' reported food skills vary by sex, FN education, living condition, and years away from their parental home. While higher abilities were reported for basic mechanical food skills, conceptual skills were significantly lower. Despite calls for mandatory food and nutrition education, few students have the opportunity to learn food skills in school (Colatruglio & Slater, 2016; Lichtenstein & Ludwig, 2010; Slater, 2013). Furthermore, the transference of food skills and meal preparation patterns may not be occurring from parent to child (Colatruglio & Slater, 2016). Results of the current study suggest that nutrition education interventions aimed at improving the food skills of university students, especially in their first year of study and/or during first year living away from home, are particularly important.

Acknowledgements

This study was funded by an internal research grant from Brescia University College.

References

American College Health Association. (2014). *American College Health Association – National College Health Assessment II: Reference Group Data Report Fall 2013*. Retrieved from American College Health Association: http://www.acha-ncha. org/reports_ACHA-NCHAII.html.

Bandura, A. (2004). Health promotion by social cognitive means. *Health Education Behaviour, 31*, 143–164.

Brevard, P. B., & Ricketts, C. D. (1996). Residence of college students affects dietary intake, physical activity, and serum lipid levels. *Journal of the American Dietetic Association, 96*(1), 35–38.

Chenhall, C. (2010). *Improving cooking and food preparation skills: A synthesis of the evidence to inform program and policy development*. Retrieved from Health Canada http://www.hc-sc.gc.ca/fn-an/nutrition/child-enfant/cfps-acc-synthes-eng.php.

Colatruglio, S., & Slater, J. (2016). Challenges to acquiring and using food literacy: Perspectives of young Canadian adults. *Canadian Food Studies, 3*(1), 96–118. http://dx.doi.org/10.15353/cfs-rcea.v3i1.72.

Colton, T. (1974). *Statistics in medicine.* New York, NY: Little, Brown and Company.

Daniels, S., Glorieux, I., Minnen, J., & van Tienoven, T. P. (2012). More than preparing a meal? Concerning the meanings of home cooking. *Appetite, 58*(3), 1050–1056. http://dx.doi.org/10.1016/j.appet.2012.02.040.

Deliens, T., Clarys, P., De Bourdeaudhuij, I., & Deforche, B. (2014). Determinants of eating behaviour in university students: A qualitative study using focus group discussions. *BMC Public Health, 14,* 53. http://dx.doi.org/10.1186/1471-2458-14-53.

Desjardins, E., & Azevedo, E. (2013). *Making something out of nothing: Food literacy among youth, young pregnant women and young parents who are at risk for poor health.* Retrieved from Public Health Ontario http://foodsecurecanada.org/sites/default/files/food_literacy_study_technical_report_web_final.pdf.

Dillman, D. A. (1978). *Mail and Telephone Surveys: The Total Design Method.* New York, NY: John Wiley & Sons.

Garcia, A. C., Sykes, L., Matthews, J., Martin, N., & Leipert, B. (2010). Perceived facilitators of and barriers to healthful eating among university students. *Canadian Journal of Dietetic Practice and Research, 71*(2), e28–e33. http://dx.doi.org/ 10.3148/71.2.2010.69.

Garcia, A. L., Vargas, E., Lam, P. S., Shennan, D. B., Smith, F., & Parrett, A. (2014). Evaluation of a cooking skills programme in parents of young children - A longitudinal study. *Public Health Nutrition, 17*(5), 1013e1021. http://dx.doi.org/10.1017/S1368980013000165.

Guo, S. S., Wu, W., Chumlea, W. C., & Roche, A. F. (2002). Predicting overweight and obesity in adulthood from body mass index values in childhood and adolescence. *American Journal of Clinical Nutrition, 76,* 653–658.

Ha, E. J., & Caine-Bish, N. (2009). Effect of nutrition intervention using a general nutrition course for promoting fruit and vegetable consumption among college students. *Journal of Nutrition Education and Behaviour, 41*(2), 103–109. http://dx.doi.org/10.1016/j.jneb.2008.07.001.

Health Canada. (2015). *A look at food skills in Canada.* Retrieved from Dietitians of Canada http://www.dietitians.ca/Downloads/Public/FoodSkills_FactSheet_ENG-FINAL.aspx.

Larson, N. I., Perry, C. L., Story, M., & Neumark-Sztainer, D. (2006). Food preparation by young adults is associated with better diet quality. *Journal of the American Dietetic Association, 106,* 2001–2007. http://dx.doi.org/10.1016/j.jada.2006.09.008.

Lichtenstein, A. H., & Ludwig, D. S. (2010). Bring back home economics education. *Journal of the American Medical Association, 303*(18), 1857–1858. http://dx.doi.org/10.1001/jama.2010.592.

Matthews, J. I., Doerr, L., & Dworatzek, P. D. N. (2016). University students intend to eat better, but lack coping self-efficacy and knowledge of dietary recommendations. *Journal of Nutrition Education and Behaviour, 48*(1), 12–19. http://dx.doi.org/10.1016/j.jneb.2015.08.005. e1.

Matthews, J. I., Zok, A. V., Quenneville, E. P. M., & Dworatzek, P. D. N. (2014). Development and implementation of FRESH – A post-secondary nutrition education program incorporating population strategies, experiential learning and intersectoral partnerships. *Canadian Journal of Public Health, 105*(4), e306–311. http://dx.doi.org/10.17269/cjph.105.4481.

Nelson, S. A., Corbin, M. A., & Nickols-Richardson, S. M. (2013). A call for culinary skills education in childhood obesity-prevention interventions: Current status and peer influences. *Journal of the Academy of Nutrition and Dietetics, 113*(8), 1031–1036. http://dx.doi.org/10.1016/j.jand.2013.05.002.

Nelson, M. C., Story, M., Larson, N. I., Neumark-Sztainer, D., & Lytle, L. (2008). Emerging adulthood and college-aged youth: An overlooked age for weight-related behavior change. *Obesity, 16*(10), 2205–2211. http://dx.doi.org/10.1038/oby.2008.365.

Plotnikoff, R. C., Costigan, S. A., Williams, R. L., Hutchesson, M. J., Kennedy, S. G., Robards, S. L., et al. (2015). Effectiveness of interventions targeting physical activity, nutrition and healthy weight for university and college students: A systematic review and meta-analysis. *International Journal of Behavioural Nutrition and Physical Activity, 12*(1), 45. http://dx.doi.org/10.1186/s12966-015-0203-7.

SafeFood. (2014). *Food Skills: Definitions, influences and relationship with health.* Retrieved from SafeFood (Food Safety Promotion Board) http://www.safefood.eu/Publications/Research-reports/Food-Skills-Definitions-influences-and-relations.aspx.

Slater, J. (2013). Is cooking dead? The state of home economics food and nutrition education in a Canadian province.

International Journal of Consumer Studies, 37(6), 617–624. http://dx.doi.org/10.1111/ijcs.12042.

Statistics Canada. (2010). *Trends in the age composition of college and university students and graduates.* Retrieved from http://www.statcan.gc.ca/pub/81-004-x/ 2010005/article/11386-eng.htm.

Statistics Canada. (2013). *Canadian postsecondary enrolments and graduates, 2011/2012.* Retrieved from http://www.statcan.gc.ca/daily-quotidien/131127/dq131127d-eng.htm.

Twells, L. K., Gregory, D. M., Reddigan, J., & Midodzi, W. K. (2014). Current and predicted prevalence of obesity in Canada: A trend analysis. *Canadian Medical Association Journal Open, 2*(1), E18–E26. http://dx.doi.org/10.9778/cmajo.20130016.

Vella-Zarb, R., & Elgar, F. J. (2009). The "freshman 5": A meta-analysis of weight gain in the freshman year of college. *Journal of American College Health, 58*(2), 161–166. http://dx.doi.org/10.1080/07448480903221392.

Waterloo Region. (2010). *Food skills of Waterloo region adults.* Retrieved from Region of Waterloo Public Health http://chd.region.waterloo.on.ca/en/researchResources Publications/resources/FoodSkills.pdf.

Western Office of Institutional Planning & Budgeting. (2014). *Common university data Ontario – 2013 Western University.* Retrieved from http://cudo.cou.on.ca/page.php?id=7&table=8#univ=42&topic=B&table_hidden=5&y=2012.

Woodruff, S. J., & Kirby, A. R. (2013). The associations among family meal frequency, food preparation frequency, self-efficacy for cooking, and food preparation techniques in children and adolescents. *Journal of Nutrition Education and Behaviour, 45*(4), 296–303. http://dx.doi.org/10.1016/j.jneb.2012.11.006.

Key and challenging words

self-efficacy, purport, paucity, jurisdiction

Questions

1. (a) In one or two sentences, explain the justification for the study in your own words; (b) Explain why the authors might have chosen to express their thesis as a statement of purpose rather than the more traditional form of a hypothesis.

2. Summarize the measures that the authors took to ensure the validity of their survey as discussed in paragraph 4.

3. Using reliable sources, briefly define "cross-sectional" survey design. Explain some of the advantages and disadvantages of the cross-sectional design in empirical (scientific) research.

4. Using critical thinking, explain the likely reasons behind one of the following findings of the study: (a) higher self-reported food skills for females than for males; (b) higher self-reported food skills for those living away from home for more than one year than for those living away from home for less than one year.

5. Choosing two paragraphs from the "Background" or "Discussion" sections of the reading, describe how the authors use related studies for support.

6. Analyze the authors' use of strategies for comprehension in paragraph 20 or 21. Is the paragraph unified, coherent, and well-developed? Strategies you could consider in answering this question include the use of topic sentences and transitions, logical sentence order, rhetorical patterns, and the like (see Chapter 5, pp. 52–54).

Post-reading

1. Argue for or against the establishment of mandatory food and nutrition courses at your university. (They would be scheduled for early in the first term, for example, four 1-hour sessions in September and October.) In your argument, consider using some of the argumentative strategies discussed in Chapter 9, p. 110.

2. Design a promotional and educational campaign, including either a poster or brochure that highlights

key information, for students at your university. The purpose is to increase awareness about the need for healthy eating. It should target first-year students, in particular, and include practical tips for developing adequate food skills. You can use some of the intervention strategies mentioned in the "Discussion" section of the reading, along with other strategies that seem appropriate and interesting to your audience.

Healthy Choice?: Exploring How Children Evaluate the Healthfulness of Packaged Foods

Charlene Elliott and Meaghan Brierley
(3,303 words)

> ## Pre-reading
>
> 1. *Collaborative or individual activity:* How important is it that school-aged children are well informed about the healthfulness of packaged foods? Discuss or debate issues relevant to this question or write a response in which you take a side and defend your point of view.
> 2. Note that in the list of References, the lead author of this study cites three other studies she has authored. Access the abstracts of two of these studies and consider how prior authorship affects her credibility as an author of the current study.

Abstract

Objectives: Today's supermarket contains hundreds of packaged foods specifically targeted at children. Yet research has shown that children are confused by the various visual messages found on packaged food products. This study explores children's nutrition knowledge with regard to packaged food products, to uncover strengths and difficulties they have in evaluating the healthfulness of these foods. **Methods:** Focus groups were conducted with children (grades 1–6). Particular attention was paid to the ways children made use of what they know about nutrition when faced with the visual elements and appeals presented on food packaging. **Results:** Children relied heavily on packages' written and visual aspects—including colour, images, spokes-characters, front-of-package claims—to assess the healthfulness of a food product. These elements interfere with children's ability to make healthy choices when it comes to packaged foods. **Conclusions:** Choosing healthy packaged foods is challenging for children due to competing sets of knowledge: one pertains to their understanding of visual, associational cues; the other, to translating their understanding of nutrition to packaged foods. Canada's Food Guide, along with the curriculum taught to Canadian children at schools, does not appear to provide children with the tools necessary to navigate a food environment dominated by packaged foods.

———

1   Supermarket food products designed to appeal to children frequently feature cartoon images (including characters from popular television shows/movies for children) and/or they promote food by using appeals to fun or play. Such packaging is designed to capture attention, not to help children make informed, healthy choices.[1] While previous research has explored the effects of advertising on children,[2-4] children's understanding of advertising's intent,[5-8] branding's influence on children's tastes[9-12] and spokes-characters' influence on children's choices,[13] this study probes how children assess the healthfulness of packaged foods. Specifically, it examines children's views on why they

Source: From *Canadian Journal of Public Health*, vol. 103, no. 6, 2012, pp. 453–8. Reprinted with permission of the Canadian Public Health Association.

selected particular packaged foods as "healthy" choices over similarly packaged edibles in the same product category.

2   Studies focusing on how children interpret food products show that the children have difficulty evaluating the healthfulness of packaged edibles.[14] Visual aspects of packages—such as colour, design and image—strongly influence children's evaluations (often incorrect) of the healthfulness of foods, and also impact the overall desirability of the food.[15] By examining children's selection of a "healthy" packaged product (out of various choices), and their subsequent discussion of what made that product the "healthy" choice, this study highlights how various symbolic appeals on packaging affect children's understanding of a product's nutritional qualities. The article concludes with recommendations on how to bolster children's interpretive strategies when it comes to evaluating packaged foods for healthfulness—and with a comment on why such bolstering (in light of marketing strategies employed by the food industry) may not be enough.

Methods

3   This study draws from data collected from a broader, federally funded research project focused on children's interpretations of packaged food products. Focus-group methodology is increasingly viewed as a productive method for discovering children's attitudes, perspectives and ideas.[16] This approach, moreover, is particularly appropriate for the question of children's interpretations of packaged foods since it allows for open-ended responses from the participants, which can be probed and clarified.

4   In 2009, 52 focus groups were conducted with a total of 225 children in three cities in Canada (Calgary, Alberta; Ottawa, Ontario; and Fredericton, New Brunswick). Children were divided according to grade with separate focus groups held for grades 1–2 (G1/2), 3–4 (G3/4), and 5–6 (G5/6), so as to reveal potential differences in opinion according to age. (Separate focus groups were held for boys and for girls, although differences according to gender were not the focus of this particular analysis.) Each focus group was an hour in length and had four to six children participants. Creating a small group setting was strategic, since it creates a space that encourages participation from shyer children.[16]

5   A moderator, following a semi-structured moderator's guide, asked questions pertaining to packaged foods targeted at children. Pertinent to this analysis, children were shown a variety of packaged food products from the same product category to examine and evaluate. Children were asked to identify the foods that they considered the most healthy, and to explain why they chose those packaged product(s) over the other options available.

6   Institutional ethics certification was granted for the study; written child and parental consent was obtained prior to the focus groups. Children were informed that they did not have to participate (or answer) questions should they choose not to, and that they could stop (or leave) at any time. Although some children said they did not know the answer to certain questions, all chose to participate. The small number of participants in the focus groups ensured that every child could respond to each question posed. The moderator addressed the children in a round-table format, varying the order in which children were asked questions, but giving each child the opportunity to explain their choice. This allowed the analysis not only to draw out themes, but to provide some (albeit generalistic) level of detail in terms of the frequency of reliance on certain themes over others according to age. The moderator probed for elaboration on answers where appropriate, and allowed for open discussion between participants. Children's responses were transcribed verbatim. Themes were identified and insights crystallized; iterative comparison and inductive coding techniques were used, following a grounded theory approach. Qualitative research software (NVivo) was used to facilitate the process.

Results

7   Children of all grades (1–6) revealed a general inability to evaluate the healthfulness of a packaged food. They used package colours, spokes-characters, pictures, and front-of-package (FOP) claims, to support their choices of healthy foods. While some children used information from nutrition facts tables and ingredient lists in their assessments, these were often used ineffectively. Figure 1 presents the breakdown of children in each grade who discussed colour, spokes-characters, FOP claims, (etc.) in their evaluation. Table 1 provides relevant quotations from the children that support the themes discussed.

Colour

8   Children across all grades used package colours to determine what comprised a "healthy choice": 22% of children from the G1/2 focus groups specifically relied on

this, as did 14% of children from G3/4 and 19% from G5/6. Indeed, colour might function as the sole criterion for judging a product as healthy or unhealthy. For G1/2 children, a packaged food was labeled healthy "maybe cause it's green" or unhealthy because (for example) the "rainbow" of colours on a box of Lucky Charms® cereal meant it was "like a rainbow of sugar." Some children in G3/4 provided more elaborate reasoning: products were deemed healthy because "they don't add like sugars and coloured stuff." The G5/6 children consistently identified colour—particularly artificial colour—as an object of critique. As one child remarked about a packaged product she deemed unhealthy: "They're not natural colours as in fruits."

9   Foods with muted colours, in contrast, were deemed more healthy. Children identified cereal boxes with "not a lot of colour" as the healthy choice. One child picked a box of Cheerios® as the healthiest option out of seven choices,

in part because "Cheerios® have no colours" (G1/2); another (older) child similarly observed that Cheerios® were healthiest because "they don't add like sugars and coloured stuff" (G3/4). Identical reasoning was provided by G5/6 children.

10   Colours on packages also represented other things children understood as being healthy, such as associating green with vegetables: "the colour green represents organic or healthy because a lot of healthy vegetables are green and organic is healthy and sometimes it's more healthy than other foods" (G5/6). These comparisons also paralleled issues of literalism (discussed below) in packaged food interpretation.

Literalism in Text and Image

11   Literalism—taking the strict interpretation of a word or image (without accounting for metaphor or exaggeration)—was present in the children's responses. Literal

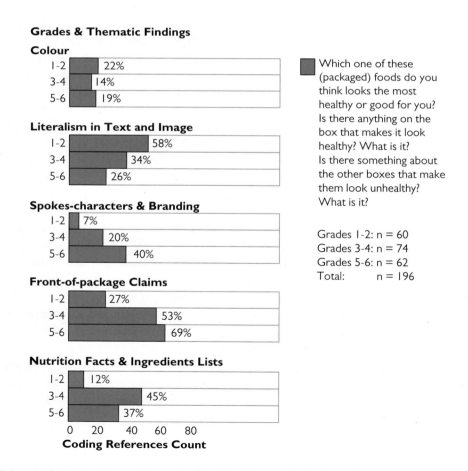

Figure 1   Breakdown of children (according to grade) who discussed colour, spokes-characters and branding, front-of package claims—and/or provided literal "readings" of text and images—in choosing healthy packaged foods

Table 1   Children Describe How They Choose Healthy Packaged Foods; Sample Quotations

Findings	Details	Moderator: Which one of these foods do you think looks the most healthy or good for you? Why? Is there something on the other boxes that makes them look less healthy? What is it?
Colour	Colour can act as a sole criterion for judging a product as healthy or unhealthy	"When there is green on the box, it means it's healthy" (G1/2) "The colour is green and green is . . . good . . . [it means the] environment and green which is good" (G1/2) "Green stands for good!" (G5/6)
	Colour can be unhealthy	"Um well some of the stuff just looks really fake and like colourful and even though that looks fun it can be really unhealthy" (G3/4) ". . . it's like different colours and that means that they put in food colouring or like something to change the colour . . . when it's healthy cereals . . . it's more white" (G5/6)
	Lack of colour indicates "healthy"	"the one that is healthy is . . . the white box" (G1/2) "the Organics® because there's not a lot of colour and made up characters on the box, it's just actually showing you what's inside" (G1/2) "because lots of healthy brands have the black writing at the top. Also, because all this stuff is usually in the white box" (G5/6)
Literalism in text and image	Children's literal interpretation of packaged foods complicates their decision-making processes	". . . that one (Life® cereal) says . . . um . . . a check on it. If it was an 'x' it would mean not healthy like sugar and a check mark means no sugar" (G1/2) "The Life® [cereal] because it has a peach on the box" (G1/2) "Crunchy Corn® because it has like strawberries in it and it's got corn" (G3/4) "I know it's healthy because there's green and that is the colour of life and plants" (G1/2) "Honey Combs [cereal] . . . um cause they have honey in them" (G5/6)
Spokes-characters branding	A spokes-character (or licensed character's) presence could be interpreted as unhealthy	"Dora's not healthy at all . . . cause it's Dora!" (G5/6) "Elmo isn't healthy . . . he's all scruffy" (G5/6) "I just laughed because Dora is not healthy and everybody laughed because we're thinking of the cartoon person on the candy. It's gummy worms or gummy bears, or gummy gummy gummy Dora" (G5/6) *Moderator: "Why do you choose this as the healthiest of the three?* ". . . because it's not from a movie?" (G1/2)
	A spokes-character or brand's presence could be interpreted as healthy	*Moderator: "Why do you choose this as the healthiest of the three?* "Cause it's Quaker® . . . and I have a bag of Quaker® flour and it says that it's really healthy on the back" (G3/4) " The Life® looks healthy, they pour the milk a certain way, and it's Quaker® – it's a popular company that lots of people like to buy" (G3/4) ". . . it has the organic thing on it, and it's the President's Choice company" (G3/4) ". . . it has that [Quaker®] dude and I am pretty sure that he's a lot of healthy food" (G5/6) "I usually look for a company that I know doesn't make treats and makes more meals. I think President's Choice" (G5/6)

Continued

Table 1   (continued)

Children use front-of-package claims to make healthy choices, yet have little understanding of their meaning	Front-of-package claims were typically understood as presenting positive characteristics of healthy food	"Um, the check mark on the Fun Bites® . . . on the corner. Helps people see that it's healthy!" (G5/6) "Fruit bars because on the box it says contains vitamin C . . . hmm . . . I'm not . . . not really . . . and it says no sugar added" (G3/4) ". . . um see that little check mark at the bottom of that Life® box . . . uh, I think it's sort of like checking off like a health list of something" (G5/6) "I think the Life® one . . . it has the little check mark thingies here — low in saturated fat, zero trans fats, source of fibre" (G3/4)
Children need help applying their knowledge to nutrition facts and ingredients lists	Children could not thoroughly interpret nutrition facts and ingredients lists due to incomplete knowledge	"sometimes on the back, it shows you what it is has in it — some people have allergies, and they need to look what they have . . . on the side or on the back" (G1/2) "the nutrient facts — how much calories it has, if they have added bad things like chemicals, preservatives, artificial things" (G3/4) "the Life® one cause I was just reading, I was looking at this . . . I thought it's sort of like a percentage and it's made with 100 whole grain oats and I was looking down here where it says no trans fat in it and source of fibre" (G5/6)

interpretations became less common as children got older, although all of the explanations held interesting insights. For example, when asked to explain why he chose Life® cereal as the healthiest of seven cereal options, a child in G1/2 explained, "Usually if they're talking, Life® is good for you because they're actually worried about your health." Another G3/4 child said "And it gives you life!" In G5/6, a child mused: "I don't know why but something struck me with the title 'Life' that it has something to do with healthy things in life . . .".

12   Other interesting instances of textual literalism emerged in G1/2 students' interpretation of "Fat Free" as meaning to get the ingredient of fat for free. Two represent-ative examples include: "because if they put *more* fat, that means they put fat free" (G1/2); and "yeah, fat free, and, and it's free."

13   The most common mistake children made, however, was thinking that packages contained particular ingredi-ents (that were not actually present) due to the pictures featured *on* the package. In the focus groups, children con-sistently identified cereal boxes featuring an image of a bowl of cereal with sliced fruit in it as the healthiest option—even though the box(es) in question did not contain any fruit. Pictures of milk on a package also prompted some children to classify the cereal itself as healthy (although this oc-curred less frequently).

Moderator: Which box of cereal is the healthiest?

- Life® cereal "because it has fruit" [points to picture of sliced peaches on the front of the cereal box) (G5/6)
- "Crunchy Corn® because it has like strawberries" [points to picture of strawberries in bowl featured on the front of the cereal box] (G3/4)

Simply put, these items *not* in the package made children of all grades claim a product was "the healthiest" out of num-erous similar options.

Spokes-Characters and Branding

14   Certain spokes-characters, such as Toucan Sam® and Lucky the Leprechaun®, were interpreted as signifying an un-healthy product, whereas other spokes-characters *explicitly associated with brand lines* were cited as indicators of healthy food. These associations, of certain spokes-characters with "unhealthy" and certain brands with "healthy" (regardless of the product), increased dramatically as children got older (i.e., G1/2, 7%; G3/4, 20%; and G5/6, 40%).

15   Older children recognized how spokes-characters might attract younger children to less nutritious prod-ucts. When spokes-characters were mentioned in terms of health, it was either in combination with a brand or, notably,

the *absence* of a spokes-character that indicated health for children. In the first case (brand spokes-characters and health), several children in G3/4 explained that a packaged food was healthy *because* "it has the Quaker® dude" on it. Some children associated the brand across individual product lines: [It's healthy] "cause it's Quaker® . . . and I have a bag of Quaker® flour and it says that it's really healthy on the back" (G3/4). In the second case (the *absence* of a spokes-character), some children used this "lack" as an indicator of health, as per the child who identified Organics Crunchy Corn® cereal as the healthy choice because "there's not a lot of colour and made-up characters on the box" (G3/4).

Front-of-Package Claims

16   When analyzed according to grade, it was evident that children in the focus groups increasingly relied on and trusted front-of-package (FOP) claims to help them to make healthy choices, yet continued to have little understanding of their meaning. The percentage of children who spontaneously referenced a FOP claim to justify why a product was healthy rose from 27% of children in G1/2 to 53% in G3/4 and up to 69% in G5/6.

17   Claims such as *Organic, Fat Free* or *Goodness Corner* were typically understood as positive characteristics, even though the product might be nutritionally lacking in other ways (i.e., low in fat but high in sugar; organic but high in sugar, etc.). Children frequently interpreted these claims literally:

- "It says fat free, so you won't get fat" (G1/2)
- "It's from the Heart and Stroke Foundation—that means that like it's good for you and it won't give you a heart attack" (G3/4)
- "Behind the O for Organics there's a leaf which is natural, so it's made from something natural" (G5/6).

One striking aspect of such claims was their influence on children's interpretations of healthy foods. FOP claims and/or nutrition "corners" found on boxes of cereals such as Honeycomb®, Alpha Bits®, Lucky Charms® and Froot Loops® successfully convinced six children in G1/2 that the cereals were a healthy choice. During group discussion (led by the moderator) about the nutrition claims, eight children in G3/4 changed their minds, subsequently labelling Honeycomb® cereal, PC Organics Crunchy Corn® cereal and Lucky Charms® cereal as a "healthy food". Four children in G5/6 similarly changed their minds to declare Life® cereal and PC Organics Crunchy Corn® cereal as the healthy choice.

Nutrition Facts and Ingredients Lists

18   In all grades, fewer children relied on nutrition facts and ingredients lists than FOP claims in making healthy food choices. Not surprisingly, when they did use nutrition facts and ingredients lists, their knowledge base was shown to be incomplete. The few G1/2 children who discussed the nutrition facts table were vague on how one might actually use it: "I would look at the label on the box. . . .Um, if you look what I did is when I looked at these and I saw the ingredients and noticed a little bit of sugar in it." These children often resorted to using FOP claims to justify their initial explanations: "that's good because there's no fat . . . no bad fat. See, it says fat free, so there is no bad fat in there" (G1/2).

19   The G3/4 age group offered no consistent "reading" or treatment of the nutrition facts table, nor was there clarity on what children felt they should be looking for: "I'm always looking for tons of different things on that side" [referring to where the nutrition facts table appears] "and it helps and it comes in handy lots, and it can tell you what kinds of things are in it" (G3/4).

20   Most children in G5/6 were equally vague about how they used the nutrition facts table and ingredients list; some children, however, were able to express its complexities:

21   "I look at the side where it says, um, calories, and, um, sodium and everything. But, um, you have to be careful because sometimes, it says like, you look on a chip bag sometimes and it says like, say the chip bag is sixty grams, it'll say like sixty calories or something per 30 grams. But you have to add . . . because if you eat the whole chip bag it's twice that right? You can't be too careful. Well, sometimes, they say sensible solution, but that's only if you add something. They're very tricky about that."

Discussion

22   Children's worlds are filled with packaged food products—yet children have not been provided the tools to evaluate packaged foods for their healthfulness. This study draws attention to some common stumbling blocks encountered by children when asked to identify and explain why a packaged food is a healthy or unhealthy choice. Children provided savvy—if incorrect—explanations of why a packaged food was healthy (or not), relying heavily on visual and associational cues. Drawing from knowledge gained (presumably from the school nutrition curricula and home) about healthy eating, children applied this knowledge to evaluate packaged edibles. While their logic was

impressive, the assessment was often flawed, as per declarations that the colour green or a picture of fruit or the absence of a spokes-character on a box signaled a healthy food. Such literal interpretations trumped children's use of the nutrition facts table and ingredients list. The study revealed, quite clearly, that children need help navigating the complexity of the visual packaged food environment. In short, *nutrition literacy* (the skills of evaluating, processing and understanding basic nutrition information) needs to be accompanied by *media literacy* (the ability to access, analyze and evaluate messages across a variety of contexts) when discussing packaged food.

23   Certainly, extensive data exist on how children understand food advertising,[3,6,7,17] and previous research has shown that cartoon characters can influence children's taste and snack preferences,[18,19] or increase a child's interest in fruit.[20] However, studies on how children interpret *packaged* foods are rare.[14] Previous research has shown, however, that children identify "serious" looking packages with healthy food,[14] and also classify "kids" food as "fun" compared to "boring" adult fare.[15]

24   When it comes to children's views on food and nutrition, focus group research has probed the "major barriers" children identified with regard to healthy eating (such as taste, appearance of food, rebellion),[21] as well as the relationship between television viewing and children's nutritional knowledge and reasoning.[22] More importantly, research has shown that children's preference for healthy foods (particularly fruits and vegetables) increases along with their cognitive abilities as they age and come to understand the importance of health.[23] Research has also found that on-package nutritional claim information sometimes had "a backlash effect" on children, "causing them to make unhealthier choices when on-package claims are present"[24]—a finding supported by the children in this study who "flip-flopped" on their choice of a healthy product after observing a FOP claim.

25   One of the core calls in policy initiatives to promote the health of Canadian children is to make the healthy choice "an available and easily recognizable option".[25] This study suggests a new, and remarkably significant, point for consideration—namely, that the school-aged children interviewed did not have the knowledge base to "easily recognize" a healthy choice when it comes to packaged foods. Their interpretive strategies were intelligent, but often contradictory or wrong-headed. At this point, it remains important to underscore that this study did not seek to document whether the children could identify some predetermined "healthier" packaged product from a range of packaged products. This type of approach transforms the line of questioning on *why* the children made the choices they did into more of a documentation of correct or incorrect answers. (Indeed, the determination of a healthiest packaged option confounds many adults, since in many instances, the difference between regular packaged goods and "better-for-you" is simply a difference of degree and not of kind. Health claims/appeals to health are sometimes more about marketing than nutrition,[26] and the argument can be fairly made that a "less-bad-for-you" processed product is still a heavily processed product.) Rather than trying to figure out whether the children could identify a predetermined "healthier" packaged product, the point of the study was to consider *how* children choose "healthy"—that is, what frames of reference they use, what semiotic, associational or linguistic cues, and what counts as relevant (or irrelevant) when asked *what they look for to know whether a packaged food product is healthy*. Although one might question whether it is reasonable to assume that children should be able to understand health claims or the nutrition facts table—Nutrition Facts is designed for adults, not children—it is important to underscore that children *are* interpreting these packaging appeals, regardless. They have clear opinions about packaging and health, and it is therefore productive to understand what interpretations they have. Moreover, the school curriculum suggests that children *should* have a complex level of reasoning when it comes to nutrition. The Government of Alberta Curriculum, for example, states that (as a learning outcome), by the end of Grade 2, children will be able to classify foods according to *Canada's Food Guide to Healthy Eating*, and "apply knowledge of food groups to plan for appropriate snacks and meals."[27] Grade 3 children are asked to deal with nutritional labels.[27] And by the completion of Grade 4, children are expected to understand the "role of protein, fats, carbohydrates, minerals, water, vitamins" in the diet.[27] This grappling with food classification, labels, and the function of key nutrients in the body demands a complex level of reasoning—reasoning that is complicated by the fact that the Canada Food Guide (on which children are supposed to base their decisions) does not deal with packaged foods in the first place. The children's answers suggest that the school curriculum, based on Canada's Food Guide and the merits of whole, unprocessed foods, does not provide children with the tools they need to navigate our contemporary foodscape, which is filled with packaged edibles.

Conclusion

26   This study demonstrated that children lack the media literacy necessary to make effective nutrition choices with regard to packaged foods. Package colours, images, spokescharacters, brands and FOP claims influenced children's ability to evaluate the products based on the nutrition facts table and ingredients list. Clear opportunities exist to move beyond merely telling children *what* foods are healthy (e.g., fruits, vegetables) to teaching them to critically evaluate packages. This means providing children with the type of information that allows them to sidestep common errors of interpretation (e.g., green or fruit on the box = healthy food) so that they may truly make the healthy choice in an environment dominated by packaged goods. Though policy changes are needed to ensure that the packaged foods promoted to consumers as healthful are indeed healthful, in the interim it would be wise to arm our youngest consumers with a tool kit that allows them to avoid the common stumbling blocks (described above) when it comes to evaluating packaged foods.

Acknowledgements

This work was supported by the Canadian Institutes of Health Research (CIHR) [funding reference number 86633] and the CIHR Canada Research Chairs program.

References

1.   Berry B, McMullen T. Visual communication to children in the supermarket context: Health protective or exploitive? *Agric Hum Values* 2008;25(3):333-48.

2.   Gwozdz W, Reisch LA, on behalf of the IDEFICS Consortium. Instruments for analysing the influence of advertising on children's food choices. *Int J Obesity* 2011;35(S1):S137-S143.

3.   Livingstone S, Helsper E. *Advertising Foods to Children: Understanding Promotion in the Context of Children's Daily Lives.* London, UK: Department of Media and Communications, London School of Economics and Political Science, 2004.

4.   Livingstone S, Helsper EJ. Does advertising literacy mediate the effects of advertising on children? A critical examination of two linked research literatures in relation to obesity and food choice. *J Commun* 2006;56(3):560-84.

5.   Andronikidis AI, Lambrianidou M. Children's understanding of television advertising: A grounded theory approach. *Psychol Market* 2010;27(4):299-322.

6.   Martin MC. Understanding of the intent of advertising: A meta-analysis. *J Public Policy Marketing* 1997;16(2):205-16.

7.   Owen L, Auty S, Lewis C, Damon B. Children's understanding of advertising: An investigation using verbal and pictorially cued methods. *Infant Child Dev* 2007;16(6):617-28.

8.   Young B, Webley P, Hetherington M, Zeedyk S. *The Role of Television Advertising in Children's Food Choices? A Critical Review of Some of the Recent Literature.* London: Ministry of Agriculture, Fisheries and Food, 1996.

9.   Connor SM. Food-related advertising on preschool television: Building brand recognition in young viewers. *Pediatrics* 2006;118(4):1478-85.

10. Ji MF. Children's relationships with brands: "True love" or "one-night" stand? *Psychol Market* 2002;19(4):369-87.

11. Jones SC, Mannino N, Green J. 'Like me, want me, buy me, eat me': Relationship-building marketing communications in children's magazines. *Public Health Nutr* 2010;13(12):2111-18.

12. Robinson TN, Borzekowski DL, Matheson DM, Kraemer HC. Effects of fast food branding on young children's taste preferences. *Arch Pediatr Adolesc Med* 2007;161(8):792-97.

13. Roberto CA, Baik J, Harris JL, Brownell KD. Influence of licensed characters on children's taste and snack preferences. *Pediatrics* 2010;126(1):88-93.

14. Elliott C. Healthy food looks serious: How children interpret packaged food products. *Can J Commun* 2009;34(3):359-80.

15. Elliott C. "It's junk food and chicken nuggets": Children's perspectives on 'kids' food' and the question of food classification. *J Consum Behav* 2011;10(13):133-40.

16. Heary C, Hennessy E. The use of focus group interviews in pediatric health care research. *J Pediatr Psychol* 2002;27(1):47-57.

17. Chernin A. The effects of food marketing on children's preferences: Testing the moderating roles of age and gender. *Ann Am Acad Polit SS* 2008;615(1):101-18.

18. Lumeng J. Cartoon characters on food packages influence taste and snack preferences in young children. *J Pediatr* 2011;158(1):170-71.

19. Lapierre MA, Vaala SE, Linebarger DL. Influence of licensed spokescharacters and health cues on children's ratings of cereal taste. *Arch Pediatr Adolesc Med* 2011;165(3):229-34.

20. de Droog SM, Valkenburg PM, Buijzen M. Using brand characters to promote young children's liking of and purchase requests for fruit. *J Health Commun* 2011;16(1):79-89.

21. McKinley MC, Lowis C, Robson PJ, Wallace JM, Morrissey M, Moran A, Livingstone MB. It's good to talk: Children's views on food and nutrition. *Eur J Clin Nutr* 2005;59:542-51.

22. Harrison K. Is "fat free" good for me? A panel study of television viewing and children's nutritional knowledge and reasoning. *Health Commun* 2005;17(2):117-32.

23. Zeinstra GG, Koelen MA, Kok FJ, de Graaf C. Cognitive development and children's perceptions of fruit and vegetables; a qualitative study. *Int J Behav Nutr Phys Act* 2007;4(30).

24. Miller EG, Seiders K, Kenny M, Walsh ME. Children's use of on-package nutritional claim information. *J Consum Behav* 2011;10:122-32.

25. Public Health Agency of Canada. Curbing Childhood Obesity: A Federal, Provincial and Territorial Framework for Action to Promote Healthy Weights. Ottawa, ON: PHAC, 2010. Available at: http://www.phac-aspc.gc.ca/hp-ps/hl-mvs/framework-cadre/intro-eng.php (Accessed March 23, 2011).

26. Elliott C. Packaging health: Examining "better-for-you" foods targeted at children. *Can Public Policy* 2012;38(2):265-81.

27. Government of Alberta. Education: Health and Life Skills Guide to Implementation. Available at: http://education.alberta.ca/teachers/program/health/resources/k-9health.aspx (Accessed August 3, 2012).

Key and challenging words

bolster, pertinent, verbatim, iterative, muted, savvy

Questions

1. In the literature review section, (a) identify the justification of the study and explain how the objectives of this study differ from other studies on the same topic; (b) identify, then summarize, the thesis statement.

2. (a) Why is the use of focus groups an appropriate and useful methodology for children, according to the authors? (b) The authors don't explain why girls and boys were separated to form focus groups (paragraph 4): why do you think this may have been the case?

3. Explain how the authors addressed the challenges of using children in focus groups.

4. Compare the Results section in "Healthy Choice?" to the Results section in a Type B essay in *The Active Reader* that uses a quantitative methodology (see Appendix B, p. 378, for a list of essay types). In your answer, include one similarity and at least two differences.

5. Choosing one of the subsections in the Results section, analyze strategies used by the authors to increase comprehension (see Strategies for Coherent Writing in Chapter 6, pp. 73–75).

6. Explain the importance of definitions to paragraphs 11 and 23; in paragraph 23, also explain the importance of definitions to the Discussion section as a whole.

7. Referring to the Discussion section, (a) analyze how the authors use related studies to help establish importance for their study; (b) analyze their use of the sources identified in notes 26 and 27 in the Reference list to make their study relevant to health concerns in society today.

Post-reading

1. ". . . [I]n the interim, it would be wise to arm our youngest consumers with a tool kit that allows them to avoid the common stumbling blocks [described in the essay] when it comes to evaluating packaged foods" (paragraph 26). Outline a strategy that could be used in a family and/or school setting. This could take the form of a short report with an introduction identifying the problem, a discussion section referring to the study "Healthy Choice?" (and perhaps other relevant studies), and a conclusion with specific recommendations.

2. Compare "Healthy Choice?" with the essay "A Ban on Marketing of Foods/Beverages to Children" on p. 297 in Part III: The Reader, using as bases of comparison the authors' purpose in writing, rhetorical strategies, and one other basis of your choice.

A Ban on Marketing of Foods/Beverages to Children: The Who, Why, What and How of a Population Health Intervention

Daniel J. Dutton, Norman R.C. Campbell, Charlene Elliott, and Lindsay McLaren
(1,766 words)

Pre-reading

1. Read the title and abstract, and scan the essay, noting headings and topic sentences. Write a one- to two-paragraph reading hypothesis (see p. 49) that considers the essay's purpose, audience, and main points.

Abstract

There is increasing recognition in Canada and elsewhere of the need for population-level interventions related to diet. One example of such an intervention is a ban on the marketing of foods/beverages to children, for which several health organizations have [developed] or are in the process of developing position statements. Considering the federal government's inaction to impose restrictions that would yield meaningful impact, there is opportunity for the health community to unite in support of a stronger set of policies. However, several issues and challenges exist, some of which we outline in this commentary. We emphasize that, despite challenges, the present and predicted future of diet-related illness in Canadian children is such that population-level intervention is necessary and becoming increasingly urgent, and there is an important role for the health community in facilitating action.

---

1   To achieve significant and sustained reduction in various health risk factors, the need for population-level intervention (i.e., intervention [policy or program] operating within or outside the health sector, that targets a whole population[1,2]) is increasingly recognized. One current example is diet. Approximately 40% of deaths from non-communicable diseases worldwide are attributed to excess consumption of saturated fats, trans fats, sugar and salt.[3] This applies to children as well: Canadian children, on average, do not eat enough fibre[4] or fruits and vegetables[5] and consume too much sodium.[6] Accordingly, it has been predicted that the current generation of children could live a shorter life span than their parents; this would be unprecedented.[7]

2   Several population-level interventions have been suggested, one of which is banning marketing to children (e.g., ref. 8). Marketing to children includes traditional forms of marketing, such as television or print advertisements, as well as internet or cellular phone-based promotion, games and contests, and in-store promotions targeting children.[9] A reasonable evidence base exists to support a ban on marketing to children, although much of the evidence to date pertains to television advertising. Advertisements appear to have a strong influence on children's preference, according to a review commissioned by the World Health Organization (WHO), which included both observational and controlled experimental trials. This review concluded that children exposed to advertising exhibit preferences towards food they see advertised, a tendency towards purchasing and requesting the foods they see advertised, and a greater consumption of those foods.[10] Cecchini et al.[11] estimated that, among various interventions used to tackle unhealthy diet and physical inactivity, the largest overall gains in disability-adjusted life years (DALYS) in a developed country would come from regulation of food advertisements to children, the benefits of which would accrue over the lifetime of the children.

3   One clear lesson from the history of public health is that even a robust evidence base often is not sufficient to ensure the adoption and implementation of specific policies—particularly those that are upstream in nature.[12] To achieve the desired population-level impact, interventions will need to have a significant structural or regulatory

component,[13] due to inherent weaknesses of a voluntary, company-initiated approach. However, the current political environment in Canada is not supportive of this: in a regime characterized by active and passive encouragement of market forces,[14] government action to regulate private industry and potentially restrict profits by corporations is unpalatable to some. This is illustrated by the federal government's preference for voluntary rather than regulatory approaches in dietary policy.[8] That government has identified diet-related health issues as a priority (www.phacaspc.gc.ca/media/nr-rp/2011/2011_0307-eng.php) yet fails to implement policy that would have the desired impact, makes the government potentially vulnerable to a health lobby. There is opportunity for the health community to unite around a call for population-level interventions that require regulation and enforcement, such as banning marketing to children. However, for such a call to have credibility, the health community needs to be cognizant of the issues and challenges, some of which we outline here.

The Who: Creating a Health Lobby

4   There is opportunity for health organizations (including professional organizations in public health and health care, and non-profit groups) to unite in favour of banning marketing to children. While some in the public health community may readily support this, other health organizations may encounter challenges. For example, the disease-specific focus of some federal or provincial non-governmental organizations lends itself to a "downstream" orientation whereby the organization's funding is predominantly for biomedical and/or clinical research activities. For these organizations, supporting a call for banning marketing to children may be viewed as "too upstream" to be consistent with the organization's mandate. Ultimately, these organizations are accountable to their donor base, so support for a ban may be achieved through increased support for upstream policies from the general public, which includes the donor base, as well as organizational leadership. To secure the buy-in of these organizations, it may be necessary to actively promote the value (i.e., evidence base, potential impact) of such population health interventions. Such promotion, or education, could occur via communication (e.g., newsletters) to membership, as well as through conventional channels such as increased media attention to the determinants of health through newspapers and other mainstream media.

The Why: "Health" May not be the Most Effective Rationale

5   Although an evidence base exists to support banning marketing to children for health reasons, health communications scholars have argued that "health" may not be the most effective rationale. In particular, the "health pitch" has been shown to be vulnerable to manipulation by industry.[15] For example, towards ostensibly aligning with health goals, some companies have been keen to brand their foods as "healthier" than alternatives by emphasizing particular characteristics of their product, though in a misleading manner. For example, a company may emphasize elevated levels of desirable content (such as fibre), while other characteristics of the product may be questionable from a nutrition point of view; alternatively, they may advertise decreased levels of less desirable content (such as sodium) "per serving," which is achieved by reducing serving size rather than through product reformulation. That health branding is vulnerable to manipulation reflects attributes of the regulatory system (i.e., manipulation would not occur if the system was designed to disallow it), and regulatory systems in turn are often developed in conjunction with industry, thus raising the broader issue of potential conflict of interest when industry is involved in the development of government-set regulations. While the expertise and advocacy of the health sector is integral to the proposed ban, an important complement is the ethical case for a ban: children are a vulnerable group. Health professionals, who are understandably accustomed to viewing health as sufficient rationale to implement an activity such as a ban, may need prompting to look beyond "health" as the only or most important rationale, and endorse the critical role of the ethical case. Further, privileging the ethical case may appeal to sectors of the general population who are not as convinced by a health rationale. There is a precedent for the value of privileging the ethical case: under sections 248 and 249 of the Consumer Protection Act, Quebec has banned advertising to children since 1980.[16] The ban was challenged by industry, but the Supreme Court of Canada upheld the ban on the basis that children are unable to critically assess advertising (which may be coercive or misleading), and thus advertising to children is not ethically defensible.[17] For a health lobby to be effective, health and health care professionals need to recognize and emphasize the ethical rationale of a ban, in addition to the health rationale. Privileging the ethical justification for a ban would also solve some of the problems with the vulnerability of existing initiatives, as noted above, to manipulation of what constitutes "healthier."

The What and How: The Nuts and Bolts of the Intervention, and Jurisdictional Issues

6   Banning "marketing" to children is, in fact, complex. Other well-known public health bans have focused more on single products (e.g., cigarettes) or mediums (e.g., television) than on target audiences. While we can avoid the complexity posed by the large diversity of products (foods/beverages) by calling for a complete ban on all products, questions remain about how to operationalize marketing to a target audience. For example, how do we determine the audience targeted by marketing, including their age? How do we ensure that all important media (i.e., television, internet, cell phones, video games, etc.) are included?

7   The Quebec case is instructional. Although there are guidelines on what constitutes advertising to children,[17] the guidelines are open to interpretation. Monitoring of the Quebec ban comes mostly in the form of complaints by advocacy groups that direct attention to potential violations of the ban, and the onus is on the complainants to emphasize that the delivery and/or content of the advertisement is directed at children (such as the Coalition Poids www.cqpp.qc.ca/en). While it is operationally easy to extend the Quebec model to every other province in Canada, it is not clear that a grassroots monitoring approach would be appropriate or effective at the national level. Without comprehensive national rules, regional discrepancies could give rise to both unequal enforcement of such a ban as well as differential interpretations across regions of what counts under the ban, which would lead to future national enforcement difficulties. The need for a national policy and enforcement is consistent with discussion of jurisdictional issues in public health generally: while public health delivery is largely a provincial responsibility, a coordinated central response federally is necessary for successful intervention, especially when the costs of the intervention are likely to be unequal across provinces.[18]

Conclusion

8   The Canadian government has identified certain diet-related health issues as priorities, yet their actions are insufficient to achieve meaningful change to the food environment. There is an opportunity for the health community to unite around population-level interventions such as a ban on marketing to children, and such a lobby could potentially be very powerful in the face of government hypocrisy. For a health lobby to be effective, there is need for cognizance of key issues and challenges, some of which we outline here. However these challenges should not be seen as reasons not to proceed, considering what is at stake. The present and predicted future of diet-related illness in Canadian children is such that population-level intervention is necessary and becoming increasingly urgent. Although the action suggested, and issues raised, in this commentary may be known to experts with regard to the relationship between health and marketing in children, we propose that this relatively small number of experts will be limited in their ability to enact change unless they have the active support of the general health community.

Conflict of Interest: Dr. Norman R.C. Campbell received financial travel support from Boehringer Ingelheim to attend hypertension meetings in 2010. Otherwise, the authors have no conflicts of interest to declare.

References

1. Rose G. *The Strategy of Preventive Medicine.* Oxford, UK: Oxford University Press, 1992. [Reprinted. *Rose's Strategy of Preventive Medicine.* Oxford: Oxford University Press, 2008.]

2. Hawe P, Potvin L. What is population health intervention research? *Can J Public Health* 2009;100(Suppl 1):S8–S14.

3. Beaglehole R, Bonita R, Horton R, Adams C, Alleyne G, Asaria P, et al. Priority actions for the non-communicable disease crisis. *Lancet* 2011;377(9775):1438–47.

4. Health Canada. Do Canadian Children Meet their Nutrient Requirements through Food Intake Alone? 2009. Cat. No. H164–112/1–2009E-PDF. Available at: www.hc-sc.gc.ca/fn-an/alt_formats/pdf/surveill/nutrition/commun/art-nutr-child-enf-eng.pdf (Accessed February 8, 2012).

5. Garriguet D. Canadians' eating habits. *Health Rep* 2007;18(2):17–32.

6. Garriguet D. Sodium consumption at all ages. *Health Rep* 2007;18(2):47–52.

7. Olshansky SJ, Passaro DJ, Hershow RC, Layden J, Cames BA, Brody J, et al. A potential decline in life expectancy in the United States in the 21st Century. *N Engl J Med* 2005;352:1138–45.

8. Sodium Working Group. Sodium Reduction Strategy for Canada: Recommendations of the Sodium Working Group. Health Canada, 2010. Available at: www.hc-sc.gc.ca/fn-an/nutrition/sodium/strateg/index-eng.php (Accessed February 8, 2012).

9. Harris J, Pomeranz J, Lobstein T, Brownell KD. A crisis in the marketplace: How food marketing contributes to childhood obesity and what can be done. *Annu Rev Public Health* 2009;30:211–25.

10. Hastings G, McDermott L, Angus K, Stead M, Thomson S. The Extent, Nature and Effects of Food Promotion to Children: A Review of the Evidence. World Health Organization, 2007. Available at: www.who.int/dietphysical activity/publications/Hastings_paper_marketing.pdf (Accessed February 8, 2012).

11. Cecchini M, Sassi F, Lauer JA, Lee YY, Guajardo-Barron V, Chisholm D. Tackling of unhealthy diets, physical inactivity, and obesity: Health effects and cost-effectiveness. *Lancet* 2010;376(9754):1775–84.

12. Siegel M, Doner Lotenberg L. *Marketing Public Health: Strategies to Promote Social Change,* 2nd ed. Sudbury, MA: Jones and Bartlett Publishers, 2007.

13. McLaren L, McIntyre L, Kirkpatrick S. Rose's population strategy of prevention need not increase social inequalities in health. *Int J Epidemiol* 2010;39:372–77.

14. Eikimo TA, Bambra C. The welfare state: A glossary for public health. *J Epidemiol Community Health* 2008; 62:3–6.

15. Elliott C. Marketing fun foods: A profile and analysis of supermarket food messages targeted at children. *Can Public Policy* 2008;34(2):259–73.

16. Éditeur officiel du Québec. *Consumer Protection Act.* 1978;248–49.

17. Jeffery B. The Supreme Court of Canada's appraisal of the 1980 ban on advertising to children in Québec: Implications for "misleading" advertising elsewhere. *Loyola of Los Angeles Law Review* 2006;39:237–76.

18. Wilson K. The complexities of multi-level governance in public health. *Can J Public Health* 2004;95(6):409–12.

Key and challenging words

unpalatable, cognizant, coercive, onus, differential, jurisdictional

Questions

1. Briefly discuss the importance of the studies mentioned in paragraph 2 to the authors' purpose.
2. Explain why the authors state that "even a robust evidence base often is not sufficient to ensure the adoption and implementation of specific policies" (paragraph 3).
3. Identify the authors' thesis, and comment on its rhetorical effectiveness; for example, you could consider language, tone, or appeals designed for the essay's audience.
4. Define *upstream* (paragraph 3) and *downstream* (paragraph 4) approaches and explain the difference between them. Try to use context to answer the question before referring to a business dictionary.
5. (a) Discuss the strategies the authors use to aid comprehension in the section "The why: 'Health' may not be the most effective rationale." You could consider organization, rhetorical patterns, transitions, and the like; (b) If you were to divide this long paragraph into three shorter paragraphs, where would you make the separations? Justify your choices and provide headings for each subsection.
6. Analyze the authors' use of precedent and one other argumentative strategy in their essay (see Kinds of Evidence in Argumentative Essays in Chapter 9, p. 105).
7. Analyze the authors' conclusion, keeping in mind the audience they are addressing.

Post-reading

1. As a group lobbying for health interventions for children, use the information and approaches discussed in this essay (along with other sources if appropriate) to create a brief report/presentation. Your audience will not be health professionals but government representatives in a position to recommend or implement the kinds of interventions discussed in the essay.

Society of Excess?

Waste Not, Want Not, Emit Less

Jessica Aschemann-Witzel

(1,125 words)

> ### Pre-reading
>
> 1. How would you define "food waste"? Give examples of ways that food can be wasted.
> 2. *Individual or collaborative activity:* As Aschemann-Witzel makes clear in her essay, food waste is a significant problem in developed countries like Canada. Do you ever think about how you, your family, or your friends waste food? Who do you think is largely responsible (e.g., governments, businesses, individuals)? In groups, discuss these or other relevant questions or, using one of these questions as a prompt, respond in one or two paragraphs.

1   Ensuring a sufficient supply of quality food for a growing human population is a major challenge, aggravated by climate change and already-strained natural resources. Food security requires production of some food surpluses to safeguard against unpredictable fluctuations (1). However, when food is wasted, not only has carbon been emitted to no avail, but disposal and decomposition in landfills create additional environmental impacts. Decreasing the current high scale of food waste is thus crucial for achieving resource-efficient, sustainable food systems (2). But, although avoiding food waste seems an obvious step toward sustainability, especially given that most people perceive wasting food as grossly unethical (3), food waste is a challenge that is not easily solved.

2   About one-third (in weight) of the world's food overall (4) or one-fourth (in kilocalories) of the world's crops (5) are lost or wasted. Food loss encompasses loss of agricultural produce—for example, when crops are damaged during production, harvest, storage, transport, and processing. Food waste refers to the wastage of items fit for human consumption—for example, when foods are discarded in the retail trade, in food service, or in households because they are regarded as "suboptimal" when close to the "best-before" date or due to minor product flaws. Some authors expand the definition and argue that crops potentially for human consumption but grown for nonfood purposes, such as animal feed or energy, should be regarded as food losses and that overnutrition leading to obesity constitutes food waste (6).

3   Food loss and waste are caused by many factors across the supply chain and differ by the country and commodity in question, but can be roughly separated into two areas of concern. Developing countries suffer the greatest loss during the early, upstream part of the supply chain. For example, 75% of food losses occur during production and postharvest in Africa. In contrast, industrialized countries waste most downstream, especially in the consumption stage. For example, household-level waste accounts for 50% of overall loss and waste of crops in North America and Oceania (5). The share of food that is lost or wasted is particularly high for perishable products such as fresh fruits and vegetables (6, 7). However, the environmental impact of wastage is especially notable for meat because of its large carbon footprint. Food loss and waste in total are greatest in Asia (4, 5), but per capita they are highest in high-income countries; great within-country differences due to income disparities are suspected (1, 5, 6).

4   In developing countries, policy recommendations for tackling food loss and waste include building better infrastructure through transfer of knowledge and technology and improving collaboration and market opportunities in the food supply chain (4, 6). Achieving this might hinge on good political governance (5) and should include locally adapted small-scale farming (6) to bring about effective and sustainable production. However, urbanization and dietary transition, especially in countries such as BRIC (Brazil, Russia, India, and China),

Source: From *Science*, vol. 352, no. 6284, 2016, pp. 408–9. Reprinted with permission from AAAS.

is expected to increase food-waste volumes and shift a greater share of it to the consumption stage in households and catering (6).

5   In developed countries, food waste in the consumption stage is influenced by societal factors such as the economic situation, technological innovation, and food legislation, but also by more immediate factors such as product and packaging characteristics and retailer marketing strategies. Furthermore, an individual's demographics and mindset can explain food-waste levels (8, 9). For example, families, younger consumers, and single households waste relatively more (6). However, levels of food waste also depend on an individual's values, attitudes, and motivation and his or her skills in food provisioning and handling (9). Moreover, culture, habits, and emotions (such as cultural norms that prescribe offering plenty of food to guests, food safety misperceptions, and exaggerated disgust) partly explain why, on average, 10 to 30% of a household's food basket is thrown away (8, 10). Often, causes of food waste boil down to a trade-off: Consumers want to avoid wasting food, but then prioritize taste, convenience, or health concerns in the day-to-day situation (9).

6   Given the complex drivers of food waste, involvement of numerous stakeholders is crucial. To reduce food waste, experts recommend that governments develop legislation to make date labels (such as sell-by, best-before, and consume-by) more user-friendly for consumers (11) and that retailers loosen aesthetic standards (12).

7   Governments can provide a supportive context, for example, by regulating retailer food waste and changing overly strict food safety laws to allow use of suboptimal foods. Producers can help with innovative product and packaging solutions, for example, to allow easy withdrawal of small amounts while the rest remains fresh (7). Retailers should act responsibly, for example, by abolishing or changing "buy 1 get 2" offers and better aligning orders with demand. Campaigners and NGOs can trigger consumer interest and action, for example, with "Feeding the 5000" events (9).

8   Food-waste reduction campaigns encourage consumers to become more aware of the extent and consequences of food waste and how adopting small, daily behavioral changes (such as checking the fridge prior to shopping) can help to tackle the problem (8). Efforts seem fruitful, so far. Consumers appear receptive to discounts on food nearing its expiration date, or to retailers advertising imperfections in fruits and vegetables as natural and lovable. Redistribution of surplus food through foodbanks has gained considerable foothold, and there are indications that societal campaigns successfully contribute to shifting social norms and consumer motivation (8, 9). However, many actions are at an experimentation stage.

9   Greater food-waste reduction requires collaborative, multifaceted mitigation actions and policies. These should work hand in hand with other food policy goals. Sometimes the solutions may be counterintuitive: When a food item has a high environmental impact, more packaging might help to reduce food waste (7). Price reductions of food close to the expiration date and alternative redistribution are not effective if they simply postpone wastage from retailers to households, but the exact relation between pricing, consumer behavior, and food waste is underexplored (9). There are also trade-offs to consider: Care must be taken that an increased societal focus on food-waste avoidance does not cause consumers to dismiss legitimate food safety concerns—such as eating fish beyond the consume-by date (11).

10   Food-waste reduction efforts should not distract public attention from the fact that buying less meat—particularly red meat—is even more effective for reducing both carbon emissions and pressure on our natural resources (13). After all, the problem of food waste is a symptom of the currently unsustainable food supply. A broad range of efforts are needed to move toward sustainable food security for all, and each individual consumer contributes both to the problem and the solution (2). The fact that consumers and stakeholders alike perceive food waste as obviously unethical makes it a good starting point for individual consumers to become engaged in sustainability.

Acknowledgments

I thank the COSUS (cosus.nmbu.no) research team for excellent collaboration and B. Stefensen, V. Kulikovskaja, L. Haahr, and T. Hessellund Nielsen for valuable feedback on the text.

References and Notes

1.   E. Papargyropoulou et al., *J. Cleaner Production* 76, 106 (2014).

2.   J.A. Foley et al., *Nature* 478, 337 (2011).

3. D. Evans, *Food Waste: Home Consumption, Material Culture and Everyday Life* (Bloomsbury, London, 2014).

4. Food and Agriculture Organization, *Food wastage footprint: Impacts on natural resources. Summary report* (FAO, Rome, 2013); www.fao.org/docrep/018/i3347e/i3347e.pdf.

5. M. Kummu et al., *Sci.Total Environ.* 438, 477 (2012).

6. J. Parftt, M. Barthel, S. Macnaughton, *Philos.Trans. R. Soc. B* 365, 3065 (2010).

7. F. Wikström et al., *J. Cleaner Production* 73, 100 (2014).

8. T. E. Quested et al., *SI: Resourceful Behaviours* 79, 43–51 (2013).

9. J.Aschemann-Witzel et al., *Sustainability* 7, 6457 (2015).

10. J. C. Buzby,J. Hyman, *Food Policy* 37, 561 (2012).

11. S.Van Boxstael et al., *Food Control* 37, 85 (2014).

12. T. Stuart, *Waste: Uncovering the Global Waste Scandal* (Penguin, London, 2009).

13. C. Hoolohan et al., *Energy Policy* 63, 1065 (2013).

Key and challenging words

disparity, provisioning, prescribe, aesthetic, mitigation, counter-intuitive

Questions

1. (a) Identify by paragraph numbers the essay's introduction; (b) In your own words, explain the justification of the essay; (c) Identify, then paraphrase, the author's thesis.

2. Discuss the use of two of the following rhetorical patterns in the essay, referring specifically to the text: (a) compare and contrast, (b) definition, and (c) cause-effect.

3. Analyze the author's use of one of the following kinds of evidence, referring specifically to at least two paragraphs: (a) statistics, (b) examples.

4. Explain why the author has devoted more space to food waste, rather than food loss, in her essay.

5. What role can individual consumers play in the efforts to reduce food waste, according to the author?

6. Of the many challenges to overcoming food waste in developed countries mentioned in "Waste Not," which two would you consider the greatest? Support your answer by using critical thinking and at least one reference to the essay.

Post-reading

1. Access the "Feeding the 5000" website (http://feedbackglobal.org/campaigns/feeding-the-5000/) (see paragraph 8) in order to (a) write/present a summary of its aims, history, and upcoming projects. You could also include the aims of its sponsoring organization, http://feedbackglobal.org *or* (b) analyze the website for its effectiveness (for example, its design, display of content, function of graphics, and the like).

2. Using suggestions mentioned in paragraphs 7–11 of "Waste Not," along with other relevant suggestions, design an informational campaign intended to prevent food waste at your college or university. Summarize the main goals and strategies of your campaign. (If you wish, you can target your campaign to a narrower audience, such as students living on- or off-campus.)

Addressing Driver Aggression: Contributions from Psychological Science

Christine M. Wickens, Robert E. Mann, and David L. Wiesenthal

(2,572 words)

Pre-reading

1. *Collaborative or individual activity:* Has aggressive driving affected you or someone you know—either as a perpetrator or a victim? What were the circumstances, causes, and/ or consequences of the incident(s)? Could anything have been done to minimize the likelihood of the incident(s) (for example, reducing driving speed, clearer signalling, etc.)?
2. Read the abstract and first paragraph to determine how this essay conforms to the conventions of a Type C (critical review) essay. Write a one-paragraph reading hypothesis (see p. 49) that establishes a plan or strategy for reading the essay.

Abstract

Aggressive roadway behavior contributes to motor-vehicle collisions, resulting in significant injuries, fatalities, and related financial costs. Psychological models have identified person- and situation-related variables that are predictive of driver aggression, and these have been used to develop strategies to alleviate aggressive roadway behavior. Future psychological research directions are discussed.

---

1   Aggressive roadway behavior increases the risk of motor vehicle collisions and is associated with greater injury severity resulting from such collisions (Galovski, Malta, & Blanchard, 2006; Paleti, Eluru, & Bhat, 2010). Although estimates of the prevalence of aggressive driving vary considerably (see Galovski et al., 2006), the AAA Foundation for Traffic Safety (2009) reported that 56% of fatal crashes in the United States from 2003 through 2007 involved at least one driver action that is typically associated with driver aggression, such as excessive speeding or reckless/careless driving. Although 78% of Americans recognize the danger and resulting health and financial impact of aggressive driving, a significant number of American drivers admit to speeding to beat a yellow light (58%), pressuring other motorists to speed up (26%), and tailgating (22%; AAA Foundation for

Traffic Safety, 2009). Given this paradox of attitude versus behavior, psychological science clearly has a role to play in furthering our understanding of what factors contribute to aggressive driver behavior and identifying potential solutions to the problem.

Defining Aggressive Driver Behavior

2   In addressing the issue of driver aggression, the first step must be to define the term. Most available statistics, including those cited in the prior paragraph, are based on a broad interpretation of aggressive driving; however, there has been controversy concerning which aggressive acts meet the inclusion criteria. Many researchers have argued that the aggressive action must be deliberate. If one motorist has an accidental lapse in judgment and does not leave enough space when pulling in front of another driver, is this an example of aggressive driving? Another definitional issue involves the nature of the intention. Must the driver be motivated by hostility toward another motorist to be considered aggressive, or can the driver be motivated by impatience or an attempt to save time? Some researchers have argued that there is a distinction between aggressive and risky driving. The former involves harmful intent directed toward another motorist, whereas the latter involves exclusively selfish motives such as time urgency or thrill-seeking

(for a thorough review of this debate, see Galovski et al., 2006; Wiesenthal, Lustman, & Roseborough, in press). For the purposes of streamlining the current review of a vast literature, *driver aggression* will be used to refer to violations of highway traffic laws (e.g., speeding, tailgating, reckless driving) and less serious anger expressions (e.g., swearing, obscene gestures) that are assumed to result from hostility directed toward another motorist; *driver violence* will be used to refer to violations of criminal laws (e.g., threatening harm, assault). These acts are not errors or lapses in judgment; they are aberrant driving behaviors (see Reason, Manstead, Stradling, Baxter, & Campbell, 1990) motivated specifically by hostility. Psychologists have postulated many theoretical models explaining driver aggression that hypothesize a combination of person-related and situational variables (e.g., Shinar, 1998).

Person-Related Contributors

Demographics

3   Person-related variables are those factors that are specific to the driver; arguably, they constitute the largest and most diverse class of contributory factors. Demographic characteristics are the most basic of these variables. Driver aggression is more common among the young and the unmarried, which may be explained by more frequent risk-taking behavior by these demographic groups. Driver aggression has also been seen more commonly among the well-educated and higher socioeconomic status groups, perhaps because they have more social engagements and may be more rushed for time, or they may be less deterred by the risk of fines should they be observed by the authorities (Wickens et al., 2012). Driver aggression has been shown to be greater among men than women, but the most significant gender difference is found with driver violence: men are much more likely to engage in this extreme behavior (Hennessy, Wiesenthal, Wickens, & Lustman, 2004).

Personality

4   Personality may affect our cognitive perception of a situation, our preferences regarding levels of arousal or stimulation, or our sensitivity to stress or threat, all of which play a role when we are driving (Matthews, Dorn, & Glendon, 1991). Drivers who frequently demonstrate high levels of verbal and physical aggression or anger in other aspects of their lives are generally more likely to do so in the driving environment (Deffenbacher, Deffenbacher, Lynch,

& Richards, 2003). Narcissistic people are recognized as arrogant, selfish, and having a sense of entitlement. Narcissists have been found to engage in more retaliatory and vengeful behavior, perhaps because they are more likely to perceive ambiguous driving altercations as intentional or unjust (Lustman, Wiesenthal, & Flett, 2010). Sensation seeking, associated with a need for novel and intense stimuli, has generally been associated with risky driving behavior. This trait has also been identified as a significant predictor of driver aggression, perhaps because sensation seekers perceive less risk in, or accept the risk associated with, roadway aggression (Dahlen, Martin, Ragan, & Kuhlman, 2005). Impulsive people demonstrate poor control over thoughts and behaviors, often initiating behavior without significant forethought, and are more likely to use the vehicle as a weapon for retaliation (Dahlen et al., 2005). Type-A personality consists of a cluster of traits relevant to driver behavior including competitiveness, hostility, achievement motivation, and a sense of time urgency (Bone & Mowen, 2006; Wickens & Wiesenthal, 2005). Not surprisingly, Type-A personality is more common among aggressive than nonaggressive drivers (Miles & Johnson, 2003). Neuroticism is associated with feelings of anxiety, anger, envy, depressed mood, and poor emotional response to stress. Drivers high in neuroticism engage in more horn honking, tailgating, and using obscene hand gestures (Bone & Mowen, 2006). Other variables that have been found to contribute to driver aggression include machismo, extraversion, ego defensiveness, and emotional instability (Bone & Mowen, 2006; Krahé & Fenske, 2002; Neighbors, Vietor, & Knee, 2002; Sümer, Lajunen, & Özkan, 2005). There are also personality variables that have been found to reduce the likelihood that a driver will engage in roadway aggression, including high levels of conscientiousness and agreeableness (Bone & Mowen, 2006; Sümer et al., 2005).

Cognition

5   How we cognitively perceive a driving event will have a major impact on how we feel and eventually respond to the event. Stress researchers conceptualize cognition in driver aggression as involving appraisal of the demands of a stressful situation and ability to cope with them. A driver caught in a stressful driving situation characterized by crowded but quickly moving traffic, time urgency, and an unexpected near-collision may assess the situation as being greater than his/her personal resources can tolerate. The motorist may experience feelings of anger and may lash out

aggressively (Matthews et al., 1991; Wickens & Wiesenthal, 2005). Attribution theorists have conceptualized the role of cognition as a series of judgments regarding why an event occurred and the level of responsibility assigned to an offending driver. If we are cut off on the highway and assume that the offending driver's actions were intentional, we feel angry and may respond in kind. However, if we attribute the driver's actions to an unintentional cause such as a sudden tire blowout causing the vehicle to swerve in front of us, then we may feel sympathy for the other motorist (Wickens, Wiesenthal, Flora, & Flett, 2011).

6   Cognitive biases can also influence the development of driver aggression. When interpreting the potentially offensive actions of other motorists, drivers tend to overestimate internal (e.g., personality) and underestimate external (e.g., situation) causes; however, drivers tend to do the opposite when making attributions for their own actions (i.e., the actor-observer bias; e.g., Herzog, 1994). Novice motorists tend to be overconfident of their driving skills (Mynttinen et al., 2009), thus lowering their tolerance for the perceived misdeeds of other motorists.

Alcohol, Drugs, and Mental Health

7   Alcohol-related problems, use of cannabis, and use of these substances immediately before driving increase one's risk of engaging in driver aggression (Butters, Mann, & Smart, 2006; Wickens et al., 2012). Drivers reporting the use of cocaine, ecstasy (MDMA), or both are more likely to commit violent roadway behavior (Butters et al., 2006). The pharmacological effect of these substances on mood and inhibition, along with personality characteristics (e.g., trait anger or aggression, sensation seeking) common to drinkers, drug users, and aggressive drivers, may also explain the overlap in these behaviors.

8   Various psychiatric disorders have also been implicated as contributors to driver aggression. Intermittent explosive disorder is an impulse control disorder characterized by extreme expressions of anger out of proportion to the provoking stimulus. In a study of treatment-seeking aggressive drivers in Albany, New York, approximately one third of these drivers met criteria for intermittent explosive disorder, significantly more than a control sample of non-aggressive drivers (Galovski et al., 2006). Attention deficit hyperactivity disorder is characterized by inattention, impulsivity, and hyperactivity and is associated with increased self-reports of driving violations, anger, and aggression (Barkley & Cox, 2007). Attention deficit hyperactivity

disorder often co-occurs with other disruptive behavior disorders, such as conduct disorder and oppositional defiant disorder. Relative to a sample of nonaggressive control subjects, these disorders have been found to be more prevalent among aggressive drivers (Malta, Blanchard, & Freidenberg, 2005). Personality disorders, such as antisocial personality disorder and paranoid personality disorder, are also more likely to be found among aggressive than nonaggressive drivers (Galovski et al., 2006). Psychiatric distress, which includes symptoms of both depression and anxiety, has been found to significantly increase the odds of perpetrated driver violence (Butters et al., 2006). Nonetheless, studies examining the impact of anxiety and mood disorders on driver aggression have generated mixed findings, providing some support for this relationship but necessitating additional research (Wickens, Mann, Butters, Smart, & Stoduto, in press). Finally, it is also important to note that medications used to ameliorate psychiatric problems may influence, and perhaps increase, driver aggression (Wickens, Mann, Butters, et al., in press).

Situation-Related Contributors

Environmental Factors

9   Sights, sounds, and smells can all play a role. The visual content of the roadside environment can influence the level of stress and negative affect experienced by drivers; urban roadways lined with commercial buildings and billboards generate more stress than rural roadways lined with natural vegetation (Parsons, Tassinary, Ulrich, Hebl, & Grossman-Alexander, 1998). Likewise, hostile cues such as aggressive billboard advertising or a gun rack in the window of a pickup truck increase driver anger and aggression (Ellison-Potter, Bell, & Deffenbacher, 2001). Sounds within the vehicle can also influence stress levels; self-selected music reduces stress experienced in heavy traffic congestion (Wiesenthal, Hennessy, & Totten, 2000). Likewise, the smell of peppermint decreases drivers' frustration, anxiety, and fatigue (Raudenbush, Grayhem, Sears, & Wilson, 2009), and rising ambient temperature increases drivers' horn honking (Kenrick & MacFarlane, 1986).

Situational Factors

10   Within the driving environment, aspects of the situation can also elicit or augment anger behind the wheel that would not otherwise have emerged. Offensive driving

by another motorist can provoke roadway anger and aggression (Wickens et al., 2011), but situational factors can further increase the likelihood of an aggressive response. Traffic congestion is a major source of roadway stress, and the resulting frustration may be directed aggressively at other motorists (Shinar, 1998). Daily hassles and job-related stresses can make traffic congestion or an offensive driver action seem much more upsetting (Matthews et al., 1991; Wickens & Wiesenthal, 2005). Likewise, time urgency can make traffic congestion or an otherwise benign traffic situation seem much more stressful (Wickens & Wiesenthal, 2005), which can lead to driver aggression.

11   Attributions of other drivers' roadway actions are influenced by the visible characteristics of that driver and the features of their vehicle. Female drivers are judged to be more careless and less aggressive than male drivers, and drivers of BMWs are judged to be more aggressive than drivers of Smart cars (Lawrence & Richardson, 2005). The relative status of vehicles also makes a difference in the likelihood of aggression; when blocked by a "middleclass" vehicle stopped at a green light, drivers of upperclass vehicles honk their horns more quickly than drivers of middle-class vehicles, who honk more quickly than drivers of lower-class vehicles (Diekmann, Jungbauer-Gans, Krassnig, & Lorenz, 1996).

Alleviating Aggressive Driver Behavior

12   Beyond bettering our understanding of the factors that contribute to driver violence and aggression, psychological science is also developing strategies to alleviate the behavior. Programs to treat aggressive drivers are now being developed using cognitive-behavioral therapy, attributional retraining, and relaxation training (Galovski et al., 2006). These programs teach drivers to identify the triggers of their roadway anger and aggression, to recognize cognitive distortions that contribute to their anger, and to control their breathing and relax their muscles when an anger-provoking event is encountered. Additional evidence-based curricula could be added, such as recognizing the tendency to overestimate our own driving skills and emphasizing the importance of roadway communication (e.g., signaling lane changes, flashing headlights as a sign of gratitude; Wickens et al., 2011). Although development of these programs is in the early stages, the success of similarly-intended programs for persons convicted of driving while intoxicated (e.g., Wickens, Mann, Stoduto, Flam Zalcman, & Butters, 2013)

suggests that these programs could substantially improve traffic safety if implemented on a large scale. These programs could also be beneficial if presented early in a novice driver's training.

13   Other attempts at behavior modification have included incentives for good driving: Instrumented vehicles or monitored traffic zones identify and reward law-abiding drivers with entries in a lottery or direct monetary compensation (Battista, Burns, & Taylor, 2010; Haggarty, 2010). Directed passenger feedback has also been used to encourage drivers to better monitor their speed and mirrors (Hutton, Sibley, Harper, & Hunt, 2002), although it is unclear how long this effect might persist, whether it could be used to reduce retaliatory aggression, and whether it is affected by the type of relationship between the driver and the passenger (e.g., teen driver and parent; see Wiesenthal et al., in press).

14   Psychological science can also advise police by identifying specific driving behaviors for enforcement campaigns and when these efforts should occur (Wickens, Wiesenthal, Hall, & Roseborough, 2013). It can inform public service and education campaigns through identification of the audience to target and the most effective focus of the public appeal (e.g., emotional versus informational; Lewis, Watson, White, & Tay, 2007). Psychological science also allows for the evaluation of various technological solutions to the driver aggression problem, including photo radar, red-light cameras, and electronic message boards over the highway for safety appeals or in the rear window of a passenger vehicle to facilitate inter-vehicle communication (e.g., Chen, Meckle, & Wilson, 2002; Retting, Williams, Farmer, & Feldman, 1999; Smart, Cannon, Howard, & Mann, 2005).

Future Directions

15   Psychology is advancing our knowledge of factors contributing to driver aggression, adding to the list of relevant variables and expanding our understanding of existing factors. Person-related and situational variables operate together; thus, it is imperative that we continue to investigate how the contributions of multiple factors combine and interact to influence aggressive roadway behavior. We also need to understand the mechanisms underlying the influence of contributory factors. Personality, cognition, and affect all influence each other, and an improved assessment of the temporal order and strength of these influences is needed. Efforts to apply this information to

modify driver aggression through policy, incentive-based approaches, psychotherapeutic programs (e.g., attributional retraining), and technological innovations to the vehicle and the roadway environment (e.g., electronic message boards) are in their infancy but possess great potential for impact.

Declaration of Conflicting Interests

The authors declared that they had no conflicts of interest with respect to their authorship or the publication of this article.

Funding

This work was supported by a grant from AUTO21, a member of the Networks of Centres of Excellence program that is administered and funded by the Natural Sciences and Engineering Research Council, the Canadian Institutes of Health Research, and the Social Sciences and Humanities Research Council (SSHRC), in partnership with Industry Canada. C.M. Wickens was supported by Postdoctoral Fellowships from the SSHRC and the Centre for Addiction and Mental Health, and R.E. Mann acknowledges ongoing funding support from the Ontario Ministry of Health and Long-Term Care.

References

AAA Foundation for Traffic Safety. (2009, April). *Aggressive driving: Research update*. Washington, DC: Author.

Barkley, R.A., & Cox, D. (2007). A review of driving risks and impairments associated with attention-deficit/hyperactivity disorder and the effects of stimulant medication on driving performance. *Journal of Safety Research 38*, 113–128.

Battista, V., Burns, P., & Taylor, G. (2010). *Using rewards to influence driving behaviour: A field operational trial*. Proceedings of the 20th Canadian Multidisciplinary Road Safety Conference, Niagara Fall, Ontario, Canada.

Bone, S.A., & Mowen, J.C. (2006). Identifying the traits of aggressive and distracted drivers: A hierarchical trait model approach. *Journal of Consumer Behaviour 5*, 454–464.

Butters, J.E., Mann, R.E., & Smart, R.G. (2006). Assessing road rage victimization and perpetration in the Ontario adult population. *Canadian Journal of Public Health 97*, 96–99.

Chen, G., Meckle, W., & Wilson, J. (2002). Speed and safety effect of photo radar enforcement on a highway corridor in British Columbia. *Accident Analysis & Prevention 34*, 129–138.

Dahlen, E.R., Martin, R.C., Ragan, K., & Kuhlman, M.M. (2005). Driving anger, sensation seeking, impulsiveness, and boredom proneness in the prediction of unsafe driving. *Accident Analysis & Prevention 37*, 341–348.

Deffenbacher, J.L., Deffenbacher, D.M., Lynch, R.S., & Richards, T.L. (2003). Anger, aggression, and risky behavior: A comparison of high and low anger drivers. *Behaviour Research and Therapy 41*, 701–718.

Diekmann, A., Jungbauer-Gans, M., Krassnig, H., & Lorenz, S. (1996). Social status and aggression: A field study analyzed by survival analysis. *The Journal of Social Psychology 136*, 761–768.

Ellison-Potter, P., Bell, P., & Deffenbacher, J. (2001). The effects of trait driving anger, anonymity, and aggressive stimuli on aggressive driving behavior. *Journal of Applied Social Psychology 31*, 431–443.

Galovski, T.E., Malta, L.S., & Blanchard, E.B. (2006). *Road rage: Assessment and treatment of the angry, aggressive driver*. Washington, DC: American Psychological Association.

Haggarty, E. (2010, December 9). Speed camera lottery pays drivers for slowing down. *The Toronto Star*. Retrieved from www.thestar.com/news/world/2010/12/09/speed_camera_lottery_pays_drivers_for_slowing_down.html.

Hennessy, D.A., Wiesenthal, D.L., Wickens, C.M., & Lustman, M. (2004). The impact of gender and stress on traffic aggression: Are we really that different? In J.P. Morgan (Ed.), *Focus on aggression research* (pp. 157–174). Hauppauge, NY: Nova Science Publishers.

Herzog, T.A. (1994). Automobile driving as seen by the actor, the active observer, and the passive observer. *Journal of Applied Social Psychology 24*, 2057–2074.

Hutton, K.A., Sibley, C.G., Harper, D.N., & Hunt, M. (2002). Modifying driver behavior with passenger feedback. *Transportation Research Part F 4*, 257–269.

Kenrick, D.T., & MacFarlane, S.W. (1986). Ambient temperature and horn honking: A field study of the heat/aggression relationship. *Environment & Behavior 18*, 179–191.

Krahé, B., & Fenske, I. (2002). Predicting aggressive driving behavior: The role of macho personality, age, and power of car. *Aggressive Behavior 28*, 21–29.

Lawrence, C., & Richardson, J. (2005). Gender-based judgments of traffic violations: The moderating influence of car type. *Journal of Applied Social Psychology 35*, 1755–1774.

Lewis, I.M., Watson, B., White, K.M., & Tay, R. (2007). Promoting public health messages: Should we move beyond fear-evoking appeals in road safety? *Qualitative Health Research 17*, 61–74.

Lustman, M., Wiesenthal, D.L., & Flett, G.L. (2010). Narcissism and aggressive driving: Is an inflated view of the self a road hazard? *Journal of Applied Social Psychology 40*, 1423–1449.

Malta, L.S., Blanchard, E.B., & Freidenberg, B.M. (2005). Psychiatric and behavioral problems in aggressive drivers. *Behaviour Research and Therapy 43*, 1467–1484.

Matthews, G., Dorn, L., & Glendon, A.I. (1991). Personality correlates of driver stress. *Personality and Individual Differences 12*, 535–549.

Miles, D.E., & Johnson, G.L. (2003). Aggressive driving behaviors: Are there psychological and attitudinal predictors? *Transportation Research Part F 6*, 147–161.

Mynttinen, S., Sundström, A., Koivukoski, M., Hakuli, K., Keskinen, E., & Henriksson, W. (2009). Are novice drivers overconfident? A comparison of self-assessed and examiner-assessed driver competences in a Finnish and Swedish sample. *Transportation Research Part F 12*, 120–130.

Neighbors, C., Vietor, N.A., & Knee, C.R. (2002). A motivational model of driving anger and aggression. *Personality and Social Psychology Bulletin 28*, 324–335.

Paleti, R., Eluru, E., & Bhat, C.R. (2010). Examining the influence of aggressive driving behavior on driver injury severity in traffic crashes. *Accident Analysis & Prevention 42*, 1839–1854.

Parsons, R., Tassinary, L.G., Ulrich, R.S., Hebl, M.R., & Grossman-Alexander, M. (1998). The view from the road: Implications for stress recovery and immunization. *Journal of Environmental Psychology 18*, 113–139.

Raudenbush, B., Grayhem, R., Sears, T., & Wilson, I. (2009). Effects of peppermint and cinnamon odor administration on simulated driving alertness, mood and workload. *North American Journal of Psychology 11*, 245–256.

Reason, J., Manstead, A., Stradling, S., Baxter, J., & Campbell, K. (1990). Errors and violations on the roads: A real distinction? *Ergonomics 33*, 1315–1332.

Retting, R.A., Williams, A.F., Farmer, C.M., & Feldman, A.F. (1999). Evaluation of red light camera enforcement in Oxnard, California. *Accident Analysis & Prevention 31*, 169–174.

Shinar, D. (1998). Aggressive driving: The contribution of the drivers and the situation. *Transportation Research Part F 1*, 137–160.

Smart, R.G., Cannon, E., Howard, A., & Mann, R.E. (2005). Can we design cars to prevent road rage? *International Journal of Vehicle Information and Communication Systems 1*, 44–55.

Sümer, N., Lajunen, T., & Özkan, T. (2005). Big five personality traits as the distal predictors of road accident involvement. In G. Underwood (Ed.), *Traffic and transport psychology: Theory and application—Proceedings of the ICTTP 2004* (pp. 215–227). New York, NY: Elsevier.

Wickens, C.M., Mann, R.E., Butters, J., Smart, R.G., & Stoduto, G. (in press). Road rage. In I. Treasaden & B. Puri (Eds.), *Forensic psychiatry: Fundamentals and clinical practice*. Boca Raton, FL: CRC Press.

Wickens, C.M., Mann, R.E., Stoduto, G., Butters, J.E., Ialomiteanu, A., & Smart, R.G. (2012). Does gender moderate the relationship between driver aggression and its risk factors? *Accident Analysis & Prevention 45*, 10–18.

Wickens, C.M., Mann, R.E., Stoduto, G., Flam Zalcman, R., & Butters, J. (2013). Alcohol control measures in traffic. In P. Boyle, P. Boffetta, W. Zatonski, A. Lowenfels, O. Brawley, H. Burns, & J. Rehm (Eds.), *Alcohol: Science, policy and public health* (pp. 378–388). New York, NY: Oxford University Press.

Wickens, C.M., & Wiesenthal, D.L. (2005). State driver stress as a function of occupational stress, traffic congestion, and trait stress susceptibility. *Journal of Applied Biobehavioral Research 10*, 83–97.

Wickens, C.M., Wiesenthal, D.L., Flora, D.B., & Flett, G.L. (2011). Understanding driver anger and aggression: Attributional theory in the driving environment. *Journal of Experimental Psychology: Applied 17*, 354–370.

Wickens, C.M., Wiesenthal, D.L., Hall, A., & Roseborough, J.E.W. (2013). Driver anger on the information superhighway: A content analysis of online complaints of offensive driver behaviour. *Accident Analysis & Prevention 51*, 84–92.

Wiesenthal, D.L., Hennessy, D.A., & Totten, B. (2000). The influence of music on driver stress. *Journal of Applied Social Psychology 30*, 1709–1719.

Wiesenthal, D.L., Lustman, M., & Roseborough, J. (in press). Aggressive driving: Current perspectives in theory and research. In A. Smiley (Ed.), *Human factors in traffic safety* (3rd ed.). Tucson, AZ: Lawyers & Judges Publishing Company.

Key and challenging words

postulate, deter, retaliatory, attribution, intermittent, ameliorate, alleviate

Questions

1. Summarize the nature of the paradox referred to in paragraph 1.
2. Why is it important that the authors define the term *driver aggression* (paragraph 2)? Paraphrase the definition given in paragraph 2.
3. Explain the importance of headings as an aid to essay organization.
4. Analyze the organization and development of paragraph 8, referring to strategies that make detailed content accessible. For example, you could consider the topic sentence, paragraph development, rhetorical patterns, logical sentence order, sentence structure, transitions, and the like.

5. The authors not only report on studies but also sometimes speculate on (infer) the reason for the findings (for example, see the first half of paragraph 4 where they infer why narcissistic and sensation-seeking drivers may drive more aggressively). Choose two findings that are not speculated on in this paragraph—for example, "machismo, extraversion, ego defensiveness, and emotional instability" are not discussed—and in one or two sentences infer why they might increase driver aggressiveness.
6. Explain which you think is the main factor in aggressive driving, choosing one of the subsections under person-related contributors or situation-related contributors. Use critical thinking and specific textual references to support your answer.

Post-reading

1. Create an educational and/or enforcement campaign to address aggressive driving. As part of your general strategy, choose the person- and situation-related contributors to aggressive driving you believe are most likely to reduce the incidence of aggressive driving. You can aim your strategy to a particular demographic if you think it will be effective to do so. (A substantial budget allows you to take a multi-pronged approach to the problem.)

Pharmaceutical Innovation: Can We Live Forever?
A Commentary on Schnittker and Karandinos

Joel Lexchin
(1,954 words)

> ### *Pre-reading*
>
> 1. Access your library's database and read the abstract for "Methuselah's medicine: Pharmaceutical innovation and mortality in the United States, 1960–2000," the basis for Lexchin's commentary. Who was Methuselah? Summarize the article's abstract in two sentences.
> 2. Does the title suggest Lexchin's thesis or approach? Scan the first two paragraphs in order to determine this information and come up with a reading hypothesis.

1　If we discover enough new drugs can we live forever, or at least for a lot longer than we currently do? This is the thesis that Schnittker and Karandinos set out to explore in "Methuselah's Medicine: Pharmaceutical Innovation and Mortality in the United States, 1960–2000" in this issue of Social Science & Medicine (Schnittker & Karandinos, 2010). More specifically, they look at the relationship between pharmaceutical innovation and life expectancy between 1960 and 2000 in the United States (US). The amount of pharmaceutical innovation is measured by the number of new molecular entities (NME) approved by the Food and Drug Administration and mortality—life expectancy at birth and age-specific mortality—is examined as a function of NME approvals within a given year. In addition to drug approvals they also consider the role that per-capita gross domestic product (GDP) and health-specific spending play in increasing longevity. Although they find that gdp has a larger association with life expectancy than NME, they also conclude that their "study demonstrates a significant relationship between pharmaceutical innovation and life expectancy at birth" (Schnittker & Karandinos, 2010).

2　This paper joins a growing list of publications, chiefly from Frank Lichtenberg (2007), that argue that the more new drugs there are the better off we are. However, just as Lichtenberg has his critics (Baker & Fugh-Berman, 2009) so too there are issues with this present paper that need to be debated and clarified before its conclusions can be accepted. Before doing that, though, let us give some new drugs their due—the antiretroviral drugs for HIV/AIDS certainly have extended the lives of people with that disease; the antithrombolitics are extremely valuable for treating patients with acute myocardial infarctions. Clearly, some new drugs are valuable but can that conclusion be generalized in the way that Schnittker and Karandinos have done?

3　All NMEs are not the same; the first angiotensin converting enzyme (ACE) inhibitor or the first proton pump inhibitor yielded significantly more benefits than the second or third or fourth in the class and many of the NMEs that have appeared in the 40 years being considered by the authors are "add-ons" to existing drug classes. Furthermore, many nmes have nothing to do with increasing life expectancy. Terbinafine is a good drug for treating toenail fungal infections, but no one dies from infected toenails. Minoxidil has some benefit in male pattern alopecia, but baldness is not a fatal disease. What percent of nme introductions since 1960 have the potential for altering mortality patterns? That question is not explored in this present study.

4　The French drug bulletin, La revue Prescrire, analyzes the therapeutic value of new drugs (and new indications for older drugs) introduced into the French market. Out of 983 new drugs or new indications for existing drugs marketed between 1996 and 2006, only 4.1 per cent offered major therapeutic gains and an additional 10.8 per cent had some value but did not fundamentally change present therapeutic practice ("A look back at pharmaceuticals in 2006: aggressive advertising cannot hide the absence of therapeutic advances," 2007). Garattini and Bertele (2002) examined 12 new anticancer drugs approved in Europe between 1995 and 2000 which contained new molecular entities or known active principles with new indications and concluded that none of the 12 offered any significant improvement in action. Of the 61 new biotechnology products introduced in Europe between 1995 and 2003 for therapeutic purposes, only 2 were approved on the basis that they were superior to existing therapies using hard clinical endpoints (Joppi, Bertele, & Garattini, 2005). According to Schnittker and Karandinos (2010), the major benefit has come from the introduction of new drugs that treat cardiovascular disease and, as I acknowledged above, certain new drugs are extremely valuable in these conditions. But, on-the-other hand, the thiazide diuretics, some of which were introduced before 1960, are at least as good and possibly superior to the much newer ace inhibitors and calcium channel blockers in preventing the complications of hypertension (The allhat officers and coordinators for the allhat collaborative research group, 2002). Aspirin, which was available long before 1960, is a major factor in decreasing mortality from cardio and cerebrovascular disease.

5　The data presented by Schnittker and Karandinos show that mortality reduction is greatest in the 15–19 year age group (Schnittker & Karandinos, 2010). What are the major causes of mortality in that group? According to the US National Center for Injury Prevention and Control the three leading causes of death in the 15–19 age group are unintentional injury, homicide, and suicide (National Center for Injury Prevention and Control, 2009). Neither unintentional injury nor homicide is preventable by pharmacotherapy and the value of antidepressants in reducing deaths by suicide is far from clear (Jureidini & McHenry, 2009). The other 7 leading causes of death in this age group, which may be modifiable by drug treatment, account for little more than 12 per cent of mortality. Even if pharmaceuticals eliminated every death in each of these 7 causes, the overall impact on deaths would be minimal.

Source: From Social Science & Medicine, vol. 70, no. 7, 2010, pp. 972–3. Reprinted with permission from Elsevier.

6   Schnittker and Karandinos note that their findings are for the US and that results in other countries may differ for a variety of reasons including how extensive health insurance is (eliminating financial barriers to prescription drugs) and the degree of innovation in the country. With these caveats in mind how do changes in life expectancy in the US compare to what has happened in other developed countries? Life expectancy in the United States in 1960 was 73.1 years for women and 66.6 years for men. In that year, the US ranked 14th among the Organisation for Economic Co-operation and Development countries for women and 20th for men. By 2000 US life expectancy for women and men was 79.5 and 74.1, respectively and the US ranked 22nd and 21st (Directorate for Employment, 2009). At the same time as the US is losing ground in life expectancy compared to European countries, the European Federation of Pharmaceutical Industries and Associations is complaining that innovation in Europe is lagging behind the US (European Federation of Pharmaceutical Industries and Associations, 2009) and other work shows that new drugs become available much faster in the US than in other developed countries (Office of Fair Trading, 2007). Clearly there are other factors involved in changes in national mortality figures, but if new drugs are helping the US then they are significantly outweighed by these other considerations.

7   Schnittker and Karandinos state that "new drugs tend to be used promptly" and "this implies a relatively quick impact on mortality" (Schnittker & Karandinos, 2010). The first statement is certainly true, and this uptake is significantly fuelled by an annual $57.5 billion promotional budget (Gagnon & Lexchin, 2008). But there is good reason to question the latter claim. Knowledge about the safety of new drugs is minimal at best because they have only been tested in highly selective populations and in patient numbers that preclude identification of less common side effects. One indication of the unrecognized dangers from new drugs is that half of the drugs withdrawn from the US market for safety reasons occur within two years of marketing (Lasser et al., 2002). The example of what happened with rofecoxib should make us sceptical of claims that new drugs lead to rapid declines in mortality. Graham and colleagues estimate that in the five years that rofecoxib was on the US market there were between 88,000 and 140,000 excess cases of serious coronary heart disease with a case-fatality rate of 44 per cent (Graham et al., 2005).

8   Finally, and more generally, the paper by Schnittker and Karandinos (2010) buys into the notion that we will be saved by innovation. On a micro level, innovation is important and many people are better off due to technological advances, but on a population level, it is harder to prove that more innovation and technology is the most important reason for better health outcomes. The US has significantly more neonatologists and neonatal intensive care beds than Australia, Canada, or the United Kingdom but does not have better birth weight-specific mortality rates than these three other countries (Thompson, Goodman, & Little, 2002). A recent systematic review that I participated in compared health outcomes in the US and Canada for patients treated for similar underlying medical conditions; in effect we were comparing higher overall expenditures and more technology (US) with a universal public insurance plan where inpatient care is almost completely delivered by private not-for-profit institutions (Canada): "Studies addressed diverse problems, including cancer, coronary artery disease, chronic medical illnesses, and surgical procedures. Of 10 studies that included extensive statistical adjustment and enrolled broad populations, five favoured Canada, two favoured the United States, and three showed equivalent or mixed results. Overall, results for mortality favoured Canada" (Guyatt et al., 2007, p. e27).

9   Drugs that are important advances in medical care are few and far between. We definitely need more of them and their development should be encouraged but, despite new drugs, I'm not counting on living to 150.

References

A look back at pharmaceuticals in 2006: aggressive advertising cannot hide the absence of therapeutic advances. (2007). *Prescrire International, 16*, 80–86.

Baker, D., & Fugh-Berman, A. (2009). Do new drugs increase life expectancy? A critique of a Manhattan institute paper. *Journal of General Internal Medicine, 24*, 678–682.

Directorate for Employment, Labout, and Social Affairs. (2009). *OECD health data 2008-frequently requested data*. Organisation for Economic Co-operation and Development.

European Federation of Pharmaceutical Industries and Associations. (2009). *The pharmaceutical industry in figures: Key data – 2009 update*. Brussels: efpia.

Gagnon, M.-A., & Lexchin, J. (2008). The cost of pushing pills: a new estimate of pharmaceutical promotion expenditures in the United States. *PLoS Medicine, 5*,e1.

Garattini, S., & Bertele, V. (2002). Efficacy, safety, and cost of new anticancer drugs. British Medical Journal, 325, 269–271.

Graham, D. J., Campen, D., Hui, R., Spence, M., Cheetham, C., Levy, G., et al. (2005). Risk of acute myocardial infarction and sudden cardiac death in patients treated with cyclo-oxygenase 2 selective and non-selective non-steroidal anti-inflammatory drugs: nested case-control study. *Lancet, 365*, 475–481.

Guyatt, G. H., Devereaux, P. J., Lexchin, J., Stone, S. B., Yalnizyan, A., Himmelstein, D., et al. (2007). A systematic review of studies comparing health outcomes in Canada and the United States. *Open Medicine, 1*, E27–E36.

Joppi, R., Bertele, V., & Garattini, S. (2005). Disappointing biotech. *British Medical Journal, 331*, 895–897.

Jureidini, J. N., & McHenry, L. B. (2009). Key opinion leaders and paediatric antidepressant overprescribing. *Psychotherapy and Psychosomatics, 78*, 197–201.

Lasser, K. E., Allen, P. D., Woolhandler, S. J., Himmelstein, D. U., Wolfe, S. M., & Bor, D. H. (2002). Timing of new black box warnings and withdrawals for prescription medications. *JAMA, 287*, 2215–2220.

Lichtenberg, F. (2007). *Why has longevity increased more in some states than in others? The role of medical innovation and other factors.* New York: Manhattan Institute.

National Center for Injury Prevention and Control. (2009). *10 leading causes of death, United States 2006, all races, both sexes.* Atlanta: Centers for Disease Control and Prevention.

Office of Fair Trading. (2007). Annexe D: global overview of the pharmaceutical industry.

Schnittker, J., & Karandinos, G. (2010). Methuselah's Medicine: Pharmaceutical innovation and mortality in the United States, 1960–2000. *Social Science & Medicine, 70*, 961–968.

The ALLHAT officers and coordinators for the ALLHAT collaborative research group. (2002). Major outcomes in high-risk hypertensive patients randomized to angiotensin-converting enzyme inhibitor or calcium channel blocker vs diuretic: the antihypertensive and lipid-lowering treatment to prevent heart attack trial (ALLHAT). *JAMA, 288*, 2981–2997.

Thompson, L. A., Goodman, D. C., & Little, G. A. (2002). Is more neonatal intensive care always better? Insights from a cross-national comparison of reproductive care. *Pediatrics, 109*, 1036–1043.

Key and challenging words

pharmaceutical, therapeutic, modifiable, caveat

Questions

1. What is the function of paragraph 1? How does it differ from introductions in the kinds of essays you might be asked to write?

2. a) What specific argumentative strategy does Lexchin use in paragraph 2? b) Paraphrase the last sentence in this paragraph.

3. Explain in your own words the problems with Schnittker and Karandinos's methodology and/or the assumptions on which part of the study is based (see paragraph 3), according to Lexchin.

4. Analyze the development of paragraph 6 (e.g., you could consider the rhetorical pattern, the placement of the topic sentence, use of deductive versus inductive development, etc.).

5. What kind of evidence does Lexchin use throughout the body paragraphs to support his claims? Pointing to at least one body paragraph show how his use of evidence provides support for his claim.

6. How does the claim in paragraph 8 differ from that of the other paragraphs? Why do you think he addresses this issue in his second-last paragraph rather than in an earlier paragraph?

7. Explain the extensive use of the Guyatt et al. study in paragraph 8.

Post-reading

1. *Collaborative activity:* (a) Discuss or debate central issues related to health care in Canada versus in the United States. (b) Could the fact that the Schnittker and Karandinos study is based on US statistics affect its applicability to Canada? If so, how?

2. Access the Guyatt et al. study mentioned in paragraph 8. Note that it is found in the open access journal *Open Medicine* (www.openmedicine.ca). (a) What are open access sources? According to the website, why is open access publishing particularly important in the field of medicine? (b) Summarize the "Discussion" section of the Guyatt et al. study in approximately 150 words (the section is 1,500 words).

3. In the same issue of *Social Science & Medicine* (volume 70, issue 7, 2010), Schnittker and Karandinos respond to Lexchin's commentary as well as to another commentary. Summarize Schnittker and Karandinos's response to Lexchin; then briefly explain whether you think it was an adequate response (make your summary and analysis 300–400 words).

Cyberbullying Myths and Realities

Russell A. Sabella, Justin W. Patchin, and Sameer Hinduja
(6,935 words)

> ## Pre-reading
>
> 1. *Collaborative or individual question:* Identify/reflect on some of your beliefs about cyberbullying. For example, you could start with the five questions, *Who?*, *What?*, *When?*, *Where?*, and *How?* (e.g., Who is a typical cyberbully or victim?; What are the causes of cyberbullying?). Then, consider where these beliefs come from (e.g., family, peers, the media, teachers).

Abstract

Bullying has long been a concern of youth advocates (e.g., educators, counselors, researchers, policy makers). Recently, cyberbullying (bullying perpetrated through online technology) has dominated the headlines as a major current-day adolescent challenge. This article reviews available empirical research to examine the accuracy of commonly perpetuated claims about cyberbullying. The analysis revealed several myths about the nature and extent of cyberbullying that are being fueled by media headlines and unsubstantiated public declarations. These myths include that (a) everyone knows what cyberbullying is; (b) cyberbullying is occurring at epidemic levels; (c) cyberbullying causes suicide; (d) cyberbullying occurs more often now than traditional bullying; (e) like traditional bullying, cyberbullying is a rite of passage; (f) cyberbullies are outcasts or just mean kids; and (g) to stop cyberbullying, just turn off your computer or cell phone. These assertions are clarified using data that are currently available so that adults who work with youth will have an accurate understanding of cyberbullying to better assist them in effective prevention and response. Implications for prevention efforts in education in light of these revelations are also discussed and include effective school policies, educating students and stakeholders, the role of peer helper programs, and responsive services (e.g., counseling).

1. Introduction

1   Teens now have in their hands the same amount of computing ability that, just a decade ago, only large businesses could afford. How does a young person manage ever-increasing access to technology and, by extension, the

power it imbues? Most students use technology responsibly, but some have chosen to use it in careless and inappropriate ways by hurting, humiliating, embarrassing, and personally attacking others (Hinduja & Patchin, 2012b; Kowalski, Limber, & Agatston, 2008; Patchin & Hinduja, 2010). This phenomenon has been termed cyberbullying, which has been defined as *"willful and repeated harm inflicted through the use of computers, cell phones, and other electronic devices"* (Hinduja & Patchin, 2009, p. 5, 2012a).

2   In several ways, cyberbullying may be perceived as more sinister than "off-line" (i.e., traditional or school-yard) bullying because the attacks can be more intense, frequent, unsuspecting, and seemingly difficult to stop (Hinduja & Patchin, 2009). Compared to traditional bullies, cyberbullies are not restrained by space or time. Some cyberbullies may hide under a cloak of anonymity, in essence allowing them to easily attack others at any time and from any place they want (Kowalski et al., 2008). With modern technology, cyberbullying can occur at the "speed of thought" and in front of much larger audiences than those behaviors confined to the schoolyard. Online bullies also can potentially be even more cruel than off-line bullies because, in addition to words, they can incorporate as part of their attacks a rich array of media including sounds, altered photos, text, video, slide shows, and polls (Li, 2007; Sabella, 2008).

3   Though it occurs in cyberspace, this problem should not be trivialized since it has been linked to real-world consequences. For example, research has found that cyberbullying is associated with negative emotions such as sadness, anger, frustration, embarrassment, or fear (Hinduja & Patchin, 2007; Patchin & Hinduja, 2011; Ybarra & Mitchell, 2007), and these emotions have been correlated with delinquency and interpersonal violence among youth and young adults (Aseltine, Gore, & Gordon, 2000; Broidy & Agnew, 1997; Mazerolle, Burton, Cullen, Evans, & Payne, 2000; Mazerolle & Piquero, 1998). Furthermore, cyberbullying has been linked to low self-esteem and suicidal ideation, recent school difficulties, assaultive conduct, substance use, carrying a weapon to school, and traditional bullying offending and victimization (Hinduja & Patchin, 2007, 2008, 2009; Schneider, O'Donnell, Stueve, & Coulter, 2012; Ybarra, Diener-West, & Leaf, 2007; Ybarra & Mitchell, 2004a). It is for these reasons that youth-serving professionals should seek to gain and share knowledge related to the identification, prevention, and response of this problem.

4   One of the dangers, however, of doing cyberbullying risk-reduction work is that, in the course of educating students, staff, parents, and others, we can unwittingly contribute to the "hype" generated by a mass media that focuses on the dramatic and erratic. Recent headlines can serve to fuel what may be a distorted and artificially inflated view of cyberbullying—one not based on reality (Magid, 2011). Without a careful review of the professional literature, counseling or educating students about cyberbullying may unintentionally stem from rumor or extreme and rare cases. Without carefully differentiating fact from fallacy, our good intentions can lead to erroneous decisions, harmful attitudes, and ineffective programmatic strategies (Kowalski et al., 2008; Willard, 2007a, 2010).

5   When working with students or others within the school community, youth educators (which may include, and from hereafter, refers to school counselors, researchers, policymakers, and, in general, youth advocates) must take care to provide accurate information and guidance supported by existing research. In this article, we seek to identify and clarify common myths surrounding cyberbullying by presenting research-supported realities that call into question some of the conventional wisdom concerning this problem. The myths included in this article were identified through various sources. First, we conducted an extensive review of the available professional literature and mass media publications. Second, we have heard these myths frequently professed through our work with thousands of educators and students while providing consultation, training, and policy development in the area of cybersafety. Finally, we informally surveyed the online community called the Embrace Civility Network (formerly the *Youth Risk Online Professional Network*)—a consortium of over 250 recognized experts in the field, as well as educators, counselors, attorneys, CEOs/CSOs of online safety organizations, scholars, and legislators. This list is not intended to be exhaustive as there are unquestionably other statements that frequently appear in popular media and professional literature that lack adequate substantiation. The current work, however, is intended to clarify some of the more commonly referenced "facts" about cyberbullying. It should also be acknowledged that even the empirical research in this area is still evolving and therefore needs to be considered with a critical eye on operationalization and methodology. We begin with myth #1 which discusses this issue and its implications for our understanding of cyberbullying even further.

2. Myth 1: Everyone Knows What Cyberbullying Is

6   Many individuals may believe that they already fully understand and can recognize what cyberbullying is. The reality, however, is that there exists much variability in the way cyberbullying is defined and considered—even among cyberbullying researchers (Menesini & Nocentini, 2009; Oblad, 2012; Ybarra, Boyd, Korchmaros, & Oppenheim, 2012). As discussed by Patchin and Hinduja (2012), some researchers use very broad definitions of the problem that include every possible experience with any form of online aggression. Others focus only on specific types of harm, such as humiliation or threats to one's physical safety, without also including other forms like name-calling, insults, or social exclusion. Some cover any and all media and venues through which cyberbullying can occur, while others may leave out a few technologies (such as webcams) or environments (such as in online gaming networks). To confuse matters even further, in many languages other than English, there is no equivalent word for the term "bullying," which can affect the reported prevalence rates, especially when considering data collected internationally (Craig, Henderson, & Murphy, 2000; Smorti, Menesini, & Smith, 2003).

7   The varied conceptualizations are not surprising because, in reality, a continuum of behaviors exists, ranging from annoying or disappointing to severe, persistent, and pervasive attacks on others. At what point on the continuum does an incident make the leap from being one of poor judgment to one that we would call cyberbullying—or even one that may be criminal? The answers to these questions are still unclear and in need of further formal inquiry and examination.

8   One problem with not having a reliable and widely accepted definition of cyberbullying is that the inconsistencies lead to different measurements of the nature and extent of harassment in cyberspace, which at best provides an incomplete picture and at worst leads to misinformation and confusion (Mishna, Pepler, & Wiener, 2006; Patchin & Hinduja, 2012). Another problem with inconsistent definitions is that the terms *bullying* and *cyberbullying* are arguably now being overused among both adults and children alike. For example, some students are claiming that they are being bullied because they were not invited to a popular party, because they were accidentally pushed in the hallways, or perhaps teased, lied about, or made fun

of *one time* (Williams & Guerra, 2007; Wolak, Mitchell, & Finkelhor, 2007). It is important for all members of the school community to understand that peer conflict does not equate to bullying. To reiterate, arguing, bantering back-and-forth, ignoring, roughhousing and fighting are not necessarily instances of bullying, whether they occur online or via traditional venues (Willard, 2007c). Instead, cyberbullying, like traditional bullying, is characterized by intention, repetition, harm, and power imbalance (Patchin & Hinduja, 2006; Wolak et al., 2007). Not every conflict meets these criteria (Baas, de Jong, & Drossaert, 2013). Educators should help students understand and differentiate between situations that would and would not be considered bullying, perhaps through the presentation of examples, scenarios, and even role-playing exercises (see e.g., Sabella, 2012b).

3. Myth 2: Cyberbullying Is Occurring at Epidemic Levels

9   Consider these actual news headlines and stories:

- "Cyber bullying is a growing epidemic in communities, including ours" (Chin, 2011).
- "Cyberbullying: A National Epidemic" (Education Insider, 2010).
- "Cyber bullying spiralling out of control in schools" (McDougall, 2011).
- "Curing Utah's 'silent epidemic': Finding a solution to teen suicide" (Wood, 2013).
- "Child advocates say a growing epidemic of 'cyberbullying'—the use of computers, cell phones, social-networking sites and other technology to threaten or humiliate others" (Billitteri, 2008).

10   These are just a few examples of the many headlines that are seen through mass media that reinforce the notion that both bullying and cyberbullying have reached sweeping proportions. To be sure, one incident of any form of bullying is too many. However, making a serious issue such as cyberbullying seem more problematic than it really is, is in itself problematic. First, some students are apt to believe that if the majority of their peers are being bullied and bullying others, then it can be considered normative behavior and consequently "not a big deal" (Hinduja & Patchin, 2012b). Second, the purported cyberbullying epidemic seems to be giving our youth a bad reputation, contributing

to what some have referred to as "*juvenoia*" (Finkelhor, 2011). Conventional wisdom suggests that "kids these days" are more violent and less respectful than a generation ago. It is doubtful that this is true, especially since every generation seems to think that the youth of today are worse than when they were growing up. In fact, strong evidence exists to suggest that violence among youth, especially in schools, has actually decreased in the last decade (Finkelhor, 2013; National Center for Education Statistics, 2013). Finally, labeling cyberbullying an epidemic leads to some level of hysteria which may contribute to overzealous adults making uninformed and unwise decisions in an attempt to control youth behavior (e.g., zero-tolerance policies; taking away cell phones or other access to technology) (Hinduja & Patchin, 2009).

11   A precise measure of the prevalence of cyberbullying among teens is impossible to determine, partly related to Myth #1 (inconsistent definitions) but also due to varied methodological approaches. Some studies ask their teen participants about *any* experience with cyberbullying, while others focus on "online youth" who experience specific types of high-tech harm within the previous 30 days. One published study found that 72% of youth have experienced cyberbullying (Juvonen & Gross, 2008) whereas other published research has put this number at less than 7% (Ybarra, 2004; Ybarra & Mitchell, 2004a). The majority of studies estimate that anywhere from 6% to 30% of teens have experienced some form of cyberbullying, while the number of youth who admit to cyberbullying others at some point in their lives ranges from about 4% to 20% (Patchin & Hinduja, 2012). Of course this means that 70–80% of youth have not been cyberbullied, and have not cyberbullied others.

4. Myth 3: Cyberbullying Causes Suicide

12   Over the last few years, there have been several high-profile incidents where teenagers and young adults have taken their own lives in part because of experiences with bullying and cyberbullying (Bazelon, 2010; Boyette, 2013; Halligan, 2006; High, 2007; Jones, 2008; Marr & Field, 2001). The viral nature of these stories in the media is especially troubling because exposure to news items on suicide has been cited as one of the numerous risk factors contributing to suicidal behavior (Beautrais, Collings, & Ehrhardt, 2005; Hawton & Williams, 2001). Also, the impact of news media reporting on suicidal behavior appears to be strongest among young people (WHO, 2000). Despite these tragedies, the vast majority of cyberbullying victims do not kill themselves, and those who do typically have experienced a constellation of stressors and other issues operating in their lives, making it difficult to isolate the influence of one specific personal or social problem as compared to others (Hinduja & Patchin, 2010a).

13   That said, research has shown that being involved in bullying (both as a victim and a bully) as a young person increases the risk for experiencing factors which are associated with suicidal thoughts, suicidal attempts, and completed suicides (Bauman, Toomey, & Walker, 2013; Campbell, Spears, Slee, Butler, & Kift, 2012; Klomek, Sourander, & Gould, 2010; Klomek et al., 2009; Rigby & Slee, 1999; Skapinakis et al., 2011). Kim and Leventhal (2008), for example, conducted a meta-analytical review of 37 different studies that examined the association between bullying and suicide, with an emphasis on the strengths and limitations of each of the study's research designs. Their review concluded that any participation in bullying increases risk factors such as depression and anxiety, which can be associated with suicidal ideation and/or behaviors in a broad spectrum of youth.

14   Recently, Hinduja and Patchin (2010a) conducted a study on teen technology use and misuse involving approximately 2000 randomly selected middle school students from one of the largest school districts in the United States. Results showed that youth who experienced traditional bullying or cyberbullying, as either an offender or a target, were more likely to report suicidal thoughts and to have previously attempted suicide than those who had not experienced such forms of peer aggression. The authors found that traditional bullying victims were 1.7 times more likely and traditional bullying offenders were 2.1 times more likely to have attempted suicide than those who were not traditional victims or offenders (Hinduja & Patchin, 2010a). Similarly, cyberbullying victims were 1.9 times more likely and cyberbullying offenders were 1.5 times more likely to have attempted suicide than those who were not cyberbullying victims or offenders. Winsper, Lereya, Zanarini, and Wolke (2012) conducted a study that focused on the prospective link between involvement in bullying (bully, victim, bully/victim) and subsequent suicide ideation in preadolescent children in the United Kingdom. These authors concluded that being a target of bullying, especially as a bully/victim, significantly increases the risk of suicide ideation in preadolescent children.

15   Given all of this research, one might ask: Why is it a myth that "cyberbullying causes suicide?" The answer to this question lies in the important difference between the nature of *correlation* and *causation*. While it is true that there exists a *relationship* between bullying and suicide (a connection or correlation), no conclusive statistical evidence has shown that a cyberbullying experience directly "leads to" or *causes* suicide. As previously stated, most youth who are cyberbullied do not take their own lives. So, the best that we can confidently say is that, among some young people, cyberbullying and suicide may be co-occurring (or are "co-related") with at least one of many other factors such as depression, social withdrawal, disability, social hopelessness, or other psychiatric morbidity (Skapinakis et al., 2011). That is, cyberbullying may aggravate the victim's already existing vulnerabilities. As Hinduja and Patchin (2010a) concluded, ". . . it is unlikely that experience with cyberbullying *by itself* leads to youth suicide. Rather, it tends to exacerbate instability and hopelessness in the minds of adolescents already struggling with stressful life circumstances" (p. 217). Unfortunately, some research findings have shown that the primary focus of news items in this context is on the technology involved in the cyberbullying and not the suicide events themselves or other important factors that may have contributed to the suicides, such as victims' mental well-being (Thom et al., 2011).

5. Myth 4: Cyberbullying Occurs More Often Now than Traditional Bullying

16   Conventional wisdom would have us believe that since technology has proliferated over the last decade and stories of cyberbullying are frequently mentioned in the news, it is likely more prevalent than traditional, schoolyard bullying. However, research demonstrates that this is not the case (at least not yet). For example, according to the National Center for Educational Statistics (2013) report, *Indicators of School Crime and Safety*, (which reported data from 2011), 27.8% of students reported being the victim of bullying during the school year while only 9% of students had been cyberbullied. Ybarra et al. (2012) recently found that 25% of students had been bullied in person while 10% had been bullied online. Overall, most research demonstrates that cyberbullying still occurs less frequently than bullying, though that could change in the future. Jones, Mitchell, and Finkelhor (2013) collected data from students across the US in 2000, 2005, and 2010 and saw a modest but steady increase in cyberbullying between 2000 and 2010 (from 6% to 11%).

17   Beran and Li (2007) reviewed several published studies, all of which suggest that cyberbullying and traditional bullying occur at a comparable rate. One possible explanation for the similar rates of traditional bullying and cyberbullying is that there seems to be a significant overlap among students who are involved in both forms (Beran & Li, 2007; Cross et al., 2009; Hinduja & Patchin, 2008; Raskauskas & Stoltz, 2007; Smith et al., 2008; Vandebosch & Van Cleemput, 2009; Ybarra & Mitchell, 2004a). For example, Beran and Li (2007) surveyed 432 students from grades 7–9 in Canadian schools about their victimization experiences, and found that one third of children bullied in cyberspace were also bullied at school. In addition, Ybarra and Mitchell (2004a) found that many cyberbullies were also cybervictims, and that almost half of the cyberbullies reported having been victims of traditional bullying. Recognizing this overlap in behaviors is important, since it affects decision-making that determines a school's goals/focus and commitment of resources. Focusing on cyberbullying as a priority at the expense of addressing traditional bullying is a mistake. Both should be addressed as different manifestations of the same underlying issues.

6. Myth 5: Like Traditional Bullying, Cyberbullying Is a Rite of Passage All Teens Experience

18   "Boys will be boys." "It'll toughen him up." "It will help her grow a backbone so she can handle life." "That which does not kill you only makes you stronger." These statements are sometimes used by both children and adults to normalize or minimize hurtful behavior among children and teens, sometimes even as a way of coping with cyberbullying after it occurs (Parris, Varjas, Meyers, & Cutts, 2012). The message that these perspectives send to our youth is that social cruelty has been common to one degree or another among past generations and, because they survived, experiencing bullying is some sort of ritual that we all must go through during the course of normal maturation. This is simply not true. In fact, U.S. President Barack Obama cogently emphasized this point during a conference on preventing bullying at the White House on March 10th, 2011 when he said:

> If there's one goal of this conference, it's to dispel the myth that bullying is just a harmless rite of passage or an inevitable part of growing up. It's not.

Bullying can have destructive consequences for our young people. And it's not something we have to accept. As parents and students, as teachers and members of the community, we can take steps—all of us—to help prevent bullying and create a climate in our schools in which all of our children can feel safe; a climate in which they all can feel like they belong. As adults, we all remember what it was like to see kids picked on in the hallways or in the schoolyard. And I have to say, with big ears and the name that I have, I wasn't immune. I didn't emerge unscathed. But because it's something that happens a lot, and it's something that's always been around, sometimes we've turned a blind eye to the problem. We've said, "Kids will be kids." And so sometimes we overlook the real damage that bullying can do, especially when young people face harassment day after day, week after week (2011).

19   In reality, no matter how prevalent or pervasive bullying has been in our history, it was not acceptable then and it is not acceptable now. In her book, *Cyberbullying: What Counselors Need to Know*, Bauman (2011) presented a significant body of evidence supporting the idea that there are negative consequences of bullying for all involved youth. She presented various relevant research studies that demonstrate that victims *and* bullies have more social, emotional, behavioral, and academic problems than others who are not involved. As described above, victims are more likely to suffer from depression, anxiety, low self-esteem, and loneliness, and these consequences are still detected when the victims are adults. Various studies that have found that peer rejection, delinquency, criminality, violence, and suicidal ideation were additional outcomes of involvement in bullying (Bauman, 2008; Farrington, 2012; Fekkes, Pijpers, & Verloove-VanHorick, 2004; Hinduja & Patchin, 2007; Mynard, Joseph, & Alexander, 2000; Sharp, 1995; Smokowski & Kopasz, 2005). Having a "thick skin" or even notable coping skills may not be enough for some youth to navigate the pain, embarrassment, humiliation, and horror of victimization. Although many students are resilient and may even summon inner strength they did not know they had in order to deal with bullying or cyberbullying, some simply are unable to do so. Besides, there is no valuable life lesson that one can learn from enduring bullying that cannot be taught in a more humane way.

7. Myth 6: Cyberbullies Are Outcasts or Just Mean Kids

20   Some seem to believe that the majority of youth who cyberbully others simply do it for the sake of inflicting harm, as some sort of antisocial or even sadistic behavior inspired by their online activity (Finkelhor, 2011). As is often the case, there is a measure of truth to this, as some adolescent developmental experts and philosophers view bullying as driven by a need for control and domination by a child who perceives that his/her actions will lead to greater peer acceptance and recognition (Adler & Adler, 1995, 1996; Faris & Felmlee, 2011; Vaillancourt & Hymel, 2006). However, the weight of the research has shown, instead, that most youth participate in cyberbullying to get revenge or because they are "just playin'" (König, Gollwitzer, & Steffgen, 2010; Sanders, 2009; Varjas, Talley, Meyers, Parris & Cutts, 2010). As Elizabeth Englander (2008) concluded after surveying youth who admitted to cyberbullying others: "Cyberbullies themselves identify their own anger and desire for revenge as the major immediate motive for engaging in cyberbullying. A second motive is identified by students who report that they engage in cyberbullying 'as a joke.'" (p. 8)

21   It seems that many cyberbullies who retaliate are often angry, frustrated, or otherwise emotionally distraught and are simply acting out using the technology that is readily at their fingertips. Others participate in cyberbullying because they want retribution by returning a hurt or injury or to seek justice and teach a lesson. Still others casually dismiss the gravity of their cyberbullying behaviors because they do not make the connection between their online behavior and the offline consequences. These aggressors have also been referred to as "inadvertent" cyberbullies (Willard, 2007c) because, although their postings were intentional, they intended no harm. At the time, inadvertent cyberbullies believed that what they were doing was benign, and they were just "having fun" or "messing around." Although those who are mean to others in real life often behave similarly online, this is not always the case. Instead, some cyberbullies may be perceived among teachers and peers as kind and responsible students while in school, even when they could be actively involved in bullying others outside the purview of adults. For example, Hinduja and Patchin (2012b) found that those students who reported earning grades of mostly A's were just as likely to be involved in cyberbullying (both as a target and a bully) as those students who reported that they typically earned

C's or D's. Just because certain students do well academically does not mean they are less likely to mistreat others. Those who subscribe to this myth may also mistakenly conclude that cyberbullies are easily identified and generally known among students and teachers. In fact, some parents and teachers would be shocked to know that some "good" students are also involved in the problem behavior.

8. Myth 7: To Stop Cyberbullying, Just Turn Off Your Computer or Cell Phone

22   It may seem logical at first to consider turning away from technology as a means to stopping cyberbullying from occurring (Englander & Muldowney, 2007). Encouraging youth to turn off or avoid technology, however, is an unrealistic and overall ineffective long-term strategy (Hinduja & Patchin, 2009). Technology is ubiquitous and now integrated in virtually all aspects of their lives (Madden, Lenhart, Duggan, Cortesi, & Gasser, 2013). Moreover, technology is an important social and educational tool for teens, and someone who is being cyberbullied should not have to miss out on all of the benefits technology has to offer (Hinduja & Patchin, 2012b). Finally, if the target of the cyberbullying didn't do anything wrong, why should he or she be punished by not being able to use their favorite electronic devices? Since when has it been appropriate to blame the victim? Advising a student to avoid technology in response to cyberbullying is like advising someone being bullied at school to quit going to school. Also consider that turning off the computer or cell phone does not stop many forms of cyberbullying (Hinduja & Patchin, 2009). A student does not need to be online for someone to create a mean or hurtful Web page about him or her. Rumors can be circulated via cell phone or online text messages without the victim being involved. A harassing online profile can be created without a target even knowing about it.

23   We need to acknowledge how essential connected technology is to teens. In particular, text messaging has become the primary way that teens reach their friends, surpassing face-to-face contact, email, instant messaging and voice calling as the go-to daily communication tool for the 14–17 year old age group (Madden et al., 2013). Being forced to disconnect for an extended period of time is not a realistic long-term solution. Second, telling a child to ignore noxious messages and postings can be difficult. Once images and negative content is witnessed,

they cannot be "unwitnessed." Asking a child to simply delete unpleasant content does not solve the problem either. To the contrary, deleting posts, texts, emails, or other aggressive content destroys the evidence often needed to eventually identify and respond to the cyberbully (Kowalski et al., 2008; Willard, 2007b).

24   In short, it is clear that avoiding technology will do little to solve the problem of cyberbullying. Instead, counselors need to educate students with information and skills they can use to effectively respond when it does happen. These might include blocking harassing messages, removing hurtful content (after it is archived), or talking with a trusted adult to get additional assistance.

9. Armed with Accurate Information About Cyberbullying, Educators Can Help

25   This article has identified and clarified several myths that are associated with adolescent cyberbullying. Existing research has helped to shed empirical light on the conventional wisdom surrounding the experiences of teens online. For instance, we know that cyberbullying is not an epidemic inducing large numbers of teens to commit suicide. However, that certainly does not exempt us from addressing it before and when it happens. Cyberbullying is a significant problem for many teens, and efforts should be taken to prevent and respond to it, and to equip youth with ways that empower them to reduce their own victimization risk (Chibarro, 2007). No one person, professional, or even organization will be able to effectively accomplish the systematic changes that need to occur and pervade our society. Cyberbullying risk reduction will require comprehensive and collaborative efforts among various youth advocates. School counselors in particular can play a critical role and can help in significant ways. For instance, Sabella (2012b) suggests that school counselors take the lead with a comprehensive approach that includes five areas, all of which have a basis in empirical support (see e.g., Pearce, Cross, Monks, Waters, & Falconer, 2011; Ttofi & Farrington, 2011). These include: (1) facilitating the development of effective school policies; (2) educating parents; (3) educating students; (4) developing peer helper programs; and (5) providing responsive services such as reporting and counseling opportunities. These efforts must include all stake holders such as teachers, school support services, educational leaders, community leaders, legislators, parents, and, of course, students.

9.1. Effective School Policies

26   According to the American School Counselor Association's position statement about bullying (ASCA, 2005), leadership in the form of policy development is an appropriate role and responsibility of the school counselor:

> Professional school counselors collaborate with others to promote safe schools and confront issues threatening school safety. Professional school counselors encourage the development of policies supporting a safe school environment, and they provide leadership to the school by assisting in the design and implementation of school wide violence prevention activities and programs.

27   Hinduja and Patchin (2009) also argue that "one of the most important steps a district can take to help protect its students and protect itself from legal liability is to have a clear and comprehensive policy regarding bullying and harassment, technology, and their intersection: cyberbullying" (p. 188). Forty-nine states have bullying laws that require schools to have policies about bullying and most of these now include requirements to address electronic forms of harassment (Hinduja & Patchin, 2012a). School counselors can suggest the development of policies as described by Franek (2006), who stated that all forms of cyberspace harassment either during school hours or after school hours should not be tolerated. An anti-cyberbullying policy should also include establishing a prevention program and an annual assessment of such a program to determine its effectiveness (Diamanduros, Downs, & Jenkins, 2008; Hamburger, Basile, & Vivolo, 2011). In addition to legislation, most state departments of education have provided model anti-bullying policies (Hinduja & Patchin, 2012a) and the United States Department of Education released a report, *Analysis of State Bullying Laws and Policies* (Temple et al., 2012), which can serve as helpful references for school counselors towards this end. It is essential that counselors review and understand their school policy concerning cyberbullying so that they are able to respond to behaviors within the appropriate framework established by the policy.

9.2. Educating School Staff and Parents

28   School counselors also can serve as key players in providing parents, guardians, and school staff with the professional development or training they need to work to reduce the risk of cyberbullying among students (Bauman, 2011;

Beale & Hall, 2007; Bhat, 2008; Maher, 2008; Winburn, Niemeyer, & Reysen, 2012). At a fundamental level, adults, including teachers and parents, need to keep pace with new technology to understand how students communicate online and how cyberbullying happens. The results of one study indicated that school adults provide limited help, which might be caused by their lack of understanding and training in how to deal with the issue (Li, 2010).

29   In collaboration with community groups and parent/teacher associations, school counselors also can enhance the way caretakers protect and inform their children by providing them with solutions from both human/relational and technological perspectives (Bradshaw, Sawyer, & O'Brennan, 2007). This is especially important given that there exists some evidence of a familial pattern to bullying whereby sometimes multiple children from the same family (and sometimes within the same school) are identified bullying perpetrators (Chan, 2006). Human/relational solutions to reducing cyberbullying include encouraging the development of relationships that facilitate trust and open lines of communication (Sabella, 2008, 2012b). School counselors also should encourage parents to learn about what their children are doing online and work to better understand the technology they are using. Understanding Facebook's privacy settings, for example, will enable parents and teachers to educate children about how to protect their personal information to the maximum extent possible (ASCA & iKeepSafe, 2011). Parents can also monitor the online activities of their children by being involved in these environments along with them such as watching a few funny YouTube videos together, "Skyping" with distant family members, using Pinterest to collect their favorite pieces of online content, or checking out Tumblr blogs from around the world.

30   School counselors can also coordinate efforts among educators and youth advocates to pass along information to parents about specific technological solutions (such as filtering, blocking, or tracking software) that may be helpful in deterring inappropriate behaviors or in collecting evidence of cyberbullying. To be sure, these products are never a replacement for active human engagement and intervention. Counselors, parents, and other adults have an obligation to help children become knowledgeable about the use (and misuse) of technology, to teach them how to make good decisions about how they use technology, and to help them to police themselves (and perhaps each other). Technological solutions can be an effective complement or

backup to how youth are educated and supervised (Ybarra & Mitchell, 2004b). These include, but are not limited to, password protecting home wireless networks, using Internet safety services/software, subscribing to a digital reputation monitoring service, and/or exploring cell phone parental controls (Kowalski et al., 2008).

9.3. Educating Students

31   In collaboration with other educators, student training (also known as classroom guidance) should be provided to confront cyberbullying by including student competencies which help youth recognize legal and personal consequences of cyberbullying, improve social problem-solving and anger management skills, encourage prosocial behavior, and increase the ability to empathize with victims (Bradshaw, Waasdorp, O'Brennan, & Gulemetova, 2011; Hazler, 2006; Limber, Kowalski, & Agatston, 2009; Lund, Blake, Ewing, & Banks, 2012; Macklem, 2003). Students who witness or learn about cyberbullying happening to others should also learn about their responsibilities and how best to support each other (Li, 2010).

32   Although an abundance of cyberbullying and Internet safety related resources are available online, few sequenced and comprehensive lesson plans exist. Moreover, none of these has been formally evaluated. That said, some promising approaches do exist (see e.g., Sabella, 2012a for a compilation of recommended cyberbullying lesson plans) which include many of the components of cyberbullying prevention education recommended by other researchers (e.g., Diamanduros et al., 2008; Hinduja & Patchin, 2009).

9.4. Peer Helper Programs

33   Together with teachers, parents, and other youth advocates, school counselors should also take advantage of the expertise that already exists in their buildings. That is, they can use students to help educate their classmates about using technology responsibly. Led by the school counselor, educators can train students to work with and educate younger peers so that they make wise decisions online starting at an early age. Students can also work with others who are "at risk" as well as with those who are experiencing typical childhood problems and concerns, and thereby play important roles in both intervention and prevention (ASCA, 2008). Myrick, Highland, and Sabella (1995) indicated that the advantages of using peer helpers in general may include: better communication and relationships among students; the generation of positive sentiments and a healthier climate across campus;

wider message delivery, higher visibility, and the promotion of positive public relations to the school; evaluation of lesson plans, content, or learning activities by those who likely have the most insight into what works and what does not; and the provision of platforms on which peer helpers can model appropriate behavior for others to emulate. Along similar lines, Mustacchi (2009) has eloquently described how her students assisted her in developing lesson plans, materials, and ultimately teaching other students about cyberbullying and other technology related issues:

> When I began implementing this curriculum the next fall, I noticed how much the 8th graders knew and were eager to impart to one another—with almost desperate urgency. As if riding a rollercoaster, students relayed stories and advice to one another, hitting highs and lows at breakneck speed. They were experts in some aspects of online interaction and risks but complete novices in others. I realized that their knowledge and thirst to exchange information provided a rare opportunity. So I charged my 8th grade students with the job of teaching my 6th graders. . . . Their talks, materials, and activities kept the younger students fully engaged. They asked questions and got their peers to think and reflect, sometimes with creative tactics (p. 80).

9.5. Responsive Services

34   Finally, school counselors, social workers, psychologists and community mental health workers (those who can provide personal/social counseling services) should provide help to both cyberbullies and their targets in the form of responsive services. This refers to specific activities designed to meet students' immediate needs and concerns such as individual or small-group counseling and crisis response (ASCA, 2012). Through these mechanisms, appropriate student support service personnel can help perpetrators to better understand the consequences of their actions, find better ways to resolve anger and conflict, and make more thoughtful and responsible choices about social interactions (Beaty & Alexeyev, 2008; Borg, 1998; Camodeca & Goossens, 2004; Haynie et al., 2001; Pellegrini, Bartini, & Brooks, 1999). Counselors also can help cyberbullying victims who may need help with issues of post-traumatic stress. Many counseling approaches exist that can be helpful in working with students involved in cyberbullying situations. Sabella (2012b) recommended three models in particular

that are effective for both victims and perpetrators: Solution Focused Brief Counseling (SFBC), Reality Therapy (RT), and Rational Emotive Behavioral Therapy (REBT). All three models can help aggressors to take responsibility for their actions and correct their behaviors while also empowering targets to successfully cope and respond.

35 It should be noted that small group counseling has been specially recognized as an effective way to help students who experience bullying. For example, Young (1998) described a procedure and process for how school counselors can conduct support groups among the victim's identified supporters, the perpetrator, and those perceived to be supporters of the perpetrator. Reber (2012) provides some evidence about the positive impact of an eight (8) session group counseling experience on the self-esteem levels of students who have been identified as the targets of bullying aggressors. In another example, Hall (2006) proposed a "Solving Problems Together" (SPT) group in which the school counselor can help students develop the knowledge, attitude, and skills that will enable them to deal more effectively with bullying. Relatedly, Perkins and Williamson (2010) described how they incorporated cyberbullying prevention groups in schools as part of a service learning project designed and implemented by counseling graduate students. These suggested efforts hold much promise if counselors can take the lead and perform the required steps to educate and enlist youth (and other educators on campus) towards the common goal.

10. Conclusion and Future Directions

36 The current work is certainly not exhaustive in its attempt to illuminate the facts and debunk the myths about cyberbullying, as other misconceptions about the behaviors of teens online exist and warrant empirical scrutiny. An even more systematic review of popular media accounts of these problems would no doubt reveal additional unsubstantiated, questionable, or patently false claims about the nature, extent, causes, and consequences of cyberbullying behaviors. It is essential to compare these assertions to the body of scientific evidence that is available to separate fact from fiction. To be sure, there is still much that is not known about cyberbullying, especially about the efficacy of efforts to intervene. For instance, as of this writing, there have been no formal process or outcome evaluations of programs designed to prevent or respond specifically to cyberbullying.

37 Anecdotally, there is much talk about "what works" and "what doesn't," but data need to be collected about the short- and long-term outcomes associated with these initiatives. And, because cyberbullying includes so many different people and organizations (e.g., students, school personnel, parents, cell phone service providers, social networking companies, gaming companies, legislators, and police), future research must be comprehensive in scope. Many important questions still remain unanswered such as: (a) What types of parental actions/responses are most effective in preventing and responding to cyberbullying? (b) How effective are peer helpers as compared to adults when delivering cyberbullying risk-reduction strategies? (c) How effective are self-led online tutorials (e.g., videos or interactive games) in reducing the prevalence and incidence of cyberbullying? (d) What reporting procedures and processes are best for preventing and responding to cyberbullying? and, (e) What specific supervising and monitoring techniques, both human and technological, work best?

38 According to Pearce, Cross, Monks, Waters, and Falconer (2011), the special characteristics of cyberbullying pose new challenges to future anti-bullying research. As mentioned earlier, these include the anonymous nature of the problem, greater breadth of audience, the lack of authority in cyberspace, and 24-h access to technology, as well rapid technological changes continually providing new means by which harm can be inflicted. These challenges, together with the rapidly changing landscape of technology, will continue to make future research in this area as difficult as it is necessary. In the meantime, educators and other youth advocates should be careful to use information, curricula, and other resources that are informed by the most current and valid research available. Otherwise, by default, they risk falling into the trap of relying on conventional wisdom and media hyperbole in their well-intentioned efforts to address cyberbullying.

References

Adler, P.A., & Adler, P. (1995). Dynamics of inclusion and exclusion in preadolescent cliques. *Social Psychology Quarterly, 58*(3), 145–162. http://dx.doi.org/10.2307/2787039.

Adler, P.A., & Adler, P. (1996). Preadolescent clique stratification and the hierarchy of identity. *Sociological Inquiry, 66*, 111–142. http://dx.doi.org/10.1111/j.1475–682X.1996.tb00213.x.

ASCA (2005). *The professional school counselor and bullying, harassment and violence prevention programs: Supporting safe and respectful schools (Position Statement)*. American School Counselor Association. <www.schoolcounselor. org/content.asp?pl=325&sl=127&contentid=178>.

ASCA (2008). *The professional school counselor and peer helping (Position Statement)*. American School Counselor Association. <http://asca2.timberlakepublishing.com// files/PS_PeerHelping.pdf>.

ASCA & iKeepSafe (2011). *Facebook for School Counselors*. <https://www.facebook.com/safety/groups/teachers/>.

ASCA (2012). *The ASCA national model: A framework for school counseling programs* (3rd ed.). Alexandria, VA: American School Counselor Association.

Aseltine, R.H., Gore, S., & Gordon, J. (2000). Life stress, anger and anxiety, and delinquency: An empirical test of general strain theory. *Journal of Health and Social Behavior, 41*(3), 256–275.

Baas, N., de Jong, M., & Drossaert, C. (2013). Children's perspectives on cyberbullying: Insights based on participatory research. *Cyberpsychology, Behavior, and Social Networking, 16*(4), 248–253.

Bauman, S. (2008). Effects of gender, grade, and acculturation on overt and relational victimization and depression in Mexican American elementary school students. *Journal of Early Adolescence, 28*, 528–554.

Bauman, S. (2011). *Cyberbullying: What counselors need to know*. Alexandria, VA: American Counseling Association.

Bauman, S., Toomey, R.B., & Walker, J.L. (2013). Associations among bullying, cyberbullying, and suicide in high school students. *Journal of Adolescence, 36*(2), 341–350.

Bazelon, E. (2010). *What really happened to Phoebe Prince?* (Retrieved 12.06.13). <www.slate.com/articles/life/bulle/ features/2011/what_really_happened_to_phoebe_prince/ the_untold_story_of_her_suicide_and_the_role_of_the_ kids_who_have_been_criminally_charged_for_it.html>.

Beale, A.V., & Hall, K.R. (2007). Cyberbullying: What schools administrators (and parents) can do. *The Clearing House, 81*(1), 8–12. http://dx.doi.org/10.3200/ TCHS.81.1.8–12.

Beaty, L.A., & Alexeyev, E.B. (2008). The problem of school bullies: What the research tells us. *Adolescence, 43*(169), 1–11.

Beautrais, A.L., Collings, S.C., & Ehrhardt, P. (2005). *Suicide prevention: A review of evidence of risk and protective factors, and points of effective intervention*. Wellington, New Zealand: Ministry of Health.

Beran, T., & Li, Q. (2007). The relationship between cyberbullying and school bullying. *Journal of Student Wellbeing, 1*(2), 15–33.

Bhat, C.S. (2008). Cyber bullying: Overview and strategies for school counselors, guidance officers, and all school personnel. *Australian Journal of Guidance and Counseling, 18*(1), 53–66. http://dx.doi.org/10.1375/ajgc.18.1.53.

Billitteri, T.J. (2008, May 2). *Cyberbullying* (Retrieved 28.02.13). <http://library.cqpress.com/cqresearcher/document.php?id =cqresrre2008050200&PHPSESSID=o6qklm45di95pqru6 uiftj3ba0>.

Borg, M.G. (1998). The emotional reaction of school bullies and their victims. *Educational Psychology, 18*(4), 433–444.

Boyette, C. (2013). *N.Y. police probe possible cyberbullying after girl found hanged* (Retrieved 12.06.13). <www.cnn. com/2013/05/23/us/new-york-girldeath>.

Bradshaw, C.P., Sawyer, A., & O'Brennan, L. (2007). Bullying and peer victimization at school: Perceptual differences between students and school staff. *School Psychology Review, 36*(3), 361–383.

Bradshaw, C.P., Waasdorp, T.E., O'Brennan, L.M., & Gulemetova, M. (2011). *Findings from the National Education Association's nationwide study of bullying: Teachers' and education support professionals' perspectives*. Washington, DC: National Education Association.

Broidy, L.M., & Agnew, R. (1997). Gender and crime: A general strain theory perspective. *Journal of Research in Crime and Delinquency, 34*(3), 275–306.

Camodeca, M., & Goossens, F.A. (2004). Aggression, social cognitions, anger and sadness in bullies and their victims. *Journal of Child Psychology and Psychiatry, 46*, 186–197.

Campbell, M., Spears, B., Slee, P., Butler, D., & Kift, S. (2012). Victims' perceptions of traditional and cyberbullying, and the psychosocial correlates of their victimisation. *Emotional & Behavioural Difficulties, 17*(3/4), 389–401. http://dx.doi.org/10.1080/13632752.2012.704316.

Chan, J.H.F. (2006). Systemic patterns in bullying and victimization. *School Psychology International, 27*(3), 352–369. http://dx.doi.org/10.1177/0143034306067289.

Chibarro, J.S. (2007). School counselors and the cyberbully: Interventions and implications. *Professional School Counseling, 11*(1), 65–68.

Chin, A. (2011). *Police try to prevent cyber bullying*. <www. kktv.com/news/headlines/Police_Try_To_Prevent_ Cyber_Bullying_121227869.html>.

Craig, W.M., Henderson, K., & Murphy, J.G. (2000). Prospective teachers' attitudes toward bullying and victimization. *School Psychology International, 21*(1), 5–21. http://dx.doi.org/10.1177/0143034300211001.

Cross, D., Shaw, T., Hearn, L., Epstein, M., Monks, H., Lester, L., et al. (2009). *Australian covert bullying prevalence study.* Safe Schools Research. <www.deewr.gov.au/Schooling/NationalSafeSchools/Pages/research.aspx>.

Diamanduros, T., Downs, E., & Jenkins, S.J. (2008). The role of school psychologists in the assessment, prevention, and intervention of cyberbullying. *Psychology in the Schools, 45*(8), 693–704.

Education Insider (2010). *Cyberbullying: A national epidemic.* <http://educationportal.com/articles/Cyberbullying_A_National_Epidemic.html>.

Englander, E.K. (2008). *Research brief: Cyberbullying & bullying in Massacusetts: Frequency & motivations.* <http://webhost.bridgew.edu/marc/MARC%20findings%20summary%202008.pdf>.

Englander, E.K., & Muldowney, A. (2007). Just turn the darn thing off: Understanding cyberbullying. In D.L. White, B.C. Glenn, & A. Wimes (Eds.), *Proceedings of persistently safe schools: The 2007 national conference on safe schools* (pp. 83–92). Washington, DC: Hamilton Fish Institute, The George Washington University.

Faris, R., & Felmlee, D. (2011). Status struggles: Network centrality and gender segregation in same- and cross-gender aggression. *American Sociological Review, 76*(1), 48–73. http://dx.doi.org/10.1177/0003122410396196.

Farrington, D.P. (2012). Childhood risk factors for young adult offending: Onset and persistence. In F. Losel, A. Bottoms, & D.P. Farrington (Eds.), *Young adult offenders: Lost in transition?* (pp 48–64). London: Routledge.

Fekkes, M., Pijpers, F.I.M., & Verloove-VanHorick, S.P. (2004). Bullying behavior and associations with psychosomatic complaints and depression in victims. *Journal of Pediatrics, 144*(1), 17–22.

Finkelhor, D. (2011). *The Internet, youth deviance and the problem of Juvenoia.* <www.unh.edu/ccrc/pdf/Juvenoia%20paper.pdf>.

Finkelhor, D. (2013). Trends in bullying and peer Victimization. <www.unh.edu/ccrc/pdf/CV280_Bullying%20&%20Peer%20Victimization%20Bulletin_1–23–13_with%20toby%20edits.pdf>.

Franek, M. (2006). Foiling cyberbullies in the new wild west. *Educational Leadership, 63*(4), 39–43.

Hall, K.R. (2006). Solving problems together: A psycho-educational group model for victims of bullies. *The Journal for Specialists in Group Work, 31*(3), 201–217. http://dx.doi.org/10.1080/01933920600777790.

Halligan, J. (2006). *Ryan Patrick Halligan* (Retrieved 23.01.08). <www.ryanpatrickhalligan.org/>.

Hamburger, M.E., Basile, K.C., & Vivolo, A.M. (2011). *Measuring bullying victimization, perpetration, and bystander experiences: A compendium of assessment tools.* Atlanta, GA: Centers for Disease Control and Prevention, National Center for Injury Prevention and Control. <www.cdc.gov/ViolencePrevention/pub/measuring_bullying.html> (Retrieved 02.03.13).

Hawton, K., & Williams, K. (2001). *The connection between media and suicidal behavior warrants serious attention 22*(22), 137–140. http://dx.doi.org/10.1027//0227–5910.22.4.137.

Haynie, D., Nansel, T., Eitel, P., Crump, A., Saylor, K., & Yu, K. (2001). Bullies, victims and bully/victims: Distinct groups of at-risk youth. *Journal of Early Adolescence, 21*(1), 29–49.

Hazler, R.J. (2006, March 18, 2006). *Essential techniques for successful intervention and prevention of bullying,* Carrollton, GA.

High, B. (2007). *Bullycide in America–Moms speak out about the bullying/suicide connection.*

Hinduja, S., & Patchin, J.W. (2009). *Bullying beyond the schoolyard: Preventing and responding to cyberbullying.* Thousand Oaks, CA: Sage Publications (Corwin Press).

Hinduja, S., & Patchin, J.W. (2012a). *School climate 2.0: Preventing cyberbullying and sexting one classroom at a time.*

Hinduja, S., & Patchin, J.W. (2012b). *Bullying and cyberbullying laws.* <www.cyberbullying.us/Bullying_and_Cyberbullying_Laws.pdf>.

Hinduja, S., & Patchin, J.W. (2007). Offline consequences of online victimization: School violence and delinquency. *Journal of School Violence, 6*(3), 89–112.

Hinduja, S., & Patchin, J.W. (2008). Cyberbullying: An exploratory analysis of factors related to offending and victimization. *Deviant Behavior, 29*(2), 1–29.

Hinduja, S., & Patchin, J.W. (2010a). Bullying, cyberbullying, and suicide. *Archives of Suicide Research, 14*(3).

Jones, T. (2008). *A deadly Web of deceit: A teen's online 'friend' proved false, and cybervigilantes are avenging her.* <www.washingtonpost.com/wp-dyn/content/article/2008/01/09/AR2008010903367_pf.html> (Retrieved 10.01.08).

Juvonen, J., & Gross, E.F. (2008). Extending the school grounds?—Bullying experiences in cyberspace. *Journal of School Health, 78*, 496–505.

Kim, Y.S., & Leventhal, B. (2008). Bullying and suicide. A review. *International Journal of Adolescent Medical Health, 20*(2), 133–154.

Klomek, A.B., Sourander, A., & Gould, M. (2010). The association of suicide and bullying in childhood to young adulthood: Review of cross-sectional and longitudinal research findings. *Canadian Journal of Psychology, 55*(5), 282–288.

Klomek, A.B., Sourander, A., Niemela, S., Kumpulainen, K., Piha, J., Tamminen, T., et al. (2009). Childhood bullying behaviors as a risk for suicide attempts and completed suicides: A population-Based birth cohort study. *Child & Adolescent Psychiatry, 48*(3), 254–261.

König, A., Gollwitzer, M., & Steffgen, G. (2010). Cyberbullying as an act of revenge? *Australian Journal of Guidance and Counselling, 20*(2), 210–224.

Kowalski, R.M., Limber, S.P., & Agatston, P.W. (2008). *Cyber bullying: Bullying in the digital age.* Malden, MA: Blackwell Publishing.

Li, Q. (2007). Bullying in the new playground: Research into cyberbullying and cyber victimisation. *Australasian Journal of Educational Technology, 23*(4), 435–454.

Li, Q. (2010). Cyberbullying in high schools: A study of students' behaviors and beliefs about this new phenomenon. *Journal of Aggression, Maltreatment & Trauma, 19*(4), 372–392. http://dx.doi.org/10.1080/10926771003788979.

Limber, S.P., Kowalski, R.M., & Agatston, P.W. (2009). *Cyberbullying: A prevention curriculum for grades 6–12.* Center City, MN: Hazelden.

Lund, E.M., Blake, J.J., Ewing, H.K., & Banks, C.S. (2012). School counselors' and school psychologists' bullying prevention and intervention strategies: A look into real-world practices. *Journal of School Violence, 11*(3), 246–265. http://dx.doi.org/10.1080/15388220.2012.682005. <www.tandfonline.com/doi/pdf/10.1080/15388220.2012.682005> (Retrieved 02.03.13).

Macklem, G.L. (2003). *Bullying and teasing: Social power in children's groups.* New York: Kluwer Academic/Plenum.

Madden, M., Lenhart, A., Duggan, M., Cortesi, S., & Gasser, U. (2013). *Teens and technology 2013.* <www.pewinternet.org/Reports/2013/Teens-and-Tech.aspx> (Retrieved 12.06.13).

Magid, L. (September 17, 2011). *Cyberbullying is a serious problem, but is it an epidemic?* Huff Post. <www.huffingtonpost.com/larry-magid/cyberbullying-is-a-seriou_b_967310.html>.

Maher, D. (2008). Cyberbullying: An ethnographic case of one Australian upper primary school class. *Youth Studies Australia, 27*(4), 50–57.

Marr, N., & Field, T. (2001). *Bullycide: Death at playtime— An expose of child suicide caused by bullying.* London: Success Unlimited.

Mazerolle, P., Burton, V., Cullen, F.T., Evans, D., & Payne, G.L. (2000). Strain, anger, and delinquent adaptations: Specifying general strain theory. *Journal of Criminal Justice, 28*, 89–101.

Mazerolle, P., & Piquero, A. (1998). Linking exposure to strain with anger: An investigation of deviant adaptations. *Journal of Criminal Justice, 26*(3), 195–211.

McDougall, B. (2011). *Cyber bullying spiralling out of control in schools.* The Daily Telegraph. <www.news.com.au/technology/cyber-bullying-spirallingout-of-control-in-nsw-schools/story-e6frfro0–1226233680802>.

Menesini, E., & Nocentini, A. (2009). Cyberbullying definition and measurement: Some critical considerations. *Zeitschrift für Psychologie/Journal of Psychology, 217*(4), 230–232.

Mishna, F., Pepler, D., & Wiener, J. (2006). Factors associated with perceptions and responses to bullying situations by children, parents, teachers, and principals. *Victims & Offenders, 1*(3), 255–288. http://dx.doi.org/10.1080/15564880600626163.

Mustacchi, J. (2009). R U safe? *Educational Leadership, 66*(6), 78–82.

Mynard, H., Joseph, S., & Alexander, J. (2000). Peer victimization and posttraumatic stress in adolescents. *Personality and Individual Differences, 29*(5), 815–821.

Myrick, R.D., Highland, W.H., & Sabella, R.A. (1995). Peer helpers and perceived effectiveness. *Elementary School Guidance and Counseling, 29*(4), 278–288.

National Center for Educational Statistics (2013). *Indicators of school crime and safety: 2012.* <http://nces.ed.gov/programs/crimeindicators/crimeindicators2012/>.

Obama, B. (2011). *Remarks by the president and first lady at the White House conference on bullying prevention.* <www.whitehouse.gov/the-pressoffice/2011/03/10/remarks-president-and-first-lady-white-house-conference-bullying-prevent>.

Oblad, T. (2012). *Understanding cyberbullying in the net generation: A meta-analytic review.* Masters thesis. <http://repositories.tdl.org/ttu-ir/handle/2346/47526>.

Parris, L., Varjas, K., Meyers, J., & Cutts, H. (2012). High school students' perceptions of coping with cyberbullying. *Youth & Society, 44*(2), 284–306. http://dx.doi.org/10.1177/0044118X11398881.

Patchin, J.W., & Hinduja, S. (2006). Bullies move beyond the schoolyard: A preliminary look at cyberbullying. *Youth Violence and Juvenile Justice, 4*(2), 148–169.

Patchin, J.W., & Hinduja, S. (2010). Changes in adolescent online social networking behaviors from 2006 to 2009. *Computers and Human Behavior, 26*, 1818–1821.

Patchin, J.W., & Hinduja, S. (2011). *Traditional and nontraditional bullying among youth: A test of general strain theory*. Youth and Society.

Patchin, J.W., & Hinduja, S. (2012). *Preventing and responding to cyberbullying: Expert perspectives*. Thousand Oaks, CA: Routledge.

Pearce, N., Cross, D., Monks, H., Waters, S., & Falconer, S. (2011). Current evidence of best practice in whole-school bullying intervention and its potential to inform cyberbullying interventions. *Australian Journal of Guidance & Counselling, 21*(1), 1–21. http://dx.doi.org/10.1375/ajgc.21.1.1.

Pellegrini, A.D., Bartini, M., & Brooks, F. (1999). School bullies, victims, and aggressive victims. Factors relating to group affiliation and victimization in early adolescence. *Journal of Educational Psychology, 91*(2), 216–224.

Perkins, G.W., & Williamson, M.L. (2010). *A service learning approach to cyberbullying prevention*. Ideas and research you can use: VISTAS 2010. <http://counselingoutfitters.com/vistas/vistas10/Article_63.pdf>.

Raskauskas, J., & Stoltz, A.D. (2007). Involvement in traditional and electronic bullying among adolescents. *Developmental Psychology, 43*(3), 465–475.

Reber, C. (2012). *The impact of group counseling on the self-esteem levels of students who have been identified as the targets of bullying aggressors*. <http://digitalcommons.brockport.edu/edc_theses/130> (Retrieved 02.03.13).

Rigby, K., & Slee, P.T. (1999). Suicidal ideation among adolescent school children, involvement in bully-victim problems, and perceived social support. *Suicide and Life Threatening Behavior, 29*(2), 119–130.

Sabella, R.A. (2008). *GuardingKids.com: A practical guide to keeping kids out of high-tech trouble*. Minneapolis, MN: Educational Media.

Sabella, R.A. (2012a). *Cyberbullying/technology safety lesson plans*. <http://bit.ly/cyberbullying-curr-table>.

Sabella, R.A. (2012b). Cyberbullying: How school counselors can help. In J.W. Patchin & S. Hinduja (Eds.), *Cyberbullying prevention and response: Expert perspectives*. New York: Routledge.

Sanders, J. (2009). Cyberbullies: Their motives, characteristics, and types of bullying. In *Paper presented at the XIV European conference of developmental psychology*, Vilnius, Lithuania.

Schneider, S.K., O'Donnell, L., Stueve, A., & Coulter, R.S. (2012). Cyberbullying, school bullying, and psychological distress: A regional census of high school students. *American Journal of Public Health, 102*(1), 171–177. http://dx.doi.org/10.2105/AJPH.2011.300308.

Sharp, S. (1995). How much does bullying hurt? The effects of bullying on the personal well-being and educational progress of secondary aged students. *Educational and Child Psychology, 12*, 81–88.

Skapinakis, P., Bellos, S., Gkatsa, T., Magklara, K., Lewis, G., Araya, R., et al. (2011). The association between bullying and early stages of suicidal ideation in late adolescents in Greece. *Psychiatry, 11*(1), 22.

Smith, P.K., Mahdavi, J., Carvalho, M., Fisher, S., Russell, S., & Tippett, N. (2008). Cyberbullying: Its nature and impact in secondary school pupils. *Journal of Child Psychology and Psychiatry, 49*(4), 376–385.

Smokowski, P.R., & Kopasz, K.H. (2005). Bullying in schools: An overview of types, effects, family characteristics and intervention strategies. *Children & Schools, 27*(2), 101–110.

Smorti, A., Menesini, E., & Smith, P.K. (2003). Parents' definitions of children's bullying in a five-country comparison. *Journal of Cross-Cultural Psychology, 34*(4), 417–432. http://dx.doi.org/10.1177/0022022103034004003.

Temple, J.R., Paul, J.A., van den Berg, P., Le, V.D., McElhany, A., & Temple, B.W. (2012). Teen sexting and its association with sexual behaviors. *Archives of Pediatrics and Adolescent Medicine*, 1–6.

Thom, K., Edwards, G., Nakarada-Kordic, I., McKenna, B., O'Brien, A., & Nairn, R. (2011). Suicide online: Portrayal of website-related suicide by the New Zealand media. *New Media & Society, 13*(8), 1355–1372. http://dx.doi.org/10.1177/1461444811406521.

Ttofi, M.M., & Farrington, D.P. (2011). Effectiveness of school-based programs to reduce bullying: A systematic and meta-analytic review. *Journal of Experimental Criminology, 2011*(7), 1. http://dx.doi.org/10.1007/s11292–010–9109–1.

Vaillancourt, T., & Hymel, S. (2006). Aggression and social status: The moderating roles of sex and peer-valued characteristics. *Aggressive Behavior, 32*, 408–596. http://dx.doi.org/10.1002/ab.20138.

Vandebosch, H., & Van Cleemput, K. (2009). Cyberbullying among youngsters: Profiles of bullies and victims. *New Media and Society, 11*(8), 1349–1371.

Varjas, K., Talley, J., Meyers, J., Parris, L., & Cutts, H. (2010). High school students' perceptions of motivations for cyberbullying: An exploratory study. *Western Journal of Emergency Medicine, 11*(3), 269–273.

WHO (2000). *Preventing suicide. A resource for media professionals. Geneva: Mental and behavioural disorders.* Department of Mental Health, World Health Organisation.

Willard, N.E. (2007a). The authority and responsibility of school officials in responding to cyberbullying. *Journal of Adolescent Health, 41*, S64–S65.

Willard, N.E. (2007b). *Cyber-safe kids, cyber-savvy teens, helping young people use the internet safely and responsibly.* San Francisco, CA: Jossey-Bass.

Willard, N.E. (2007c). *Cyberbullying and cyberthreats: Responding to the challenge of online social aggression, threats, and distress.* Champaign, IL: Research Press.

Willard, N.E. (2010). *School response to cyberbullying and sexting: The legal challenges.* Center for Safe and Responsible Internet Use. <http://csriu.org/documents/documents/cyberbullyingsextinglegal_000.pdf>.

Williams, K., & Guerra, N.G. (2007). Prevalence and predictors of Internet bullying. *Journal of Adolescent Health, 41*, S14–S21.

Winburn, A., Niemeyer, R., & Reysen, R. (2012). Mississippi principals' perceptions of cyberbullying. *Delta Journal of Education, 2*(2), 1–15. <www.deltastate.edu/PDFFiles/DJE/Niemeyer%20Final%20for%20Publication.pdf>.

Winsper, C.C., Lereya, T.T., Zanarini, M.M., & Wolke, D.D. (2012). O-61—Involvement in bullying in childhood and suicide ideation at 11 years: A prospective birth cohort study. *European Psychiatry, 271* http://dx.doi .org/10.1016/S0924–9338(12)74161–5.

Wolak, J., Mitchell, K., & Finkelhor, D. (2007). Does online harassment constitute bullying? An exploration of online harassment by known peers and online-only contacts. *Journal of Adolescent Health, 41*, S51–S58.

Wood, B. (2013, Feburary 24). *Curing Utah's "silent epidemic": Finding a solution to teen suicide.* Desert News. <www.deseretnews.com/article/865574056/Curing-Utahs-silent-epidemic.html> (Retrieved 28.02.13).

Ybarra, M.L. (2004). Linkages between depressive symptomatology and Internet harassment among young regular Internet users. *CyberPsychology and Behavior, 7*(2), 247–257.

Ybarra, M.L., Boyd, D., Korchmaros, J.D., & Oppenheim, J. (2012). Defining and measuring cyberbullying within the larger context of bullying victimization. *Journal of Adolescent Health, 51*(1), 53–58.

Ybarra, M.L., Diener-West, M., & Leaf, P.J. (2007). Examining the overlap in internet harassment and school bullying: implications for school intervention. *Journal of Adolescent Health, 41*, S42–S50.

Ybarra, M.L., & Mitchell, J.K. (2004a). Online aggressor/targets, aggressors and targets: A comparison of associated youth characteristics. *Journal of Child Psychology and Psychiatry, 45*, 1308–1316.

Ybarra, M.L., & Mitchell, J.K. (2004b). Youth engaging in online harassment: Associations with caregiver–child relationships, Internet use, and personal characteristics. *Journal of Adolescence, 27*(3), 319–336.

Ybarra, M.L., & Mitchell, K.J. (2007). Prevalence and frequency of internet harassment instigation: Implications for adolescent health. *Journal of Adolescent Health, 41*, 189–195.

Young, S. (1998). The support group approach to bullying in schools. *Educational Psychology in Practice, 14*(1), 32–39. http://dx.doi.org/10.1080–0266736980140106.

Key and challenging words

ideation, erroneous, pervasive, purport, overzealous, exacerbate, proliferate, cogently, resilient, emulate, debunk, efficacy

Questions

1. (a) Identify the essay's justification and its thesis; (b) Paraphrase the passage in the introduction that discusses the essay's limitations.

2. What do the authors mean by *conventional wisdom* (see, for example, paragraphs 5 and 16)? Explain the term in your own words.

3. Although the authors primarily summarize the results of studies, they often use lengthy direct quotations (see, for example, paragraphs 9, 18, 26, and 33). Explain the importance of direct quotations in the essay, using at least two examples from the text.

4. In the abstract, the authors identify their audience as "adults who work with youth." Find two examples in the essay itself where members of this target audience are addressed, and explain the contribution of each to the section in which it occurs.

5. Clear organization is an important feature of Type C (review) essays. Show how (a) the essay's organization facilitates comprehension (e.g., use of markers, such as headings and section summaries; order of points; repetition; and prompts); (b) choosing either section 3 or section 8, discuss organization and/or rhetorical strategies that make the section easy to follow (some of the above features could apply, along with topic sentences, diction, transitions, and the like).

6. The authors do not usually just dismiss the "myths" they discuss; rather, they use critical thinking to analyze their validity. Show how the authors achieve their balanced and objective approach to the myth discussed in the section "Myth 6: Cyberbullies Are Outcasts or Just Mean Kids."

Post-reading

1. Explain which of the five approaches mentioned in section 9 of the article you think will best help combat cyberbullying. Justify your answer by using critical thinking and information in the article, along with your own observations, if applicable.

2. In paragraph 37, the authors pose some unanswered questions about cyberbullying. Design an experiment in order to attempt to answer one of these questions. Include a hypothesis (see p. 19) and a one-paragraph summary of the method you would use to test the hypothesis.

3. *Collaborative or individual activity:* You are a member of the Canadian citizens' group, "Anti-bull Canada," whose mission is to dispel myths about bullying, especially cyberbullying, while promoting anti-bullying strategies and actions. Using information from section 9 and/or other parts of "Cyberbullying Myths and Realities," along with other sources, if appropriate, design a campaign for a specific group—for example, parents, school counsellors, government, etc.

The More You Play, the More Aggressive You Become: A Long-Term Experimental Study of Cumulative Violent Video Game Effects on Hostile Expectations and Aggressive Behavior

Youssef Hasan, Laurent Bègue, Michael Scharkow, and Brad J. Bushman
(2,814 words)

Pre-reading

1. *Collaborative or individual activity:* Using your observations and other kinds of anecdotal evidence, discuss/reflect on the link between violent video games and aggressive behaviour. Is it a causal relationship; that is, do you believe that playing video games causes violent behaviour? If so, do you believe the link is weak or strong, short-term or long-term?

Abstract

It is well established that violent video games increase aggression. There is a stronger evidence of short-term violent video game effects than of long-term effects. The present experiment tests the cumulative long-term effects of violent video games on hostile expectations and aggressive behavior over three consecutive days. Participants ($N = 70$) played violent or nonviolent video games 20 min a day for three consecutive days. After gameplay, participants could blast a confederate with loud unpleasant noise through headphones (the aggression measure). As a potential causal mechanism, we measured hostile expectations. Participants read ambiguous story stems about potential interpersonal conflicts, and listed what they thought the main characters would do or say, think, and feel as the story continued. As expected, aggressive behavior and hostile expectations increased over days for violent game players, but not for nonviolent video game players, and the increase in aggressive behavior was partially due to hostile expectations.

Introduction

1   In a classic Calvin and Hobbes cartoon, Calvin is shown watching a violent television program. He has the following internal dialog: "Violence in the media. Does it glamorize violence? Sure. Does it desensitize us to violence? Of course. Does it help us tolerate violence? You bet. Does it stunt our empathy for our fellow beings? Heck yes. Does it *CAUSE* violence? . . . Well, that's hard to prove. The trick is to ask the right question."

2   Contrary to what Calvin thinks, experimental studies do allow for causal inferences. Although it is not ethical for researchers to allow assaults, rapes, and murders to occur in laboratory settings, numerous experimental studies have shown a causal relationship between violent media exposure and less serious forms of aggression (Anderson & Bushman 2002a). One problem with experimental studies, however, is that they typically last less than 1 h, although there are some exceptions (e.g., Bushman & Gibson 2011).

3   It is not so much the immediate short-term causal effects of media violence that are of concern, but rather the cumulative long-term causal effects. Long-term effects are generally assessed in longitudinal studies. However, because longitudinal studies employ correlational methods, it is difficult to make strong causal inferences based on longitudinal data. Although single-session experiments allow one to make causal inferences about violent video game effects, they do not allow one to test whether violent video games have a cumulative effect on aggressive thoughts and behaviors. The present research is the first experiment to test the cumulative causal effects of violent video games on aggression over a relatively long period of time—three days.

4   Smoking provides a useful analogy for the importance of this work. Smoking one cigarette will probably not cause lung cancer, but repeatedly smoking cigarettes for days, weeks, months, and years, greatly increases the risk. Similarly, playing a violent video game once will probably not cause a person to become more aggressive, but repeatedly playing violent games for days, weeks, months, and years may increase the risk. In the ideal experiment, participants would be randomly assigned to play violent or nonviolent video games for weeks, months, or years. However, it is not feasible (or ethical) to do such an experiment. Thus, we limited our experiment to three days. If the effects accumulate over three days, they may accumulate even more over weeks, months, and years.

Theoretical Foundation

5   There are theoretical reasons to predict that repeated exposure to violent video games has cumulative effects over time. According to cognitive neoassociative-theory (Berkowitz 1990), human memory can be thought of as a network represented by nodes and links. The nodes represent concepts and the links represent relations among concepts. Once a concept is processed or stimulated, activation spreads out along the network links and primes (activates) associated or related concepts as well. In addition, thoughts are linked, along the same sort of associative lines, not only to other thoughts but also to emotional reactions and behavioral tendencies. Thus, exposure to violent media can prime a complex of associations consisting of aggressive ideas, angry feelings, and the impetus for aggressive actions. According to this theory, repeated exposure to media violence over longer periods of time can create a rich, intricate network of aggressive associations that can be more easily primed by violent media.

6   Cognitive information-processing models also posit that exposure to violent media should have a cumulative effect over time. One model emphasizes scripts, beliefs, and observational learning (Huesmann 1988, 1998; Huesmann & Eron 1984). In a play or movie, scripts tell actors what to say and do. In human memory, scripts define situations and guide behavior: The person first selects a script for the situation and

Source: From *Journal of Experimental Social Psychology*, vol. 49, no. 2, 2013, pp. 224–7. Copyright 2013, with permission from Elsevier.

then assumes a role in the script. Scripts that produce good outcomes become more likely to be used again. Scripts that produce bad outcomes become less likely to be used again. Scripts can be learned by direct experience or by observing others, including mass media characters. According to this theory, repeated exposure to media violence results in the practice and rehearsal of aggressive scripts, and the creation and reinforcement of a hostile worldview over time.

7   Another model emphasizes attributions (e.g., Dodge 1980; Dodge & Frame 1982; Fite, Goodnight, Bates, Dodge, & Pettit 2008). Attributions are the explanations people make about why others behave the way they do. For example, if a person bumps into you, a hostile attribution would be that the person did it on purpose to hurt you. Repeated exposure to violent media can lead people to develop hostile attribution biases. People who consume a heavy dose of violent media eventually come to view the world as a hostile place.

8   The General Aggression Model (e.g., Anderson & Bushman 2002b; DeWall, Anderson & Bushman 2011) encompasses all of these models.

Mediating Role of Hostile Expectations

9   As a possible causal mechanism of the link between exposure to violent video games and aggression, we focus on the hostile expectation bias, defined as the tendency to expect others to react to potential conflicts with aggression (Dill, Anderson, Anderson, & Deuser 1997). When people expect others to behave aggressively, they should be more likely to behave aggressively themselves. In the General Aggression Model (Anderson & Bushman 2002b), hostile expectations are conceptualized as mediators of violent video game-related aggression. Our previous research has supported these theoretical predictions. Playing violent video games increases hostile expectations (Bushman & Anderson 2002), and hostile expectations, in turn, are positively related to aggressive behavior (Hasan, Bègue, & Bushman 2012).

Overview

10   Participants in the present experiment were exposed to violent or nonviolent video games for three consecutive days. We predict that violent games (but not nonviolent games) will increase hostile expectations and aggressive behaviors, and the effects will become stronger each day. That is, we expect a cumulative effect of violent video games on both hostile expectations and aggressive behaviors over time. We also predict that hostile expectations will mediate the effect of violent games on aggressive behaviors.

Method
Participants

11   Participants were 70 French university students (50% female; M_{age} = 24.4, SD = 13.4). They were paid 10€ ($13) each day for three consecutive days.

Procedure

12   Participants were told that the researchers were conducting a 3-day study on the effects of brightness of video games on visual perception. After informed consent was obtained, participants were randomly assigned to play a violent or nonviolent game for 20 min. To increase the generalizability of findings (Wells & Windschitl 1999), we used three violent games (*Condemned 2*, *Call of Duty 4*, and *The Club*; all rated 18+) and three nonviolent games (*S3K Superbike*, *Dirt 2*, and *Pure*; all rated 10+). By the flip of a coin, participants played either a violent game or a nonviolent game for 20 min each day for three consecutive days. They played a different game each day. The order of games was randomized.

13   After playing the game, participants completed one of three ambiguous story stems each day (Dill et al. 1997). For example, in one story a driver crashes into the back of the main character's car, causing a lot of damage to both vehicles. After surveying the damage, the main character approaches the other driver. Participants are asked: "What happens next? List 20 things that the (main character) will do or say, think, and feel as the story continues." They completed a different story stem each day. The order of the story stems was randomized.

14   Next, participants were told that they would compete with a same-sex opponent (actually a confederate) on a 25-trial computer game in which they had to respond to a visual cue faster than their partner, with the loser receiving a noise blast through a pair of headphones. Participants thought they were playing against a different same-sex opponent each day. The intensity and duration of the noise were determined by each individual at the beginning of each trial, from 60 dB (Level 1) to 105 dB (Level 10; about the same level as a smoke or fire alarm). A nonaggressive no-noise level was also offered (Level 0). Participants could also determine how long their opponent suffered by setting the noise duration from 0 to 5 s, in 0.5-second increments. The noise was a mixture of sounds that many people find very unpleasant, such as fingernails scratching a chalkboard, dentist drills, and

ambulance sirens. The intensity and duration of the noise participants gave the confederate were used to measure aggression. The opponent set random intensity and duration levels across the 25 trials. Participants lost half the trials (randomly determined). Basically, within the ethical limits of the laboratory, participants controlled a weapon that could be used to blast their opponent with unpleasant noise. The construct validity of this task is well established (Anderson & Bushman 1997; Bernstein, Richardson, & Hammock 1987; Giancola & Zeichner 1995). It has been used for decades as a reliable and valid measure of laboratory aggression (Taylor 1967).

15   Next, participants rated how absorbing, action-packed, arousing, boring, difficult, enjoyable, entertaining, exciting, frustrating, fun, involving, stimulating, and violent the video game was (1 = *not at all* to 7 = *extremely*). They also rated how bright the display was, which was the ostensible purpose of the study. The violent rating was used as a manipulation check. The other ratings were used as possible covariates to control for the differences between video games besides violent content. To control for habitual exposure to violent video games, participants also listed their three favorite games, and we counted the number of violent games rated 18+ (for players 18 years and older). Because the same pattern of results was obtained with and without the covariates, we used the simpler analyses that excluded the covariates. A debriefing followed, which included a probe for suspicion. No participant expressed suspicion about the study.

Results

Preliminary Results

Exemplars of violent and nonviolent video games

16   There were no significant differences among the three violent video games, or among the three nonviolent video games, on hostile expectations or aggressive behaviors. Thus, the data were collapsed across exemplars of video game types for subsequent analyses.

Manipulation check of violent content of video games

17   As expected, violent video games were rated as more violent than nonviolent video games on all three days (p's < .0001, d's > 1.75). Thus, the violent game manipulation was successful.

Reliability of story stem completions

18   Independent coders, blind to experimental conditions, counted the number of aggressive behaviors, thoughts, and feelings the participants listed when completing the story stems. The intraclass correlations were .81, .86, and .74, for aggressive behaviors, thoughts, and feelings, respectively (Shrout & Fleiss 1979). Because the intraclass correlation coefficients were relatively high, the scores from the two raters were averaged.

Sex differences

19   There were no significant main or interactive effects involving sex of participant on either hostile expectations or aggressive behaviors, so the data from men and women were combined.

Primary results

20   Noise intensity and duration levels across the 25 trials were significantly correlated on all three days (r's > .90), so noise intensity and duration were standardized and averaged to form a more reliable measure of aggression.

21   As can be seen in Fig. 1, hostile expectations and aggressive behaviors both increased over time for violent video game players but not for nonviolent video game players. Latent growth curve analysis (Muthen & Curran 1997) shows that playing a violent game had a significant positive effect on both the intercept (b = 0.46, β = .38) and the slope (b = 0.49, β = .94) for hostile expectations. Violent game players start off with more hostile expectations than nonviolent game players on day 1, and hostile expectations increase on subsequent days. There is no increase in hostile expectations for nonviolent game players. Turning to aggressive behavior, the intercept is significantly higher than in the nonviolent video game group (b = 1.11, β = .38), and there is also a significant effect on the slope factor (b = 1.05, β = .33). Thus, violent game players start off more aggressive than nonviolent game players on day 1, and become even more aggressive on subsequent days. There is no increase in aggression for nonviolent game players. Finally, a cross-sectional model showed that hostile expectations mediated the effect of violent video game exposure on aggressive behavior (b = 0.17, 95% bootstrap CI: .01 to .62, which excludes the value zero; Hayes 2009).

Discussion

22   In the cartoon cited at the beginning of this article, Calvin asked a question that many others have asked: "Do

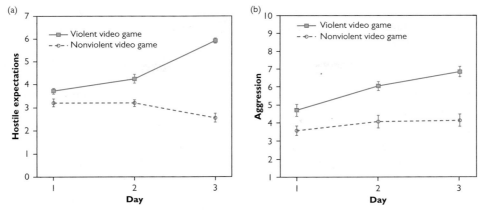

Figure 1   (a) Effect of video game content on hostile expectations over time. Capped vertical bars denote 1 standard error. (b) Effect of video game content on aggressive behavior over time. Capped vertical bars denote 1 standard error.

violent media cause violence?" Although one cannot determine whether violent media cause criminal acts of violence (e.g., rape, assault, murder), because it is unethical to study such behaviors in laboratory settings, one can determine whether violent media cause an increase in less serious forms of aggressive behavior (e.g., blasting a person with loud, unpleasant noise through headphones) and on aggression-related thoughts and feelings (e.g., hostile expectations). Importantly, one can also test whether these causal effects are cumulative. The present research clearly showed a cumulative effect of violent video games on hostile expectations and aggressive behaviors. Because we used the experimental method, we can infer that playing violent video games caused both hostile expectations and aggressive behaviors to increase over the three-day study period. These findings are consistent with cognitive neoassociative-theory (e.g., Berkowitz 1990) script theory (e.g., Huesmann 1988), attribution theory (e.g., Dodge 1980), and the General Aggression Model (e.g., Anderson & Bushman 2002b). All of these models propose that exposure to violent media can have a cumulative effect of aggressive thoughts and behaviors over time.

23   In addition, replicating our previous work (Hasan et al. 2012), hostile expectations mediated the link between exposure to violent video games and aggression. Violent video games increased hostile expectations. Hostile expectations, in turn, were positive related to aggression.

Limitations and Future Research

24   The present experiment is not without limitations. One limitation is that we only considered one possible underlying mechanism in the link between exposure to violent

video games and aggression—hostile expectations. We chose to focus on hostile expectations because we expected hostile expectations to cumulate over time. We also wanted to replicate our previous findings showing that hostile expectations mediate the effect of violent video games on aggression (Hasan et al. 2012). However, there are surely other important mediators of violent video game-related aggression that we did not consider, such as angry feelings, physiological arousal, and brain processes. Future research can examine whether other mediators also accumulate over time in response to violent game play in the way that hostile expectations do.

25   Another limitation is that our experiment lasted only three days. We wish we could have conducted a longer experimental study, but that was not possible for practical and ethical reasons. Although we predict violent video game effects to cumulate beyond three days, we cannot be sure, nor can we be sure of the shape of the curve. During our three-day study, the increase was linear for both hostile expectations and aggressive behaviors, but over a longer period of time the curves might asymptote or possibly even decrease (although we can think of no theoretical reason why it would decrease). Future research should examine the cumulative effects of violent video games on aggressive behaviors and aggression-related thoughts and feelings over a more extended period of time.

Conclusion

26   Although previous experiments have shown that violent video games can cause a short-term, immediate increase in aggression, until now no experimental study has

tested the long-term cumulative causal effects of violent video games on aggression. Although longitudinal correlational studies can investigate cumulative effects of violent video exposure, they cannot be used to make strong causal statements. The present 3-day experiment showed that violent video games increased both hostile expectations and aggression, and the effects increased each day. As predicted, hostile expectations mediated the effect of violent video game exposure on aggression. When people expect others to behave aggressively, they are more likely to behave aggressively themselves. In sum, violent video games do cause an increase in aggression, and the effects are cumulative and can be relatively long-lasting.

References

Anderson, C.A., & Bushman, B.J. (1997). External validity of "trivial" experiments: The case of laboratory aggression. *Review of General Psychology 1*, 19–41.

Anderson, C.A., & Bushman, B.J. (2002a). Media violence and societal violence. *Science 295*, 2377–2378.

Anderson, C.A., & Bushman, B.J. (2002b). Human aggression. *Annual Review of Psychology 53*, 27–51.

Berkowitz, L. (1990). On the formation and regulation of anger and aggression: A cognitive-neoassociationistic analysis. *American Psychologist 45*, 494–503.

Bernstein, S., Richardson, D., & Hammock, G. (1987). Convergent and discriminant validity of the Taylor and Buss measures of physical aggression. *Aggressive Behavior 13*(1), 15–24.

Bushman, B.J., & Anderson, C.A. (2002). Violent video games and hostile expectations: A test of the General Aggression Model. *Personality and Social Psychology Bulletin 28*, 1679–1689.

Bushman, B.J., & Gibson, B. (2011). Violent video games cause an increase in aggression long after the game has been turned off. *Social Psychological and Personality Science 2*, 29–32.

DeWall, C.N., Anderson, C.A., & Bushman, B.J. (2011). The general aggression model: Theoretical extensions to violence. *Psychology of Violence 1*(3), 245–258.

Dill, K.E., Anderson, C.A., Anderson, K.B., & Deuser, W.E. (1997). Effects of aggressive personality on social expectations and social perceptions. *Journal of Research in Personality 31*, 272–292.

Dodge, K.A. (1980). Social cognition and children's aggressive behavior. *Child Development 51*, 620–635.

Dodge, K.A., & Frame, C.L. (1982). Social cognitive biases and deficits in aggressive boys. *Child Development 53*, 620–635.

Fite, J.E., Goodnight, J.A., Bates, J.E., Dodge, K.A., & Pettit, G.S. (2008). Adolescent aggression and social cognition in the context of personality: Impulsivity as a moderator of predictions from social information processing. *Aggressive Behavior 34*(5), 511–520.

Giancola, P.R., & Zeichner, A. (1995). Construct validity of a competitive reaction-time aggression paradigm. *Aggressive Behavior 21*, 199–204.

Hasan, Y., Bègue, L., & Bushman, B.J. (2012). Viewing the world through "blood-red tinted glasses": The hostile expectation bias mediates the link between violent video game exposure and aggression. *Journal of Experimental Social Psychology 48*, 953–956.

Hayes, A.F. (2009). Beyond Baron and Kenny: Statistical mediation analysis in the new millennium. *Communication Monographs 76*, 408–420.

Huesmann, L.R. (1988). An information processing model for the development of aggression. *Aggressive Behavior 14*, 13–24.

Huesmann, L.R. (1998). The role of social information processing and cognitive schema in the acquisition and maintenance of habitual aggressive behavior. In R.G. Geen, & E. Donnerstein (Eds.), *Human aggression: Theories, research, and implications for policy.* (pp. 73–109). New York: Academic Press.

Huesmann, L.R., & Eron, L.D. (1984). Cognitive processes and the persistence of aggressive behavior. *Aggressive Behavior 10*, 243–251.

Muthen, B.O., & Curran, P.J. (1997). General longitudinal modeling of individual differences in experimental designs: A latent variable framework for analysis and power estimation. *Psychological Methods 2*, 371–402.

Shrout, P.E., & Fleiss, J.L. (1979). Intraclass correlations: Uses in assessing rater reliability. *Psychological Bulletin 86*, 420–428.

Taylor, S.P. (1967). Aggressive behavior and physiological arousal as a function of provocation and the tendency to inhibit aggression. *Journal of Personality 35*, 297–310.

Wells, G.L., & Windschitl, P.D. (1999). Stimulus sampling and social psychological experimentation. *Personality and Social Psychology Bulletin 25*, 1115–1125.

Key and challenging words

cumulative, longitudinal, attribution, confederate (n), replicate, asymptote

Questions

1. After reading the first four paragraphs, explain why the authors might have chosen to begin the way they do with a joke from a *Calvin and Hobbes* cartoon.
2. Identify the two main problems facing researchers exploring a link between video game playing and aggression.
3. (a) Briefly explain the function of the section "Theoretical foundation" to the essay as a whole; (b) Summarize paragraph 5 or 6 in one or two sentences.
4. (a) Explain why so much detail is needed in the "Method" section; (b) Explain the purpose of the "manipulation check" (you may need to read the "Results" section to answer this).
5. Using figures 1a and 1b, along with textual information, explain the results of the subjects' hostile expectations and aggression measures.
6. Show how the "Discussion" section fulfils the requirements of an experimental study (Type B essay), identifying at least three of the features mentioned in Chapter 3, p. 23.

Post-reading

1. Referring to the subsection "Limitations and future research" in "Discussion," come up with a hypothesis that could be the basis of an experiment to remedy a limitation or extend the finding of the current study. Then, give a two-sentence description of the design of such a study—i.e., give a brief description of its methodology. (See the section titled "Method" in this essay, and Chapter 3, Type B essays.)

Intersections with Science

The Social Dilemma of Autonomous Vehicles

Jean-François Bonnefon, Azim Shariff, and Iyad Rahwan
(2,767 words)

> ### Pre-reading
>
> 1. What is a "social dilemma"? Using reliable sources, explain this term, giving examples of situations in which a "social dilemma" is involved.
> 2. *Collaborative or individual activity:* What is your opinion of autonomous cars? Do you believe that their use will be commonplace in the near future? What are some problems to be overcome before self-driving cars become feasible on our roads? In groups, discuss issues related to autonomous cars, or explore this topic in writing, answering the above and other related questions.

Abstract

Autonomous vehicles (AVs) should reduce traffic accidents, but they will sometimes have to choose between two evils, such as running over pedestrians or sacrificing themselves and their passenger to save the pedestrians. Defining the algorithms that will help AVs make these moral decisions is a formidable challenge. We found that participants in six Amazon Mechanical Turk studies approved of utilitarian AVs (that is, AVs that sacrifice their passengers for the greater good) and would like others to buy them, but they would themselves prefer to ride in AVs that protect their passengers at all costs. The study participants disapprove of enforcing utilitarian regulations for AVs and would be less willing to buy such an AV. Accordingly, regulating for utilitarian algorithms may paradoxically increase casualties by postponing the adoption of a safer technology.

———

1   The year 2007 saw the completion of the first benchmark test for autonomous driving in realistic urban environments (1, 2). Since then, autonomous vehicles (AVs) such as Google's self-driving car covered thousands of miles of real-road driving (3). AVs have the potential to benefit the world by increasing traffic efficiency (4), reducing pollution (5), and eliminating up to 90% of traffic accidents (6). Not all crashes will be avoided, though, and some crashes will require AVs to make difficult ethical decisions in cases that involve unavoidable harm (7). For example, the AV may avoid harming several pedestrians by swerving and sacrificing a passerby, or the AV may be faced with the choice of sacrificing its own passenger to save one or more pedestrians (Fig. 1).

2   Although these scenarios appear unlikely, even low-probability events are bound to occur with millions of AVs on the road. Moreover, even if these situations were never to arise, AV programming must still include decision rules about what to do in such hypothetical situations. Thus, these types of decisions need be made well before AVs become a global commodity. Distributing harm is a decision that is universally considered to fall within the moral domain (8, 9). Accordingly, the algorithms that control AVs will need to embed moral principles guiding their decisions in situations of unavoidable harm (10). Manufacturers and regulators will need to accomplish three potentially incompatible objectives: being consistent, not causing public outrage, and not discouraging buyers.

3   However, pursuing these objectives may lead to moral inconsistencies. Consider, for example, the case displayed in Fig. 1A, and assume that the most common moral attitude is that the AV should swerve. This would fit a utilitarian moral doctrine (11), according to which the moral course of action is to minimize casualties. But consider then the case displayed in Fig. 1C. The utilitarian course of action, in that situation, would be for the AV to swerve and kill its passenger, but AVs programmed to follow this course of action might discourage buyers who believe their own safety should trump other considerations. Even though such situations

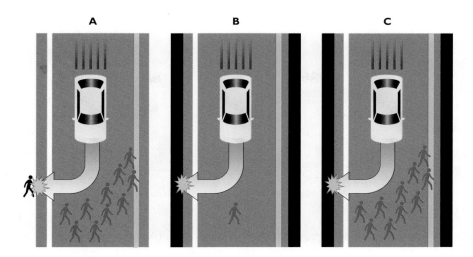

A   **B**   **C**

Figure 1   Three traffic situations involving imminent unavoidable harm. The car must decide between (A) killing several pedestrians or one passerby, (B) killing one pedestrian or its own passenger, and (C) killing several pedestrians or its own passenger.

may be exceedingly rare, their emotional saliency is likely to give them broad public exposure and a disproportionate weight in individual and public decisions about AVs. To align moral algorithms with human values, we must start a collective discussion about the ethics of AVs —that is, the moral algorithms that we are willing to accept as citizens and to be subjected to as car owners. Thus, we initiate the data-driven study of driverless car ethics, inspired by the methods of experimental ethics (12).

4   We conducted six online surveys (n = 1928 total participants) between June and November 2015. All studies were programmed on Qualtrics survey software and recruited participants (U.S. residents only) from the Amazon Mechanical Turk (MTurk) platform, for a compensation of 25 cents each. Studies described in the experimental ethics literature largely rely on MTurk respondents, with robust results, even though MTurk respondents are not necessarily representative of the U.S. population (13, 14). A possible concern with MTurk studies is that some participants may already be familiar with testing materials, particularly when these materials are used by many research groups. However, this concern does not apply to our testing materials, which have never been used in a published MTurk study to date.

5   In all studies, participants provided basic demographic information. Regression analyses (see supplementary materials) showed that enthusiasm for self-driving cars was consistently greater for younger, male participants. Accordingly, all subsequent analyses included age and sex

as covariates. The last item in every study was an easy question (e.g., how many pedestrians were on the road) relative to the traffic situation that participants had just considered. Participants who failed this attention check (typically 10% of the sample) were discarded from subsequent analyses.

6   Detailed statistical results for all studies are provided in the supplementary materials (tables S1 to S8). Overall, participants strongly agreed that it would be more moral for AVs to sacrifice their own passengers when this sacrifice would save a greater number of lives overall.

7   In study one (n = 182 participants), 76% of participants thought that it would be more moral for AVs to sacrifice one passenger rather than kill 10 pedestrians [with a 95% confidence interval (CI) of 69 to 82]. These same participants were later asked to rate which was the most moral way to program AVs, on a scale from 0 (protect the passenger at all costs) to 100 (minimize the number of casualties). They overwhelmingly expressed a moral preference for utilitarian AVs programmed to minimize the number of casualties (median = 85) (Fig. 2A). However, participants were less certain that AVs would be programmed in a utilitarian manner (67% thought so, with a median rating of 70). Thus, participants were not worried about AVs being too utilitarian, as often portrayed in science-fiction works. If anything, they imagined future AVs as being less utilitarian than they should be.

8   In study two (n = 451 participants), participants were presented with dilemmas that varied the number of pedestrians' lives that could be saved, from 1 to 100. Participants

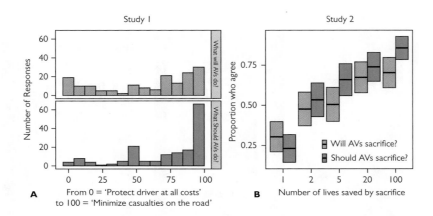

Figure 2   Considering the greater good versus the life of the passenger. (A and B) In studies one and two, when asked which would be the most moral way to program AVs, participants expressed a preference for AVs programmed to kill their passengers for the greater good. This preference was strong, provided that at least five lives could be saved [(A) shows detailed results for 10 lives]. On average, participants were more confident that AVs should pursue the greater good than whether AVs would actually be programmed to do so. In (B), boxes show the 95% CI of the mean.

did not think that AVs should sacrifice their passenger when only one pedestrian could be saved (with an average approval rate of 23%), but their moral approval increased with the number of lives that could be saved (P < 0.001), up to approval rates consistent with the 76% observed in study one (Fig. 2B).

9   Participants' approval of passenger sacrifice was even robust to treatments in which they had to imagine themselves and another person, particularly a family member, in the AV (study three, n = 259 participants). Imagining that a family member was in the AV negatively affected the morality of the sacrifice, as compared with imagining oneself alone in the AV (P = 0.003). But even in that strongly aversive situation, the morality of the sacrifice was still rated above the midpoint of the scale, with a 95% CI of 54 to 66 (Fig. 3A).

10   Still, study three presents the first hint of a social dilemma. On a scale of 1 to 100, respondents were asked to indicate how likely they would be to buy an AV programmed to minimize casualties (which would, in these circumstances, sacrifice them and their co-rider family member), as well as how likely they would be to buy an AV programmed to prioritize protecting its passengers, even if it meant killing 10 or 20 pedestrians. Although the reported likelihood of buying an AV was low even for the self-protective option (median = 50), respondents indicated a significantly lower likelihood (P < 0.001) of buying the AV when they imagined the situation in which they and their family member would be sacrificed for the greater good (median = 19). In other words, even though participants still agreed that utilitarian

AVs were the most moral, they preferred the self-protective model for themselves.

11   Study four (n = 267 participants) offers another demonstration of this phenomenon. Participants were given 100 points to allocate between different types of algorithms, to indicate (i) how moral the algorithms were, (ii) how comfortable participants were for other AVs to be programmed in a given manner, and (iii) how likely participants would be to buy an AV programmed in a given manner. For one of the algorithms, the AV would always swerve when it was about to run over people on the road. Figure 3B shows the points allocated to the AV equipped with this algorithm, in three situations: (i) when it swerved into a pedestrian to save 10 people, (ii) when it killed its own passenger to save 10 people, and (iii) when it swerved into a pedestrian to save just one other pedestrian. The algorithm that swerved into one to save 10 always received many points, and the algorithm that swerved into one to save one always received few points. The algorithm that would kill its passenger to save 10 presented a hybrid profile. Like the high-valued algorithm, it received high marks for morality (median budget share = 50) and was considered a good algorithm for other people to have (median budget share = 50). But in terms of purchase intention, it received significantly fewer points than the high-valued algorithm (P < 0.001) and was, in fact, closer to the low-valued algorithms (median budget share = 33). Once more, it appears that people praise utilitarian, self-sacrificing AVs

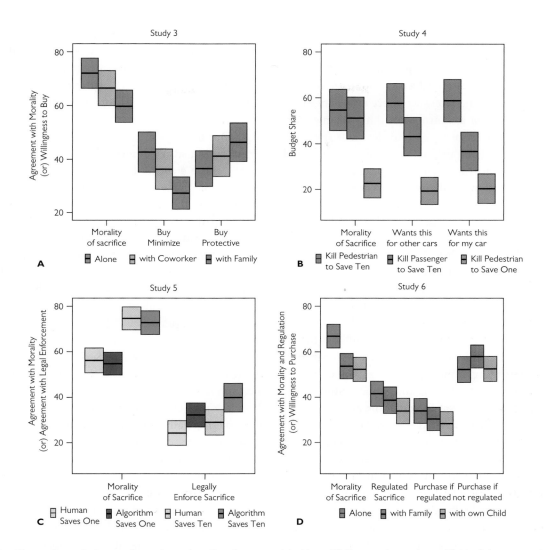

Figure 3   Toward regulation and purchase (studies three to six). (A to D) Boxes show the 95% CI of the mean. In all studies, participants expressed a moral preference for AVs sacrificing their passengers to save a greater number of pedestrians. This moral preference was robust for situations in which participants imagined themselves in the av in the company of a co-worker, a family member, or their own child. However, participants did not express a comparable preference for buying utilitarian AVs, especially when they thought of family members riding in the car [(A) and (B)]. Additionally, participants disapproved of regulations enforcing utilitarian algorithms for AVs and indicated that they would be less likely to purchase an AV under such regulations [(C) and (D)].

and welcome them on the road, without actually wanting to buy one for themselves.

12   This is the classic signature of a social dilemma, in which everyone has a temptation to free-ride instead of adopting the behavior that would lead to the best global outcome. One typical solution in this case is for regulators to enforce the behavior leading to the best global outcome. Indeed, there are many similar societal examples involving trade-off of harm by people and governments

(15–17). For example, some citizens object to regulations that require children to be immunized before starting school. In this case, the parental decision-makers choose to minimize the perceived risk of harm to their child while increasing the risk to others. Likewise, recognition of the threats of environmental degradation have prompted government regulations aimed at curtailing harmful behaviors for the greater good. But would people approve of government regulations imposing utilitarian algorithms in AVs, and would they be more likely to buy AVs under such regulations?

13   In study five (n = 376 participants), we asked participants about their attitudes toward legally enforcing utilitarian sacrifices. Participants considered scenarios in which either a human driver or a control algorithm had an opportunity to self-sacrifice to save 1 or 10 pedestrians (Fig. 3C). As usual, the perceived morality of the sacrifice was high and about the same whether the sacrifice was performed by a human or by an algorithm (median = 70). When we inquired whether participants would agree to see such moral sacrifices legally enforced, their agreement was higher for algorithms than for human drivers (P < 0.002), but the average agreement still remained below the midpoint of the 0 to 100 scale in each scenario. Agreement was highest in the scenario in which algorithms saved 10 lives, with a 95% CI of 33 to 46.

14   Finally, in study six (n = 393 participants), we asked participants specifically about their likelihood of purchasing the AVs whose algorithms had been regulated by the government. Participants were presented with scenarios in which they were riding alone, with an unspecified family member, or with their child. As in the previous studies, the scenarios depicted a situation in which the algorithm that controlled the AV could sacrifice its passengers to minimize casualties on the road. Participants indicated whether it was the duty of the government to enforce regulations that would minimize the casualties in such circumstances, whether they would consider the purchase of an AV under such regulations, and whether they would consider purchasing an AV under no such regulations. As shown in Fig. 3D, people were reluctant to accept governmental regulation of utilitarian AVs. Even in the most favorable condition, when participants imagined only themselves being sacrificed to save 10 pedestrians, the 95% CI for whether people thought it was appropriate for the government to regulate this sacrifice was only 36 to 48. Finally, participants were much less likely to consider purchasing an AV with such regulation than without (P < 0.001). The median expressed likelihood of purchasing an unregulated AV was 59, compared with 21 for purchasing a regulated AV. This is a huge gap from a statistical perspective, but it must be understood as reflecting the state of public sentiment at the very beginning of a new public issue and is thus not guaranteed to persist.

15   Three groups may be able to decide how AVs handle ethical dilemmas: the consumers who buy the AVs; the manufacturers that program the AVs; and the government, which may regulate the kind of programming manufacturers can offer and consumers can select. Although manufacturers may engage in advertising and lobbying to influence consumer preferences and government regulations, a critical collective problem consists of deciding whether governments should regulate the moral algorithms that manufacturers offer to consumers.

16   Our findings suggest that regulation for AVs may be necessary but also counterproductive. Moral algorithms for AVs create a social dilemma (18, 19). Although people tend to agree that everyone would be better off if AVs were utilitarian (in the sense of minimizing the number of casualties on the road), these same people have a personal incentive to ride in AVs that will protect them at all costs. Accordingly, if both self-protective and utilitarian AVs were allowed on the market, few people would be willing to ride in utilitarian AVs, even though they would prefer others to do so. Regulation may provide a solution to this problem, but regulators will be faced with two difficulties: First, most people seem to disapprove of a regulation that would enforce utilitarian AVs. Second—and a more serious problem—our results suggest that such regulation could substantially delay the adoption of AVs, which means that the lives saved by making AVs utilitarian may be outnumbered by the deaths caused by delaying the adoption of AVs altogether. Thus, car-makers and regulators alike should be considering solutions to these obstacles.

17   Moral algorithms for AVs will need to tackle more intricate decisions than those considered in our surveys. For example, our scenarios did not feature any uncertainty about decision outcomes, but a collective discussion about moral algorithms will need to encompass the concepts of expected risk, expected value, and blame assignment. Is it acceptable for an AV to avoid a motorcycle by swerving into a wall, considering that the probability of survival is greater for the passenger of the AV than for the rider of the motorcycle? Should AVs account for the ages of passengers and pedestrians (20)? If a manufacturer offers different versions of its moral algorithm, and a buyer knowingly chose one of them, is the buyer to blame for the harmful consequences of the algorithm's decisions? Such liability considerations will need to accompany existing discussions of regulation (21), and we hope that psychological studies inspired by our own will be able to inform this discussion.

18   Figuring out how to build ethical autonomous machines is one of the thorniest challenges in artificial intelligence today (22). As we are about to endow millions of vehicles with autonomy, a serious consideration of

algorithmic morality has never been more urgent. Our data-driven approach highlights how the field of experimental ethics can provide key insights into the moral, cultural, and legal standards that people expect from autonomous driving algorithms. For the time being, there seems to be no easy way to design algorithms that would reconcile moral values and personal self-interest—let alone account for different cultures with various moral attitudes regarding life–life trade-offs (23)—but public opinion and social pressure may very well shift as this conversation progresses.

Acknowledgments

J.-F.B. gratefully acknowledges support through the Agence Nationale de la Recherche–Laboratoires d'Excellence Institute for Advanced Study in Toulouse. This research was supported by internal funds from the University of Oregon to A.S. I.R. is grateful for financial support from R. Hoffman. Data files have been uploaded as supplementary materials.

References and Notes

1. B. Montemerlo *et al.*, *J. Field Robot.* 25, 569–597 (2008).
2. C. Urmson *et al.*, *J. Field Robot.* 25, 425–466 (2008).
3. M.M. Waldrop, *Nature* 518, 20–23 (2015).
4. B. van Arem, C.J. van Driel, R. Visser, *IEEE Trans. Intell. Transp. Syst.* 7, 429–436 (2006).
5. K. Spieser *et al.*, in *Road Vehicle Automation*, G. Meyer, S. Beiker, Eds. (Lecture Notes in Mobility Series, Springer, 2014), pp. 229–245.
6. P. Gao, R. Hensley, A. Zielke, "A roadmap to the future for the auto industry," *McKinsey Quarterly* (October 2014); www.mckinsey.com/industries/automotive-and-assembly/our-insights/a-road-map-to-the-future-for-the-auto-industry.
7. N.J. Goodall, in *Road Vehicle Automation*, G. Meyer, S. Beiker, Eds. (Lecture Notes in Mobility Series, Springer, 2014), pp. 93–102.
8. K. Gray, A. Waytz, L. Young, *Psychol. Inq.* 23, 206–215 (2012).
9. J. Haidt, *The Righteous Mind: Why Good People Are Divided by Politics and Religion* (Pantheon Books, 2012).
10. W. Wallach, C. Allen, *Moral Machines: Teaching Robots Right from Wrong* (Oxford University Press, 2008).
11. F. Rosen, *Classical Utilitarianism from Hume to Mill* (Routledge, 2005).
12. J.D. Greene, *Moral Tribes: Emotion, Reason, and the Gap Between Us and Them* (Atlantic Books, 2014).
13. S. Côté, P.K. Piff, R. Willer, *J. Pers. Soc. Psychol.* 104, 490–503 (2013).
14. J.A.C. Everett, D.A. Pizarro, M.J. Crockett, *J. Exp. Psychol. Gen.* 145, 772–787 (2016).
15. N.E. Kass, *Am. J. Public Health* 91, 1776–1782 (2001).
16. C.R. Sunstein, A. Vermeule, *Stanford Law Rev.* 58, 703–750 (2005).
17. T. Dietz, E. Ostrom, P. C. Stern, *Science* 302, 1907–1912 (2003).
18. R.M. Dawes, *Annu. Rev. Psychol.* 31, 169–193 (1980).
19. P.A.M. Van Lange, J. Joireman, C.D. Parks, E. Van Dijk, *Organ. Behav. Hum. Decis. Process.* 120, 125–141 (2013).
20. E.A. Posner, C.R. Sunstein, *Univ. Chic. Law Rev.* 72, 537–598 (2005).
21. D.C. Vladeck, *Wash. Law Rev.* 89, 117–150 (2014).
22. B. Deng, *Nature* 523, 24–26 (2015).
23. 23 .N. Gold, A.M. Colman, B.D. Pulford, *Judgm. Decis. Mak.* 9, 65–76 (2014).

Key and challenging words

saliency, utilitarian, aversive, allocate, degradation, intricate, liability

Questions

1. Analyze the introductory paragraphs (1–3), commenting on the section's and individual paragraphs' structure and development, referring to common features of introductions (see Chapter 2, pp. 18–20), along with other relevant features.

2. The authors chose not to divide their essay according to the IMRAD format common in Type B essays: (a) Why do you think they made this choice? (b) Identify the first paragraph in which the authors explain their method and the first paragraph in which they begin to explain results.

3. Explain why "study three presents the first hint of a social dilemma," according to the authors (paragraph 10).

4. Using the information in the text about study four (paragraph 11) along with the corresponding graph in Figure 3 *or* the information in the text about study six (paragraph 14) along with the corresponding graph in Figure 3, explain the purpose, results, and significance of the study in one or two paragraphs.

5. Analyze paragraph 12 for its rhetorical effectiveness. As well as specific strategies for coherence, consider the ways it provides a transition between paragraphs 11 and 13.

6. Explain why the authors' studies of moral algorithms may not represent the true complexity of the issues surrounding AVs (see paragraph 17).

7. Although the authors of this essay conduct surveys as part of their empirical approach to their topic (See Type B essays, p. 23 in Chapter 3), they also use argument selectively. Identify passages from the Introduction (paragraphs 1–3) and the Conclusion (paragraphs 16–18) where argument is used, pointing to argumentative purpose and argumentative strategies (see Chapter 9).

Post-reading

1. In paragraph 4, the authors mention that they recruited subjects from the Amazon Mechanical Turk platform. Using reliable sources, describe in one paragraph what MTurk is and comment on whether it appears to be a credible source for the authors' surveys.

2. Form focus groups of four to six participants each in order to discuss issues raised in "The Social Dilemma of Autonomous Vehicles" and other issues related to AVs. In focus groups, participants express their perceptions and opinions on an issue without restrictions—except that they remain on topic. (If appropriate, one group member could act as facilitator, and the session could be recorded.) For more about focus groups, see p. 24.

Taking Race Out of Human Genetics: Engaging a Century-Long Debate about the Role of Race in Science

Michael Yudell, Dorothy Roberts, Rob DeSalle, and Sarah Tishkoff
(1,486 words)

Pre-reading

1. What did the sequencing of the human genome involve? What was the Human Genome Project? Using a reliable source, such as The National Human Genome Research Institute website (https://www.genome.gov/12011238/an-overview-of-the-human-genome -project/), answer these questions.

2. The term *race* is familiar to most people, but the concept may be challenging to define. Give a one-sentence definition of *race* as you understand it.

1   In the wake of the sequencing of the human genome in the early 2000s, genome pioneers and social scientists alike called for an end to the use of race as a variable in genetic research (1, 2). Unfortunately, by some measures, the use of race as a biological category has increased in the postgenomic age (3). Although inconsistent definition and use has been a chief problem with the race concept, it has historically been used as a taxonomic categorization based on common hereditary traits (such as skin color) to elucidate the relationship between our ancestry and our genes.

Source: From *Science*, vol. 351, no. 6273, 2016, pp. 564–5. Reprinted with permission from AAAS.

We believe the use of biological concepts of race in human genetic research—so disputed and so mired in confusion—is problematic at best and harmful at worst. It is time for biologists to find a better way.

2   Racial research has a long and controversial history. At the turn of the 20th century, sociologist and civil rights leader W. E. B. Du Bois was the first to synthesize natural and social scientific research to conclude that the concept of race was not a scientific category. Contrary to the then-dominant view, Du Bois maintained that health disparities between blacks and whites stemmed from social, not biological, inequality (4). Evolutionary geneticist Theodosius Dobzhansky, whose work helped reimagine the race concept in the 1930s at the outset of the evolutionary synthesis, wrestled with many of the same problems modern biologists face when studying human populations—for example, how to define and sample populations and genes (5). For much of his career, Dobzhansky brushed aside criticism of the race concept, arguing that the problem with race was not its scientific use, but its nonscientific misuse. Over time, he grew disillusioned, concerned that scientific study of human diversity had "floundered in confusion and misunderstanding" (6). His transformation from defender to detractor of the race concept in biology still resonates.

3   Today, scientists continue to draw wildly different conclusions on the utility of the race concept in biological research. Some have argued that relevant genetic information can be seen at the racial level (7) and that race is the best proxy we have for examining human genetic diversity (8, 9). Others have concluded that race is neither a relevant nor accurate way to understand or map human genetic diversity (10, 11). Still others have argued that race-based predictions in clinical settings, because of the heterogeneous nature of racial groups, are of questionable use (12), particularly as the prevalence of admixture increases across populations.

4   Several meetings and journal articles have called attention to a host of issues, which include (i) a proposed shift to "focus on racism (i.e., social relations) rather than race (i.e., supposed innate biologic predisposition) in the interpretation of racial/ethnic 'effects'" (13); (ii) a failure of scientists to distinguish between self-identified racial categories and assigned or assumed racial categories (14); and (iii) concern over "the haphazard use and reporting of racial/ethnic variables in genetic research" (15) and a need to justify use of racial categories relative to the research questions asked and methods used (6). Several academic journals have taken up this last concern and, with mixed success, have issued guidelines for use of race in research they publish (16). Despite these concerns, there have been no systematic attempts to address these issues and the situation has worsened with the rise of large-scale genetic surveys that use race as a tool to stratify these data (17).

5   It is important to distinguish ancestry from a taxonomic notion such as race. Ancestry is a process-based concept, a statement about an individual's relationship to other individuals in their genealogical history; thus, it is a very personal understanding of one's genomic heritage. Race, on the other hand, is a pattern-based concept that has led scientists and laypersons alike to draw conclusions about hierarchical organization of humans, which connect an individual to a larger pre-conceived geographically circumscribed or socially constructed group.

6   Unlike earlier disagreements concerning race and biology, today's discussions generally lack clear ideological and political antipodes of "racist" and "nonracist." Most contemporary discussions about race among scientists concern examination of population-level differences between groups, with the goal of understanding human evolutionary history, characterizing the frequency of traits within and between populations, and using an individual's self-identified ancestry to identify genetic risk factors of disease and to help determine the best course of medical treatments (6).

7   If this is what race in contemporary scientific and medical practice is about, then why should we be concerned? One reason is that phylogenetic and population genetic methods do not support a priori classifications of race, as expected for an interbreeding species like *Homo sapiens* (11, 18). As a result, racial assumptions are not the biological guide-posts some believe them to be, as commonly defined racial groups are genetically heterogeneous and lack clear-cut genetic boundaries (10, 11). For example, hemoglobinopathies can be misdiagnosed because of the identification of sickle-cell as a "Black" disease and thalassemia as a "Mediterranean" disease (10). Cystic fibrosis is underdiagnosed in populations of African ancestry, because it is thought of as a "White" disease (19). Popular misinterpretations of the use of race in genetics also continue to fuel racist beliefs, so much so that, in 2014, a group of leading human population geneticists publicly refuted claims about the genetic basis of social differences between races (20). Finally, the use of the race concept in genetics, an issue that has vexed natural and social scientists for more than a century, will not be obviated by new technologies. Although the low cost of next-generation sequencing has

facilitated efforts to sequence hundreds of thousands of individuals, adding whole-genome sequences does not negate the fact that racial classifications do not make sense in terms of genetics.

8   More than five decades after Dobzhansky called on biologists to develop better methods for investigating human genetic diversity (21), biology remains stuck in a paradox that reflects Dobzhanky's own struggle with the race concept: both believing race to be a tool to elucidate human genetic diversity and believing that race is a poorly defined marker of that diversity and an imprecise proxy for the relation between ancestry and genetics. In an attempt to resolve this paradox and to improve study of human genetic diversity, we propose the following.

9   Scientific journals and professional societies should encourage use of terms like "ancestry" or "population" to describe human groupings in genetic studies and should require authors to clearly define how they are using such variables. It is preferable to refer to geographic ancestry, culture, socioeconomic status, and language, among other variables, depending on the questions being addressed, to untangle the complicated relationship between humans, their evolutionary history, and their health. Some have shown that substituting such terms for race changes nothing if the underlying racial thinking stays the same (22, 23). But language matters, and the scientific language of race has a considerable influence on how the public (which includes scientists) understands human diversity (24). We are not the first to call for change on this subject. But, to date, calls to rationalize the use of concepts in the study of human genetic diversity, particularly race, have been implemented only in a piecemeal and inconsistent fashion, which perpetuates ambiguity of the concept and makes sustained change unfeasible (16). Having journals rationalize the use of classificatory terminology in studying human genetic diversity would force scientists to clarify their use and would allow researchers to understand and interpret data across studies. It would help avoid confusing, inconsistent, and contradictory usage of such terms.

10   Phasing out racial terminology in biological sciences would send an important message to scientists and the public alike: Historical racial categories that are treated as natural and infused with notions of superiority and inferiority have no place in biology. We acknowledge that using race as a political or social category to study racism and its biological effects, although fraught with challenges, remains necessary. Such research is important to understand how structural inequities and discrimination produce health disparities in socioculturally defined groups.

11   The U.S. National Academies of Sciences, Engineering, and Medicine should convene a panel of experts from biological sciences, social sciences, and humanities to recommend ways for research into human biological diversity to move past the use of race as a tool for classification in both laboratory and clinical research. Such an effort would bring stakeholders together for a simple goal: to improve the scientific study of human difference and commonality. The committee would be charged with examining current and historical usage of the race concept and ways current and future technology may improve the study of human genetic diversity; thus, they could take up Dobzhansky's challenge that "the problem that now faces the science of man [sic] is how to devise better methods for further observations that will give more meaningful results" (21). Regardless of where one stands on this issue, this is an opportunity to strengthen research by thinking more carefully about human genetic diversity.

Acknowledgments

All authors contributed equally to the conceptualization of this paper. M.Y. wrote the first draft and revised it based on comments from coauthors. Special thanks to E. Arana for research assistance.

References and Notes

1. F. Collins, *Nat. Genet.* 36 (suppl.), S13 (2004).
2. M.W. Foster, R.R. Sharp, *Nat. Rev. Genet.* 5, 790 (2004).
3. P.A. Chow-White, S.E. Green Jr., *Int. J. Commun.* 7, 556 (2013).
4. W.E.B. Du Bois, *The Health and Physique of the Negro American* (Publ. no. 11, Atlanta Univ. Publications, Atlanta, GA, 1906).
5. T. Dobzhansky, *Genetics and the Origin of Species* (Columbia Univ. Press, New York, 1937).
6. M. Yudell, *Race Unmasked: Biology and Race in the 20th Century* (Columbia Univ. Press, New York, 2014).
7. E.G. Burchard et al., *N. Engl. J. Med.* 348, 1170 (2003).
8. Y. Banda et al., *Genetics* 200, 1285 (2015).
9. C.E. Powe et al., *N. Engl. J. Med.* 369, 1991 (2013).
10. D. Roberts, *Fatal Invention: How Science, Politics, and Big Business Re-Create Race in the Twenty-First Century* (The New Press, New York, 2012).

11. D. Serre, S. Pääbo, *Genome Res.* 14, 1679 (2004).
12. P.C. Ng, Q. Zhao, S. Levy, R.L. Strausberg, J.C. Venter, *Clin. Pharmacol. Ther.* 84, 306 (2008).
13. J.S. Kaufman, R.S. Cooper, *Am. J. Epidemiol.* 154, 291 (2001).
14. T.R. Rebbeck, P. Sankar, *Cancer Epidemiol. Prev.* 14, 2467 (2005).
15. L.M. Hunt, M.S. Megyesi, *J. Med. Ethics* 34, 495 (2008).
16. A. Smart, R. Tutton, P. Martin, G.T.H. Ellison, R. Ashcroft, *Soc. Stud. Sci.* 38, 407 (2008).
17. G. Lettre et al., *PLOS Genet.* 7, e1001300 (2011).
18. K. Bremer, H.E. Wanntorp, *Syst. Biol.* 28, 624 (1979).
19. C. Stewart, M.S. Pepper, *Genet. Med.* (2015).
20. G. Coop et al., *New York Times*, 8 August 2014, p. BR6.
21. T. Dobzhansky, *Mankind Evolving: The Evolution of the Human Species* (Yale Univ. Press, New Haven, CT, 1962).
22. S.M. Fullerton, J.H. Yu, J. Crouch, K. Fryer-Edwards, W. Burke, *Hum. Genet.* 127, 563 (2010).
23. L. Braun, E. Hammonds, *Soc. Sci. Med.* 67, 1580 (2008).
24. W.C. Byrd, M.W. Hughey, Ann. *Am. Acad. Pol. Soc. Sci.* 661, 1 (2015).

Key and challenging words

taxonomic, elucidate, disparity, heterogeneous, stratify, circumscribe, antipodes, obviate, proxy, unfeasible

Questions

1. In your own words, summarize the problem referred to in paragraph 1 that the authors seek to resolve.

2. (a) Explain the roles that W.E.B. Du Bois and Theodosius Dobzhansky played in racial research in the twentieth century (see paragraph 2); (b) Why do you think the authors devote more space to Dobzhansky's role than Du Bois's?

3. (a) What rhetorical pattern is prominent in paragraphs 3 and 4? (b) paragraph 5? (See "Rhetorical Patterns and Paragraph Development," in Chapter 6, pp. 77–80.) (c) Choosing one of these rhetorical patterns, explain how it aids in paragraph development.

4. How does the way scientists use the term *race* differ from its previous uses? (See paragraph 6.)

5. Analyze the authors' use of comprehension strategies in paragraph 7. In your answer, you can refer to such strategies as topic sentences, prompts, rhetorical patterns, transitions, repetition, word choice, and other methods to enhance the reader's understanding of content. In your analysis, also consider any strategies the writers use to connect this paragraph to the preceding and following paragraphs.

6. (a) Find three examples of direct quotations consisting of more than two words and discuss why the authors might have chosen to integrate some of their sources this way; (b) Explain the use of brackets in the direct quotation in paragraph 11.

7. Analyze the effectiveness of the argument presented in paragraphs 9–11. In your analysis, refer to at least two specific strategies discussed in Chapter 9 (summarized on page 118).

Post-reading

1. *Collaborative activity:* What are some of the racial stereotypes that you have heard or been exposed to? Did the article change your perception about race? If so, how? Do you believe that a shift in focus from race to racism (see paragraph 4) would have practical benefits to society? In groups, discuss the concept of race as described in "Taking Race out of Human Genetics," using these or other race-related questions as prompts.

2. Respond to one of the ideas mentioned in the last three paragraphs, supporting your argument by your experiences, observations, critical thinking, or points made by the authors.

Speed That Kills: The Role of Technology in Kate Chopin's "The Story of an Hour"

Jeremy Foote
(1,564 words)

> ## Pre-reading
>
> 1. Read the short story that is analyzed by the author of the essay below (see pp. 348–349), noting themes, characters, setting, tone, language, and relevant techniques common to literary analyses. Summarize the story's theme(s) in one or two sentences.
> 2. *Collaborative or individual activity:* Reflect on the role of technology in our society today. Generate a list of the pros and cons; choosing one or two items from the list on each, explore their significance to you and your peers either orally or in writing.

1   Kate Chopin's "The Story of an Hour" has been taught and analyzed almost exclusively from a feminist perspective. As Lawrence Berkove writes, "There has been . . . virtual critical agreement on what the story says: its heroine dies, ironically and tragically, just as she has been freed from a constricting marriage and has realized self-assertion as the deepest element of her being" (1). Louise Mallard's sense of joy at her husband's apparent death, and her own death at his return, have become an archetype of feminine self-realization and the patriarchy that is always there to extinguish it (e.g., Harlow 501). Indeed, the feminist images of the story are so powerful that I believe critics have overlooked another theme. "The Story of an Hour" can be read as a protomodernist text. As also seen with later modernist writers, technology and the societal changes caused by technology play important roles in Chopin's story.

2   "The Story of an Hour" was first published in *Vogue* in 1894. More than a century later, now in the midst of our own technological revolution, it is difficult to grasp how fundamentally nineteenth-century technologies were altering the world in Chopin's time. Before the railroad, traveling was extremely difficult and dangerous. In the 1850s, it took an average of 128 days to traverse the Oregon Trail (Unruh 403), with a mortality rate of 4 per cent to 6 per cent (Unruh 408). The transcontinental railroad, completed in 1869, allowed the same journey to be made, safely and much more comfortably, in less than a week (Cooper). Perhaps more importantly, during the 1890s trains started to become part of daily life. In 1889 the first interurban electric rail lines were laid, and by 1894 hundreds of miles of track were being added every year (Hilton and Due 186–87).

3   Communications underwent an even more dramatic acceleration. The completion of the first successful transatlantic cable in 1866 meant news that had previously taken a week or more to travel between Europe and the Americas could now be sent nearly instantaneously. Like the railroad, while the initial invention had occurred years earlier, in the 1890s telegrams went from novel to quotidian. In 1870, Western Union relayed 9 million telegrams. By 1893, they were sending more than 66 million telegrams annually (United States Bureau of the Census 788).

4   Later writers would explore the effects of these and other technologies. In his 1909 "Futurist Manifesto," Filippo Marinetti gushes, "Time and Space died yesterday. We already live in the absolute, because we have created eternal, omnipresent speed." Not all writers would be as optimistic as Marinetti. A few decades after "Hour" was published, World War I would provide striking evidence of the destructive power of new technologies, and writers like Ezra Pound and T.S. Eliot would lament the new world that man had created. In "Hugh Selwyn Mauberly," for example, Pound claims that the world experienced "Fortitude as never before / Frankness as never before, / Disillusions as never told in the old days" (81–83). Pound felt that technology led to a world "as never before" but that these changes led to a "botched civilization" instead of a technological utopia (89).

Source: From *The Explicator*, vol. 71, no. 2, 2013, pp. 85–9. Reprinted by permission of the publisher (Taylor & Francis Ltd, wwwinformaworld.com).

5   "The Story of an Hour" can be read as a precursor to these more technophobic works. The story begins with news of Mr Mallard's death in a railroad disaster—received by telegram. This may be a commentary on the literal danger of riding trains in the 1890s, but we can also see the railroad's role in the story as a more subtle warning. While we don't know for certain why Mr Mallard would have been riding a train that day, Chopin describes him later as "a little travel-stained, composedly carrying his grip-sack and umbrella," bringing to mind the image of a commuter returning home from a day at the office (Chopin). The railroads, and the urbanization and industrialization that they symbolized and enabled, were changing how and where people worked. In Chopin's St. Louis, for example, the population had quintupled in her lifetime, as people moved away from their farms and into the cities (Gibson). Railroads meant that where people lived and where they worked could be far apart, giving rise to the commuter lifestyle (and the word *commuter*) (Paumgarten). Time that in previous generations had been spent with family was now spent apart, as family members sped away from one another. These changes certainly affected marital relationships and the experience of womanhood. Women were spending more and more time by themselves, with time to pursue their own interests. Perhaps it is these hours alone each day that leave Louise wanting more autonomy, dreaming of "no one to live for during those coming years" (Chopin).

6   In fact, the story gives evidence that Louise's emotions are affected by the physical absence of her husband. After recognizing the joy she feels upon learning of her husband's supposed death, Louise reflects on her feelings: "She did not stop to ask if it were or were not a monstrous joy that held her. . . . She knew that she would weep again when she saw the kind, tender hands folded in death; the face that had never looked save with love upon her, fixed and gray and dead" (Chopin). Confronted with her husband's body, she knows that she will feel differently. Her joyous reaction is to a distant, faceless death, unimpeded by the reality of an actual corpse—unattached to an actual person. The railroad provides this catalyst for Louise's self-realization, because it "killed" Mr Mallard both quickly and distantly. Indeed, the speed and remoteness of Mr Mallard's death seem to be primary causes of the speed and intensity of Louise's emotions. Instead of taking care of an ailing husband and preparing for his death, death is thrust upon her, forcing her to confront her entire reaction to his passing all at once.

7   While Brently's death and Louise's joyful reaction are enabled by the railroad, the story would be equally impossible without the technology of the telegraph. At the beginning of the story, Mr Mallard's friend hears of a telegram listing Brently Mallard as deceased. He decides to break the news to Louise, after having "taken the time to assure himself of its truth by a second telegram" (Chopin). Before telegrams, information could not travel faster than people. Mr Mallard would have arrived home, safe and sound, long before the news of his death could have reached his wife. "Slow" communications (i.e., everything before the telegraph) also had to be relayed person to person. Having people as part of the medium helped maintain the veracity and the context of messages. To send a telegram, on the other hand, words are converted into electrical impulses and then reinterpreted at their destination. They travel at the speed of light, without any substance, as disembodied information. "Hour" seems to be warning us that there are dangers in this separation of message from medium: the more information is isolated, the more meaning comes from the recipient's interpretation. The telegram that Louise receives is an example of this danger. There may very well have been a Brently Mallard killed in the railroad disaster, so the disembodied information was true, but the substance of the information—that it was her husband who had been killed—was false. Even a second telegram was not enough to verify the truth, because the needed truth was found in the context, not in the information, and telegrams can only relay information.

8   "Hour" is not only about the danger of communications moving too quickly but also a warning about the overall increase in the speed of life. These technologies that were speeding up how people moved and communicated naturally sped up their lives, including their emotional lives. As the title tells us, this is a story about time; the rate at which things happen is important. Louise Mallard goes from devastation to euphoria to shock, all within an hour. Arguably, her death is more a result of how quickly her emotions occur, rather than the emotions themselves. Living in a time with twenty-four-hour news and ever-scrolling Twitter feeds, we know something of the dangers of not having enough time to process what is happening. The time needed to experience and analyze emotions has been eliminated, and the body (and soul) cannot keep up with that kind of schedule. Louise is forced to confront the great questions of life—death and love and self-actualization—in the space of an afternoon. It is no wonder that there are repercussions.

9   "The Story of an Hour" has long been heralded as a wonderful feminist text, which it is. The issues of male

The Story of an Hour

by Kate Chopin

Knowing that Mrs Mallard was afflicted with a heart trouble, great care was taken to break to her as gently as possible the news of her husband's death.

It was her sister Josephine who told her, in broken sentences; veiled hints that revealed in half concealing. Her husband's friend Richards was there, too, near her. It was he who had been in the newspaper office when intelligence of the railroad disaster was received, with Brently Mallard's name leading the list of 'killed'. He had only taken the time to assure himself of its truth by a second telegram, and had hastened to forestall any less careful, less tender friend in bearing the sad message.

She did not hear the story as many have heard the same, with a paralyzed inability to accept its significance. She wept at once, with sudden, wild abandonment, in her sister's arms. When the storm of grief had spent itself she went away to her room alone. She would have no one follow her.

There stood, facing the open window, a comfortable, roomy armchair. Into this she sank, pressed down by a physical exhaustion that haunted her body and seemed to reach into her soul.

She could see in the open square before her house the tops of trees that were all aquiver with the new spring life. The delicious breath of rain in the air. In the street below a peddler was crying his wares. The notes of a distant song which someone was singing reached her faintly, and countless sparrows were twittering in the eaves.

There were patches of blue sky showing here and there through the clouds that had met and piled one above the other in the west facing her window.

She sat with her head thrown back upon the cushion of the chair, quite motionless, except when a sob came up into her throat and shook her, as a child who has cried itself to sleep continues to sob in its dreams.

She was young, with a fair, calm face, whose lines bespoke repression and even a certain strength. But now there was a dull stare in her eyes, whose gaze was fixed away off yonder on one of those patches of blue sky. It was not a glance of reflection, but rather indicated a suspension of intelligent thought.

There was something coming to her and she was waiting for it, fearfully. What was it? She did not know; it was too subtle and elusive to name. But she felt it, creeping out of the sky, reaching toward her through the sounds, the scents, the colour that filled the air.

Now her bosom rose and fell tumultuously. She was beginning to recognize this thing that was approaching to possess her, and she was striving to beat it back with her will—as powerless as her two white slender hands would have been.

hegemony and feminine independence are dealt with in an important and powerful way. Chopin helps us realize, however, that other subtle factors are at play. This is a cautionary tale about a world that is speeding up; it is a warning about lives that move too quickly. The tragedy of Louise Mallard's death occurs not only because she is a woman but because she is a modern woman. This story would have unfolded very differently without the technologies of the railroad and telegraph; by exploring the effects of these technologies within a purposely feminine text, Chopin shows us that even such "timeless" issues as male and female relations can only be fully understood within the time and place in which they occur.

Works Cited

Berkove, Lawrence I. "Fatal Self-Assertion in Kate Chopin's 'The Story of an Hour'." *American Literary Realism* 32.2 (2000): 152–58. Print.

Chopin, Kate. "The Story of an Hour." *Wikisource*. Web. 19 Jul. 2011. <http://en.wikisource.org/wiki/The Story of an Hour>.

Cooper, Bruce C. "Riding the Transcontinental Rails: Overland Travel on the Pacific Railroad—Introduction." *Central Pacific Railroad Photographic History Museum*. 2004. Web. 2 May 2011. <http://cprr.org/Museum/Riding the Rails Intro.html>.

When she abandoned herself a little whispered word escaped her slightly parted lips. She said it over and over under her breath: "free, free, free!" The vacant stare and the look of terror that had followed it went from her eyes. They stayed keen and bright. Her pulses beat fast, and the coursing blood warmed and relaxed every inch of her body.

She did not stop to ask if it were or were not a monstrous joy that held her. A clear and exalted perception enabled her to dismiss the suggestion as trivial.

She knew that she would weep again when she saw the kind, tender hands folded in death; the face that had never looked save with love upon her, fixed and grey and dead. But she saw beyond that bitter moment a long procession of years to come that would belong to her absolutely. And she opened and spread her arms out to them in welcome.

There would be no one to live for her during those coming years; she would live for herself. There would be no powerful will bending hers in that blind persistence with which men and women believe they have a right to impose a private will upon a fellow creature. A kind intention or a cruel intention made the act seem no less a crime as she looked upon it in that brief moment of illumination.

And yet she had loved him—sometimes. Often she had not. What did it matter! What could love, the unsolved mystery, count for in face of this possession of self-assertion which she suddenly recognized as the strongest impulse of her being!

"Free! Body and soul free!" she kept whispering.

Josephine was kneeling before the closed door with her lips to the keyhole, imploring for admission. "Louise, open the door! I beg; open the door—you will make yourself ill. What are you doing, Louise? For heaven's sake open the door."

"Go away. I am not making myself ill." No; she was drinking in a very elixir of life through that open window.

Her fancy was running riot along those days ahead of her. Spring days, and summer days, and all sorts of days that would be her own. She breathed a quick prayer that life might be long. It was only yesterday she had thought with a shudder that life might be long.

She arose at length and opened the door to her sister's importunities. There was a feverish triumph in her eyes, and she carried herself unwittingly like a goddess of Victory. She clasped her sister's waist, and together they descended the stairs. Richards stood waiting for them at the bottom.

Someone was opening the front door with a latchkey. It was Brently Mallard who entered, a little travel-stained, composedly carrying his grip-sack and umbrella. He had been far from the scene of the accident, and did not even know there had been one. He stood amazed at Josephine's piercing cry; at Richards' quick motion to screen him from the view of his wife.

But Richards was too late.

When the doctors came they said she had died of heart disease—of joy that kills.

Gibson, Campbell. "Population of the 100 Largest Cities and Other Urban Places in the United States: 1790 to 1990." Population Division Working Paper No. 27. U.S. Census Bureau. 1998. Web. 19 Jul. 2011. <www.census.gov/population/www/documentation/twps0027/twps0027.html>.

Harlow, Barbara. "From the Women's Prison: Third World Women's Narratives of Prison." *Feminist Studies* 12.3 (1986): 501–24. Print.

Hilton, George W., and John F. Due. *The Electric Interurban Railways in America.* Stanford, CA: Stanford UP, 2000. *Google Books.* Web. 21 Jul. 2011.

Marinetti, F.T. "The Futurist Manifesto." 1909. Web. 8 May 2012. <http://cscs.umich.edu/~crshalizi/T4PM/futurist-manifesto.html>.

Paumgarten, Nick. "[Annals of Transport:] There and Back Again." *The New Yorker,* 16 Apr. 2007. Web. 2 May 2012. <www.newyorker.com/reporting/2007/04/16/070416fa factpaumgarten>.

Pound, Ezra. "Hugh Selwyn Mauberley." 2007. *Project Gutenberg.* Web. 25 Apr. 2013.

United States Bureau of the Census. *Historical Statistics of the United States: Colonial Times to 1970.* Vol. 2. Washington, DC: U.S. Department of Commerce, Census Bureau, 1975. *Google Books.* Web. 21 Jul. 2011.

Unruh, John D. *The Plains Across: The Overland Emigrants and the Trans-Mississippi West, 1840–60.* Urbana: University of Illinois, 1993. *Google Books.* Web. 18 Jul. 2011.

Key and challenging words

patriarchy, quotidian, utopia, technophobic, precursor, autonomy, veracity, disembodied, euphoria, repercussion, hegemony

Questions

1. (a) Summarize the essay's justification; (b) Paraphrase its thesis.
2. Discuss the importance of primary sources in Foote's essay, using at least two specific examples as support (one of the examples should be from a text other than "The Story of an Hour").
3. At what point does the author explicitly connect the story's themes to propose a unified reading of the text? Comment on the placement and effectiveness of this passage.
4. Does Foote's essay stress primarily the pros or the cons of technology during the 1890s? Explain your answer by referring specifically to the text.
5. Analyze paragraph 6, focusing on the rhetorical and/or organizational strategies used by the author. These could include language, parallel structures, repetition, sentence length/variety, paragraph structure, use of transitions, and the like.
6. Today's literary essays often look beyond the text being analyzed to embrace other disciplines and perspectives. Show how Foote uses non-literary sources to enrich his reading of "The Story of an Hour."

Post-reading

1. Foote makes many comparisons between Chopin's age and our own. Identifying one or two of these comparisons, discuss his success (or lack of it) in making the story relevant to today's reader.

Psychology's Essential Role in Alleviating the Impacts of Climate Change

Robert Gifford
(5,347 words)

Pre-reading

1. Scan the abstract, introduction, and headings in order to determine the essay's purpose (expository or argumentative?) and intended audience. From this information, formulate a reading hypothesis.
2. How might the IPCC Report, mentioned in the first sentence, have affected the timing of Gifford's essay?

Climate change is occurring: where is psychology? The conventional wisdom is that amelioration of the impacts of climate change is a matter for earth and ocean science, economics, technology, and policy-making. This article presents the basis for psychological science as a key part of the solution to the problem and describes the challenges to this both from within psychology and from other points of view. Minimizing the personal and environmental damage caused by climate change necessarily is a multidisciplinary task, but one to which psychology not only should, but must contribute more than it has so far.

Keywords: climate change, role of psychology, Canada

*

1   By now, the issue of whether or not climate change is occurring has been resolved for quite some time, and the fourth report of the Intergovernmental Panel on Climate Change (IPCC), in November 2007 has reiterated its conclusion. It is happening. Some may wish to debate the relative extent of natural and human causes of the change, but little doubt exists that human activities have been, and continue to be, one important force driving climate change. One can imagine that climate change might have some positive consequences for some people in some places, but according to many experts, climate change already is having, and will have many more, negative consequences for many people in many places.

2   The present thesis is that psychology, in concert with other disciplines, has an important role to play in easing the pain caused by climate change. Were this thesis widely recognized, the present article would be unnecessary. Unfortunately, the thesis is not broadly acknowledged. Anecdotally, I can report that I sat through a recent meeting of scientists from a variety of disciplines concerned with climate change and heard a leading natural scientist state that the large interdisciplinary grant proposal being discussed should not include any input from "fluff," by which he apparently meant the social sciences. More formally, the emerging discipline of sustainability science, clearly a first cousin to climate-change studies, has been advocated and defined by some authors (e.g., Clark & Dickson, 2003) without the slightest reference to possible contributions by psychologists. Are these assertions and omissions justified?

A Bit of Background

3   Each person on the planet, whether as an individual or as part of an organization, curates a stream of natural resources that are converted into products; the conversion process often creates greenhouse gases. Thus, as psychologists have long recognized, the fundamental unit of analysis for the human-caused portion of climate change is the person (Ehrlich & Kennedy, 2005; Gifford, 1987). Thus, ultimately, amelioration of that part of environmental problems such as climate change over which we have some potential control occurs at the individual level (Clayton & Brook, 2005).

4   Psychologists have long been concerned with individuals' behaviour that contributes to climate change.[1] In particular, environmental psychology, a child of 1960s idealism, was conceived to solve environment-related problems through scientific evidence-based research. Research on energy conservation and other environmental problems has been going on for 35 years (e.g., Buckhout, 1972; Pallak & Cummings, 1976; Seligman & Darley, 1977). Derived in part from Kurt Lewin's mantra that nothing is so practical as a good theory, it has always been an approach that seeks to combine quality research with applications aimed at personal and organizational change. In doing so, it has developed a wide range of theories, models, and principles that can be used to design action research techniques for changing behaviour (e.g., Bechtel & Churchman, 2002; Gifford, 2007). A stream of special issues in journals on environmental problems has appeared since the 1980s (see Vlek & Steg, 2007, for a list), and they are the tip of an iceberg that includes hundreds of individual journal articles. In 40 years of existence, environmental psychologists have developed an extensive toolbox of ideas and techniques (e.g., Bechtel, Marans, & Michelson, 1987). They are based on hundreds of articles published in its two primary journals, the *Journal of Environmental Psychology* and *Environment and Behaviour,* and numerous allied journals, which form a very extensive information base for designing programmes and solutions to a variety of problems (Gifford, 2002b), including sustainability problems.

---

1 Ironically, this probably precedes the concern for climate change on the part of most of the 2000 or so natural scientists whose work was used by the Intergovernmental Panel on Climate Change, and thus basked in the shared glory of the 2007 Nobel Prize, with the notable exception of Al Gore himself.

Source: From *Canadian Psychology*, vol. 49, no. 4, 2008, pp. 273–80. © 2008 Canadian Psychological Association. Reprinted by permission of the Canadian Psychological Association.

So Why Then Has Psychology Not Been a Climate-Change Player?

5   Discourse on climate change in the media and amongst policy-makers is virtually silent on the role of psychology. The conventional wisdom in the wider world of climate-change thought is that psychology has no important role to play. Why?

6   First, we must lay the blame in part on ourselves. Psychology, in general, has been accused of ignoring the environment by treating people as if they existed in a vacuum (nicely embodied in the blank four walls of the laboratory). As noted by Kidner (1994), the psychological scientist too often "perpetuates and legitimizes a world view in which the individual is seen as separate from the environment" (p. 362). Even environmental psychologists have largely kept their focus on individual-level influences on environment-related behaviour: values, attitudes, motives, intentions, goals, social comparison, habits, and similar constructs. We have left the making of connections between these constructs—which *are* important, and policy—which is essential—to others. We write in our discussion sections that "someone" should take into account these important findings of ours. However, unfortunately, for the most part policymakers and natural scientists do not read our discussion sections. This is one reason sustainability science can be defined without reference to psychology.

7   Second, the kinds of effort needed to combat the consequences of climate change do not suit the academic context in which most established psychologists work. In this forum I need not elaborate on the ways and means needed to find an academic position, earn tenure, and win grants: usually it is to conduct many parametric experiments in laboratories with those handy introductory psychology students. This is not to blame graduate students and young PhDs who find themselves in this situation: the levers to success were not created by them.

8   Third, most policymakers in ministries and departments concerned with environmental problems were not trained in the behavioural sciences. Reser and Bentrupperbaumer (2001) estimate that functionaries in resource-related government agencies and departments trained in the natural sciences outnumber those trained in the social sciences by at least 50 to 1. With less or no social-science experience, these policymakers are unlikely to understand what the social sciences have to offer, and even if they were sympathetic to the idea, they would have difficulty understanding many of the concepts and results. This leads to fundamental misunderstandings of such concepts as values, valuation, and social impacts (Reser & Bentrupperbaumer, 2001). Some excellent but isolated progress has been made toward finding ways for natural and social scientists to communicate (e.g., Miller, 1985), but uneven numbers and inadequate communication and understanding remain serious problems.

9   Fourth, the role of psychology in climate change has so far been particularly neglected in Canada. Although discourse on the role of psychological science and climate change has been less than robust anywhere, it has at least existed in the United States and Germany (Oskamp, 2000; Schmuck & Schultz, 2002; Stern, 1993), Australia (Reser, 2007), the Netherlands (Vlek, 2000), Sweden (Lundqvist & Biel, 2007), and the United Kingdom (Uzzell, 2007). I am unaware of any substantive previous discussion of psychology's role by a Canadian psychologist concerning the Canadian context. The leading proponent of environmental action in Canada was trained as a geneticist in a fruit-fly lab. How can psychologists expect to be players when we are silent?

The Basis for Psychology's Role

10   Each person, whether an average citizen or a CEO, has some level of choice and control over sustainability-related behaviours and actions. As Paul Stern (2005) has pointed out, these choices often are heavily constrained by contextual factors and one's own habits. Stern posits a hierarchical set of forces in which structural factors above or external to the individual usually are much more powerful influences on behaviour than individual-level influences.

11   Although one must acknowledge the power of context, and that Stern's hierarchy often accurately describes environmental behaviour choices, I maintain that individuals truly are the ultimate key to climate-change amelioration: policies, programmes, and regulations themselves do not change anything. For one thing, to be acceptable and efficacious to individuals; policies must be "bought into" by individuals. In short, policy beckons or even commands, but persons accept or refuse its demands. Behavioural change does not occur until this happens.

12   Many people do resist the temptation to engage in self-serving behaviours that contribute to climate change. Yet, admittedly, many do yield to the temptation. What will it take to change these people's behaviour?

As a start—but only a start—understanding environment-related motivations, attitudes, social and organizational perceptions, rationales, biases, habits, barriers to change, life-context, and trust in government will help. Certainly, psychologists are already engaged in the effort on their own. For example, some have investigated the psychological dimensions of global warming (e.g., Dresner, 1989–90; Heath & Gifford, 2006; Nilsson, von Borgstede, & Biel, 2004). However, the major thesis of the present article is that we psychologists must do more.

13   I do not wish to argue that environmental psychology is, or even could be, a stand-alone panacea. For example, Schmuck and Vlek (2003) advocate that we work more closely with environmental scientists. However, I believe that we must work with at least four other groups to be effective: natural scientists, technical experts, policy experts, and local citizens' committees.

14   Fortunately, environmental psychologists have a history of interdisciplinary collaboration, beginning with geography and architecture, embodied in the collaborations between Robert Sommer, Humphry Osmond, and Kiyo Izumi in 1950s Saskatchewan (Sommer, 1983), or between Raymond Studer and David Stea in the United States (1966). More recently, and more pertinent to current concerns, fruitful collaborative work is being done in sustainability research (e.g., Schoot Uiterkamp & Vlek, 2007), including some collaborations that represent new bridges. Schoot Uiterkamp and Vlek (2007) describe five instances of collaborations, and their account is particularly valuable for its advice about the practicalities of engaging in multidisciplinary studies. This collaboration trend has been influenced, one suspects, by policies at national and international grant agencies that, for better or worse, virtually require interdisciplinary collaboration. In terms of influencing policy, collaborative efforts not only have "face credibility" based on the very breadth of their approach, but also success that is legitimately based on the increased validity of policy suggestions that emerge from studying a given problem with multiple valuable perspectives.

15   Gattig and Hendrickx (2007) bring perspectives from economics and behavioural decision theory into the mix. Discounting, the tendency to reduce the importance of an outcome with greater "distance" (temporally, socially, geographically, and probabilistically), is seen to be an important component of thinking about sustainability-related thinking. Fortunately, environmental problems appear to be less subject to discounting than some other matters.

Although they incorporate some concepts from economics, Gattig and Hendrickx demonstrate why using those concepts in the same way that traditional economists do could lead to ineffective policies (cf. Stern, 1986). "Rational" discount rates are not the same as those of the public which, to its credit, seems to discount environmental impacts less than in other domains. This helps to illustrate why other disciplines need psychology as much as psychology needs them.

16   Turning the policy issue upside down, some psychologists are examining the effects of policy strategies, as opposed to conducting studies that they hope will inform policy. Jager and Mosler (2007) are amongst those who use modeling to understand the outcomes of different policy choices. This form of active modeling offers the attractive advantage of trying out various policies before they are implemented and understanding why they might or might not work, thereby potentially avoiding expensive mistakes in policy-making. As Jager and Mosler point out, modeling can also be used to train policymakers. The very act of modeling encourages the idea that many policy alternatives exist, when often only a few may occur to a policymaker.

Technosalvation?

17   Technology is often promoted as the solution to many problems, including those related to climate change. Amongst these are biofuels, wind power, and solar power. Suspicion about the value of technology (e.g., Frank, 1966; Osborn, 1948) is longstanding and is justifiable in part. For example, growing biofuels requires the use of pesticides, reduces biodiversity, creates atmospheric pollution when burned, and has already caused large increases in food prices. Wind power creates noise, kills many birds, is unsightly, and negatively affects the rural lifestyle. Solar power requires the manufacture of photovoltaic cells, which creates a waste stream of cadmium, lead, and other heavy metal by-products. The downside of technology (pollution, health impacts, landfill contributions, accidents, energy consumed in production, and impacts on flora and fauna) is often overlooked in the touting of its benefits. As just one example that is not widely recognized, air pollution kills about 800,000 people each year (Kenworthy & Laube, 2002), and most air pollution is caused by technology in one form or another.

18   Of course, technology has another side to it, and as Midden, Kaiser, and McCalley (2007) clearly show,

psychological scientists must deal with it because it is very unlikely to go away. It will not disappear because, despite its negative effects on people and the environment, it undoubtedly has improved the quality of life for millions of other people, particularly when one thinks in terms of decades and centuries past (Simon, 1981). Assuming individuals have the motivation and appropriate skills, technology can assist in the goal of reducing greenhouse gas emissions. However, Midden et al.'s (2007) quite valid point is that the mere introduction of some new technology does not guarantee that it will be accepted and used by citizens, or that further investigation will not reveal that the cure is worse than the disease. Thus, policies aimed at facilitating the use by citizens of salutary technology must be encouraged, and the basis for such policies lies with research by environmental psychologists, who have the tools to understand why, whether, and when technology is accepted or not by citizens.

Three Models and Some Other Contributions of Psychology to Policy

19   Environmental psychologists share an interest in modeling with scientists in some other disciplines. The value of models is that they postulate relations amongst key influences and help to represent complex systems in understandable ways. They can stimulate investigation of the properties of the system and suggest predictions of future outcomes.

20   One such approach, Stern's (2000) values-beliefs-norms model (see Figure 1), postulates that behaviour is determined in part by a causal sequence that begins with deep-seated and quite-stable values, which strongly influence the more-mutable beliefs that one has, which set up the person's behavioural norms.

21   A second general approach is the social dilemma paradigm, which originated with Robyn Dawes' (1980) seminal article and has been expanded by Charles Vlek (1996). In essence, this paradigm asserts that individuals may act in self-interest or in the community interest; if they are amongst a few who act in self-interest they will prosper, but if many or most people act in self-interest, the environment (and they themselves) will suffer.

22   For the last several years, I have set myself the goal of integrating the many influences on, and outcomes of, social dilemmas into a coherent and comprehensive model (Gifford, 2002a, 2008). Initially, I considered that influences on proenvironmental behaviour could be grouped into those associated with (a) the natural resource itself, such as its abundance or regeneration rate, (b) the decision-makers, such as their values and experience, (c) relations amongst decision-makers, such as trust and communication, and (d) the structure of the dilemma, such as the rules that govern environment-related actions (Gifford, 1987). Since then, the model has been expanding and relations amongst these categories of influence have been described and investigated (see Figure 2). In a meta-analysis Donald Hine and I (1991) conducted, about 30 different influences could be identified. This gradually led to the attempt to create a more comprehensive and organized model.

23   The model includes five categories of antecedent influences on a person's decisions, as shown in Figure 2: geophysical, governance (policies), interpersonal, decision-maker characteristics, and problem awareness. These influences are presumed to determine the different strategies or heuristics that individuals as decision-makers

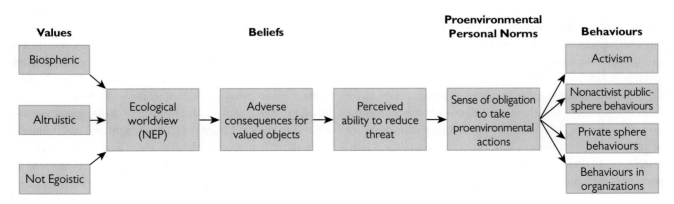

Figure 1   Stern's (2000) values-beliefs-norms model.

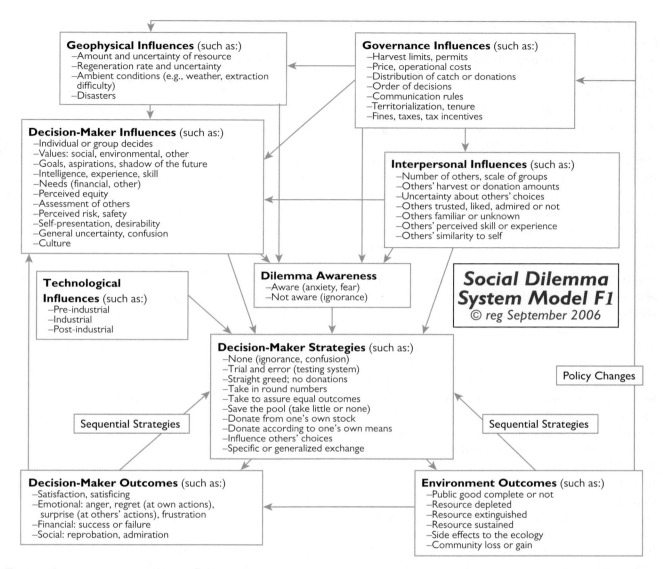

Figure 2 A model of the social dilemma approach to environmental problems that focuses on the decision-making of individuals (Gifford, 2008).

actually employ. Finally, two kinds of outcomes may be distinguished: those for decision-makers and their intimates, and those for the environment (the resource itself, the environment in general, and for other people in the community). Each element in the model includes numerous specific influences, which may be seen in Figure 2. A complete description of these influences may be found elsewhere (Gifford, 2007).

24 A mere listing of influences and outcomes is fairly straightforward; postulating and testing links amongst them is both more interesting and more challenging. For

example, some decision-makers' strategy is geared toward sending a message to other decision-makers; the explicit message of some participants in our resource dilemma studies has been, for example: "Look, I am making sustainable choices, and I want you to do the same." Hence, a causal link exists between decision-maker strategies and interpersonal influences. At the larger social scale, consequences for climate change (environmental outcomes) often are reflected in changes in policies or regulations (governance influences). These hypothesized links between categories, and the conditions under which influence occurs or does not occur, represent the heuristic value of the model. Other direct and feedback links amongst the model's elements could be hypothesized and tested by psychologists, who alone amongst the climate-change players possess the necessary methodological tools to do so.

25   One recent example of this is provided by the work of Eek and Garling (2008). Social values (decision-maker influences) generally are thought to be associated with cooperative choices in resource dilemmas. One school of thought is that cooperation is actualized by a person's goals or aspirations (another decision-maker influence) that results in maximized outcomes for self and other (decision-maker outcomes). However, Eek and Garling convincingly make the case that a different goal, namely equal outcomes for all decision-makers, often is more influential than the joint maximization goal. Thus, choices presumably are a function of social values and goals, reflecting the model's implicit assertion that climate-change actions are multi-determined.

26   Another possibility is that over the course of time, different influences are regnant at different times (Gifford & Hine, 1997). This is reflected in the "sequential strategy" note in the model. Nevertheless, however helpful a comprehensive model might be for visualizing the big picture in the model, the challenge for psychologists is to find ways to encourage those influences that promote behaviours that result in less greenhouse gas emissions.

27   Decision-makers usually are investigated as individuals by environmental psychologists, but in the everyday world decisions are sometimes, perhaps usually, made by groups such as boards of directors or government committees. Groups may be largely unified in their goals and decisions, or not, which opens the door to group dynamics researchers, who often are psychologists. For example, Kazemi and Eek (2008) demonstrate the importance of considering the group as a decision-maker. Group goals (as well as individual goals) can affect the decisions made in the face of environmental problems. Clearly, given the ecological validity of the group as a decision-maker, this is an important direction for research to take. The model's decision-maker influences category obviously must include groups as well as individuals as the decision-makers. Its decision-maker strategies category includes several popular strategies used by decision-makers, and a link is necessary from that category to the interpersonal influences category, thereby postulating that strategies used by decision-makers will influence such within-group factors as trust, admiration, and perceived similarity to self.

The Challenges

28   Even a sustainability science that does include psychology must deal with several important human-nature challenges. The first is what has been called in other contexts mindlessness (Langer, Blank, & Chanowitz, 1978) or proximal cognition (Björkman, 1984), or what Dawes (1980) described in a more relevant context as limited-processing theory. Each of these constructs broadly asserts that humans often act without much reflection or rational planning. A few years earlier, I reported a little study in which university students were forced to navigate a path through some classroom desks that had been deliberately arranged to be difficult to navigate as they entered and left a classroom. Virtually all the students struggled through the desks, squeezing and turning, but when interviewed afterward, were almost completely unaware of their struggles. Their attention was largely allocated to thinking about the laboratory assignment they were conducting and probably other matters. I called this phenomenon "environmental numbness" (Gifford, 1976).

29   The notion of environmental numbness probably can be extended to the current climate-change crisis, in that most people, most of the time, simply are not thinking at all about climate change. Instead, they are (understandably) thinking about their work, their friends and family, or the big game. The crucial challenges are to get as many people around the world as possible actively thinking about climate change, and to stimulate informed, evidence-based policy that creates accepted structural solutions, so that greenhouse gas emissions can be reduced whilst the rest of the people march, numb to the environment, through their days.

30   A second challenging element of the social dilemma is trust, or the lack of it (e.g., Brann & Foddy, 1987; Foddy & Dawes, 2008). When decision-makers remove less of the resource than they could have, or donors make a sizable contribution, many of them are trusting in a norm of fairness and reciprocity that, unfortunately, is not always shared by other decision-makers. Defectors or free-riders sometimes then see an opportunity for personal gain, and by acting in self-interest they harm the climate-change cause. For example, laboratory studies show that stealing from others in the commons is frequent (Edney & Bell, 1984). Lack of trust leads easily to reactance and denial. Read any online newspapers story about climate change, and below it will be comments deriding the scientific consensus that climate change is happening.

31   Third, a sense of community or group identity is important (Dawes & Messick, 2000). Where it is lacking, and around the globe it is tragically lacking, cooperation in our planetary commons is imperilled. For example, in one lab study, when harvesters thought of themselves more as individuals than as group members, they were more likely to overharvest the resource (Tindall & O'Connor, 1987). Another lab study did suggest that not much is required to create enough group identity to improve cooperation. In it, the only difference between "high-identity" and "low-identity" participants was that the high-identity participants came to the lab and received their instructions as a group (as opposed to singly), yet the high-identity harvesters cooperated more (Samuelson & Hannula, 2001). Unfortunately, given human history and current events, one is forced to wonder about the ecological validity of this encouraging finding. In December, 2007, China was rejecting mandatory emissions cuts because it said that the wealthy nations created the problem (Casey, 2007); this shows that people can have a strong identity (e.g., with their nation), but lack sufficient identity with the environment to avoid destructive attitudes and behaviour.

32   A fourth challenge is that of human aspiration. Before we condemn the defectors and free-riders in our commons, we must confess that self-improvement is an essential part of human nature. This is the motive that Julian Simon (1981) celebrated as the solution to human problems. The "ultimate resource" that he believed in essentially was human ingenuity. When combined with the improvement motive, it has led to all the wonderful inventions that we enjoy today. However, in others, it also leads to venal self-aggrandizement (aided and abetted, of course, by the vast apparatus of persuasion that has been constructed in the modern consumption-oriented society). What to do? Use psychological science to reframe aspiration toward climate-amelioration ends. The other disciplines in sustainability science do not have the tools for this task, so it is up to us.

33   The fifth serious challenge problem is uncertainty, which can take several forms, such as in the absolute or relative amount of one's greenhouse gas emissions, the intentions of other decision-makers, the number of other decision-makers, the correct cost of a carbon credit, and so forth (e.g., Hine & Gifford, 1997). In fact, uncertainty can be a factor in every part of the model, from uncertainty about geophysical influences to uncertainty about quantitative and qualitative outcomes. For example, if someone drives 100 km in a particular car, it would not be difficult to measure the amount of greenhouse gases emitted. However, uncertainty about the effect of this emission on the atmosphere or whether the driver was wrong to drive at all is not easily decided. In sum, certainty may exist only under highly specific or highly aggregated conditions. For that reason, ecological validity in this area demands more studies of uncertainty in all the categories of the model.

34   A sixth challenge is that of perceived equity and justice, and the procedures designed to achieve these goals. Probably every researcher in the area, and certainly myself, has heard at least figurative and sometimes literal cries of revenge or anguish from participants who found the actions of others reprehensible. Therefore, justice-related issues cannot be ignored in social dilemma contexts. Four justice systems may be discerned: distributive, procedural, restorative, and retributive (Schroeder, Bembenek, Kinsey, Steel, & Woodell, 2008). Each system may be imposed from above (governance influences), or agreed-upon by decision-makers (interpersonal influences) but then are implemented as rules and regulations, thus creating a link between those two categories. Schroeder et al. (2008) believe that procedural justice systems will be more stable and cooperation-inducing than distributive justice systems, and explicitly argue that although such systems are best created through communication and agreements amongst those most affected (the decision-makers), they should become instituted as structural (i.e., rules and regulations) solutions to the eternal problem of transgressions in the commons. Clayton and Opotow (2003) discuss how justice is related to group and individual identity, and suggest that group identity promotes intergroup conflict, whereas its absence may allow individuals to experience their relation to nature as direct, which should lead to more pro-environmental behaviour.

35   The seventh challenge is the heavy weight of momentum. Although many people speak of changing their lives, the reality is that many people fail to achieve their goal of altering their behaviour patterns. Habit is not an exciting concept, but it is one important reason for the well-known gap between attitude and behaviour.

36   The eighth challenge is a widespread lack of a sense of efficacy, or perceived behavioural control. Many are hampered by the belief that they alone cannot change the global situation by anything that they do. Some acknowledge the truth that "every vote counts" without being able to muster the motivation (and often, the increased cost or

inconvenience) of changing their behaviour in ways that would help to slow the forces that drive climate change.

37   The ninth challenge, and a potentially fatal one, is that of population size; this was central to Hardin's (1968) perspective, and current social scientists (e.g., McGinnis & Ostrom, 2008) quite naturally ask whether the often optimistic results obtained by those who work at the small-group level on common-resource problems would apply at larger scales. Of course, this question has been haunting psychologists for many years (e.g., Edney, 1981), particularly when many studies show a decline in cooperation as the size of the harvesting group grows, even in fairly small groups (by societal standards) of 3 versus 7 (e.g., Sato, 1989). Nearly every study of group size has found that behaviour in resource management tends increasingly toward self interest as group size increases. Cooperation declines both as the number of decision-makers rises and as the number of groups within a commons with a constant total membership rises (Komorita & Lapworth, 1982). Good reasons for this are easy to list. As group size increases, the harm from any one participant's greed is spread thinner amongst the other participants: no single other decision-maker is badly hurt. Also, violations of sustainability or failures to donate are often less visible to others in larger groups. In addition, in large groups, the effect of the harm done to other decision-makers often is less visible to the violator (Edney, 1981); it is easier to inflict pain if one does not have to watch the victim experience pain. Finally, negative feedback or sanctions to violators or free-riders are increasingly difficult to manage in larger groups.

The Opportunities and Imperatives

38   If psychological science is to become recognized as an essential part of sustainability science and as an important player in the struggle to ameliorate the impacts of climate change, it must move toward a more serious engagement with the problem. If we do not, we run the danger of being viewed from the perspective of future citizens as the science that fiddled whilst the planet burned. One can either adopt the pessimistic view expressed by Garrett Hardin (1968) in his famous *Science* article, which most environmental psychologists have implicitly rejected by continuing to try to solve environmental problems, or one can adopt the view expressed in a more recent *Science* piece by Paul Ehrlich and Donald Kennedy (2005) that we "can organize fair and sustainable rules" (p. 563) to solve the problem.

39   Here is what we should do. First, obviously, we should conduct more research that bears directly on the many problems described above. Probably the central area of psychology for this task is environmental psychology, but we are a small group (about 650 worldwide who self-identify at least in part as environmental psychologists, according to a census I have undertaken this year, with only about two dozen in Canada). Other psychologists can help: how do people make climate-change-related decisions (cognitive and decision-science psychologists)? How can aspirations be reframed from owning more and more material goods to defining "improvement" as adopting climate-change amelioration behaviours (consumer psychologists)? How can helpful attitudes and lifestyles be more effectively taught (health psychologists)? How is acceptance of change related to the life cycle (life span psychologists)?

40   Second, we must engage policymakers (Clayton & Brook, 2005). A number of psychologists (e.g., Paul Stern) already are fully occupied in this crucial enterprise, and others have strongly advocated it (e.g., Vlek, 2000), but not enough of us are stepping off campus to do it. Green and green-leaning politicians now exist in much larger numbers in many countries, and these legislators both want and need quantified, substantiated information that they can use to enact more enlightened legislation. "Brown" politicians too should be our targets, perhaps more than green ones. Fritz Steele's (1980) notion of environmental competence includes knowing which political buttons to push, and psychologists have not done much button-pushing on climate change so far. The admirable fad in governments today is "evidence-based" policy (e.g., Davies, Nutley, & Smith, 2000). This new hunger for evidence-based policy is a huge opportunity for psychology, because of our methodological and research experience.

41   Because much in the way of needed change will occur (or not) at the level of individual citizens, environmental psychology is essential. Psychologists can serve as the key link between individuals—our traditional level of analysis—and policymakers. We can, and should, do the fundamental research on individuals and climate change, assess the acceptability of proposed policy and structural changes, and assess the impact of these changes on the behaviour, well-being, stress, and quality of life of individuals.

42   Third, we must seek out and interact with the other sustainability science players. We must tell the economists, technologists, and climate modellers what psychology can do. The climate scientists are merely the messengers, the technologists merely make machines, and the economists

still think largely in terms of pricing. Without the help of psychological science, these disciplines, although valuable in their own ways, will not be able to ameliorate the impacts of climate change.

*

I wish to acknowledge the contributions of Paul Stern, Joseph Reser, and Charles Vlek to my thinking on this issue. Naturally, however, I take responsibility for any views or fallacies expressed in this article that would not flatter them. I thank Donald Hine for his unintended challenge, and Brenda McMechan, Reuven Sussman, Leila Scannell, and Mary Gick for their comments and suggestions.

References

Bechtel, R. B., & Churchman, A. (2002). *Handbook of environmental psychology.* New York: Wiley.

Bechtel, R. B., Marans, R. W., & Michelson, W. (1987). (Eds.), *Methods in environmental and behavioral research.* New York: Van Nostrand Reinhold.

Björkman, M. (1984). Decision making, risk taking and psychological time: Review of empirical findings and psychological theory. *Scandinavian Journal of Psychology, 25,*31–49.

Brann, P., & Foddy, M. (1987). Trust and the consumption of a deteriorating common resource. *Journal of Conflict Resolution, 31,*615–630.

Buckhout, R. (1972). Pollution and the psychologist: A call to action. In J. F. Wohlwill & D. H. Carson (Eds.), *Environment and the social sciences* (pp. 75–81). Washington, DC: American Psychological Association.

Casey, M. (2007). China rejects mandatory emissions cuts. *The Globe and Mail,* December 8, p. A21.

Clark, W. C., & Dickson, N. M. (2003). Sustainability science. *Proceedings of the National Academy of Sciences, USA, 100,*8059–8061.

Clayton, S., & Brook, A. (2005). Can psychology help save the world? A model for conservation psychology. *Analyses of Social Issues and Public Policy, 5,*87–102.

Clayton, S., & Opotow, S. (2003). Justice and identity: Changing perspectives on what is fair. *Personality and Social Psychology Review, 7,*298–310.

Davies, H. T. O., Nutley, S. M., & Smith, P. C. (2000). *What works? Evidence-based policy and practice in public services.* Bristol, United Kingdom: Policy Press.

Dawes, R. M. (1980). Social dilemmas. *Annual Review of Psychology, 31,*169–193.

Dawes, R. M., & Messick, D. M. (2000). Social dilemmas. *International Journal of Psychology, 35,*111–116.

Dresner, M. (1989–1990). Changing energy end-use patterns as a means of reducing global-warming trends. *Journal of Environmental Education, 21,*41–46.

Edney, J. J. (1981). Paradoxes on the commons: Scarcity and the problem of equality. *Journal of Community Psychology, 9,*3–34.

Edney, J. J., & Bell, P. A. (1984). Sharing scarce resources: Group-outcome orientation, external disaster, and stealing in a simulated commons. *Small Group Behavior, 15,*87–108.

Eek, D., & Garling, T. (2008). A new look at the theory of social value orientations: Prosocials neither maximize joint outcomes nor minimize outcome differences but prefer equal outcomes. In A. Biel, D. Eek, T. Garling, & M. Gustaffson (Eds.). *New issues and paradigms in research on social dilemma*(pp. 10–26). New York: Springer.

Ehrlich, P. R., & Kennedy, D. (2005). Millennium assessment of human behavior. *Science, 309,*562–563.

Foddy, M., & Dawes, R. M. (2008). Group-based trust in social dilemmas. In A. Biel, D. Eek, T. Garling, & M. Gustaffson (Eds.), *New issues and paradigms in research on social dilemma*(pp. 57–71). New York: Springer.

Frank, J. D. (1966). Galloping technology, a new social disease. *Journal of Social Issues, 12,*1–14.

Gattig, A., & Hendrickx, L. (2007). Judgmental discounting and environmental risk perception: Dimensional similarities, domain differences, and implications for sustainability. *Journal of Social Issues, 63,*21–39.

Gifford, R. (1976). Environmental numbness in the classroom. *Journal of Experimental Education, 44,*4–7.

Gifford, R. (1987). *Environmental psychology: Principles and practice*(1st ed.). Newton, MA: Allyn & Bacon.

Gifford, R. (2002a). *Managing natural resources: A matter of life and death.* Keynote address to the International Congress of Applied Psychology, Singapore, July.

Gifford, R. (2002b). Making a difference: Some ways environmental psychology has improved the world. In R. Bechtel & A. Churchman (Eds.), *Handbook of environmental psychology* (2nd ed.). New York: Wiley.

Gifford, R. (2007). *Environmental psychology: Principles and practice*(4th ed.). Colville, WA: Optimal Books.

Gifford, R. (2008). Toward a comprehensive model of social dilemmas. In A. Biel, D. Eek, T. Gärling, & M. Gustaffson (Eds.), *New issues and paradigms in research on social dilemmas*(265–280). New York: Springer.

Gifford, R., & Hine, D. W. (1997). Toward cooperation in commons dilemmas. *Canadian Journal of Behavioural Sciences, 29,*167–179.

Hardin, G. (1968). The tragedy of the commons. *Science, 162,*1234–1248.

Heath, Y., & Gifford, R. (2006). Free-market ideology and environmental degradation: The case of beliefs in global climate change. *Environment & Behavior, 38,*48–71.

Hine, D. W., & Gifford, R. (1991). *The commons dilemma: A quantitative review.* Canadian Psychological Association annual meetings, Calgary, June.

Hine, D. W., & Gifford, R. (1997). Individual restraint and group efficiency in commons dilemmas: The effects of two types of environmental uncertainty. *Journal of Applied Social Psychology, 26,*993–1009.

Jager, W., & Mosler, H.-J. (2007). Simulating human behavior for understanding and managing environmental resource use. *Journal of Social Issues, 63,*97–116.

Kazeemi, A., & Eek, D. (2008). Promoting cooperation in social dilemmas via fairness norms and group goals. In A. Biel, D. Eek, T. Garling, & M. Gustaffson (Eds.), *New issues and paradigms in research on social dilemmas*(pp. 72–92). New York: Springer.

Kenworthy, J., & Laube, F. (2002). Urban transport patterns in a global sample of cities and their linkages to transport infrastructures, land use, economics and environment. *World Transport Policy and Practice, 8,*5–20.

Kidner, D. W. (1994). Why psychology is mute about the environmental crisis. *Environmental Ethics, 16,*359–376.

Komorita, S. S., & Lapworth, C. W. (1982). Cooperative choice among individuals versus groups in an N-person dilemma situation. *Journal of Personality and Social Psychology, 42,*487–496.

Langer, E., Blank, A., & Chanowitz, B. (1978). The mindlessness of ostensibly thoughtful action: The role of "placebic" information in interpersonal interaction. *Journal of Personality and Social Psychology, 36,*635–642.

Lundqvist, L. J., & Biel, A. (2007). From Kyoto to the town hall: Making international and national climate policy work at the local level. Sterling, VA: Stylus.

McGinnis, M., & Ostrom, E. (2008). Will lessons from small-scale scale up?. In A. Biel, D. Eek, T. Garling, & M. Gustaffson (Eds.), *New issues and paradigms in research on social dilemmas*(pp. 189–211). New York: Springer.

Midden, C., Kaiser, F., & McCalley, T. (2007). Technology's four roles in understanding individuals' conservation of natural resources. *Journal of Social Issues, 63,*155–174.

Miller, A. (1985). Cognitive styles and environmental problem-solving. *Journal of Environmental Studies, 26,*535–541.

Nilsson, A., von Borgstede, C., & Biel, A. (2004). Willingness to accept climate change strategies: The effect of values and norms. *Journal of Environmental Psychology, 24,*267–277.

Osborn, F. (1948). *Our plundered planet.* Boston: Little, Brown.

Oskamp, S. (2000). The psychology of promoting environmentalism: Psychological contributions to achieving an ecologically sustainable future for humanity. *Journal of Social Issues, 56,*378–390.

Pallak, M. S., & Cummings, W. (1976). Commitment and voluntary energy conservation. *Personality and Social Psychology Bulletin, 2,*27–30.

Reser, J. (2007). Psychology and the natural environment: *A position paper for the Australian Psychological Society.* Melbourne, Australia: Australian Psychological Society.

Reser, J. P., & Bentrupperbaumer, J. M. (2001). "Social science" in the environmental studies and natural science arena: Misconceptions, misrepresentations, and missed opportunities. In G. Lawrence, V. Higgins, & S. Lockie (Eds.), *Environment, society, and natural resource management: Theoretical perspectives from Australasia and the Americas.* Northampton, MA: Edward Elgar.

Samuelson, C. D., & Hannula, K. A. (2001). *Group identity and environmental uncertainty in a sequential resource dilemma.* Unpublished manuscript, Department of Psychology, Texas A&M University.

Sato, K. (1989). Trust and feedback in a social dilemma. *Japanese Journal of Experimental Social Psychology, 29,*123–128.

Schmuck, P., & Schultz, W. P. (Eds.) (2002). *Psychology of sustainable development,* London: Kluwer Academic.

Schmuck, P., & Vlek, C. (2003). Psychologists can do much to support sustainable development. *European Psychologist, 8,*66–76.

Schoot Uiterkamp, A. J. M., & Vlek, C. (2007). Practice and outcomes of multidisciplinary research for environmental sustainability. *Journal of Social Issues, 63,*175–197.

Schroeder, D. A., Bembenek, A. F., Kinsey, K. M., Steel, J. E., & Woodell, A. J. (2008). A recursive model for changing justice concerns in social dilemmas. In A. Biel, D. Eek, T. Gärling, & M. Gustaffson (Eds.), *New issues and paradigms in research on social dilemmas*(pp. 142–158). New York: Springer.

Seligman, C., & Darley, J. M. (1977). Feedback as a means of decreasing residential energy conservation. *Journal of Applied Social Psychology, 62,*363–368.

Simon, J. (1981). *The ultimate resource.* Princeton, NJ: Princeton University Press. Sommer, R. (1983). *Social design: Creating buildings with people in mind.* Englewood Cliffs, NJ: Prentice Hall. Steele, F. (1980). Defining and developing environmental competence. In C. P. Alderfer & C. L. Cooper (Eds.), *Advances in experiential social processes*(Vol. 2), 225–244.

Stern, P. C. (1986). Blind spots in policy analysis: What economics doesn't say about energy use. *Journal of Policy Analysis and Management, 5,* 220–227.

Stern, P. C. (1993). A second environmental science: Human-environment interactions. *Science, 260,*1897–1899.

Stern, P. C. (2000). Towards a coherent theory of environmentally significant behavior. *Journal of Social Issues, 56,*407–424.

Stern, P. C. (2005, September 21). *Psychological research and sustain-ability science.* Keynote address to the 6th Biennial Conference on Environmental Psychology, Bochum, Germany.

Studer, R., & Stea, D. (1966). Architectural programming and human behavior. *Journal of Social Issues, 12,*1–14.

Tindall, D. B., & O'Connor, B. (1987, June). *Attitudes, social identity, social values, and behavior in a commons dilemma.* Presentation at the Canadian Psychological Association Conference, Vancouver, BC.

Uzzell, D. (2007). How the science of psychology can make a contribution to sustainable development. Working paper, British Psychological Society.

Vlek, C. (1996). Collective risk generation and risk management: The unexploited potential of the social dilemmas paradigm. In W. B. G. Liebrand & D. M. Messick (Eds.), *Frontiers in social dilemmas research*(pp. 11–38). New York: Springer-Verlag.

Vlek, C. (2000). Essential psychology for environmental policy making. *International Journal of Psychology, 35,*153–167.

Vlek, C., & Steg, L. (2007). Human behavior and environmental sustain-ability: Problems, driving forces, and research topics. *Journal of Social Issues, 63,* 1–19.

Key and challenging words

amelioration, parametric, functionary, substantive, salutary, postulate (v.), antecedent, heuristics, regnant, reciprocity, deride, venal, aggrandizement, retributive

Questions

1. What is the function of the section "A Bit of Background"?

2. Why is it important to study the behaviour of individuals in a global phenomenon like climate change?

3. What is environmental psychology? How could it be a "player" in climate change policies? Why has it not been?

4. "We [psychologists] write in our discussion sections that 'someone' should take into account these important findings of ours. However, unfortunately, for the most part policymakers and natural scientists do not read our discussion sections" (paragraph 6): a) Why do you think Gifford included this criticism of psychologists? b) What are stereotypes that are applied to psychologists? To what extent do you believe these stereotypes are responsible for the lack of credibility Gifford addresses in this paragraph?

5. Summarize paragraphs 10–11, in which the author explains his disagreement with Stern.

6. In no more than two sentences provide a more complete caption for Figure 2, using the explanation in paragraph 23. Then, in about two additional sentences explain the nature of the relationship between any two parts of the diagram, using one of the examples that refer to Figure 2 in paragraphs 24–27.

7. Analyze one of the paragraphs in the section "The Challenges," showing how the writer creates a coherent, unified, and well-developed paragraph (do not analyze paragraphs 29, 35, or 36, as they are too short).

8. Which do you consider are the two most crucial challenges for psychologists among the nine discussed in this section? Write one paragraph each explaining why you believe it is so important in alleviating the effects of climate change.

9. In one or two paragraphs, analyze the rhetorical effectiveness of the concluding section, "The Opportunities and Imperatives," referring to specific passages.

Post-reading

1. *Collaborative or individual activity:* "The Tragedy of the Commons" (see paragraph 38) refers to an analogy used by Garrett Hardin of an open pasture in which herdsmen overuse a resource by applying a process of "rational" (though selfish) thinking. According to Hardin, each herdsman attempts to maximize his own profit by asking, "What is the utility *to me* of adding one more animal to my herd?" His reasoning is that if he adds one animal to the pasturage, he will be able to sell an additional animal at the market, whereas the group cost will be shared among all the herdsmen. Hardin concludes that "Each man is locked into a system that compels him to increase his herd without limit—in a world that is limited," which creates the tragedy. Hardin believed that humans are doomed by the tragedy of the commons, which makes it impossible to solve all such problems of the commons, like that of world overpopulation. Discuss the apparent strengths and flaws in this concept, using, if possible, realistic examples from your own experience or observation about shared resources (for example, car-pooling lanes). Before discussing or debating this issue, you could read Hardin's essay, accessing it through a library database or at www.sciencemag.org/cgi/content/full/162/3859/1243.

2. Do you believe the gap mentioned between academic studies and policymakers first mentioned in paragraphs 7 and 8 applies to social science research in general? Write a response to one of the following prompts: (a) Social science research done at universities is remote from the concerns of everyday life; *or* (b) Research in the social sciences done at universities could be made more relevant to everyday life and/or could affect policy decisions if. . . .

3. *Collaborative activity:* Do you believe that individuals are, in fact, the key to addressing climate change or that the key lies with politicians and other policy-makers, rather than with individuals? What can individuals do to help alleviate climate change?

Community Perspectives on the Impact of Climate Change on Health in Nunavut, Canada

G.K. Healey et al.

(4,359 words)

> *Pre-reading*
>
> 1. *Collaborative or individual activity:* What specific concerns or issues are you aware of concerning the effects of climate change on northern communities in Canada? Using a pre-writing technique (individual) or through discussion, come up with a list of at least five concerns or issues.

Abstract

The purpose of this study was to explore community perspectives on the most important ways that climate change is affecting the health of northern peoples. The study was conducted in Iqaluit, Nunavut, using a participatory action approach and the photovoice research method. Participants identified themes and patterns in the data and developed a visual model of the relationships between the themes identified. Five themes emerged from the data: the direct impacts

Source: From *Arctic*, vol. 64, no. 1, 2011, pp. 89–97. Reprinted by permission of the Arctic Institute of North America.

of climate change on the health of individuals and communities, the transition from past climates to future climates, necessary adaptation to the changing climate in the North, the call to action (individual, regional, and national), and reflection on the past and changing knowledge systems. A climate change and health model was developed to illustrate the relationships between the themes. Participants in this study conceptualized health and climate change broadly. Participants believed that by engaging in a process of ongoing reflection, and by continually incorporating new knowledge and experiences into traditional knowledge systems, communities may be better able to adapt and cope with the challenges to health posed by climate change.

Introduction

1   The evidence that the climate is changing and that these changes can be attributed to human activities has become stronger in recent years (Hegerl et al., 2007). A recent report published by the Lancet Commission on Climate Change found that climate endangers health in six key ways: through changing patterns of disease and mortality, extreme weather events, food insecurity, water scarcity, heat waves, and threats to built structures, including housing and public infrastructure (Costello et al., 2009). The Arctic Climate Impact Assessment (ACIA) suggests that future climate change will be experienced earlier and more acutely in polar regions (ACIA, 2004). Indigenous peoples of the North are being affected by climate change, and future changes in climate are likely to pose serious challenges (World Health Organization, 2003; ACIA, 2004). However, the health-related impact on communities in northern Canada is not yet fully understood. Northern communities hold a close relationship with the land. Seals, whales, walrus, caribou, and other species provide highly nutritious food (Kuhnlein and Soueida, 1992) and provide a deep connection to the natural environment (Watt-Cloutier, 2004). The environment and the country foods that come from the land, lakes, rivers, and sea remain central to the way of life, cultural identity, and health of northern people (Egan, 1998; Duhaime et al., 2004; Watt-Cloutier, 2004; Van Oostdam et al., 2005). Hunting lies at the core of Inuit culture, teaching such key values as courage, patience, tenacity, and boldness under pressure, qualities that are required for both worlds—the modern and the traditional—in which Inuit live (Watt-Cloutier, 2004). For Inuit communities, sea-ice travel is critical to accessing wildlife resources and

traveling between communities during winter months. Uncharacteristic weather patterns, storm events, and ice conditions are undermining the safety of travel and hunting or fishing activities (Furgal and Seguin, 2006). The increased risks to safety, as well as the longer traveling distances, are challenging the harvesting of country foods (Furgal and Seguin, 2006). The increasingly unpredictable weather patterns affect access to health services by threatening medical evacuation procedures that rural and remote areas rely upon for emergency and high-risk patient care. In addition to posing threats to livelihood and food security in the North, warming temperatures may be contributing to an increase in reports of never-before-seen species of biting flies and insects. Climate change is also proposed to pose the threat of increased vector-borne disease; however, this increase has not yet been clearly demonstrated (Kovats and Haines, 2005). Furthermore, permafrost melting attributable to a warmer climate will have serious implications for the structural integrity of northern houses and buildings (Furgal and Seguin, 2006). Northern community members have shared the concern that climate change, and the resulting changes in the environment and communities, may further compound existing health issues, including mental health and wellness, nutritional deficiencies, rates of respiratory illness, livelihood and economic stability, safety, and the spread of disease (Furgal and Seguin, 2006).

2   Research on the health impacts of climate change in northern Canada is a newer field. To date, the literature has largely focused on the collection of local indigenous knowledge and observations about weather patterns, land and sea-ice conditions, animal behaviour, and species sightings (Furgal et al., 2002; Furgal and Seguin, 2006; Laidler, 2006; Laidler et al., 2008; Weatherhead et al., 2010); risk and community vulnerability to climate change (Ford and Smit, 2004; Ford et al., 2006; Ford, 2009; Laidler et al., 2009); and adaptation and adaptive capacity (Berkes and Jolly, 2001; Natural Resources Canada, 2004). Current approaches include a focus on indigenous knowledge and local observations of environmental change, as well as scientific assessments of the impacts associated with these and other forms of change (Furgal and Seguin, 2006).

Community-Led Research

3   Research that strives to understand how climate change affects the health of northern communities must elicit meaningful community involvement in the research

process. Moreover, community participation and social mobilization are essential for identifying the factors that enhance or inhibit local adaptive capabilities in the face of climate change. The data presented here resulted from an initiative by Qaujigiartiit Health Research Centre, an independent community organization located in Iqaluit, Nunavut, in response to community requests for a forum in which to gain technical knowledge and hands-on experience of research. The Centre's mandate is to enable health research to be conducted locally, by Northerners and with communities, in a supportive, safe, culturally sensitive, and ethical environment, as well as to promote the inclusion of both Inuit *Qaujimajatuqangit* and Western science in addressing health concerns, creating healthy environments, and improving the health of Nunavummiut. The Centre is governed by a board of directors, whose members represent Nunavut-based research bodies, Inuit organizations, territorial and municipal governments, community members, and youth. This project was part of a research skills workshop held in Iqaluit on 12–14 May 2009, which included training in interviewing, survey administration, Inuit and community perspectives on ethics in research, and photovoice methodology. The photovoice research study presented in this paper took place over the course of that workshop.

4   This study explored community perspectives on the impact that climate change can and will have on the health of northern peoples. We combined a research project with an educational opportunity in order to build confidence and capacity so that Northerners may participate meaningfully in projects that come to their communities and eventually lead their own research projects on health, climate change, or both, in the future.

Methods

5   This exploratory, qualitative study used the photovoice research method. Six community participants from Nunavut communities (Gjoa Haven, Chesterfield Inlet, and Iqaluit), and two visiting graduate students took part in the training, data collection, and analysis of the study in Iqaluit, Nunavut. The participants were recruited through an open invitation sent by fax and e-mail to health centres, community organizations, and government and nongovernment agencies in Nunavut. The six participants volunteered to take part, and travel was provided to Iqaluit for the volunteers from other communities. The role of the

graduate students was to learn about the research method and process and to record the discussion. The Participatory Action Research (PAR) approach (Macaulay et al., 1999) affords individuals the opportunity to participate directly in a study by sharing their knowledge and providing their perspectives on the research question. Participatory research attempts to negotiate a balance between developing valid, generalizable knowledge and benefiting the community that is being researched and to improve research protocols by incorporating the knowledge and expertise of community members. Collaboration, education, and action are the three key elements of participatory research. An advantage of a PAR approach in the North is that it stresses the relationship between researcher, participants, and community; capacity building in the community through research involvement; and the direct benefit to the community of the potential research outcomes (Macaulay et al., 1999). A goal is that research participants and collaborators should "own" the research process and use its results to improve the quality of life in the community. Photovoice (originally termed "photo novella") is referred to as an educational tool, an advocacy tool, and a participatory action research method (Wang and Burris, 1994, 1997; Wang et al., 1998). Rooted in the tenets of participation, empowerment, accessibility, and self-documentation, photovoice is a technique for eliciting community perspectives and capturing everyday life experiences through photography (Moffitt and Vollman, 2004).

6   The photovoice technique was used to explore the impacts of climate change on health in Nunavut from the perspective of community members. The participants were the researchers and photographers: they own the data, and they were full participants in the analysis. Community participants were each provided with a camera and asked to photograph what they understood to be the most important effects of climate change on the health of the people in their communities. The photographs served to elicit individual perspectives and experiences in a group discussion about the effects of climate change on health. Participatory analysis emphasizes process, and participants are made central to this process (Moffitt and Vollman, 2004). Participants were asked to describe the rationale behind their photographs and to share the stories, perspectives, and experiences represented in these images. The printed photos were discussed one at a time, and the group members collaborated to select a "message" or "title" that they felt represented the photo. The photos were then grouped (and re-grouped) according to patterns the participants began to identify in

the images. Photographs that they considered similar were placed together, and the messages attached to each photo at the beginning of the process formed the basis for the themes identified. This process led them to develop a visual model of relationships between these themes. With the group's permission, a written record of the discussion was kept.

7   As the participants in the project are the researchers and this project was initiated in Nunavut by Nunavummiut, this project was not eligible for review by a governing or legislative body. Therefore, a detailed discussion about community and Inuit perspectives on ethics was part of the process, and a locally developed "ethics checklist" was used as a guiding framework (Qaujigiartiit Health Research Centre, 2010). Additionally, the project adhered to the ethical principles developed by the Association of Canadian Universities for Northern Studies (ACUNS) and the Canadian Institutes of Health Research (CIHR) Guidelines for the Ethical Conduct of Health Research with Aboriginal Peoples (ACUNS, 2003; CIHR, 2008). Most importantly, the participants agreed to adhere to the Inuit principle of *Inuuqatigiittiarniq*, working in an environment of respect and appreciation for one another. The participants collectively decided how to share the results of the study with their communities, the research community, and the public in general. They have used local newspaper and radio interviews, a research report, and an exhibit at the Nunatta Sunakkutaangit Museum in Iqaluit (all in both English and Inuktitut), as well as a poster presentation at an academic conference and the present paper.

Results

8   Five themes emerged from analysis and discussion of the photographic data: reflection on past and changing knowledge systems, direct impacts of climate change on health, transition from past climates to future climates, necessary adaptation to the changing climate in the North, and a call to action. The participants created a model of the themes identified during the analysis to illustrate visually the relationships they felt were crucial to understanding their perspective on climate change and health in their communities.

Reflection and Changing Knowledge Systems

9   Participants identified the theme of reflection and changing knowledge systems as central to the relationship between climate change and health. In the words of one participant, "We need to think about the past, reflect on our

experiences, and look forward to the future." Participants saw the capacity to reflect on the past and preserve Inuit *Qaujimajatuqangit*(Inuit knowledge) as essential to coping with the effects of climate change on health (Fig. 1). They also recognized the importance of new knowledge about the changing environment and its implications for the land and for community health: in their view, incorporating new information into traditional knowledge systems is essential to managing the health effects of climate change.

The Impacts of Climate Change on Health

10   Direct effects of climate change on health were a prominent theme in group discussions. Participants thought that climate affects health in six key ways: through contamination of food, contamination of water, changes in weather patterns, melting permafrost, isolation due to restricted mobility, and loss of their way of life and their livelihood. One participant reflected that access to country food will be altered profoundly by climate change. Participants felt that community members will have to travel farther, in more dangerous conditions, and using different modes of transportation, in order to ensure country food security and maintain a traditional diet. The participant who photographed the ski-doo (Fig. 2) said, "We'll being seeing more of this . . . more machines for sale. We won't be able to use them any more when it warms up," highlighting her concern not only that ways of hunting will change, but also that people may not be able to hunt at all in the future.

The Transition from Past Climates to Future Climates

11   Participants reported that the transition from cold to hot was a particularly salient theme for the North, where history, health, and well-being are so intimately associated with colder environments. Figure 3, an image of ice and sand, is meant to represent the participants' perspective on the melting environment and the change from cold to warmer climates. Notions of change and transformation were discussed, and with these ideas emerged expressions of vulnerability. One participant said, "I feel vulnerable to the changes that may come. The snow is melting, the ice is melting. It will be different." Participants described feelings both of personal vulnerability (highlighted by the need to travel in dangerous conditions, for example) and of collective vulnerability (highlighted by the sense of collective cultural demise). Participants associated the sense of loss they feel with climate change in the North. For many, the

Figure 1   A participant reading information about the historical context of the area displayed on a signpost outside of Iqaluit. This photo generated discussion about changes over time in the way knowledge is transmitted, as oral history was traditionally the primary means of sharing knowledge among Inuit, and now information comes in many forms, including written form.

Figure 2   This photo of a ski-doo with a "For Sale" sign was meant to convey the very real and immediate impact of climate change on community members if it results in a warming Arctic. Snowmobiles will become useless, and hunting practices and patterns may change. The group expressed grief at the idea that this photo may represent future events.

transition from colder to warmer environments means a loss of livelihood, a loss of tradition, and a loss of preferred activities, such as snowmobiling, hunting, and camping.

Necessary Adaptation

12   Building upon the conclusion that transition is nearly inevitable, the participants highlighted the importance of adaptation for health and well-being in light of climate change. Participants proposed a variety of strategies for coping with climate change and reversing its ill effects. For example, referring to the image of the stop sign (Fig. 4), the photographer said, "I took this picture because it shows we can recycle things. The old oil drum is being re-used to help hold up signs. There are many more ways we can recycle if we think about it." These ways included improving personal choices, promoting sustainability, discouraging waste, cleaning up our own communities, and advocating for hope

Figure 3   This photo shows the meeting place of land and sea ice along a ski-doo trail on the beach in Iqaluit. The participants felt it was a metaphor for the receding ice in the Arctic.

Courtesy Arctic Institute of North America

and survival in the face of adversity. The participants felt that collectively, Northerners can make changes to adapt to the changing climate and make lifestyle choices that may help reduce the effects of human-induced climate change.

The Call to Action

13   One participant, showing a picture of a sewage truck (Fig. 5), told the story of a recent event in her community. The local river eroded during the spring melt, washed out the bridge, and obstructed the route of the sewage-removal truck to the community. As a result, the community was forced to dump its sewage into the sea. The contamination of sea waters with sewage was a serious concern to community members. The participant told this story to illustrate her feelings of being "stuck between a rock and a hard place," since communities in the North often have few alternatives, and thus little capacity to live more sustainably. Participants further indicated that geographic and environmental conditions in the North necessitate resource- and energy-intensive practices (such as sea-lift shipment, air cargo and air travel) and hinder environmentally friendly practices (such as recycling). The paucity of environmentally favourable alternatives for communities in the North was deemed, by participants, to be a call to action. One participant spoke of the need for action to protect our children from any harm or hazard that comes from human-induced climate change. In the context of the photo of a tricycle stuck in the snow (Fig. 6), this participant said: "This bike is stuck in the snow. Our children will be stuck in the future, too. They are stuck with what we leave for them. If we do nothing, they will be stuck with our mess."

14   Participants highlighted that action on an individual level can be two-pronged, involving education and responsible living. First, they suggested that information and education are essential to ensuring that individuals are knowledgeable about the effects of climate change in the North and can participate in meaningful, informed decision making on these issues. Secondly, they thought that individuals ought to be responsible for reducing consumption and living sustainably.

15   At the community level, it was believed that planning and consultation were essential to ensure successful management of climate-change effects on health. Engaging communities in political action was deemed imperative, and mechanisms of redistribution, or community sharing, ought to be strengthened to ensure more equitable access to country foods for communities whose access has been limited.

Courtesy Arctic Institute of North America

Figure 4   This photo of a stop sign anchored into place with an old oil drum demonstrates the recycling of old products. Many of the street signs in the Arctic can't be placed into the ground because of the permafrost. Anchoring the signs with old oil drums filled with rocks has been an innovative way to meet needs and re-use old materials.

Courtesy Arctic Institute of North America

Figure 5   This photo shows a sewage truck removing waste from a home. Most homes in Nunavut are equipped with a water tank and a waste tank. Water is delivered to the home by truck and stored in the water tank. Used water and waste water are collected in the waste tank and removed by these trucks throughout the week. This photo prompted the telling of the story about river erosion in a community that blocked sewage trucks from accessing the treatment plant in 2008.

Figure 6   This photo of a child's tricycle stuck in the snow near a play area in Iqaluit was viewed by participants as representing how our children are "stuck" with what we leave them. They will inherit a planet, a land, and an environment that we are responsible for keeping in the best possible condition for them.

16   Participants associated a reduction in consumption with sustainable practices that would help mitigate the effects of climate change, and they stressed the need for investment in waste management services on a regional level, to ensure that recycling and compost programs have the capacity to operate throughout the territory. They felt it was also important to invest in territorial search-and-rescue programs, given the increasingly unpredictable weather patterns and sea-ice traveling conditions. Correspondingly, engaging policy makers was seen as essential to the promotion of environmentally friendly practices in Nunavut.

17   Finally, participants believed that the call to action on a national level involves a strengthening of knowledge sharing, consciousness-raising, and communication about the effects of climate change in the North. They believe that national policy makers can enforce corporate accountability and ban the dangerous chemicals that contaminate the environment and country foods in the North. Finally it was thought that investment should be made, at a national level, into alternative energy sources and innovative environmental practices.

The Climate Change and Health Model

18   The climate change and health model is a visual representation of the themes that emerged through the photovoice analysis process (Fig. 7). The model was created by the participants in the project. The placement of the themes around and within a circle, signifies interaction and overlap between ideas and messages. The theme of reflection and changing knowledge systems was identified as central to the relationship between climate change and health. The participants felt that knowledge, both past, present, and future, is one of the most important factors in mitigating the effects of climate change on health. From this central concept emerged four extensions: the themes of impacts, transition, adaptation, and action. Participants felt that the direct impacts of climate change both result from and contribute to the transition of the land, environment, and way of life of northern peoples. This transition has and will continue to promote action at the individual, community, regional, and national levels. Action may take the form of an individual lifestyle change (i.e., using more energy-efficient light bulbs) or advocacy on a national political level. The actions are part of our collective adaptation to the changing climate. The adaptive capacity of communities will be affected by the level and extent of the actions undertaken. These adaptations could then potentially change or mitigate the continuing and future impacts of climate change on health in this cyclic model.

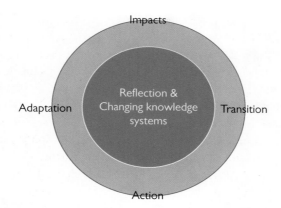

Figure 7   The Climate Change and Health Model developed by the study participants to visually represent how the themes identified in the data analysis process relate to each other. The model illustrates how the impacts of climate change can lead us to take action (or lead to inaction), which in turn changes the influence or impact. They interpreted these processes as cyclical, with the quality and accuracy of the knowledge available being one of the central influences in the entire process.   (Redrawn courtesy of the Arctic Institute of North America.)

Discussion

19   Northern communities have figured prominently in recent research on climate change. However, little is known about the health effects of climate change in the North. What is more, community perspectives regarding these effects are largely absent from the literature. Our findings document the experience of a small group of community participants in Nunavut. Participants in this study conceptualized health and climate change broadly and identified the theme of reflection and changing knowledge systems as central to the relationship between the two concepts. They believe that by engaging in a process of ongoing reflection, and by continually incorporating new knowledge and experiences into traditional knowledge systems, communities may be better able to adapt and to cope with health-related challenges posed by climate change. It was in light of these ideas that the four additional themes emerged, and that the action plan was formulated. The five thematic areas identified by the participants in this study confirm, for the most part, the current, limited body of evidence on climate change and health.

20   Participants discussed personal and collective vulnerability in the context of the present climate transition. The concept of vulnerability to climate change has been discussed somewhat in the literature. Ford and Smit (2004) conceptualize vulnerability as a function of exposure to climatic stresses and the adaptive capacity to cope with these stresses. They argue that in order to identify needs and improve adaptive capacity, the process must begin with an assessment of the vulnerability of the group of interest, in terms of who and what are vulnerable, to what stresses, and in what way, and what capacity exists to adapt to changing risks. The results of the present study add to this body of work by highlighting the need to explore individual vulnerability to climate change and the mental, emotional, and spiritual impact of climate change on the health of Northerners, as well as the collective vulnerability of all northern indigenous peoples, communities, and cultures.

21   Models of climate change and its impact on the health of northern peoples are fairly new in the literature. Existing models explore vulnerability to climate change, exposure-sensitivity of a community to climate change effects, adaptive capacity to deal with exposures, and risks (including but not limited to those associated with climate change). They include buffering factors such as the nature of the community in question and its economy, location, and population (Ford et al., 2006). The model developed by participants in this study highlights the importance of community perspective, knowledge, and the cyclic nature of the relationships between events and reactions to climate change. This model also reflects well-known Inuit perspectives of the integral connection between personal and community health and the environment.

22   The theme of reflection and changing knowledge systems is important in the context of the literature reporting indigenous knowledge and perspectives on climate change. The participants in this study placed importance on the roles of both traditional and new Inuit knowledge about the land, changing environment and climate, and adaptations to these changes. How knowledge is gained, transmitted, and shared within and between northern communities has changed over time with globalization and increasingly accessible telecommunications technology and media. Reflection upon these changes and critical analysis of the information available were viewed as important responsibilities for community members in exploring adaptation to climate change.

23   The perspectives shared in this study are not meant to represent all northern communities. Our purpose was to shed light on the impact of climate change and health through the eyes of Nunavut community members with an interest in climate change research. The particular photographs, stories, and messages that emerged through this research process reflect a unique community perspective, rendering these findings particularly relevant to the North and significant for compelling community action around the issue of climate change. The findings show that perceived effects of climate change on health are varied and multifaceted. Accordingly, responsive action to these effects must transpire at multiple socio-ecological levels, ranging from individual choices to community, municipal, provincial or territorial, and federal strategies. The multilateral approach assumed in the participants' call to action reflects the multidimensional nature of the issue, as well as the varied opportunities for adaptation in the North.

Conclusion

24   Livelihood changes are predicted to continue and further alter Inuit communities and well-being (ACIA, 2004; Ford, 2009; Laidler et al., 2009). There will always be uncertainty about the magnitude of the adverse effects of climate change, and the burden of those effects will most probably fall predominantly on populations that have contributed little to the problem (Kovats and Haines, 2005). While the health impacts of climate change are not yet fully understood, this study contributes to the literature on perceived health effects of climate change in Inuit communities by identifying some community priorities surrounding this issue.

25   The culture, economy, and way of life of Inuit are under threat from human-induced climate change (Watt-Cloutier, 2004). The destruction of the age-old hunting economy presages destruction of the very culture of Inuit. The seriousness of the issue means that Inuit have to use every available avenue to bring their perspectives to the attention of decision makers who have the power to affect change (Watt-Cloutier, 2004; Kovats and Haines, 2005). This study further highlights the importance of participatory research and the merits of the photovoice technique in eliciting community perspectives and promoting social action from the individual to national level. Building social capacity, thereby empowering communities to gain a sense of control, is essential to managing the health effects of climate change (Costello et al., 2009). Our findings support this notion and suggest that an investment in community is an essential strategy for mitigating the ill effects of climate change on health.

26   This study provides the foundation for continuing community-led research projects exploring the land-health environment relationship. Further community-led research using creative and participatory methods is needed to improve our understanding of the health implications of climate change in the North and to reduce health disparities between northern communities and the rest of Canada. This project provided community members with the opportunity to learn and apply new research skills and contribute to a growing body of knowledge about the effects on climate change on the health of Northerners. Given the health threats posed by climate change, further work should be done to bolster community involvement in these issues and to actualize change at multiple socio-ecological levels. It is by strengthening capacity that northern communities will be able to cope with, and potentially reverse, the effects of climate change on health in the North.

Acknowledgements

The community participants/researchers in this project shared incredible stories and experiences that cannot be articulated in the limited scope of this paper. For the opportunity to share and learn from each other, we are grateful. The funding for this research came from the Health Canada First Nations and Inuit Health Branch program entitled Climate Change and Health Adaptation in the North.

References

ACIA (Arctic Climate Impact Assessment). 2004. Impacts of a warming Arctic. Cambridge: Cambridge University Press.

Association of Canadian Universities for Northern Studies. 2003. Ethical principles for conduct of research in the North. http://acuns.ca/website/ethical-principles/.

Berkes, F., and Jolly, D. 2001. Adapting to climate change: Social-ecological resilience in a Canadian western Arctic community. Conservation Ecology 5(2): 18. [online] URL: www.consecol.org/vol5/iss2/art18/.

CIHR (Canadian Institutes of Health Research). 2008. CIHR guidelines for health research involving Aboriginal people. www.cihr-irsc.gc.ca/e/29134.html.

Costello, A., Abbas, M., Allen, A., Ball, S., Bell, S., Bellamy, R., Friel, S., et al. 2009. Managing the health effects of climate change. The Lancet 373:1693–1733.

Duhaime, G., Chabot, M., Fréchette, P., Robichaud, V., and Proulx, S. 2004. The impact of dietary changes among the Inuit of Nunavik (Canada): A socioeconomic assessment of possible public health recommendations dealing with food contamination. Risk Analysis 24:1007–1018, doi:10.1111/j.0272–4332.2004.00503.x.

Egan, C. 1998. Points of view: Inuit women's perceptions of pollution. International Journal of Circumpolar Health 57 (Suppl. 1):550–554.

Ford, J.D. 2009. Vulnerability of Inuit food systems to food insecurity as a consequence of climate change: A case study from Igloolik, Nunavut. Regional Environmental Change 9:83–100, doi:10.1007/s10113–008–0060-x.

Ford, J.D., and Smit, B. 2004. A framework for assessing the vulnerability of communities in the Canadian Arctic to risks associated with climate change. Arctic 57:389–400.

Ford, J.D., Smit, B., and Wandel, J. 2006. Vulnerability to climate change in the Arctic: A case study from Arctic Bay, Canada. Global Environmental Change 16:145–160, doi:10.1016/j.gloenvcha.2005.11.007.

Furgal, C., and Seguin, J. 2006. Climate change, health and vulnerability in Canadian northern Aboriginal communities. Environmental Health Perspectives 114:1964–1970.

Furgal, C., Martin, D., and Gosselin, P. 2002. Climate change and health in Nunavik and Labrador: Lessons from Inuit knowledge. In: Krupnik, I., and Jolly, D., eds. The earth is faster now: Indigenous observations of Arctic environmental change. Washington, D.C.: Arctic Research Consortium of the United States and Arctic Studies Centre, Smithsonian Institution. 266–300.

Hegerl, G.C., Zwiers, F.W., Braconnot, P., Gillett, N.P., Luo, Y., Marengo Orsini, J.A., Nicholls, N., Penner, J.E., and Stott, P.A. 2007. Understanding and attributing climate change. Chapter 9. In: Solomon, S., Qin, D., Manning, M., Chen, Z., Marquis, M., Avery, K.B., Tignor, M., and Miller, H.L., eds. Climate change 2007: The physical science basis. Contribution of Working Group I to the Fourth Assessment Report of the Intergovernmental Panel on Climate Change. Cambridge: Cambridge University Press.

Kovats, R.S., and Haines, A. 2005. Global climate change and health: Recent findings and future steps. Canadian Medical Association Journal 172:501–502, doi:10.1503/cmaj.050020.

Kuhnlein, H.V., and Soueida, R. 1992. Use and nutrient composition of traditional Baffin Inuit foods. Journal of Food Composition and Analysis 5:112–126, doi:10.1016/0889–1575(92)90026-G.

Laidler, G.J. 2006. Inuit and scientific perspectives on the relationship between sea ice and climate change: The ideal complement? Climatic Change 78:407–444.

Laidler, G.J., Dialla, A., and Joamie, E. 2008. Human geographies of sea ice: Freeze/thaw processes around Pangnirtung, Nunavut, Canada. Polar Record 44:335–361, doi:10.1017/S003224740800750X.

Laidler, G.J., Ford, J.D., Gough, W.A., Ikummaq, T., Gagnon, A.S., Kowal, S., Qrunnut, K., and Irngaut, C. 2009. Travelling and hunting in a changing Arctic: Assessing Inuit vulnerability to sea ice change in Igloolik, Nunavut. Climatic Change 94: 363–397, doi:10.1007/s10584–008–9512-z.

Macaulay, A.C., Commanda, L.E., Freeman, W.L., Gibson, N., McCabe, M.L., Robbins, C.M., and Twohig, P.L. 1999. Participatory research maximizes community and lay involvement. British Medical Journal 319:774–778.

Moffitt, P., and Vollman, A.R. 2004. Photovoice: Picturing the health of Aboriginal women in a remote northern community. Canadian Journal of Nursing Research 36:189–201.

Natural Resources Canada. 2004. Climate change impacts and adaptation: A Canadian perspective. Edited by D.S. Lemmen and F.J. Warren. Ottawa: Climate Change Impacts and Adaptation Division, Natural Resources Canada. http://adaptation.nrcan.gc.ca/perspective/profile_e.php.

Qaujigiartiit Health Research Centre. 2010. Reviewer health research ethics checklist (draft). Iqaluit, Nunavut: Qaujigiartiit Health Research Centre. www.nunavut.arctichealth.ca/apps/Docs/displayDocs.aspx.

Van Oostdam, J., Donaldson, S.G., Feeley, M., Arnold, D., Ayotte, P., Bondy, G., Chan, L., et al. 2005. Human health implications of environmental contaminants in Arctic Canada: A review. Science of the Total Environment 352:165–246.

Wang, C., and Burris, M.A. 1994. Empowerment through photo novella: Portraits of participation. Health Education Quarterly 21:171–186.

——. 1997. Photovoice: Concept, methodology, and use for participatory needs assessment. Health Education and Behavior 24:369–387.

Wang, C.C., Yi, W.K., Tao, Z.W., and Carovano, K. 1998. Photovoice as a participatory health promotion strategy. Health Promotion International 13:75–86.

Watt-Cloutier, S. 2004. Climate change and human rights. Human Rights Dialogue: "Environmental Rights." Series 2(11). New York: Carnegie Council.

Weatherhead, E., Gearheard, S., and Barry, R.G. 2010. Changes in weather persistence: Insight from Inuit knowledge. Global Environmental Change 20:523–528, doi:10.1016/j.gloenvcha.2010.02.002.

World Health Organization. 2003. Climate change and human health—Risks and responses: Summary. Edited by A.J., McMichael, D.H. Campbell-Lendrum, C.F. Corvalán, K.L. Ebi, A.K. Githeko, J.D. Scheraga, and A. Woodward. Geneva, Switzerland: World Health Organization. www.who.int/globalchange/publications/cchhsummary/en/.

Key and challenging words

tenacity, mandate, protocol, adhere, salient, paucity, equitable, mitigate, advocacy, presage, disparity

Questions

1. Explain why the introduction is divided into two sub-sections and analyze the functions of each.
2. (a) Which study of those mentioned in the Introduction appears closest to the authors' study? Explain. (b) Identify, then paraphrase, Healey et al.'s thesis.
3. In your own words, (a) define participatory research; (b) explain its importance as a research method; (c) explain its value to the community.
4. For the "Results" section, (a) discuss the importance of organization, identifying strategies that aid the reader's understanding; (b) focusing on any two of the first four sub-sections within "Results," identify specific strategies that aid the reader's comprehension of those sections.
5. Compare and contrast the "Results" section in this essay with the corresponding section in Hasan's essay "The More You Play, the More Aggressive You Become" on p. 329 of this Reader. For the general characteristics of Type B essays and the differences between those with quantitative and qualitative methodologies, see Chapter 3, p. 23, and Appendix B.
6. Explain the way in which the health model emerged from the photovoice analysis process and its importance to the study as a whole.
7. Referring to at least one paragraph in the "Discussion" section, show how the Healey et al. study contributes to the literature on climate change and health in northern communities.
8. Do you think the authors are essentially positive or negative about the ability of northern communities to meet the challenges posed by climate change? In your answer, refer to specific passages in the text.

Post-reading

1. *Collaborative activity*: After re-reading paragraphs 5–6 of the study, break into groups of six members each. Plan a qualitative study in which you address a problem at your university using the participatory research method and the photovoice technique. After identifying the problem and key research question(s), discuss what an "Introduction" and a "Methods" section would include. Group members should take photographs that

reflect their concerns with the problem. Meet during a later class to choose representative photographs and discuss their significance in terms of the problem/research questions. Finally, identify "themes" emerging from the discussion (see paragraphs 6 and 8).

2. Write a brief (500- to 750-word) evaluative report (stressing assessment) or informational report (stressing content) on a website dedicated to the study of climate change in the Canadian Arctic. One such site mentioned in the article is ArcticNet; this site also contains links to similar sites that you could consider. Organize your report by appropriate formal or descriptive categories. Formal categories could include introduction, methods (basis of your evaluation), results, and conclusion. You could consider the website's purpose, credibility, main menu, links, navigation aids, accessibility, organization, visual appeal, quality and depth of information, use of charts to enhance understanding, and so on.

A Note on Statistics

The Active Voice

What Do Students Need to Know about Statistics?

1 There are two main types of research: qualitative and quantitative. Both types help us to describe or explain a phenomenon (e.g., the experience of war veterans); however, each method goes about describing the situation in very different ways. Qualitative research uses non-numerical data, such as words or pictures, in order to describe a phenomenon. In-depth interviews and/or extensive observations are typically used in order to collect this type of data. An interview with a war veteran about his experience during the war is an example of a qualitative research approach. Quantitative research, on the other hand, uses numbers in order to describe or explain a phenomenon and typically investigates the relationship between variables (e.g., the relationship between war veterans and depression). Quantitative research typically includes questionnaires with large samples of participants and uses a strict methodology in order to control all factors that are related to the data and therefore may affect the interpretation of that data. A questionnaire mailed out to a random sample of 500 male war veterans across Canada between the ages of 65 and 85 who have no family history of depression is an example of a quantitative research approach.

2 The decision to use qualitative versus quantitative methods depends on the research question that you ask and the type of information you want to obtain. Qualitative research provides rich and detailed words to describe a phenomenon, but the data is situation- and context-specific. By contrast, quantitative research provides numerical data to describe the relationship between variables, and these relationships may be generalized to the population as a whole. In this essay, we will describe why and how quantitative research methods may be used to answer a research question.

3 In the social sciences, we conduct research because we are interested in better understanding human behaviour (e.g., frequency of drinking, reaction time, level of intelligence). Most of the time, however, we do not limit ourselves to describing just that behaviour, but we also want to know whether (and how) it is related to some other feature of the person or the situation. For example, suppose you are interested in studying the level of intelligence (IQ) of undergraduate students in linguistics. You might be wondering whether female and male students will have, on average, the same IQ or whether it varies depending on gender. That is, do female students have higher or lower IQ than males? In this case, IQ is what we call the dependent variable, and the feature in your study that you think has an influence on it—gender—is the independent variable.

Mean and Variance

4 Now suppose you recruit 10 male and 10 female students from one of your classes to answer this question. After administering an intelligence test to your 20 participants (N=20), you realize that each has a different IQ level. For some participants, their IQ value is 100, for others 130, and for still others 110. Because you want to compare the IQ of two groups (females versus males), you need a unique value, representative of each group, that would allow you to make this comparison. The best way to create that value is by averaging the individual IQ values within each group, creating the mean IQ for each group.

Continued

5   Because the mean is only an average of individual IQ values, it will not tell us much about each value from which it was calculated. For example, suppose the mean IQ of both the male and female groups is the same (e.g., 115). The single values used to compute those means could nonetheless be very different. Some males, for example, may have values of 90 and others 130, averaging out to 115, whereas the IQ values of females may be in general closer to the mean (e.g., some 115 and others 120) but also averaging out to 115. In other words, the group of males may have more variation in their IQ values than the group of females.

6   As you can probably infer by now, the mean becomes less trustworthy as an estimate of the group's IQ when the variation is greater. Therefore, it is useful to have information about how much the single values used to calculate the mean differ from this mean (i.e., a general measure of how spread these values are from the mean). You can obtain this information by calculating the variance.

7   Once you have the information about the mean IQ and the variance for each of your groups, you can use a statistical test of inference to determine whether the means of the two groups are actually different from each other. Recall that you were interested in determining whether, on average, females in your class have higher or lower IQ than males. If the mean IQ for males and females is exactly the same, you would intuitively conclude that females and males are equally smart (as measured by IQ). If they differ by one or two points, your conclusion would probably be the same, because you would consider those one or two points to be random and unimportant. However, what would you conclude if the two means differed by 10 points? How would you determine whether the two means are meaningfully different and that their difference is not just due to chance?

8   Researchers consider two means to be significantly different when there is a very small probability (less than .05 or less than 5 in 100 times) that these two means are different only by chance. In order to determine this probability there are a number of statistical tests you can use (see below, Correlation and Prediction). Returning to our example, if the mean IQ for female students was 130 and the mean IQ for male students was 120, and if the test you used indicated that there was a less than 5 in 100 probability that these two values differed by chance, then you could (sadly or happily) say that the girls in your class have a significantly higher IQ value than the boys. The standard of 5 in 100 for "statistical significance" is an arbitrary but useful convention in research. It does not refer to the social or practical significance of the result, because that is not a statistical issue.

9   If you had obtained the 20 participants from your class (i.e., your sample) using a random procedure, you could generalize the results of your study to your entire class (in this case, your population). However, notice that very rarely do researchers randomly select subjects to participate in their studies and, instead, the selection depends on other factors (e.g., those people who agree to participate in the study).

Correlation and Prediction

10   Say we want to know the relationship between high school GPA and university GPA. Our research question could be, What is the relationship between GPA in high school and GPA in university? A simple bivariate correlation can be used to answer this question. Correlations describe the extent to which two variables co-vary (e.g., as high school GPA goes up, so does university GPA).

11   However, say we determine that mothers' university GPA, fathers' university GPA, age, gender, and parents' income are also related (correlated) to GPA, and we want to know which factors influence university GPA the most. We can use multiple regression to answer this question. In multiple regression, all of the variables are entered into a regression (mathematical) equation, which then determines which factors most strongly influence university GPA when controlling for all other factors that were entered into the equation. Let's say fathers' university GPA and mothers' university GPA are revealed as the strongest factors influencing a university GPA. We can then use this information to screen and/or predict who will do the best in university based on their scores on the predictor variables. For example, if a student's mother and father had a high university GPA, we would predict that the student would have a high university GPA.

12   Another common statistical procedure is called an ANOVA (analysis of variance), which allows us to compare groups. Say we want to compare basketball players, volleyball players, and soccer players on their GPA. A t-test can be used to compare two groups (e.g., basketball players and volleyball players); however, an ANOVA

will allow us to compare more than two groups (e.g., basketball, volleyball, and soccer players).

13 For many people, statistics seem intimidating and overwhelming. However, the importance of statistics cannot be understated. At the most basic level of statistics, there are means, medians, modes, and percentages that tell us basic descriptive information (e.g., can describe the current situation). At the more complex level of statistical analysis used by most researchers, statistics allow us to answer some very interesting questions and to make important predictions about human behaviour.

—**Rachel Dean, Ph.D.,** and **Agustin Del Vento, M.Sc.**

Characteristics of Type A, Type B, and Type C Essays

Feature	Type A	Type B	Type C
Methodology	qualitative (ideas, values, qualities); may have theoretical base	usually quantitative; centred on data that are generated, observed, and recorded	qualitative: organizes studies by categories, such as approaches to subject; summarizes and analyzes them
Author	often single author	often two or more authors	varies
Abstract	sometimes	yes	sometimes
Purpose	variable: may inform, generate new knowledge, or seek to interpret knowledge in a new way	generates new knowledge	evaluates what has been written; finds gaps in the research and suggests future directions
Audience	other scholars and advanced students in the humanities	other scholars/researchers and advanced students in the social sciences and sciences	other scholars/researchers and advanced students in all disciplines, especially the social sciences; other educated and interested readers
Length	variable; tend to be longer than Type B and C; paragraphs may be lengthy due to discursive nature	variable; qualitative studies are often longer than quantitative ones	variable
Structure	may use content headings	formal, standardized headings and sections	may use content headings
Introduction	includes thesis, key question(s), or essay plan; justifies need for study and often includes literature review; claim is interpretive[1]	includes hypothesis to be tested or question to be answered; justifies need for study and includes literature review; claim is fact-based[1]	essay plan, key question(s), or thesis; justifies need for review but no special review section as the entire article reviews the literature; claim is fact-based
Primary sources	interprets/analyzes them; often uses direct quotation	generates raw (numerical) data in order to test hypothesis, arrive at conclusions; primary sources often appear in tables/charts	focuses on results/findings of secondary sources
Secondary sources	interprets/analyzes them; uses both direct quotation and summary	refers to them in literature review; uses summary	refers to/analyzes secondary sources (studies) throughout; uses summary more than direct quotation

Feature	Type A	Type B	Type C
Source treatment	uses analysis and synthesis throughout essay	uses analysis in "Results" and/or "Discussion" section; uses synthesis in literature review and in "Discussion" or "Conclusion"	uses synthesis throughout; analyzes and critically evaluates studies, often using compare and contrasting pattern; definition and division are also common
Voice	variable: may be relatively detached (humanities) or involved (some social science research involving group observation; active voice preferred	objective, detached; may use passive voice occasionally	objective
Style	variable: may be discursive and complex; longer sentences and paragraphs; sentence variety; moderate/difficult language level	straightforward, direct; simple sentence structure	variable: straightforward, direct; simple sentence structure; may at times be discursive in analyzing/evaluating studies
Terminology	specialized diction but may borrow terms from other disciplines and define their specific usage in essay; may use terms applicable to a particular theory	specialized diction; assumes reader familiarity with terms as well as experimental and statistical processes	specialized diction; may explain key terms
Ancillary material	may be included in some disciplines, such as history or Greek and Roman studies; illustrations may be used in book chapters	charts, graphs, tables, figures, photos, appendices are common	sometimes includes figures or other illustrations to summarize content
Conclusion	may summarize or focus on implications of the study's findings	indicates whether hypothesis is proved/disproved or how question has been answered; often suggests practical applications/further research directions	may summarize and/or suggest future research directions or specific ways to apply the studies reviewed; may make recommendations

1 In an interpretive claim, the author weighs and interprets the evidence of the primary or secondary sources, using close analysis and sound reasoning. In a fact-based claim in a Type B study, the author presents his or her hypothesis and proceeds to test it under controlled conditions. An interpretive claim could use factual material as evidence; similarly, the evidence in a fact-based claim could be interpreted various ways.

Glossary

abstract A condensed summary used in an empirical study; it is placed before the essay begins and includes at a minimum purpose, methods, and results.

academic (scholarly) journal A type of periodical containing scholarly content (articles, reviews, and commentaries) by experts for a knowledgeable audience in related fields of study.

academic writer A specialist in his or her subject area who is familiar with what has been written and is able to assess the strengths as well as the limitations of others' work.

active construction (active voice) A way of constructing a sentence to show that the subject performs the action of the verb.

analogy A systematic comparison between the topic item and another one that is like it in the relevant point but is otherwise unlike the first one; it can be used to make the first item more easily understood.

analysis In analysis, you break up a whole in order to (1) closely examine each part individually and/or (2) investigate the relationships among the parts.

annotated bibliography An expanded bibliography that includes not only the information of standard bibliographies but also highly condensed summaries of related works.

annotation (verb annotate) A note that explains, expands on, or comments on a written text.

appeal to ethos The strategic use of ethics or morality in order to help convince a reader. Intrinsic ethos demonstrates the writer's credibility, for example, through knowledge or fairness; extrinsic ethos is shown by the writer's character or abilities as perceived by others.

appeal to logos The strategic use of reason and logic in order to help convince a reader.

appeal to pathos The strategic use of emotion in order to help convince a reader.

audience Whom you are writing to; includes one or more readers with common interests, knowledge level, and/or expectations.

brainstorming A pre-writing technique in which you list your associations with a subject in the order they occur to you.

case study A carefully selected example that is analyzed in detail in order to support a writer's claim.

circular conclusion Reinforces the thesis.

claim An assertion about the topic appearing in the thesis statement and in topic sentences.

clustering A pre-writing technique that works spatially to generate associations with a subject and connections among them.

coherence A principle of paragraph construction in which ideas are logically laid out with clear connections between them.

common ground An argumentative strategy in which you show readers that you share many of their values, making you appear open and approachable.

concession An argumentative strategy in which you concede or qualify a point, acknowledging its validity, in order to come across as fair and reasonable.

conclusion The last paragraph or section of an essay whose main function is to summarize the thesis and/or main points in the body of the essay.

connotation (verb connote) The implications or additional meanings of a word; a word's context may suggest its connotations.

conventions Recurrent patterns that direct and organize the behaviour of specific groups of people and that, applied appropriately, help us communicate with our audience.

credibility Along with evidence, helps support a claim. Credibility can be demonstrated by an author's knowledge, reliability, and fairness.

deductive reasoning Reasoning based on a generalization, which is applied to a specific instance to draw a conclusion.

denotation (verb denote) The meaning of a word, for example, as defined in a dictionary.

descriptive (content) headings Headings usually consist of a phrase summarizing the content of the section that follows.

digital object identifier (doi) A number-letter sequence that begins with the number 10 often found on journal articles; it serves as a persistent link for digital material.

discursive Expansive, or covering a wide area.

documentation style Guidelines for documenting sources put forth in style manuals and handbooks for researchers and other academic writers.

dramatic opening A technique for creating reader interest by beginning with a question, illustration, anecdote, quotation, description, or other attention-grabbing technique.

ellipsis Three or four spaced dots in a direct quotation, indicating that one or more words have been omitted.

empirically based study Data or information based on an experiment or on observation; it can be verified.

essay plan A form of a thesis in which main points are outlined in the order they will occur in the essay.

extrinsic ethos What an audience knows about the speaker or writer outside of the argument itself.

focused reading A reading strategy in which close attention is paid to sentences and words in order to extract detail, tone, style, relevance, etc.

freewriting A pre-writing technique in which you write on a subject without stopping to edit.

graph Represents relationships between two variables.

hypothesis A prediction about an outcome; used in essays in which an experiment is set up to prove/disprove the prediction.

inductive reasoning Reasoning that relies on facts, details, and observations to draw a conclusion.

inference A conclusion based on what the evidence shows or points to. More than one inference might be possible in a given situation, but the most probable one is said to be the best inference.

intrinsic ethos The impression of the speaker or writer shaped within the argument.

irony   The existence in a text of two levels of meaning, one surface and literal, the other deeper and non-literal.

jargon   Discipline-specific language used to communicate among members of the discipline.

justification   Announces reason for undertaking the study; may focus on what it will add to previous research or what gap in the research it will fill.

literature review   A condensed survey of articles on the topic arranged in a logical order, usually ending with the article most relevant to the author's study.

logical fallacies   Categories of faulty reasoning.

logical opening   A technique for creating reader interest by beginning with a generalization and narrowing to the thesis.

mixed format   A method of source integration in which you combine significant words of the source, placed in quotation marks, with your own words.

monograph   A highly specialized scholarly work or treatise in book form.

open-access journal   A kind of journal (usually scholarly) that is available online without a fee.

order of points   The way in which points are presented in an essay. Climax order is the order of points that proceeds from the weakest to the strongest; other orders include inverted climax order and mixed order.

original research   Research in which the author(s) conducts an experiment to generate raw data or uses available data to prove/disprove a hypothesis or answer a research question.

outline   A linear or graphic representation of main and sub-points, showing an essay's structure.

paragraph wrap   Sums up the main idea in the paragraph, re-calling the topic sentence. It usually appears in the last sentence of a paragraph.

paraphrase   A method of source integration in which you put someone else's ideas in your own words, keeping the length of the original.

passive construction (passive voice)   A way of constructing a sentence to show that the subject is being acted upon.

peer-reviewed journal   A type of journal in which submissions are reviewed by experts before publication; it is an authoritative source for scholarly research.

periodical   A kind of publication that is issued periodically, at regular or semi-regular intervals; academic journals and magazines are examples of periodicals.

policy claim   An assertion about a topic that advocates an action (e.g., to fix a problem or improve a situation).

precedent   A kind of example that refers to the way a situation was dealt with in the past in order to argue for its similar use in the present.

primary sources   Original material in a field of study; examples include literary texts, historical documents, and interviews.

process-reflective draft   A draft that emerges from a flexible engagement with what you are writing, one that reflects the connections between thinking and writing.

prompt   A word, phrase, or clause that directs readers to important content rather than containing important content itself.

purpose   Why you are writing; variables affecting purpose include your topic and your audience.

questioning   A pre-writing technique in which you ask relevant questions about the topic.

reader-based prose   Clear, accessible writing designed for an intended reader.

refutation   An argumentative strategy of raising opposing points in order to counter them with your own points.

rhetoric   The study and use of linguistic and stylistic resources in order to communicate effectively to convince an audience.

rhetorical or critical analysis   A writing activity concerned with breaking down a text to examine its structure, reasoning, rhetorical strategies, significance, and other features.

rhetorical pattern   A method for organizing and presenting information in essays and paragraphs; examples include cause–effect, classification, comparison and contrast, cost–benefit, and definition.

scanning   A form of selective reading in which you skim sections or an entire text. In a general scan, you try to determine the gist of a text—for example, by locating main ideas; in a targeted scan, you look for specific concepts or topics by keywords or phrases.

secondary sources   Commentary on or interpretation of primary material; examples include academic studies, reports, and presentations.

selective reading   A reading strategy designed to meet a specific objective, such as scanning for main points or reading for detail.

signal phrase   Introduces a reference by naming the author(s) and usually includes a "signal verb" (e.g., *states, argues, explains*).

spiral conclusion   Suggests applications or further research.

subject index   A list of important words in a text, ordered alphabetically and usually placed at the end of the text.

summary (verb summarize)   A broadly inclusive term for representing the ideas of a writer in a condensed form, using your own words.

support   Evidence to help prove a claim.

syllogism   A logical three-part structure that can be used to illustrate how deductive conclusions are made.

synthesis   Writing in which elements of a work or other studies about a work are brought together, usually in order to draw a conclusion or interpret a claim you wish to assert about the work.

table   Presents detailed information in matrix format, in columns and rows that are easily scanned.

thesis statement   A statement that includes the main point of your essay or what you will attempt to prove; it is placed at the end of your introduction.

topic sentence   A sentence that states the main idea in the paragraph; it is usually the first sentence.

trade books   Books published by non-academic presses for general readers about topics of interest to them.

transitional words and phrases   Words and phrases that connect ideas in a sentence or paragraph, or between paragraphs.

unity   A principle of paragraph construction in which only one idea is developed throughout the paragraph.

university press   A university-affiliated publisher, usually of books or journals; an authoritative source for scholarly research.

value claim   An assertion about a topic that appeals to its ethical nature (e.g., good/bad or fair/unfair).

Subject Index

The Subject Index includes essays in *The Active Reader* organized by 27 subject categories.

Index of Essay Types

Academic Essays

The following categories apply to the academic essays in this book. If the primary focus is on argument rather than exposition, the essay is listed under Argument.

Type A

Anderson (228); Dyer (272); Foote (346); McLeod (194); Ouellette (266)

Type B

Arbour-Nicitopoulos et al. (175); Barker et al. (163); Bonnefon et al. (336); Elliott and Brierley (288); Hasan et al. (329); Healey et al. (362); Kobayashi and Preston (203); Tavernier and Willoughby (257); Wilson et al. (277)

Type C

Boksa et al. (216); Dysart-Gale (241); McMurdo (213); Sabella et al. (314); Snow (158); Stegemann (248); Wickens et al. (304)

Argument

Aschemann-Witzel (301); Dutton et al. (297); Gifford (350), Lexchin (310); Shade (235); Young (182); Yudell et al. (342)

Non-academic Essays

Kingwell (187); Lackenbauer (199); Miyagawa (221); Toope (191)

Index

Classification of Readings by Rhetorical Mode/Pattern

Most essays in *The Active Reader* employ the problem–solution rhetorical pattern; in addition, virtually all essays use some form of analysis and most use examples. However, writers use other rhetorical patterns to develop their main points. These patterns are listed below. Readings may make use of other patterns than just those listed.